ᴬRʏ   ᴶᴼ ᴿ
ᴸ ORIGINS.

MORRIS DICTIONARY
OF WORD AND PHRASE ORIGINS

MORRIS
DICTIONARY
OF WORD AND
PHRASE ORIGINS

William and Mary Morris

Foreword by Edwin Newman

1817

HARPER & ROW, PUBLISHERS

NEW YORK, HAGERSTOWN, SAN FRANCISCO

LONDON

This book is dedicated to
Elizabeth Jones Davis
who gave a special love of
the Mother Tongue and its
lore to all her sons
and daughters

FIRST EDITION

Designed by Sidney Feinberg

Library of Congress Cataloging in Publication Data

Morris, William, date
   Morris Dictionary of word and phrase origins.
   "Four-in-one volume of Dictionary of word and phrase origins" which includes vols. 1–3 previously published 1962–1972.
   Includes index.
   1. English language—Etymology—Dictionaries.
2. English language—Terms and phrases. I. Morris, Mary Davis, joint author. II. Title. III. Title: Dictionary of word and phrase origins.
PE1580.M6 1977   422'.03   77–3763
ISBN 0–06–013058–X

77 78 79 80 81 10 9 8 7 6 5 4 3 2 1

Foreword
by
Edwin Newman

Those of you who have heard or read my views on the likely demise of literate English know how strongly I feel about making every effort to preserve precision in communication. True, I learned to curb my criticism of colleagues' conversation when it became evident that, if I failed to do so, I would be doomed forever to have lunch alone. But the battle against inaccuracy, infelicity and downright impropriety in the use of our mother tongue continues, even with an occasional luncheon recess, and I am delighted that William and Mary Morris are adding another powerful new weapon to the small arsenal those of our persuasion can draw upon.

At first glance it may seem odd that a dictionary of word and phrase origins should claim to contribute to the cause of linguistic precision. But a knowledge of a word's history is likely to assure its accurate use. As Morton Bloomfield wrote in the introduction to the *American Heritage Dictionary*, "Modern English has developed a vocabulary of great extent and richness, drawn from many languages of the world. . . . Above all it is a supple and variegated language, which its native speakers should cherish and which provides them with their hold on the past, their contact with the present, and their claim on the future."

In this volume you will find thousands of word histories based upon sound research but presented in lively, eminently readable fashion. The Morrises continue to demonstrate, as they did in the *American Heritage Dictionary* and the *Harper Dictionary of Contemporary Usage*, that learning the subtleties and nuances of our common tongue can be not only instructive and rewarding, but fun.

Introduction

The statement that English is incalculably the richest of the world's languages is by now a cliché. It's the richest language because it has borrowed freely from virtually every other language spoken on the face of the earth. Our aim in the *Morris Dictionary of Word and Phrase Origins* is to trace the histories of several thousands of the more interesting words and phrases, some borrowed from other tongues, others the product of quick-witted invention. Though the tone of many entries is casual, even light-hearted at times, rest assured that careful scholarship buttresses every entry.

English as a distinct, spoken language may be said to have begun early in the Christian era with the rude dialects of the Angles, Jutes and Saxons, supplemented by occasional additions from the Viking sea rovers on their sporadic invasions of the British Isles from Scandinavia.

The Roman legions had occupied England, seizing London (which they called Londinium) in 43 A.D., but, though their occupation continued for nearly four centuries, it seems to have had remarkably little influence on the language spoken by the common folk. Traces remain in place names ending in "caster" (Lancaster) and "chester" (Winchester), both from the Latin word for camp, "castra." But otherwise the direct Roman influence on English seems nil.

Centuries later, at the time of the Norman Conquest in 1066 A.D., William the Conqueror's invading troops brought many thousands of French and Latin terms into the language, but the original Roman army of occupation had infinitely less influence on the language than the American troops quartered in Britain fifteen centuries later.

Among the contributions of the Vikings are many simple, everyday nouns —words like *root, dirt, leg, gate, freckle, seat, bull, birth* and *trust*. They also contributed such monosyllabic verbs as *call, crawl, nag, guess, gasp, scream, skulk* and *take*. Among the earthy adjectives that were part of the Viking contribution we find *awkward, tattered, ugly, rotten, ill* and *odd*.

With the coming of the Normans we find the first great enrichment of the language. To that time and to the centuries during which the Normans consolidated their control of England, we can trace the arrival of *parliament, chancellor, ministry, nativity, prayer, discipline, penalty, attorney, traitor* and *sacrifice*. These words, you will note, tend to be longer, more ornate than the rude and simple words the early Angles and Saxons had used. Many of them show clearly their Latin origin (*sacrifice*, for example, from Latin *sacer* plus *facio*, make sacred).

Still others reflect a concern for elegance and beauty unknown to the relatively uncultured plain folk of Great Britain. Among the elegant cotributions from the courtly world of the Normans we find *palace, ornament, castle, tower, beauty* and *mansion*. Even nine centuries ago the French were much interested in food, as indicated by such verbal contributions to English as *pastry, feast, sauce* and *roast*.

The next few centuries saw a vast enrichment of the language and its molding into an instrument of unique power and beauty by such as Spenser, Marlowe, Jonson, Shakespeare and Milton. Early on, the tendency to borrow from other languages was manifest.

Over the centuries the British did battle with just about every nation on the continent of Europe but they didn't allow hostility to interfere with their borrowings from the languages of their enemies. The Spanish, Italian and Dutch languages made many useful contributions to English during these centuries. Ultimately, also, the influence of great works of classical Greece and Rome was evident. Many of the classics of Homer, Vergil and Horace had been known to scholars in British and Irish monasteries before the Normans came, but it was not until these classics had been Englished by Shakespeare and his contemporaries that they became part of the culture of the average man.

Later, as English explorers and trders traveled the trade routes and eventually established the British Empire, they borrowed thousands of words from the peoples with whom they did business. From India, long a bastion of the Empire, came *bungalow, madras, punch, coolie* and *faker*. The seemingly perennial wars with the Dutch produced such borrowings as *schooner, scum, scour, landscape* and *freight*. Spain supplied *armada* (of course!), *potato, cargo, tobacco* and *hurricane*.France has made many contributions to English, such as *dull, bombast, progress, volunteer, bizarre* and *redingote*. The last is a charming oddity for it was originally the English "riding coat." French fashion designers borrowed it to describe a style of full-length unlined cloak, Frenchifying it to *redingote* in the process. Then British designers borrowed both the style and the French name.

The next great stage in the expansion of English was undoubtedly the result of the colonization of America. As H. L. Mencken has pointed out in *The American Language*, early settlers had to invent a lot of Americanisms in order to describe the unfamiliar circumstances surrounding them in the New World. From the Indians they soon borrowed animal names for creatures never seen in Britain, such as *raccoon, opossum, moose* and *skunk*. Other unfamiliar objects soon added new words to the vocabulary of the settlers: *hickory, squash, terrapin, persimmon* and *pecan*. Not all of these words are precisely the way they appeared in the original Indian dialects, by the way. In an effort to make the strange Indian sounds resemble familiar English words, Piligrims made the Indian *otcheck* into *woodchuck* and *seganku* into *skunk*.

From other Indian dialects we have, during the centuries, made hundreds of other borrowings: *moccasin, powwow, toboggan, succotash*, to say nothing of such expressions as *medicine man, pipe of peace* and *bury the hatchet*.

The next enrichment of the American language came from the Dutch who settled New Amsterdam (now New York) and left there many words that are still a lively part of our language—*cruller, cole slaw, spook, snoop, dope, waffle, boss* and, of course, *Santa Claus*. Interestingly enough, the very first Yankees were Dutchmen, for *Yankee* was derived from the name *Jan* and *kees*(cheese), so the word originally was a derisive nickname *John Cheese*.

Although many of the islands in the West Indies had been occupied by the Spanish, relations between them and the British were not friendly and there were few borrowings from Spanish at this period, though later the American cowboy took much of his lingo from his Mexican Spanish counterpart, including *desperado, incommunicado, bronco, lasso, coyote, cinch, stampede* and *rodeo*. Among the notable words taken from Spanish during the earlier colonial period, however, were two that we use every summer: *mosquito* and *barbecue*.

After the American Revolution and throughout the nineteenth century, our language grew at an amazing rate, and some of the most colorful and characteristic American expressions were born. *Okay*, which also appears as *O.K.* and sometimes as *Okeh*, is one word whose origin has puzzled scholars almost since its first appearance in the early 1800s. For a long time it was thought to be a Choctaw Indian word. President Woodrow Wilson supported this theory. Then someone theorized that it was an abbreviation for *Orl Kerrect*, used by Andrew Jackson as a youthful law clerk. Still a later theory was that it was from the initials of the Old Kinderhook political club which supported Martin Van Buren, "the Kinderhook fox," for president. Still newer theories are discussed later in this volume under *O.K.*

Though the scholars still argue about where *O.K.* came from, there's no question that it is as American as the hot dog—and it might interest you to know that the ordinary hot dog can cause serious arguments among scholars. One group says that the first hot dogs were sold at New York's Coney Island amusement park about 1869, while another claims that the name was first used about 1900 at the Polo Grounds baseball park. Both could be right, because the frankfurter certainly existed before it came to be called the hot dog.

All the while, our language had been steadily enriched by borrowings from all parts of the world. Among common words we use every day, for example, there are *denim* from the expression *serge de Nîmes*, from the city of Nîmes, France; *slogan* from the Gaelic *slaugh* (army) and *gairm* (shout)—adding up to *battle cry; dungaree* from the Hindustani *dungri,* a fabric first used for tents, later for sails and eventually for sailors' work clothes; *jeans* form Genoa, where the fabric was first woven; and *galoshes* from a special sandal worn on rainy days (*galoche*) by courtiers of the French kings Louis XIV.

It is doubtful, however, if the language has ever seen such a fantastic growth as in the years since World War II. One of the world's leading scientists used the term *quantum jump* (itself a recent coinage) to describe the altogether incredible growth of language in this period. Scientific *breakthroughs* (another recent term) have brought with them entirely new vocabularies. Most of the technical terms will remain, of course, in the lexicons of the scientists themselves. But hundreds have come into everyday use. It's hard to believe, but true, that *radar* was a military secret until 1945, *transistors* were known only in laboratories until 1955, the *laser* and *maser* are products of post-1960 research—and *quasar,* a key word in a whole great branch of astronomy, first appeared in 1964.

But it is not solely to science that we owe the enorous expansion of English and American English in recent years. Many words have come into our language as a result of vastly increased trade with all parts of the world. Today English is indisputably the world's first language both in trade and in intellectual interchange between nations and scholars.

Lest we be accused of endings on a note of *chauvinism* (from Napoleon's most fanatical supporter, Nicolas Chauvin), note that today you will find in your daily newspaper such terms as *aficionado* and *mañana* (Spanish); *ambiance, apéritif, avant-garde, bon vivant, bête noire* and *bon voyage* (French); *gemütlich, gesundheit, blitzkrieg* and *schmaltz* (German); *skoal, slalom* and *smorgäsbord* (Danish, Norwegian and Swedish); and even *banzai* (Japanese) and *vox populi* (Latin). Though these terms have been taken into our language without change—except sometimes in their pronunciation—you should find each of them in your general dictionaries.

The purpose of this volume—if it may be said to have a purpose other than to entertain and enlighten—is to lay before you some of the results of many years of exploration of the more casual byways of the fascinating science, etymology.

William and Mary Morris

NOTE: Material not found in alphabetical listing should be checked in the index.

Acknowledgments

Our first words of thanks go to the thousands of readers of our daily syndicated column "Words, Wit and Wisdom" whose questions and comments—mostly favorable, some sharply critical—have kept us on our toes these past twenty-five years. Almost every page of this *Morris Dictionary of Word and Phrase Origins* bears testimony to the contributions our readers make, whether by asking probing questions or by helping us to answer the really difficult ones.

The hundreds of people who worked very closely with us on the *American Heritage Dictionary of the English Language* were, directly or indirectly, responsible for the many of the items and anecdotes in the pages that follow. And let's note parenthetically that the "us" in the previous sentence is a word carefully chosen, for Mary Morris—though nowhere accorded byline credit in the *American Heritage Dictionary*—was very much a part of the group working on the project. She worked, indeed, on the basic concepts of its editorial approach years before the American Heritage people ever gave any thought to publishing a dictionary.

Over the years we have had special reason to be grateful to the various editors who handled our copy at the syndicates that distributed our column to papers throughout the United States, Canada, Mexico and Japan. Notable among them we count Elmer Roessner of Bell-McClure, Pat McHugh of the L. A. Times Syndicate, and, currently, Sid Goldberg and Martin Linehan of United Feature Syndicate. At Harper & Row Joseph Vergara and William Davies have displayed patience and forbearance far above the call of duty, and Dolores Simon, William Monroe and Marjorie Horvitz have been everlasting vigilant at the onerous chores of copyediting and checking proofs. And a special salute to Miss Delight Ansley who did a superb job of indexing.

A-1 was first used in the *Register of British and Foreign Shipping,* issued by the great maritime insurance firm Lloyd's of London. They rate the world's merchant shipping by a combination of letters to indicate the condition of the hull, and numbers to indicate the condition of the equipment. Thus *A-1* means that the hull is excellent and so is all the ship's gear.

A.B./AB is nautical shorthand for "able-bodied seaman," the rank above "apprentice" or "ordinary seaman" and below "boatswain's mate" in the merchant services of Great Britain and the United States.

A.B./B.A. In college bulletins some professors are listed as having *A.B.* degrees, others as having *B.A.* degrees. The degrees are the same, but *A.B.* may be an abbreviation of the Latin *Artium Baccalaureus,* while *B.A.* is an abbreviation of the English "Bachelor of Arts."

abacus comes from the Greek *abax,* a tablet for writing or ciphering. The bead-and-frame gadget that we call an *abacus* was originated by the Chinese and called *suan pan.* Amazingly fast and intricate computations can be made by skillful users of the instrument.

a-borning merely means "in the state of being born." The prefix *a-* occurs fairly often in such words as *"asleep"* or such expressions as "The frog he would *a-wooing* go."

aboveboard was originally gamblers' language and referred to their insistence on keeping hands, cards and markers on the board or table rather than below. It's now most commonly heard in the phrase "honest and *aboveboard,"* which may be redundant but certainly makes its point. Incidentally, as an indication that gamblers and gambling have long been with us, the *Oxford Dictionary* records the appearance of *aboveboard* in print as early as 1616, the year of Shakespeare's death.

above (below) the salt. Back before the time of the first Queen Elizabeth, the ruling families of Great Britain started a custom that is now reflected in this expression. In those days salt was a fairly rare item, in marked contrast to today. So the saler, or salt cellar, was the most important feature of the table setting. So important was the saler that it established the social order at medieval feasts. The host was seated above the saler and with him were the most important guests. Lesser fry and minor family dependents were seated below the saler.

abracadabra, much favored by magicians when practicing their sorcery, has a very long history, going back to the Greek *abrasadabra,* a word used by members of a Gnostic (early Christian) sect when invoking divine help. It may have come from the name of a leader of one of these sects, Abrasax, or from the initial letters of three Hebrew words: Ab, the father, Ben, the son, and Acadsch, the holy spirit.

absence makes the heart grow fonder is an expression which first appeared in a song by Thomas Haynes Bayley early in the nineteenth century. It's a sentiment not universally held to be true. Dr. Samuel Johnson once wrote that "Friendship, like love, is destroyed by long absence, though it may be increased by short intermissions." And Homer, many centuries earlier, · wrote: "Out of sight, out of mind." Then there was the cynic, reported by Franklin Pierce Adams (F.P.A.), who amended Bayley's line thus: "Absence makes the heart grow fonder—for somebody else." And S. J. Perelman, in a script for an early Marx Brothers film, had this variation on the theme: "Absinthe makes the heart grow fonder."

absquatulate (pronounced ab-SKWOT-yoo-layt) is one of a number of elaborate slang terms popular midway through the nineteenth century. It was fabricated, in imitation of a Latin compound verb, of *ab* and *squat*—and means the opposite of *squat,* that is, to depart in a hurry, especially in a secretive fashion. The *-ulate* ending is tacked on only to make the word sound more impressive.

absurd has had quite a history, evolving from the ancient Latin adjective *surdus,* meaning "mute." *Absurdus,* literally "away from muteness," came to mean "discordant" and was used in music as a term signifying "out of harmony." Then *absurd* came into general use as describing anything out of harmony with logic or reason, and finally to its present meaning of "ridiculous, illogical and silly."

a cappella (pronounced ah kah-PEL-uh), originally Italian for "from the chapel," means "without accompaniment."

accessory before (after) the fact. An *accessory before the fact* (of a crime) is one who is aware that such an act is being planned but is not himself present at the commission of the crime. An *accessory after the fact* is one who, knowing of the commission of a crime, helps the criminal to evade justice. The hostler who held the horse John Wilkes Booth used to make his getaway after assassinating Lincoln could be called an *accessory after the fact.* Of course, if he had been informed in advance of the plot on the President's life he would also have been an *accessory before the fact. Accessory* came into English from the Medieval Latin *accessorius,* "helper."

accolade, a word which today means "award or expression of high praise," comes from the Latin *ad,* meaning "to," and *collum,* meaning "neck"— and with good reason, since an *accolade* was originally a ceremony in which knighthood was conferred, an embrace being part of the ceremony.

accommodation ladder is a ladder, usually made of heavy rope or flexible cables with wood or metal crosspieces, that is hung from a large port or gangway opening in the side of a ship. It is used mostly by pilots embarking (or disembarking) while the ship is under way. In heavy seas this can be very chancy.

according to Hoyle. Edmund Hoyle was an eighteenth-century British clubman and games expert. One of the most popular games of the time was whist, which continued in popularity until the advent of auction and contract bridge. Hoyle was the first person to prepare a really authoritative handbook on it: *A Short Treatise on the Game of Whist.* Later he added rules for other card games and he became accepted as the final authority on the playing of card games. To this day the phrase "played *according to Hoyle*" means "played in accordance with the rules of the game."

ace in the hole, in stud poker, is an ace whose face is turned to the table, while most of the other cards are exposed. Thus, an *ace in the hole* is a secret source of power.

Achilles' heel/tendon. Achilles, the hero of Homer's *Iliad,* was invulnerable save for one part of his anatomy, his heel. According to legend, his mother, Thetis, took him, while still an infant, and dipped him in the river Styx to make him impervious to all mortal wounds. However, the heel by which she held him remained untouched by the magic waters and he was eventually slain in the siege of Troy by an arrow that struck his heel. To this day the tendon running from the heel bone to the calf muscle of the leg is known as the *Achilles' tendon.*

acid test, meaning a sternly critical examination, one designed to reveal even the slightest flaw, comes from the use of nitric acid to test gold. Inferior metals may be decomposed by the acid—but not gold.

acknowledge the corn goes back to the early 1800s and means, simply, to admit losing an argument or minor contest. One story of its origin has to do with a farmer who went to New Orleans to sell his crops and fell among gamblers. Before they got through with him, he had lost all his money and his two barges, one full of corn, the other loaded with potatoes. Next day, waking with a fine hangover, he rushed down to the river, hoping to be able to retrieve his goods. When he got there, he found that the barge full of corn had sunk and was utterly worthless. So he decided to halve his losses, saying, "I *acknowledge the corn*—but I'll be darned if you get the potatoes."

acrimonious, a word used to describe bitter or biting remarks, is one of the many English words which have a clear origin in Latin. It derives its spelling and meaning from the Latin *acrimonia,* meaning "sharpness."

acronym. Probably the most interesting and widespread recent development in our changing language has been the vast popularity of acronyms. *Acronym* (pronounced AK-roh-nim) is the name for a word formed by combining the initial letters or syllables of a series of words—for example, *Jato* (Jet Assisted Take-off) or *Basic* (British-American Scientific International Commercial) English. It comes from the Greek *akros* (tip) and *onym* (name).

The earliest *acronyms* are not known, though some scholars claim to have located examples in ancient Hebrew scriptures. *Acronyms* are found among nineteenth-century British and American word coinages, but their appearance in profusion dates from World War I, when *Anzac* (Australian–New Zealand Army Corps) and *WAAC* (Women's Army Auxiliary Corps) were coined. The full tide of popularity of *acronyms* in America, however, came with the advent of the New Deal and World War II. The custom of referring to the "alphabet agencies," such as *WPA* and *NLRB,* by their initials undoubtedly accelerated the trend toward naming organizations and offices by pronounceable combinations of letters. The U.S. Navy was especially prolific in coining acronyms, such as *Bupers* (Bureau of Personnel) and the ill-chosen *Cincus* (Commander in Chief, U.S. Fleet), which was abruptly changed after the disaster at Pearl Harbor.

During World War II, *acronyms* ranging from technical labels like *Radar* (Radio Detection and Ranging) to slang terms like *Snafu* (Situation Normal; All Fouled Up) became commonplace. During the years since World War II no single classification of word coinages has proliferated so rapidly.

We're inclined to think that the vogue for *acronyms,* which has recently burdened the language with such lunacies as *EGADS* for Electronic Ground Automatic Destruct System and *MOUSE* for Minimum Orbital Unmanned Satellite of Earth, may be petering out. Who with a straight face could possibly invent an *acronym* that could match the one much in the news during Watergate—*CREEP,* for Committee for the Re-Election of the President.

acrophobia, meaning fear of heights, is derived from the Greek *akros* (at the point, end or top) and *phobos* (fear).

actuary. An *actuary* today is a person who calculates insurance risks and premiums and the relationship between the two. It comes from the Latin *actuarius,* for "clerk." The first *actuaries* were those clerks who took care of the payroll of the Roman army.

adamant, a word that has been part of our language since Chaucer's time, has quite an interesting background. It was originally coined by the ancients from the Greek words *a* (not) and *damao* (I tame) to describe a mineral of incomparable hardness. For many centuries it was regarded as synonymous with "diamond"—the hardest of gems. The two words, indeed, come from precisely the same Greek root. It is now used chiefly in the senses of "unyielding and immovable."

Adam's ale is water—the theory being that the first man would have had nothing else to drink.

Adam's off ox. On Cape Cod you can still hear many unusual expressions. One that keeps coming back to us was said by a Hyannis native speaking about the reception given President Kennedy on one of his flights from Washington. "He was all smiles," said the Cape Codder, "and he waved to me and said hello even though he didn't know me from *Adam's off ox.* " The *off ox* in a team of oxen is the one on the right. Since he is farther from the driver, the presumption is that he can't be so well seen and may get worse footing than the ox on the left. Thus *off ox* came to be farmer's slang for a clumsy person.

The late Charles E. Funk reported that the expression "poor as God's off ox"—meaning very poor indeed—was common on Nantucket. It's reasonable to guess that *Adam* was substituted as a euphemism for "God" when the expression reached the mainland. Certainly the expression "didn't know him from Adam's off ox," meaning "to have no knowledge whatever of a person," is common throughout New England.

A.D./B.C. A.D. is the abbreviation for the Latin *anno Domini,* "in the year of the Lord." It refers to dates in the Christian era and should precede the date (A.D. 2000). B.C. is the abbreviation for "before Christ" and indicates time in the pre-Christian era. It customarily follows the date (44 B.C.).

Addisonian termination. This odd phrase was once a term of critical abuse in the world of letters. It seems that Joseph Addison (of Addison and Steele renown) was addicted to ending sentences with prepositions. According to the classically oriented scholars of his day, this was a most reprehensible practice, the more so since Addison had long demonstrated his ability to write both well and persuasively. But since Latin virtually never tolerated sentences ending with prepositions (most ended with verbs) the wise men said that English should be hammered into the same mold—a proposition that Addison took a dim view of. As do we, obviously.

The creator of the term *Addisonian termination,* by the way, was an Anglican bishop, Richard Hurd. His other contributions to literature, if any, are long forgotten, while Addison is still read, at least in our schools and colleges. It would appear that the Hurdian termination was somewhat more final than the Addisonian.

ad hoc. An *ad hoc* committee is one organized to direct attention to a single particular situation, usually without regard to the broad picture. Thus members of a university faculty might organize an *ad hoc* committee for the defense of one of their number who they feel has been unfairly discharged, without regard to the general problem of academic freedom or tenure or whatever other broader concepts might be involved. The term comes from the Latin *ad* (to, for) and *hoc* (this thing).

adieu. The French word for "goodbye" is interestingly a direct parallel of its English equivalent. *Adieu* is a shortened form of an Old French expression meaning "I commend you to God," just as the English "goodbye" is a shortened version of "God be with you."

ad infinitum (pronounced ad in-fin-EYE-tum) is taken direct from Latin and means a thing or an action that seems and does go on endlessly—to infinity. As Jonathan Swift wrote: "So, naturalists observe, a flea hath smaller fleas that on him prey; and these have smaller still to bite 'em; and so proceed *ad infinitum.*"

Admirable Crichton. Actually there were two *Admirable Crichtons*—one fictional and one real—and it's hard to tell which was the more fascinating. One is the hero of James M. Barrie's play of the same name, first performed in 1902 and revived many times since. In it, Crichton, the very model of the typical British butler, serves in the household of Lord Loam, who likes to believe that class distinctions are silly stuff. To prove his point he insists, one day each year, on serving Crichton and the other servants at tea, an eccentricity that horrifies Crichton. Later the household is shipwrecked on a desert island and Crichton, as the man best qualified to manage things, takes over and becomes the unquestioned leader of the group. He even proposes to marry his former lord's daughter. A rescue party comes to the island, however, and Crichton—again the very model of a proper British manservant—reverts to his former menial status.

The earlier, real-life Crichton was born in 1560 and was the outstanding physical and mental prodigy of his age. By the time he reached fifteen he had taken his Master of Arts degree and at twenty was reported to have mastered a dozen languages and to be knowledgeable in all the then known sciences. The British Isles were obviously too small a theater for a lad of his gifts, so he went first to France, where he dazzled the best brains of the Sorbonne, served a year or two with the French Army, then went on to Italy. There he became tutor to sons of dukes and princes, dazzling everyone with his beauty, brilliance and ability as a swordsman. While still in his early twenties, he was rash enough to steal the love of a prince's lady and was treacherously assaulted by three masked men. Thus he died—not wholly admirably, perhaps—one of history's most fabled prodigies.

admiral is a word borrowed into English from the Arabic *amir*, "lord or commander." At first it was used to refer to any leader, as Caxton in the fifteenth century could refer to the "son of an admiral of Babylon." Indeed, in its Latin form, *admirabilus*, it meant anything so outstanding as to be marveled or wondered at. However, since shortly after its adoption into English it has been largely restricted to designating leaders of fleets.

ad nauseam is a Latin term, meaning "to the point of nausea." It occurs in sentences like: "The speaker rambled on and on and on *ad nauseam.*"

adroit. We get *adroit* from the French phrase *a droit,* "to the right." When we use *adroit* today it means skillful, dexterous, deft—especially when under pressure or handling a difficult situation. *Adroit* is another example of the way English always seems to discriminate against left-handed people. Like "dexterous," from Latin *dexter,* "right," it implies cleverness or skillfulness, while words like "sinister" (from the Latin word for "left") and "gauche" (from the French word for "left") have decidedly unpleasant and unflattering implications. Even the word "gawky" originally came from the dialect expression "gawk-handed," meaning "left-handed."

aegis. We suspect that very few diplomats who use phrases like: "We act under the *aegis* of the United Nations" realize that that high-sounding word *aegis* originally meant "goatskin." Zeus, who was the supreme deity of the Greeks, was suckled in infancy by a goat named Amalthaea, whose skin was subsequently used to cover the great shield of Zeus. Since this shield was the symbol of the power of the greatest of the gods, a person who acted "under the *aegis*" was one who had the omnipotent power of the gods supporting him.

aerobics is a system of building up the body by means of exercises which develop the use of oxygen by the body. It comes from two Greek words, *aer,* meaning "air," and *bios,* "life." The adjective form *aerobic* has been around for a while, used to describe organisms that can function only in the presence of oxygen. But the system of *aerobics* is quite new. Its first recorded appearance in print was in 1969.

aesthete's foot. John Chapman, late dean of New York's drama critics, once commented on the odd medical fact that gout usually afflicts people of distinctly higher-than-average intelligence and education. "You might call it," said Chapman, *aesthete's foot.*

aesthetic/esthetic. *Aesthetic* comes from the Greek word *aisthetikos,* meaning "perceptive." Thus an *aesthete* is one who perceives—but today it is applied chiefly to a person with a keen appreciation and love of the beautiful, especially in art, music and poetry. There has been a marked tendency over the past few decades to spell words from the Greek with *e* rather than *ae.* "Anesthesia" has replaced "anaesthesia," for example. However, a survey by linguists at Brown University shows that the spelling *aesthete* appears at least four times as often as *esthete* in American books and magazines. So while *esthete* is an acceptable spelling, *aesthete* is still preferred.

afeard appears frequently in Shakespeare, and the *Oxford Dictionary* traces it back to Middle English—the language spoken in England roughly from 1150 to 1500. However, it has long been considered "dialectal," by which we mean that it is a variety of speech different from the standard tongue and usually limited to a particular region or social class. In the Carolinas, West Virginia and Kentucky, regional dialects have changed very little over the centuries and a claim can be made that since terms like *afeard* were common in Elizabethan England, the speech of some of our mountain folk is closer to "true" English than what most of us commonly use.

affiliate/subsidiary. In business, it is common to speak of a smaller company which has been bought out by or created by a larger company as its *affiliate.* If you believe your Latin, this makes the smaller company the adopted son of the larger one (from the Latin *affiliatus,* past participle of *affiliare,* "to adopt as a son"). If the *affiliate* enjoys a better relationship with the parent company than a *subsidiary* of the parent company, that is because *subsidiary* comes from the Latin *subsidere,* meaning "to sit down and remain" —which certainly puts the *subsidiary* in its place.

affluent (pronounced AF-loo-ent) today usually means "rich." Thus, "The mink-upholstered limousine belongs to an *affluent* newcomer from Texas." Derived from the Latin *ad* (to) and *fluere* (flow), it literally means "flowing abundantly"—like the *affluent* oil wells which may well have made our Texas newcomer financially *affluent.*

affront (pronounced uh-FRUNT) means "to insult or to offend by disrespect." It is perhaps more commonly met in the passive than the active voice, in sentences like: "The congressman was *affronted* by the lobbyist's lack of respect." *Affront* comes from the Latin words *ad* (to) and *frons* (forehead). Its original meaning was to confront a person face to face. Nowadays, however, it has the special meaning of to insult a person openly and deliberately. You may insult or offend another person in private, but you can *affront* him only in public. *Affront* is also a noun, in such a sentence as: "Your action in snubbing me at the dance constituted an *affront.*"

afghan. It's curious, but the way the name *afghan* came to be applied to the familiar knitted woolen blanket has not previously been documented in any standard reference book. That it is derived from *Afghan,* a native or product of Afghanistan, is obvious, but it does seem odd that a name coming from such a faraway corner of the world, deep in Asia, should have been used for so long for such a homely item typically found in the American cedar chest. One characteristic of the *afghan* is that, in the words of the *Modern Textile Dictionary,* it is made with a series of stripes, zigzag effects, or squares, varying in size and vivid colorings." This characteristic is shared, of course, with *afghan* rugs, which also feature geometric patterns and vivid colors. So the likelihood is that the *afghan* blanket was named for its resemblance to these Oriental rugs, which enjoyed such a great vogue in America during the latter part of the Victorian era.

aficionado (pronounced ah-fee-shuh-NAH-doh) is a Spanish word, much affected by people who want to add a little highfalutin tone to their talk or writing. It simply means "devotee," especially an enthusiastic, amateur follower of an art form.

agape (pronounced either AH-gah-pay or AG-uh-pee) goes back to the earliest days of Christendom but has returned to common use in recent writings of a religious nature. Originally it described a Christian love feast, complete with the Eucharistic service and the giving of offerings to the poor. Over a period of two or three centuries scandalous elements crept into the service and it was officially banned toward the end of the fourth century A.D. Now it is used to indicate a completely spontaneous and selfless outpouring of love, the highest manifestation of Christian brotherhood.

agnostic is a relative oddity among words, one whose creation (like those of "moron" and "googol") can be quite precisely dated and credited to a single person. *Agnostic* was created by Thomas Henry Huxley, the eminent British biologist and advocate of Darwin's theory of evolution. Searching for a word to describe a person who would neither accept nor reject the existence of a God, since he deemed the proposition incapable of proof, he combined the Greek *a* (not) with *gignoskein* (to know). Thus an agnostic is simply a person who says, in effect, this all may very well be true but, as for me, "I do not know."

à go-go is a phrase ("dancing *à go-go*" and the like) which is borrowed from French. Meaning "in a fast or lively manner" originally, it has come to be loosely used as a sort of synonym for sophisticated, as in "*à go-go* boutique" or "*go-go* styles of dress." It is thought to be a reduplication of the second syllable of the French word *agogue,* meaning "merriment."

agony originally was the Greek *agonia,* meaning "contest," especially any athletic contest, and this in turn came from *agon,* the stadium in which the contests took place. Since at least one party—the loser—in an athletic contest usually suffers some pain or anguish, the word gradually came to mean what it does today: intense suffering, whether physical or mental.

agony column, now more common in British papers than American, is simply a column devoted to short advertisements for missing relatives and friends. Behind each ad is a story of personal anguish.

agronomist. Before the days of specialization, the man who toiled in the fields was simply a farmer, and the size of his crops seemed to depend not only on the weather but on how "good" or "poor" a farmer he was. Many of today's farmers are *agronomists* or consult bearers of that title. Derived from the Greek *agros,* "field," and *nomos,* "to manage," *agronomist* means "specialist in land management and crop production."

ailurophile. A lover of cats is an *ailurophile,* from the Greek *ailouros,* meaning "cat," and *philos,* meaning "loving or fond of."

Alabamian/Alabaman. An old friend and associate of ours came originally from Alabama and he tells us: "We used to call ourselves *Alabamians.* However, I usually see *Alabaman* in print, especially in stories about political figures." Adaptations of place names to designate residents of the various towns and states follow no special rules, though attempts have been made to codify them. Some years ago George R. Stewart, whose *American Place Names* is the best book ever written on the subject, reported that "if a name ends with '-i,' '-an' is added; if it ends in '-a,' not preceded by 'i,' the common rule is to add '-n.'" According to this, *Alabaman* would be preferred. But the fact of the matter is that natives of Alabama overwhelmingly prefer *Alabamian.* Indeed, the editor of the *Dothan* (Alabama) *Eagle* went on record with this statemente: "If there is any merit in the rule of spelling a proper name just as the possessor spells it, then we are *Alabamians.*" So the weight of evidence supports a preference for the pleasanter-sounding *Alabamian.*

Neither of these names, incidentally, would even begin to qualify as an oddity among place names. Natives of Cambridge are known as Cantabrigians or Cantabs—from the Roman name for Cambridge, England. Natives of Glasgow are Glaswegians and of Liverpool, Liverpudlians. In Idaho there are two schools of thought as to whether natives are Idahovians or Idahoans. At one time the faculty at the State University (in Moscow, Idaho) indicated a preference for Moscovite or Muscovian as the proper designation for a resident of their town. But the natives themselves would have none of this verbal elegance—they prefer Moscowite. And so it goes.

albatross, famed in legend and verse, gets its name from the Arabic words *al* (the) and *ghattas* (white-tailed sea eagle). It was viewed with awe by early sailors in southern latitudes because its extraordinary wingspan gave it the ability to soar for great distances. Thus, it seemed to sailors, the *albatross* was a bird that could fly without flapping its wings. So it was endowed with mystical abilities and seamen believed that to shoot this semi-sacred bird would bring disaster or death. Coleridge's *Rime of the Ancient Mariner* (1798) is the best-known account of a tragic destiny induced by killing an albatross.

Albion. There are a variety of theories about how England got to be called *Albion* in the first place. The most likely one is that the Romans called it that from the Latin word *albus,* meaning "white"—in reference to the famous white cliffs of Dover. But one really wild legend has it that a Syrian king had fifty daughters, the oldest named Albia. They were all married on the same day in what must have been one of the most massive weddings on record. But that was only the beginning. Every single one of the daughters took a knife to the neck of her husband on the wedding night, with the result that, come dawn, there were fifty newly made widows. The king, understandably, took a dim view of the proceedings and banished all fifty of the girls. After much drifting about, they finally landed on the wild shores of England and named it after their leader, Albia. And there, as if to prove that they weren't indiscriminate man-haters, they took unto themselves new husbands from among the natives, "a lawless crew of devils," according to one account—but more to their liking than the men the king had chosen for them. This little story could be Chapter 1 in the History of the Women's Liberation Movement—but we hasten to add that it is just that, a story, a legend, a myth.

Alexander's beard is no beard at all. In other words, a man with Alexander's beard is clean-shaven. Presumably the expression derives from the fact that Alexander the Great (356–323 B.C.), conqueror of the Persian Empire, is customarily pictured as beardless.

Alexandra limp. Queen Alexandra, the wife of Edward VII of England, once suffered an accident which resulted in her walking with a very slight limp. Many women of the court, presumably in an effort to make her limp even less noticeable than it was, imitated her way of walking.

al fresco. Eating *al fresco* is an old Italian custom which has been adopted by the Americans in the form of the barbecue. *Al fresco* means "in the fresh or the cool," and it is used to indicate any event taking place outdoors; but is most commonly associated with outdoor eating.

alibi. In law an *alibi*—Latin for "elsewhere"—is the plea that a person accused of a crime could not have committed it because he was someplace other than at the scene of the crime when it was committed. In popular usage, *alibi* usually carries with it the implication that there is something spurious about the explanation given. We speak of a person trying to *alibi* his way out of an embarrassing situation. *Alibi* also implies a desire to shift blame or avoid punishment.

all Greek to me goes back to Shakespeare. The line was first spoken by Casca, one of the conspirators against Caesar in the first act of *Julius Caesar.* He was speaking of the comments made by Cicero after Caesar three times refused the crown of emperor. Cicero actually did speak in Greek, using that language as a device to make sure that casual passers-by did not understand his remarks. Today the expression "It's *all Greek to me"* simply means that what has been said is beyond the speaker's understanding.

all hands and the cook. Cowboys of the Old West gave us this expression to refer to a situation of extreme danger. When, for example, a herd of cattle stampeded, it was the responsibility of every cowhand—including even the cook—to saddle up and work at the job of rounding up the rampaging herd. The expression is also common among New England seafaring men. As long ago as the days when whaling ships sailed from New Bedford, when it came time to "cut in" on a whale the call would go out for *all hands and the cook* because the work had to be done rapidly, before decomposition could set in. We're told that it is still commonly used by fishermen to describe a successful trip: "We had *all hands and the cook* on deck."

almanac. We all know such publications as the *Old Farmer's Almanac* and have heard of *Poor Richard's Almanack* and the like, probably without realizing that such compendiums of dates, seasons, witty sayings, astronomical data and long-range weather forecasts actually go back in time to long before Gutenberg invented movable type. In medieval monasteries monks first compiled such annual collections of fact and fantasy. The word itself comes to us from the Medieval Latin *almanachus,* and may very well have been derived from the Spanish-Arabic *al* (the) and *manakh* (sundial).

almighty dollar. The first person to use *almighty dollar* was Washington Irving, in a book called *The Creole Village,* published in 1836. He was writing about the settlements along the banks of the Mississippi in Louisiana and commented that "the *almighty dollar,* that great object of universal devotion throughout the land, seems to have no genuine devotees in these peculiar villages." The phrase caught on and became so popular that Irving later felt forced to explain that he meant no irreverence by the phrase, making it clear that he as much as anyone regarded the dollar as a fit object of worship.

alter ego is a Latin phrase which literally means "another I." It is used as a noun: "George is Tom's *alter ego*"—meaning that the two men think alike, react alike and have the same tastes.

alumnus/alumna. *Alumnus* and *alumna* are simply the Latin words for "foster son" and "foster daughter." Though used in Great Britain to mean "pupil," in America they describe only former students or graduates of a school or college. Incidentally, the plurals of these two words often cause trouble. They retain the original Latin endings, but the accepted American pronunciations of these endings happen to be precisely transposed from the classical Latin sounds. Thus *alumni* (men graduates) in Latin was pronounced uh-LUM-nee and *alumnae* (women graduates) was uh-LUM-nye. However, present-day pronunciation throughout the English-speaking world is uh-LUM-nye for *alumni* and uh-LUM-nee for *alumnae*.

-ama. *Foodorama, Bowlerama, Pizzarama*—the *"ama* addicts" have got completely out of hand. As Wolcott Gibbs once wrote in another connection, "Where it all will end knows God." But if no one can predict when the craze for such "nonce words" will end, we can tell pretty well where it started. Specifically, though the coinage was in imitation of *panorama*, the first such word was Futurama, a trademarked name devised by the General Motors people to describe their "World of Tomorrow" exhibit in the New York World's Fair of 1939. Then the suffix *ama* went into temporary eclipse for a few years, only to be revived in 1952 by *Cinerama*, one of the more spectacular wide-screen movie techniques. After that the deluge: *sporteramas, bowleramas, chickeneramas* (where "bar-b-q" chicken is sold, of course) and countless others.

amanuensis is a word borrowed without change from the Latin, which created it from the elements of *servus a manu*, "one who serves by the hand"— hand, in this case, meaning handwriting. It has been in the language at least since 1619, according to the *Oxford Dictionary*, but we can date quite precisely the first time it swam into our ken.

The year was 1934 and William had a summer job as chauffeur-companion to George Pierce Baker, founder of Harvard's famous 47 Workshop, where his students included Eugene O'Neill, Thomas Wolfe, George Abbott, Sidney Howard and many more of the nation's leading playwrights. In August of that year Mr. Baker (he always scorned the title "Doctor," though several universities had conferred the degree on him in recognition of his work both at Harvard and at Yale, where he founded the School of the Drama) was invited to be a judge of a one-act play tournament held in Dorset, Vermont. The other judges were Alfred Kreymborg, a poet of distinction, and Alexander Woollcott, a sometime drama critic and then celebrated as radio's "Town Crier."

Baker cordially detested Woollcott, especially because of his habit of arriving just at or after curtain time at Broadway first nights and bowing and waving salutations to all his acquaintances as he moved down the aisle. The procession was very gratifying to Woollcott's supreme ego—and equally devastating to the play and players. "Watch him, William," said Baker to Morris. "Even up in a small town like this, Woollcott will run true to form."

And sure enough, he did. Kreymborg, Baker and Morris were well settled in their seats ten minutes before curtain time, but not Woollcott. Minutes passed. The curtain was held for the great man. "Now do you understand why I have such a great scunner [which see] to him?" asked Mr. Baker somewhat rhetorically.

Then, with a flourish, the legendary Woollcott made his traditional entrance with a wave of the hand and peck on the cheek of those of his acquaintances who happened to have aisle seats. When he reached our row, he leaned over me—no easy task since Woollcott was the original "five by five" man—and effusively greeted Mr. Baker with many a "Doctor" interlarded in his remarks. Then he paused a moment, motioned to a slim young man behind him, and said, "And, Dr. Baker, may I introduce my secretary, Mr. Sweeney?"

"Pleased to meet you," said Baker. "May I introduce my *amanuensis,* William Morris!"

And that, we think, can serve to illustrate not only *amanuensis* but a fine sample of "gamesmanship" or "one-upmanship."

amateur. An *amateur* is—or was originally—a person who loves a game or subject. The word comes from the Latin *amare* (to love). Thus a painter like Sir Winston Churchill may properly be called an *"amateur* painter" for, though his works may indeed have genuine artistic merit, he painted them primarily for the sheer love of painting.

"Love" in tennis and other racket games is directly derived from this idea of amateurism. A person who "plays for love," in the age-old expression, is literally playing for nothing—at least nothing in the form of a tangible reward. Thus the figure *O* has for more than two centuries been called "love"—and the person who remains on the "love" end of many sets of tennis must truly be called *amateur* in all the senses of that much-abused word.

ambiance, sometimes also spelled *ambience,* means "surroundings or environment." It's borrowed from French and ultimately from Latin *ambiens,* of the same meaning. It is sometimes used in literary and artistic contexts to indicate the totality of patterns surrounding and enhancing the central elements of a design.

ambiguous (pronounced am-BIG-yoo-us), an adjective, and the noun *ambiguity* (pronounced am-big-YOO-ih-tee), both come from the Latin words *ambi-* (around) and *ago* (go) and have the meaning of evasion or "going around" an issue. If you say that a person's answer to a question is *ambiguous,* you mean that he has been evasive and that his answer has two or more possible meanings. He has been guilty of *ambiguity* in his reply.

ambition. The *ambitious* young man is traditionally the alert fellow who is everlastingly making the rounds—ever on the move to impress his employer with his earnestness. In these actions he is, probably unwittingly, fulfilling the original meaning of the word *ambition,* which comes from Latin. The Romans knew the type and recognized the quality that today's businessmen still admire, for they made their own word *ambitio,* and tabbed their eager-beaver politicians with it. *Ambitio* alluded to scurrying around to curry favor in the form of votes.

ambulance. Through most of mankind's wars, men injured in battle were allowed to lie where they fell until, under cover of night, doctors or medical aid men could reach them. During Napoleon's campaigns, medical men devised a quicker means of bringing help to the wounded—a light, readily portable, covered litter, fitted out with bandages, tourniquets and other first-aid equipment. This was called an *hôpital ambulant,* literally a "walking hospital." Because of the speed with which they functioned, these portable aid stations became known as *ambulances volantes* (flying travelers). When the British Army adopted the system, the name of the vehicles was shortened to *ambulance.*

Amelia is generally associated with ladies of gentle breeding, so it's something of a shock to learn that in ancient Rome it meant "industrious or laboring." The ancient Roman family of Amelius also interpreted it as meaning "eloquent or flattering," doubtless after some noted orator in the line. Nowadays the form *Emily* is more common.

ameliorate. Coming directly from the Latin *ad* (to) and *melior* (better), *ameliorate* means "to make better, to improve."

American dream. We doubt if any one person can take credit for coining this phrase. It almost certainly appeared in print as long ago as the classic study of nineteenth-century America by Alexis de Tocqueville in 1835. The phrase may well have appeared even earlier in the writings of Jefferson, Madison and others of the founding fathers. More recently, the phrase figured in the often-quoted speech by Dr. Martin Luther King, Jr., delivered in August 1963 from the steps of the Lincoln Memorial: "I have a dream . . . It is a dream deeply rooted in the *American dream* . . . I have a dream that one day in the red hills of Georgia, sons of former slaves and the sons of former slave-owners will be able to sit down together at the table of brotherhood."

American English. Why was English chosen as our language after we broke from England? Why wasn't it Indian or something else? At first glance these look like frivolous questions, but it may surprise you to know that at the time of the founding of this nation many of its leaders debated very seriously whether or not English should be carried forward as the official language of the United States, as it had been of the colonies. Never was there any serious consideration of an American Indian language as a substitute for English. For one thing, the various Indian dialects were spoken tongues. Not until Sequoyah, in the early nineteenth century, devised an alphabet for the Cherokee language, did an Indian tongue become a written language.

But the bitterness of the colonists against the British was strong enough for many to feel that they should rid themselves of the British tongue, as well as of "the tyrant's rule." So some members of the Continental Congress solemnly proposed that English be banished and Hebrew substituted. The fact that few colonists could read or speak Hebrew and that it had not been a living language for centuries sufficed to kill that suggestion. Another proposal was that Greek be adopted as our official language. That idea lasted only long enough for one patriot to remark that "it would be more convenient for us to keep the language as it is and make the English speak Greek."

What finally happened, of course, was that we continued to speak our own brand of English, which, after a century or so, became known as "American English" or "The American Language." The differences between our version and that spoken in the British Isles are great. Even the influences of movies, magazines and television have not removed many of the inconsistencies between the two versions of the language. In the end Britain and America find themselves, in George Bernard Shaw's paradoxical phrase, "one people divided by a common language."

America's Cup. After an interruption by World War II, leading yachtsmen of Great Britain, Australia, and America have been competing for a hundred-year-old mug that symbolizes international supremacy in yacht racing. Many a sportswriter and many a proofreader have had to learn that the cup at stake is not the *American* but the *America's Cup.*

To know the significance of that particular *'s,* we have to go back more than a hundred years to the time when the cup was known as the *Hundred-Guinea Cup* and was offered by the Royal Yacht Squadron as a trophy for the winner of an international yacht race. None of the proud members of the squadron dreamed that an upstart American could successfully challenge craft of the empire that had for centuries "ruled the waves." But that's just what the yacht *America* did. She sailed the broad Atlantic, bested the finest British yachts, and brought the coveted cup back with her. Then, compounding the chagrin felt by the vanquished British, the cup's new owners proudly renamed it the *America's Cup.*

The original *America,* incidentally, went on to an illustrious career after her initial triumph. During the Civil War she served as a dispatch carrier for the Confederate forces, was seized by the Union navy and sent to Annapolis, where she served as a training vessel. Refitted for racing after the war, she competed for her cup in 1870 but came in fourth. Eventually she was berthed at Annapolis and finally was broken up during the 1940s.

amethyst is a semiprecious stone, often used in necklaces, rings and the like, and purple or violet in color. But the origin of the word indicates that, for the Romans at least, it was once regarded as a very precious stone indeed. Its name comes from the Latin word *amethystus,* which in turn came from the Greek words *a* (not) and *methuskein* (to intoxicate). So generations of Greek and Roman wives thought that serving wines in goblets made of amethyst would ensure that their husbands could not become intoxicated and thus would be less likely to stray.

amicus curiae. This Latin phrase means "friend of the court." According to the general principles of Anglicizing legal Latin, one would expect the pronunciation of the second word of the phrase to be KYOOR-ee-ee; but lawyers, like everyone else, can be inconsistent. Their usual pronunciation is KYOOR-ee-eye.

amortize. There is a certain grim humor in the origin of *amortize,* a word which to many of us constitutes an uncomfortable reminder of the monthly payment on the mortgage on the house. The earliest origin of the word is found in the Latin *ad,* meanining "to," and *mors,* meaning "death." With today's long-term mortgages, this seems an apt definition. However, there is another legal meaning of the word, which goes back for centuries: "to give or sell property in mortmain." And *mortmain,* literally meaning "dead hand," refers to the acquisition or ownership of property by a corporation, such as a school or religious organization, which will hold it in perpetuity.

ampersand. The sign & is called the *ampersand.* It comes from the practice of British schoolchildren, when reciting the alphabet, of giving all twenty-six letters plus the & sign, which they describe thus: "X, Y, Zed and per se [by itself] and." The last phrase was gradually slurred into *ampersand.* The symbol is a corruption of *et,* the Latin word for "and." This is most clearly apparent in the italic version of &, where the *e* and the cross-line of the *t* may be clearly seen.

anachronism, from Greek *ana,* "backward," and *kronos,* "time," refers to the depiction of something as existing at a time when it did not. The most celebrated *anachronisms* are the celebrated "striking clocks" in Shakespeare's *Julius Caesar.* Striking clocks were not invented until some fourteen centuries after Caesar was assassinated.

Anadama bread. A charming story came to light as the result of a query from David W. Scott of Sewickley, Pennsylvania. He wrote:

From out of the misty past, recalling my youth in New England, I am haunted by an old yarn. It concerned a gruff sea captain who invariably, albeit benignly, referred to his wife as "Anna, damn 'er." Among her many attributes Anna had the knack of baking bread that would not mold or spoil for long periods. For this she was widely known and admired by crews who had no way of getting fresh supplies.

It was natural for the men to pick up the skipper's phrase, and it became a byword: "Anna damn 'er's bread." In fact, years after she had gone to her reward, a commercial bakery produced the product under the trade name "Annadammer" or maybe "Annadama." An interesting sidelight to this story is the epitaph the captain had cut on her tombstone: "Anna was a lovely bride, but Anna, damn 'er, up and died."

This has been bugging me for at least forty years, and I come to you only after exhausting every reference at my disposal. Can you shed light? Is it fact or fancy?

We went through dozens of reference books without success until, with a gleam in her eye, Mary said, "How about *The American Heritage Cookbook?*" And there we found a different story—and a recipe. Here is the *American Heritage* version: "One story that was repeated in Massachusetts in the 19th century was of a fisherman who became enraged at his wife. All she gave him for dinner was corn meal and molasses—day after day. One night he tossed flour and yeast into the corn meal and molasses, put it all into the oven and sat down to eat a loaf of bread that had no name, mumbling 'Anna, damn her!' " At least this version confirms the relationship of *Anadama* (preferred spelling) *bread* to seafaring men and their wives.

an Alphonse and Gaston comes from an old comic strip featuring two Frenchmen who tried to outdo each other in politeness. Each strip would end with them saying to each other: "After you, my dear Alphonse!" "No, after you, my dear Gaston!" When a sportscaster reports that two players have "pulled *an Alphonse and Gaston*" he is referring to a play in which two outfielders running to catch the same fly each pull back to let the other make the play—with the result that the ball falls safe between them.

anathema is a word that has changed very considerably in meaning down through the centuries. Originally it meant anything devoted to the gods, coming as it does from the Greek word of the same spelling meaning a votive offering. In time, however, its meaning changed and came to mean only something devoted to an accursed purpose, so that now *anathema* means either a formal ecclesiastical ban, a strong denunciation or a person so cursed. "She's *anathema* to me."

anemophobia. Derived from the Greek *anemos* (the wind) and *phobos* (fear), *anemophobia* is the dread of hurricanes and cyclones.

angel. A financial backer of a theatrical production, without whom the show could not be opened, has long been known as an *angel.* A fascinating, albeit somewhat incredible, theory of the origin of the term is that the original *angel* was named Luis de Santangel, and he was the one who *really* put up the money for Christopher Columbus's voyage to America. It seems that Queen Isabella and King Ferdinand stalled so long that Columbus took de Santangel's money and left, allowing the Queen to keep her jewels. So to the many questions as to whether Columbus really did discover America, we can add the question of who paid for the trip.

Angry Young Men. During the 1950s a group of British writers, notable chiefly for their iconoclastic rebellion against the mores of the time, earned for themselves this epithet. It derives from the title of a play by one of the leaders of the group, John Osborne: *Look Back in Anger.*

animosity (pronounced an-ih-MOSS-ih-tee) is intense dislike, amounting sometimes to open hostility. It comes from the Latin word *animus,* which originally meant "soul or driving force" and came in time to mean "passion." Nowadays only one kind of passion is represented in *animosity*—the passion of hatred.

ankh. Pronounced like "tank" without the *t, ankh* is an ancient Egyptian symbol of life, a cross with a loop at the top.

annex is taken directly from the Latin *annexum*—that which is tied or bound to something else. Readers have queried as to whether the proper plural might not be *annexa.* But since we use English—not Latin—as our method of communication, there seems to be no justification in using the Latin plural, *annexa,* in place of the English form *annexes.*

Annie Oakley. We have long known the theatrical term *Annie Oakley,* for a free ticket. It is so called because it has a hole punched in it, to ensure that it cannot be traded for cash at the box office. The allusion is to the great sharpshooter of the old Buffalo Bill Wild West shows. She also had another item of cardboard named after her—one that the general public could not be aware of. In the jargon of circuses and carnivals, meal tickets are also called *Annie Oakleys,* because a hole is punched whenever a meal is eaten. So as the meal ticket is used up, it gradually resembles more and more one of the cards that were perforated by Annie in her sharpshooting act.

John Rochford of Washington, D.C., tells us of another use of this term. "I am a writer/editor in the U.S. Naval Oceanographic Office," he writes. "For intra-office correspondence a large manila envelope is used. It has two columns for listing senders and recipients. By crossing out the last entry, the envelope can be used until it falls apart or all the blank spaces are used. Two sets of holes are punched in the envelope so that one can see if it's empty and so available for use and also to ensure that it's not thrown away while there is still something in it. These envelopes are almost universlly known as *Annie Oakleys.* I don't know if this informal term is unique to our office. I suspect it's widely used in the federal government, but I have never heard it used in private industry."

annuit coeptis is the motto on the Great Seal of the United States, and the quickest place to find it—right under your nose—is on the back of any dollar bill. It means "He [God] has favored our undertakings" and comes from the *Aeneid* of Vergil, Book 9, line 625. A similar thought appears in Vergil's *Georgics* (Book 1, line 40): *"Audacibus annue coeptis,"* meaning "Be favorable to bold beginnings."

anodyne. All those animated television commercials showing hammers pounding away inside your head are really trying to sell you on the *anodyne* properties which various competing aspirin compounds are claimed to have. Usually the announcer talks of "pain-killing ingredients"—which is exactly what *anodynes* are. The word is made up of the Greek *an-* (without) and *odynē* (pain). It can be used either as an adjective or as a noun.

anomie is an elegant word for alienation. It's a word popular with sociologists to describe the feelings of one who has been rejected by society, whether because of age or antisocial behavior.

anonymous. Our unknown friend "Mr. Anonymous" goes all the way back to ancient Greece, where the word *anonumos,* from *an,* "without," and *onoma,* "name," was used as the by-line for a work whose author was unknown.

another Richmond in his field. The expression comes from Shakespeare's *Richard III.* The King, speaking of Henry of Richmond, who later became Henry VII, says: "I think there be six Richmonds in the field; Five have I slain today, instead of him—A horse! a horse! my kingdom for a horse!" The meaning is that still another, and unexpected, opponent has turned up to do battle.

antebellum. *Ante* means "before" in Latin and *bellum* is the Latin word for "war." So *antebellum* simply means "before the war." It is used in the United States only in reference to the Civil War. However, the new Supplement to the *Oxford English Dictionary* reports that in the United Kingdom *antebellum* is also used in connection with the South African War of 1899–1902 (what we call the Boer War) and both World Wars, which the British simply label "The War of 1914–1918" and "The War of 1939–1945."

anticlimax. When a series of statements seemingly building to a climax has the effect spoiled by a final item of little importance, the last item is an *anticlimax.* Often an *anticlimax* is unintentional. Fowler, in *Modern English Usage,* cites a case of this sort: "The rest of all the acts of Asa and the cities which he built, are they not written in the books of the chronicles of the kings of Judah? Nevertheless in the time of his old age he was diseased in his feet." The late Monty Woolley, star of *The Man Who Came to Dinner* and one-time teacher of theater at Yale, once remarked that the classic American *anticlimax* is: "For God, for country and for Yale."

antidisestablishmentarianism. This word's chief claim to fame is the legend that it is the longest word in the English language. There are several of greater length, but we are concerned here with the origin of the word. The efforts of Prime Minister Gladstone of England to effect the *disestablishment* of the Church of Ireland (that is, to separate it from the Church of England) led to the coinage of the word. Gladstone referred to opponents of his measure as believers in *antidisestablishmentarianism.* Whether awed by the label or impressed by his logic, they finally capitulated, and Gladstone's proposals carried.

antimacassar. A century ago, long before today's greaseless hair tonics had been devised, it was the fashion for dandies to slick down their locks with fragrant pomades and oils, the better to charm their fair ladies. One of the favorite lotions contained a large percentage of macassar oil. In England, indeed, the word "Macassar" was trademarked as the name of a proprietary brand of hair oil. Here enters the practicality of women. Wishing neither to blight the vanity of their gentlemen callers nor to spend hours trying to remove hair oil from their upholstered furniture, they devised attractive yet practical lace coverlets and pinned them on the furniture to absorb the Macassar oil. Hence the name, *anti-* (against) *Macassar.*

any man who hates dogs and small children can't be all bad was a remark made *about* W. C. Fields, not by him, as most people think. The occasion was a testimonial banquet in Hollywood given by the Friars Club in 1938 to honor Fields's fortieth anniversary in show business. The evening wore on, with speaker after speaker outdoing one another in praise for the great Fields. The late H. Allen Smith, reporting the scene, said: "Orators like Eddie Cantor and Georgie Jessel stood up and let the tears flow down their cheeks until it was almost necessary to club them to the floor to stop them." Finally, at about two in the morning, the master of ceremonies insisted on calling one more speaker. The crowd, including Fields, groaned because the speaker was referred to as a Ph.D. and they expected some long, dull doctoral dissertation on Humor in the Twentieth Century. Instead the speaker, Dr. Leo C. Rosten, gave a one-sentence speech: "It is my opinion that any man who hates dogs and little children can't be *all* bad." It brought down the house.

Rosten later wrote: "It was one of those happy 'ad libs' God sends you. I didn't have the faintest inkling that I would be called upon to make any remarks, and those I made were uttered in an almost total daze."

A-O.K. was invented by a NASA public relations officer, Colonel "Shorty" Powers. The occasion was our first suborbital flight in May 1961 and the astronaut involved was Alan Shepard. But Powers, relaying to newsmen and the radio audience what he heard from Shepard, mistook a simple "O.K." for *A-O.K.* He fancied the sound of the term so much that he repeated it several times and it caught on with newspaper headline writers, if not with the astronauts themselves. According to our best information, no astronaut ever used the term and it has been notably absent from radio and TV reports of subsequent space flights.

Apache. Pronounced uh-PACH-ee in its American use, this is the name of a famous tribe of nomadic Southwestern American Indians. Its most famous chief was probably Geronimo (1829–1909), whose name is still used as a war cry by U.S. paratroopers when jumping from their planes. For reasons unknown, *apache* (pronounced ah-PASH) had a great vogue in France in the early years of this century, when the *"apache* dance," a sinuous and eventually quite violent cabaret dance, was popular. The term was also applied to members of the Parisian underworld, none of them remotely resembling the American Indians of the same name.

apartheid (pronounced uh-PART-hite) is a South African Dutch word descriptive of the policy of segregation of white and colored races promulgated in the Union of South Africa. It is derived from two Dutch words, *apart* and *heid* (hood). Thus it literally means the state of being apart or segregated. The first recorded appearance of the word in print was in 1949 and to date its use seems to have been limited to that government's policy of segregation. It has not, we believe, been used as yet in reference to segregation in any other part of the world.

Aphrodite/aphrodisiac. The goddess Aphrodite was and remains a symbol of feminine beauty, indeed the goddess of beauty. She gets her name from the Greek *aphros* (foam), from the legend that she sprang from the sea's foam. From her name we also take the word *aphrodisiac* to describe drugs or other substances that heighten one's amatory desires.

apocryphal/Apocrypha. *Apocryphal* (pronounced uh-POK-ruh-ful) is an adjective derived from the Greek words *apo* (from) and *kryptein* (to hide). Thus it meant originally "hidden from," but today it means "of doubtful authenticity" or even counterfeit. The most famous *apocryphal* writings are the fourteen books of the Septuagint Bible which were not found in the Hebrew Old Testament. Regarded by some scholars as of doubtful authenticity, they are called the *Apocrypha.*

a posteriori/a priori. Here are two Latin phrases still much in use. An *a posteriori* finding is one that is deduced after the fact. If one sees footprints on freshly fallen snow, one may deduce that a person has recently passed. An *a priori* assumption is one based upon the advance evaluation of the facts in hand. Thus one could have concluded on the basis of statistical evidence in hand that the New York Mets baseball team of 1969 could not possibly win their league's pennant, let alone the world championship. That conclusion, obviously, was false—and that's why, if you must jump to conclusions, it's much wiser to do it *a posteriori* than *a priori.*

apothecary. Until the turn of the century—and still in England today—the *apothecary* shop or, as the British have it, *chemist's,* was a place where medicines alone were sold. A complete revolution has occurred since those simple days and today it sometimes appears that medicines are the least important products dispensed by the *apothecary.* Many a wail has been heard from those purists who want things always to remain as they were. Many are the complaints that the drugstore should sell drugs, not radios, scrambled eggs and all the rest. But from the standpoint of language alone, there's not much to support this view. For the *apothecary* shop originally was simply a warehouse—dispensing a wide variety of wares. That's the meaning of the Greek word *apothēkē,* from which our word comes. In fact, it wasn't until the seventeenth century that Britain's druggists and grocers arrived at an agreement whereby the *apothecaries* would sell only drugs and the grocers only food, household supplies and the like. If such a division of spoils were agreed upon today, the government would certainly start a restraint of trade action. However, as anyone who has seen aspirin and toothpaste in supermarkets and detergents in the *apothecary* shop well knows, there's no limit to the competition between America's grocers and druggists. They both run smartly styled warehouses.

Appalachia. The use of *Appalachia* in referring to the major mountain system in the eastern part of the United States dates back to the late nineteenth century. But there's a lot more to the story than that. In his fascinating book *American Place Names,* George Stewart tells us that the Spanish explorer Cabeza de Vaca recorded "Apalachen" as an Indian name for a province, and the word got on various maps and charts as a vague name for the mountainous interior of the country. The English then adopted the name, changing its spelling to "Appalachian," and applied it to the southern part of the range. By the nineteenth century, mapmakers had extended it to apply to the entire range from southern Quebec to central Alabama. Then, late in the century, scholars mistakenly decided that because "Appalachian," ended with an *n,* it was an adjective—although, as we have seen, it was spelled with an *n* from the very beginning. So they arbitrarily lopped off the *n,* creating *Appalachia.*

Appaloosa. The *Appaloosa* is a very rugged saddle horse bred in the western United States from Spanish stock. It has a spotted hide and probably gets its name from the Palouse Indians.

apparel, now used to mean almost any kind of clothing, originally meant elegant embellishments of wearing apparel. Indeed, it once meant the fancy devices added to adorn ecclesiastical vestments. Its origin is in the Latin *ad* (toward) and *parare* (prepare or make ready).

apple of one's eye. The first *apple of the eye* was the pupil, which in ancient days was thought to be a round object similar to the apple. As recently as Anglo-Saxon times, the same word, *aeppel,* meant both "eye" and "apple." It goes without saying that the pupil of one's eye is very precious indeed —and that's how the expression *the apple of one's eye* came to mean something greatly treasured.

apple-pie order has little to do with the culinary arts. It is, in fact, a corruption of the French phrase *nappe plié,* meaning "folded linen." It is applied to dinner napkins, and perhaps the transition from the dining room to the kitchen is not so very far fetched, after all. The expression *apple-pie bed,* meaning one in which prankish bunkmates have folded the sheets so that a person cannot stretch his legs full length, likewise comes from this French phrase.

One widely held theory is that *apple-pie order* comes to us from our historic past, from the early days of New England. One of the colonial housewives was in the habit of baking seven pies ahead for the new week just starting. When she had her pies all baked and cooled, she then placed them on her pantry shelves just so: the pie that was to be eaten on Monday was set on the first shelf, the one for Tuesday right next to it, and so on. Being a meticulous housekeeper, she always checked to make sure they were lined up just right, hence the phrase *apple-pie order.* That's a nice little story and we don't suppose it will do anyone any harm to believe it. The only trouble is that there isn't a shred of truth in it, since the one point that all authorities agree on is that the term *apple-pie order* was commonly used in England long before it appeared in this country. And anyway, wouldn't that seventh pie have been pretty stale after sitting on the shelf for a week?

appreciate. Originally *appreciate* meant "to estimate the quality or worth of something." That's a meaning it still has today, of course, in such a sentence as "Father certainly *appreciates* fine chamber music." But this basic meaning (from the Latin *appretiare,* "to value") has long since been broadened to include the idea of being grateful for favors or services rendered. So when the master of ceremonies says, "We certainly *appreciate* your being here to talk to us tonight," he is not violating standards of proper usage. *Appreciate* has still another, rather special meaning: "to increase in value." In this sense it is the opposite of *depreciate.*

après moi le déluge means literally "After me, the flood." The popularity of the phrase stems from its use by Madame de Pompadour, celebrated beauty and intimate of King Louis XV of France. The French court at the time was famed for its lavish and wasteful extravagances. When Pompadour, whose philosophy was "Live for the minute—who cares what happens when we're gone?" was reproved for these excesses, she replied, *"Après nous le déluge."*

April. The fourth month of the year takes its name from the Latin *aprilis,* which may well mean "the month of Venus." It is believed that this word came into Latin by way of the Etruscan *apru* from the Greek *Aphro,* a shortened form of Aphrodite. An earlier theory, that April came from *aperire,* "to open," and referred to the budding of trees and flowers, is now discounted by scholars.

April Fool's Day is the day for childish pranks, the day when the gullible and unwary are fair game for the inventive and enterprising among us. There seem to be almost as many theories about the origin of All Fool's Day, as the British call it, as there are pranks to be played. One account traces it back to Roman mythology. It seems that Proserpina, daughter of Ceres, the goddess of agriculture, was playing happily in the Elysian Fields and had just plucked a lapful of daffodils when she was seized by Pluto, king of Hades, and carried off to rule as his queen. Her mother heard the echo of her screams and went in search of Proserpina, but it was a fruitless errand. Thus, say some, began the custom of sending gullible people on fools' errands.

Perhaps the soundest theory of the day's origin traces it back to the time when the Gregorian calendar (the one we now use) replaced the Julian calendar, which had been in use since Roman times. During the Middle Ages most Christian countries celebrated the start of the new year with a festival beginning March 25 and ending April 1. Traditionally, the last day of this period was devoted to the bearing of gifts to one's friends and neighbors. When the Gregorian calendar was finally adopted by England in 1752, New Year's Day was moved back to January 1. But some practical jokers continued to make calls and give mock gifts on April 1 and thus, so the story goes, April Fool's Day was born.

The Scots have an amusing phrase to describe the chap sent to fetch a left-handed monkey wrench or a can of cold steam. He's said to be "hunting the gowk"—and "gowk" is the cuckoo bird. In France the victim of such pranks is called *poisson d'Avril* (fish of April). The April fish is newly hatched and thus naïve and easily trapped.

apron is one of those words that, somewhere along the way, either lost or gained an *n* through merging with *a* or *an*. The original *apron* was *napperon* in Old French, becoming *napron* in Middle English. Through faulty separation of *a napron,* we now have *an apron.*

apron-string tenure. When Governor George Wallace of Alabama, prohibited by law from succeeding himself for another term, named his wife as candidate for the office, he was making a bid for a kind of *apron-string tenure.* Here the *apron string* is that of a wife—not of a mother—and *apron-string tenure* is the right to hold property or office because of one's wife. While Wallace did not actually hold the office, he made it clear that he intended to continue to hold the authority through his wife.

aqua, when used as the name of a color, is a shortened form of "aquamarine" and means, in the words of *Webster,* a "color, green-blue in hue, of low saturation and medium brilliance."

aquanaut. Man's unceasing struggle to extend the limits of his habitation is reflected in *aquanaut,* a name for one who pursues the scientific study of man's capacity for living and working under water by spending long periods beneath the sea in a specially designed steel vessel, occasionally venturing outside by using scuba gear. *Aquanaut* was coined from the Latin *aqua,* "water," and Greek *nautes,* "sailor."

arachnid is a technical term for a large order of invertebrates which includes spiders and scorpions, but it has a charmingly feminine origin in Greek mythology. Minerva, the daughter of Jupiter, was goddess of all the useful and ornamental arts, including spinning, weaving and needlework. A princess of the ancient maritime province of Lydia who was named Arachne became so renowned in the arts of spinning and weaving that she decided to challenge Minerva to a weaving contest. The goddess, angered and insulted, disguised herself as an old woman and appeared before Arachne to demand that she apologize to the goddess. On Arachne's refusal, Minerva disclosed her identity and the contest began. Minerva's canvas included many scenes involving the gods and goddesses, some of them meant as warnings of displeasure with criticism of the immortals. Arachne failed to heed the warnings and so infuriated Minerva that the goddess destroyed Arachne's weaving. Finally filled with remorse, Arachne hanged herself, and as she hung suspended, the goddess changed her into a spider.

Arah is a name from the Bible (I Chronicles 7:39), where it appears as the name of one of the sons of Ulla—"heads of their father's house, choice and mighty men of valor." The feminine form is commonly spelled *Ara* and can mean either "eagle heroine" or "fair altar," depending on whether a Teutonic or Latin source is accepted.

arbitrary is a rather difficult word to pin down, since synonyms for it in standard dictionaries run the gamut from "absolute" and "autocratic" to "capricious" and "uncertain." An *arbiter,* of course, is one who has the authority to decide between two conflicting points of view. Thus there is a discretionary element in any *arbitrary* decision. But the fact that the decision is final and conclusive accounts for the "absolute" element in the word's meaning. Hence, *arbitrary* in current usage has come to mean "conclusive but based on the judgment or whim of an individual."

arcane (pronounced ar-KANE) is derived from the Latin word *arcanum,* which meant anything hidden from the masses of men, especially any of the great secrets of nature. In medieval times alchemists tried to discover such great *arcana* as the means by which base metals could be transformed into gold.

argy-bargy is a Scottish term for an argument—especially a drawn-out quarrel.

Arlene is one of various feminine variants—*Arleen, Arlana, Arline* and *Arlina* are others—of the Celtic name *Arlen,* meaning "a pledge." The widespread popularity of the name in its various spellings is probably due to the tremendous success scored by the heroine Arline of Balfe's nineteenth-century opera *The Bohemian Girl*—from which, incidentally, comes the famous song "I Dreamt I Dwelt in Marble Halls."

armada. The original *armada* was the Spanish Armada, sent by King Philip II to attack England in 1588. It was considered to be the world's most powerful attack force, but it was soundly defeated by the British fleet, with

Sir Francis Drake among its commanders. The Spanish ships fled all the way up the coast, around the tip of Scotland and down the west coast of Ireland. Along the way several ships were wrecked and the sailors took refuge on the shore. Some of those Spanish sailors who landed in Ireland and Wales were Moors, conscripted into the service of the Spanish king. And that is how our name Morris became so common in Wales and Ireland. It's simply a centuries-old version of "Moorish."

Armageddon. Originally a combination of the Hebrew word *har* (mountain) and *Megiddon* (the plain where decisive battles traditionally were fought), *Armageddon* appears in the Bible (Revelations 16:16) as the scene of the final catastrophic battle between the forces of good and evil. "And there fell upon men a great rain out of heaven . . . and there were thunder and lightnings . . . and there was a great earthquake, such as was not since men were upon the earth, so mighty an earthquake and so great . . . and every island fled away and the mountains were not found."

Arms, as used in the names of many apartment buildings, goes back to the ancient British country inns, which often took their names from the name of the chief member of local nobility and displayed his coat of arms on the signpost. Thus, if the local seigneur was Lord Hammersmith, the inn might well call itself Hammersmith Arms. The practice of naming apartment houses in this fashion began in the early 1900s and it was especially popular in the various boroughs of New York. According to research reported by H. L. Mencken in *The American Language* about apartment listings in the 1947 telephone directories of Manhattan, the Bronx, Queens, Brooklyn and Staten Island: "the names favor a few banal patterns. Something between a quarter and a third contain the word 'Arms' or 'Court' and a great many of the rest include 'Hall,' 'Manor,' 'Towers' and the like. In them Americans are seen turning to British life for connotations of prestige and security."

Army (Navy/Air Force) brat. We first heard the expression during the 1930s at Annapolis—as *Navy brat,* of course. At the time it seemed to be limited to the offspring of officers, but we gather that with the vast expansion of the services and the increased number of married people in the enlisted ranks, it may well have been expanded to include all the offspring of members of the armed services. A *brat* is, of course, a spoiled child, usually unbearably conceited and both impudent and unruly. It goes without saying that many if not most of the offspring of servicemen do not deserve such a label. However, in the years between the two world wars the officer corps of the Navy, Army and Marines were a very clannish lot who reared their children to believe that they were something very special. Quite possibly they were, but our experience, as civilians meeting *Navy brats,* was that the label seemed to fit most of them rather well.

arraign/arrange. *Arraign* (pronounced uh-RAYN) comes from the Latin *ad* (to) and *ratio* (judgment) and means "the summoning before the bar of justice of a person accused of crime." At the *arraignment* (uh-RAYN-ment) a prisoner may plead guilty or not guilty. *Arrange* comes from the old French word *arangier* and literally means "to place in order or rank." This meaning still is common as in such phrases as "to *arrange* flowers." So although *arraign* and *arrange* look alike, their meanings differ and their origins are totally unrelated.

Ars Gratia Artis, "Art for Art's Sake," was for many years the slogan of the mighty Metro-Goldwyn-Mayer motion picture company, appearing with Leo the Lion to introduce each of their pictures. Like many other aspects of the movie business, this was essentially phony because MGM was always more interested in money than in art. Even the Latin involved is inaccurate. It should have read *Ars Artis Gratia.* The alteration of the elements was probably the work of an art director, more interested in balance and symmetry than accuracy.

artesian well gets its name from Artois, formerly a province in northern France, where such wells were first drilled. Actually the spelling *artesian* comes from the Old French name of the province, Arteis. An *artesian well* is one which is drilled through one or more impermeable strata until water or oil is reached, whereupon the fluid spurts up spontaneously, forced by underground pressure.

artichoke. Efforts to eat the entire leaf of an *artichoke,* rather than just the tender part, have led in the past to such folk etymology as: "You have to expect a choke in *artichoke,* for there's where the name came from." However, there is no connection between choking and the vegetable. The first *artichokes* were Arabian and called *al-kharshuf*—which, said aloud, is more like a sneeze than a choke. The Italians made this word into *articiocco,* from which comes our *artichoke.* In present-day Italy the *artichoke* is known by the name *carciofo.* Incidentally, the *artichoke* is technically an herb, not a vegetable, but it is cooked and served as a vegetable.

ascent to Parnassus. Mount Parnassus, now called Liákoura, was regarded as sacred to Apollo, handsomest of the gods and the god of the sun, prophecy, music, poetry and medicine. So when one makes the *ascent to Parnassus* or takes the road to Parnassus, one is embarking on a career in the arts, usually as poet or musician.

ascetic/asceticism/aestheticism. *Ascetic* (pronounced uh-SET-ik) is an adjective meaning "self-denying, rigorous and austere." Interestingly enough, it came from the Greek word *askein,* meaning "exercise," and originally referred to the rigorous self-denial practiced by an athlete when in training. In the early days of the church, an *ascetic* was a person who removed himself from all worldly temptations and devoted himself to a life of contemplation and austerity. The religious doctrine followed by those sects who hold that a closer approach to divine grace is achieved by self-denial and abstinence from worldly things is called *asceticism. Asceticism* (pronounced uh-SET-uh-siz'm) should not be confused with *aestheticism* (sometimes spelled *estheticism*), which means "devotion to beauty and good taste in the arts." *Aestheticism* (pronounced es-THET-uh-siz'm) comes from the Greek *aisthetikos,* meaning "sensitive," and an *aesthetic* person is one whom we consider especially sensitive in matters of beauty and art.

ascob is a word you might run into in dog-breeding circles. It is an acronym meaning "assorted colors other than black"—as in "an *ascob* spaniel."

as good as George-a-Greene is said of a person who determinedly does his duty, regardless of difficulty or consequences. George-a-Greene was the mythical poundkeeper of Wakefield in *Tales of Robin Hood,* who, when Robin Hood, Little John and Will Scarlett attempted to "commit a trespass" in his village, confronted them single-handedly.

Ashes. *The Ashes* is the mythical prize for which cricket teams from England and Australia compete annually in the famous test matches. The story goes that a British sporting publication, on the occasion of Australia's triumph in 1882, wrote a farewell salute to British cricket and noted that its body would be cremated and the ashes shipped Down Under.

Ashmolean. When Frank Loesser wrote "The New Ashmolean Marching Society" for the musical show *Where's Charlie?* he may or may not have been aware that behind that wonderful word *Ashmolean* there lurked a real person, Elias Ashmole (1617–1692), who created the Ashmolean Museum, designed and built by Sir Christopher Wren and famed as the first museum of "curiosities" in all England. He gave it to Oxford University and it has now been supplanted by a "New" Ashmolean Museum and includes the Arundel (or "Oxford") marbles—which have nothing to do with what you and we think of as marbles but are chiefly items of Greek and Cretan statuary merrily plundered from their homelands by the British while their ascendancy in the Mediterranean went unchallenged.

ask not what your country can do for you. At the Warren G. Harding home in Marion, Ohio, is a speech in what is labeled Harding's own handwriting. For all to read, since it is under a magnifying glass, is the phrase "think not what your country can do for you . . ." and so on.

When President John F. Kennedy said: "And so, my fellow Americans, ask not what your country can do for you; ask what you can do for your country," he was echoing a thought that had occurred to other political figures, Harding among them. In a speech before the Republican National Convention in 1916, Harding said: "In the great fulfillment we must have a citizenship less concerned about what the government can do for it and more anxious about what it can do for the nation."

It's not likely that Kennedy took his inspiration from Harding, however. Arthur M. Schlesinger in *A Thousand Days* noted that "the thought had lain in Kennedy's mind for a long time. As far back as 1945 he had noted down in a looseleaf notebook a quotation from Rousseau: 'As soon as any man says of the affairs of the state, What does it matter to me? the state may be given up as lost.' " It's more probable that Kennedy may have drawn his inspiration from Oliver Wendell Holmes, Jr. Many years earlier Holmes had said: "It is now the moment when we pause to recall what our country has done for each of us and to ask ourselves what we can do for our country in return."

as queer as Dick's hatband. The *Dick* in this old expression is Richard Cromwell, son of the lord protector, Oliver Cromwell, who ruled England from 1653 to 1658. By all accounts, Richard was an amiable chap but totally ineffectual as a leader. After his father's death he took over his title, but lasted less than a year before he was forced to abdicate. The meaning of the phrase *as queer as Dick's hatband* is that few things have been more ridiculous than the elevation and abdication of Richard Cromwell, *hatband* being a satirical reference to his crown. Richard was also mocked as "Tumbledown Dick."

assassination. Simply put, an *assassination* is always a murder, but a murder need not be an *assassination.* The broader term is "murder," taking another person's life in a criminal fashion. It is usually premeditated and may result from any of hundreds of motives, though revenge and money are probably the most common. An *assassination* is the deliberate murder of a person, usually but not always a figure of importance, for political motives. Often the *assassin,* as in the case of John Wilkes Booth, thinks he is killing a tyrant and that the well-being of the nation itself depends upon his success in the effort. The *assassin* of Lincoln was, as such persons often are, a fanatic. It's interesting to note that *assassin* itself comes from the name of a secret band of fanatics who were called *hashashin* because they fired up their fanaticism by eating or smoking hashish before making their attacks. And hashish is none other than dried hemp, which, under the name *marijuana* and such nicknames as *pot, reefers* and *muggles,* is still very much with us today.

ass waggeth his ears/ass-eared. When an unknowledgeable man expounds at great length on a subject about which he knows little, the old proverb *The ass waggeth his ears* applies. The ass is no great student of music, but when he hears it he wiggles his ears as if in appreciation. The notion that an ass has no taste for music goes back to ancient times. In the tales of mythology, Apollo and Pan had a contest to determine which was the better musician and chose Midas as the judge. Midas decided in favor of Pan; and Apollo, in anger and disgust, changed Midas's ears to those of an ass. Hence the phrase *ass-eared* for one who has no ear for music.

asterisk comes not from the aster flower but from the Greek word which gave both of them their names: *aster* for "star." It is, obviously, a starlike sign, just as the aster flower has a starlike pattern. The *asterisk* (*) is used chiefly in printing to indicate a reference to a footnote.

as the crow flies means the shortest distance between two points. The crow flies straight to its destination.

astronaut/cosmonaut. Our word *astronaut,* from the Greek words *astron* (star) and *nautes* (sailor or seaman), aptly labels a person who sails among the stars. But the stars are not the whole of our cosmos (from the Greek *kosmos,* meaning "universe"). So it would seem that *cosmonaut* is more all-encompassing than *astronaut.* Perhaps *cosmonaut* was chosen by the Russians with a thought to its propaganda implications, since cosmos implies not merely the universe but specifically a universe conceived as an orderly, harmonious system.

at first blush. In this phrase *blush* means merely "glance," a sense which was common enough three centuries ago but now survives only in this one expression. The other *blush,* meaning "to flush crimson," records varying stages of embarrassment. Keats put it rather neatly: "There's a *blush* for won't, and a *blush* for shan't and a *blush* for having done it."

at sixes and sevens. The expression *"everything is at sixes and sevens"* originated in a dice game so ancient that it is reported by Chaucer in the *Canterbury Tales.* We're not gamblers, but we're told that in today's game of craps, *making eleven*—rolling a six and a five—is very hard indeed. Apparently the dice used by the Canterbury pilgrims had numbers somewhat higher than those in use today. At any rate, it was possible to attempt to roll for a six and a seven. This was known to be a very hard point to make and was attempted only by headstrong or careless players. So the present-day meaning of *at sixes and sevens*—"all disorder and confusion" —may have come from the fact that only a confused or disorganized person would roll for this point.

Attic salt. *Attic* in this phrase is not the storage place at the top of a house; it refers to Attica, the state of ancient Greece whose capital was Athens. In both Latin and Greek, *salt* was used as a term for "wit." Since the men of Athens were noted for their wit and ability to express themselves in elegant fashion, such wit is known as *Attic salt.*

au courant (pronounced oh koo-RONǴ) is a French phrase which means literally "with the current." It is applied to a person who is up to date and fully informed in matters of current events.

auction. As most of us who have succumbed to the tantalizing lure of *auctions* well know, the element that is essential to their charm is the steadily increasing level of price of the object being auctioned. The ever-present hope is that you can bid the item in before the price increases too much. So it's not surprising to learn that the word *auction* itself comes from a Latin verb, *augere,* meaning "to increase." Indeed, the Romans themselves held public sales which bore the label *auctio.*

August. The eighth month of the year takes its name from Augustus Caesar (*Augustus mensis* in Latin).

auld lang syne is a Scottish term meaning literally "old long since." Freely translated, it means "long ago" and thus it lends itself with singular appropriateness to New Year's Eve, when we review the joys and sorrows of the past and prepare to face the challenge of the year to come. Incidentally, the last word should be pronounced as spelled *(syne)*, not, as all too often it is, as if it were spelled "zyne."

auspices. "Under the *auspices*" means "under the protection or under the patronage of." The significance of the phrase in today's use is that the organization under whose *auspices* an affair is held usually guarantees to sell tickets, arrange the entertainment and otherwise guarantee the success of the show. It was not always thus. In ancient Roman days, soothsayers —roughly the equivalent of today's poll-takers—used to predict the future by studying the flight of birds through the sky. The direction they took would determine the forecast for the future. In battle only the commander in chief was allowed to determine the portents for the future. If an underling achieved victory, he did it under the *auspices* of the chief. *Auspices* comes from two Latin words: *avis* (bird) and *spicere* (to see). When the seers found the omens favorable to your mission, you were "under good *auspices.*"

automation. The general principle of using machines to do jobs once handled by manpower seems to be the central characteristic of automation. Now, then, who invented this obviously very important word? Most dictionaries say only that it is made up of "automat" plus "ion"—which leaves one precisely nowhere. Many sources credit this word to John Diebold, one of the nation's foremost management consultants, an authority on the cybernetic revolution of which *automation* is a result and author of two books on the subject. The first, *Automation, the Advent of the Automatic Factory,* was published in 1952 and undoubtedly did much to popularize the word. However, R. S. Fetters, writing in the *Saturday Review,* challenges Diebold's claim to invention of the word. He reports that D. S. Harder, a vice-president of the Ford Motor Company, was the actual creator. He is reported to have first used the word in 1936, when in the employ of General Motors, and defined it as "the automatic handling of parts between progressive production processes."

autopsy/biopsy. Both *autopsy* and *biopsy* refer to the close examination, often by microscope, of body tissues. There are, however, two chief points of difference. First, an *autopsy* is performed on dead tissue, while a *biopsy* is performed on living tissue. Second, the purpose of the *autopsy* is to determine the cause of death, while the *biopsy* is a clinical and diagnostic examination whose chief purpose is to help determine the proper treatment for a diseased organ. Both words are derived from the Greek root *opsis,* meaning "sight." The prefix *auto* is from the Greek *autos* (self). Thus an *autopsy* is literally "a seeing for oneself." The combining form *bio* in *biopsy* is from the Greek *bios* (life), so that a *biopsy* is literally a "looking at" or study of living flesh.

avant-garde. A literal translation of the French words making up *avant-garde* would be "before the guard." The English modification of it is "vanguard," meaning a group in the leading position in any field. Today the original French phrase is used to designate leaders in political and intellectual fields. In this use it also usually connotes a deviation from the normal pattern, as in the case of *avant-garde* poetry, *avant-garde* art and so on.

awful. The first meaning of *awful* is not "bad" or "ugly," as many people think. It is "inspiring awe or reverence." Thought of in this way, there is nothing inconsistent in the expression "awfully good." However, it has come to be accepted as a colloquial expression simply meaning "very good" or "extremely good." You will find it fairly common even in the speech of literate and well-educated people.

ax to grind. The creation of this phrase is attributed to Benjamin Franklin, who used it in an article entitled "Too Much for Your Whistle." It means a private or selfish motive behind a request or action—something which is not obvious at first glance. The story is that of a man who had an ax which needed to be sharpened. He pretended to young Franklin that he didn't know how a grindstone worked and asked Franklin to show him. Many turns of the handle later Franklin was weary, the ax was beautifully sharp and the man, having gained his objective, only jeered at Franklin for having been hoodwinked.

azaleas, among the most beautiful and varicolored of spring-flowering shrubs, get their name from Greek *azaleos,* meaning "dry." The *azalea* was thought to flourish in dry soil.

azure was brought into English as a term of heraldry representing the color blue. It comes from the Arabic *allazaward,* meaning lapis lazuli, a deep-blue gemstone. Nowadays it is considered a poetic term, used chiefly in reference to the color of the skies.

babel, meaning any confusion of sounds, especially meaningless chatter, comes from the Biblical reference (Genesis 11:7) to the ancient people of *Babel* who tried to build a tower reaching to heaven. Until that time all mankind had spoken the same language, but the Lord decided to "confound their language, that they may not understand one another's speech." And thus were the many languages—and the resulting confusion—born. Modern scholarship identifies *Babel* as Babylon.

Interestingly enough, linguistic scholarship postulates the existence in prehistoric times of a single Indo-European tongue from which virtually all languages of our Western culture have been derived. Included are the Germanic languages (including English, of course), Celtic, Italic (including Latin, French, Italian, Spanish and Portuguese), Baltic, Slavic, Greek, Armenian, Hittite, Tocharian, Iranian and Indic (including Sanskrit, Urdu, Hindi and many others). And to round out what may be much more than a simple coincidence, Babylon was in Mesopotamia (literally "the land between the rivers"), bordered by the Euphrates and Tigris rivers, pretty much where present-day Iraq is located. Right in the heart of the hypothetical "Indo-European" area, in short.

Our *American Heritage Dictionary of the English Language* is the only general dictionary to devote extensive coverage to the Indo-European origins of English.

babes in the woods. Nowadays when we speak of people as being "mere *babes in the woods,*" we mean that they are incredibly naïve and innocent, blind to the evils of the world about them. The original story of "Babes in the Wood" goes back to the time of Shakespeare. About 1595, there was a popular ballad on a very sad, indeed tragic, theme. It told of a wealthy gentleman of Norfolk, England, who arranges on his deathbed for his infant son and daughter to inherit his property. Until they come of age, they are to be cared for by their uncle, his wife's brother. However, if they die before coming of age, the uncle inherits the estate. After pondering this situation for a year or so, the uncle succumbs to temptation and hires a pair of thugs to do away with the children.

One of the thugs is soft-hearted, so instead of killing the babes, he murders his partner and leaves the infants to fend for themselves in the wood. They die during the night and Robin Redbreast comes and covers their bodies with leaves. The wicked uncle then suffers all sorts of troubles. His own sons die, his barns, with all the cattle inside, burn down, and finally he ends in jail. The whole tragic tale winds up with the arrest of the surviving thug, who is taken in for highway robbery. He then confesses to his part in the plot and is condemned to death.

bacchanalia is a drunken party or orgy. When capitalized, the word refers to the Roman celebration honoring Bacchus, the god of grape-growing and wine.

bachelor. From its earliest origin, *bachelor* has had the connotation of "novice," a sense that is reflected also in the other major use of *bachelor*—in such phrases as *"bachelor* of arts" to designate the first degree awarded by a college or university. In the Middle Ages a *bachelor* was a young knight serving a period as vassal to a member of the landed gentry. In fact, the original *bachelor* was little more than a glorified cowhand—*baccalaris* being the Latin term for "one who cares for cows."

Technically today, a *bachelor* is simply an unmarried man, not necessarily a man who has never been married. But here, as in so many other areas of language, the scales seem tilted in favor of the male. A woman who has been married and divorced is labeled a "divorcee," while a man under similar circumstances is a *bachelor* and enjoys all the prerogatives that carefree label carries with it. There is, of course, the male form "divorcé" (pronounced div-or-SAY), but we have never seen it used in print because of the obvious confusion with the noun "divorce" (pronounced dih-VORSS).

bacitracin, a common antibiotic, is what the dictionary calls an arbitrary blending of "bacillus" and the last name of the American girl (Margaret Tracy) from whose wounds the bacteria was isolated in 1945. It is used primarily as a salve for bacterial infections of the skin.

back and fill is a term from the language of sailing men. It describes a maneuver of tacking when the tide is running with your craft and the wind against it. Obviously not much progress is made under these circumstances. The end result is that there's a good deal of motion fore and aft—much shifting of ground, so to speak—but the boat stays just about where it was. So to *back and fill* has been taken into popular speech as synonymous with "to vacillate" or "to be irresolute."

backbencher is a very junior member of the British House of Commons and he gets his nickname from the fact that he is seated on one of the rear benches. The more important positions, on the front benches, are occupied by leading members of the party in power and their opposite numbers in the party out of power.

back formations. Our guess is that all of you readers have been using *back formations* all your lives, without having heard the technical name for them. Take *ad,* a back formation from "advertising." Likewise, "phone" from "telephone," "commute" from "commuter," "photo" from "photograph" and, one which still gives purists the pip, "enthuse" from "enthusiasm."

backroom boys are the unsung heroes in the field of technological and scientific research—men whose work is not known to the public and hence not generally appreciated. Lord Beaverbrook coined the phrase in a speech on war production in March 1941, in which he said, ". . . to whom most praise must be given . . . to the boys in the backroom."

backs—football. How did the terms *fullback, halfback* and *quarterback* originate? First you have to forget everything you have learned about the way backfields are organized today. We're going all the way back to the 1890s to dig up the origin of these names. In those simpler days the line consisted of three men on each side of the center—seven men in all. The backfield consisted of one man directly behind the center (actually behind and slightly to one side), two men flanking him but positioned several feet to the rear, and one chap quite a distance farther back and directly behind the center. This chap who was all the way back was called the *fullback* (fully back from the line). The two flanking backs were half the fullback's distance back and so were logically called *halfbacks.* Equally logically, the man closest to the line was only one quarter as far from it as the fullback. So he became a *quarterback.* Those names don't make very much sense in reference to the game as it is played today. Indeed, some of them—like many of the linemen's names—are seldom used nowadays.

backstairs influence/gossip. Because royal palaces usually had more than one set of stairs to the upper floors, anyone able to reach the monarch by way of the back stairs could avoid being forestalled by officers of the court. Inevitably this involved bribing or otherwise winning over the servants, who routinely used the back stairs. Having done so, the briber had direct access to the monarch and could exert his *backstairs influence.* Of almost equal value to him was *backstairs gossip,* the gossip of the servants, who, by the nature of their work, were the best-informed people in the castle.

back to Blighty originated among British soldiers stationed in India and was used by them to refer to their home country. It is a corruption of the Hindustani word *bilayati,* meaning "foreign country." The one foreign country to which British soldiers—the Tommy Atkinses of Kipling's poems—wanted to be sent from India was, of course, home. So *Blighty* became England in the jargon of servicemen. During World War I it also meant a wound serious enough to cause a soldier to be returned home.

back to the wall. A person with his/or her *back to the wall* is usually fighting against odds and has backed up to the wall to eliminate one direction from which he/or she might be attacked. The term also implies desperation, for obviously there is no way to retreat.

backup man is a product of the space program. The *backup man* in an astronautical team is the man who replaces a pilot if the person scheduled to make a flight is unable to do so.

bad cess. The expression *"bad cess* to ye" is, to be trite about it, as Irish as Paddy's pig. It means "bad luck to you; a curse be upon you." There are two theories of its origin. One is that it's a contraction of "assessment" or tax—and taxes have never been popular with anyone anywhere. The other thought is that it may be a contraction of "success"—though the idea of "bad success" seems pretty farfetched to us.

badger/badger game. A badger is a burrowing animal with a broad back and thick short legs, and it is from this ungainly creature that the term *to badger* acquired the meaning of "persistently annoy or torment." The meaning of the verb stems from a so-called sport, formerly popular in England, which consisted of putting a *badger* in a barrel or box or tub and then allowing a number of dogs to drive him from his refuge. Once driven or dragged out, he was allowed to retire to safety momentarily, then the dogs were turned loose again. Repeated until spectators wearied, the game was known as badger-baiting. For figurative use, it was shortened to *badger.* From the same cruel sport comes the term *badger game,* which is not a game at all but criminal blackmail. A woman entices a man to her room with the assurance that enjoyable hanky-panky awaits him. Soon her male accomplice enters and demands money from the man on the threat of exposure if he doesn't pay up. Obviously the "mark," as he's called, doesn't have a chance—any more than the *badger* does.

bad penny. The phrase usually is heard in this country as "A *bad penny* always turns up," meaning that a no-good person can be counted upon to come back again and again. The expression was originally English and the unit of currency referred to was the shilling. Sir Walter Scott, in one of his early-nineteenth-century novels, wrote: "Bring back Darsie? Little doubt of that. The bad shilling is sure enough to come back again."

bad time/good time. In army lingo, *good time* is time served with honor and good conduct, counted toward eventual termination of enlistment. *Bad time* is time served without pay because of infringement of regulations. *Bad time* may be served in stockade or hospital or by confinement in barracks.

bag. A person's *bag* is her personal enthusiasm or hobby, his personal interest or avocation. Our *bag* is words.

bagel and lox. *Bagel and lox* with cream cheese is as popular a breakfast delicacy in America's Jewish community as doughnuts and coffee in the nation as a whole. And, incidentally, many non-Jews have learned to savor this gustatory treat. The *bagel*—which has been described as "a doughnut with a Jewish education"—is similar to the doughnut in shape but is made of an unsalted yeast dough which is first simmered in water and then baked. It gets its name from the Yiddish word *beigen,* meaning "to bend or twist."

The *bagel* is split before serving, spread well with cream cheese and then topped with *lox.* And what is *lox,* you ask? Simply thin-sliced, salty smoked salmon. Usually the Nova Scotia variety of salmon is served in New York but Alaskan or West Coast salmon may be served in other parts of the country. *Lox* comes from another Yiddish-German word, *lachs,* which is closely related to the Anglo-Saxon *leax,* also meaning "salmon." There is a legend that *bagels* were first made in the form of stirrups—*begel* or *buegel* being German for "stirrup"—in Vienna in 1683. The bakers chose that form to show their gratitude to the King of Poland, who liberated them, in commemoration of the fact that many of those liberated clung to the stirrups as the king rode through on horseback.

bagman is an old slang term for a commercial traveler who toted his samples in a bag or bags. Before the day of the automobile, the salesman often arrived on horseback with his wares in saddlebags. In present-day slang, a *bagman* is one to whom graft is paid.

Bailey Bridge is a portable bridge made of prefabricated steel sections in the form of lattices. It was named for its inventor, Donald Coleman Bailey, of the British Ministry of Supply in World War II. So successful was his invention that he was knighted in 1945.

bailiwick. In general use, *bailiwick* has come to mean your own province, particularly one in which experience or knowledge gives you special authority or freedom to act. However, it has had a very definite legal sense for centuries: the area of jurisdiction of a bailiff (sheriff's assistant). It goes back to Middle English *bailie,* meaning "bailiff," and *wick,* meaning "village." If you trace the origin of *bailiff* back to Latin, the poor chap suffers a loss in dignity since *bailiff* is derived from *bajalus,* the Latin word for "porter."

baker's dozen. There are many theories about the origin of this phrase. The most commonly accepted theory dates back to fifteenth-century England. It seems that bakers had long had a reputation—whether deserved or not—for short-weighting their bread. As a result, very strict laws were passed, regulating the weight of the various breads, muffins and cakes. But, as every cook knows, it's not possible—especially when cooking with the primitive ovens then available—to have the loaves absolutely uniform in weight. So the practice developed of giving thirteen loaves on every order for twelve, thereby guaranteeing that there would be no penalty for shortages.

Another theory is that the phrase developed by analogy from "printer's dozen," for in the early days of publishing it was the custom of printers to supply the retailer with thirteen copies of a book on each order of twelve. Since the retailer was billed at list price, the return on the thirteenth book represented his profit on the transaction. As a sidelight on this medieval selling technique, by the way, we may note that today one of the most prevalent practices of the book trade is for the publisher to offer retailers "one for ten" or one free book with every ten ordered, thereby increasing the retailer's margin of profit and, of course, the number of books sold by the publisher.

Then there's still another theory. It seems that the bakers of the medieval period had such a bad name that the words *baker* and *devil* were sometimes used interchangeably. Thus the term *baker's dozen* may have evolved from *devil's dozen,* which was a common folk phrase meaning thirteen. And thirteen was the number of witches usually present at meetings summoned by Old Nick.

baker's knee. If you have *baker's knees,* you are knock-kneed. In the days before the baking industry was mechanized, bakers were said to develop knock-knees as the result of standing in one position for long periods while kneading the bread.

baksheesh. *"Baksheesh,* for the love of Allah" is the plaintive plea of beggars throughout the Middle East. *Baksheesh,* the tourist soon learns, means alms or charitable handouts. But when he comes to write this in his diary, he finds that the dictionary-makers give him no fewer than four different ways to spell this word: *baksheesh, backsheesh, bakshish* and *backshish.* If his evening meal includes the regional specialty shish kebab, he'll find that the learned gentry who put together the wordbooks haven't been able to make up their minds on how that should be spelled, either. "Kebab," "kabab," "cabob" and "kabob"—any of these spellings will pass muster with the editors of one or another of America's great dictionaries.

Balaam's ass. Nobel laureate George Wald, author of a notable speech entitled "A Generation in Search of a Future," appeared one evening on a TV talk show to discuss some of the ramifications of public reaction to his talk. As an outspoken opponent of our Vietnam involvement and a person much concerned about the increasing alienation of our youth, Professor Wald noted that he found himself "fulfilling the function of *Balaam's ass.*" The reference is to the Old Testament Book of Numbers (22:31–33), in which is told the story of Balaam, who saddled his ass and rode in quest of worldly riches in defiance of the wishes of God. An angel of the Lord stood in his way and three times the ass strayed from the proper path because it could see the angel, while Balaam could not. Finally Balaam in his wrath beat the offending donkey, not realizing that it was actually saving him from the avenging angel. Eventually, "The Lord opened the eyes of Balaam, and he saw the angel of the Lord . . . his sword drawn in his hand . . . and the angel of the Lord said unto him . . . the ass saw me, and turned from me three times: unless she had turned from me, surely now also I had slain thee." Professor Wald obviously saw himself in the thankless role of trying to persuade mankind to change a course which may lead to doomsday.

bald as a coot. An uncomplimentary term for a man who has lost his hair, *bald as a coot* likens him to the bald coot of Europe, an aquatic bird whose bill extends well up its forehead.

balderdash goes back to Shakespeare's time and originally meant an incongruous mixture of liquors, such as wine mixed with beer. The word gradually came to mean pretentious, bombastic and essentially senseless prose. During the 1920s the word was a great favorite of Henry L. Mencken, who used it often to describe the orations of congressmen and senators of the period. There are those among us who feel that *balderdash* remains an apt term for much of the prose flowing from Washington in these times, too.

balk comes from the Anglo-Saxon *balca,* "wooden beam," and refers to the huge timbers used to bar outer doors, thus *balking* an enemy's onslaught.

balletomane is an enthusiast for ballets. The word, which was coined in France, is from the words *ballet* and *manie* (mania). Thus a *balletomane* (pronounced bal-LET-uh-mayn) is one whose devotion to the dance is roughly equal to a baseball fan's enthusiasm for a pennant contender in mid-August—and *fan,* in case you have forgotten, is often thought to be a shortened form of "fanatic."

balling the jack is a phrase from the jargon of railroadmen and simply means going at top speed. It also has acquired the meaning in gambling circles of risking everything on a single throw of the dice or turn of a card.

ballistics. It's a long way from Roman warfare to the intercontinental ballistic missile, but the word *ballistics* has survived the trip. In Latin, *ballista* was a military machine for throwing large stones, one of their most effective weapons. We're still firing objects through space as a means of attack, but now the projectiles are bullets, rockets and bombs; and *ballistics* has come to mean the science of the firing of such projectiles, their motion and impact.

ballot. We take this word from the Italian *ballotta,* literally "small ball." Centuries ago voting was done by dropping small balls into a box or other receptacle. A white ball designated a "yes" vote, while a black ball indicated "no."

banal is related to the *ban* of medieval days—a ruling of the king. Serfs forced to labor under the royal ban lived a very trite and commonplace existence. So *banal* came to mean "trivial, trite, commonplace."

bandbox. The bands in question here are entirely unmusical. They were clerical bands—the little square linen tippet worn around the neck by ministers, especially those of the Presbyterian faith. So the *bandbox* was a box in which clergymen kept their vestments, which were invariably spotless and neatly pressed. And a person looking as if he had just stepped out of a *bandbox* was neat, spruce and spotless.

bandy. "I'll not *bandy* words with you" is a fairly common remark, meaning: Let's not waste time kicking the conversational ball around; let's get down to business. The figure of speech employed is really quite accurate, since the original meaning of *bandy* came from the Old French *bander,* meaning "to bat the ball back and forth" in a primitive form of tennis.

bane of my existence. *Bane* was originally a deadly poison and came from the Anglo-Saxon *bana,* meaning "murderer or slayer." Used in the phrase *bane of my existence,* it means something which is a constant, serious problem—something which ruins life as it should be.

bangtail. The *bang* in *bangtail* has the same origin as the *bangs* in a hairdo. It simply means "cropped or cut short." So the original *bangtails* were horses whose tails were docked. Now it means any race horse. The word has been current in sports slang since about World War I. The earliest recorded appearance in print is in 1921, but it probably had been around awhile before then. The Wentworth-Flexner *Dictionary of American Slang* notes that it is "becoming obsolescent"; but as long as sportswriters need a snappy synonym for race horse, you'll be seeing *bangtail* in print.

bankrupt. In medieval Italy, moneylenders operated from *bancas*—benches or shelves. When a moneylender was forced to suspend his business from lack of funds, his *banca* was broken up and he was given the name *bancarotto.* From this beginning the word *bankrupt* eventually came to mean any insolvent person, especially anyone who had been legally declared unable to pay his debts.

bankrupt worm. *Bankrupt* may seem a wild word for a worm, but there is such a worm. It's a roundworm of the genus Trichostrongylus, and it gets its name from the effect it has on farmers unlucky enough to have a cattle herd infested by this particular parasite.

banned in Boston. During the 1920s the phrase *banned in Boston* became famous because the long-established Watch and Ward Society of the so-called Hub of the Universe was forever getting the city censor to ban books from sale. Many publishers actively sought to have their books *banned in Boston* because they knew that label would increase their sales in the rest of the country.

So H. L. Mencken, then editor of the avant-garde *American Mercury* magazine, decided to take action when the society moved to ban the sale of an issue of the magazine which contained a short story about a lady of easy virtue. He openly challenged the secretary of the society, the Reverend J. F. Chase, to meet him at high noon on Boston Common and purchase from Mencken a copy of the magazine. When Chase appeared and handed over a silver half dollar, Mencken, who was always quite a showman, bit the coin to be sure it was legitimate, handed over the magazine and surrendered to the head of the vice squad. The next day a judge dismissed the charges against Mencken, and though the society continued in existence for several more years, it never again wielded the power it had in its earlier days.

The general level of censorship in Boston in those days may be gauged by the fact that the theatrical censor (who banned Eugene O'Neill's plays) got the job because (1) he was a cousin of the mayor and (2) he had lost an arm and could no longer play drums in the pit band of a burlesque show.

banshee. Most of us associate *banshee* with the unearthly wails of a female spirit foretelling a death in the family. But in the original Gaelic, the *banshee* was usually depicted as a beautiful woman, not a hag.

bantam. This nickname for a small but courageous, even pugnacious, person comes from the *bantam* cock or rooster, renowned for its ability to best other gamecocks of greater size. The breed of fowl was thought to have originated in the town of Bantam in northwest Java.

banzai. The war cry *"Banzai!"* meant "May you live ten thousand years!" The Japanese, with a logic incomprehensible to Western minds, used to shout it when launching a suicide attack.

barbecue comes to us from the Spanish and Haitian word *barbacoa,* meaning "framework of sticks." Originally a *barbecue* was a device for roasting a whole animal over an open fire. Now it means any meat cooked over an open fire without the use of a utensil and, by extension, the occasion on which such food is eaten.

barber/barber pole. The *barber* gets his name from the Latin word for "beard," *barba.* Roman barbers, by the way, were called *tonsores,* a word which gave us the elegant "tonsorial parlor"—the Victorian name for barbershop. During the Middle Ages, the *barber* was also a surgeon. Since surgery was something less than a fine art at the time, it involved a good deal of bloodletting. And that's where the symbolic red-and-white-striped *barber pole* came from. The *barber*-surgeon simply draped his bloodstained bandages around a white pole to dry.

Barbers, like taxi drivers, regard themselves as all-knowing—and that, too, goes back to the ancients. Horace, in one of his satires, wrote *"Omnibus, notum tonsoribus"*—"known to every barber"—which translates more freely into the English proverb "Every barber knows that."

Barkis is willin'. Barkis was the character in Charles Dickens's *David Copperfield* who proposed to Clara Peggotty by sending her the message that *"Barkis is willin'."* The saying has been widely adopted as a means of indicating willingness on any score.

bark up the wrong tree. Raccoon-hunting usually takes place at night, and the hunters have to rely on their dogs to force the raccoon up a tree and stand there barking until the hunters arrive. A dog that *barks up the wrong tree* is certainly on the wrong track and is wasting his energy. Hence a person who *barks up the wrong tree* is directing his attention wrongly and may be placing the blame where it doesn't belong.

barley duck. It is a comparatively easy matter to trace down *barley duck* and discover that it is a tangy preserve made of gooseberries or currants, frequently served as an accompaniment to the main roast meat course at dinner. But where did the strange name come from? It's what the language experts call a "corrupted" pronunciation of *Bar-le-Duc* (pronounced bar-luh-DYOOK), which is the name of the French town where this preserve is thought to have originated.

barn burner. According to an old story, there was once a Dutchman who was so bothered by the rats in his barn that he burned down the barn to get rid of them. Thus a *barn burner* became one who destroyed all in order to get rid of a nuisance. In the 1840s and 1850s there was a faction of the Democratic party in New York State opposed to the extension of slavery in the territories, and the name *Barnburners* was given them by their opponents. Most of the Barnburners later became Free-Soilers.

barnstorming. This term, though now almost exclusively a political word meaning to travel rapidly about the country making speeches wherever people will gather, was originally a theatrical term. It described itinerant stock companies whose repertory and talent were not topflight and who had to appear in second-rate auditoriums and even occasionally in barns. Since such itineraries as they had were usually hastily improvised, they gave the impression of *storming* (moving impetuously) around the country.

baron of beef is a double sirloin—two sirloins not separated at the backbone. There is a theory that the sirloin was named by an English king who so liked the cut that he tapped it with his sword and dubbed it "sir." Indeed, the otherwise estimable *Larousse* French dictionary perpetuated this untrue etymology with this comment: "King Henry VIII, who was a big eater, was very fond of roast beef. One day, enraptured by the sight of a magnificent sirloin, he conferred knighthood upon it. The noble title bestowed on this piece of beef by word of royal mouth has been sanctioned by custom and the cut is known to this day as sirloin."

Now, this is all very well but completely untrue, since "sirloin" was originally a French word, *surloigne,* from *sur* (over) and *longe* (loin). Furthermore, according to the *Oxford English Dictionary,* it appeared in English well before the reign of Henry VIII. But there is evidence that *baron of beef* got its name from a group of English clubmen of the eighteenth century who believed the story about the origin of "sirloin." As a joke, they named the double sirloin *baron* because a real baron, being a member of the fifth rank of the peerage, ranks one up on an ordinary "sir."

barrage. Here's a word we all know in its military sense of a curtain of artillery fire, designed to protect troops, especially when advancing. It also has acquired the extended sense of a sudden outpouring of any kind, such as a *barrage* of questions. So it comes as a bit of a surprise to discover that the original *barrage* was a sort of dam, designed to contain large amounts of water, rather than to cause widespread outpouring. It's from the French word of the same spelling, meaning "barrier."

barristers/solicitors. Generally speaking, *barristers* are lawyers who practice in the superior courts in England. Indeed, there are two classes: the simple *barrister,* an attorney admitted to the bar, and a higher order known as "King's Counsel." The latter are said to *"take silk"* when appointed "K.C." because they thenceforth wear silk gowns while junior counsel *(barristers)* wear gowns of ordinary cloth. *Solicitors* are lawyers who are not members of the bar and do not plead cases in higher courts.

Bartholomew pig/doll. In Shakespeare's *Henry IV,* Falstaff, in referring to himself, says he is "a little tidy *Bartholomew pig"*—meaning that he is a very fat person. The phrase comes from the famous—or, if you will, infamous—annual Bartholomew Fair held for centuries in Smithfield, London, on or about St. Bartholomew's Day. Among its many attractions was *Bartholomew pig,* which was roasted whole and sold in piping-hot chunks to the fairgoers. There were many amusements, sideshows and refreshment stands, and life at the fair became more dissipated every year. Eventually the Puritans tried to control the situation, but to no avail. The fair, which began in 1133, was finally moved to Islington in 1840 and fifteen years later died. *Bartholomew doll,* in the meantime, became a name for a flashy or overdressed woman whose dress was similar to that of the dolls sold at the fair.

baseball jargon. The sport pages are a daily reminder that no American activity has developed so colorful and extensive a vocabulary as baseball. Ever since the days of Abner Doubleday, sportswriters and the players themselves have coined graphic and picturesque phrases to describe all aspects of the National Game. We assume that everyone knows the difference between a base hit and an out, so we'll pass over the standard terms and concentrate on the colorful "slanguage" of baseball reporters and sportscasters.

Aboard—On base. When there are three men on base, the bases are *loaded* and there are *three men aboard.*

Bad ball—A ball pitched well outside the strike zone. A batter who habitually "goes after" such pitches is known as a *"bad ball* hitter."

Baltimore chop—A ball that hits the ground just in front of the plate and takes a long, high bounce, slow enough to enable the batter to reach first base. This term is now almost obsolete. In fact, it's so far out it may soon be "in" again.

Bases loaded—The situation when there are runners on first, second and third bases.

Bean ball—A ball pitched directly at the batter's head, to force him back from the plate. Technically illegal, it is resorted to fairly frequently, though not so often as indignant batters would have you believe.

Bench jockey—A player or coach who taunts members of the opposing team from his place on the bench. Most notable *bench jockey* in recent years has been Leo "The Lip" Durocher.

Bleeder—Kissing cousin of the *blooper* (which see) except that it spends most of its time on the ground. Usually it's a weak grounder that takes a bad bounce just outside the reach of an infielder. It's also called a *scratch hit.*

Blooper—A weak fly which falls beyond the infield and short of the outfield. It's also called a *banjo hit* and, in the old days, was named a *Texas leaguer.*

Change-up or *change of pace*—A slow ball pitched after one or more fast balls, but with the same motions of delivery. What used to be called a "slow ball" is now referred to by most sportscasters as a *change-up,* even when the pitch is the first one delivered to the batter.

Clutch hitter—The kind of hitter who can be counted on to deliver a hit when it is most needed.

Cousin—A pitcher whom a batter finds consistently easy to hit. Even very great pitchers sometimes find an occasional opposition batter who can fathom their trickiest deliveries.

Cripple—Ball pitched when the count on the batter is three balls and one strike, so called because the pitcher usually needs to *groove it* for a strike and therefore eliminates trickery from his delivery.

Dust or duster—The pitcher's term for the pitch a batter calls a *bean ball.* It's a pitch thrown hard and close to the batter, designed to make him step back from the plate.

Fireman—A relief pitcher who comes in to put out the "fire" caused by the opposing team's getting men on bases.

Gopher ball—A pitch the batter hits for a home run.

Grand slam—A term borrowed from bridge; it is, of course, what batters cherish most: a home run with three men on base.

Homer—A home run, of course. Also an umpire whose decisions consistently favor the home team.

Hot corner—Third base.

In the hole—A batter is *in the hole* if the count is two strikes and no balls; a pitcher is *in the hole* if the count is three balls and no strikes.

Keystone sack—Second base.

Life—Another chance. If a batter hits a foul which a fielder should catch, but doesn't, he gets a *life*. Similarly, if he gets on base through an error, he gets a *life*.

Meat hand—The one a player doesn't have a glove on. Except in unusual circumstances—such as the World Series—most players are understandably loath to try catching hard-hit balls with their *meat hands*.

Money player—One who can always be counted upon to perform well when most is at stake.

Mound, rubber or hill—The slightly elevated pitcher's box in the center of the diamond.

No-hitter—A game in which one side fails to make any hits.

Payoff pitch—The pitch delivered when the count is three balls and two strikes. Unless the batter fouls out of play, a *payoff* decision—hit, base on balls or out—must result from this pitch.

Peg—A throw, especially a long one from an outfielder to a base or home plate in order to trap a base runner.

Pick-off—A surprise play in which a base runner who has been taking a long lead is caught away from the base by a sudden throw from the pitcher or catcher.

Pick-up—A ball caught immediately after it strikes the ground.

Platter—Home plate.

Rhubarb—An argument on the playing field, especially a noisy, vehement one involving an umpire and players from both teams.

Run-down—One of the most exciting plays in the game, when a base runner is caught between bases by two fielders who throw the ball back and forth several times before tagging him for the put-out. Occasionally, of course, the trapped runner outwits the fielders, but then the play should not properly be called a *run-down*.

Shut-out—A game in which the losing team fails to score any runs.

Southpaw—A left-handed player, especially a pitcher.

Sun field—That portion of the outfield where the fielder has to face the sun directly.

Switch-hitter—Mickey Mantle was the most proficient *switch-hitter* in many years. He could bat with equal ferocity from either side of the plate, batting right-handed against left-handed pitching and left-handed against right-handed pitching, thereby eliminating the theoretical advantage that pitchers have against batters who stand on the same side of the plate that they deliver their pitches from.

Texas leaguer—A fly ball which falls just beyond the infield and results in a base hit. Sometimes called a *blooper.*

Twin bill or double-header—Two games played between the same two teams on the same day.

Twi-night double-header—Two games between the same teams on the same day, the first starting in late afternoon, the second being played under lights at night.

bash originally meant a jam session—a gathering of musicians who played together for their own enjoyment. Nowadays it is loosely used to mean any high-spirited social gathering.

Basic English. In the late 1920s, the noted English scholar C. K. Ogden and a number of collaborators devoted a lot of time to the selection of what they considered the basic words of our language. The final list, labeled *Basic English,* consists of 850 words—600 nouns, 150 adjectives, and another 100 of what they called "structural" words. The purpose of these scholars was to develop a skeletonized English language which could be easily learned by foreigners and would, they hoped, become a truly international language. English is today the most international of languages, but it seems that the credit for this fact goes not so much to Ogden as to the pervasive American influence in all parts of the globe. By that we mean the influence of American businessmen as well as of American servicemen.

The vocabulary of *Basic English* is given in full in two encyclopedias published by Grolier, Inc., *Encyclopedia International* and the *Grolier Universal Encyclopedia.* It may very well be given in other reference books also, but we can certify to its appearance in these two sets, to which we contributed. Another fascinating source book on the most common words in the language is the *Standard Corpus of Present-Day Edited English* by W. Nelson Francis and Henry Kucera, published by Brown University. Professors Francis and Kucera fed into a computer random selections— 500 words in length—from a vast variety of materials published in 1962. Magazines, books and newspapers all provided source material and, through the computer, the professors were able to analyze the frequency of appearance in print of many thousands of words. One amusing sidelight revealed by the Francis-Kucera study is that newspapermen tend to have larger and more versatile vocabularies than scholars.

basil, a commonplace herb in every well-ordered kitchen, has an extraordinarily elegant etymology. Its name comes from the Greek *basilikos,* meaning "royal," because it was thought to have been used in making perfume for royalty.

baste, in the cooking use, comes from the Old French word *basser* (to moisten), and thus accurately describes the basting process of moistening meat during roastings. *Baste,* as used in sewing, comes from the Old High German *bastjan,* meaning "to sew with bast"—and bast, in turn, is a heavy fiber used in making ropes. Thus any stitches taken with such fiber would be long and loose. The two words are homonyms—words similar in sound and sometimes in spelling, but of different origin and meaning. Incidentally, there's still a third homonym of *baste*—meaning "to strike or beat" —and it comes from still another root, this one Old Norse.

Bastille. The *Bastille* of French history must be one of the most famous fortresses and prisons of all time—and yet its name, which has come to be synonymous in English with jail or prison, originally simply meant "building." The Parisian *Bastille* was built in the fourteenth century by Charles V as a royal chateau. Henry IV used it as a treasury, but by the eighteenth century it was used solely as a prison, with a number of noted political prisoners, including Voltaire, incarcerated there. The storming of the *Bastille* on July 14, 1789, marked the start of the French Revolution and, for more than a century past, July 14, *Bastille* Day, has been the great French national holiday.

bastion (pronounced BASH-chun or BASS-tee-un) means "stronghold or defensive bulwark." Originally a French word dating back to the great ages of chivalry, castles and knightly warfare, it denoted a projection in the wall of a fort, designed to give the defenders a wider firing range—hence, an improved defense.

Bath chair is not a chair in which ill or handicapped persons can take baths. It's simply a hooded wheelchair, used to move invalids about. It gets its name from the fact that it was first used at the spa in Bath, England.

Bath Oliver is an unsweetened biscuit, so named because it was invented by a Dr. William Oliver, who practiced in Bath, England. Dr. Oliver seems to have been one of the early food-fad doctors, like his fellow countryman Dr. J. M. Salisbury, who invented the Salisbury steak, and our own Dr. Sylvester Graham, who invented the Graham cracker and Graham bread.

bathos/pathos. *Bathos* (pronounced BAY-thos) is not synonymous with *pathos,* though the two are closely related. *Pathos,* properly speaking, is the quality in an experience which moves the onlooker to pity or compassion. *Bathos,* by contrast, is a false, synthetic, exaggerated appeal to the emotions. It comes direct from the Greek *bathos,* meaning "depth." *Pathos* in Greek meant "passion" or "suffering."

bats/batty, used in reference to a person who is eccentric or even crazy, originally was expressed as "he has *bats* in his belfry." It was coined early in this century, probably by Ambrose Bierce. It refers to the eccentric flight of bats disturbed by the ringing of bells in a church bell tower (belfry). The analogy is to the human head as the belfry, and the bats to the wild disorder of thoughts in the mind of a mentally deranged person.

battery. Most familiar as part of the term "assault and *battery,*" *battery* itself comes from the Latin *battuere* (to beat) and means in this connection illegal beating or touching of another person.

battle royal. A term from the now outlawed sport of cockfighting, *battle royal* refers to a kind of elimination tournament common to the cockpit. First, sixteen cocks are pitted against one another. The eight victors are similarly matched. Then the four survivors are pitted and finally the two cocks remaining fight it out to find the winner of the *battle royal.* This same sport has given us at least one other term current in everyday speech. We often speak of two baseball teams being *pitted* against each other in an important series, little realizing that we are using a metaphor from cockfighting, where the contestants are literally dropped into a pit to fight out their bloody battle.

bayou is the Louisiana French version of *bayuk,* used by earlier inhabitants, the Choctaw Indians, to describe small streams and inlets. Although *bayous* are associated in the public mind with Louisiana almost as closely as the French Quarter is with New Orleans, the truth is that there are *bayous* in other states as well. In parts of northern Arkansas and southern Missouri a brook or rivulet rising in the hills is called a *bayou,* though these have none of the romance and charm of the Cajun *bayous* of old Louisiana.

Bay State for the Commonwealth of Massachusetts derives from the fact that its colonial name was the "Colony of Massachusetts Bay."

bazaar/bizarre. There seems to be no etymological relation between *bazaar* and *bizarre. Bazaar,* meaning a marketplace or a shop where a variety of goods is sold, comes from the Persian word *bazar. Bizarre,* meaning odd or unusual in appearance or behavior, comes from the Spanish *bizarro* (brave or gallant).

bazooka. One of the most successful weapons of modern land warfare is the *bazooka,* a portable, smoothbore device for firing armor-piercing rockets. All dictionaries solemnly record that it was named after a primitive funnel-type musical instrument created and popularized by the now deceased radio comedian Bob Burns, who punctuated his homespun monologues with occasional solos on his horn. That's all very well, so far as it goes, but it doesn't go far enough. Harken to a transplanted Arkansawyer (Burns came from Arkansas, too) named C. E. Warford, now resident in Kearney, Nebraska. "Bob Burns did not invent the *bazooka,* though he did adapt it into a musical instrument and possibly made some modifications so that it would serve as a musical instrument. The original *bazooka* was an agricultural device for use in accurately hand-planting commercial fertilizer and/or small grain. It was a peculiarly shaped funnel, having a flared bell, a large tube about three feet long, and ending in a smaller opening at the lower end. The fertilizer or grain was carried in a shoulder bag, and the *bazooka* was pointed into the furrow while the material was dribbled into it. So what actually happened is that Bob Burns took an Arkansas farm implement and made a fortune out of using it as a musical instrument."

B.C./A.D. Obviously no one—least of all the Romans, who were pretty much in control everywhere at that time—suddenly awakened on the day of Christ's birth and announced: "From now on we're going to number our years differently." So how did it happen that we number our years either B.C. or A.D.? It all goes back to the sixth century. A scholarly monk in Rome, named Dionysius Exiguus, wrote a treatise named *"Cyclus paschalis"*—"Cycle of Easter." In it he announced that henceforth the numbering of years should begin with the year of Christ's birth. He decided that that year would have been 753 in the Roman calendar, so he determined that the Roman year 754 would henceforth be called the first year of the Christian era (A.D. 1). As it happened, he was a little off in his calculations. Later students of the Bible say that the actual date was between two and six years earlier than he figured, with most of them agreeing that Christ was actually born in 4 B.C.

Because this monk renumbered the calendar, the Christian era is occasionally called the Dionysian era—which is sort of funny, if you happen to be a student of ancient history. The original Dionysius (called Bacchus in the Roman mythology) was the most riotously pagan of the Greek gods. Dionysian revels were orgies of feasting, wine-bibbing and all sorts of licentious goings-on. Scarcely a model for Christian conduct.

BCU, in television language, is a "big close-up" of an actor in a picture so greatly magnified that only his face shows.

beak/beakie. *Beak* was originally British and Irish underworld slang for magistrate or constable. In American union lingo, *beakie* means the police used to spy secretly upon members of a union.

beal. Webster's *New International* (1934) defines *beal* as "to swell and become infected" and notes that it is "obsolete, except as a dialect term." Wentworth's *American Dialect Dictionary* reports that it once was widely used, chiefly in spoken language, in rural areas of Pennsylvania, West Virginia and Ohio. It often occurred in the expression "a *bealed* ear," meaning an inflammation of the inner ear.

bear by the tail. Here is a very colorful metaphor—particularly if you have a good imagination. It means you are in a terrible spot. If you have a *bear by the tail,* what is the choice? If you hold on to the tail, you are in grave danger; but to let go might be even more dangerous.

beard. In ancient times and, indeed, as late as the nineteenth century, beards were a characteristic facial adornment of men of distinction, leaders in civic and educational affairs. After a period during which, in America at least, virtually every man was clean-shaven, beards returned as a symbol among the young of rebellion against convention. In earlier ages, especially among Jews, it was considered highly offensive for one man to touch, much less tug, another's beard. So when one *bearded* another man, one was boldly confronting him, often defying or insulting him.

bear's service. In Russian the phrase *bear's service,* meaning that a person has performed a disservice to you while trying to be helpful, is a household expression. Its popularity comes from the fact that a certain fable has appeared for many years in Russian schoolbooks. Here is how it goes: A man lives in a deserted place and is very lonesome. One day he meets a lonely bear and they become friends. The bear tries to be helpful. When the man rests at noon, the bear sits by his side and chases the flies away. One impudent fly comes back again and again. The bear becomes angry, grabs a stone and throws it at the fly. The fly is crushed—but so is the man's skull. Hence the phrase *bear's service.* The closest we can come to an English equivalent would be the often-heard expression: "With friends like him, who needs enemies?"

beat/beatnik. *Beat* as a slang word goes back to the jargon of black musicians in the 1930s, perhaps as far back as the 1920s. Then it meant simply "exhausted, worn out." "Man, I'm *beat,*" would be a typical remark at the end of a long session. In the late 1940s and early 1950s a West Coast cult of writers, low in talent but high in publicity potential, labeled themselves "The Beats" or "The Beat Generation." At this point, unshaven faces and untidy clothing became a part of the uniform of the *beats,* and one of them —Kerouac, we believe—had the consummate bad taste to invent an origin for the term. *Beat,* he opined, was short for "beatified," thus sanctifying himself and his talentless fellow travelers.

Then came the first Soviet satellite, *sputnik,* bringing into prominence the suffix *-nik,* which had hitherto been used in this country chiefly as a Yiddish term meaning "a person engaged in or connected with some trade." Thus a "real-estatenik" was a Yiddishism for "real estate agent."

Then someone put the *beat* together with the *-nik* and, presto, *beatnik* was a label for anyone connected with the *beat* group. With the passage of years the West Coast *beats* have either disappeared or become respectable.

beat around the bush. The real meaning of *beat around the bush* is not so much to evade an issue entirely but to approach it cautiously and indirectly. "Stop *beating around the bush!* Get to the point," goes back many centuries and comes from the language of the huntsman. It was once the custom to hire beaters to beat bushes and arouse game birds for the hunter to shoot at. So the beater stirred up the action, but the hunter got to the point.

beatific (pronounced be-uh-TIFF-ik), from the Latin words *beatus* (happy) and *facere* (make), literally means "making blissfully happy." It also means rapturously or exaltedly happy and is often used in a religious context, as one might say, "St. Joan's face was wreathed with smiles of *beatific* rapture."

because it's there. Sir Edmund Hillary is credited by many as originating this retort to questions as to why he wanted to climb Mount Everest. Hillary may have said it, but it was already a tired cliché by the time he made his historic ascent of Everest in 1953. The first man to make the remark was George Leigh Mallory, who made two unsuccessful efforts (1922 and 1924) to scale Everest. On the second try he and a companion were lost from sight when only a few hundred feet from the summit. No one knows whether they reached the peak before they died.

bêche-de-mer. In one of Jack London's later novels certain of the characters speak a sort of pidgin English, a blend of the native dialects of the west Pacific islands and English. The name of the language is *bêche-de-mer* and it literally means "worm of the sea." Here's how this lingua franca—or hybrid language—got its name. The *bêche-de-mer,* also called the trepang or sea cucumber, is much prized as an item of food by natives of the islands of the western Pacific. It is a water animal with a leathery skin and a mouth surrounded by tentacles. Doesn't sound very appetizing, does it? However, it is chiefly used as a base for soups—and the Chinese make a highly esteemed soup from birds' nests, so you never can tell.

During the late eighteenth and nineteenth centuries, when trading developed between English-speaking colonists and seamen and the Melanesian natives, a language was needed and one gradually developed that combined elements of English and the various native dialects. Since a prime item of commerce was *bêche-de-mer,* the new hybrid tongue was called by that name—and that's how the language widely spoken in the far Pacific has the same name as the lowly sea cucumber.

bedbug letter. If you are one of the thousands of people who have cause to complain about poor products, poor service or inaccurate billing, you may, if you are ignored by the computer, be lucky enough to receive what some corporations call the *bedbug letter.* The phrase comes from the folklore of the hotel industry. It seems that a hotel guest, after exterminating one large bedbug, did not rest very soundly the rest of the night because he feared that other such creatures might be present. On his return home, he wrote an irate letter to the president of the hotel chain. In short order he received a very apologetic letter stating shock that such a thing could have happened, claiming that it had never happened before and promising that it would never happen again. The only hitch: his original letter was accidentally enclosed with the reply. Penciled across the top of the letter of complaint was the instruction: "Send him the *bedbug letter.*"

bedlam, meaning "noise and confusion," is a contraction of *Bethlehem,* the name of a London lunatic asylum. In the fifteenth century it was one of the sightseeing spots of London. For a modest fee, people could watch the inmates behind the bars, much as we view animals in the zoo, except that onlookers would tease the poor souls with jeers and taunts.

bee. Apparently the busyness of the ordinary honeybee as she works coopera-
tively with her fellow bees to fill the community hive was the inspiration
for such phrases as *sewing bee, husking bee, spelling bee* and *raising bee.*
This sort of social gathering where all work for a common, and often
charitable, purpose is nothing new. They were well known to the yeomanry
of England during the Middle Ages, but the name *bee* seems to have been
an American invention. One reason for the great popularity of such *bees,*
especially among young folk, is that they are usually followed by refresh-
ments and dancing and thus are in the nature of a community-wide celebration. During the rough-and-ready days when our Western frontier was
being opened, the word *bee* was used in several less socially commendable
combinations. Thus one might have read in Sam Clemens's *Virginia City
Enterprise* or Bret Harte's *Overland Monthly* accounts of such community
activities as *lynching bees, shooting bees,* and even *hanging bees.*

beefcake is a show business expression coined by analogy to "cheesecake," a
term long used to designate semi-clad feminine pulchritude. *Beefcake* is
simply display of the male torso.

beefeater. One widely held theory of the origin of this word runs so: "In 1485
when the Tower of London was one of King Henry's palaces, the corps of
the Yeomen of the Guard was formed as the King's bodyguard. Some of
these men were used to wait on table, and, being under a certain French
influence, these men were called Buffetiers, which the London cockney in
due time corrupted into Beefeaters." But this is a farfetched notion, for this
particular theory has been denied by all leading authorities on language.
The *Oxford English Dictionary*—and surely there is no higher court of
appeal on a word like this—says explicitly that "beefeater [is] not connected with buffet." *Brewer's Dictionary of Phrase and Fable* says: "There
is no evidence whatever for the old guess that the word is connected with
the French 'buffet,' and signified 'an attendant at the royal buffet.' " So
what does *beefeater* mean? Simply what it says: eater of beef—for substantial portions of beef have regularly been included among the rations of the
Yeomen of the Guard except, perhaps, during England's "austerity" years.

beer and skittles. *Skittles* is a version of the old-fashioned game of ninepins.
It's not bowling as we know it today, because the "ball" thrown at the pins
was not a ball at all, but a thick, flattened disk that was hurled across grass.
In centuries past, the average British yeoman's idea of paradise on earth
was not "a jug of wine, a loaf of bread and thou beside me in the wilderness." Rather he was content with a mug of beer and a friendly game of
skittles with his fellow farmers—and he'd be just as happy, thank you, if
"thou" would stay home tending the children.

before the mast. In the days of sailing ships, ordinary sailors had bunks in the
forecastle, the forward section of the ship, and so were literally *before the
mast.* There is another use of the same expression. In the navy a sailor who

is accused of a violation of a regulation is called to appear *before the mast.* On certain mornings of the week the culprits are escorted to the "mast," where the captain of the ship holds court and determines, after a hearing, what punishment should be meted out. Then the culprit is taken into custody by the ship's police officer, generally a chief master at arms (nicknamed "Johnny Legs"), and he'll see that the punishment is carried out.

beggar is often used, especially by the British, simply to mean "rascal or scoundrel" with no direct reference to the act of begging. In *Beau Geste,* for example, the hero was practically singlehandedly defending a desert camp against hordes of attacking sheiks. At a critical point he called to his aide: "Look at the *beggars* come!"

begonia is a plant originally found in the tropics, with brightly colored leaves and flowers of various colors. It takes its name from Michel Bégon, French governor of Santo Domingo and an enthusiastic amateur botanist.

beg the question has a sense seemingly rather far removed from the basic sense of "beg"—to entreat, to plead, especially for money. To *beg the question* means to avoid an issue. In debating it has the special meaning of taking as a basic assumption something which has not been proved, thereby avoiding the matter at issue. It is a very old expression, dating to Shakespeare's time, and may very well have developed as a sort of loose translation of *petitio principi,* a Medieval Latin term for taking for granted that which has not been proved. *Petitio* comes from the Latin verb *peto,* meaning "to seek or ask," so the connection is not farfetched.

beguile (pronounced be-GILE) is a combination of the Anglo-Saxon prefix *be-* and *guile,* meaning "deceit or cunning," which came unchanged from French, probably at the time of the Norman Conquest. *Beguile* still has the meaning of "to cheat or deceive" and even in the fairly common phrase *"beguile* the time away" retains the meaning of cheating, since the aim is to make time pass unnoticed. The verb *to beguile* and the noun *beguilement* are often used today with the connotation of pleasurable deceit.

behemoth. The original *behemoth,* from the Hebrew word of virtually the same spelling, meaning "great animal," was described (Job 40:15–24) as having bones like "strong pieces of brass" and "bars of iron . . . He moveth his tail like a cedar . . . Behold, he drinketh up a river, and hasteth not: he trusteth that he can draw up Jordan into his mouth." Allowing for a certain amount of literary license, that makes him sound like a very formidable beast indeed. That's why most modern scholars suspect that the hippopotamus is being described. In contemporary use, however, *behemoth* (pronounced beh-HEE-muth) can be used to describe anything of enormous size, from military tanks to superjet airplanes.

behind the eight ball comes from the game of Kelly pool. In one version of this game the player is required to pocket the balls in numerical rotation, except for the black ball, which is numbered eight. If another ball hits the eight ball, its player is penalized. So a position directly behind the eight ball is a position of great hazard.

belfry. Nowadays we know *belfry* solely as a church steeple, usually one in which bells are located. But the original *belfries* had nothing whatever to do with bells or with churches either. They were instruments of warfare, huge towers which were pushed up to the walls of medieval cities so that missiles, torches and the like could more easily be hurled upon the city's defenders. The church steeple gets the name *belfry* from its resemblance to these portable siege towers.

bell, book and candle refers to a solemn form of excommunication from the Roman Catholic Church. When the sentence denying further participation in the sacraments or rituals of the church is pronounced, a bell is rung, the book is closed and a candle extinguished—this last to symbolize the spiritual darkness in which the person sentenced must abide in the future.

belling the cat, meaning to take on a dangerous task for the benefit of others, has been traced back to Aesop's Fables. There you'll find the tale of the mice who held a meeting to decide what to do about a cat that had been killing off too many members of their clan. One sage old mouse suggested that a bell be put around the cat's neck, so that its tinkle would act as a warning to the mice. "Splendid idea," agreed one of the younger mice, "but who's to *bell the cat?*"

bellwether has been the designation since Anglo-Saxon times of the *wether* or eunuch sheep which carries a bell around its neck and acts as leader of the herd.

belly-timber. The word *belly* is one of the oldest English words, traceable to Anglo-Saxon and considered perfectly proper for most of the centuries since. However, it fell under the ban of Victorian "nice-nellyism." "Stomach"—which doesn't mean the same thing at all—came to be used as a euphemism for *belly*. To many people *belly* still sounds slightly indelicate. The phrase *belly-timber,* however, is another dish of tea. Originally a perfectly serious phrase, it is now used only in jest, as a rather pompously facetious synonym for food.

belly up is borrowed from fishing. A fish that floats *belly up* is dead.

below the belt. A blow *below the belt* is a manifestly unfair attack. The phrase originated in the rules for fisticuffs promulgated by the Marquis of Queensberry (John Sholto Douglas, 1844–1900), the same person who—in the view of some—struck Oscar Wilde rather a low blow by precipitating the libel suit that led to Wilde's downfall and imprisonment.

Ben Bolt/sweet Alice. There never literally was such a person as *Ben Bolt,* but in a sentimental ballad of the Victorian era, he was beloved by a maiden named *Alice,* who was to become a famous figure in song and drama. "Don't you remember *sweet Alice, Ben Bolt?*" was the first line of a song written just a few years after Victoria came to the throne of England—in

1843, to be precise. It was an American song, set to an old German tune and originally used in a play. It would be nice to report that *sweet Alice* was an instant hit, but that was not the case. The lyrics went like this: "Oh, don't you remember *sweet Alice, Ben Bolt?/Sweet Alice,* whose hair was so brown,/Who wept with delight when you gave her a smile,/And trembled with fear at your frown?" Even the sentimental Victorians weren't quite ready for that mushy a lyric, so the song languished almost unknown for half a century.

Then George Du Maurier quoted it in his best-selling novel *Trilby* and *sweet Alice* was off to the races. The novel, you'll recall, dealt with a lovely Parisian artist's model named Trilby who became a famous singer under the influence of Svengali, who was able to mesmerize her into singing beautifully. When Svengali died, her career died with him—and soon thereafter, so did she. *Trilby* was a great tear-jerking success and was adapted into a play, which ran in stock company productions for many years, and later into several films. The most notable movie version, as we recall, cast John Barrymore as Svengali—a role that brought out all the ham in that legendary actor.

Incidentally, while neither *Alice* nor *Ben Bolt* have made their way into the pages of current dictionaries, both *Ben Bolt* and Svengali are recorded in the 1934 edition of the *Merriam-Webster New International Dictionary*. Our guess is that the editors of that earlier work could still remember how their own heartstrings were tugged by the sentimental saga of *sweet Alice* and the object of her affections, *Ben Bolt.*

bench mark was originally a surveyor's term and referred to a marking made on something that has a permanent position and known altitude, like a rock outcropping, that is then used as a reference point for determining other altitudes. By extension, *bench mark* has come to be used as a general term for a standard of merit or achievement.

bend with the wind. In Sophocles' *Antigone* you will find this passage: "In flood time you can see how some trees bend, and because they bend, even their twigs are safe, while stubborn trees are torn up, roots and all." This must be one of the earliest examples of the trite but true expression *bend with the wind.* We find only one version that we can be reasonably sure was written earlier—this by the Chinese sage Confucius. "The relation between superiors and inferiors," he wrote, "is like that between the wind and the grass. The grass must bend when the wind blows across it." Sophocles lived from about 496 B.C. to 406, while Confucius lived from 551 to 479 B.C. Though there's a bit of overlap here, we think the odds favor Confucius as likely to have uttered the thought first.

benedict. Originally a *benedict* was a perennial bachelor, one sworn to a life of celibacy in the tradition of St. Benedict, the founder of the Benedictine order of monks. But William Shakespeare created in *Much Ado About*

Nothing a character who, though an avowed bachelor, is entrapped into matrimony—and Shakespeare, with one of those plays upon words which the Elizabethans dearly loved, named him Benedick. As a result, the two words *benedick* and *benedict* have become interchangeable, with the latter spelling much more common today. So a *benedict* today means not a bachelor but a married man—especially one who has only recently become married.

benny. In the lingo of the jazz musician, a *benny* is a pawnbroker.

berk. In a magazine article, Dudley Moore, who was co-starring with Peter Cook in the Broadway show *Good Evening,* wrote about Cook: "It is hard to distinguish sometimes whether Peter is being playful or merely a *berk.*" *Berk* is British slang—originally a bit of Cockney rhyming slang—meaning "fool."

berm. If you see SOFT BERM—KEEP OFF on a sign, it's simply another way of saying "soft shoulder." Most commonly used in the Central and Southern states, it is occasionally encountered in other parts of the country—sometimes with the spelling *berme.* It is not, as you might think, a regional dialect term. Indeed, *berm* has a history dating back to the romantic days of knightly chivalry. A *berm,* in Norman times, was the ridge between the edge of the moat around a castle and the fortress wall itself. Thus its use to designate the shoulder of a road is not at all farfetched.

berserk. In Norse legend, a *berserkr* was a warrior who fought with the fury and ferocity of a wild beast. He was said to wear a coat of bearskin, from which he got his name (*ber* for "bear" and *serkr* for "coat"). As a matter of fact, *Berserker* was the name of a legendary hero of the eighth century, who was so named because he refused to wear the traditional protective coat of mail. We inherited the word as *berserk* and we use it as an adjective or adverb meaning "in or into a state of wild or violent frenzy."

bespoke, a British term meaning "custom-tailored or made to measure," is a variant form of "bespoken," which in turn is the past participle (are you following us?) of "bespeak," which means "to speak for or order in advance."

best bib and tucker. When one puts on his *best bib and tucker,* he dresses his finest. This term originated shortly before 1700. The *bib* was an item of apparel not unlike a child's bib of today—and it served a similar purpose: keeping the clothes clean while eating. The *tucker* was an ornamental item, usually of lace or muslin, which women tucked into the necks of their dresses. It hung long and loose enough to cover the neck and shoulders. Thus a couple dressed in their *best bib* (the man) *and tucker* (the woman) was all spruced up for a fancy occasion.

best is yet to be. This optimistic phrase is from the first lines of *Rabbi Ben Ezra* by Robert Browning. The stanza runs: "Grow old along with me! The best is yet to be, The last of life, for which the first was made."

best man is of Scottish origin and goes back many centuries to the times when a prospective groom simply kidnaped the woman of his choice and carried her away with him. Such a venture required courage and audacity as well as a good deal of manpower. So the groom selected the bravest of his friends to accompany him. They were known as "groomsmen"—a term still used in some parts of the country to describe ushers at a wedding. The closest and most valiant of the bridegroom's associates became known as the *best man*. Similarly the bridesmaids were originally the closest friends of the bride, the ones who helped or pretended to help the bride defend herself against her abductors. Thus the customs of a savage and primitive society are echoed in the names used today for the participants in that most formal and civilized of ceremonies, the church wedding.

bête noire (pronounced bet nwar) is a French phrase that literally means "black beast." It is used figuratively in both French and English to refer to a person or thing which is disliked or feared—and which is to be avoided if possible. The phrase can also mean any sort of stumbling block—a person or thing which consistently interferes with one's life and which is seemingly unconquerable.

be there with bells on. Arriving *with bells on*—meaning happy and delighted to attend—goes back to the days before automobiles, when it was the custom to deck out with the fanciest harness the horse that drew the carriage for special occasions. That, of course, was the harness *with bells on*.

better than a poke in the eye with a stick. At the request of one of the readers of our newspaper column we passed on to other readers a query about the origin of the expression *better than a poke in the eye with a stick*. We noted that it paralleled a much more widely heard expression involving a kick in the posterior. But we didn't know the origin of the *poke in the eye* version and asked for help. George Grade of McLean, Virginia, had a suggestion. "It smacks of bittersweet Jewish humor," he wrote, "and that's a very rich type. The first time I heard or read it was in a novel in the Travis McGee mystery series by John D. MacDonald. Therein T.M.'s hairy friend, Meyer, who in swim trunks resembles Smokey Bear without his hat, commented on T.M.'s cash windfall: 'Five thousand dollars in the pocket is *better than a poke in the eye with a stick.*'"

better to light a candle than to curse the darkness. The author of the phrase is generally believed to be the Reverend James Keller, founder of the Christophers. It appeared in the preface of his book *One Moment, Please,* and was adopted as the motto of the Christopher Society, a Roman Catholic organization whose purpose is to "motivate people to get beyond self and bring spiritual values into the mainstream of modern life." That is true, as far as it goes. But Dr. Otto Phillips of Pittsburgh decided to take it one step further. He wrote Father Richard Armstrong, director of the organization, and received this comment: "Our motto is an ancient Chinese proverb. However, even scholars have been unable to attribute it to any specific person." So there the matter rests. Like many another saying of the sages of ancient China, it remains a bit of wisdom to be cherished and acted on.

Perhaps the most eloquent use of the expression was in Adlai Stevenson's tribute to Eleanor Roosevelt at the time of her death in 1962. "I have lost more than a friend," said Stevenson, "I have lost an inspiration. She would rather *light candles than curse the darkness* and her glow has warmed the world."

between Scylla and Charybdis is a very dangerous spot because avoidance of one can result in destruction by the other. Literally, *Charybdis* is a whirlpool off the Sicilian coast. Across the Strait of Messina is *Scylla,* a huge rock. In Greek mythology they were both personified as female monsters, intent on the destruction of any sailors who came near them. *Scylla* was believed to live in a cave in the rock and when a vessel came within reach she would thrust out her long necks (she had six heads) and grasp a sailor in each mouth, then drag them all back into her den. *Charybdis,* the monster in the whirlpool, meant certain death to all who came within reach of the swirling waters. During the wanderings of Ulysses for ten years after the fall of Troy, he had to pass between the two. Circe, the enchantress, had warned him and he could hear the roar of the waters of *Charybdis.* While he and his sailors were busy steering away from the whirlpool, *Scylla* silently reached out and carried away six of his sailors. On the other hand Aeneas, leader of the Trojans, who fled after his city was sacked, was warned of the dangers of the pass and managed to avoid it by taking a different route.

between the devil and the deep blue sea, meaning having little choice between two perils, is nautical in origin. The *devil* in this case is not the evil one himself, but a heavy plank (gunwale) fastened to the side of a ship as a support for guns. It was difficult of access and, once you were there, a perilous place to be, but better than the *deep blue sea.*

between you and me and the lamppost is an old expression—at least two centuries old, because Charles Dickens used it in *Nicholas Nickleby.* It often appears as *between you and me and the gatepost.* The meaning of the expression is that what is about to be said is being said in confidence—just the two of us and an inanimate object like a fence post will know what we say. It usually precedes a particularly juicy bit of gossip.

bev, ev, mev and cutie pie are creations of perhaps the most serious-minded and dedicated group of professional workers in America today, the nation's atomic energy researchers. Just as every trade, industry and profession gradually develops its own special language or jargon, so the workers on the newest and most challenging frontier of science have been creating their own body of language to describe the techniques and materials used in their work. Characteristically, they have in one short decade developed a vocabulary of many hundreds of words. Here are just a handful.

An *ev*, to begin with, is an electron volt, a measurement of the amount of energy gained by an electron when it is acted upon by one volt. An *ev* doesn't really represent much energy—but that's only the beginning. From the *ev* we go to the *mev*—a million electron volts—and beyond that to the *bev*, a billion electron volts. Now we are really cooking with nuclear gas, because an electron possessing one *bev* of energy is traveling almost as fast as the speed of light—186,000 miles per second.

Naturally, when scientists are dealing with power of this magnitude, all sorts of precautions must be observed. So it's perhaps not surprising that the thick-walled lead container in which radioactive materials are transported is called, somewhat morbidly, a *coffin*. The material carried in the coffin is usually designated *hot*—meaning highly radioactive—and when it reaches its destination it may well be stored in a *pig*—another name for a thick-walled container. The capsule used to carry samples in and out of an atomic reactor is known as the *rabbit*. And *cutie pie?* Well, that's a portable instrument used to determine the level of radiation in an area— mighty important work for a device so flippantly named.

Anyway, it's reassuring to know that these scientists, charged with researches of the utmost significance to the future of us all have not mislaid that most stabilizing of influences—a sense of humor.

beyond the pale. The *pale* in such phrases as *outside the pale, beyond the pale* and even *within the pale* has nothing whatever to do with the adjective meaning "whitish or colorless." The *pale* we are talking about when we use these phrases is actually a stake or fence post, a meaning which has come to us unchanged from the original Latin word *palus.* Since stakes or "palings" are generally used to mark off restricted areas, the word *pale* came in time to have the figurative meaning of a territory or district.

Back in the fourteenth century the areas of Ireland which had been colonized by the British were collectively known as the British *Pale.* The area, which included Dublin, Cork, Drogheda, Waterford and Wexford, was considered to be under British law, so that anything that took place *outside the pale* would be beyond British jurisdiction. Thus when we say that a person is *"outside the pale* of the law" we mean that by his actions he has forfeited the protection that the laws provide to law-abiding citizens. No one needs to be told that the Irish regarded British supervision as rather less than a mixed blessing. So it's not surprising that the area known as the British Pale contracted steadily and, by the sixteenth century, included only an area of about twenty miles around Dublin.

Incidentally, there were two other English *pales* in sixteenth-century Europe—one the city of Calais in France, which had been in English hands for centuries, and the other in Scotland, which, like the Irish domains, had been but recently acquired.

Today, of course, the British *Pale* is merely a phrase to be found in the history books, but the common phrases which it made part of our language —*beyond, outside* and *within the pale*—are still in daily use.

bialy. Now we will introduce you to a first cousin of the bagel, the *bialy.* Pronounced bee-AH-lee, it's a flat, round baked roll topped with onion flakes and lacking the hole characteristic of the bagel. It got its name from Bialystok, an industrial city in northeastern Poland. Naming foods for places has been going on for centuries. Boston baked beans, for instance, or to take a socially high-toned first cousin of the *bialy,* how about the Parker House roll, born on Tremont Street in Boston?

bibliomania/bibliophilia. One of these words will probably accurately describe a disease afflicting most readers of this volume. We trust it's the latter, for *bibliophilia* merely means "love of books"—a very healthy thing, we say—while *bibliomania* describes a passion for the printed word bordering on lunacy.

b.i.d. and **t.i.d.** on prescriptions are abbreviations for the Latin terms *bis in die* (twice a day) and *tres in die* (three times a day).

Big Apple. Most of us know that there was a popular dance of the 1930s called the *Big Apple* and that New York has for generations been known as the Big Town. But just how the Big Town received the nickname the *Big Apple* is unclear. In 1976 William had occasion to introduce New York City's Mayor Beame at a luncheon. Here surely, he thought, was the perfect opportunity to get a truly authoritative answer. So during lunch he asked the mayor what he knew about the origin of the nickname. "Well," replied Beame, "there was that dance back in the thirties, of course, but how it got connected to New York City I have no idea." If any reader has the true clue, we'd like to know—and we'll pass it on to the mayor.

Big Ben. The famous clock in London's Houses of Parliament which has been used for many years as a symbol of the empire, sounding the hours on BBC broadcasts aimed throughout the world was named after Sir Benjamin Hall, who was chief commissioner of works when the bell was cast in 1856. If Sir Benjamin has any other claims to fame, they have gone unrecorded in the history books.

Big Bertha was one of the greatest guns ever built, with a claimed range of 75 miles. It was built at the Krupp works during World War I with the announced intention of bombarding Paris from safe within the German lines. The name, a translation of the German *dicke Bertha* (fat Bertha), was a rather unflattering reference to Bertha Krupp von Bohlen und Halbach, owner of the works where it was made. The real-life Bertha outlived the gun named for her; indeed, she neatly survived both World Wars, dying in 1957 at the age of seventy-one.

big brass. Originally a military term, alluding to the gold braid on the hats of officers, *big brass* has carried over into civilian life as referring to top-ranking executives in business.

big butter-and-egg man is credited to a nightclub owner and mistress of ceremonies named Texas Guinan. One night in 1924 a chap appeared at her speakeasy-cabaret, called for rounds of drinks for the house and wound up giving fifty-dollar bills to all the chorus girls and other entertainers. Naturally Texas wanted him to take a bow, but he refused to identify himself further than to say he was in the dairy business. So Texas, moving him into the spotlight, called for "A great big hand for my *big butter-and-egg man*" —and the phrase was born.

bigger they are, the harder they fall is an expression from the prize ring. Back in 1902 "Ruby Robert" Fitzsimmons, one-time heavyweight champion of the world, said this on the even of his fight with James J. Jeffries, a much bigger man. That's not the way things came out, by the way. Jeffries won.

bigot. There are two theories of the origin of the word *bigot.* One holds that it was originally a contraction of two old English words, *bi God* (by God). Since bigots are people who are narrow-minded and hold blindly and intolerantly to their beliefs, they may well feel that they are acting by God. Another idea is that it is derived from the Spanish *hombre de bigote,* meaning "man with a mustache." A man so endowed was presumably more obstinate than his fellows, though in our own experience we have known as many bigots without mustaches as with.

A patently inaccurate theory of its origin has been advanced by a writer of Philippine history, who holds that it comes from the name of Chief Bigotillos, the Moro chief of Sulu in 1730. However, *bigot* appeared in print first in 1598—almost a century and a half before the Moro chief.

In top-secret World War II code *bigot* was used to mean something entirely different. In England in the tense weeks and months prior to the Normandy invasion, those members of Allied headquarters staff who were engaged in planning for the operation and hence were privy to the greatest secret of the war were known by the code name *bigot.* It was probably the only time in history when the label *bigot* was a mark of honor.

bigotty, is one of the most widespread of American dialect terms, but we do not wonder if you are uncertain of its spelling. Wentworth's *American Dialect Dictionary* lists six different spellings, which have appeared in our literature from Mark Twain to Marjorie Kinnan Rawlings: *biggity, biggety, bigotty, briggity, brigaty* and *brickety.* The clue to its origin will be found in the third version, *bigotty,* for the word originally meant "very bigoted." Hence, in the words of Webster's *Unabridged Dictionary,* Second Edition: "conceited or conceitedly self-important; saucily impudent." Wentworth gives other meanings: "proud, haughty, stubborn and snooping." So no matter how you spell it, *bigotty* is a useful word indeed and we wish it a long life as a tangy regional colloquialism.

bigwig is a person of importance or, at least, a person who thinks he is important. The name comes from the wigs worn by British barristers and judges. To some of them, no doubt, it seemed that the bigger the wig, the more important the office.

bikini. A summer fashion of the distaff side is the scanty two-piece bathing suit named the *bikini.* As many of its young wearers may be only dimly aware, it takes its name from an atoll in the Marshall Islands where the United States held its first post–World War II tests of the atomic bomb. We may assume that it got its name from the comparatively scanty attire of the original inhabitants of Bikini atoll, but the Merriam-Webster *Third International* tells us, in solemn dictionaryese, that it's "from a comparison of the effects wrought by a scantily clad woman to the effects of the atomic bomb." Ah, for the life of a lexicographer!

bilk—meaning to cheat or defraud—is a variant form of *balk.* It was first used in cribbage, meaning to spoil your opponent's score and thus, by sharp play, to defraud him of points he has earned. During the nineteenth century the term came into wide general use in this country and a *bilker* was once defined by a boardinghouse keeper as a man "who never missed a meal and never paid a cent."

bill. A *bill* is $100 in thieves' argot—and in show and garment business talk, too. So 5,000 *bills* is actually $500,000. A $100 bill is also called a *C-note* or a *yard;* $500 is *five bills, five C's* or *half a G*—the *G,* obviously, being a *grand,* or $1,000. Incidentally, the little old dollar bill has dozens of slang names: *buck, buckeroo, one-spot, shekel, simoleon* and *single,* to name only a few.

billikins. When we were quite young there were dolls called *billikins.* They were the kind that toppled over easily and rolled on a weighted round base. We also used to call obese people *billikins. Billikin* is thought to be a combination of the nickname "Billy" plus *-kin,* a suffix indicating affection —as in "lambkin." The old *Funk & Wagnalls* Unabridged Dictionary has a rather more menacing description. It says that the *billikin* is a "grotesque figure used as a fetish; the god of things as they ought to be." Be that as it may, we recall the *billikins* as being a lot of fun. No matter how you pushed or tossed them, they always ended right side up!

billingsgate is a term for foul language and comes from the name of a section of London, *Billingsgate,* for centuries the site of a great fish market. Its workers—including female peddlers called *fishwives*—have long been noted for the violence and vulgarity of their language.

According to legend, *Billingsgate* got its name as a contraction or corruption of *Belin's Gate,* one of the earliest gates of London. Belin was thought to be the son of King Lud, the mythical founder of London (Lud's Town). All this must be viewed with some skepticism, for it is based on the writings of Geoffrey of Monmouth, a Welsh chronicler writing nearly two thousand years after the reigns—if any—of Lud and Belin.

More logical, perhaps, is the theory based on the writings of the Roman historian Tacitus reporting the Roman invasion of Britain. According to him, one of the tribes called itself the *Billings.* In any event, this once noble plot of land has long been graced by the foulest tongues of Britain.

Billingsgate pheasant, named for the London fish market, is a term that the British use jokingly for the common red herring or bloater in much the same way that a dish of melted cheese is called Welsh rabbit.

billion. In America and France a *billion* is a thousand million. In Great Britain and Germany it is a million million. Moral: If you want to be a billionaire, stay right here in America.

bindle stiff was and is a migrant worker who carries his own bedroll with him. *Bindle* is a dialect variation of "bundle," a reference to the bedding he carries. The term was much more commonly heard in the early days of this century when the IWW, commonly called the Wobblies, was a force to be reckoned with. The union, a radical outfit, had special appeal for immigrant factory workers and for migrant farm workers, and it was in the latter group that the *bindle stiffs* were to be found. The union took a strong antiwar position in World War I and the public's reaction was overwhelmingly hostile to it. After a trial in 1917, in which the leader "Big Bill" Haywood and nearly a hundred others were convicted of sedition, the strength of the union was broken. Jim Tully, an ex-prize fighter and hobo, whose writings were popularized by H. L. Mencken in the twenties, once explained the various classes of men who chose a life "on the road." Said Tully: "I was a *bindle stiff.* That's the class that will do some work once in a while. The grifters are the desperate characters; the hobos are the philosophers."

bird. A recent item of British slang, somewhat voguish in America as well, is *bird,* to describe a young girl, especially one who may be classed as a bit of a swinger. There's really nothing new about the use of *bird* to refer to young females, though the type of girl to whom it was applied in centuries past was not quite of the same order as today's *birds.* In Middle English and Old English the word was *brid,* from which we also get "bride." By a semantic shift known as metathesis, the *i* and the *r* became transposed and *bird* resulted. Originally meaning only our various feathered friends, it later came to mean a young lady as well.

birdiebacking. The trucking industry has added at least two bright terms to the lexicon of business English—*piggybacking,* to describe trailers loaded aboard flatcars and transported by rail to their destination, and more recently, *fishybacking,* the transportation of loaded trailers by boat. Now there is a third new coinage—*birdiebacking.* That's right—now they load the trailers aboard airplanes and fly them to their destination.

birds and bees. Perhaps the answer to how this phrase became a euphemism for "sex" lies in these verses by Samuel Taylor Coleridge: "All nature seems at work . . . The bees are stirring—birds are on the wing . . . and I the while, the sole unbusy thing, not honey make, nor pair, nor build, nor sing." In past times, when schools touched on such matters at all—which was seldom—sex was usually handled in classes with titles such as Hygiene or Health. The facts of reproduction of the species were presented by analogy—telling how birds do it and how bees do it and trusting that the youngsters would get the message by indirection.

bite the bullet. The expression comes from the medical profession. During the nineteenth century surgeons were often called on to perform amputations and the like on the battlefield when no anesthesia was available. So the patient would be given a bullet and told to bite hard upon it. The theory was that this creation of a counterirritant would serve to distract somewhat from the attention paid by the patient to the pain of the operation. The basic meaning of the expression *bite the bullet* is that one must act with courage and avoid any show of fear. Rudyard Kipling said it well in his "The Light That Failed": "Bite on the bullet, old man, and don't let them think you're afraid."

bite the hand that feeds them. This expression, meaning utter ingratitude, first appeared in the writings of Edmund Burke, one of the greatest British parliamentarians and certainly one of the finest orators of all time. In an essay published after his death, he wrote: "And having looked to government for bread, on the very first scarcity they will turn and bite the hand that fed them."

blab school. Abraham Lincoln is recorded as once having attended a *blab school*—an elementary school usually with several grades in a single room, in which pupils recited and sometimes studied aloud. *Blab* means, of course, "to speak out." Often, in a *blab school,* a group of pupils would recite a lesson in unison, over and over, until even the dullest one could recite it by rote.

blackball refers to the practice once common of having members of a private club vote on prospective candidates for admission by dropping colored balls in a box. If, at the end of the voting, all the balls were white or red, the candidate was admitted. But one single black ball would cause his exclusion.

Black Belt. Many news stories about the South have referred to the states from South Carolina west to Louisiana as the *Black Belt,* implying that the name derives from the fact that blacks outnumber whites in this area. While this statistic is undoubtedly true, that's not how the name originated. The *Black Belt* was first so called because of the rich black soil that predominates in the area. Such soil was ideal for the raising of cotton. Slaves were imported to harvest the crops, and in time the numerical preponderance of blacks became a reality.

black book. A dashing young bachelor may pride himself on his *black book,* in which he claims to have the names and addresses of dozens of beautiful females. But the first famous *black book* was one of far more sinister implications for people whose names appeared in it than the one the office Casanova boasts about. It was compiled by Henry VIII during his long struggle with Rome. He planned to take control of the Church and its holdings in England, and to support his case with Parliament, he made a list of British monasteries and used allegations of sinful misconduct on the part of their occupants. As a result, those properties were assigned to the Crown.

Over the centuries since that event there have been many *black books* compiled by officials, especially law-enforcement officers. The one common denominator of all these *black books* was that any name entered in them was the name of a person held in disfavor. Why, then, should the office gallant be speaking of his little *black book* of names that he obviously holds in very high regard? This radical alteration in meaning can be traced at least as far back as one of the Fred Astaire–Ginger Rogers musical films of the 1930s, when Astaire, seeking to arouse jealousy in Miss Rogers, whisked out a tiny black notebook and extolled the charms of the girls whose names were listed in it. Since Fred Astaire was the very paragon of charm and sophistication, his example was imitated by thousands of would-be charm boys.

black comedy, which originated in French as *comédie noire,* is a dramatic form in which the humor is based on morbid or grotesque situations and activities. One example cited in the Barnhart *Dictionary of New English* will give you a pretty good idea of what *black comedy* is like. In a quotation from a review that appeared in a British paper, we read that "Hal Prince's 'Something for Everyone' is a *black comedy* about a handsome young man who transforms the lives of a family of down-at-the-heels aristocrats by seducing them all."

Black Jack Pershing. The World War I American Expeditionary Force Commander, General John Pershing, got the nickname *Black Jack* while he was an instructor at West Point in 1897. Before being assigned there, he had been an officer in the Tenth U.S. Cavalry, a famous Negro regiment that later came to the rescue of Theodore Roosevelt and his Rough Riders in the Spanish-American War. Because Pershing had served five years with this outfit before coming to the Point, he was first nicknamed "Nigger Jack" but the sobriquet was later softened to *Black Jack.*

black list, which is in our language today as both a noun and a verb (to *blacklist*), has its origin in practices which go back as far as medieval times. Early records of such British universities as Oxford and Cambridge show that black books were used to record all cases of misconduct on the part of students, and anyone whose name appeared in them was, at least temporarily, in disgrace. Henry VIII used his version of the black book with great success in his fight with Rome (see BLACK BOOK). Later merchants used black books for recording the names of people with poor credit ratings, and the first *black lists* were lists of men who had gone bankrupt.

Before the Wagner Act made them illegal, *black lists* were used in various industries. Men who joined unions were put on "don't hire" lists circulated among employers. Shortly after World War II, a number of Hollywood writers claimed that they had been *blacklisted* by the industry for alleged leftist leanings. Then, in the early 1950s, similar complaints were heard in the television industry. Actors, producers and writers claimed that they were being denied employment because their names were on an industry *black list*.

blackmail. *Black* here merely means "evil or sinful or bad." The *mail* part, though, is interesting because it has nothing to do with the post office, though *blackmail* demands are often delivered through the mails. In this case the *mail* means "rent or tax" and refers to the tribute demanded by and paid to freebooters along the Scottish border who demanded *blackmail* as the price for passage and freedom from molestation.

black sheep. "There's a *black sheep* in every family," goes the old expression, meaning that there's sure to be one disreputable chap in every assemblage. A *black sheep* was held to be valueless by the shepherd. Also, according to widely held belief, a *black sheep* was an outcast because its color frightened other sheep.

Black Shirts was the popular name of the elite corps of the Nazi army, so named because *black shirts* were part of the uniform. The official name of the outfit was *Schutzstaffel* or *SS Corps*. *Black Shirts* was also applied to members of Mussolini's and other fascist groups wearing them as part of their uniform.

black shoe navy refers to the traditional seaborne navy, as differentiated from its newer airborne arm. More specifically, it is a term often used by officers of the fleet air arm—most of whom are alumni of naval training stations, rather than of Annapolis—in deprecatory reference to Naval Academy alumni, who, they feel, exercise too much control over promotions to flag rank. The origin of the term goes back to the time when all naval uniforms were either blue or white, and black shoes were part of the prescribed attire. The uniform of naval aviators, which permitted use of brown shoes, was the first deviation from the traditional modes of naval dress.

black velvet is a drink composed of equal parts of Guinness stout and champagne. *Black* refers to the color of the stout and *velvet* to the smoothness of the concoction when drunk.

bladders. In circus jargon, balloons are called *bladders;* the man who sells them is the *rubber man.*

blanket. In one of his novels Thomas Costain devoted quite a bit of space to his theory as to how the word *blanket* for the ordinary bedcover was originated. He stated that among the weavers in Britain during the Middle Ages there was one who wove coverlets of surpassing fineness. His name was *Blanket,* an Anglicized version of the Flemish *Blanquette,* according to the tale; and so splendid were his bedcovers that in time his name became the generic term applied to all. With all due respect to Costain, whose historical novels we admire, we suspect that he was indulging in a bit of whimsy on this occasion. According to all authorities, *blanket* is simply derived from the French *blanc,* meaning "white," and its first meaning (before 1400) was simply "undyed or white cloth."

blarney. The Blarney Castle, located a few miles north of Cork, Ireland, is famous for its *Blarney stone,* a triangular piece of limestone very difficult to reach. It is said that anyone brave enough to hang by his heels to kiss the stone is rewarded by the gift of a blandly persuasive manner of speech. A man who has kissed the *Blarney stone* is reputed to be able to charm, coax and cajole his fellow humans so long as he lives.

The legends that have grown up about the stone are legion. One theory is that it was brought from ancient Tyre and Carthage by a band of adventurers centuries before Caesar and his legions invaded the British Isles. More credible is the story about McCarthy Mor, the lord of the castle, who in 1602 was defeated after a long siege and agreed to surrender to British troops under Sir George Carew. Day after day poor Carew waited for the terms to be fulfilled; day after day the lord of the castle would put him off with some new, fanciful excuse. At last Carew became the butt of jokes from his fellow members of Queen Elizabeth's court. Finally the Queen herself took a hand in the proceedings, but all she could get was a long, windy and evasive letter, about which she is reported to have said: "This is more of the same *blarney*"—and a word was born.

blatant. Edmund Spenser, English poet of the sixteenth century, coined *blatant* to describe a monster in his *Faerie Queene.* The *Blatant* Beast, as it was called, possessed one hundred tongues and a sting and was supposed to be a personification of slander. Spenser probably made the word from the Latin *blaterare,* meaning "to babble." It has come to mean offensively loud and noisy and, by extension, too obvious, crudely conspicuous or in bad taste.

blazer. This sports jacket gets its rather remarkable name from the fact that the first *blazers,* worn by the Lady Margaret (St. John's College, Cambridge) crew in the late nineteenth century, were made of brilliant red cloth, so bright that at a distance the crew seemed almost literally ablaze.

bleb. A word seldom seen outside a dictionary, *bleb* comes unchanged from the Middle English *bleb* (the sound produced by forming a bubble with the lips) and now means "blister."

blend words. Words that are really combinations of two words are generally called *blend words,* though the most illustrious inventor of such words

called them *portmanteau words.* He was Lewis Carroll, whose pages spar-
kled with such inventions as " 'Twas brillig and the slithy toves did gyre
and gimble in the wabe," in a language he labeled "Jabberwocky." In
Through the Looking Glass, Carroll explains that he chose the word *portmanteau*—a then fashionable term for a kind of suitcase—because there
are two meanings "packed up" in such a word. Among his most vivid
concoctions were *slithy,* a blend of "lithe" and "slimy," and *mimsy* from
"miserable" and "flimsy." Some of Carroll's other coinages have become
part of Standard English. For example, *squawk* from "squeal" and
"squall" and *chortle* from "chuckle" and "snort." But the native American
genius for creation of *blend words* has been in evidence at least since 1812,
when *gerrymander* (from "Gerry" and "salamander") was coined. Perhaps
the moral to all this comes from another of Lewis Carroll's creations,
Humpty-Dumpty, who said: "When I use a word, it means just what I
choose it to mean—neither more nor less."

blind pig/blind tiger describe illegal establishments where alcoholic beverages
are sold. During the Prohibition era such places were generally called
"speakeasies" on the theory that the prospective customer should modu-
late his voice when speaking to the man behind the entrance door. *Blind
pig* and *blind tiger* considerably antedate Prohibition. They go back as far
as 1857, when the following account appeared in a sportsmen's gazette
called *Spirit of the Times:* "I sees a kind of pigeon hole cut in the side of
the house and over it a sign *Blind Tiger,* ten cents a sight.' Says I to the
feller inside, 'here's your ten cents. Walk out your wild-cat.' I'll be dod-
busted if he didn't shove out a glass of whiskey. You see that *'blind tiger'*
was an arrangement to evade the law, which won't let them sell licker
there." For the record, the first time *blind pig* appeared in print was about
fifteen years later.

blind robin is the unusual name, once common in western Pennsylvania, for
the kind of herring the British call a bloater. One correspondent's somewhat clinical explanation for the name follows: "Since the *blind robin* was
first cleaned and then smoked whole, with head and tail attached, the first
thing you would notice would be that cold eye staring at you. No wonder
it was called *blind.* The skin was smoked to a beautiful golden color and
was so loose that it would peel off as though it were parched paper. But
the real treat was inside. The meat had a deep rose color and came off the
bones so easily that the entire bone structure would remain intact. And the
taste—most delicious. Now then, suppose that someone as enthusiastic as
I am about bloaters took a look at that blind eye and the color of the meat,
which could easily remind him of a robin's red breast, and then combined
the two ideas. Presto! He'd call it *blind robin.* "

blitz. Hitler made *blitz* an international word when he began his plan to
conquer the world. *Blitz* is the German word for "lightning or flash" and,

combined with *krieg* (war), it aptly described the military strategy of
Hitler's armies. Since then, however, *blitz* has been Americanized to mean
any quick triumph, whether in games or in business.

blizzard. Allen Walker Read of Columbia University reported more than
thirty years ago that the editor of an Estherville, Iowa, paper was the first
to use *blizzard* (in 1870) to describe a fierce snowstorm. This report has
been challenged many times since and this particular editor's claims must
now be regarded as a bit shaky. What is certain is that *blizzard*—probably
derived from the German *blitz,* "lightning"—was in use many years earlier
in different senses. For example, Davy Crockett used it to mean a volley
of shots ("I took a *blizzard* at one of the bucks and he tumbled").

blockhouse. Any viewer of films concerning frontier days is familiar with the
small building in a frontier fort called the *blockhouse.* Why was it so
named? Simply because of its square shape—like a block—and the fact that
it was built of squared timber or logs.

bloodhound. *Bloodhounds* are so called because theirs was the first breed
whose "blood" or breeding records were maintained. The first chronicles
of the genealogy of this breed were maintained by the monks of St. Hubert's
Abbey in France in the ninth century.

blood money. The earliest meaning of *blood money*—dating back to 1535—
is money paid to an informer, one who gives testimony leading to the
conviction of another. In this sense it could be said that the pieces of silver
paid to Judas to betray Jesus were the very first *blood money. Blood money*
is also used to describe the money paid to the next of kin of a person
murdered, especially such sums in the form of pensions paid to policemen
or servicemen killed in the line of duty. In the underworld, the expression
describes the sum paid to a hired killer. Now we have the newest meaning
—money paid to a blood donor.

blood, toil, tears and sweat. When the matter of tracing a quotation comes up,
we often turn to our friend and editorial associate Bruce Bohle, editor of
the sprightly *Home Book of American Quotations.* Here are his comments
on Winston Churchill's famous phrase:

> It is a curious fact that many of us who are ready to grant a man status as a
> hero are quite chary about accepting his credentials as the coiner of something
> as good as the blood-sweat-tears combination. Few would begrudge Churchill
> the title of architect of British survival in World War II, but quite a few would
> suspect that he had some help in putting together the quotation at hand.
>   The quotation in question was spoken by Churchill on the floor of the House
> of Commons, May 13, 1940: "I have nothing to offer but *blood, toil, tears and
> sweat.* " It was the first public statement by the man just commissioned by the
> Crown to form a new government, thirteen days before the start of the Dunkirk
> evacuation.
>   Though the wording is not new, the sentiment was probably never stated more

effectively, even by Churchill himself, who knew a good thing when he wrote it. Nine years earlier, in *The Unknown War* (1931), referring to the Russian armies prior to the Revolution, Churchill observed, "Their sweat, their tears, their blood bedewed the endless plain."

Since he was a man with a flair for vivid expression, and an avid reader of good things, Churchill may well have been aware of John Donne's "An Anatomie of the World" (1611), in which appears: " 'Tis in vain to dew, or mollifie/It with thy teares, or sweat, or blood." Perhaps he had read Byron's "The Age of Bronze" (1823): "Year after year they voted cent per cent,/Blood, sweat, and tear-wrung millions—why? for rent!" And in 1919, Lord Alfred Douglas's *Collected Poems* contained this line: "It [poetry] is forged slowly and patiently, link by link, with sweat and blood and tears."

In any case, Churchill got *blood, toil, tears and sweat* into subsequent major addresses on Oct. 8, 1940; May 7, 1941; Dec. 2, 1941; Jan. 27, 1942; and Nov. 10, 1942. Thereafter, the state of the war justified something less despairing (but it is interesting that it inspired nothing so lasting).

bloody until recently was considered censorable in English, a sort of British equivalent of some of the four-letter words that still cannot appear in a family newspaper. To linguists, such words are simply labeled "intensives," meaning that they have no literal significance beyond strengthening the power of the expression they are part of. There are many theories of the origin of *bloody* in its distasteful aspects, including references to Mary I of England as *Bloody* Mary and that it may be a vulgar corruption of "By our Lady." None of the theories seems convincing.

bloomers. There is a story behind bloomers—a story more than a century old. It was Mrs. Amelia Bloomer, one of New York's earliest and most vehement suffragettes, who first tried to get American women to wear trousers. The costume she advocated consisted of loose-fitting trousers, gathered tight at the ankle, with a knee-length outer skirt. The fashion never met with great success, but much later, after the turn of the century, the billowing, knee-length pants which some of us remember as *bloomers* were devised for girls to wear while exercising. Ironically, Amelia Bloomer insisted to her dying day that she was not the person who invented the first *bloomers.* She always credited the style to a Mrs. Elizabeth Miller, daughter of a New York congressman. But the public liked the word *bloomers* —and *bloomers* they remain.

blooper is a slang term of fairly recent origin meaning "blunder or error." It usually has the connotation of an inadvertent error, such as a slip of the tongue, which exposes a prominent or pompous person to ridicule. *Blooper* is also used in baseball slang in quite a different sense, to mean a weakly hit fly ball which drops just beyond the infield. Years ago this was called a "Texas leaguer."

bloviate. Francis Russell's biography of President Warren Harding, *The*

Shadow of Burning Grove, says that Harding and his friends back in Marion, Ohio, used to spend a lot of time sitting around *bloviating.* There was—indeed, there is—such a word as *bloviate,* but you have to do a lot of searching to find it. The 1913 *Funk & Wagnalls* Unabridged lists *bloviation* and defines it as "loud, defiant, boastful talk." The current *Merriam-Webster Third International* defines *bloviate* as "to orate verbosely and windily." It's a dandy word and one that should not be allowed to wither on the vine, not so long as long-winded political orators exist—and that they still do.

It's a particularly appropriate word for Warren Gamaliel Harding, for he was the very epitome of that characteristically American phenomenon, the politician who makes a handsome, impressive appearance and talks impressively at great length, without ever managing to say anything of real substance. Harding's rhetoric was much commented on in his own time. Henry L. Mencken once observed that "Harding's style was so bad that a sort of grandeur crept into it." And the poet e.e. cummings once dashed off a verse about "Warren Gamaliel Harding/ The only man, woman or child/ Who could make seven grammatical errors/ In a simple declarative sentence."

blow his (her) stack. We suspect that this refers to the "stacks" on old-time riverboats. If the ship's boiler got badly overheated, it might *blow the stack* and wild confusion and widespread damage would result. There are dozens of similar expressions for "letting off steam" or venting one's anger. "Blow a fuse," "blow your top" and "blow your cork" are just three of them.

bluchers. Field Marshal Gebhart Leberecht von Blücher was a notable Prussian general who rates much more than a footnote in the accounts of the Napoleonic campaigns because he was instrumental in the defeat of the Little Corporal at Waterloo. But his lasting fame, so far as word students are concerned, is that, like Raglan and Cardigan—a brace of British generals of Crimean War fame—his name lives on in the language of wearing apparel, as the name for a kind of heavy half boots.

bludgeon can be used as a verb in either a literal or a figurative sense to mean "to beat into submission." It takes its meaning from the Middle French word *bougen,* a diminutive of *bouge,* meaning "club." Used as a noun, it means a short club with a weighted end.

blue. According to the *Dictionary of American Slang,* "blue" in the sense of risqué or bordering on the obscene has been current since about the turn of the century and it suggests that *blue* got this meaning "perhaps because the color blue is associated with burning brimstone." Well, perhaps—but that explanation doesn't seem to square with its use by people in show business, especially the more raffish kinds of show business like nightclubs and burlesque. In the days before congressmen made stripteasers respectable, it was standard practice to change the color filters on spotlights when the star dancer went into the gamier parts of her act. A favorite color used during these portions of her act was blue, so "dipping into the *blue,*" as the common expression went, may well have come from this change in color of the spotlights.

blue-bellied Yankees is a term of contemptuous jest first used by the British in referring to the colonists at the time of the American Revolution. The red-coated British soldiers took an old Scottish tune and named it "Yankee Doodle," giving it lyrics derogatory to the colonials, who were dressed in homespun. During the Civil War, Confederate soldiers applied the term to the men of the Northern army, whose uniforms were blue.

blue-chip stock comes from the chips used in gambling games like poker. These chips or counters range in value from red (cheapest) through white to blue (most valuable—usually worth ten times the red). So a *blue-chip stock* is one likely to give the greatest return on an investment.

blue funk is, as one of our readers puts it, "an expression that I have heard my mother use many times to describe what advertisements call 'the blahs.' " She complained that she got both "Noah" and "Funk" out and that they described *funk* as "fright."

We were just as surprised as she to find that many dictionaries don't record the meaning of *blue funk* as what we might call "mental depression, usually of short duration." That's the sense both of us Morrises have known all our lives and it's passing strange that Noah Webster and, especially, Isaac Funk didn't have it.

However, Noah Webster's successors, the editors of the *Merriam Third International,* have caught up with this sense of *funk* and in their new dictionary say this: "a depressed state of mind, as 'in a deep *blue funk* about life in the city.' "

Blue Hen State. The regiment furnished by Delaware in the Revolutionary War was known, because of its intense combativeness, as the Game Cock Regiment. Its commander, one Captain Caldwell, was a famous breeder of gamecocks who held that the very finest fighting cocks were those born of blue hens. So the Delaware warriors, first known as Caldwell's Game Cocks, later were known as the Blue Hen's Chickens—and Delaware became the *Blue Hen State.*

blue jeans. In any contest to select the item of wearing apparel most popular among American youth there's not much question but that *blue jeans* would be the winner. Boys and girls alike wear them at work and play the year around—and many a grownup dons them when heavy chores are in prospect. In the West, especially among cattlemen, they are usually called *Levis* and everywhere you hear *jeans* and *denims.* Interestingly enough, there is a story behind each of these names—and it's hard to tell which is more unusual.

Take *jeans,* for example. Although thousands of girls named Jean have worn them, there is no connection at all between the girl's name and the name of the garment. It's actually an altered form of "Genoa," where the cloth was once woven. Similarly, *denim* comes from the phrase *serge de Nîmes,* after the city of Nîmes, France. *Levis,* derive their name from Levi Strauss, a San Francisco clothing merchant of Gold Rush days. His great contribution was the addition of rivets to the corners of pockets, so that they would not tear out when miners loaded them with samples of ore. As his fame spread throughout the West, *Levis* became the popular term for these durable work clothes—just as "Stetson" or "John B." (both from the John B. Stetson hat-manufacturing company) became the accepted terms for the cowpuncher's ten-gallon hat.

blue law is a law restricting activities, particularly those of a commercial or recreational nature, at specified times, especially on Sunday. Such laws were originally enacted during our colonial period. The very first such laws were enacted in the early days of the New Haven colony, with the result that Connecticut was known at one time as the *Blue Law* State. In a story about widespread defiance of such laws by supermarkets and similar stores that insist on seven-day-a-week operation, the *New York Times* reported that "the name derives from Puritan legislation, regulating Sabbath conduct, printed on blue paper in the theocratic New Haven colony in the 17th century." That's a nice story, but the truth is simpler. The *blue* in *blue law* is simply a synonym for "puritanical" or "strict."

blue Monday. It is an unquestioned fact that during the Middle Ages the Monday before the beginning of Lent was called *Blue Monday*—but there are two schools of thought as to why it got that name. One holds that the churches were decorated in blue on that day. Another believes that because so many people spent the weekend before Lent in drunken revels, they woke up mighty "blue" and hung over on that Monday morning. And then there's a later version of the origin of *blue Monday,* this one stemming from the days of sailing ships. Monday—any Monday—was flogging day. Errant sailors were brought before the mast and flogged until they were black and blue.

blue ribbon. The color blue has traditionally been associated with eminence in all fields of endeavor. Perhaps because the blue skies were thought to be the abode of the gods of ancient times, the color has long been associated with royalty—hence, "royal blue." In Britain the *blue ribbon* is the badge of the Order of the Garter, the highest honor bestowed by the crown. In France the *cordon bleu* was once the emblem of the highest order of knighthood, a member of the Order of the Holy Ghost. Today it is also used to designate a chef of the very first order. Throughout the Western world *blue ribbon* signifies "highest honor."

blues. The matter of just where the term *blues* came from is much in dispute. The most widely held theory is that it is an abbreviation of "blue devils"

—hallucinations, like pink elephants, popularly believed to accompany delirium tremens. The mood of acute depression following an attack of the d.t.'s would surely be depressing enough to cause the moans of anguish which may first have given birth to the *blues*. At any rate, that's more likely than the popular song's theory about the "breeze in the trees" inspiring the first *blues*.

Incidentally, the term *blue* in the sense of melancholy, depressed or despondent has been an element of slang, especially black slang, since midway through the past century. According to one authority, the *blues* was common as a form of work song in the cotton and tobacco fields as early as 1870. The earliest published *blues* was the work of that self-styled genius of the piano, Jelly Roll Morton. With his customary modesty, Morton named it "The Jelly Roll Blues" in 1905.

blue stocking. When we were preparing for a trip through Wales, we acquired a travel guide for that charming country, and one of the points of interest was the town of Llangollen, situated by the River Dee. It is there that the annual International Eisteddfod is held, with more than twenty-five countries competing for awards for singing and dancing. According to this travel guide, the phrase *blue stocking,* used to describe ladies of literary bent, was originated there. It seems that late in the eighteenth century, two romantic and eccentric young ladies named Lady Eleanor Butler and the Honorable Sarah Ponsonby moved from Ireland to a Llangollen house called Plas Newyald. Determined to lead an intellectual life and vowing never to marry, they seem to have spent much of their time, according to the travel guide, knitting blue stockings and "creating a new English expression." They were said to have been visited by "notable people such as Wellington, De Quincey, Scott and Wordsworth, all of whom brought gifts to add to their collection." Some of this must be true—although we never did get to investigate—because the house inhabited by the two ladies is open to tourists every day of the year.

The one thing that isn't true is that the phrase *blue stocking* originated there and then, although it was undoubtedly applied to these intellectual young ladies. As long ago as 1400, ladies and gentlemen in Venice formed a society called *della calza,* whose members were distinguished by the color of their stockings. By 1590 the fashion had spread to Paris, where it became the rage. It took almost two centuries to reach England, where Mrs. Elizabeth Montague, an English writer and society leader, wore the badge of the *bas bleu* club at the literary evenings which she held in her home. So the two "Ladies of Llangollen," as they were called, had probably just joined the club, rather than coined the phrase.

blurb. Originally *blurb* meant a statement of lavish praise quoted on the dust jacket of a book. More recently, it has come to mean any exaggerated advertising claim. The word was coined by the late great humorist Gelett Burgess, who also used "bromide" to describe a person addicted to the use of clichés. Burgess also created the Purple Cow (which see).

board of directors. The "board" in *board of directors* is the same word that is used to describe a long, flat piece of lumber. It refers to the fact that such groups usually hold their formal meetings around a wooden table. The "chairman of the board" title goes back to the early days of our colonial history. At that time chairs were comparatively rare. Most people made do with stools or benches. So when the leaders of a colony sat around the "board" to confer on matters of state, the leader was the man seated in the chair. Hence, "chairman of the board."

boat/ship. There's a distinction here which no old salt will ever forget—and no landlubber ever seems able to learn. The dictionary puts it this way: "A ship is a vessel of considerable size navigating deep water and not propelled by oars, paddles or the like—distinguished from 'boat.' " A more up-to-date definition would also note that *boats* may be powered by outboard motors—but the basic distinction remains this: a *ship* is big and travels the sea lanes; a *boat* is relatively small and stays mostly in shallow or sheltered waters. *Boat* comes from Old Norse *batr,* while *ship* was the Old English *scip.*

bobbitt. The only clue to *Bobbitt* as a child's nickname that we can track down is its use in a Scottish song celebrating the game of bobbing for apples. Just in case there is anyone so unfortunate as never to have bobbed for apples, be it known that there are at least two ways to approach the task. One is to have a large tub of water on the floor (better do this in the kitchen) in which apples are set afloat. Children then kneel beside the tub and try to bite an apple. The child catching the biggest apple or the greatest number of apples is the winner. The other way of bobbing is to hang an apple from a hook over a doorway. The string is then twisted and, as the apple twirls about, children take turns trying to get bites from it. So much for child's play. In an old Scottish song celebrating this activity there's a line: "If it isn't weel *bobbit,* we'll bob it again."

bobby pin. Until women started cutting their hair short in the flapper era, the word *bob* had been used chiefly to describe docking horses' tails. We suppose the first hairpins designed to hold the newly cut hair may have been called *bob pins,* but the well-known penchant for the terminal *-ie* or *-y* soon made itself felt, and the pins became *bobbie pins* or *bobby pins.*

Bob's yer uncle. This takes us back to the halcyon days of radio, when an English comedian named Pat O'Malley used to tell Yorkshire-dialect stories on the Ray Noble show. Among the favorites was a series about "The Lion and Albert," recounting the misadventures of an impossible brat named Albert who managed to get swallowed by the lion in a zoo—"after we'd paid to come in." The humor doesn't translate very well to the printed page, but the high point came when the lion, irked at Albert's pushing a stick in his ear, pulled the lad into the cage and "before you could say *Bob's yer uncle* had swallered the little lad whole."

All of which brings us no closer to the explanation of *Bob's yer uncle*— but be patient. According to *Brewer's Dictionary of Phrase and Fable:* "*Bob's yer uncle* means 'That'll be all right, you needn't bother any more.' The origin of the phrase is unknown; it was certainly in use in the 1880's, but no satisfactory explanation of who Bob was has been brought forward." It appears, then, that *Bob's yer uncle* is another of those nearly meaningless slang expressions that enjoy a brief vogue for no ascertainable reason. In this country, at various times, "So's yer old man," "Twenty-three skiddoo" and "Go fly a kite" have had similar brief periods of popularity.

boche/kamerad. In World War II *boche* was a term used by the French to show their contempt for their German foes. It may be loosely and politely translated as "cabbage head." *Kamerad* is simply the German word for "comrade" and was reportedly used by deserting German soldiers as they made their way toward the Allied forces to assure them that they were surrendering.

bodacious/boldacious. *Bodacious* is a term applied to a person who is bold, audacious or even impudent. In any event, a *bodacious* person is one who is full of daring. Originally it was spelled *boldacious,* and a good guess is that it was a blend of *bold* and *audacious.* It first appeared in British slang centuries ago. You can take your choice of spellings.

body English. This expression probably originated with the game of billiards —and in America. At any rate, the first examples of it in print, including one by Mark Twain in 1859, so use it. To apply *English* to a billiard or pool ball is to strike it to the right or left of its center, thereby causing it to spin to the right or left after it strikes an object or a rail. It's said that in the early days of baseball, around 1880, a keen billiard fan named McConnell discovered that a somewhat similar effect could be obtained by imparting spin to a pitched ball. According to legend, he organized a ball club, coached his pitchers to apply *English* to the ball, and the team went undefeated for several seasons until the other teams' pitchers caught on.

Why is *English* used in this connection? Well, it may simply have been that the rosin applied to cue tips was originally imported from England. A smart stylist with the cue would "apply a bit of the English" before making his stroke, and this expression may eventually have been transferred to the unusual motion resulting from stroking the ball off center.

Another theory, perhaps more persuasive, is that the word *English* was used in this way to refer to the tricky or deceitful effects of such a stroke. Throughout history people have used the names of their enemies to describe underhanded or socially unacceptable practices. The English themselves were famous for insulting their Dutch rivals with such expressions as *Dutch treat* (implying cheapness), *Dutch courage* (false courage derived from liquor) and *doing the Dutch* (committing suicide). So since we were not overly friendly with the English at the time when our first billiard players were stroking the ball, this bit of trickery may well have got its name in this fashion.

boffo is show business slang for a hit. Originally it was a belly laugh—a comedian's finest reward. Then it came to mean any kind of smashing success.

Bohemian as a designation for raffish nonconformists of an earlier vintage comes logically and directly from the place name Bohemia. Before World War I, Bohemia was a part of Austria and many centuries earlier it was mistakenly believed to be the home of the Gypsy tribes which roamed through Western Europe as early as the fifteenth century. Actually, Gypsies were wandering tribes from the Caucasus and are believed to be of Hindu origin. But popular superstition was stronger than fact—which could not have been easy to determine in any event—so *Bohemian* and Gypsy became virtually synonymous and the latter's connotations of aimless wandering and disregard for conventions were soon attached to *Bohemian* as well. Thackeray fixed the label once and for all on *avant-garde* thinkers and others who scorn social proprieties when he called Becky Sharp, his headstrong heroine of *Vanity Fair,* a "*Bohemian* by taste and circumstances . . . of a wild, roving nature."

Bombay duck is dried bummalo fish, imported from Bombay, heated to crispness and served crumbled over curry. Our guess is that it got its name just the way Cape Cod turkey (codfish) and Scotch woodcock (scrambled eggs on anchovy-buttered toast) acquired their names—as semihumorous terms for dishes people couldn't afford applied to dishes they could afford.

bone to pick. When we say we have a *bone to pick* with someone, we mean that we have a very touchy problem to discuss—one that may very well lead to argument, discord and injured feelings. The expression unquestionably started among dog owners, well aware of the fact that two dogs plus one bone is a fine formula for starting a dog fight.

bon vivant (pronounced bong vee-VONǥ) is the French term for a man who loves good food and the other pleasures of life. It also means "a boon companion, someone who is a pleasure to be with."

booby hatch, meaning a wooden hood over a hatch leading to the forepeak of a sailing vessel, was common during the last century and it is probable that its present meaning of "insane asylum" may have derived from the practice of confining deranged sailors in the *booby hatch.* Certainly credit for the widespread popularity of the phrase must go, however, to cartoonist Milt Gross, who used to draw one of the most hilarious and meaningful of Sunday strips. Many readers will remember the character who each week was freed from the asylum, spent a day being horrified by the antics of "normal" beings in the outer world, and in the last panel was always to be seen hurrying back to the asylum, saying, "Back to the dear old *booby hatch.*"

boodle/boodlers. Part of the political slang of the nineteenth century, *boodle* was a bribe and a *boodler* one who dealt in bribes, especially in an effort to fix elections.

boojum. Lewis Carroll, the author of *Alice in Wonderland,* also penned *The Hunting of the Snark* in which *boojum* first appeared. The snark is a wholly imaginary creation by Carroll, the word being a blend of "snake" and "shark." In the story the snark was the cause of all sorts of mischief, so hunters pursued it, finally tracking it down—whereupon it proved to be not a snark at all, but a *boojum.* And what's a *boojum?* Well, originally it was just another imaginary creation of Carroll's, but now its name has been given to a grotesque spiny tree found in Lower California. The tree has the somewhat dubious distinction of sometimes arching over so far that its branch tips touch the ground and take root.

bookie. The first *bookies*—or *betting commissioners* as they were sometimes grandly labeled—used to record wagers in notebooks. The books noted the amount wagered, the odds and the eventual settlement of the bets. This recording was known as "making book," and the commissioner became first a "bookmaker" and then, less formally, a *bookie.*

boomerang was coined by Australian aborigines to describe the unique, fly-back weapon which they created—and which American youngsters discovered as a plaything. The word may have had some such significance in aboriginal lingo as "weapon that flies through the air and returns to part the thrower's hair"—but that's just a guess.

boondocks. During the occupation of the Philippines, many terms from the native language, Tagalog (tah-GAH-log), found their way into the slang of our soldiers and Marines and often, as in this case, the meaning became somewhat broader in translation. Whereas the Philippine native meant simply "mountain" when he said *bandok,* American servicemen used the term to apply to any kind of rough back country, eventually making *boondocks* a rough-and-ready synonym for "sticks."

Boondocks first came into general public knowledge during an investigation of harsh methods of training employed by some Marine noncoms at Camp Lejeune. According to reports then current, recruits were ordered on night marches into the *boondocks,* which included swamp areas where at least one recruit drowned. So, in current application, it appears that *boondocks* may apply to any back-country area, from the original Philippine mountain to sea-level swamps.

boondoggling, in governmental use, was first applied to the "make-work" projects of the first Franklin Roosevelt administration, which many critics thought were wasteful. The term was reported earlier as a slang expression common in the Ozarks and, in 1929, was used by a scoutmaster as a name for ornamental thongs made by Boy Scouts under his direction.

boot camp is navy slang for a training station for recruits. The term is thought to have originated in the 1890s. At that time it was a point of pride with experienced seamen to scrub down a ship's decks in their bare feet, no matter what the weather. Recruits from the Midwest did not take kindly to frozen feet, so they went to town and bought rubber boots, thereby earning the scornful label "rubber boot sailors." Then recruits were called "rubber boots," which eventually was shortened to simply *boots.*

boot hill. In Westerns, the cemetery is always labeled *boot hill* because most of its occupants are cowboys who died with their boots on. As Ramon Adams notes in his *Western Words:* "There ain't many tears shed at a *boot-hill* burying," and it is "full of fellers that pulled their triggers before aimin'."

bootlegger originated from the fact that the first *bootleggers* carried illicit merchandise in the legs of high boots when making deliveries. In this sense the word was common in the middle nineteenth century. Since the most easily made and profitably sold commodity was illicit liquor, *bootlegger* gradually became applied to distributors of illegal booze.

bootstrapper. "Attention *Bootstrappers*" is a heading sometimes seen in the want-ad sections of newspapers. It is based on the familiar expression "He raised himself by his own bootstraps," meaning that he succeeded in his endeavor solely on his own power, unaided by any outside source or person. So a *bootstrapper* is a very ambitious young person, working hard to advance in the world.

booze. A friend of ours has an old whiskey bottle, in the shape of a log cabin, which bears the name "E. S. Booz" as the distiller. He says that's where *booze* came from. Others claim it is a word from the roaring twenties. Both theories are about five centuries away from the right answer. It's true that Mr. Booz's bottles had much to do with popularizing the word during the last century, but the Dutch had been using it many centuries earlier, certainly as early as when they settled New Amsterdam. Moreover, a variant form has been in the language as far back as Edmund Spenser (1590) and the *Oxford Dictionary* says "boozy—affected by drinking" was in use in 1529.

booze terms. Among the most numerous and colorful slang terms developed in this country in the course of its history are those dealing with strong drink and resulting intoxication. Anyone who has watched Western movies knows that *firewater* was the whiskey that Indians drank, at least in the minds of scriptwriters. One of our favorites, among the many terms for alcoholic stimulants which date back to pre–Civil War days, is *nose-paint.* Presumably its origin was in the belief that chronic guzzlers would be marked by reddened noses. Of the same vintage, according to H. L. Mencken's *The American Language,* are: *panther sweat, red eye, corn juice, forty rod, mountain dew, coffin varnish, bust head* and *stagger soup.*

borax is a term of Yiddish origin used to describe furniture that is cheaply made but flashy and ornate in appearance. It is the stock in trade of the ten-dollars-down-and-the-rest-when-we-catch-you merchandisers.

born to the purple. Purple has been emblematic of royalty and hence of great wealth ever since the days of ancient Rome when the emperor's robes were dyed purple. As a result, purple came to symbolize wealth and power. Even today we sometimes speak of people like the various Rockefellers as *born to the purple,* meaning that they inherited vast riches and power.

"born with the gift of laughter and a sense that the world was mad" is from the first line of the novel *Scaramouche* by Rafael Sabatini, author of many popular but not highly regarded novels of the 1920s. It appears, rather surprisingly, inscribed over the inside of a gate at Yale University's Hall of Graduate Studies. How did a quotation from one whose own contemporaries considered him a "trashy" writer appear so permanently inscribed in such an illustrious position at one of the nation's leading universities?

It was the work of John Donald Tuttle, a young architect working on the plans—and not at all happy about his assignment. He wrote later that he chose the quotation, rather than something from a celebrated Greek or Latin writer, as his form of protest against the ersatz Gothic style that had been decided on. It was, he said, "a type of architecture expressly designed for allowing archers to shoot arrows from slits in its surface and to enable yeomen to pour molten lead through slots on their enemies below. As a gift to my gods for this terrible thing I was doing, and to make them forget by appealing to their sense of humor, I carved the inscription over the door."

When it was discovered, the Yale faculty was mystified. Savants studied the classics in an effort to find the source of the quotation without success, until finally a young member of the faculty who had obviously misspent part of his youth reading trashy literature pointed out the source in *Scaramouche.* Someone leaked the story to Alexander Woollcott, who devoted two of his "Shouts and Murmurs" pieces in *The New Yorker* to it—and faces were red on the New Haven campus.

borscht circuit is the name for a group of predominately Jewish hotels in the Catskill Mountains of New York State. In the 1930s it was customary for entertainers to "play the *borscht circuit,*" traveling from one hotel to another every few days. Today these hotels, which then were little more than glorified rooming houses, are multimillion-dollar establishments, running year round and employing highly paid entertainers. Still the nickname persists, especially inside show business. The *borscht* in the title refers to the kind of Russian beet soup once a staple on the menus at these hotels.

Borstal Boy. Borstal is the location of the first modern reform school in

Britain, established just after the turn of the century. Its theory is that youthful offenders can more readily be prepared for reentry into society by education and technical training, rather than by mere imprisonment. One of Britain's angry young men, Brendan Behan, named his autobiographical book *Borstal Boy* in reference to the time he spent at this institution. Behan —may his soul rest in the peace he seldom knew on this earth—was in the news when the play *Borstal Boy*, by and about Behan, received the Tony Award, Broadway's equivalent of the Hollywood Oscar. Everyone who ever met this brilliant, gifted, unruly Irishman has a story to tell about him. The one we cherish has to do with the time he was being interviewed by a *New York Times* reporter. Behan drew a parallel between his own career and that of the legendary French prisoner-poet François Villon. "That name," he told the reporter, "is spelled *V-i-l-l-o-n*." "You don't have to tell a *Times* reporter how to spell Villon," said the newspaperman, folding his notebook and stuffiing it into his pocket. "Ah, but you don't understand," replied Behan. "I thought you might be interested in the fact that a lad who spent his teen years in Borstal Reformatory could spell Villon." We also remember with admiration Behan's explanation of why he loved cities. "In a city," he said, "you're less likely to be attacked by a maddened deer."

bosh. Here's an oddity, a word that looks characteristically British, so much so that one can scarcely think of hearing it from any but British lips. Yet it actually comes from the Turkish word *bos*, meaning "empty or useless." It is usually used as an exclamation: "Oh, bosh!" meaning "What nonsense!"

boss, derived from the Dutch word *baas*, meaning "master," is equally common today in business and politics.

botanophobia, meaning an intense dislike of flowers and plants, stems from the Greek *botane* (plant or herb) and *phobos* (fear).

boudoir, borrowed without change from French and pronounced boo-DWAHR, is a fairly elegant designation for a lady's most intimate dressing room, the one to which—in the Victorian phrase—she would "repair to complete her toilette." But it wasn't always so. In the original French it simply meant a room in which to pout or sulk. When *boudoir* was first introduced to English, at about the time of the American Revolution, it was sometimes also applied to a man's den.

bought the farm. There are several theories of the origin of the expression "He *bought the farm*," common among the military to indicate that a soldier has been killed in action. Several readers have commented to us on a very likely origin of the expression. Here are the words of Mrs. George Warn of Toledo, Ohio. "I think," she writes, "that the expression comes from the civilian soldiers who were in the war and hated it. They dreamed in their spare time of going home to peace and tranquillity—and what would their ideal life be except back home and buying their own farm? They probably even talked about it to their fellow soldiers. So when they were killed, they found peace and tranquillity (let us hope). No more horrors of war. The soldiers of today still dream of coming home. (My son does.)"

And G. R. Waldron of Lodi, New Jersey, commenting in the same vein, recalls World War II bull sessions. "Almost invariably two questions arose," he writes. "What did you do before you got into the army, and what do you plan to do when you get out? More times than not a fellow would have come from a rural family; his girlfriend was awaiting his return so they could marry, buy those fifty acres down the road from dad, and settle down to raising corn and kids (not necessarily in that order). The original statement was a philosophical comment. Upon learning of the death of a friend, the final remark was 'Well, he's *bought his farm,*' wryly commenting on humanity's unfulfilled aspirations."

bouillabaisse is perhaps the most famous fish soup ever devised. Originated on the Mediterranean coast of France, it contains a variety of fish and shellfish and is cooked in white wine and water with plentiful herbs for seasoning. Its name comes from the joking admonition of the chef to the pot: "First boil [*bouille*] and then settle [*abaise*]." Just as Les Halles of Paris was famous for the onion soup served in the early morning hours to marketmen and visitors, so the many waterfront cafés of Marseilles are noted for the excellence and variety of their *bouillabaisse.*

bouillon/consommé. Any good cook can tell you that a true *consommé* and a *bouillon* are very similar, though today's *bouillon* is all too often merely hot water and a cube of beef concentrate. Both words originally came from the French and in themselves tell a good deal about the process of cooking soups in years gone by. A good soup had to be, first of all, the product of long, slow boiling. *Bouillon* comes from the French word *bouillir* (to boil), and *consommé* is from the verb *consommer* and literally means "finished." In the word you can almost hear the sigh of relief of a French cook that the long task of preparing the perfect, clear soup is finally finished.

bounce is derived from the Dutch word *bonzen,* meaning "to thump or strike."

bourbon and branch/bourbon and ditch. A *branch* in regional usage means a small stream, usually slightly smaller than a creek. Water from a *branch,* according to legend at least, is clearer, cooler and more refreshing than ordinary water. Nowadays the term probably survives because the alliterative phrase *bourbon and branch* falls pleasantly on many ears. The truth of the matter is that in almost every instance nowadays the so-called *branch* water is just city water from the tap.

Mrs. Don Sanford of Freeland, Michigan, adds: "My former home was near Billings, Montana. That is a country of irrigation ditches, and naturally when anyone orders a bourbon, he just says *bourbon and ditch.* I might add that the water is from the tap—not from an irrigation ditch."

For the record, *bourbon* (pronounced BER-b'n) is a whiskey that takes its name from Bourbon County, Kentucky, where it was first distilled.

boutique was borrowed from the French to mean "a small specialty shop," especially one featuring women's dresses, jewelry and accessories.

bowdlerize means to censor printed matter by expurgating material considered offensive to the person or group doing the censoring. The word comes from the proper name Bowdler and every reference book in our library, including several we ourselves have written or edited, reports that *bowdlerize* is formed from the name of Thomas Bowdler, who, in 1818, published an expurgated edition of Shakespeare called *The Family Shakespeare.*

It now appears that every one of those reference books is wrong. The original *bowdlerizer* was not Thomas Bowdler but his sister Henrietta Maria, known as Harriet. Writing in the London *Times* (March 30, 1976), Susan Shatto of the Shakespeare Institute in Birmingham summons up a wealth of detail to prove the case for Harriet.

The first edition of *The Family Shakespeare* was published in Bath in 1807 with an unsigned preface and no editor's name on the title page, though, reports Ms. Shatto, "Harriet's family and friends knew the work to be hers." A revised and enlarged second edition was issued in 1818 and this one was signed by Thomas Bowdler as editor. That assured him of the fame that came to him because of the success of this edition.

Why did Harriet not take the credit that was her due? As Ms. Shatto points out: "As a spinster past middle age, she might not want the public to know that her understanding of Shakespeare was sufficient to expurgate it."

And that puts us in mind of the remark that Samuel Johnson made to a pair of ladies who congratulated him for omitting the four-letter words from his dictionary. "I find it interesting to note that you have been looking for them." Miss Bowdler not only looked for them. She found them and expurgated them.

Bowery is the name of a street and a district in New York City. Now known chiefly as the final refuge of drunken riffraff, it was once the sunniest, healthiest part of the city. Indeed, its name came from the Dutch word for "farm" *(bouwerij)* and in the early days of New Amsterdam the *bowery* was a place of open fields, grazing cattle and frolicking, happy-faced children.

bowie knife, a single-edged hunting knife, is generally thought to be named after Colonel James Bowie, hero of the Alamo. Not true. The first such knife was made by a Louisiana blacksmith working from a design by Colonel Bowie's brother, Rezin Pleasant Bowie. There is no doubt that Jim Bowie used the knife often and his great popularity did much to spread its fame.

bowler is the common British name for what Americans call a "derby." That's a bit amusing in itself, because the derby is so named from a British race held at Epsom Downs, which in turn was named after the twelfth Earl of Derby, who started the whole race business in 1780. To confuse matters even more, the British call the race a DAR-bee, while we call the hat a DER-bee.

But back to *bowler.* There are a couple of theories of its origin, one being the dull and not very likely idea that it is named from its presumed resemblance to a bowling ball. Much more persuasive is the story that the hat was actually designed by a huntsman named William Coke, who became weary of having his top hat knocked off by low-hanging branches as he tallyhoed after the fox and hounds. A round-topped or oval-topped headpiece, he reasoned, would slide under the branches. So he called in his favorite hatmaker, a Frenchman named Beaulieu, told him what he wanted, and Beaulieu complied. The resulting low-crowned hard felt hat was initially named for its creator, the *beaulieu,* but the British would have none of this Frenchification of the mother tongue and quickly corrupted the name to *bowler.* Rumor has it that the hatmaker, seeing that the inevitable was at hand, bowed to it and changed his own name from "M. Beaulieu" to "Mr. Bowler."

bowling. Some say that *bowling* was first done by the Dutch who settled New York City; others believe it started in England, where they used to bowl on the grass. Neither is correct. While it is true that the British and Dutch both "played at bowls," as the expression went, the game itself goes back farther than recorded history. Indeed, when the first pyramids were explored in Egypt, archaeologists discovered bowling apparatus believed to be at least seven thousand years old. Our word *bowl* comes from the Latin *bulla* for "bubble," hence "bowling ball."

Box and Cox is a British expression going back to a popular farce of the mid nineteenth century. Two men, one named Box and the other Cox, lived in the same room, one by day, the other by night, and neither knew of the other's existence. In 1867 it was adapted as a comic opera called *Cox and Box,* with music by Sir Arthur Sullivan. Though W. S. Gilbert had nothing to do with it—the text being by Francis Burnand—it is often performed as part of the Gilbert and Sullivan repertory. So *Box and Cox* as an expression simply means "alternating or in turn."

Boxing Day. The *boxing* in *Boxing Day,* a British holiday, has nothing to do with fighting. It refers to the custom of giving gift boxes to faithful employees on the day after Christmas. In earlier times this was also the day when church almsboxes were opened and the contents distributed to the needy members of the parish.

box office. On a guided tour of London the guide told the following story about the origin of the term *box office.* It seems that in the days of the first Queen Elizabeth, theater audiences were admitted to the "pit"—what

Americans call the "orchestra"—without paying in advance. Then an attendant would pass among them with a box on the end of a stick, collecting the admission charge. From this "box" came our phrase *box office*. Charming, but not true. According to the *Oxford English Dictionary*, a *box office* is "an office in a theatre for booking seats (originally for hiring a box)." So we're afraid the "box" in *box office* is the traditional theatrical box.

boycott. Captain Charles Cunningham Boycott, a retired English Army officer, was land agent in Ireland's County Mayo for the estate of an absentee owner, the Earl of Erne. Now, any son of the Old Sod will tell you that there is no love lost between natives of Ireland and those they would label the "English usurpers." But Boycott seemed bound and determined to bring upon himself the concentrated hatred of the entire populace.

Insisting upon the very letter of the law—despite the fact that crop scarcity in the mid nineteenth century had made the natives poor indeed—he refused to reduce rents and attempted to evict any tenants who could not pay in full. As a result, he was completely ostracized, his servants departed en masse, and attempts were even made to cut off his supply of food. By harvest time, public opinion was so inflamed against him that he had to import several hundred British soldiers to protect the harvesters—who themselves had been brought in from Northern Ireland. The Irish Land League, an organization of tenants, finally made life so completely miserable that Captain Boycott fled to England—thereby making the first *boycott* a success. Ever since that day, to *boycott* a person has meant to combine with one's neighbors in refusing to deal with him, in order to force him to change a position previously taken. A *boycott* may also, of course, be organized against a business firm.

Boy Scouts were founded in England in 1908 by Sir Robert Baden-Powell and it wasn't until two years later that the movement came to the United States, though Canada had its first Scouts in the same year they started in England. In 1977 the American organization was renamed Scouting/USA.

brack. A reader who signed herself a "loving granddaughter" wrote that her grandmother, who would be 130 years old if she were alive, used to say, "I'm not doing away with this coat. There's not a *brack* in it." *Brack* is an English word going back to at least 1550. It's a variation of "break" and is used particularly to refer to a flaw in woven fabric. So her grandmother was saying that she would not discard the coat because there were no flaws in it. *Brack* is now labeled "dialect" in dictionaries, indicating that it may still be heard in the speech of country folk.

braggadocio (pronounced brag-uh-DOH-she-oh) is a loud-mouthed boaster, one who—in the popular idiom—can talk up a storm but is notably short on performance when the chips are down and he is challenged to make good on his boastful claims. The word comes from a character in Spenser's *Faerie Queene*, supposedly inspired by the Duc d'Alençon, who was one of many who sought the hand of the Virgin Queen, Elizabeth I of England.

braille, the method of printing and writing for the blind by the use of raised dots that can be identified by touch, takes its name from its inventor, Louis *Braille*. A primitive method of "night writing" had been developed in the French army. It involved combinations of raised marks on paper or cardboard which could be passed in darkness and decoded by sentries on duty, thus avoiding the use of any illumination, which might expose the sentry's position. Braille, a young man of uncommon brilliance, refined the method into the system we now know. An accomplished organist, he also composed music with the help of his method.

brain trust was first coined by a *New York Times* political reporter, James M. Kieran, and its original form was *brains trust*. However, popular use and the need for economy in the number of letters used in headlines soon reduced the label to *brain trust*.

brand-new has a long and honorable history. It dates back to the Middle Ages and earlier, when *brand* meant "flame or torch"—as it does in the still current phrase "snatching a *brand* from the burning." The description *brand-new* in those days was applied to products—usually made of metal —newly taken from the flames in which they were molded.

brands/trademarks. The practice of *branding* animals for the purpose of identification is so old that its exact origins are unknown. We do know, however, that *brands* were first used on humans—criminal and slaves. According to the *Oxford Dictionary*, the practice of *branding* animals to indicate ownership was well established in England before Shakespeare's time and the term *trademark* for the word or symbol chosen by a manufacturer to identify and distinguish his product was in use before 1838. Official registration of *trademarks* by the U.S. Patent Office did not begin, however, until 1870.

brass/scrambled eggs/fruit salad. *Brass* is a shortened form of *brass hat*, a term originally used in the British Army as long ago as 1890. The allusion is to the gold braid worn on officers' hats as an insignia of rank. During World War I the term *brass hat* was commonplace in American Army circles—usually in the form of contemptuous references by enlisted men to their top-ranking officers. In World War II the term was shortened to *the brass*, sometimes *the big brass* or *the top brass*. With the return of thousands of ex-servicemen to civilian life, it was inevitable that the term would be carried over and applied to top-ranking executives in business. Incidentally, the actual braid adorning the hats of top-ranking officers is usually called *scrambled eggs*, just as a collection of service and combat ribbons worn on the chest is known as *fruit salad*.

brass ring. In the amusement parks of our youth the merry-go-rounds often had a gimmick whereby rings were fed into a slotlike device located at shoulder height about two feet from the edge of the rotating platform where the wooden horses whirled about. Brave young people—among whom we were surely to be numbered—could risk a bad tumble by reaching out to catch a ring as they raced past. If you were lucky and caught a *brass ring,* you turned it in for a free extra ride. So "he grabbed the *brass ring"* translates into "he had a bit of good luck."

bread, as a term for money, has been current in popular musicians' slang for years. Since much teen-age jargon comes from musicians' argot, it's not surprising that the young people have picked up *bread.* As a matter of fact, a very closely related sense of *bread,* meaning one's livelihood, has been in accepted usage for many years. In one episode of Sherlock Holmes, for example, Conan Doyle has a blackmailer, Milverton, say: "Here's how I make my humble *bread.*"

break a leg. In the theater the customary way to wish an actor good luck as he makes his first entrance in a show is to pat him on the back and say, *"Break a leg!"* If it happens to be an actress instead of an actor, the routine varies a bit. First there's one of those fake kisses we see so often on the television talk shows—the careful brushing of cheeks so that makeup and hairdo will not be mussed. Then the well-wisher says, *"Break a leg,* darling!"

But why *break a leg?* asked a reader. She passed on a few theories she had heard, including one about the fact that "the divine Sarah" Bernhardt had only one leg, so the idea was that one would be lucky to emulate this famous actress. Since none of the theories was very convincing, we asked other readers for the answer. Several came up with the same very persuasive explanation—and we'll quote Mrs. David Forden of Puerto Vallarta, Jalisco, Mexico, on the subject.

"I don't know the expression as actors' slang or any other kind of slang —in English," she writes. "In German it is commonly used to wish someone good luck in any undertaking: *'Hals-und-Beinbruch'*—'May you break your neck and your leg.' But I am not proposing a German answer to your question. My ear says *break a leg* comes into the American theater from Yiddish. Furthermore, I would guess that in Yiddish the explanation has general application, as it does in German. Perhaps its identification as theater slang in the United States is due to the influence of the Yiddish theater and of Jewish-descended directors and actors in stage and film work."

breathalyzer. Because of the large number of motor crashes charged to overindulgence in drink, British bobbies are now equipped with a device called the *breathalyzer.* It's a little tube containing chemical crystals through which the suspected drunk must breathe. If the crystals turn green, he's slapped in the poky, given a fat fine and deprived of his license for a year.

bridge is derived from a Russian game, *biritch,* which was introduced to Western cultures as "Russian whist." The name *biritch* was soon transformed to *bridge* (by a process known as folk etymology) and so it has remained.

brief/debrief. One newscaster said, "We will shortly be getting a detailed *brief* of what was said." Logically there is no such thing as a detailed *brief.* If it's brief, it's brief. If it's long, it's long. But, as so often happens, logic has nothing to do with the evolution of the language. The trouble here began when lawyers began submitting *briefs* to courts—such *briefs* frequently running to many pages because their purpose is to sum up for the court every bit of essential information about an action. So a lawyer's *brief* became a catalogue of all the essential points of a case. After that, a *brief* was no longer necessarily brief.

Then the military took up the word and, by World War II, *brief* was the standard verb for imparting to members of a military mission the essential facts about the nature of an attack, the resistance to be expected, the terrain to be covered and so forth. These *briefing* sessions, like lawyers' *briefs,* were frequently very long indeed, since the safety of all concerned depended upon their knowing every possible contingency.

More recently—though this, too, may date back to World War II—we have heard of *debriefing* sessions wherein a returning envoy or space cadet is *debriefed* or interrogated by his superiors so that all pertinent information may be recorded while it is still fresh in mind.

brighten a room by leaving it. Fred Allen once referred to a celebrated television M.C., noted for his expressionless manner of presenting acts, as "the only man I know who can *brighten a room by leaving it.* " Perhaps unconsciously, Allen was echoing a sentiment that has been part of the language since before the time of Shakespeare. The *Oxford Dictionary of Proverbs* reports that in 1579 a collection of witty sayings entitled *The Marriage of Wit and Wisdom* carried this gem: "I had rather have your room as your company," and Walter Scott in an 1822 novel called *The Fortunes of Nigel* wrote: "The waterman declared he would rather have her room than her company".

bring home the bacon. As so often happens, there are two theories of the origin of this phrase. The first is that it refers to the fact that the winner of the greased pig contest at country fairs traditionally keeps the pig and thus *brings home the bacon.* An earlier story goes all the way back to A.D. 1111 and the town of Dunmow in England. A noblewoman, wishing to encourage marital happiness, decreed that "any person from any part of England going to Dunmow and humbly kneeling on two stones at the church door may claim a gammon [side] of bacon, if he can swear that for twelve months and a day he has never had a household brawl or wished himself unmarried." So the "Dunmow flitch," as the side of bacon was called, became a symbol of domestic felicity and a man *bringing home the bacon* would be a rare and happy fellow. Let cynics make what they will of the record that in a period of five centuries (1244–1772) there were only eight claimants of the prize.

brinjalls. The vegetable hiding behind the unfamiliar name *brinjalls* is none other than the common garden variety of eggplant. *Brinjall* is a corruption of the Portuguese word *bringella.*

brinkmanship. Some claim that *brinkmanship* was invented by Eisenhower's Secretary of State, John Foster Dulles, and the others say that it was coined by Adlai Stevenson. The chaps who bet on Dulles are wrong, and those who bet on Stevenson may or may not be right. Even Stevenson himself was not sure.

Here is the story. In 1956 *Life* magazine carried an article quoting Dulles as saying that he would not hesitate to "go to the *brink*" if the best interests of his country were served thereby. Mr. Dulles's sister, in a recent memoir of her brother, denies he ever said this and lays his refusal to deny the quote to loyalty, perhaps misguided, to the reporter who wrote the article. Be that as it may, the word *brinkmanship,* coined in imitation of Stephen Potter's "gamesmanship" and "one-upmanship" began to appear in the papers as a label indicating willingness to bring a nation to the very edge of catastrophe in furtherance of a diplomatic policy.

In the revised edition of Fowler's *Modern English Usage,* Sir Ernest Gowers writes: "*Brinkmanship* is said to have been coined by Adlai Stevenson. Few such pleasantries are likely to prove more than jocular and transitory slang but *brinkmanship* is evidently felt to supply the need for a word denoting the qualities or character associated with one whose conduct of his country's foreign policy puts anxious spectators in mind of a man precariously balancing himself on the edge of a precipice."

Whether Adlai Stevenson coined the word even he could not say definitely, though it is clear that he used it in a speech within a few weeks of the *Life* article's appearance. When asked, Stevenson replied: "I cannot claim authorship of *brinkmanship.* I am not sure whether I read it or heard it or dreamed it up. I am reasonably sure I did not invent it."

British was *Bruttische* or *Bryttische* in Middle English and can ultimately be traced back to the Latin *Britto,* the name used by the Roman invaders for the members of the Briton tribe. This was simply the closest approximation the Romans could arrive at for the word used by the tribesmen themselves. In the *Anglo-Saxon Chronicle* it appeared simply as *Brit* or *Brett.*

broad is simply a variant spelling of "bawd," a word that goes back to before Shakespeare's time. It referred to a woman who—to use a euphemism—ran a house of ill repute, sometimes called a bawdy house. Oscar Hammerstein lent a certain respectability to *broad* when he wrote the lyric Mary Martin sang in *South Pacific* about the *broad* who was "*broad* where a *broad* should be *broad.*" However, many women consider it still to be a derogatory term.

broadcloth/Pima cotton/Sea Island cotton. In case you've wondered where *broadcloth* got its name, the answer is really quite simple. It's made on a loom broader than the standard 29-inch width. *Pima cotton* gets its name from Pima County, Arizona, and *Sea Island cotton* is so called because it's grown only on certain islands of the Caribbean—isolated so it won't cross-breed with more plebeian cottons.

broderick. *To broderick,* as synonymous with "to clobber," comes from the name of John Joseph Broderick, a first-grade detective on New York City's police force whose crime-fighting activities earned him the title "the world's toughest cop." On the force from 1923 to 1947, he subdued many gangsters with his fists and left the force with eight medals for valor. Jack Dempsey, who had on occasion used him as a bodyguard, is said to have admitted that Broderick was the only man he would not care to fight outside the ring.

bronco. The *bronco, broncho* or *bronc* of Western folklore and of today's rodeos is a wild or semi-wild horse and the task of the bronco-buster is to break him to the saddle. He comes by his name honestly enough, since *bronco* is simply the Mexican-Spanish word for "wild or rough."

Brontë. Just how did the Brontë sisters—Charlotte, Emily and Anne—get a double dot over the final *e* of their name? So far as we can tell, this is unique among English family names. If they were of German descent, the umlaut or dieresis would be understandable. But these were three normal (well, not quite normal) English girls.

The father of these incredibly talented girls was an Irishman from County Down named Patrick Brunty, the son of an Irish farmer. At the age of twenty-five (in 1802) he enrolled at Cambridge University and signed himself as Patrick Brontë. The great British naval hero Horatio Nelson had recently been given the honorary title Duke of Bronte (no dieresis) in Sicily. Apparently young Patrick decided that the way for an Irishman to succeed in England was to out-English the English. In a way he seems to have succeeded, for he became an Anglican priest in 1806 and later moved to a "perpetual curateship" at Haworth, where the three girls wrote most of their novels. Beginning writers can take some encouragement from the fact that the first collaborative effort of the girls, who were later to number *Wuthering Heights* and *Jane Eyre* among their works, was a book of poems that was a dismal failure. It sold only two copies.

brooch. The name of a lady's dress ornament, *brooch* is pronounced as if it were spelled "broach" because it originally *was* spelled "broach." This ornament with a clasp—usually worn at the neck of a dress—gets its name from the pin that holds it together. The *broaches* of old were sharp-pointed spits or skewers, similar to but larger than a shish-kebab skewer and used for roasting oxen over huge fires. When milady's jewelry was fashioned, the resemblance between the pin and the broach was obvious, so it was called *broach,* later *brooch.*

brougham has become a fancy name for a four-door sedan in the world of auto dealers, who usually pronounce it *brome.* The original *brougham* was a closed four-wheel carriage with an open seat in front for the driver. It was named after Henry Peter Brougham, a Scottish-born member of Britain's Parliament, who designed the first one. Brougham was a notably eccentric fellow, but the design of what he called "a garden chair on wheels" was very successful, though we suspect the drivers, sitting out in the cold and rain, may not have been wildly enthusiastic about it.

brouhaha was borrowed directly from the French, where it originally meant "noisy chattering," and acquired the same meaning of "fuss" or "argument" that it has in English today. It's a fairly recent borrowing, being recorded by *American Speech* magazine as first appearing in the popular press in 1943.

brown as a berry seems an odd phrase if you think in terms of fruit berries, which become brown only when rotten. But the berries referred to need not be the fruit berries with which we ordinarily associate the word—blueberries, raspberries, strawberries and the like. Though we have no way of proving this, we think the berries referred to in this expression are those of the brown-berried cedar and juniper trees.

brownout serves as a good example of how a word may come into the language to fit a particular situation, drop out of sight when the situation changes and then reappear when the need next arises. *Brownout* was coined during World War II to describe a partial blackout of a city as a defense against possible bombing raids. During the early stages of World War II many coastal cities in the United States were supposed to observe *brownouts*—that is, electric advertising signs and all other unnecessary lights were supposed to be extinguished. Midway through the war it became obvious that Germany and Japan were much too busy in other areas of war to consider bombing the American homeland, so the word disappeared. Now *brownout* is back, with the new sense of deliberate curtailment of electric power to avoid too heavy a drain on generators and other sources of power. When an entire community or city suffers from a total power failure, as happened in New York City in the mid 1960s, it is a "blackout."

browse. The original meaning of *browse* had nothing to do with *browsing* in stores, for it came from the Old French word *brouz,* meaning the twigs and leaves an animal could feed on. There is still a very nice distinction between *browsing* and "grazing" in that an animal who *browses* eats only foliage from trees and bushes, while a grazing animal eats grass from the ground. So *to browse* literally means to nibble at. It also has the related meaning of glancing in casual fashion through a book or the various books in a library—nibbling, so to speak, at learning. Many of our bookstores today carry signs in the window inviting passers-by to "come in and *browse* around." Quite possibly this is where some get the idea that the use of *browse* should be limited to places like libraries and bookstores.

brummagem is an adjective meaning "cheap, tawdry or meretricious." Pronounced BRUM-uh-jem, it is a corruption of Birmingham (England), a town that built itself quite a reputation in the seventeenth century for manufacturing cheap and flashy jewelry for peddlers to hawk.

brunch, a meal combining elements of breakfast and lunch and customarily eaten about noon, is one of a class of words known as "portmanteau" or "blend" words. At one time, indeed, *brunch* became so widely popular that some scholars labeled the whole category *"brunch* words." Lewis Carroll's *slithy*—from "slimy" and "lithe"—was probably the first such word. No one seems to know for sure when *brunch* first attained popularity, though H. L. Mencken reports that it appeared in England around 1900. He adds that "it was thirty years later before it began to make headway on this side of the water." In any event, *Merriam-Webster* entered it for the first time in their 1934 revision, so Mencken's notion of the date of its first use in America would appear to be fairly well founded.

brush-fire war. A completely accurate definition of *brush-fire war* would have to come from an expert in military science, but the general sense of the phrase is a localized war, especially one in which nuclear weapons are not used. The phrase has been used on several occasions by spokesmen for the Atomic Energy Commission, who take the position that such small local wars are probably inevitable but that the deterrent threat of nuclear bombs will prevent any of the major powers from allowing these minor actions to develop into worldwide warfare. Needless to say, not all authorities support this relatively optimistic viewpoint.

brusque/brusquerie. "As blunt as a butcher's broom" might well be a definition for *brusque* when you consider the origin of the word. Brought into English from French without change, it was taken by the French from the Italian *brusco,* meaning "rude." The Italians, in turn, had formed the word from the Latin *ruscus,* meaning "butcher's broom." Today it means "abrupt, blunt or curt in speech or manner."

buck meaning "dollar" is a slang term from that favorite American indoor sport, poker playing. Originally the *buck* was a marker or counter placed before a player to remind him that his was the next turn to deal. In the gambling dens of the early West, silver dollars were often used as such markers, and in time the name *buck* came to be applied to both silver and paper dollars. Despite the fact that *buck* has been in our language for upward of a hundred years, it is still labeled "slang." An alternate theory of the origin of *buck*—one which has some support among scholars—is that it is short for "buckskin," used as a unit of barter with Indians.

bucket shop. Brokerage firms have been fighting for more than a century to get rid of the name *bucket shops* as a term for stock-exchange brokerage offices or investment firms. Indeed, they thought they had succeeded, since such firms are now forbidden by security and exchange laws.

The first *bucket shops* are thought to have been created in Chicago in the years immediately following the Civil War. Even then they were at least illegitimate, if not downright illegal. What's more, they never actually bought and sold stocks. They merely handled bets on the probable rise or fall of prices in stocks and commodity "futures," as in grain, sugar, beef cattle and the like. The customer would bet that a certain item would rise to such and such a price. The *bucket shop* operator would take his bet, ostensibly to purchase the stock but not actually doing so. If the customer had guessed right, he got his profit, less commission. If he guessed wrong, he lost whatever security he had posted.

One theory of the origin of the term *bucket shop* is that some of them were such shoestring operations that instead of dealing in tons of grain, as legitimate operators did, they dealt in buckets of the commodity. Another theory is that, in the words of the *American Heritage Dictionary,* it was where "small amounts of commodity gambling transactions took place and where the customer could buy liquor in buckets." As the *New York Post* reported in 1881: "A *bucket shop* in New York is a low ginmill or distillery where small quantities of spirits are dispensed in pitchers and pails (buckets). When the shops for dealing in one-share and five-share lots of stocks were opened, these dispensaries of smaller lots than could be got from regular dealers were at once named *bucket shops.* "

buckeye. The study of words—philology—is supposed to be an objective science. But the subjective element occasionally creeps in. Witness the famous definition of "oats" in which Dr. Samuel Johnson showed his disdain for the Scots people. "Oats," he wrote, "is a grain which in England is generally given to horses but in Scotland supports the people."

Allow for a little subjectiveness in our comments on *buckeye* as a synonym for "corny," for the buckeye nut is the symbol of the state of Ohio. And Ohio is, with perhaps the exception of Texas, the most staunchly proud of all our United States. It is also the birthplace of the feminine co-author of this book.

No matter where they wander, the Ohio natives remain proud and voluble about the beauties of their birthplace. The mental attitude of émigré Ohioans is reflected in a couple of true stories about two famous Ohio alumni. Milton Caniff, the distinguished cartoonist, once told us of the head of a leading New York ad agency, also an Ohioan, and his method of choosing copywriters. "If the applicant had a *magna cum laude* in English from Harvard, with four years experience on the *Crimson,* " said Caniff, "he would be considered. But if an Ohio State Journalism School grad with a C average applied at the same time, *he* got the job!"

And James Thurber never tired of talking and writing about the wonders of Ohio and the uniqueness of its citizens. "If everything about Ohio is so wonderful," he was asked once, "why did you leave?" "Simple," replied Thurber. "The competition back there was too keen."

So no matter how *buckeye* is used elsewhere, it is *not* a synonym for "corny" in this lexicon.

buddy, meaning "friend," is more than a century old. The *World Webster* reports it as appearing in print about 1850 and says that it is derived from an earlier British dialect word, *butti,* of the same meaning. On the other hand, the *Merriam-Webster* says that *buddy* is probably a baby-talk version of "brother." So you may take your choice. As so often happens in matters of word origins, even the authorities can't agree with each other.

buff. BUFFS BARRED FROM BLAZES, ran a headline in a leading New York newspaper. The story concerned an order by New York City's Fire Commissioner banishing all unauthorized persons from the immediate scenes of fires. The commissioner, complaining that "you can't get to the fire because of the *buffs,* " said that the *buffs,* who originally came to fires to dispense coffee and sandwiches to the fire fighters, had become carried away by enthusiasm and had taken to fighting the fires themselves. "They're all over the place, making a nuisance of themselves," the commissioner continued. This is not a new problem, especially in New York, where Fiorello H. La Guardia ranked as the No. 1 fire *buff* throughout his several terms as mayor. Actually, *buffs* have been nearly as much nuisance as help ever since the days when New York had only volunteer fire departments —the days when the *buffs* first got their name.

A fire *buff* is a person who drops everything when he hears the fire whistle or the shriek of sirens and pursues the clanging engines to the scene of the blaze. *Buff,* you see, is short for "buffalo robe"—favorite cold-weather covering of amateur fire fighters midway through the last century. Also, these early volunteer companies attracted wealthy young men by the dash and danger of the assignment—and their favorite winter coats were made of buffalo skins. So we can credit to the nearly extinct bison the origin of the word *buff* to describe an enthusiast, especially one who delights in attending fires in a semiofficial capacity. He is by no means to be confused with the fire *bug,* who, known to the police by the more formal names of "incendiary" and "pyromaniac," is a person who starts fires for the thrill of seeing buildings burn.

A true fire *buff* prides himself on being the first civilian to arrive at the scene of the blaze and, especially in a small town where a large fire may tax the resources of the regular fire department, he can be of great help to the official firemen. He usually makes it a point to become well acquainted with the fire department officers and with all the complex routine of running a fire department, and is regarded by many chiefs as a welcome amateur assistant.

buffalo. The city of *Buffalo* did not get its name until 1810 (at first it was called New Amsterdam). Long before that, plainsmen had discovered and hunted the *buffalo;* indeed, *buffalo* rugs and blankets were probably used by the earliest settlers of the area which came to be the city of *Buffalo.*

The name *buffalo* is a misnomer when applied to the American bison. It is, nonetheless, the popular name for the animal. However, the Indians had nothing to do with coining it. *Buffalo* comes from Portuguese *(bufalo)* and can be traced to the Latin *bufalus* (wild ox).

buffoon. Jimmy Durante was often referred to as "America's most beloved *buffoon.*" This is a remarkably appropriate label for Jimmy, since it comes to us from the land to which the Great Schnozzola traced his ancestry, Italy. In the *commedia dell'arte* of the Middle Ages, one of the most beloved stock characters was *buffone,* whose specialty was puffing out his cheeks, then collapsing them suddenly. The resultant noise was not unlike the raucous Bronx cheer (more elegantly called the "raspberry"), which long was a staple of the sort of roughhouse cabaret comedy in which Jimmy himself was reared.

bugbear. Here is one of the few words which the Welsh have given to the English language, possibly because the Welsh language is so full of consonants that transition to English is not easy. *Bwg,* the Welsh for "hobgoblin" or "ghost," was made *bug* in English and used for some time to mean the same thing. The English added *-bear,* just to indicate an animal, and a *bugbear* became an imaginary but terrifying monster described to naughty children to make them behave. By extension, the word acquired the meaning of anything causing fear beyond reason.

Incidentally, Wales is very much a bilingual nation. English is taught in their schools, but the Welsh, being very proud people, see that their children learn the native tongue also. (CO-AUTHOR'S NOTE: And in case you hadn't guessed, Mrs. Morris is of Welsh descent.)

bug boy. When you look down a list of entries on a racing program, you will notice that there is an asterisk beside the names of some of the jockeys. Occasionally there will be two or three such asterisks, or "bugs," as they are called by both turfmen and printers. A *bug boy,* therefore, is simply an apprentice jockey.

The chief reason for the bugs is to alert the bettor that because the rider is an apprentice, he will be granted an allowance in the amount of weight his horse must carry in the race.

The weight allowances vary slightly from state to state, but for most major tracks they run like this: The apprentice is allowed a reduction of ten pounds (a triple bug on the program) until he has ridden five winning

horses. Then his allowance is reduced to seven pounds (a double bug) until
he rides thirty more winners. After he has ridden thirty-five winners, he
gets an allowance of five pounds for the balance of his first year in racing.

build a better mousetrap. Ralph Waldo Emerson, Elbert Hubbard and Mrs.
Sarah S. B. Yule make a rather formidable trio of chief actors in a long-
lasting dispute about who first uttered the nonsense about mousetraps: "If
you *build a better mousetrap,* the world will beat a path to your door."
Generally it is credited to Emerson, though Hubbard claimed to have said
it first, and there is no record in Emerson's published writings of this
precise phrase—though a similar idea is expressed in a paragraph of windy
rhetoric in one of his, speeches. Mrs. Yule gets into the picture because,
years before Hubbard made his claim, she published a book, *Borrowings,*
in which she quoted the mousetrap remark as having been made by Emerson in a speech she had heard years before.

bull meaning "mistake" comes from the French *boule,* which originally was
a lie, especially when made in the form of a bragging statement. Over the
centuries, the meaning changed somewhat, so that a *bull* nowadays means
"a boastful but unwittingly mistaken statement." Also, it's usually one that
is so obviously wrong that any listener knows at once that the maker of
the *bull* has made an utterly absurd remark.

bull band. In rural America during the nineteenth and early twentieth centuries, the custom of celebrating a wedding night with noisy revelry and
practical jokes was widespread. It had many names, the most formal of
which is "charivari," which is defined as "a noisy mock serenade to newlyweds." Interestingly enough, this word comes from the Latin word for
headache—and many a bride and groom woke up with just that after a
long, loud night. Some idea of how widespread this custom was can be seen
in the wide variety of names for it. Harold Wentworth, in his *American
Dialect Dictionary,* lists "belling, horning, callathump, skimmelton, tin-
kettling and bull-banding." And, reports Wentworth, the phrase *"bull
band,* calithumpian band" turned up in a newspaper published in 1916 in
Frederick County, Maryland.

bulldogging. In the slang of cowboys, *bulldogging* a steer means to get a grip
on its horns and twist its neck until it hits the ground.

bulldozer. Originally *bulldose* (as it was then spelled) meant a severe beating
or, as the expression used to be, a good sound thrashing. The thought is
that such a beating would be a "dose" suitable for a "bull" or administered
by a bullwhip. Then the verb *bulldoze* came to mean intimidating a person
by threatening violence. Later a *bulldozer* was the term applied to a big
pistol or revolver. Its application to earth-moving tractors came during the
1920s, apparently by extension of the idea of changing people's minds by
threats to changing the contours of the earth by pressure.

bullion, meaning bars of gold or silver, comes from the French word *billion,* the name of a small coin, and this word in turn came from *bille,* "stick or bar."

bull pen. There are a lot of theories about the origin of *bull pen,* including the obvious one based on the resemblance between the cages where relief pitchers warm up and the enclosures where bulls are kept before being sent charging into the bull ring. However, we discussed this some years ago with our friend Moe Berg, the only life member of the Linguistic Society of America ever to play big-league ball. Matter of fact, Moe played fifteen seasons in the majors, mostly in the American League, winding up with the Boston Red Sox in the late 1930s, when he doubled in brass as a panelist on the *Information, Please* radio show. We'd like to be able to say that Moe was one of the outstanding players of all time, but the fact is that he was a pretty good catcher and one of the most anemic hitters ever to make the majors. One year, and only one, he hit over .300, but that was the year he appeared in only ten games.

We go into all this background to show that it's safe to say that Moe spent more time in *bull pens* than any other catcher of his era. As a brilliant student of language (a Princeton Ph.D.), he had plenty of time to think about the origin of the name *bull pen* while he was warming up the second-string pitchers. It was Moe's conclusion that none of the highfalutin theories of the word's origin was even close to the mark. The true explanation, he told us, is that in baseball's early days the *bull pen* was usually located in left field, and standard equipment in ball parks of the period was a huge billboard on the left-field fence advertising Bull Durham tobacco.

bulls and bears. The *bull* is an investor who purchases stock in anticipation of a rise in its value and a *bull* market is one in which the majority of investors act on the assumption that their stocks will continue to increase in value. Various theories are advanced concerning the origin of the term and the most likely is that it refers to the bull's habit of tossing its head upward.

Bears, conversely, buy in anticipation of a slump in the market. Like its counterpart, *bull,* this term has been in use at least since 1700 and no one is quite sure how the term first got its meaning. Most plausible is the theory that it comes from the old axiom about "selling the skin before you've caught the *bear.*" A trader who operated in this fashion was once known in England as a "bearskin jobber."

bum. *Bums,* according to Jeff Davis, self-styled Emperor of the Knights of the Road and King of America's Hobos, are like tramps but are drunkards as well. The term is considered vulgar by dictionary editors and is a corruption of "bottom" for "buttocks" in British slang.

bumbershoot/parachute. *Bumbershoot* is late-nineteenth-century slang. It's a combination of the *umber* part of umbrella and the *chute* from *parachute.* For some reason our ancestors seem to have been very umbrella-conscious.

Harold Wentworth records in his *American Dialect Dictionary* more than fifteen other variations—*bumbershoot, bumbersell* and *umbershoot* among them.

If you're skeptical about parachutes being known in the nineteenth century, here's a surprise. The word *parachute,* in precisely the same meaning it has today, first appeared in print in 1785! The reason? Well, they needed a way to get out of balloons when trouble loomed—and balloons were commonplace long before the Wright brothers conquered the air in heavier-than-air craft.

bumpkin. When you speak of someone as a "country *bumpkin,*" you're implying that he's not very bright, something of a blockhead, in fact. And you couldn't be more accurate, because *bumpkin* is a borrowing from the Dutch *boomken,* meaning "small tree." The British, never notably fond of the Dutch, once used *bumpkin* as a pejorative for "Dutchman."

bunco is generally thought to come from *buncombe,* though its present-day meaning—"swindle or confidence game"—has much more distasteful connotations than does *bunk* (which see). A *bunco steerer* is a swindler's accomplice who "steers" the unwary to a crooked or fixed game of cards, chance or pool. Incidentally, though *bunco* was common in the latter part of the nineteenth century and appears often in the works of Bret Harte, O. Henry and other writers, it is still a part of today's underworld jargon.

bungalow is a borrowing from the Hindi word *bangla,* literally "of Bengal." The word dates back to the times of Britain's imperial greatness and originally described a one-story building not unlike the contemporary ranch house, except that the original Indian *bungalow* had a thatched roof to act as insulation against the hot midday sun, into which, in Noel Coward's memorable phrase, only "mad dogs and Englishmen" would venture.

bunk/bunkum. According to well-authenticated legend, Congressman Felix Walker of Buncombe County, North Carolina, made a speech in 1820 which was notable—even by the extraordinarily tolerant standards of our House of Representatives—for its windiness and general nonsensicality. As member after member rose to leave the floor of the House, the Honorable Felix became gradually aware of the fact that, in today's theatrical parlance, he was "laying an egg." With remarkable humility for a congressman, he interrupted his speech to remark, "You're not hurting my feelings, gentlemen. I am not speaking for your ears. I am only talking for Buncombe." Congressman Walker's candor was so relished by his colleagues that they adopted the phrase "talking for Buncombe" as a synonym for talking nonsense. Over the years the spelling was simplified by popular usage to *Bunkum.* In time, of course, the capital *B* was changed to lower case and the terminal *um* was lost. Thus *bunk,* which we all know so well, is in reality an abbreviation of "Buncombe County, North Carolina."

Bunthorne manner. In the *Hartford Courant* dated June 26, 1887, the Boston correspondent (a man named Templeton) alludes to an Irish protest meeting in Faneuil Hall regarding a proposed banquet to be held there in honor of Queen Victoria's birthday. Mr. John Boyle O'Reilly led the protest and, according to Templeton, "cursed Faneuil Hall for the future, after the most approved Bunthorne manner, because it was to be desecrated by the gathering of admirers of Queen Victoria."

While this was well before our time, we beg to differ with Mr. Templeton. In the comic opera *Patience* by W. S. Gilbert and Sir Arthur Sullivan, first produced in 1881, a leading character was named Bunthorne. He was a deliberate caricature of Oscar Wilde, who was just then achieving fame as a writer and as a personality of a decidedly effeminate cast. In the words of one authority, Bunthorne was a youth "who adopts the most extravagantly aesthetic and lackadaisical style."

Templeton, the author of this dispatch, certainly grossly misjudged John Boyle O'Reilly. Though a poet and editor of the Catholic diocesan newspaper *The Pilot*, O'Reilly had been a member of the Fenian Brotherhood in Ireland and had enlisted in the British Army for the express purpose of spreading anti-British sentiment among the ranks. Indicative of his success is the fact that he was sentenced to death for high treason, a sentence which was finally commuted to twenty years of penal servitude in Australia. He escaped from the prison colony after a couple of years and made his way to Boston, where he soon became a leader in the Irish community. If further evidence of O'Reilly's virility be needed, note that he was a second to the Boston Strong Boy, John L. Sullivan, when he defeated Jake Kilrain for the heavyweight championship of the world in a 75-round bare-knuckles match at Richburg, Mississippi, in 1889.

And how do we happen to know all this? Well, one of Father Morris's favorite law clients (she called him her "solicitor") was the daughter of John Boyle O'Reilly. The first great woman war correspondent of World War I, Mary Boyle O'Reilly ("M.B.O'R." to her friends) ran the Scripps London bureau during that conflict, was an intimate friend of many world leaders, notably Tomáš Garrigue Masaryk of Czechoslovakia, and—in later days—the inspiration for the younger Morris, your author, to enter the newspaper business.

burble is actually two different words, each with its own meaning and origin. Used to mean "to confuse or perplex," it is a Scottish dialect word. The second *burble,* an English word of much more recent vintage, is what word experts call an echoic word—that is, it tries to spell out the sound it represents. Originally *burble* meant the noise made by a gurgling stream. Then, by extension, it came to mean the noise made by a speaker who gushes out his speech.

burgeoning. An ad warning against certain unscrupulous dog breeders who palm off mutts as AKC-registered canines contained these statements:

"Their business would wither away were it not for America's *burgeoning* prosperity. The booming economy has brought a vast increase in disposable income."

Burgeoning means "budding," not "mushrooming." It has been much in vogue—in the wrong sense—during the past few years. Whether it will come to be used in this new sense by people who observe the niceties of language remains to be seen. *Burgeon* comes from Middle English *burjon,* "bud."

burgoo. Offhand one would be hard put to think of anything more characteristically Southern than this rich stew, a blend of various meats and vegetables, slowly simmered until it gives off an aroma and taste calculated to warm the most recalcitrant voter's heart—which is why it has so long been a staple at political rallies in the Deep South. So would you believe that at least one source, the *American Heritage Dictionary* (of all authorities!), suggests that *burgoo* may have got its name from the Arabic *burghul,* which the Arabs in turn took from an identical Persian word, meaning "bruised grain"? Well, maybe—but we'd hate to have to convince a Southern politician that the staple stew served at his vote-gathering barbecues started life in Persia! We find more persuasive the suggestion of historian Clark Kinnaird that it may be "a Negro pronunciation of barbecue, for which Negroes were generally the chefs, servers and incidental consumers."

burke means "to murder by suffocation," especially in such a fashion that the body of the deceased is not marred and hence is suitable for clinical dissection by medical students. It comes from one William *Burke,* an Irishman who found his destiny in Edinburgh supplying corpses on order to the medical school of the University of Edinburgh. Estimates vary as to how many cadavers he turned in, but there were at least fifteen. Finally caught, he was hanged before a crowd in a public square in 1829 to enthusiastic cries of *"Burke* him! *Burke* him!" *Burke* subsequently acquired the extended meaning of, as the *American Heritage Dictionary* puts it, "to suppress quietly and unceremoniously."

Burke/Jefferson. Samuel Johnson once summed up his opinion of *Edmund Burke* in these words: "You could not stand five minutes with Burke beneath a shed while it rained, but you must be convinced you had been standing with the greatest man you had ever seen." Nearly two centuries later, John F. Kennedy used somewhat similar phrases when he spoke at a dinner honoring Nobel Prize winners at the White House in 1962: "I think this is the most extraordinary collection of talent, of human knowledge that has ever been gathered together at the White House," said Kennedy, "with the possible exception of when *Thomas Jefferson* dined alone."

Burke and *Jefferson,* interestingly enough, were contemporaries and, while *Burke* did not share *Jefferson's* revolutionary fervor, he did strongly oppose measures taken by the British government to oppress the American colonists.

bury the hatchet. *Burying the hatchet* was, quite literally, the gesture made by Indians in New England when they made peace with the white men. In 1680, for example, Samuel Sewall wrote: "Meeting with the Sachem [Indian chiefs], they came to an agreement and buried two axes in the ground, which ceremony to them is more significant and binding than all the Articles of Peace, the hatchet being the principal weapon."

bus is a shortened form of "omnibus." The first omnibuses were put in service in England in 1829. They were horse-drawn wagons, much like the stage-coaches that we knew in our own West a few years later. They carried a half dozen or so people inside and three or four on the roof. The name was borrowed from the French *voiture omnibus* (vehicle for all). *Omnibus* is the dative plural form of the Latin adjective *omnis,* and means "for everyone."

bush is a contraction of the old baseball expression *bush league,* used to describe minor and semiprofessional leagues of ball clubs. *Bush* has a dictionary definition of "uncultivated country." Since most of the players in such leagues are either inexperienced or past their prime, the expression *bush leaguer* has a connotation of amateurishness or incompetence.

busman's holiday originated in the close relationship between horse teams and their drivers in the days when London's omnibuses were horse-drawn. Almost invariably the regular driver would report to the starting point on his day off to see to it that proper care was used in harnessing his team. If he had any reason to suspect that the substitute driver was negligent in handling the horses, the regular busman might unobtrusively sit among the passengers to observe the new driver's behavior. These rides—beyond the call of duty and without extra pay—came to be called *busman's holidays.*

busy as a bee. The origin of this well-known expression is probably many thousands of years old, since *bee* is one of a handful of words found in every one of the languages we now trace to a common Indo-European source. In other words, bees were known throughout Europe and western Asia from the dawn of civilization, and the earliest men must have wondered at their incredible industry. The first mention of the phrase in its present form is in Chaucer's *Canterbury Tales,* where we find: "For aye as *busy as bees* been they."

but and ben. In Scotland the *ben* is the inner room or parlor of a house, while the *but* may be either the entranceway or an outer part of a house—such as a porch. Thus a Scotsman's *but and ben* is his entire house.

but for the grace of God. John Bradford, a leading Protestant minister and martyr of sixteenth-century England said, as he saw a criminal passing by: "There, *but for the grace of God,* goes John Bradford." Bradford was burned at the stake for alleged heresies in 1555, shortly after the accession of Queen Mary I ("Bloody Mary"), only child of Henry VIII and Catherine of Aragon.

butterfly. The word *butterfly* obviously might better be "flutterby," but equally obviously it isn't. All the way back to Anglo-Saxon, the insect's name remains essentially the same, though the spelling differs a bit. It's simply *butter* plus *fly.* Why? Well, there is no lack of speculation, and the theory we like best suggests that the name may go back to medieval folklore and tales that fairies and witches in the form of butterflies stole butter in the dark of the night.

butter wouldn't melt in his (her) mouth. A person in whose mouth *butter would not melt* is one who looks supremely innocent—but probably is not. He or she may, to use another popular expression, be like the cat who just ate the canary—and assume a beguiling air of injured innocence. The expression first appeared in print in a collection of proverbs published by John Heywood in 1546—but the likelihood is that it goes much further back than that. Heywood, like other collectors of proverbs, including our own Ben Franklin, who put a lot of them into *Poor Richard's Almanac,* was merely publishing a collection of pithy and witty sayings that may have been passed along for centuries. So the person who first said *"Butter wouldn't melt in her mouth"* was our old friend Anon—and he may well have said it in Chaucer's time.

buying a pig in a poke, meaning "buying blind," has an amusing origin. The expression comes from a ruse practiced for centuries at country fairs in England. A trickster would try to palm off on an unwary bumpkin a cat in a burlap bag, claiming it was a suckling pig. If the "mark"—or victim —was brighter than the sharper expected him to be, he would insist on seeing the pig and thus "let the cat out of the bag." *Poke,* meaning "bag or sack," is now chiefly heard in regional dialects in this country and England, though it has a long and honorable history, and indeed is the word from which "pocket" was derived.

buzz session/buzz word. A few years ago the expression *buzz session* was very big among educational groups. Programs for organizations like the American Library Association and the National Council of Teachers of English regularly scheduled *buzz sessions,* involving several "discussants," and usually following a lecture or panel program. They amounted to little more than verbal post-mortems on the subjects previously discussed. *Buzz,* then, was taken over from the private jargon of the educators and now seems to be used as synonymous with "in"—that is, a *buzz word* is one known to and used by specialists in communications. As such, a word like "demographics" (which see) would certainly qualify.

by and large. It's difficult to fix a precise meaning for *by and large,* since it means "generally speaking" or "on the whole." But originally the phrase had a very precise meaning in the language of sailors. In the days of sailing ships, when a vessel was running close-hauled, the man at the helm would usually be given one of two orders, "full and by" or *by and large.* The first command, used with a skillful helmsman, meant "sail as close to the wind as you can." The second, *by and large,* meant "sail slightly off the wind" and was given to the inexperienced helmsman since this tack would leave him in less danger of being "taken aback." So the phrase *by and large* has come to indicate imprecise generalities. A person speaking *by and large* about a subject can be considered to be something less than entirely expert on it.

bye is a term which has been used for many years in such competitions as tennis, bridge and chess tournaments. In each of these it is standard practice to pair competitors who will then battle each other to move ahead to the next stage of the tournament. If there is an odd-numbered group of competitors, the odd man draws a *bye*—that is, he automatically goes ahead to the next stage of the tournament without having to play a match.

bye and bye God caught his eye. We have for years quoted the "Epitaph for a Waiter" without knowing its author. Now we learn that it's David McCord, long the wit behind Harvard University's legendary and enormously successful fund appeals. Our hat is off to him. And the Epitaph? *"Bye and bye God caught his eye."*

bye-bye. The childish farewell *"bye-bye"* has become a television trade term for that point in the program when the star announces, "Now we're going to have to say so long."

by hook or by crook. When a person needs something desperately, he will manage to obtain it *by hook or by crook.* In doing so, he is figuratively following the example of the peasants of feudal times who, though in dire need of firewood, were allowed only to take those tree branches which hung low enough to be pulled down or cut off *by hook or by crook.*

by Jove/holy jumping Jupiter. The practice of using the name of a god profanely goes back to the Greeks and Romans, who had a considerable pantheon of gods whose names would serve the purpose. Some of them still survive as mild expressions of surprise or anger.

by the grapevine, meaning "by unofficial means," is the way gossip and rumor most often travel. In America's Civil War, the speed of the *"grapevine* telegraph" was legendary, just as were "latrine rumors" and "scuttlebutt" in later wars. The expression probably comes from the legendary speed with which jungle tribes—and our American Indians—were able to pass word.

by the great horned spoon. The earliest known appearance of *by the great horned spoon*—an imprecation about as powerful as "Great Caesar's ghost!"—is in a song popular around 1840. Spoons were, of course, made from the horns of cattle in centuries past, just as the original shoehorns were. But just how any horn spoon became "great" is the point that has puzzled researchers. One ingenious scholar suggests that the phrase is really a translation of *gros cornes* (great horns), which was the name given to Rocky Mountain bighorn sheep by the early explorers. And Francis Parkman, great historian of the opening of the West, noted that Indians made from the horns of these sheep spoons capable of holding more than a quart. So perhaps this theory of the origin of this frontier expression is not so farfetched after all.

by the skin of my teeth, meaning "just barely" or "by a hair's breadth," comes from the Book of Job (19:20): "My bone cleaveth to my skin, and to my flesh, and I am escaped with the *skin of my teeth.*"

Byzantine logothete. Theodore Roosevelt once described Woodrow Wilson as a *Byzantine logothete.* Actually a *logothete* was an officer—either treasurer or chancellor—of the Byzantine Empire. What T.R. meant was that in his opinion Wilson was an official who talked a lot but did nothing. He used the expression at a time when T.R. thought we should enter World War I, but Wilson still advocated vigilant neutrality.

cab/cabriolet. The *cab* in *taxicab* is a shortened form of *cabriolet,* a word that readers with long memories will recall as part of the elegant language of motoring in the years before Detroit decided America wanted *Furies* and *Spyders* and *Mustangs* more than phaetons, limousines and cabriolets. *Cabriolet,* by the way, was a French word, a diminutive of *cabriole,* meaning "goatlike leap or caper." Anyone who has been jolted by a New York hackie's quick response to a light change may agree that the original meaning still applies.

cabal. A widely held but erroneous notion of the origin of this word for a group of persons working together from somewhat hidden or devious motives is that it comes from the first letters of the names of five cabinet ministers of Charles II. But the word is much older than that. Indeed, it may be traced back to a Hebrew word of similar meaning.

While it's true that the word was popularized during the reign of Charles II, the *Oxford Dictionary* reports its appearance in print as early as 1616, nearly sixty years before the cabinet of Clifford, Arlington, Buckingham, Ashley and Lauderdale. Thanks to the coincidence that their last initials spell *cabal,* the word came into great vogue and was thought to be one of the earliest acronyms (a word made up of the first letters of a group of words).

In point of fact, however, *cabal* was borrowed directly from the French *cabale,* where it meant a club or society of intriguers. Eventually it can be traced through Latin to the Hebrew *qabbalah*—the doctrines received from Moses and handed down through the centuries by word of mouth.

During the Middle Ages the possessors of these doctrines were believed to possess secrets of magical power, and thus the word *cabal* acquired its implications of stealth and mystery.

caboose. *Caboose* sounds like a characteristic bit of American railroad jargon, perhaps derived, like "vamoose" and "hoosegow," from Spanish by way of Mexico. But that is not the case. *Caboose* was originally a Dutch word, or rather two Dutch words, *kaban huis,* meaning "cabin house or ship's galley." In time the two words blended into one, *kabuys,* and even before our Revolutionary War, the term *caboose* was commonly used on British ships to designate the cook's quarters. The word has been traced back as far as 1862 in its current American meaning of the last or trainmen's car on a freight train. Incidentally, it has never been used by British railroaders. To them a *caboose* is a "brake van."

cache. Pronounced KASH, this word comes from the French *cacher* and retains its original meaning of "to hide away or conceal." See also STASH.

caddy. Golf *caddies* were originally "cadets." The word *caddie* has been used in Scotland for centuries to mean an errand boy, so it was entirely logical that it be used to designate the boy who carries the clubs, watches the ball and, generally speaking, runs errands for the golfers. In America today the usual spelling is *caddy.* The word was introduced into Scotland by French-born, golf-playing Mary, Queen of Scots. Her "cadets" were no errand boys, but noble-born pages.

caduceus. The medical symbol of a stick with a pair of snakes wrapped around it is called the *caduceus* (pronounced kuh-DOO-see-us). It has been the symbol of the medical profession since ancient times. Its white staff was originally carried by Roman warriors when they desired to ask the enemy to discuss truce terms—just as the white flag is used by peace negotiators today. It was also carried by Mercury, the wing-footed messenger of the gods.

The snakes come from the tradition that Aesculapius, the Roman god of medicine, appeared during a plague in Rome in the form of a snake. The ancients also believed that snakes had discovered the secret of eternal life, interpreting the snake's seasonal sloughing off of its skin as a return to youth. What's more, they credited snakes with being able to search out health-giving medicinal herbs. Thus the combination of the snakes as symbols of health and the staff representing both speed and peace adds up to a meaningful emblem for the medical profession.

Caesar/czar/kaiser all have the meaning of leader, the first in ancient Rome, the second in Russia of pre-Revolutionary times, the third in imperial Germany of the period ending with the end of the First World War. *Caesar* may actually be traced back to a family name of Etruscan origin. The surgical operation known as the Caesarean section, performed to extract a fetus, is so called because of a legend that Julius Caesar or one of his ancestors was born by this method. The child was described as *ā caeso mātris ūtere*—"from the incised womb of his mother"—*caesus* being the past participle of the verb *caedere,* "to cut."

Caesar salad. We once mentioned in our column that the *Caesar salad* was the invention of "Prince" Mike Romanoff, whose restaurant in Hollywood was the favorite hangout of writers and celebrities during the great days of the films. Mike was, of course, not a prince at all, simply a transplanted New Yorker with a king-size supply of chutzpah.

But this proved to be less than accurate. Romanoff did a great deal to popularize the salad, but he did not invent it. That was the work of one Caesar Gardini, who ran a restaurant called Caesar's Place in Tijuana, Mexico. One day many more hungry tourists than expected stopped at his place on their way north from the bullfights, races, beaches and other Baja California attractions. So he improvised a salad from ingredients on hand. The result was the *Caesar salad,* made of romaine lettuce, garlic-flavored olive oil, lemon juice, grated Parmesan cheese, coddled egg, Worcestershire sauce and garlic-flavored croutons, all tossed lightly before serving.

There have been many variations on this formula over the years. Romanoff added anchovies and others often add bleu or Roquefort cheese. But it was modest restaurateur Caesar Gardini who gave it its name—not imperial Julius Caesar and certainly not less-than-regal Prince Mike Romanoff.

Caesar's wife must be above suspicion. Caesar had three wives, but only one of them—Pompeia, the second wife—was responsible for this particular saying. Here's how it came about. At two seasons of the year—in May and December—the leading women of Rome gathered for sacred services in honor of their favorite goddess, Bona Dea—"the good goddess."

In 62 B.C. Caesar's home was chosen for the ceremony, which was to be attended only by women. Shortly after the rites began there were sudden shouts of alarm and several of the celebrants fell upon one of the group— veiled and clad like the others—stripped off part of her costume, and revealed a man in their presence. And not just any man—but Publius Clodius, a notorious rake whose name had been linked with that of Pompeia. There is no clear evidence that there actually had been any hanky-panky between the two and it is a fact that Caesar never claimed that there was. Nevertheless, the devotions to the goddess had been pro- faned and Caesar's wife was in charge at the time the profanation took place. So a shadow of suspicion had been cast on her and Julius, with a political career at stake, uttered the Latin equivalent of "Caesar's wife must be above suspicion"—and divorced her.

Cajun. If you remember Longfellow's "Evangeline," you'll recall that the French settlers of what is now Nova Scotia (then called Acadia) were deported by order of the British in 1755. Many of them settled in Louisiana, where the name Acadian gradually became corrupted to *Cajun*. In theory, the term is restricted to Louisianans of Acadian French ancestry.

cakes and ale. This British expression is roughly akin to "beer and skittles." Life, runs the aphorism, is not all *cakes and ale.* The expression is of some literary interest because W. Somerset Maugham used it as the title of a novel (1930) which many contemporaries regarded as a rather spiteful lampoon of Thomas Hardy. The expression appears in Shakespeare's *Twelfth Night* when Sir Toby Belch says to the Puritan Malvolio: "Dost thou think, because thou art virtuous, there shall be no more *cakes and ale?*"

calaboose, meaning "jailhouse," was borrowed by cowboys from their Mexican counterparts. Just as "hoosegow" was a corruption of *jusgado,* so *calaboose* was originally the Spanish word for dungeon, *calabozo.*

Calamity Jane is a term applied either to a woman who always has a tale of woe or to one who seems to bring trouble with her, much as Typhoid Mary (which see) does. The real *Calamity Jane* had none of these characteristics. She was an American frontierswoman noted for her markmanship with both rifle and revolver, who threatened "calamity" to any man who offended her. She was born Martha Jane Canary in Princeton, Missouri, about 1852. In 1864 her parents took her to Virginia City, Montana, where they later separated and left her on her own. She dressed like a man, moved from one boom town to another and eventually went with the Gold Rush to the Black Hills of South Dakota, where she lived until she died in 1903. Despite her fame, her history is a little clouded. The then governor of New Mexico claimed that she was a prostitute in Hays City, Kansas, when he was there. She claimed to have been the sweetheart of Wild Bill Hickock. Some believed that she served as a scout for Generals Custer and Miles. Certainly she performed men's jobs, including those of bullwhacker and Indian fighter. Reference books give her married name as Burke but make no mention of a husband. An admirer paid her the ultimate frontiersman's tribute: "She'd look like hell in a halo."

calculate/calculus come from the same Latin word, *calculus,* meaning "pebble." In Roman times the last word in computers was the abacus. Today's abacus—a device still widely used in the Orient—consists of a wooden frame with beads that slide back and forth on wires. The beads have varying values, and their positions on the board have special significance. But the abacuses of ancient Rome were more primitive affairs, consisting of boards with slots or grooves in which pebbles *(calculi)* were moved back and forth to keep track of the reckoning. So a person who *calculated* was originally a Roman pebble-pusher.

call a spade a spade. The first spade-caller is lost in antiquity, for the coiner of the Latin proverb *"Ficus ficus, ligonem ligonem vocat"* is unknown, though Menander and Plutarch are both credited with it. As long ago as the early part of the sixteenth century, John Knox, Scottish Protestant reformer, gave an English version: "I have learned to call wickedness by its own terms: a fig a fig, and *a spade a spade.*"

Words you use when you don't want to *call a spade a spade* are "euphemisms." The heyday of the euphemism in our language and culture was undoubtedly the Victorian era. When the names of many items of wearing apparel were inadmissible in polite society, the mention of shirt, trousers or—worse yet—breeches was a symptom of utmost depravity. As one versifier noted: "I've heard that breeches, petticoat and smock/Give to thy modest mind a grievous shock/And that thy brain (so lucky its device)/ Christened them 'inexpressibles,' so nice." In those days, of course, the word "leg" was entirely inadmissible in polite society and even piano "limbs" were decorated with frilled trousers—or "inexpressibles."

call him (her) every name in the book. The book referred to in this expression is not the phone book nor yet the Bible. It's the dictionary—the one book that has all the names and quite a few derogatory adjectives, too.

calligraphy. From the Greek *kalli-* (beautiful) and *graphein* (to write), *calligraphy* quite literally means "beautiful writing." In this modern age when the doom of even the printed word has been sounded by some avant-garde prophets, examples of fine calligraphy are hard to find. The art reached perhaps its finest flowering in the Cursive Chancery handwriting of papal scribes of the fifteenth century. However, as late as the nineteenth and early twentieth centuries Spencerian handwriting was much in vogue, and a few diehards—implacable foes of the typewriter—occasionally display it today.

calliope. From the Greek *kalli-* (beautiful) and *ops* (voice). Calliope was the goddess of epic poetry in ancient Greece. In American circuses and carnivals, to say nothing of nineteenth-century showboats, the *calliope* was something else again. It was a keyboard instrument that emitted, through a set of steam whistles, some weird and wonderful sounds that those who loved it called music. Though purists might shudder, the noise was loud and, in its way, unique. When you heard the *calliope,* you could be mighty sure the circus was in town. Incidentally, while the name of the Greek muse was pronounced kuh-LY-uh-pee, circus and carnival hands without exception called the steam-whistle contraption the kal-ee-OHP.

callipygian is or is not a flattering word, depending on your ideas of feminine beauty. It's derived from the Greek *kallos* (beautiful) and *pyge* (buttocks).

Callithumpian band. Isn't that a darlin' phrase! You can almost hear the sounds such a band made just from saying it aloud. Here's a description of such a band in action, from *Bartlett's Dictionary of Americanisms,* published in 1848: "It is a common practice in New York, as well as other parts of the country, on New Year's Eve, for persons to assemble with tin horns, rattles, bells and similar instruments, and parade the streets, making all the noise and discord possible. This party is called the Callithumpian

Band." The word is probably made from a combination of "calliope," the steam-whistle music-maker we know from circuses and carnivals, and "thumping."

calumny (pronounced KAL-um-nee) comes direct from the Latin *calumnia* and means a false and defamatory accusation, one deliberately intended to hurt another person's reputation.

cambric tea, also called "hot water tea," is a concoction formerly given to children when adults were having tea. It consisted of hot water, milk, sugar and sometimes a dash of actual tea. The idea behind its concoction was to make the children feel part of the social group. It gets its name from the fabric *cambric,* which is thin and white, like the tea. It's an American invention, quite unknown in England, where menus in restaurants catering to families may sometimes list the concoction as "a dash of tea," but never as *cambric tea.*

camellia. The *camellia* is named after George Joseph Kamel, a Moravian Jesuit missionary who brought back the first shrubs from the Orient.

camelopard. The *camelopard,* famed in medieval folklore, is actually the giraffe—tall as a camel, spotted like a leopard.

camel through needle's eye. The origin of this expression is in the words of Christ as recorded in Matthew 19:24: "It is easier for a camel to go through the eye of a needle, than for a rich man to enter into the kingdom of God."

Similar expressions may be found in other religious works. For instance, the Koran contains this: "This impious shall find the gates of heaven shut; nor shall he enter till a camel shall pass through the eye of a needle." Note here, though, that it's the "impious" who are barred, not the rich. However, the basic idea of the metaphor remains the same: the sheer impossibility of a camel's ever being able to go through the eye of a needle.

But there is still some hope for the rich man. Note Mark 10:24: "How hard is it for them that trust in riches to enter into the kingdom of God!" So the basic idea, we think, is not that a man of wealth is necessarily barred, but that those who feel they can gain admission solely because of their wealth will not be admitted.

cameo bit/role. The expression *cameo bit* or *cameo role* to describe a bit part played by a famous actor was widely publicized by Mike Todd in his production of *Around the World in 80 Days,* in which Marlene Dietrich, Frank Sinatra and other famous players took roles that required their appearance on screen for only four or five minutes. Under such an arrangement, the producer gets the advantage of having a lot of star names to parade in his ads, the spectator has the piquant excitement of wondering, "Now can that really *be* So-and-so?" and the actor, presumably, gets a lot of money for very little work.

An earlier and slightly different use of *cameo* dates back to about ten years before Todd's highly successful experiment. A very popular afternoon TV show called *Cameo Theatre* presented hour-long condensations of popular plays. Because a different play was given every day, the budget was necessarily limited, and the sets were not elaborate. In order to compensate for these shortcomings, many of the camera shots were facial close-ups—known in the trade as *cameos.*

Camorra was a nineteenth-century forerunner of the Mafia or Black Hand, Italian terrorist societies, notable for its blackmailing and gambling activities. It took its name from the smocklike blouse *(camorra)* worn by its members, who were known as Camorrists.

Canada. According to the best authority, *canada* was originally a word in the Huron-Iroquois language meaning "a collection of lodges." Thus the first *canada* was an Indian village. *Canada* first appeared in the narrative of Jacques Cartier in 1535. According to one well-attested story, Cartier talked with an Indian chief, who waved his arms about as if to include all the land that stretched far beyond the horizon, exclaiming, "Kanata." Cartier thought the chief meant that Kanata was the name for the entire country. Actually, it was only a reference to a nearby village.

canapé/hors d'oeuvre. According to a leading cookbook, "The phrase *hors d'oeuvre* is used to describe savory little appetizers or relishes other than *canapés.*" *Canapés,* in turn, are defined as "savory appetizers made with a bread, cracker or pastry base, so that they can be picked up with the fingers and eaten in one or two bites." *Hors d'oeurves,* then, include the whole range of cocktail-time tidbits except *canapés.*

Both terms come from the French and each has an interesting background. Would you have guessed, for instance, that *canapé* originally meant a canopy of mosquito netting over a couch or bed? In time it came to mean the bed or divan itself—whence it was taken into English with its present meaning of a bit of bread or cracker over which a tasty mixture of cheese, meat or fish is spread. *Hors d'oeuvre*—which means literally "outside the work"—came to its present meaning because the appetizers referred to are almost invariably served outside of and in advance of the main meal.

Both words, incidentally, offer some challenge in the matter of pronunciation. None of us is likely to stray so far from the correct pronunciation as the legendary new-rich oil millionaire who demanded "horses' doovers," but it's worth taking the trouble to be right. Say or-DERV for *hors d'oeuvre* and kan-uh-PAY for *canapé.*

canard. This term for "lie, hoax or exaggerated account" comes from the French word of the same spelling meaning "duck." It is believed to have had its origin in the French expression *vendre des canards à moitié,* "to sell half-ducks," and thus to swindle or deceive or make a fool of a person.

cancel. When the post office *cancels* a stamp or a bank *cancels* a check, it is doing it in the true Roman tradition by making a lattice of lines across the stamp or check. *Cancelli* in Latin meant "lattice," and the Romans themselves used it to make the word *cancellare,* "to strike out writing by making a lattice of lines across it." By extension, *cancel* also means "to invalidate in any way or to abolish."

candidate. In the course of one of our quadrennial political frenzies, with politicians exchanging charges and countercharges with ever-increasing recklessness, it is almost amusing to reflect on the fact that the word *candidate* originally meant a man clad in spotless raiment, a person immune from tawdry mud-slinging. In Roman days a person *candidatus*— "clothed in white"—was a man seeking elective office. The white toga, of course, was intended to indicate that the candidate's motives were as pure and spotless as the gown he wore.

The politics of ancient Rome have given us other words now heard in daily use among our legislators. A *senator,* for instance, was originally one of the elder wise men, and the body in which they met—the *senate*—took its name from *senex,* the Latin word for "old." A *legislator,* logically enough, was one who brings laws, from the Latin words *lator* (bringer) and *lex* (law). *Congress* is a group which "comes together," from the Latin *congredi,* while a *parliament* is, almost too aptly, a place where people talk —from the French *parlement* (talking).

candid camera. Dr. Erich Salomon, using one of the first Leica 35–millimeter cameras, in 1928 took a series of unposed pictures of world-famous statesmen at a League of Nations meeting in Geneva. When published in the London *Graphic,* they created a sensation because they were so unlike the customarily stiff and formal group photographs taken at such assemblies. The word *candid* was used to describe Salomon's photos by the *Graphic* and the word soon came into general use to describe the miniature cameras and photographs taken while the subject was unaware and "off guard."

Candlemas Day (February 2) derives its name from the church mass on that day when all candles to be used in the church during the coming year are blessed. The feast is in commemoration of the purification of the Virgin Mary and the candles are symbols of Jesus Christ as "light of the world." But to many people Candlemas Day is now known only as Groundhog Day because they are unaware of the historical connection. The origins of the legend that the groundhog comes out of his hibernation hole on Candlemas Day extend far back into history, long before astute publicists decided to focus attention on Punxsutawney, Pa., by calling in camera crews and staging a show on that day.

As a matter of fact, the history of this legend goes back centuries and it didn't always involve the groundhog or woodchuck. In ancient Germany it was a badger who, in the words of an old proverb, "peeps out of his hole on Candlemas Day and, if he finds snow, walks abroad. But if he sees the sun shining, he draws back into his hole."

The Scotch have a centuries-old proverb, not involving any particular animal but stating the case for weather forecasting on that day: "If Candlemas Day be dry and fair,/The half o' winter's come and mair./If Candlemas Day be wet and foul,/The half o'winter was gone at Youl."

Incidentally, Missouri, the "show me" state, always noted for its independence, celebrates Groundhog Day on February 14.

cannibalize has been standard mechanics' jargon since World War II. It is entered in most dictionaries, with the meaning of salvaging parts from abandoned vehicles to put others into working order. The *Air Force Dictionary* has still another definition—a bit closer to the original jungle sense of the word: "to obtain personnel from other units to build up an organization's strength."

can of worms. "Don't try to pass me that *can of worms*" has been a staple item in the jargon of advertising agency types for decades. The meaning is clear: don't try to fob off a complicated, perplexing problem on me. A variation of the standard phrase appears in a novel by Allen Drury in which a newly elected U.S. President says: "I arrived in Washington and found that I had inherited a large basketful of slippery eels and it will take me some time to cull them out."

cant. In the eighteenth century *cant* or *canting words* were terms used by dictionary editors to designate a variety of vulgar terms. Several dictionaries of the period, notably that of Nathaniel Bailey (from which Dr. Johnson borrowed heavily) and one by the Reverend John Ash, published in London in 1775, included such words. During the nineteenth century, under the influence of Bowdler (who expurgated Shakespeare) and of Queen Victoria, such words were taboo, and only recently have they begun to reappear.

Johnson, incidentally, did not include them in his dictionary. They say that a pair of very proper ladies approached him at a literary tea and declared: "We see, Dr. Johnson, that you do not have those naughty words in your dictionary!" To which he replied: "And I see, dear ladies, that you have been looking for them!"

Cantab. *Cantab* is a shortened form of Cantabrigian, an adjective formed from *Cantabrigia,* the Latin name for the city of Cambridge, England. Since the Massachusetts city, like the one in England, houses one of the nation's distinguished universities, it's not surprising that the name was adopted—though in abbreviated form—to describe the athletes of Harvard. *Cantab* has the added virtue of fitting snugly into a newspaper headline. Incidentally, Boston papers also use *Cantab* to describe undergraduates of the Cambridge High and Latin School. See also LIVERPUDLIAN.

canteen. The name of this small flask, slung over the shoulders of hundreds of thousands of Boy Scouts, has a rather interesting history. The first *cantina* was an Italian wine cellar. Indeed, the same word, carried into

Spanish without alteration, was used in the Southwestern United States and in Mexico to designate a bar or saloon. For many years the soldiers' *canteen* has been the place to which they repair for drink, food and casual relaxation. Gradually it came also to mean the portable flask in which liquids could be carried.

can't hold a candle to. This expression has nothing to do with the method of testing the freshness of eggs by holding them before a candle's flame. Instead it goes back to Shakespeare's time, before there was any such thing as street lighting. In those days a person returning home from a tavern or theater would be accompanied by a linkboy, who carried a torch or candle. These linkboys were considered very inferior beings, so to say that Tom couldn't *hold a candle to* Harry meant that Tom was very much inferior to Harry.

can't see the forest for the trees. A person who *can't see the forest for the trees* is one who is so concerned with trivial matters that he can't grasp the big problems. If he were a writer, for instance, he might be more concerned with getting every sentence precisely correct grammatically than working to make sure that the book as a whole impressed its readers the way he wanted it to. The expression first appeared in the works of Christoph Martin Weiland, a German poet and novelist, who wrote: "Too much light often blinds gentlemen of this sort. *They cannot see the forest for the trees.*"

Cape Cod turkey is a New England name for baked codfish, in the same spirit in which Welsh rabbit and Billingsgate pheasant were named.

capricious means changeable, guided by a sudden whim or notion, mercurial. It is an Anglicized form of the French word *capricieux,* while the French *caprice* comes to us unchanged. Originally it referred to a curled or frizzled head (Latin *caput,* meaning "head," and *riccio,* meaning "curled or frizzled").

captain of the head. In navy parlance the *head* is a washroom and the *captain of the head* is the enlisted man assigned to keep it tidy.

carafe was a French word before it came into English, but earlier it was the Spanish *garrafa* and the Italian *caraffa.* Most likely it came originally from the Arabic verb *gharafa,* meaning "to draw water."

carbonize. A trend in government prose is the creation of useless verbs, apparently under the impression that they make already heavy prose more impressive. A pair of examples are *folderize,* for "put papers in a folder," and *reliablize, for* "make reliable." We guess one *reliablizes* a table by replacing a broken leg. Our favorite, though, is *carbonize.* When you have your memo ready for typing, you have to decide which of your associates you want to *carbonize*—that is, send carbon copies to. Any day now we will hear of people being *Xeroxed*—put on a list for Xerox copies.

cardigan/raglan. The Earl of Cardigan gave his name to the popular knitted woolen front-buttoning sweater. Lord Raglan's fame in menswear circles hangs upon his invention of the *raglan* coat, in which the sleeves continue in one piece to the collar, without the shoulder seam found in other coats. It's ironic that their fame should now rest on such homely articles, for in their lifetime they were among the most celebrated—and bumble-headed —of the military leaders. It was Cardigan who led the doomed Charge of the Light Brigade at Balaklava in the Crimea, while Raglan was in supreme command of the British forces during that war. Though praised by Queen Victoria for his services, he was sharply criticized by military experts for his handling of the campaign.

carnival has acquired several meanings through the process of extension, but its original and basic meaning is that of feasting and revelry in the period before the fasting of Lent. Scholars theorize that it comes from the Latin words meaning "remove meat" and that it is "associated by folk etymology with the Middle Latin *carne vale,* meaning "flesh, farewell." Its extended meanings include any kind of revelry, a traveling show and an organized program of sports events.

carnival talk. *Hurry, hurry, hurry! Step right up and take your pick of the glass pitch, the glider, the girl show or the high-striker. The grinder's in front of each pitch and the bally comes loud and fast. Will you end the day happy or hurt? Will the pitches be gimmicked or gaffed so the marks will be properly taken?*

Gibberish? Perhaps. But not to anyone who has lived in the colorful, fast-paced world of side shows and carnivals—*carnies,* as they're known in the trade. For these are all expressions common to the jargon of *carny* workers. Like all private languages, this one exists partly so that members of the trade can converse in the presence of outsiders without being understood by them.

A colorful part of small-town life in the summer months has long been the arrival of the traveling carnival show, and earnest students of the folkways of American speech have chronicled the rough, savory and colorful language of its performers. Here are some of the words and phrases characteristic of the med shows, mud shows and side shows.

A *med show* is a medicine show, while a *mud show* is a small wagon show playing one-night stands in back country where roads may still be unpaved. A *mud show* is no place for a *dry-weather trouper*—which is the label carny folk use in place of "fine-weather friend."

Improbable though it sometimes must seem to the operators, traveling tent shows are supposed to make money—or *lettuce*—and the boss must keep a sharp eye out for the *O.P.C.*, "office percentage," and make sure it gets a cut of the *H.O.*—"holdout" or the agent's graft from the concessions.

This sometimes necessitates *laying the note*—duping the customer by interchanging bills of different denominations—and an operator specially skilled in this technique is said to be *on the whizz*. Naturally he must use a number of *shills*—confederates in the audience, also called *sticks*—and he must have an ample supply of *cush*—money that the shills are permitted to win in order to stimulate interest among the *marks*. And a *mark*, dear reader, is you—the general public, often referred to less elegantly as *suckers*.

A person who travels with a tent show is *kicking sawdust*. Performers are called *kinkers* and their living quarters are known as *kinkers' row*. The spun cotton candy which every child remembers from his visit to the carnival is known as *floss*, while the cheap gimcracks used as prizes at the concessions are *slum*.

The *glass pitch* is the familiar side-show concession where the *mark* tries to win a prize by pitching coins into glassware.

The *glider* is the so-called *chairplane*—miniature planes hung on chains from a revolving tower, which spins the planes upward and outward.

The *girl show* needs no introduction to the men in the audience, at least, and most males, at one time or another, have probably tried to impress their fair companions by belting away with a heavy mallet on the *highstriker*.

The *grinder* is the spieler, barker or come-on man who gives you the "hurry, hurry" spiel in front of the *pitches*—or concessions. *Bally*, of course, is his message—or *ballyhoo*.

"Are you happy or hurt?" is the carny operatives' way of asking, "Did you win or lose?"

A *pitch* that is *gimmicked* or *gaffed* is a game of chance whose wheel or other mechanical device has been so rigged that the *mark* cannot possibly win—and an *ungimmicked* wheel is about as common as a nine-dollar bill.

See also CIRCUS JARGON.

carouse. To *carouse* is, of course, to indulge in boisterous merrymaking to the accompaniment of strong drink. The word came into English from the German *garaus*, meaning "completely" or "entirely." The word was used pretty much as we say "Bottoms up!" today, meaning "drain the glass entirely."

carpetbagger, which has become a lasting symbol of political trickery and venality, is a term first used for unscrupulous Northern politicians who roamed the South after the Civil War, carrying their belongings in carpetbags and taking advantage of impoverished Southerners.

carrot and stick. A riddle that seems to have confounded many students of language is the origin of the *carrot and stick* expression. Research in Aesop's *Fables,* the *Uncle Remus* folk tales and other such sources didn't turn up any answers. Then we found that it was said by Winston Churchill in a press conference, May 25, 1943: "We shall continue to operate on the

Italian donkey at both ends, with a carrot and with a stick." But the suspicion would not die that the expression was not original with him.

Then came a letter from a reader of our column: "I am thinking of an old Humphrey Bogart movie, perhaps *The Maltese Falcon* (1941) or possibly *Across the Pacific* (1942). Sidney Greenstreet offers a deal to Bogart and the dialogue runs like this:

"Bogart: Why should I do this?

"Greenstreet: For the same reason a donkey with a carrot in front and a stick in back goes forward instead of backwards.

"Bogart: (after a pause) Tell me about the carrot.

"If this was indeed *The Maltese Falcon,* the dialogue may have come direct from the original novel. In either case, it predates the Churchill quotation." True, for Dashiell Hammett wrote this superb mystery and suspense tale in 1930.

History records that when Prime Minister Churchill visited President Roosevelt at the White House during World War II, they occasionally relaxed with a private showing of a Hollywood film. It's intriguing to speculate on the possibility that the P.M. might have heard this bit of Greenstreet dialogue and added it to his incomparable store of rhetoric for use when the time was right.

carry coals to Newcastle. Newcastle upon Tyne is the capital of Northumberland, England, a city of more than a quarter-million population. It has long been famous as a center of coal mining, so to *carry coals to Newcastle* simply means to "supply something already abundant."

carte blanche means giving someone blanket permission to do what he thinks best. In French the phrase simply means "white card." But *carte blanche* means a rather special kind of white card—specifically, one bearing only the signature of a person in authority. The bearer of such a card can, of course, fill in above the signature whatever instructions or conditions he wishes.

Nowadays in America a home-grown idiom that exactly parallels *carte blanche* is coming into general use. It is, of course, *blank check*—which you will find in such statements as: "Congress today gave the President *blank-check* authority to proceed with his disaster relief program."

case the joint. Originally thieves' jargon, this phrase means to examine a place carefully, especially in anticipation of committing a crime on the premises. Nowadays it's used lightheartedly to mean any kind of inspection of tavern, club or place of entertainment.

cashier may either mean an employee who handles financial matters, especially the person handling cash transactions in a store or restaurant, or mean dismissing a person from a position of rank and importance. The two actually are not the same, since they come from different routes into English. The first *cashier*—the one you'll see at your friendly local supermarket, where she's more likely to be called a "check-out clerk"—gets her name from the French *caisser,* meaning "money box." The second *cashier* ("As the result of the court-martial, the colonel was *cashiered* from the service") comes from Old French *casser,* "to discharge or annul," and that came from the Latin *quassare,* "to shake or break into pieces."

castanet comes from the Spanish word for chestnut, from the resemblance of the small, hollowed pieces of hardwood or ivory to empty chestnut shells. They originated in Spain and are held in the hand by a connecting cord or ribbon looped over the thumb. The noise is made, of course, by clapping together the two halves of the *castanet.*

casting pearls before swine. "Do not cast your pearls before swine," meaning don't offer anything of value and merit to people incapable of appreciating it, can be traced to the earliest writings in English. In Langland's *Vision of Piers Plowman,* for instance, we find "Noli mittere Margeri—perles Among hogges" and in the King James Bible (Matthew 7:6) we find this injunction: "Give not that which is holy unto the dogs, neither cast ye your pearls before swine, lest they trample them under their feet, and turn again and rend you."

catalyst/catalysis. *Catalyst* (pronounced KAT-uh-list) comes from the Greek *katalysis,* which meant "dissolution." *Catalysis* (kuh-TAL-ih-sis) is a term common in chemistry, meaning the process of starting or speeding up a chemical reaction by the addition of a substance which is not itself changed or affected by the reaction.

catamaran. As Dr. Johnson remarked to a lady who detected an error in his dictionary, the cause was "Ignorance. Sheer ignorance." In our blissful naïveté, the only *catamarans* we were aware of are the twin-hulled sailing craft which originated in the southwest Pacific and Indian oceans but are now to be seen in practically every harbor and lake in these United States. And we fail to be convinced—Webster to the contrary notwithstanding— that *catamaran* in the sense of a quarrelsome woman is the same word as the name of the boat, which comes from a native Tamil word meaning "logs tied together." According to the *Dictionary of American English,* this *catamaran* has been around since the time of the American Revolution and probably is a variant of (or, at least, influenced by) "catamount." And a catamount, as you need not be told, is a wildcat or mountain lion.

catbird seat. The best explanation of the phrase *in the catbird seat* was given by James Thurber in a story titled "The Catbird Seat," which appears in his book *The Thurber Carnival.* In it a mild-mannered accountant is driven to the point of contemplating the murder of a fellow employee because she continually heckles him with silly questions like: "Are you lifting the oxcart out of the ditch?" "Are you tearing up the pea patch?" And of course, "Are you sitting *in the catbird seat?*" One of the meek man's fellow employees explains: "She must be a Dodger fan. Red Barber announces the

Dodger games and he uses these expressions—picked them up down South. 'Tearing up the pea patch' means going on a rampage; 'sitting *in the catbird seat'* means sitting pretty, like a batter with three balls and no strikes on him."

In a letter to Thomas Middleton of the *Saturday Review* in 1976, Barber recalls how he acquired the expression *catbird seat.* In a stud poker game, he got the deal and determined to raise and re-raise, hoping to force others to drop out. He succeeded with all but one player, who kept meeting every raise and raising back. When the final showdown came, Barber had only a pair of eights with nothing in the hole. His opponent had an ace showing and, as it turned out, an ace in the hole. Said he to Barber: "Thanks for all those raises. From the start I was sitting *in the catbird seat."* Adds Barber: "Inasmuch as I had paid for the expression, I began to use it. I popularized it, and Mr. Thurber took it." To complete the record, be it noted that the man sitting *in the catbird seat* that night was one Frank Koch.

catcalls, boos and hisses. If a new opera or instrumental piece is adversely received by the audience, almost invariably the report will say that it was greeted by *"boos, hisses and catcalls."* *Boos* and *hisses* are obvious, but not so *catcalls.* The *catcall* is not simply a "meow." Rather it is a high-pitched whistle, the kind some people can make by placing thumb and forefinger between their teeth and blowing hard. In America this sound used by itself without the *boos* and *hisses* is often an indication of approval. In England and much of the rest of the world, the whistle is an indication of strong disapproval.

catch a crab is an expression common to oarsmen, especially those rowing on crews in competition. An oarsman can *catch a crab* in one of two ways—either by failing to dip his oar into the water and then making his stroke, or by failing to lift the oar completely free of the water in making his recovery from the stroke. In either case, the boat is thrown slightly or completely off beat. Many a crew race has been lost because a *crab* was caught.

Catch-22 is the title of a novel by Joseph Heller which has enjoyed enormous readership since its publication in 1961. It has been described as a grotesquely comic tale that satirizes military illogic—which indeed it does. The *catch-22* occurs in the course of a psychiatric examination and renders invalid all the questions that have gone before. The hero, Yossarian, tries to convince the shrink that he is mentally unfit for service and should be given a discharge. But *catch-22* is that if he is intelligent enough to know that he is crazy, he is fit enough for continued service, since it's all insane anyway.

cater-corner/cater-cornered/catawampus/cattywampus. The correct spelling of this term is either *cater-corner* or *cater-cornered,* though two variant forms, *kitty-corner* and *katty-corner,* are often heard in our various regional dialects. Actually the word *cater* comes from the French *quatre* and thus the term originally meant "four-cornered." But by a process known to language students as "folk etymology," the ordinary users of the term thought they detected an analogy to the ordinary domestic feline. Hence *cater* soon became *catty* and eventually even *kitty.*

The variations on this phrase are too many to list, but our favorite has long been *catawampus* or *cattywampus,* a dialect term heard throughout the South, from the Carolinas to Texas. You'll often hear the expression: "He walked *cattywampus* across the street," and down in Tennessee a college professor of mathematics was once heard to say: "You might call a rhombus a *catawampus* square."

Still another sense of *catawampus* and *cattywampus* was common in some sections of the antebellum South. It meant goblin, sprite or, sometimes, fearsome beast. Slaveowners were known to warn slaves they thought might be planning to run away that *catawampus cats* were lurking in wait for them. They sometimes also made fearsome noises in the night, which they claimed were the bloodthirsty roars of the *catawampus cats.*

cat has nine lives is one of the oldest English proverbs, being recorded in Heywood's collection in 1546 and being certainly much older even than that date would indicate. The allusion is probably to the cat's legendary ability to land on all four feet when dropped or tossed from a height that would mean death to any other animal. Heywood's version goes like this: "No wife, no woman hath nine lives like a cat." And in *Romeo and Juliet* (Act III, Scene 1) there is the following interchange between Tybalt and Mercutio: "What wouldst thou have with me?" asks Tybalt. "Good King of Cats, nothing but one of your nine lives," replies Mercutio.

Catherine means "pure" and comes from the Greek *katharos*—"pure and unsullied." It was one of the most popular girls' names among early Christians—as, indeed, it remains today. *St. Catherine,* the first to bear the name, was a maiden of noble heritage in Alexandria. At a public feast held by Emperor Maximinus, she proclaimed her Christian faith. For this she was condemned to death on a torture wheel. She survived the ordeal and was later beheaded.

Possibly no name has more variant spellings and nicknames than *Catherine.* A few of them are: *Katrina, Katrine, Kit, Kitty, Cassie, Kate, Kathy, Katharine* and *Trina.*

cat on a hot tin roof. "As nervous as a *cat on a hot tin roof*" is a phrase common in the popular idiom for at least half a century—probably since tin roofs were invented. It derives originally from the British expression *like a cat on hot bricks,* meaning "very ill at ease."

cat's meow/pajamas/whiskers. These are slang expressions from the 1920s, all designating excellence. Clara Bow, the "it" girl of those long-gone days, was the *cat's meow,* in the opinion of her millions of silent-screen admirers.

In Percy Marks's once-famed but now forgotten novel, *The Plastic Age* (1924), occurs this eminently forgettable passage: "It's a good poem. It's the *cat's pajamas.*" Before these expressions gained wide popularity in the "jazz age," they were apparently well known in girls' schools. We have an authenticated report of their currency in Wellesley in 1918 and one report that they were common in a ladies' seminary in Philadelphia in the mid-nineteenth century.

cat's-paw. A *cat's-paw* is a person easily tricked into performing a dangerous task for someone else. It goes back to an ancient fable that appears in the collections of both Aesop and La Fontaine. It seems a monkey wanted to get some chestnuts out of a fire, so he persuaded a cat to do it for him. Result: one singed paw and one new word—*cat's-paw.*

Caucasian. One of the earliest anthropologists, Johann Blumenbach, divided all mankind into five races: Caucasian, Mongolian, Ethiopian, American and Malayan. The best-proportioned skull in his collection was from the Caucasus, so he chose the name *Caucasian* as symbolizing the finest type of the white race. Blumenbach also thought that the Caucasus was the original home of the hypothetical race known as "Indo-Europeans," to whom most Western and some Eastern cultures trace their language origin. These theories of Blumenbach are, in the words of the *World Webster Dictionary,* "now not scientific and often tinged with racism; however the word [*Caucasian*] is used in default of a better."

caucus. The first *caucus* was probably held before this land of ours was discovered—certainly before it was colonized. The word comes from an Algonquin Indian word, *cau-cau-a-su,* meaning "adviser." John Smith in 1624 reported that the word was used in connection with powwows of Indian tribal leaders.

In the early 1700s a backstage political action group (involving Sam Adams's father) was organized in Boston and known, at least informally, as The Boston Caucus-club. By the time of the Revolution, the idea of political factions meeting in *caucus* to decide on candidates and campaign issues was well established, and *caucus* remains a favorite political device to this day.

The British borrowed this word early in the nineteenth century, but as the *Oxford Dictionary* says, it was "grossly misapplied." Instead of referring to a small group of leaders meeting to chart a program, the British use *caucus* to designate the controlling organization of a party—something rather like the Republican and Democratic National Committees in America.

Caudillo is the Spanish equivalent of the German *Führer* and the Italian *Duce,* meaning "leader." While Spain's General Francisco Franco was certainly not the first dictator to give himself the title *El Caudillo,* he was the most famous and long-lived.

caught red-handed. In the phrase *caught red-handed,* the analogy is to a murderer trapped so soon after committing the crime that his hands are still smeared with blood. The expression appeared in print first around 1800, but the idea is as old as Lady Macbeth's anguished cry "Out, damned spot."

caul. The superstition about a child who is born with a *caul* over his head dates back to the time of the Romans. The *caul* is the membrane that contains the fetus before birth. Sometimes a part of the membrane remains at the time of birth, enveloping the head of the newborn child. This has, since ancient times, been regarded as a good-luck omen. In the Middle Ages it was considered to be a charm against any possibility of death by drowning.

caution. Originally a Yankee phrase, *she's/he's/it's a caution* was widely used on the American frontier to designate a person or event that was or might prove to be a source of unexpected excitement or surprise. As one writer used the term: "She was just a little thing, Babe was, but it was a *caution* how just having her near could brighten the general drabness of life." It is sometimes also used in the phrase "a caution to," as "The way I'll kick you will be a *caution* to the rest of your family." And in the Old West, the word *caution* was sometimes used euphemistically. T.H. Gladstone, in his chronicle *The Englishman in Kansas* (1857), wrote: "On a piece of paper nailed to a tree appear the words: 'This is Jim Barton's claim; and he'll shoot the first fellow as comes within a mile of it.' Such an announcement is technically called a 'caution.' " Yessiree, that feller Barton sure was a *caution!*

caveat has a rather precise and technical meaning in legal language, but in a sentence such as "Let me enter a *caveat* on that," it merely means a warning or a caution. It's derived direct from the Latin *caveat,* meaning "let him beware." The best-known *caveat* is certainly *Caveat emptor*—"Let the buyer beware"—which was common business advice in the years before Better Business Bureaus, the Federal Trade Commission and the various consumer protection agencies stepped in to guard buyers against their own folly.

caviar to the general. The *general* involved is the general public, the masses who would not be expected to know or appreciate a rare delicacy like caviar. The line comes from Shakespeare, when Hamlet addresses the leader of the strolling players, saying, "the play . . . pleased not the million; 'twas *caviar to the general;* but it was, as I received it . . . an excellent play."

cellophane was first developed around 1900 by a Swiss chemist named Brandenberger, who was trying to combine viscose with cotton to make material that would resist dirt and staining. He invented the name *cellophane* from the first syllables of *cellulose* and *phanein* (the Greek word for "appear" or "see through"). In 1913 Brandenberger made an arrangement with Du Pont to manufacture cellophane by his patented process, but nothing much was done with it until it was made moisture-proof. Then, about 1930, it was introduced as a wrapping material for cigarette packages, and the boom was on. The word *cellophane,* originally a trademark, was declared a generic term by a court decree in 1941. It had proved so uniquely appropriate to the product that the courts declared that no other word or combination of words could describe it.

Celsius/hertz. *Celsius* is not a different way of measuring temperature, merely another name for centigrade. The original Celsius, a Swede named Anders Celsius, was the man who devised the first centigrade thermometer in 1742. Celsius was quite a figure in the world of science, being head of the leading observatory in Sweden and a participant in at least one polar expedition. In 1948 leaders of today's scientific community decided to honor his achievement by abandoning "centigrade" for *Celsius.*

Along about the same time scientists decided that the cycles and kilocycles by which we had measured radio waves since Marconi's time should be renamed *hertz,* after Heinrich Rudolph Hertz, a German physicist who had worked during the nineteenth century on electromagnetic phenomena. The second change has worked rather more successfully than the first. Perhaps because the layman doesn't have much to do with kilocycles, "kilo*hertz*" is now standard. But everyone is concerned with the weather and we predict it will be a long time before the man in the street describes a cold morning as "subzero *Celsius.*"

Centaur. The *Centaurs* (a word derived from the Greek *Kentauros,* the name of an ancient Thessalian tribe known for their superb horsemanship) were the figures of Greek legend depicted as half-man, half-horse. Any creatures with this sort of makeup were bound to create some hair-raising legends and these lived up to their promise. Invited to a wedding feast, some of them, in one historian's delicate words, "behaved with great rudeness to the women." The Lapithae men, outraged that this should happen at the marriage of their king, behaved with something more than mere rudeness and drove them clear out of the country.

Centennial State is Colorado, for the reason that it achieved statehood in 1876.

cents/pennies. Why are *pennies* called *cents* in America? As part of the trend to de-English our language at the time of the Revolution, Gouverneur Morris proposed the word *cent*—one hundredth of a dollar—to replace the British word *penny.* The attempt was not entirely successful, for *penny* is still widely heard in the U.S. *Penny,* incidentally, goes all the way back to Anglo-Saxon and is probably related to, if not derived from, the German *pfennig,* which in turn was borrowed from the Latin *pannus,* meaning "cloth." It seems that in barbarian Europe of the Dark Ages, pieces of cloth were used as a medium of exchange.

c'est magnifique! This French expression, literally meaning "It's magnificent!" has been used millions of times but never more trenchantly than by Pierre Jean François Joseph Bosquet, marshal of France, who served with distinction in the Crimean War. Commenting on the ill-fated Charge of the Light Brigade at Balaklava (1854), he said: *"C'est magnifique, mais ce n'est pas la guerre"*—"It's magnificent, but it isn't war."

chairman of the board. One of the most illustrious titles in the power of American business to bestow is *chairman of the board.* Generally speaking, it means that its holder has reached the pinnacle of achievement within his company and rates with the elite of the business world. And where did the title come from? Well, for an answer we turn to Marshall Davidson, author of the *American Heritage History of Colonial Antiques:* "It is hard to realize that when Elder William Brewster of the Plymouth Plantation was a lad in England, even such elementary devices as chimneys, solid and permanent bedsteads, glass windows, wooden floors and pewter tableware were relatively novel features of the ordinary English house. Chairs were not widely used. As in the Middle Ages, they were generally reserved for persons of importance; the others sat on stools or benches. At a time when tables often consisted of removable boards set on trestles, he who occupied the principal seat had that distinction we recall in the phrase *'chairman of the board.'* "

chaise longue is a direct borrowing from French and means, literally, "long chair." The correct pronunciation is SHAYS LONG, but the vast majority of people misread the second word, as if it were "lounge." As a result, the pronunciation "shays lounge" is very common, especially in the furniture industry. Partly to avoid confusion, you'll find that this now fairly uncommon item of furniture is usually advertised simply as a *chaise.*

chalk player is a bettor who waits for the late odds on a race before placing his bet. The term is also more loosely used to describe a bettor who always plays the favorite. He's sometimes called a "chalk eater."

Why all this talk about "chalk"? Because in the days before parimutuel betting, bookmakers (bookies) at trackside used to post the odds on various entries using chalk on blackboards. As the volume of betting on a particular horse mounted, the odds would usually drop and the bookie would erase the old odds and write in the new. A *chalk player,* by waiting until the last minute, might obtain better odds than if he had placed his bet early. And, of course, he might not. That, as the saying has it, is horse racing.

Incidentally, bookmakers still post their odds this way at the Royal Ascot in England, or at least they did when last we visited, just a few years ago. We don't recall whether our betting practices were those of chalk eaters, but we do remember coming out slightly ahead on the afternoon's betting. That's no small feat, considering that we knew nothing whatever about any of the horses and that, to confuse matters still further, the races were all run backward—clockwise on the course, rather than counterclockwise, as in America.

cham was the eighteenth-century British form of *khan,* the name for Turkish and Tartar rulers. The "great *Cham* of literature" was, of course, our fellow lexicographer Dr. Samuel Johnson (1709–1784).

chancery. Technically, *in chancery* means having a lawsuit hung up in the London court presided over by the Lord Chancellor (*chancery* is a shortened form of "chancellery"), where litigation was usually protracted. Indeed, it may have been here that the famous expression "Justice delayed is justice denied" was born. In any event, the term was borrowed into wrestling to describe a headlock in which the head is secured against one wrestler's chest by one arm in such a fashion that—if the rules permit—the head can be pummeled at will. Nowadays the phrase *in chancery* may also be used merely to describe any situation involving prolonged mental or physical anguish.

changeling. In medieval times many simple folk believed that unless babies were carefully watched, fairies would spirit away a healthy infant and put in its place a *changeling*—invariably a weak and sickly child. In those days it was easier to blame illness on the fairies than on improper diet or sanitation.

chaperon. In grandmother's day a well-bred young lady seldom ventured out, at least in the evening, without being accompanied by an older woman, often a relative, who acted as guide, protector and *chaperon.* It comes from the French word *chape,* meaning "hood or head covering" and hence "protector."

Charge of the Light Brigade. The legendary charge of the gallant and doomed "Six Hundred" took place at Balaklava (now in the U.S.S.R.) on October 25, 1854. An account of the incredibly bumble-headed leadership that committed these gallant men to their fate is given in Cecil Woodham-Smith's *The Reason Why,* one of the finest historical works of our time.

Charing Cross. The area of London known as *Charing Cross* bears a name that is a corruption of *Chère Reine Croix,* after Good Queen Caroline, who "dipped her head in turpentine."

charisma/charismatic. Originally *charism* or *charisma* meant literally "a gift of God"—a special favor, talent or grace granted by God. In more recent times it has been used, in the words of one reader, "in reference to those able to sway masses by the force of their personality, such as Hitler, William Jennings Bryan and Sinclair Lewis's Elmer Gantry."

One mystery has been why this particular word should have been plucked from the pages of unabridged dictionaries, where it has languished in merited obscurity for many centuries. A Washington reader wrote what seems to be an especially persuasive explanation for this phenomenon: "I strongly suspect that the present popular usage stems from its employment as a technical term by Max Weber, the German sociologist. In my college years, at least (Harvard 1955), Weber was widely read and every student was familiar with the phrase '*charismatic* leader,' a figure whose power stemmed from his popular appeal rather than his institutional position. While there have been good *charismatic* leaders as well as bad, Hitler probably was the *charismatic* leader nonpareil."

charity begins at home. The earliest appearance of the basic idea that *charity begins at home* was in a play by the Roman comic dramatist Terence. He wrote *"Proximus sum egomet mihi."* That, of course, is Latin, not English, and you may wonder, as we do, why the word *domus,* meaning "home," is not in it. Nevertheless, *Hoyt's Familiar Quotations* advises us that *"Charity begins at home"* is an accurate, if free, translation.

Then another playwright, or rather a brace of playwrights, picked up the idea. They were the Elizabethan team of Beaumont and Fletcher, and the expression appears in a play of theirs called *Wit Without Money.* Even earlier, in 1380, the English divine John Wycliffe wrote: "Charity should begin at himself." That's pretty close—close enough so that we can agree that the idea, if not the precise wording, is very nearly as old as the written word.

A couple of Victorian writers fiddled about with the expression, with amusing results. Dickens wrote: "Charity begins at home, and justice begins next door." And Horace Smith summed it up rather neatly: "Our charity begins at home, and mostly ends where it begins."

charlatan is a fine-sounding word meaning "quack, impostor, fraud or phony." It comes from the Italian *ciarlatano,* a native of the village of Cerreto, near Spoleto. Long famous for its quacks and frauds, Cerreto now has entered the language through a back door, so to speak, with *charlatan* to its somewhat dubious credit.

charley horse is a painfully strained muscle in the leg or arm of an athlete. Nobody is quite sure where the expression originated, but the general theory is that the first victim was a lamed race horse named Charlie or Charley.

Charley Noble. Sometime in the shrouded reaches of early maritime history there was a notable ship's cook named Charley Noble. At any rate, so the story goes. Another story has it that a New England skipper was so proud of the brass pipe standing up from the galley that he kept it brightly shined and other sailors, seeing it, would call out: "There goes *Charley Noble.*" What we know for sure is that the smokepipe on a ship's galley is called the *Charley Noble.*

chauffeur. Today's *chauffeur,* more often than not, rides around in air-conditioned comfort, which makes his name—from the French *chauffer,* "to warm up, to heat"—seem quite ridiculous. However, the first *chauffeurs* in France drove the French equivalent of our Stanley Steamer automobiles and their first task was quite literally to heat the engine until a sufficient head of steam had built up to propel the car.

And propel it the steam did! Fanciers of steam-driven autos claim that no one ever dared to run one of them at its maximum possible speed. With roads and tires in the condition they were in then, it would have been simply too hazardous. Even so, speeds upward of 100 miles per hour were commonplace. So the early *chauffeur* had to be fireman, engineer and devil-may-care, especially if he had a speed demon for a boss.

chauvinism. Most of us dream of making so lasting an impression on our fellow human beings that we will be remembered long after our passing. Not many of us ever achieve this high ambition and among those who do attain lasting fame, there is always a handful who "sought not fame but had it thrust upon them." So it is with the people whose names have been immortalized in our language by becoming common nouns and verbs.

Take Nicolas Chauvin, for instance. He was a gallant soldier of Napoleon I, wounded in battle and everlastingly devoted to his peerless leader. By his own standards, he was one of the few true patriots remaining in France after his hero's exile and he was not shy about expressing his continuing high regard for Napoleon. It is ironic that his excessive zeal in behalf of a cause most of his fellow countrymen thought well lost resulted in his becoming an object of ridicule.

Perhaps, though, Nicolas Chauvin has the last laugh, for though all those who mocked him are long forgotten, his name remains a part not only of his native French but of other languages, including our own. So blind and unreasoning was this patriot's devotion to the lost imperial cause that the word *chauvinism* was coined to describe his fanaticism—and it remains in our language today as the one best word to indicate militant, boastful and wholly unreasoning devotion to one's country or race.

In the twentieth century the term *male chauvinism* appeared and was used to describe an attitude of absolute conviction that the male is superior to the female in every respect. Women's Liberationists of the sixties and seventies used the expression as an epithet, often in the phrase *"male chauvinist* pig."

chaw has been a part of our tongue at least since 1530, according to the *Oxford Dictionary.* It means "to chew," especially to chew some substance which is not to be swallowed, such as tobacco. It also appears as a noun in such phrases as "a *chaw* of tobacco."

cheapskate. The "skate" in *cheapskate* has nothing at all to do with the metal runners that you glide on across the ice—nor, for that matter, with the ball-bearing wheels you wear in a roller rink. This "skate" comes from a wholly different source and originally (spelled "skite") meant a contemptible chap. Nowadays it's simply a synonym for "chap," as in such commonplace expressions as "He's a good skate."

Incidentally, there's still a third kind of skate—a kind of flat fish. All three "skates" are what linguists call homonyms—words that are spelled and pronounced the same but have wholly different origins and meanings.

cheesecake. There are many theories of the origin of this term, but the one most sanctified by time holds that the word was first uttered by James Kane, photographer for the *New York Journal* in 1912.

The story runs that Kane was a notable enthusiast for cheesecake, a delicacy which many New Yorkers regard as the most delectable of desserts. On a gusty summer afternoon, Kane was posing a toothsome actress in the conventional railside pose on an incoming ocean liner. Just as he shot the picture a gust of wind ruffled her skirts, with the result that—as H. L. Mencken put it—the final picture "included more of her person than either he or she suspected."

Developing the plate later in the darkroom, Kane was pleasantly surprised at the exposure and, searching for the utmost in superlatives to express his delight, exclaimed: "That's real *cheesecake!*"

Well, that's one theory and, as we have noted before, the one of earliest origin. However, we theorize that the term may actually have developed without any reference to the bakery *cheesecake.* Note for the moment that photographers for years have instructed their models to say "Cheese!" just as the exposure is being made, in order to force the lips into an attractive smile. In fact, the standard instruction, once the positioning of model and lights was completed, was: "Wet your lips and say 'Cheese!' "

Consider further that slang words like *cupcake* and *cookie* were popular terms of endearment at the time *cheesecake* allegedly was first used for the fair sex, and *cake-eater* was the virtually standard epithet for "ladies' man." Thus we have a logical explanation for *cheesecake* being used to describe the sort of *cupcake* any photographer worth his salt would be sure to have say "Cheese!" before taking the picture.

chenangoes are a special group of longshoremen who transfer cargo from railroad barges to ships or piers. Many years ago these workers were recruited from the farms of Chenango County, New York. Nowadays few if any of the *chenangoes* hail from upstate farmlands, but the name sticks.

cherry picker. A man who runs a *cherry picker* need not be in the fruit business at all but may work for the telephone company, for *cherry picker* has long been the slang term for the canvas-covered platform swung on cranes to enable linesmen to work at the top of telephone poles.

chess is a sophisticated board game which may quite literally be called the game of kings, not only because two kings are among the pieces used in the game but because the name itself comes from the French *échecs,* which in turn came from the Arabic *shah,* meaning "king."

chesterfield. The *chesterfield,* a single-breasted, velvet-collared topcoat worn on formal occasions, is named after a nineteenth-century Earl of Chesterfield.

Chevy Chase. Of the suburb of Washington (D.C.) called *Chevy Chase,* we have to guess that the original settlers were landed gentry of British heritage who liked to ride to hounds. "Chevy" or "chivvy" is a huntsman's call meaning "chase or harass the fox." But that's not all the story. Back in the fifteenth century some unknown minstrel created a song called "The Ballad of Chevy Chase," which told the story of the battle of Otterburn in 1388. Otterburn was a small village near the border between Scotland and England and here the English under the Percys were soundly defeated by the Scots under Douglas. The battle had started over a hunt (chase) near the Cheviot Hills, a range extending a short distance along the border. Percy, the Earl of Northumberland, had vowed to hunt for three days across the Scottish border in spite of the fact that he knew this would arouse the anger of the Scots. The result was an awesome slaughter on both sides, with both leaders slain in the fighting. And that's the colorful, if bloody, ancestry of *Chevy Chase.*

chic. The French, who it seems have always been fashion-conscious, gave us the word *chic* to mean "smartly and properly dressed, with a certain flair for style in clothing and manner." It comes from a Middle High German word meaning "manner, form or appearance." Although fashion magazines may use *chic* to describe clothing or accessories, its proper use is confined to the woman herself.

chicane. Ever hear the word *chicane?* No, not "chicanery," but simply *chicane.* Well, the chances are your grandmother, if she was the whist-playing sort, knew it well. *Chicane* is the seldom-used bridge whist name for a hand without trumps. Most present-day bridge players have never heard the term, and on the unhappy occasions when *chicane* would accurately describe their hands, they're more likely to say they are "void" or have "drawn a blank" in trumps.

chicanery. A few dishonest French golfers may have been responsible for *chicanery,* meaning "trickery." The word comes from the French *chicane* or *chicanerie,* meaning "a kind of golf." Scholars can only adduce that its present meaning came from a bit of cheating at the game, and hence any kind of trickery.

Chicano. This designation for Americans of Mexican descent is thought by some to be a contraction of a Spanish phrase meaning "I am not a boy." However, a more persuasive explanation comes, courtesy of the *Denver Post,* from Marcella Trujillo, language expert at the University of Colorado. "The word comes from the ending of the word 'Mexicano' " she writes, "as pronounced by the Aztecs and spelled by the Spaniards. The Aztecs pronounced this word 'Meshicano.' From the ending of the word came 'xicano' which was pronounced 'shicano' and which passed to 'chicano.' "

chickens will come home to roost. The expression *his chickens will come home to roost* means that someday he will have to pay for his present behavior.

The original version of this proverb was "Curses, like chickens, come home to roost," meaning that one who curses others will eventually himself be cursed.

chief justice. A *chief justice* is sometimes referred to as chief justice of the Supreme Court and sometimes as chief justice of the United States. Is there a difference? Yes, though traditionally both offices have been held by the same man. As *chief justice* of the United States, he is charged with direction of all federal courts. As *chief justice* of the Supreme Court, he is *primus inter pares,* the first among equals.

Children's Crusade was one of the most extraordinary and ill-fated ventures of idealistic youth in all our history. Challenged by the failure of the early crusades to free the Holy Land from the Moslem invaders, a shepherd boy, Stephen of Vendôme, preached that only the pure and sinless could succeed in such a crusade. Beginning in 1212, he moved southward through France gathering recruits by the thousands as other children were raised to a high pitch of religious fervor by his preachings.

Although the King of France forbade the march and many parents and priests joined in the protest, the children continued their march and by the time they reached Marseilles they numbered at least fifty thousand. According to one theory, they expected the waters of the Mediterranean to part and allow them to pass over to the Promised Land, as the Red Sea did before the ancient Israelites. Instead they were seized and sold as slaves in Egypt.

A second Children's Crusade, made up chiefly of German children and led by Nicholas of Cologne, was met by Pope Innocent III, who persuaded them to return home. Some scholars believe that this second crusade was the inspiration for the legend of the Pied Piper of Hamelin.

Chiltern hundreds. In Great Britain a *hundred* may mean a subsection of a shire or county having its own court. The *Chiltern Hundreds* are something else again and marvelously illustrate the British penchant for legal fictions. Under law a duly elected member of Parliament may not resign his post so long as he is physically qualified to occupy it. However, there is also a provision of British law that a person occupying "an office of profit under the Crown" must vacate his seat in Parliament.

Centuries ago footpads and robbers abounded in the *Chiltern Hundreds,* so stewards (constables) were appointed to restore law and order. In time the need for these stewards disappeared but the office remained, though now a wholly honorary one. So when an M.P. desires to resign he merely requests appointment to the "Stewardship of the *Chiltern Hundreds,*" and as an officer of the crown, he may no longer serve in Parliament. So far as we know, these stewardships are unpaid, so the "office of profit" stipulation is clearly what the *Oxford Dictionary* calls "a legal figment."

chimera (pronounced kuh-MEER-uh or ky-MEER-uh) comes direct from the

Greek *chimaira,* and originally meant a fire-breathing monster with a lion's head and a goat's body. Nowadays it means any wild and foolish fancy. The adjective *chimerical* means visionary, fantastic or wildly improbable. In the space world of today we know that many of the inventions of Jules Verne, which were thought to be *chimerical* in their day, have proved to be practical realities.

Chinaman's chance. A person with only a *Chinaman's chance* is one with practically no chance at all. The history of this phrase is indeed a curious one, since it seems probable that originally the word *Chinaman* did not mean a Chinese person or a native of China at all! Back in the sixteenth century, traders with the Far East brought back to Europe the first examples of the fine porcelainware we call *china.* The first merchants to deal in this merchandise were called *chinamen* and their stores were called *china shops.* So the phrase *a Chinaman's chance* accurately describes the odds against a merchant of china if he were to find *a bull in his* china shop!

Chinese home run. One of the more colorful phrases from the slang of America's national game is *Chinese home run*—meaning a hit that in most parks would be an easy out but, because of a short fence or some other peculiarity of the field, scores as a homer. The late, great cartoonist T. A. Dorgan, better known as "Tad," brought the phrase east with him from the California of an earlier day, when Chinese coolie labor was a subject of great controversy. Since the word *Chinese* was then synonymous with "cheap," the label *Chinese home run* was self-explanatory. Sportswriters have coined a number of fanciful synonyms for *Chinese home run—homer foo young, chow mein smash* and *egg roll bingle* among them. One even nicknamed the New York Polo Grounds the *Harlem joss house* because of its notoriously short fences.

chintzy. This slang term for "cheap, tawdry, trashy and meretriciously vulgar" has astonishingly elegant antecedents. It comes, indeed, from the Hindi word *chint,* which in turn was derived from the Sanskrit *citra,* meaning "bright or many-colored." Eventually *chintz* became the name of a printed and glazed cotton fabric which, perhaps unjustly, was associated in the public mind with mediocre decorations and upholstery. Hence, *chintzy*—a far cry from its ancient and honorable origin.

chiropody/podiatry. *Chiropody*—which was labeled a "barbarism" by H. W. Fowler—is made from the Greek words *cheir* (hand) and *podos* (foot). As you might guess, it originally meant one who treated both hands and feet. However, in the somewhat condescending words of the *Oxford English Dictionary,* a *chiropodist* is "now usually one who treats corns and bunions." In a sense, therefore, *podiatry,* from *podos* and *iatros,* the Greek word for "physician," is more accurate than *chiropody,* since it indicates the treatment of the feet alone, not of the feet and hands.

chit is the clubman's favorite phrase for the voucher or *tab* to be signed after the service of drinks. It's a word borrowed from Hindustani. The Hindi word for "note" or "letter" is *citthi.* This, in the vocabulary of British colonial officers, soon became *chitty* and finally *chit.*

chitlins/chitterlings. Most dictionaries insist that the word should be spelled *chitterlings,* but all agree that they are hog's innards, fried or boiled. Popular chiefly in the Southeastern part of the country, they are also known as far west as Missouri and Arkansas and may be bought in markets in the Negro sections of Northern cities.

A simple, Southern dialect word, to all intents and appearances, is *chitlins.* Yet to language students it is a word that can readily be traced back to Middle English, where it was used to describe similar organs in the human body. Moreover, it can be ultimately traced to the German *kutteln,* of the same meaning, and is probably related to the Danish *kuit,* meaning "fish roe."

cholesterol. Starting from the end, *-ol* is a suffix used in chemistry to denote an alcohol. *Ster-* is from the Greek *stereos,* meaning "solid." *Chole-* is the same word in Greek and means "gall" or "bile." So *cholesterol* is a crystalline fatty alcohol found in animal fats and bile. Some gallstones are almost pure cholesterol.

chopper. When helicopters first came on the scene they were usually called "whirlybirds." The name was a little too cute, but it certainly was descriptive. As time went on, reports almost invariably referred to them as *choppers.* The *chopper* label comes from the noise made by the rotors—an irritating and very loud "chop-chop" sound.

chow. This slang term for food is a borrowing from pidgin English, which in turn took it from the Chinese *ch'ao,* "to fry or cook." It probably was first used in the U.S. by Chinese laborers on the transcontinental railroads in the nineteenth century. In the military the call *"Chow* down" means that food is ready.

chowderhead. The *chowder* in *chowderhead* is neither fish nor clam, not Boston nor Manhattan. Indeed, it's simply not that kind of chowder at all. Actually, this *chowderhead* is a variation of *cholterhead,* which in turn was originally *jolterhead*—a term much used in Shakespeare's time but now completely obsolete. A *jolterhead,* as you might guess, was simply a stupid dolt, a blockhead.

Christmas words. *Yuletide* for "Christmastime" is a term derived from the yule log, which in olden days was a huge log used as the foundation of the holiday fire. *Bringing the yule log in* was, as recently as the nineteenth century, as much a part of the pre-Christmas festivities as putting up an evergreen tree today. Indeed, one authority reports that it was Queen Victoria's consort, Albert, who was responsible for the substitution, in English-speaking countries, of the German Christmas tree custom for the hitherto traditional yule log.

Yule itself can be traced back to the Middle English *yollen* (cry aloud) and is thought to date from early Anglo-Saxon revels in celebration of the discovery (after the winter solstice, December 22) that nights were becoming shorter and thus that Satan's eternal darkness had been averted for yet another year.

Santa Claus, is austerely labeled by the dictionaries a "corruption" of the Dutch "Sant Nikolaas." But bear in mind that our learned dictionary editors—generally a humorless lot—are here using "corruption" in a purely technical, linguistic sense and are by no means traducing *Santa*.

Behind the word *mistletoe* lie the Anglo-Saxon words for "bird dropping" and "twig." In spite of its somewhat drab word history, the mistletoe was highly respected by the Druids and Celts as a bearer of magical health-bringing powers. This belief carries down to the present day in the romantic custom of kissing under the mistletoe.

Christy Minstrels. Edwin Christy organized one of the earliest blackface minstrel shows, which played with great success during the 1840s and 1850s throughout America and in England. He is credited with having fixed the various conventions of this long-obsolete entertainment form: end men, interlocutors and the like. During Christy's enormously successful career Stephen Collins Foster composed a number of songs for the troupe.

chug/chug wagons. *Chug,* an onomatopoetic word for the noise made by an old locomotive engine, has been in print in America since 1866, according to the *Dictionary of Americanisms.* It also records what must have qualified for the Worst Pun of the Year Award in 1900: early autos were called—brace yourself, now—*chug wagons.*

chug-a-lug. Our first record of this expression dates back to college campus slang of the mid or late thirties. It is an onomatopoetic word, derived from the sounds made by a person downing an entire beaker or bottle of beer. Usually *chug-a-lugging* resulted from a dare or bet, when one chap challenged another to down a full container of liquid without stopping for breath.

chunnel. The *chunnel* is the long-planned tunnel under the English Channel from England to France. It was first projected in the mid-nineteenth century, but its construction was deferred at the insistence of military leaders on both sides of the Channel, all of whom feared that it would be used as an avenue of invasion in case of war. Now that nuclear weapons have made obsolete such concepts of defense against aggression, both high commands have agreed that the tunnel no longer represents a threat to security.

churchwarden pipe is the name of a pipe of clay with a very long, gently curving stem, which was smoked by wardens of the Anglican Church when they met to tot up the collections and check the parish roster. A number of London restaurants make a practice of keeping a rack of such pipes for their favored customers and one New York restaurant, the legendary

Keen's Chop House, did likewise. Pipe fanciers—among whom your authors are not to be numbered—report that the length of the stem accounts for a fine cool smoke. *Chacun*, as we say, *à son goût.*

chutzpah is a word of Yiddish origin and is pronounced HUTZ-puh, with the initial consonant sounded as if you were clearing your throat. A person with *chutzpah* is a person with gall, moxie, nerve and audacity compounded with brazen assertiveness and a complete disregard for the sensibilities of others. It was *chutzpah* that made Sammy run, for instance—and resulted in his being one of the most colorful and least likable characters in modern fiction.

A well-known definition of *chutzpah* runs something along these lines: a lad with real *chutzpah* is one who would kill both his parents and then demand leniency of the court on the ground that he is an orphan.

cinch in the sense of a "sure thing" has Western origins. While a dude saddle had a buckled *cinch* and was used on a gentle horse, the half-wild cow-pony saddle was tied up tight and sure. You bet your life on the *cinch,* so it had to be a sure thing. So any sure thing became a *cinch.*

Cinderella's slipper. The Cinderella legend is probably as durable a folk tale as ever has existed, but it has a stern challenger in one somewhat cynical four-year-old. "But, Mommy," she said, "how on earth could anybody wear a *glass* slipper? Are you sure it wasn't plastic?" The mother tried to explain that this all happened long before plastics were invented, but to a child reared in today's world, existence without plastics is as unthinkable as a world without television. Anyhow, it seems to be a pretty good question. Just how *did* that girl wear a glass slipper—without breaking it and cutting her feet, that is?

Now it can be told. The slipper wasn't really glass at all—it was made of fur. The whole mix-up resulted from one of the most horrendous mistranslations in literary history. The French phrase was *pantoufle en vair*— "slipper of fur or sable"—and the translator read it as *en verre*— "of glass."

Cinque Ports were originally five ports given special privileges by Edward the Confessor (1004–1066), the last Anglo-Saxon king, in return for their aid in defending the coast against invasion. The ports were Hastings, Sandwich, Dover, Romney and Hythe, and a measure of their usefulness may be noted in that baleful date 1066–the year of the successful invasion by the Normans, leading to the defeat of the British at Hastings. However, the ports retained their special privileges until the seventeenth century and even later. The *cinque,* incidentally, is given characteristically British treatment and is pronounced the same as the sink in your kitchen.

circadian rhythm. A person's *circadian rhythm,* popularly known as one's "body clock," is the pattern that each of us, sometimes unconsciously, sets up for governing our routine of working, eating and sleeping through a twenty-four-hour period. Most of us aren't even aware of the degree to which we have routinized our lives, until we dislocate the rhythm by taking an overnight flight to Europe or the Orient with little or no sleep en route. When we try to conduct our normal activities on the day we arrive, the resulting mental and physical dislocation can be severe. Because this phenomenon was almost unknown until air traffic entered the jet age, it is often referred to as "jet lag." *Circadian* is derived from the Latin words *circa* (about) and *dies* (day).

circus jargon. No craft or trade has a more colorful and interesting private language than the world of circus and carnival. Many words and phrases that originated here have come into wide general use. *Pitchman,* for example, originally meant the hawker who stood on a platform outside a tent and made the "spiel" to induce passers-by to enter. Nowadays a *pitchman* may be any kind of extravagant or boastful salesman, including those television announcers noted within the industry for their "persuasive pitch."

But the best of circus and carnival jargon remains almost impossible for outsiders to understand—and that's the way the troupers want to keep it. In their world, for instance, a contortionist or acrobat is a *kinker,* and that chap who winds up on top of the human pyramid is, logically enough, the *high man* or *top mounter.*

Members of that admirable institution the circus band are known irreverently as *windjammers,* and the beautiful girls who ride horses and elephants in the grand spectacular finale are, simply, *spec girls.*

Believe it or not, you might find *convicts* in a *dog and pony show,* for to circus people a *convict* is a zebra and a *dog and pony show* is any small circus. A show *gone Sunday school* is one from which all gambling concessions have been eliminated, so there would presumably be less need for a *grouch bag*— a money bag concealed inside one's clothes.

Lot lice are townspeople who hang around the lot while the big top is being set up. *Lumber* are loads of seats and poles. And the *main guy* is not the circus owner, but the guy rope that holds up the center pole in the big top.

Hey, Rube! traditionally is the rallying cry of circus people when a fight breaks out with townies—only circus folk don't have fights, they call them *clems.* And a *clem* usually develops only when the *luck boys* (gamblers) have *kifed* (swindled) too many *suckers* (circusgoers).

The come-on man who entices the suckers into the games of chance is, of course, the *shill.* The *rubber man,* though, isn't part of the side show. He's the fellow who sells balloons—which are always called *bladders,* by the way.

The circus clown is always called *Joey* backstage, in honor of the first great modern clown, Joseph Grimaldi, who flourished about 150 years ago in England. The life of the first *Joey,* appropriately enough, had its years of triumph and ended in bitter tragedy.

Joeys are divided into three main groups. The *Auguste* is the garden variety of clown, the one with the brightly painted face, any of a wide variety of costumes and a bent for slapstick humor. He's the fellow who gets laughs by pretending to hit other clowns with a baseball bat. Next higher on the scale is the *Grotesque,* who wears weirdly padded or inflated costumes, ridiculous hats and often carries an incongruously small parasol. The elite among clowns are the *Characters*—of whom Emmett Kelly is the most famous. These are the sad, Chaplinesque hobos, perpetually frustrated in their efforts to impress the audience.

Of all the words in the colorful jargon of the circus, one is our own special favorite. Can you guess what circus folk call the fellow who stands at the bottom of the human pyramid—that formation so traditional with generations of acrobats? Well, with perfect logic and wonderful directness, they call him the *understander.* See also CARNIVAL TALK.

cisatlantic. Anyone who slaved, as high school students did of yore, through Caesar's *Gallic Wars* would not have to guess at the meaning of this word, for nearly every page of that exhausting epic carried a reference to *cisalpine* Gaul. The prefix *cis,* which we take direct from Latin, means "on this side of." Thus *cisatlantic* merely means on this side of the Atlantic.

Occasionally, though rarely, the prefix is used to express a relationship in time, as well as in space. Thus *cis-Elizabethan times* would be the centuries since the end of the reign of Britian's earlier Elizabeth.

citizen's arrest is an arrest by a private citizen—and it is authorized under the Bill of Rights of the Constitution, though the limits of lawful arrest vary considerably in different jurisdictions. Broadly speaking, a private person may arrest when a felony (any of a variety of serious offenses, such as burglary or murder) has been committed or is being committed and the person making the arrest has reasonable grounds to believe the person arrested committed it. But it is a very risky business indeed and, unless your evidence stands up in court, you are virtually certain to face a suit for damage to the reputation of the person arrested.

City of Brotherly Love. There have been periods in the history of Philadelphia when this catch phrase for the city has seemed more ironic than accurate. Still it has always been precisely appropriate, at least from an etymological viewpoint, since the name is made up of two Greek words: *philos* (love) and *adelphos* (brother). The city has always had a reputation for tranquility bordering on somnolence, perhaps because of the influence of its founders, the Friends, or "Quakers" as they are better known. It has long been the butt of jokesters. ("First prize: a week in Philadelphia. Second prize: two weeks in Philadelphia," and the reported inscription on the tombstone of W. C. Fields, a Philadelphia native: "On the whole I'd rather be in Philadelphia.")

Civil War. "My grandmother was reared in Georgia," wrote a Pittsburgh reader, "and to this day she bridles when she hears the term *Civil War* used to describe the hostilities between North and South. She says this is a 'Northern' expression and that, so far as she's concerned, it remains the *War Between the States.* Do you have any arguments I can use to persuade her to adopt the phrase everyone else uses?"

We're afraid that no "argument" could persuade her grandmother to change a usage so deeply ingrained in her mind by birth and tradition. Nor do we see any particular need to try. The phrase *War Between the States* has been used in Southern States for nearly a century and appears often in books and articles about the conflict. Ironically, the Confederate States, which had hoped to be recognized as a separate nation and receive help from Britain, were disappointed when England called it *War Between the States* in recognizing a state of belligerency in 1861. The phrase *Civil War* has, however, been generally accepted by historians both North and South as the standard designation for the war.

There have been many other phrases used to describe the war—each of them betraying a certain prejudice on the part of its user. There are, for example, the *War for Southern Independence,* the *War of Secession,* the *War of Rebellion* and the *Second War of Independence.*

claptrap is literally a device to trap claps—handclaps, that is. It was originally a theatrical term and referred to a showy trick designed solely to secure applause. Because the trickery had nothing to do with the main action of the show, the word *claptrap* came (about 1700) into general language to mean any showy, artificial gesture designed, with an utter lack of sincerity, to gain applause.

claque comes from the French *claquer,* meaning "to applaud," and according to Brewer's *Dictionary of Phrase and Fable,* the term was coined in 1820 by a Parisian entrepreneur who undertook to supply the appropriate number and variety of *claqueurs.* A genius at organization, this M. Sauton could supply on demand *rieurs,* who would laugh whenever laughter was indicated, *pleureurs,* who would cry on cue, *bisseurs* who cried *bis, bis* at the end of arias, and even a group called *commissaires,* who had committed the entire opera to memory and could loudly point out its merits.

clarinet came into English from French just about the time the United States was being founded. It first appeared in print in 1796 but was part of the spoken language of musicians for decades before that. The instrument— first called *clarionet*—was invented in Germany by Johann Christopher Denner. *Clarinet* is a diminutive form of *clarine,* a long obsolete trumpet-like instrument with a clear tone and high register. The word is also related to *clarion,* which also was a kind of trumpet producing sharp, sometimes shrill tones.

claustrophobia. Based on the Latin *claustrum* (enclosed place) and the Greek *phobos* (fear), *claustrophobia* is the abnormal fear of being confined.

clean as a whistle. The whistle referred to is not one of the modern metal affairs. This whistle, like the expression itself, goes back quite a few years. In those days they were whittled out of wood, usually a reed of some sort. To produce a clear, true sound, the whistle had to be absolutely clean. And that's how "clean as a whistle" came to mean spotlessly pure, absolutely without fault.

cleanliness is next to godliness. This ancient proverb is said by some to have come from ancient Hebrew writings. However, its first appearance in English—though in slightly altered form—seems to be in the writings of Francis Bacon. In his *Advancement of Learning* (1605) he wrote: "Cleanness of body was ever deemed to proceed from a due reverence to God." Nearly two centuries later John Wesley in one of his sermons (1791) indicated that the proverb was already well known in the form we use today. Wrote Wesley: "Slovenliness is no part of religion . . . 'Cleanliness is indeed next to Godliness.' "

clean the Augean stables. It is hard to imagine a worse mess than stables that house three thousand oxen and have not been cleaned for thirty years. Such were the stables of King Augeus of Greek mythology, and the task of cleaning them was one of the twelve heroic feats performed by Hercules. His solution was to turn a river through them, thus cleaning away the accumulated filth. The phrase has been used for centuries to connote the huge task of clearing away massive corruption of one sort or another.

cleave. A puzzlement to many has been the riddle of how *cleave* could simultaneously mean "to cling to" and "to separate from": "their tongue *cleaved* to the roof of their mouth" (Job 29:10) and "Abraham . . . *clave* the wood for the burnt offering" (Genesis 22:3). And here we have the cause of the trouble. They are, of course, two entirely different words. In Middle English the first word (cling to) was spelled as "clevien" and came from the Old English *cleofian*. At the same period of the evolution of English (Middle English), the second word (separate from) was spelled "cleven" and had evolved from the Old English *cleofan*. The scholars who translated the King James version of the Bible decided, rightly or wrongly, to ignore that single letter *i*, which had differentiated the two words in the earlier phases of their linguistic evolution. They rendered both as *cleave*—and that's why what appears to be a single word has two utterly contradictory meanings.

clerihew is a four-line humorous verse about a person who is named in the first line. It was invented by E. *Clerihew* Bentley. Two, from the pen of the inventor himself, follow: "Sir Christopher Wren/Said 'I'm going to dine with some men./If anyone calls,/Say I'm designing St. Paul's' " and "It was a weakness of Voltaire's/To forget to say his prayers,/And one which, to his shame,/He never overcame."

clew/clue. A word with dual spelling is *clew,* which usually appears in mystery stories as *clue.* This has a fascinating history, for originally *clewe* was a Middle English word meaning "ball." In time it came to mean specifically a ball of thread or yarn—and then, even more specifically, the ball of yarn used to guide one's way out of a labyrinth. So we come to today's meaning of *clue*—anything that gives an indication of how to solve a puzzle or mystery.

cliché (pronounced klee-SHAY) is borrowed from the French, where it means a stereotype plate. Thus its basic meaning is the same as that of our word "stereotype" when used to describe an expression everlastingly repeated in the same form. We have all listened to dull, *cliché*-ridden speeches—bored nearly to tears (there's a *cliché* for you) by the everlasting repetition of trite expressions. But this is worth remembering: most *clichés* became popular over the years because they express a thought aptly and concisely.

Our advice is to avoid trite and threadbare expressions whenever possible. But if the right word or phrase comes to mind—the expression that says precisely what you want it to say—don't avoid it merely because thousands of others have used it before. Remember what Mark Twain said —and this, too, is near to becoming a *cliché* by now: "The difference between the right word and the almost right word is the difference between lightning and the lightning bug."

climb on the bandwagon. The *bandwagon,* in a literal sense, was a high wagon large enough to hold a band of musicians. It was horse-drawn through the streets as a means of publicity for an upcoming event. Political candidates used to ride the bandwagon through the town, and those who wished to publicly show their support for the candidate would *climb on the bandwagon* and ride with the candidate and the loud-playing band. Once the rush started, it often happened that others followed suit just to be doing the popular thing. Often there was a motive of personal benefit behind such public expression of support. The one who climbed on the bandwagon hoped that his action would mean that the candidate, if elected, would be in his debt to some extent. Today the phrase is used almost exclusively in the figurative sense, but those who *climb on the bandwagon* of a candidate or a cause still do so for one of two reasons: to join the crowd or to reap personal gain.

clinic. *Clinicus,* the Latin word from which our *clinic* comes, originally meant a person confined to bed by illness. Then it came to mean a doctor whose practice was largely made up of visiting bedridden patients. In time it acquired the meaning of a technique of teaching medicine by examining and treating patients in the presence of medical students. A further refinement of meaning was the development of *clinics* as places where groups of doctors practiced—either each in his own specialty, as at the *Mayo Clinic,* or a group specializing on a single disease, as a *cancer clinic.*

Cliometrics is formed from the name Clio, the Greek Muse of history, and "metrics," which in this instance has nothing to do with metrical verse but with the the functions of computers. It seems that there is now a school of historians calling themselves *cliometricians* or sometimes "economic historians" who employ computers to determine the accuracy of historical research. The end result of their work has been somewhat slightingly defined as "history fed through computers."

clone. *Cloning* may, just possibly, be a vital force in the future of the human race. It's asexual reproduction or propagation. At first it was confined to bulbs, cuttings and the like. But more recent laboratory experiments have duplicated frogs, for example, without the customary cooperation of a member of the opposite sex. Whether "cloning" of the human animal is within even the remotest range of possibility is something you'll have to take up with laboratory researchers, not these wordsmiths.

cloud nine. The expression "up on *cloud nine*" to describe a feeling of euphoric exaltation and joy is based on actual terminology used by the U.S. Weather Bureau. Clouds are divided into classes and each class is divided into nine types. *Cloud nine* is the cumulonimbus cloud that you often see building up in the sky in a hot summer afternoon. It may reach 30,000 to 40,000 feet, so if one is up on *cloud nine,* one is high indeed.

The popularity of *cloud nine* as a catch phrase, though, may be credited to the *Johnny Dollar* radio show of the 1950s. There was one recurring episode, like Fibber McGee's famous opening of the closet door. Every time the hero was knocked unconscious—which was often—he was transported to *cloud nine.* There Johnny could start talking again.

coaches—railroad and football. There is a connection between an athletic *coach* and a railroad *coach,* but the most remarkable thing of all about this common word is that it came to English from Hungarian. A less likely source would be hard to imagine, but here's how it came about. In the city of Kocs, Hungary, not far from present-day Budapest, the first *coaches*— large carriages for the conveyance of several passengers—were invented. First called *kocsi* or *kotczi,* their name spread throughout Europe and by 1550 had been Anglicized to *coach.* During the 1840s the nickname *coach* was applied to university tutors in England, perhaps from the idea that with their guidance the students were "carried" along. Then, about 1880, the word came into general use to describe a person who trains athletes.

coal. As might be expected of a fuel that has been known ever since cave man times, the origins of the word *coal* go back further than recorded history. It is thought to be derived from an Indo-European stem, *geu,* from which we also derive words like "glow." Of course, Indo-European itself is only a speculative or hypothetical language constructed largely by linguistic theorists. What we do know for sure is that a direct predecessor of our word *coal* is to be found in the language of our Anglo-Saxon ancestors, where it was usually spelled "col."

coast is clear is simply a password used by smugglers at least since the time of Shakespeare to mean that whatever coastal guardians may routinely have been anticipated either had deserted or been "taken care of."

cobbler/cobblestones. The fruit *cobbler* of our youth was baked with a biscuit-dough crust inside a deep pan, filled with a mixture of berries, fresh-churned butter, sugar and spices, alternated with layers of dumplings and covered with a cinnamon-coated crust. There are two theories about the origin of the baked *cobbler*. The first, a rather unimaginative one, is that a cobbler or his wife baked the original. The theory we prefer goes back to one of the ingredients mentioned—the layers of dumplings. If our memory serves, the top crust of a *cobbler* is thick and somewhat uneven. Now try to think back to the cobblestone streets you may recall from your youth or certainly have seen in pictures. Couldn't the name *cobbler* have been suggested by the somewhat uneven surface of a cobblestone pavement?

And how did the *cobblestone* get its name? Well, these naturally rounded stones, used for paving, were called *cobelstons* in Middle English, from *cob*, meaning a rounded lump, and *stone*, meaning just what it does today.

COBOL is a programming language, similar to English, used for data processing. It is an acronym of CO(mmon) B(usiness) O(riented) L(anguage). What's more, it was devised by CODASYL, the C(onference) O(f) DA(ta) SY(stems) L(anguages).

cobweb originally was *copweb*, from the Anglo-Saxon word *coppe*, meaning "spider." The change from *p* to *b* evolved over the centuries, resulting in the form we use now: *cobweb*.

-cock (suffix). The *-cock* in such names as *Hancock* and *Adcock* merely means "descendant of." Specifically, *Hancock* means "descendant of little Hane," a pet form of John, and *Adcock* means "a descendant of little Ad," which, in turn, was a pet form of Adam.

cock-and-bull story. The origin of this phrase, meaning a rambling, fanciful tale, probably goes back at least as far as Aesop's fables. From the earliest days of recorded history, man has used talking animals in his fables. The folk literature of all lands is full of stories in which animals walk and talk and act like humans. Indeed, in medieval times throughout Europe these tales were collected into tomes called "bestiaries."

The French have a phrase *coq à l'âne*—"cock to donkey"—to describe such rambling yarns, and it is likely that the English form was influenced by it, the bull being substituted for the donkey. In any event, the phrase was fixed once and for all in our language by one of the most imaginative and surely the most disconnected novel ever written in English, *Tristram Shandy* by Laurence Sterne, whose last lines read: "What is all this story about?—A cock and bull, said Yorick—and one of the best of its kind I ever heard."

cock a snook means, literally, to thumb the nose at someone. Figuratively, it means to hold someone up to derision or contempt. The "snook" or, as it sometimes appears, "snoot," is related to "snout" or nose. Incidentally, the British have another very elegant name for this gesture of putting thumb to nose and spreading the fingers. They call it "Queen Anne's fan."

cocker spaniel. The *cock* in *cocker spaniel* comes from "woodcock," a small European game bird related to the snipe. This particular breed of spaniel was widely used for hunting the woodcock because its ability to start and retrieve such small game is almost unparalleled. *Spaniel* itself, incidentally, means *Spanish dog*—and not because the breed was first developed in Spain, either. During the Middle Ages, Spaniards, justly or unjustly, were widely regarded by their enemies as servile, fawning and "meanly submissive." The long, silky, drooping ears of the spaniel and his gentle soulful eyes apparently led to the label *Spanish dog*—though anyone familiar with the breed knows that there's nothing "meanly submissive" about spaniels. Incidentally, spaniels were popular in England as early as Chaucer's time. In the *Canterbury Tales,* he writes: "For as a spaynel, she wol on hym lepe" —"For like a spaniel she would on him leap."

cockles of the heart have nothing to do with the cockles and mussels Sweet Molly Malone used to sell.

The cockles of the old ballad are what the dictionaries call "edible bivalve mollusks"—shellfish. In appearance they are not unlike our scallops, having a somewhat heart-shaped, ribbed shell. The *cockles of your heart,* on the other hand, are its ventricles and thus, by extension, the innermost depths of one's heart or emotions. The word comes from the Latin phrase *cochleae cordis,* meaning "ventricles of the heart," while the shellfish *cockle* comes from the Latin *conchylium,* meaning "conch shell."

cockney. The original *cockney* was a "cock's egg"—one without a yolk and hence of little value. In time the term came to be applied to any spoiled young man, especially an effeminate one. Then, gradually, it was applied to citified youths and, in time, to those living in what came to be called the Cockney section of London. Traditionally now a *cockney* is anyone born within the sound of the Bow Bells. The *cockney* dialect—"dropped haitches" and the like—has long been a staple of British music hall comedians.

cockney rhyming slang was originally British thieves' jargon, designed to be a secret language. Thus *head* became *lump o' lead, crook* was *babblin' brook* and *girl* became *twist and twirl.* This last expression, by the way, is where we get our slang term *twist* for a girl who is, as the Victorians used to say, no better than she should be.

cockpit. Originally this word meant only the pit in which fighting cocks did battle. Then it came to mean any small place where many battles have been waged—as in the old saying: "Belgium is the *cockpit* of Europe." By obvious analogy, World War I aviators began calling the pilot's cramped quarters the plane's *cockpit,* and now it has come to mean any space on plane or boat used by the steersman.

cocktail. Over the years we have collected and reported many versions of the origin of *cocktail.* Our own favorite is that it is a version of the French word *coquetel* and was first popularized as *cocktail* by Antoine Peychaud, a New Orleans restaurateur, who also created Peychaud's bitters. But there are almost as many theories of the origin of *cocktail* as there are varieties of *cocktail*—and there's always room for one more.

Russell Guinn of Culpeper, Virginia, has been researching the question in the musty files of the *Culpeper Exponent.* Under the date October 7, 1898, he found this report:

> The cocktail was the invention of Col. Carter of Culpeper Court House, Va. Many years ago in that locality there was a wayside inn named "The Cock and Bottle," the semblance of an old English tavern.
>
> It bore on its swinging sign a cock and bottle, meaning that draft and bottled ale could be had within—a "cock" in the old vernacular meaning a tap. He who got the last and muddy portion of the tap was said to have received the "cocktail." Upon one occasion, when Col. Carter was subjected to the indignity of having this muddy beverage put before him, he threw it angrily upon the floor and exclaimed: "Hereafter I will drink cocktails of my own brewing."
>
> Then and there, inspired evidently by the spirit of Ganymede, he dashed together bitters, sugar, the oil of lemon peel and some Old Holland gin, and then and there was the first cocktail concocted.

That's a fine story, so let's raise a glass to Col. Carter—and drink a toast to Ganymede, while we're at it. Just in case the classical allusion eludes you, Ganymede was the cupbearer to the gods in ancient mythology.

H. L. Mencken reported once that he and a friend employed a mathematician to figure out how many cocktails could be concocted of the materials to be found at any first-rate bar. The number they arrived at was in excess of seventeen million. Mencken reported further: "We tried 273 at random and found them all good, though some, of course, were better than others." Our own calculations put the number of theories of the origin of *cocktail* in the vicinity of 273, but we'll spare you the others.

C.O.D. "Cash On Delivery" is the British interpretation. In America the initials properly stand for "Collect On Delivery."

coffee was borrowed from the Italian *caffè,* which in turn came from the Arabic *qahwah,* meaning "a drink made from berries."

coffee klatch was originally *kaffee-klatsch,* which is German for "informal conversation over coffee," but the Americanized form *coffee klatch* is more often seen and heard in this country. *Klatsch,* by the way, simply means "gossip."

coffin, a word that stems from the Greek *kophinus* (basket) and has long meant a box for burial, has acquired a new meaning among the nation's atomic energy researchers. No less grim than its original meaning, the term is now used to designate the thick-walled lead container in which radioactive materials are transported.

cognac, in the strict meaning of the word, designates a fine French brandy distilled from wine in and around the French village of *Cognac*. However, the word has come to be applied to any French brandy and even to any liquor distilled from wine. Here is a case of a proper name becoming a generic term, in that the capitalization has been dropped and the word generally applied to any product similar to the genuine or original one.

cohort originally referred to a division of a Roman legion numbering between three hundred and six hundred men. Today it is widely, and some feel inaccurately, used to indicate a companion or associate. A detailed discussion of the use and abuse of *cohort* may be found in the *Harper Dictionary of Contemporary Usage.*

cold deck. The expression *cold deck* goes back at least to Gold Rush days. It worked this way. The card game got under way with a standard deck (pack) of cards. This was known, especially after play had run on for a bit, as the *warm deck.* Secreted nearby, though, was a previously "stacked" deck, known as the *cold deck.* On signal, the victim's attention was distracted long enough for the *cold deck* to be substituted—and one pigeon was plucked.

cold duck. In 1971 a beverage named *cold duck* gained almost instant popularity. It is made up of a mixture of two sparkling wines, usually domestic burgundy and domestic champagne, and there seems little logic to its being called *cold duck.* Language expert Charles Berlitz supplies the explanation: "The expression was originally German and came from the somewhat distressing practice of waiters taking wine and beer left by customers and mixing it all together to drink after the end of a banquet. The original expression was *kalte ende,* meaning 'cold end,' which indeed it was. Gradually, by folk etymology, the phrase became *kalte ente,* which translates as *cold duck.* "

cold shoulder. When knighthood was in flower, a wandering knight would be received at any castle with a sumptuous hot meal. However, the common traveler would do well to be offered a plate of cold meat. Since mutton was a common food of the times in England, he would be likely to get the *cold shoulder.* Today, when we "turn the *cold shoulder*" to anyone, we treat him with disdain bordering on contempt. This is an especially appropriate phrase if the person was once on friendly terms with us.

cole slaw. Even though *cold slaw* appears on far too many menus, the correct spelling is *cole slaw.* The term comes from the Latin word *colis,* meaning "cabbage," and a Dutch word, *sla,* meaning "salad."

colloquial versus slang. In the matter of informal or, as it's more properly called, *colloquial* English versus slang there is a widespread misconception that the two are, if not identical, at least very much alike. It's true that there is a considerable area where the two overlap. It's also true that last year's *slang* word may become next year's acceptable *colloquial* idiom. But there is as much difference between *colloquial* English and *slang* as there is between the casual informal conversation of your local minister and the equally informal but far less literate chatter of a teen-ager. Indeed, that's precisely where the difference lies.

Colloquial English is, in the words of the editors of the Merriam-Webster *New International Dictionary, Second Edition,* "acceptable and appropriate in ordinary conversational context, as in intimate speech among cultivated people, in familiar letters, in informal speeches or writings, but not in formal written discourse." The editors then cite "flabbergast," "go slow" and "harum scarum" as examples of expressions that would be admissible in colloquial English but not in formal English. They note further that "*colloquial* speech may be as correct as formal speech."

So you see that *colloquial* means exactly what an examination of its Latin roots—*com* (together) and *loqui* (to speak)—would indicate: the kind of language used by people talking together.

The last word on *colloquial* speech was the acknowledgment by Harvard's famed Shakespearean authority George Lyman Kittredge that "I always speak *colloq.* and often write it."

But *slang* is something else again. It contains the flashy novelties of language and is, in the words of one authority, "not appropriate for public affairs or the use of educated people." In other words, *slang* may be fun —but it's not good English.

colonel. The explanation of how *colonel* came to be pronounced KER-nel is a complicated one and involves at least four centuries of British military history. Back in the sixteenth century the word was spelled "coronel" and pronounced with three syllables, pretty much as spelled. Gradually, thanks to the British talent for streamlining pronunciations (Cholmondoley is pronounced "Chumly"), the word "coronel" acquired a two-syllable pronunciation: KOR-nel and eventually KER-nel. The spelling was later altered to what we know today, but the pronunciation has remained the same.

Colonel Bogey and his march. During the First World War, according to one British authority, "Troops on the march were forbidden to sing a catchy song called 'Colonel Bogey' as the words they substituted for the real ones were not considered edifying." The same spirited march served as the theme music of the film *The Bridge on the River Kwai.*

Who is the Colonel Bogey immortalized in this tune? Well, he's a wholly mythical character from the world of sports. He's the average game player —originally in golf—who never quite makes par but whose score is a fair guage of the ordinary player's ability. A committee sets for each hole the score that is the lowest a good average player can make it in, usually one above par. Thereafter to *beat Bogey* or *beat the colonel* you must play it in a fewer number of strokes.

colophon (pronounced KOL-uh-fon) has two applications in book publishing. Originally it described a note at the end of a book wherein such data as the size and style of type, the name of the book's designer, and the name and location of the printer were recorded. Today it is also loosely used to indicate the publisher's symbol (in the case of this book a torch and the date 1817) which appears on the title page and sometimes on the binding of a book. The word comes from the Greek word *kolophon,* meaning "summit" or "finish." According to Greek legend, warriors from the town of Colophon in Ionia were such superb fighters that whenever they took part in battle the side they supported won. Thus to add the *colophon* came to mean to add the finishing stroke to any enterprise.

columbine is a plant with varicolored flowers notable for five conspicuously spurred petals. Ancients thought these petals resembled doves, so they chose the name *columbine* from the Latin *columba,* "dove."

come a cropper is from the jargon of horse racing and polo playing and means a head-over-heels tumble from a horse. The phrase "neck and crop," meaning "completely" or "entirely," has long been a common term in British slang and *come a cropper* is probably a variation on that phrase.

come day, go day, God send Sunday. This expression, virtually unknown in the U.S., is quite commonly used in England to refer to a shiftless, lazy person. It has been around a long time. The *Oxford Dictionary of English Proverbs* reports its appearance in print as long ago as 1616, the date of Shakespeare's death. It was "spoken to lazy, unconscionable servants, who only mind to serve out their time and get their wages." It has been called "the sluggard's daily prayer."

There's a sort of parallel to be found in the U.S. When we were serving our time at American Heritage and other publishing houses, we were keenly aware of the existence of a numerically large employee group who called themselves members of the T.G.I.F. Club—"Thank God, it's Friday!" What most of them never realized is that membership in this club automatically qualified them for membership in management's L.I.F.O. Club—"Last In, First Out."

comedy. Originally *comedy,* from the Greek *komoidos,* "singer in the revels," referred to the singers and the songs involved in Dionysian revels, which were notable for the licentiousness of the actions of the participants. In time the festivals became fairly well organized and about 400 B.C. Aristophanes gave us the first of the true comedies in the sense we use the term today.

comeuppance is in general colloquial use, though its first recorded appearance —according to the *Dictionary of American English*—was in 1859. It generally means "merited punishment" or "just desserts." One authority reports that it is occasionally used to mean "due reward" but we have never encountered it except in the sense of deserved punishment or retribution.

commando goes back to the Boer War (1899–1902). The word is, of course, ultimately derived from the Latin *commandare* (to command), but in its special sense of a small striking force trained to make quick, devastating raids on enemy-held positions, it began with the Boers. Originally, as indicated, a *commando* was the troop itself. Now, however, we tend to think of a *commando* as an individual member of such a group and refer to "*commando* forces" or "*commando* units."

comme il faut (pronounced kom eel FOH), when translated literally from the French, means "as it should be"—or fitting and proper. This phrase is usually used after a negative, and it is a mark of good manners and breeding to avoid any action which is not *comme il faut.*

commencement/graduation. *Commencement,* from the Latin words *cum* and *initio,* "to go into together," quite literally means a beginning. The reason it is used to designate the day on which college education ends is that the ending is also a beginning—the start of the new career or vocation for which college has trained the student.

Grade and high schools, by contrast, usually and properly designate their ceremonies *graduation.* From the Latin *gradus* (step or grade), this word indicates that a pupil has completed an important step toward his educational goal but that more remains to be done.

commensurate (pronounced kuh-MEN-shoor-it) is an adjective derived from the Latin *com-* (with) and *mensurare* (to measure). It has two distinct but related meanings. The original meaning, and one which is still used in the sciences, was the relationship between two or more items which could be measured by the same standard or in common units. A more popular current meaning is that of being equal or at least proportionate in extent or value. "The salary offered was not *commensurate* to the work involved."

commentary. Originally *commentary,* from the Latin *commentum* (a commentary), meant a written memoir or record of events—especially one hastily written as a sort of memorandum for future reference. Recently it has come into wide use as the term for the spoken narration that accompanies films, television shows and so on. In this sense it has even spawned a new verb, *to commentate,* and one of our major newspapers recently shocked the purists among its readers by noting that a famed fashion stylist was going to *commentate* his new models at a fashion show.

common crackers. On a trip to New England we stayed at a pleasant inn where we were served clam chowder with what the host called *common crackers.* They were rather plain, thick crackers, unsalted and easily split so they floated on top of the chowder. We suppose they get their name because that's precisely what they are—*common* in the sense of plain and simple. If you feel like using a slightly more elegant name, call them Boston crackers. They're the same thing.

commons/cafeteria. The name *commons* is appropriate for the traditional college or university dining hall, where students sit together at identical tables and are served the same—"common"—meal. *Cafeteria* lacks the quiet elegance of *commons,* but it seems much more appropriate for college restaurants that do not serve the same food to all, nor charge all at the same price. *Cafeteria* has its origin in the American Spanish spoken in early California. The first *cafeterias* were retail coffee stores, from which evolved the uniquely American self-service restaurants we know today.

commonwealth. Pennsylvania, Massachusetts, Maryland, Virginia and Kentucky are called *commonwealths* instead of *states* simply because the word *commonwealth* was used in the original royal charter of land. (Kentucky was then part of Virginia.) The residents liked the word and its connotations, so kept the label *commonwealth* even after becoming states.

companion. A *companion* is, literally, a person with whom you share bread. The word comes from two Latin words, *cum* (together, with) and *panis* (bread).

company. We tend today to think of *company* in its business connotations— as part of the name of a firm or business association. But originally it meant simply "companions." Indeed, we took the word into English from the French word *compain,* meaning "companion," at the time of the Norman conquest.

compere (pronounced kom-PARE) is a British expression, roughly equivalent to our "Master of Ceremonies" or "MC." It may be used as either a noun or a verb. *Compere* was borrowed from the French, where it means "godfather" and was first used as the title for a person who organized vaudeville —in England "variety"—shows.

compleat goes back to a classic book on fishing and fishermen, *The Compleat Angler* by Izaak Walton. Published in 1653, it has rightly been called "one of the monuments of English literature." When Walton used *compleat* he was simply using the spelling current in his time—and the word had the sense of "fully equipped or endowed, especially as regards some art or occupation."

The spelling "compleat" is archaic now. But it's worth noting that the newly published Supplement to the *Oxford English Dictionary* reports it has been recently "revived in imitation of its 17th-century use" and quotes from Mary McCarthy's 1963 novel *The Group:* "She writes and sings and paints and dances and plays I don't know how many instruments. The *compleat* girl."

complex, in the sense of a group of buildings serving a common purpose (a hospital *complex,* for example) seems to have first appeared in print during the 1930s. It was widely used in reports of wartime bombing raids by the RAF. The *OED* gives as an example: "dropped 100 tons of high explosives on the rail bridge *complex.* "

complicity. Generally used to denote participation in some form of wrongdoing, *complicity* is made up of the Latin *com-* (with) and *plactere* (to weave). So if one man's actions are woven into the wrongdoing of another, both are guilty.

comptroller/controller. *Comptroller* is a word that has remarkably little reason for existence. In meaning it differs not at all from the more common *controller*. Both simply designate officials who control funds, whether for a private firm or for a department of government. Both words ultimately derive from the Latin *contrarotulare,* "to check by counter roll or duplicate register." *Comptroller* is thought to have been influenced in its spelling by the French *compte,* "account." In any event, it is pronounced precisely the same as *controller*. We suspect that the popularity of *comptroller* stems from an understandable but no less regrettable desire for a more important-looking title.

compunction (pronounced k'm-PUNK-sh'n) is a noun from Latin, its origin being *compunctus,* past participle of *compungere,* the intensified form of the verb for "to prick or sting." Used only to apply to the conscience, it has the meaning of uneasiness of conscience and, thus, scruple or remorse.

conclave. Coming from the Latin *con-* (together) and *clavis* (key), this word originally referred to a series of cubicles or small rooms in which are housed the cardinals assembled at the Vatican to choose a new Pope. All the rooms can be opened with a single key. By extension *conclave* came to mean any solemn convocation of dignitaries and now, by still further extension, it can mean any sort of secret meeting.

condign punishment is a penalty suitable to the crime committed, the sort of treatment Gilbert and Sullivan had in mind when their Mikado announced: "My object all sublime I shall achieve in time—to let the punishment fit the crime." *Condign* (pronounced kun-DINE) comes from the Latin *condignus,* meaning "worthy or well deserved."

condominium is made up of the Latin words *con-* (together) and *dominium* (property), but it's a word no Roman ever saw. In the sense of joint control of a territory by two or more states, it has been around since the early 1700s, according to the *OED.* But as a term for an apartment building in which the apartments are owned by tenants, rather than rented, it seems to have made its first appearance in print about 1960. Since it's an English word, the plural is formed normally by adding *s,* as *condominiums,* not— as would be the case if the word were actually Latin—by using the nominative plural ending *a*—"condominia."

condone (pronounced kun-DOHN) is a verb meaning "to pardon or forgive." It can also mean "to overlook" and by so doing to act as though no offense had been committed. It is derived from the Latin *condonare,* whose root word, *donare* (to give), has been combined with the intensifier *con-*. Generally seen in such statements as "We cannot *condone* such actions on his part," the word is used most often in the sense of "overlooking," except in legal usage, where it seems to keep its meaning of forgiveness.

Conestoga wagons were the covered wagons used by early settlers in America. "The first ones were built in Conestoga, Pennsylvania, in the mid 1700s. The so-called prairie schooners (from a distance across the prairie they looked like ships at sea), which carried most of the settlers in the transcontinental wagon trains along the Oregon and Overland trails, were lighter adaptations of the *Conestogas.*

Coney Island. Did *Coney Island* at one time have a large rabbit population? In any event, according to George Stewart's *American Place Names,* the "coney" in Coney Island is "an Anglicization of the Dutch word for rabbit." The Dutch, at the time they named the island, could never have guessed that it would eventually become famous as the gaudiest tourist trap on the East Coast, a place where gimmicked games of chance abounded and where, as Barnum noted in another connection, a sucker was born every minute. And what do you suppose was the Old English term for duping a man or playing him for a sucker? It was *"coney*-catching."

Coney Islands. Throughout the Midwest you will see signs advertising *Coney Islands.* These, for the benefit of the uninitiated, are frankfurters in rolls on which are heaped successively mustard, relish, raw onions and catsup —a rare feat of culinary ingenuity and very possibly one reason why the American ulcer rate per capita is the world's highest. Don't ever try to buy a *Coney Island* at Coney Island, New York, though! They never heard of such a mixture. The thought of catsup on a hot dog would make a Brooklyn native blanch with horror—mustard or, at most, sauerkraut, mustard and relish will serve him nicely, thanks.

confidence. Made up from two Latin words, *con-* (with) and *fidere* (faith), *confidence* means literally "faith in oneself."

confused beetles. Did you know that beetles may be—in fact, are—officially labeled *confused* and *depressed?* We didn't either until one fine day when an editor friend sent us a note about the matter. "Last January," he wrote, "the U.S. Department of Agriculture sent out a release mentioring the *confused flour beetle.* As a confused editor, I sought the name in dictionaries and, while I found the *depressed flour beetle,* I could not find the confused beetle, even though I thought confusing was depressing. I wrote the USDA for an explanation—and now I have the answer and the interesting derivation of the names of the two beetles."

He enclosed a letter from an information specialist for the USDA, shedding light on this confusing topic: "The red flour beetle *(Tribolium castaneum)* and the confused flour beetle *(Tribolium confusum)* look very nearly alike. The only visible difference is in the shape of the area around the eye. Back in the nineteenth century when the red flour beetle was first described, the description was a mixture of the two beetles. When it was discovered that they were two distinct species, someone began calling one species the *confused flour beetle* because of the earlier confusion in identifying it. The *depressed flour beetle* gets its name from its appearance; to a layman certain areas appear to be flattened or depressed." Is all confusion now clarified and all depression relieved?

congeries is a word from a vocabulary level far above the attainment of the average reader. A check of three popular desk dictionaries which reflect the vocabulary range of the literate high school graduate shows that none of the three enters and defines *congeries*. The college and unabridged dictionaries, of course, do list it. But, as the late Frank Colby wrote, "it is what one might call a 'book word' for it does not occur except in very learned or pedantic discourse."

Curious about its meaning and origin? Well, *congeries* merely means "a collection of things or parts massed together." It comes from the Latin verb *congerere,* meaning "to bring together or pile up." It is pronounced kon-JER-eez, in case you want to dazzle your friends with your erudition.

Congeries shares with "shambles" and "kudos" the distinction of having both singular and plural forms identical—and ending in *s.* This causes no end of confusion to some writers, who are forever trying to award a single kudo or describe the scene of one bloody shamble.

conk/conch. An intriguing example of how words change meaning as they move from British to American English is found when we look into the various meanings of the slang word *conk.* To most Americans *conk* is most familiar as a verb in one of two senses. If you *conk* a person, you hit him on the head. If you *conk out,* you fall asleep or unconscious. Similarly, if an airplane's motor *conks out,* it suddenly fails to operate.

But this is only part of a change in word meanings which led to the creation of an amusing but not quite accurate account of how *conk* got one of its present American meanings. This theory—that Florida Indians used to put conch shells on their hands before engaging in fisticuffs (sort of super brass knuckles)—is very interesting, and we surely wouldn't want to be *conked* by an Indian or anyone else using conch shells as brass knuckles. The only trouble with the theory is that *conk*—originally as a slang term for nose and later for the whole head—has been common in England since about 1800. The word's use as a verb, meaning to hit a person on the head, dates back almost as long, certainly long before the Everglades Indians had any need to *conk* invading white men with conch shells. So though most authorities agree that *conk* in the sense of head or nose originally was a variant spelling of *conch,* the direct connection to Florida Indians is fanciful but inaccurate.

The other sense of the word—as when a motor *conks out*—is entirely unrelated to *conch.* It was coined in World War I by military aviators in imitation of the coughing noise their engines made just before stopping completely.

conniption/conniption fit. The expressions *conniption* and *conniption fit* have been common in the American language for a century and a half. Nobody knows where they originated, except that they are thought to be the fanciful invention of some frontiersman who wanted an elegant Latin-sounding word to describe a tantrum—for that's really what a *conniption fit* is.

connoisseur comes directly from French and indirectly from the Latin *cognoscere* (to know). A *connoisseur* (and that's a word that belongs in every spelling bee) is a knowledgeable chap, a good judge of quality, especially in the arts.

conscientious objector. Under English law a "conscience clause" was a clause in an Act of Parliament "to relieve persons with conscientious scruples from certain requirements in it." For the most part the conscience clause related to religious matters, but when, in 1898, Parliament passed the Compulsory Vaccination Act, there was such wide rebellion against it that the term *conscientious objector* came to be applied almost exclusively to those who swore legally that their consciences prevented them from being vaccinated. With the outbreak of World War I, men who objected to military service for reasons of conscience acquired the name, and it has been used in that sense, both here and in England, since that time.

conservatory. The first conservatories (in Italian *conservatorio)* were homes for foundlings who were "conserved" or protected by being given a musical education. Later the term was extended to include hothouses where flowers and plants are similarly "conserved."

conspiracy of silence. This phrase was coined by a namesake of ours, Sir Lewis Morris, a minor poet of the Victorian era. He aspired to the post of Poet Laureate but never attained it. He claimed that the critics were jealous of him and, as a result, damned his poetry when they bothered to mention it at all. He once complained at length to Oscar Wilde of this treatment, finally saying: "Oscar, there's a *conspiracy of silence* against me. What shall I do?" Replied Wilde: "Join it!"

constable. Any time you feel like putting down your friendly local constable —a tactic which we emphatically do not recommend—just remind him that the original constables were stable grooms, mockingly called "counts of the stables," from the Latin *comes stabuli.* They gradually rose in rank, however, and occasionally were entrusted with the charge of the castle when the king was away. Then began the slide downhill until nowadays in this country a *constable* is a peace officer of relatively limited authority and power.

Contract, as an item of Mafia language, means pretty much the same thing as an expression that was part of the language of the Old West: "There's a price on his head." In other words, the criminal organization will pay a specified fee for proof that an enemy has been eliminated—permanently.

The word is not new to underworld slang. For decades corrupt police and politicians have referred to a bribe or "the fix" as a *contract.* The specific application of the word to a payment for murder can probably be traced to the fact that the Mafia has a penchant for operating legitimate businesses, either as fronts for their nefarious activities or as straightforward moneymaking enterprises. So the language of legitimate business is well known to underworld leaders and it's the most natural thing in the world for them to disguise the ultimate crime—murder—under the genteel euphemism *contract*.

contrail is a contraction of "condensation trail" and describes the vapor trail left in the sky by certain airplanes, notably jets. In the words of the *U.S. Air Force Dictionary*, a *contrail* is "vapor formed in supercooled air when disturbed by the passing of an airplane. It also forms from the water content of the exhaust in cold air."

contrite (pronounced kun-TRITE) is an adjective made up from the Latin *con-* (together) and *terere* (to rub), and has the meaning of being remorseful. The conscience is "rubbed" by a sense of guilt and remorse sets in.

conurbation/megalopolis. *Conurbation* means the gradual fusion of urban areas together into what some city planners call a *megalopolis*. Taking the long view, some people claim that before the end of this century the area from Boston to Washington, encompassing such major cities as Providence, New York, Philadelphia and Baltimore, will comprise such a *megalopolis* or *conurbation*. *Conurbation* (pronounced kon-ur-BAY-shun) is a recent coinage from the Latin *con-* (together) and *urbs* (city). *Megalopolis* is formed from the Greek *mega-* (large or great) and *polis* (city).

cookies. From the name, it might appear that *cookies* are so called because they are cooked. But lots of things are cooked, so why them? Good question. Actually, the word comes to us from the Dutch word *koekje,* meaning "small cake." So while cookies are cooked (rather, baked), that fact has nothing to do with their name.

cook their goose. There is a legend that the burghers of a besieged town in the Middle Ages decided to show their contempt for the attackers by hanging a goose from a tower—the goose having long been a symbol of stupidity and futility. This time, however, the taunt backfired. The attacking force was so enraged at the insult that they burned the whole town—cooking the goose in the process, of course. That's an interesting story—but alas, no more than that. In truth, the expression seems not to have appeared in English until 1851, when in a London street ballad referring to charges of "Papal Aggression" appeared these lines: "If they come here we'll cook their goose,/The Pope and Cardinal Wiseman."

coolie originally applied to any unskilled laborer from the Orient. The word was originally the Hindi *kuli* and it is thought to have originated in the name of an aboriginal tribe in Gujarat, India. The word *coolie* became well known in this country when many thousands of them were imported in the nineteenth century to work on the transcontinental railroad.

cool one's heels, meaning "be forced to wait," is an expression that goes back to the days when the horse was the main means of transportation. When a long trip resulted in the horse's hoofs becoming heated, the horseman had to interrupt his journey while his carrier's hoofs cooled a little.

coolth. A reader asked why, if we have "warmth," we do not have *coolth.* The answer is that the word exists. Indeed, it has existed, according to the *OED,* at least since 1547. For some reason—perhaps because there's so much unwanted *coolth* in the British climate—it never caught on the way "warmth" did. The *OED* now calls *coolth* "jocular and colloquial," while *Funk & Wagnalls* labels it "humorous and dialectal."

cop. The word *cop* long was a source of irritation to J. Edgar Hoover, and the nickname *nation's top cop* must have proved especially galling because of the frequency with which it turned up in newspaper and magazine articles. All of us know, of course, that any policeman responds more agreeably to the title "officer" than to *cop,* but some people ask whether this attitude on the lawmen's part is justified. Is it the result of inherited prejudice or is there good reason for disliking the nickname *cop?*

Well, good reason there is—in abundance. Though many people think that *cop* is merely a shortened form of "copper," from the buttons once worn by British bobbies, this is untrue. In the first place, "bobbies" did not exist until Sir Robert Peel secured the passage of Britain's first modern Police Act in 1828. But the word *cop* in the sense of "one who captures or snatches" is recorded as early as 1704. Indeed, an ancestor word, *cap,* with the same meaning, came into English from French at the time of the Norman Conquest and can be traced all the way back to ancient Rome's *capere* (to capture).

But there seems nothing derogatory about this meaning of *cop*—one who seizes or captures. However, over the centuries, the word *cop* has been used by unsavory underworld characters in many different meanings. To steal, for instance: an auto thief *cops a heap.* To assault from the rear by stealth: a crook *cops a sneak.* And of course, there's the well-known *cop a plea*— to plead guilty to a lesser crime in order to get a lesser penalty.

copacetic/copasetic. This slang word for excellent, topnotch or first-rate was labeled in one of our earlier books the probable invention of Bill "Bojangles" Robinson, one of the great black entertainers of this century and certainly one of the greatest tap dancers who ever lived. At least one reader challenged that attribution, saying that he had heard comedian Joe Frisco use the term in 1911. That well may be, but since Bojangles was probably active also at that time, all we can prove is that the word was well known in show business circles and that, while Robinson may not have invented it, he surely did much to popularize it. Incidentally, regardless of spelling, it's pronounced koh-puh-SET-ik.

copper a bet has to do with placing a penny on a bet previously laid, after action has started but before it is complete. Here's a definition from an edition of Hoyle published in 1866: "If a player wishes to bet that a card will lose (that is, win for the bank), he indicates his wish by placing a cent upon the top of the stake. It is called 'coppering' because coppers were first used to distinguish such bets." This phrase is now used to designate a bet made against oneself, in order to cut losses. A person who has bet $100 on a football team decides he can't afford to lose that much; he then bets $50 (thereby coppering his bet) on the other team. In that way he cuts his potential losses (and winnings) to $50.

copperheads. The copperhead snake *(Agkistrodon contortrix)* is a lethally poisonous snake common in the Eastern United States and characterized by reddish-brown markings, from which it gets its *copperhead* name. It is especially menacing in that, unlike the rattlesnake, it gives no warning of its approach. It is this characteristic, together with the fact that its coloration blends easily into the foliage, allowing it to go undetected, that led to the use of *copperhead* as an opprobrious epithet for the very considerable number of Confederate sympathizers and supporters in the North during the American Civil War. Carl Sandburg, in his elegy for Lincoln, "Cool Tombs," wrote: "When Abraham Lincoln was shoveled into the tombs, he forgot the copperheads and the assassin . . . in the dust, in the cool tombs."

During World War II Franklin D. Roosevelt used the term on at least one occasion to describe American citizens who supported the propaganda line of the Hitler-Mussolini Axis. And as recently as 1945, an editorial in *The Nation* magazine spoke of "the copperhead press which slyly apologized for Nazi aggression."

Incidentally, there is evidence of the use of the *copperhead* label by the early colonists in referring to the American Indians and later in reference to the Dutch settlers in and around New York. Its first really widespread use, however, came with the Civil War.

cord of wood. The English word *cord,* meaning "a small rope made by twisting several strands together," comes from the Latin *chorda,* meaning "catgut or cord." The use of the word in *cord of wood* comes from the old practice of measuring a stack of firewood with a cord of a certain length. A *cord of wood* occupies 128 cubic feet and is usually arranged in a stack four feet high, four feet wide and eight feet in length.

cordon bleu. If you are eating in a fine restaurant and have the services of a *cordon bleu* chef, you are being offered a truly fine cuisine. *Cordon bleu* means "blue ribbon," and the blue ribbon has long been the sign of supremacy. In the days when ocean liners vied with each other to win the title of fastest ship on the transatlantic run, the award was a blue ribbon and the fastest ship was advertised as the "blue-ribbon winner." The color blue has been associated with royalty and power ever since ancient times when gods and goddesses were believed to live in the heavens up above the blue skies. In England the highest order of knighthood is the Order of the Garter, represented by a blue ribbon. In France the Knights of the Holy Ghost wore an insigne suspended around the neck by a *cordon bleu*. In years past these knights, like many other Frenchmen, developed tastes for fine foods and wines. When they were served an especially superb meal, they rewarded the chef by calling his meal *un repas de cordon bleu* and decorating him with a blue ribbon. That's how the highest order of French chefs came to be called masters of *cordon bleu* cuisine.

corduroy. Of all fabrics used for clothing none—save, perhaps, denim—is so sturdy, so well able to withstand the abusive rough-and-tumble wear that young people give it, as *corduroy*. It is truly the plebeian workhorse of today's fabrics—and yet its name means "cord fit for the king"! Originally *corduroy* (from the French *corde du roi*) was woven from silk and was used exclusively by the kings of France as part of their hunting costumes.

corduroy road is one made by laying logs across a path, usually through a swamp or marshy bog. This results in a roadway ribbed somewhat like the ribs of the fabric corduroy.

corned beef. The *corn* in *corned beef* goes back to a time when the vegetable we know as *corn* was called "maize"—as it still is in England today. Originally a *corn* was any small substance or particle—especially a seed or kernel. When beef was laid down in a brine to cure, it was sprinkled with *corns* of coarse salt. So the process came to be known as *corning* the beef and the end product was *corned beef*. The same use of *corn* to mean a grain or particle remains in words like *peppercorn*—whole black peppers—and *barleycorn*.

corny, originally a contraction of "corn-fed," was first used by actors and vaudevillians to describe audiences in "the sticks." To a show business professional of the early days of this century "every town outside New York was Bridgeport," by which he simply meant that away from the main stem, audience reactions were unsophisticated—in a word, *corn-fed*. So that great entertainer George M. Cohan once pointed out in a well-remembered song, "only forty-five minutes from Broadway" you would find "hicks" and "jays" galore. Since these *corn-fed* audiences relished a broad and unsubtle brand of humor, it became known as *"corn-fed* humor"—a phrase which now is simply *"corny* joke."

corrupt and contented. Lincoln Steffens was one of the leaders in the muckraking movement in the early years of this century, when he and other crusading journalists tried to expose forces of corruption and greed. And with some success, it should be reported. At the time Steffens coined a memorable phrase to describe conditions in the Cradle of Liberty around the turn of the century. "Philadelphia," he wrote, "is *corrupt and contented."*

cotillion. We think of the *cotillion* as the most elegant and proper formal dance of the antebellum South, so it comes as a bit of a shock to learn that the primary purpose of the dance itself was to enable young ladies to reveal their underclothing. The word is taken from the French *cotillon,* meaning "petticoat," and one of the figures in the dance had the ladies lifting their gowns to show their petticoats. Tush, tush, and for shame!

cotton to. When we say we *cotton to* a person or idea, meaning that we have taken a fancy to it, we are referring directly to the way cotton can cling to our clothing. If you have ever tried picking cotton lint from a wool suit, you'll understand the origin of the phrase.

Council of Nicaea was the first ecumenical council of Christian churches, held at Nicaea in Bithynia, Asia Minor, in A.D. 325. At this council the Nicene Creed was promulgated as a formal statement of the tenets of the Christian faith and chiefly of the doctrine of the Trinity. This creed is still widely used in Christian churches.

countdown. Intriguingly enough, the creator of the *countdown* technique is motion picture director Fritz Lang, whose chief claim to fame was his direction of the silent-film classic *M.* In the late 1920s Lang directed one of the very earliest science fiction films, *The Lady in the Moon.* A highlight was the launching of a mammoth rocket. It occurred to Lang that greater suspense could be obtained by switching from the conventional "one-two-three" to exactly the reverse. Later science was to imitate art.

counterwords. The technical name for words like *cute* and *grand* and *darling* that are used so much that they have lost their original meanings is *counterwords. Webster's New World Dictionary* defines *counterword* as "any word freely used as a general term of approval or disapproval without reference to its more exact meaning."

country mile is just as long as a city mile—but it seems longer because the spaces are more open in the country. *Country mile* is generally used loosely to mean any long distance. "Her voice was so loud that it could be heard a *country mile.*"

coup de grâce. This term (pronounced koo-deh-GRAHS) means the finishing stroke, often the blow that ends a man's life. So it is a bit of a surprise to learn that the literal translation of the term is "blow of mercy." In medieval times, and even later, it was common practice to torture a condemned prisoner on the rack or torture wheel for protracted periods before finally dispatching him with a *coup de grâce.* By that time the blow quite literally was a blow of mercy.

course of sprouts. This expression has been traced by the *Dictionary of American English* to 1851 and means, of course, stern discipline or training. It probably was originally a *course for sprouts—sprouts* being any offshoot, including offspring of a family.

Cousin Jack comes from the slang of British coal miners. It means a Cornish mine worker or, by extension, any native of Cornwall. *Cousin,* in this phrase, is probably a corruption of "Cornish."

couth. One of the oddest things about our language is the way words will flourish for a while, then seem to die—or at least pass from general use—

only to enjoy a sudden, lively rebirth. During the past few years such long-established words as *ecumenical, arcane* and *charisma* have enjoyed such revival. They were all resting in the limbo of the small type in unabridged dictionaries, but it took the research of scholars and then the sudden quirk of popular fancy to bring them back into vogue.

An even odder case is that of *couth. Couth* actually is a very old word, appearing in Anglo-Saxon as *cuth,* meaning "known or familiar." Indeed, the word was still listed in the 1936 Fifth Collegiate in this sense, but labeled "obsolete." During the Middle Ages the negative form "uncouth" had appeared, at first in the sense of "unfamiliar or unknown." Since people tend to fear the unknown and since much of the unknown bordered on the barbarous in those days, "uncouth" soon came to mean "outlandish, repellent and boorish"—meanings it still has.

But when word play about "lost positives" became popular in the 1950s, John Crosby, then writing a TV column for the lamented *New York Herald Tribune,* and Dick Maney, the legendary theatrical press agent, did much to popularize the quest for words like *sidious, nocuous, gruntled* and *ept.* We did our bit in furthering the fad—and behold the result. *Couth* now makes a dramatic reappearance, no longer meaning "known" but now defined as the opposite of "uncouth"—"polished and sophisticated."

coven, also spelled "covin," was the same word as "convent" in the sixteenth century and was used in reference to any group or assemblage of people. Now "convent" refers only to a group of nuns and the place where they reside. Strictly speaking, a *coven* of witches is a group of thirteen of them —and that's another indication that the tradition that "thirteen is unlucky" dies hard, despite the efforts of dedicated triskaidekaphiles like us. (A triskaidekaphile is simply a person who likes the number 13. The word is made from two Greek words, meaning "thirteen" and "love.")

Coventry. There are several theories as to how *Coventry* came to symbolize a place for persons in disgrace. One goes back to the British Civil War between Charles I and Parliament. Since *Coventry* was a stronghold of the Parliamentary forces, the most difficult Royalist prisoners were sent there for safekeeping.

Much more persuasive is a second theory. This is that the townspeople of *Coventry* traditionally disliked having soldiers quartered in their town. So strong was their disaffection for the military that any girl seen talking to a soldier was automatically ostracized. So service in *Coventry* soon became what any serviceman would call "dull duty," and assignment to *Coventry* meant a one-way ticket to disgrace and boredom.

The story of Lady Godiva and Peeping Tom goes further to strengthen the meaning of the phrases *send to Coventry* and *in Coventry.* See PEEPING TOM.

cowboy is an American term, which, incredibly enough, was being used during Revolutionary times. The *cowboys* of those years, however, were a very different lot—guerrilla bands of Tories operating in what is now Westchester County, New York. According to one authority: "The *cowboys* were the worst kind of Tories; they went around in the bushes armed with guns and tinkling a cow-bell so as to beguile the patriots into the brush hunting for cows."

cowboy jargon. One of the most colorful jargons is that of the American cowboy. In the early days of the opening of the West, the trail rider had to be a pretty tough customer and most of them simply didn't have much time for "book learning."

As a result, they talked a salty and colorful lingo—a language all its own. Over the years it has contributed *hoosegow, maverick, hoodlum* and many other fresh and lively words to the working vocabulary of all Americans. But there's a lot more to cowboy jargon than this. For example, do you know what a cowboy means when he says he's *on the prod?* If you don't, partner, watch out because it means he's fighting mad and it's just not healthy to stay in the vicinity. If he says he's *on the peck* he means the same thing. But if he tells you he's *on the drift,* there's nothing to worry about because he just means he's out of work and riding the grub line (i.e., picking up free meals at ranch after ranch) until he can find another job.

A *cow waddy* nowadays means nothing more than a cowboy, although the term originally was used chiefly for rustlers and for third-rate cowhands who could get jobs only when ranches were shorthanded, usually at the time of spring and fall roundups. *Rustlers,* of course, are cattle thieves —the villains in countless thousands of Western movies. Curiously enough, though the term *waddy* was originally applied to thieves and has come to mean an honest cowhand, *rustler* originally meant only a very hard-working *hustling* cowhand. When he began *hustling* (or *rustling*) mavericks and cattle that didn't belong to him, his name fell into disrepute.

A *lariat* (from Spanish *la reata*) is not quite the same as a *lasso.* Originally, at least, the *lariat* was a rope used for hobbling and tethering cattle. The *lasso* (correctly pronounced LASS-oh, not lass-OH), of course, has a running noose on one end and is used for roping cattle and horses.

Nowadays the closest contact most of us have with cowboys reared and accoutered in the great tradition of the early West is when we go to see the rodeo. Here, too, the working cowpoke has developed a special lingo for the rodeo, which, like every other sport, has a language all its own and its technical terms may well prove puzzling to the "dudes" among us. So here are a few of the more common items in the jargon of the rodeo contestant:

Association saddle—Saddle adopted by the rodeo association and required in all official contests. It is designed so that, as the riders say, "it gives the horse all the best of it."

Blow a stirrup—To let the foot come out of the stirrup. In rodeo contests this disqualifies the rider.

Dally—In roping, to take a half hitch around the saddle horn, using the leverage thus obtained to loosen or take up on the rope, as the situation demands.

Git-up end—A horse's hind end.

Notch in his tail—Used of a man-killing bronc who has, like gunfighters notching the handles of their six-shooters, put a *notch in his tail* for each man he has killed.

Op'ry house—The top rail of the breaking corral, where ranch hands sit and watch the *buster* at work.

Pile driver—A horse that, in bucking, comes down with all four legs stiff.

Scratching—With boots and spurs raking the forequarters of the horse. In bronc-riding contests, under rodeo rules, each entrant must *come out scratching.*

And when a cowboy talks about his *John B.* and *hair pants* he means his sombrero and chaps. When you stop to think about it, *hair pants* is a perfectly simple and straightforward description of the ornamental angora-hide chaps worn by cowboys as sort of dress uniform. The *John B.* comes from the first part of the name of the John B. Stetson Company of Philadelphia, who made the best broad-brimmed hats known in the early West.

cowpoke, as a synonym for "cowboy," owes its origin to the simple, rather prosaic, fact that a lot of cowboys rode trains, not horses. Their job was to walk along the line of cattle cars whenever the train stopped and poke the steers through the open slats to make sure they were alive and standing up. They jabbed the cattle with a steel-tipped prod—and that's where the range expression "on the prod" came from. This particular part of the cowboy's job was dirty, tiring and dull. As a result, tempers were short and flare-ups were common among the cowpokes. So a cowhand who's "on the prod" is one that's mean, ornery and looking for trouble.

cowslip is a pretty plant of the primrose family, with large yellow flowers. It is sometimes called the "marsh marigold." One of its characteristics is that it may grow wild in fields or meadows. Its name in Middle English was *cowslyppe,* meaning "cow dung," from the frequent appearance of the flower in fields where cows graze.

Coxey's Army was an army of jobless workers organized in 1894 to march on Washington to get the government to provide public-works employment for victims of the financial panic and depression of 1893. It was led by an Ohioan named Jacob S. Coxey, self-styled "general," and numbered about five hundred marchers.

cozen. If someone tries to *cozen* you, his aim is to cheat or deceive, especially in a petty fashion. To the French, who gave us the word from their *cousiner,* he is trying to act like a cousin and mislead you through a claim of relationship.

c.q. In a death notice in a weekly paper, *c.q.* was printed in small letters after the name of the deceased. The *c.q.* in this use has a meaning, but its appearance in the paper was an error. The symbols originally represented the sounds (dah-dit-dah-dit-dah-dah-dit-dah) used by radio operators at the start of transmission. This *c.q.* alerts other listening operators that a message is to follow. As used by proofreaders, however, it is a warning to typesetters that a spelling that seems unusual or even erroneous is to be followed because, despite its appearance, it is correct. For example, if a first name had the unusual spelling "Lilyan," a copy editor might well follow it with *c.q.* in parentheses or encircled as a signal to the typesetter to follow copy. The error, in this case, was that the *c.q.* itself was set into type.

This reminds us of the ancient proofroom legend of the zealous and now lamented proofreader so devoted to his task that he followed copy—even when it blew out the window.

cracked up to be. A well-established colloquial usage is *crack up,* meaning to extol or praise highly. Also we often use the adjective *crack*—as in *crack shot*—to mean some person or thing that is absolutely at the top of its class. So when you say that something isn't what it is *cracked up to be,* you merely mean that it doesn't merit the high reputation it has obtained. The first recorded use of the phrase in this country appears in Davy Crockett's direct and candid comment on a fellow politician who at the time was far better known than Crockett but who has since become one of the forgotten men of American politics. "Martin Van Buren," wrote Davy in 1835, "is not the man he's *cracked up to be.*" History has certainly supported his verdict.

cracklin'. For all his occasional boastfulness, Davy Crockett had moments of earnest and becoming modesty. Once, drawing on the vocabulary of his native Tennessee, he remarked, "I looked like a pretty *cracklin'* ever to get to Congress!" *Cracklin'* in this sense has nothing to do with the *crack up* discussed above. *Cracklings* are the bits of crisp rind left after lard has been rendered, usually by frying. Esteemed by Southern epicures—especially when used in *cracklin' bread*—they remain a relatively unimportant by-product and Davy's estimate of himself as a pretty *cracklin'* is one that few Americans would accept.

cradle board/papoose board. The over-the-shoulder baby carriers popular with young mothers are very similar to the devices used by Indian women, who called them *cradle boards* or *papoose boards.* One difference: the Indian mothers wrapped the babies in skins and then laced them onto the *cradle boards.*

crambo, a word familiar to few others than Scrabble players, is the name of a word-rhyming game. Its origin is found in the Latin word *crambe* (cabbage) and more particularly in the Latin phrase *crambe repetita* (cabbage served repeatedly).

craps. This game, played by rolling two dice, gets its name from one of two sources—both of them firmly embedded in the Creole French of Louisiana.

The more colorful theory has it that a Creole gambler named Bernard Marigny but nicknamed Johnny Crapaud introduced the game in New Orleans about 1800. Known first as "Crapaud's game," the label was soon shortened to *craps.*

Incidentally, in taking the name Johnny Crapaud, Marigny was using the generic name given to French soldiers by British soldiers in the Napoleonic Wars—very much the way Confederates were called "Johnny Reb" and soldiers in World War II were "G.I. Joe." Since soldiers have been known to shoot craps ever since Roman soldiers diced for Christ's robe, it's entirely possible that *craps* came into the language as a soldier's corruption of Crapaud.

A more scholarly theory of the origin traces it to the French word *crabs* or *craps,* which was the term for the lowest possible throw in an obsolete dice game called "hazard." Since the term *craps,* or "crap out," is still used to indicate the lowest possible throw (two) in the contemporary game, the latter theory seems more sound, if less colorful.

And, not in order to encourage low living among our readers but to satisfy the curiosity of the few of you who may be as yet untutored in the niceties of this game, here are the rules. A first throw of 7 or 11 wins whatever stakes have been pledged. A first throw of 2, 3 or 12 loses the bet. A first throw of any other number (your "point") must be repeated before a 7 is rolled, for that will cost you not only the bet but the possession of the dice.

cravat. The original *cravats* were simply scarves worn around the necks of Croatian mercenary soldiers serving in Austria some four centuries or more ago. The word itself was originally *Khrvat,* a native of Croatia, and that, in case you have forgotten your geography, was a region of southeastern Europe on the northeastern coast of the Adriatic. Along about 1636, the French army set up a regiment of light cavalry, dressed in elegant imitation of the Croatians' uniforms, including fancy *cravats.* The fashion was quickly adopted by the fancy dressers of Paris—and men have been doomed to wear *cravats* or neckties ever since.

craven. The evolution of the word *craven* as a synonym for "cowardly or excessively afraid" hints that the derivation is based on the figurative rattling of the bones of a coward. This word is found in Middle English and Old French as *cravant,* which in turn evolved from the Latin *crepare,* meaning "to rattle, crack or creak."

crazy as a bedbug. How does it happen that people say So-and-so is *crazy as a bedbug?* Are bedbugs any crazier than other bugs? Quite to the contrary. We called a local exterminator, thinking he'd be an authority on the subject, and he told us that they are among the brightest bugs around. Ingenious, too. When one sets pots of water at each bedpost to act as a sort of midnight moat, the pesky things climb to the ceiling and drop down to the bed. However, he added, they are rapidly being eliminated in most parts of the country by the, entomologically speaking, lethal sprays.

Stopped by "entomological"? Well, sit still a minute for the favorite joke of dictionary editors. "Pop," says the lad, "what's an etymologist?" "Son," answers learned father, "an etymologist is a man who knows the difference between an etymologist and an entomologist."

What's an entomologist? Simple. A bug expert.

credence (pronounced KREE-d'ns), from the Latin *credere* (to trust or believe), is applied usually to the claims or statements of another person. You can *give credence to* or *have credence in* or *place credence in* his statements. Any such expression shows that you believe him. At the same time, it is possible for circumstances or proven facts to *lend credence to* what he says.

creep/give you the creeps. The simplest definition of a *creep* is that he or she is a person who *gives you the creeps*—and that phrase has been in our language since about 1860. Originally *the creeps* signified an unpleasant sensation of things creeping over one's body. In this sense the *Oxford Dictionary* labels it "colloquial."

The label *creep* first appeared during the 1930s, and it was undeniably an unflattering designation. Like many other slang terms, it turned up first in the jargon of show business. Definitions range from "stupid and tiresome person" to "objectionable . . . a drip . . . a wet blanket."

A conversation between Quentin Reynolds and Heywood Broun, in 1938, went like this:

Broun: What is this thing called *creep?*

Reynolds: Why, a *creep's* a *creep.* If you don't know when you meet one, I'm afraid I can't describe the species for you.

Broun: But how am I to decide?

Reynolds: Any sensitive person can't be mistaken. The knowledge comes to you through a kind of curdling sensation in the marrow of your bones.

cricket. At a meeting of the celebrated New York Dutch Treat club, the Right Honorable Lord Bancroft demonstrated that though the British may have lost their empire, they still retain their wit. *"Cricket,"* according to Lord Bancroft's definition, "is a game which the British—not being a spiritual people—had to invent in order to have some conception of eternity." Later, referring to some of his own experiences in international diplomacy, Lord Bancroft described himself as an expert in "dentopedology—the art of opening your mouth and putting your foot in it."

crocodile tears. The *crocodile* was a favorite figure in ancient Greek and Egyptian folklore. Indeed, its name comes directly from the Greek *krokodeilos.* The legend was that this giant lizard attracted its victims by loud moaning and then shed tears while it devoured them.

crowbar. The crowbar is a handy tool with which you can pry almost anything loose. Most crowbars are wedge-shaped at one end, but the other end is in the form of a two-pronged fork which someone, somewhere along the way, thought resembled the foot of a crow.

crust, in expressions like "He has some *crust,*" meaning he is very brash, bold or uppity, is somewhat dated slang. Newer items like "chutzpah" (which see), borrowed from Yiddish, are in greater vogue today. The way *crust* got this special sense is that it indicated a callous disregard for other people's feelings—an imperviousness that resembled the hard crust on some people's pies.

crying towel originated as part of army slang during World War II. It appeared most frequently in the phrase "Get out the *crying towel* for him," said in derision about a chronic complainer. Every unit, no matter how small, had its gripers, for whom calamity was either in the near offing or right at hand. Most soldiers and sailors had nothing but contempt for these chronic complainers, so the cry "Toss him the *crying towel*" was often heard in barracks.

The idea of providing a towel for the complainer to dry his tears may have come from the custom of tossing a towel into the prize-fight ring to indicate that the manager of one of the fighters conceded his defeat.

cryogenics/Cryovac. *Cryogenics* is the branch of physics that concerns itself with extremely low temperatures. At one time it was known as *cryogeny,* but the *-ics* ending is currently standard. The *cry-* part comes from *kryos,* the Greek word for "cold" or "frost." *Genics,* is, of course, from the same Greek root as "generate." The prefix also appears in such terms as "cryotherapy," the use of cold to reduce temperatures in certain forms of illness. There is even a packaging material much used for poultry and other meats called *Cryovac.* This is a combination of Greek and Latin roots, *cryo* (cold) and *vac* (from "vacuum"). The *Cryovac* method involves creating a partial vacuum in a plastic bag while freezing the meat, and though the blending of Greek and Latin in a single word may horrify linguists, the method itself seems to work just fine.

cubbyhole/cuddy. A small closet beneath the stairs—too small for a grown person to stand in—is called a *cubbyhole.* A sloop's small cabin—not high enough to stand in—is called a *cuddy.* There is a close relationship between *cuddy* and *cubby,* both of which come from the same Anglo-Saxon word, *cofa,* meaning "cave or cell." As a matter of fact, the word *cuddy* in British dialect means not only a small cabin aboard ship but any kind of small closet. In other words, *cuddy* and *cubbyhole* not only have the same root but are virtually synonymous. Since *cubbyhole* was originally a word used by British children, it's possible that the two were originally the same and the variant developed, as so often happens, from a child's mispronunciation.

cue in/clue in. We have heard the expression *Cue me in* for many years and suspect that it probably originated in theatrical jargon. In our time in the theater, actors in rehearsal were forever looking for an unoccupied prop man or fellow actor to *cue* them in their lines.

The expression *Clue me in,* however, first came to our attention in the early 1950s. It probably started as a variant form of *Cue me in,* with the *clue* gaining quick currency with teen-agers because of the popularity of crime and detection shows like *Dragnet.*

Perhaps the simplest explanation of the difference between the two phrases today may be given in the slang of teensters themselves. Most of them would regard *clue you in* as *hip,* while *cue you in* is *square,* the kind of talk used by *prehistorics* (anyone over twenty).

culpable. From the Latin root *culpa* (blame) *culpable* gets its meaning of "deserving of censure, blameworthy."

cummerbunds were first adapted by British colonial officials from an item of native Indian dress. Originally the Hindustani word for loincloth was *kamarband.* Later the word was applied to a sash worn around the waist and eventually it came to mean the sort of demiwaistcoat worn as a part of formal dress today.

cupboard love is love that has more than a bit of self-interest involved. It can best be described as the love of a child for an older person who may be in a position to gratify its whims with presents of delicacies from her cupboard.

cup of tea/dish of tea. One often hears the expression *not my cup of tea* or *not my dish of tea.* It has long been common in the British Isles, where tea —properly brewed—is the favorite drink. *Not my cup (or dish) of tea* simply means "not what I would want."

curfew. No one knows when the first *curfew* took place, for the custom was common throughout Europe during the Middle Ages. At that time the danger of fire spreading through a village or town was obviously very great, so at a given hour of night a signal—usually a loud bell—was sounded, warning all citizens to put out their fires. The word *curfew* comes direct from the French *couvre feu* (cover the fire). Legend has it that the practice was introduced into England by William the Conqueror, as a method of political repression, but there seems little evidence to support this theory.

curry favor is a variation (or "corruption," to use the technical term) of the Middle English expression *to curry Favel.* Favel was a chestnut horse in a medieval satire called *Roman de Favel,* which was a sort of parallel of the better-known fable of "Reynard the Fox." Favel, sometimes spelled Fauvel, was a symbol of cunning duplicity. Therefore, anyone *currying Favel* would be trying to gain favor by resorting to duplicity, especially insincere flattery.

curvaceous a blend of "curve" and "-aceous," and means "characterized by curves."

cut a dido. No one knows for sure where the expression *cut a dido* originated.

The first recorded appearance of this phrase was in the early nineteenth century and it may well be the forerunner of such common phrases as today's *cutting up* or *He's a great cut-up.* All these expressions, of course, have to do with pranks and pranksters.

One theory—and it's as good as any—is that the *dido* of this phrase was the legendary queen of Carthage, the same who committed suicide when Aeneas broke off their love affair and sailed for home in one of the more touching episodes of Vergil's *Aeneid.* When Dido was a young princess, newly come to Africa, she made a deal with the natives whereby she bought a piece of land that could be enclosed by a bull's hide. After the deal had been agreed on, she cut the hide into one continuous hair-thin thread— long enough to encompass a huge tract of land. According to legend, this land later became the walled city of Carthage. So Dido was the first—but assuredly not the last—real estate operator to *cut a dido* on some unwary landowners.

cutlass came into English from the French *coutelas,* which in turn came from the Latin *cultellus,* meaning "knife." This source also gave us the common word *cutlery* and the currently less common *cutler,* which survives today chiefly as a proper name but once was widely used to designate a person who made or sharpened knives and scissors for a living.

cut off your nose to spite your face appeared first in the writings (in Latin) of Peter of Blois, a French churchman who served in England in the court of Henry II. The expression finally made its way into English by 1796, when Francis Grose put this item into his *Classical Dictionary of the Vulgar Tongue:* "He cut off his nose to be revenged to his face. Said of one who, to be revenged of his neighbor, has materially injured himself."

cut of his jib. If you judge a man by the *cut of his jib,* you are basing your judgment on his general appearance, manner or way of doing things. Here is a term which goes back to the days of sailing ships, when a skipper would try to identify an oncoming vessel by the rigging of the *jib,* a triangular sail which projected ahead of the foremast. Each nation had its own peculiar —and recognizable—way of cutting and rigging the jib. A pirate ship would have a still different *cut of the jib*—and if the skipper didn't like the *cut of the jib,* he would change course to avoid the other ship.

cut prices. Anyone who purchases fuel for his automobile is aware of one little item that all gas companies have in common. The price always ends in .9 cents. The genius who devised this method of pricing may well be the same Mr. Anonymous who prices canned goods in supermarkets, four for 97 cents, so that you have to pay 25 cents for a single can. We asked a somewhat rhetorical question about who first had the idea of pricing items at odd figures like 98 cents instead of a dollar. Wilfred Payne of the Municipal University of Omaha tells us that J. C. Penney, founder of the Penney stores, did it not to lure customers seeking cut-rate bargains but to force his salespeople to ring up the sale on the cash register to get small change for the customer. Thus he ended the practice of dishonest clerks' simply pocketing the dollars.

cut the Gordian knot. This phrase means to solve an extremely complex problem with one simple brilliant action. It goes back to Phrygia, an ancient country in Asia Minor, where a peasant named Gordius was chosen king. To show his gratitude for the honor, he dedicated his wagon to Jupiter, then tied its yoke to a beam with a knot of bark, entwined so ingeniously that no one could untie it. Gradually the legend grew that whoever could untie the knot would become ruler of all Asia. When Alexander the Great passed through the town, now named Gordium, he studied the knot for a moment or two, then drew his sword and cut it in two.

cut the mustard was originally a Western expression, popular among cowboys during the late nineteenth century. If something was "the proper mustard," it was O.K., the genuine article. Andy Adams used the expression this way in his famous *Log of a Cowboy,* when he wrote that "for fear the two dogs were not the proper mustard, he had that dog man sue him in court to make him prove the pedigree." And Carl Sandburg once wrote: "Kid each other, you cheapskates. Tell each other you're all to the mustard." The expression *cut the mustard* then came into vogue, meaning to come up to expectations, to be of good quality. In one of his short stories, written around the turn of the century, O. Henry described a pretty girl in these words: "She *cut the mustard* all right." Nowadays the expression is usually used in the sense of being successful. Of a leading businessman, you might hear it said that "he really *cuts the mustard.*"

cut to the quick. Historically, both the noun *quick* and the adjective and adverb forms come from the same root, the Anglo-Saxon *cwicu,* meaning "alive or living." Thus the phrase "the *quick* and the dead," from the King James Bible, merely means the living and the dead. During the Middle Ages, farmers customarily referred to their herds of livestock as *quickstock* and a hedge was a *quickfence,* signifying that it was a growing thing as contrasted with a stone fence. Then, just as we have today such phrases as "look alive" and "step lively," the common folk began to use *quick* in phrases like "move *quickly*" and "she has a *quick* wit." Soon this usage became standard, as it has now been for many centuries. The phrase "You have *cut me to the quick*" is a holdover from the original meaning of the word. Literally, it means to cut through the skin to the living tissue; figuratively, "You have hurt my feelings."

cutty/cutty sark/cutty stool. *Cutty* is simply a Scottish dialect version of *cut* and means short or abbreviated. The Scots call their short shirts *cutty sarks.* Another common use of the word is in the phrase *cutty stool,* which was a short-legged bench in Scottish churches where sinners were required to sit while being publicly rebuked by the minister.

cynic. In ancient Greece, a *Cynic* was a member of a school of philosophers founded by Antisthenes, a pupil of Socrates. The *Cynics* held that virtue was the highest good and were contemptuous of worldly needs and pleasures. One of the most famous of the *Cynics* was Diogenes. The sect took its name from the Gymnasium (school) called *Cynosarges,* which in Greek meant "white dog," where Antisthenes and his pupils met. A white dog had once carried off part of a sacrifice which was being offered to Hercules in the school, hence the name. Since *Cynics* were extremely critical of the rest of society and were scornful of public opinion, the word came to mean anyone who questions the motives or actions of others.

cynosure (pronounced SY-nuh-shoor) is a remarkable word. Literally it means "a dog's tail"—hardly an object that a beautiful woman would like to be likened to. Here's how it comes about. The Greek word *kynosoura* (dog's tail) was used for the constellation of Ursa Minor, which includes the North Star. Navigators since the dawn of recorded history—and probably beyond—have used the North Star in plotting their courses. So *cynosure* became the point toward which all eyes are inevitably drawn and that, by extension, is why any person or thing that attracts widespread interest is called the *"cynosure* of all eyes."

Cynthia. Originally, *Cynthia* was one of the names of the Greek moon goddess, Artemis, and thus it means "of the moon." It was derived from Cynthus, a mountain in Delos which was the birthplace of Apollo and Artemis. The name is also closely associated with Diana, who, in the mythology of Rome, held a parallel position—as goddess of the moon, of hunting and virginity.

d. had considerable significance for many centuries in British-speaking countries because it was the abbreviation for "pence" or "pennies." This was the cause of some confusion to tourists, for the logical abbreviation for either of those words would be "p." The explanation is that the British abbreviation went all the way back to the days of the Roman occupation of Britain, when *d.* was the abbreviation for the Latin *denarius* and "L," the abbreviation for "pound," was short for *libra.*

Britain's monetary reform (1971) includes new values for pound, shilling and pence, with the new abbreviation "p." for pennies. And an end to the long-lived *d.*

dacoit is a word that, like "thug" and "assassin," we have borrowed from the Hindi language of India. It means a robber, especially one of a gang—generally consisting of at least five—who usually add physical assault to the crime of robbery. It's pronounced duh-KOIT.

dad is simply a baby-talk version of "father." It has appeared in similar form in every spoken language. In Greek and Latin it was "tata," in Old High German it was "todo" and in Welsh it is "tad." Just as "ma" or "mama" is the nearly universal child's name for its mother, so *dad,* with slight variations, means "father" everywhere.

dago/guinea/wop/nigger. All four terms are, of course, derogatory. If you hear *guinea* freely and almost affectionately used among people of Italian descent in your community, it's because they have reached a station in life where they can make fun of derogatory slurs that once much offended them. Thus an Irishman may label himself a *mick* with mock pride. So, too, the Jews are certainly at their storytelling best when telling anecdotes about members of their race that would be deeply insulting if coming from the lips of a non-Jew. Perhaps the most bitterly resented epithet in our nation is *nigger.* Yet the black comedian Dick Gregory used this derogatory term as the title of his autobiography, with the wry observation that "Now any time a white man says *nigger,* he's advertising my book."

The history of these epithets is cloudy. Each of them now means something other than it meant originally. *Guinea* originally meant a Negro from Guinea. When and how it became applied to Italians is unclear. *Wop* comes from the Italian dialect word *guappo,* meaning "a big, handsome fellow." And *dago* confused even the late, great George Lyman Kittredge of Harvard, who once wrote despairingly, "*Dago* is a queer misnomer. It must come from the Spanish *Diego,* yet is usually applied to Italians."

daguerreotype. The earliest form of photography that produced reasonably clear and lasting results was the *daguerreotype.* Pronounced duh-GAIR-uh-tipe, it was invented by Louis J. M. Daguerre in 1839. Though it was soon rendered obsolescent by newer photographic devices, a method similar to daguerreotyping was used by itinerant photographers at county fairs and the like until the Polaroid camera made the technique obsolete.

dahlia is a plant native to Mexico, with tuberous roots and variously colored flowers. It was named by Carolus Linnaeus, Swedish botanist and taxonomist after one of his pupils, Anders Dahl. See LINNEAN TAXONOMY.

dais, the name of a raised platform from which speakers may address audiences, comes to us from the Middle English *deis* and ultimately from the Latin *discus,* originally a platter but in Late Latin a table. It is pronounced DAY-is, though an astonishing number of otherwise literate people insist on calling it a DY-is. It is often confused with "podium," which, properly speaking, is a raised platform for a single speaker or performer, such as an orchestra conductor, and "podium," in turn, is often mistakenly used when "lectern"—a small reading stand, usually with a light—is intended.

damask. We suppose it's a betrayal of age to confess that we remember with delight Beatrice Lillie's incomparable rendition of the song about the dozen double damask dinner napkins—a high point in our memories of the musical comedy theater matched only by the same great lady's account of the fairies at the bottom of her garden and Noel Coward's account of mad dogs and Englishmen who go out in the midday sun. The *damask* in those napkins was, of course, the cloth and it took its name from the fact that in the Middle Ages *pannus di damasco* was already legendary as the most richly patterned linens and silks. Originally woven in Damascus, Syria, the patterns were imitated by French and Flemish weavers and finally introduced by the latter into England. And the "double" in Bea Lillie's song means a heavier, more finely woven cloth with the pattern showing through to the reverse side of the fabric.

Dan Cupid. The *Dan* in *Dan Cupid* is not so much a name as a title. Comparable to the Spanish *Don,* it was used as an honorific in the early days of English writing and meant "Sir" or "Master." Among the memorable lines of our early literature are these of Spenser saluting his most eminent predecessor: "Dan Chaucer, well of English undefiled,/On Fame's eternal beadroll worthy to be filed." Cupid, of course, was the Roman god of love.

dandelion. One of the most delightful books that has come our way is a lighthearted chronicle of an Italian-American family growing up in the New York of the 1930s and 1940s. Called *Love and Pasta,* it is the story of how Joe Vergara, its author, and his two brothers sought to explain America and its ways to their stubbornly "old-country" father. One problem, of course, was language. Vergara reports: "Around the house, Pop spoke his own personal language, a kind of fritto misto, including selected words from English and Italian. In the process, both vocabularies became enriched. Many Italian words crept unnoticed into his English speech—'giornale' (journal, newspaper), 'trene' (train), 'scuola' (school), 'ufficio' (office). . . . In the spirit of fair play he incorporated many English words into his Italian speech—'ice-a boax' (icebox, refrigerator), 'bashimento' (basement, cellar), 'bock-owsa' (backhouse, i.e., toilet)."

And from Pop Vergara we Morrises learned at least one interesting word origin. One of his sons finds him, as he thinks, weeding the lawn and asks why. " 'You call-a weeds!' exclaims Pop. 'Mamma mia, what you learn in American scuola—nothing? These we call dente di lione—how you say, teeth of the lion. Make-a best salad you ever taste.' And sure enough, that night we had dandelion salad."

daps is a word from the language of the black community. It refers to a rather elaborate and ceremonial greeting between soul brothers, involving the slapping of hands in ritualistic fashion and ending with a semiembrace. It's an extension of the hand-slapping procedure common among blacks a couple of decades ago following the salutation "Slip me some skin, brother."

Darby and Joan were an elderly couple whose devotion to each other was immortalized in a ballad published in 1735. Since then writers of lyrics have used the pair as symbols of beautiful and steadfast love, though the original version was something less than idyllic. Here's how the author Henry Woodfall described the romantic duo: "Old Darby with Joan at his side,/You've often regarded with wonder;/He's dropsical, she is sore-eyed,/Yet they're ever uneasy asunder."

dark and bloody ground. This name for Kentucky is widely and mistakenly thought to refer to the battles fought there during the Civil War. Since Kentucky was a border state, with strong sentimental attachments to the South and equally strong commercial ties to the North, many families were rent by the conflict and what has been called "The Brothers' War" was an epithet literally true there.

However, the *dark and bloody ground* epithet long antedates the Civil War. Indeed, it is thought by some to go back in time even to the period before the white man ever saw Kentucky. In the words of Henry L. Mencken (*American Language,* Supp. II, 627), the phrase "alluded, not to battles between Indians and the first white settlers, but to contests between Northern and Southern tribes of Indians."

dark horse comes from horse racing, obviously, and refers to a long shot, a relatively unknown contender in any kind of competition.

Darwin's Bulldog was a nickname for Thomas Henry Huxley, the most brilliant and fervent defender in nineteenth-century England of Charles Darwin's theory of evolution. Huxley greatly enjoyed debating fellow members of the British Association for the Advancement of Science (popularly called the "British Ass") in defense of Darwin. Indeed, he told Darwin: "Get on with your work and leave the wrestling to me."

Davis Cup, emblematic of the team championship of what used to be known as amateur tennis, was established in 1900 by Dwight F. Davis, himself a one-time U.S. national doubles champion. For most of the years since its establishment, the cup has shuttled between the United States, Great Britain and Australia, though for one five-year period (1927–1932), during the great years of Borotra, Lacoste and Cochet, France was its custodian. As an international symbol of athletic prowess, the Davis Cup ranks with The Ashes and the America's Cup (which see).

Davy Jones' locker is nautical jargon for the ocean's depths. There are a lot of theories about the original Davy Jones. We'll pass them on to you and let you take your pick. The first is that the legend is based on Jonah's maritime excursion in the belly of the whale. The trouble with that idea is that Jonah survived his ordeal and wound up not in *Davy Jones' locker* but on dry land, unharmed, three days after his watery adventure began.

Second theory: A London pubkeeper named Davy Jones catered to sailors. He was believed to keep more than just ale in the lockers in the rear of the pub. Indeed, there were those who thought his pub was just a front for shanghaiing unwary seamen—giving them knockout drops from which they would awaken only after the ship they had been shanghaied to was well at sea. So, goes that story, sailors would have plenty of reason to fear *Davy Jones' locker.*

Another theory is that the expression started with West Indian sailors because there is a word *duppy,* meaning "devil" in their dialect. This we find hard to believe—not nearly as plausible as the idea that Davy Jones was a fearsome pirate who was not above making uncooperative captives walk the plank. That's the theory we favor.

One thing we can say with certainty is that *Davy Jones' locker* has been part of sailor slang for more than two centuries. Tobias Smollet wrote in 1751: "Davy Jones is the fiend that presides over all the evil spirits of the deep."

days of the week. Sunday is taken from the Anglo-Saxon *sunnan daeg,* day of the sun. Monday is from *monan daeg,* day of the moon. Tuesday is *Tiwes daeg,* the day of Tiw, god of war. Wednesday is *Wodnes daeg,* the day of Woden, chief deity. Thursday comes from the Old Norse *Thorsdagr,* Thor's Day. Friday is from *Frigedaeg,* the day of the goddess Frig, wife of Woden. Saturday was *Saeterdaeg,* day of Saturn, Roman god of agriculture.

D.C./D.F. *D.C.* is known to every American as the abbreviation for District of Columbia. Less familiar is *D.F.,* which appears in Mexico City addresses. This is the abbreviation for Distrito Federal, and indicates that the capital city of Mexico, like the capital city of the United States, is a federal district.

D-day. The *D* in *D-day* has so simple an explanation that it's perhaps not surprising that so few people know it. It simply stands for "day," so *D-Day* literally means "Day-day." The term was first used in World War I, as the code designation for the Allied offensive at Saint-Mihiel. The most important D-day was June 6, 1944, the day Allied forces began their invasion of Western Europe.

dead as a doornail is an expression most of us learned first in Dickens's *A Christmas Carol.* Actually, it's much older than that, having appeared in the fourteenth-century *Vision of Piers Plowman* and in Shakespeare's *Henry IV,* Part 2. Until now all word experts—including us—have been explaining that the doornail referred to is the heavy stud in the middle of a wooden door against which a knocker is struck. Since this happens many thousands of times—with a well-exercised knocker, at any rate—the doornail may well be considered "dead" from the abuse it takes.

Ha, ha, says William Wagner of Falls Church, Virginia. It's pretty obvious that you experts on words are not experts on carpentry. "The dictionary," he writes, "defines a doornail as 'a large-headed nail, easily clinched, for nailing doors, through the battens.' Now the 'clinching' makes the nail 'dead.' It cannot be easily withdrawn. 'Dead-nailing' is a term most any carpenter is familiar with. It is a technique frequently used in constructing doors for log cabins, construction shanties and the like—and it antedates the ready availability of screws and more sophisticated fastening devices. It would seem that you have gone somewhat far afield to explain a phrase derived from the simple action of bending the end of a nail to provide a secure fastening."

Far afield indeed have we wandered. And thanks to you, Mr. Wagner, for spiking the old story, which we hereby label—you should forgive the expression—*dead as a doornail.* The dickens with it!

dead men's prices. As struggling young painters know, many artists do not have their worth recognized during their lifetime and it is only after they are dead and gone that their paintings sell for much more than a pittance. Hence *dead men's prices.*

debacle came to us direct from the French. Originally it was a geologist's term meaning the sudden breaking up of ice in a river. At the time of an early spring thaw, a sudden breaking of the ice may cause a violent rush of water, bearing with it stones and other debris, making a *debacle.* This technical term was later applied, about 1850, in a figurative sense to any catastrophic rout or stampede. Recently its meaning has been extended still further to cover any great catastrophe.

debilitate (pronounced dih-BIL-ih-tayt) is easily traced to the Latin. Coming from the word *debilitare* (to weaken, make feeble), it carries the same meaning into English usage. "The prisoner was *debilitated* by his long hunger strike."

debt. It's something of a pity that we can't change the spelling to "det," because that was the way it was originally spelled, way back at the time of the Norman Conquest. The English borrowed the word from the French *dette,* knocked off the last two letters and wound up with "det." So far so good. But then a century or so later medieval scholars began tampering with the word, and thinking that it had come from the Latin *debita,* inserted the *b.* In those days, before Gutenberg had invented the printing press, the monks in their priestly cloisters had practically complete control of the way language was "writ down."

debunk. William E. Woodward is generally credited with creating the word *debunk* in a novel titled *Bunk,* which exposed the pretentiousness in the family and social life of a wealthy automobile-maker. Woodward later *debunked* George Washington (here Parson Weems's cherry-tree legend went into the discard), General Grant, Lafayette and other historical figures. Quite a band of imitators, noting the popularity of these "unvarnished" biographies, which reflected the twenties' mood of cynicism, delightedly took up the task of exposing all the petty aspects in the careers of our great men. On the whole, the movement was probably a healthy one: the truly great figures of our past suffered no permanent damage and a few who had been extolled beyond their true importance were reduced to proper stature. Biography today is generally candid, less given to glossing over minor defects of a subject's character, than was the case before the debunkers enjoyed their brief turn in the spotlight. See also BUNK.

decapitate is a less dramatic version of the Queen of Hearts' dictum "Off with their heads!" in *Alice in Wonderland*. It comes from the Latin *caput* (head) and *de-* (off).

December. The twelfth month in the year takes its name from the Latin word *decem* (ten), because it was the tenth month in the Roman calendar.

decimate is a word we borrowed from the Romans. One of their quaint habits, after winning a battle, was to line up the remaining enemy soldiers, choose one out of each ten by lot and kill him. Thus one tenth of the enemy was *decimated*—from the Latin *decem* (ten).

déclassé. It is not uncommon for a once-elegant hotel to become *déclassé* because of poor upkeep or a change in the character of the neighborhood. *Déclassé,* originally a French word, simply means that a person or thing has lost the class or social status it once enjoyed.

deep six seems to have two meanings, each quite final in its own way. In sailors' lingo it means "to drown," the *six* being six fathoms deep. In general slang of the past two decades it has come to mean simply a grave.

Defender of the Faith is a title borne by British kings and queens since 1521. There's more than a little irony in it, since it was first bestowed by Pope Leo X on Henry VIII in thanks for a treatise he wrote attacking Martin Luther. Then Henry himself strayed off the reservation—taking a few extra wives with him—and the papacy had second thoughts about the matter. So Pope Paul III rescinded the title—only to have the British Parliament hastily restore it. So since 1544 British monarchs have continued to proclaim themselves *Defenders of the Faith*—even though it's a faith slightly different from the one for which the title was originally intended.

defend to the death your right to say it. The version used by the old *New York World* on its editorial page was: "I do not agree with a word that you say, but I will defend to the death your right to say it." Generally attributed to Voltaire, this statement does not appear verbatim in his published works. The closest he came was in this letter to Madame du Deffand: "I disapprove of what you say, but I will defend to the death your right to say it." Apparently even this quotation was actually a paraphrase by one of Voltaire's biographers (S. G. Tallentyre) of these words from Voltaire's *Essay on Tolerance:* "Think for yourself and let others enjoy the privilege to do so, too."

defenestration comes from the Latin *fenestra* (window) and *de-* (out of). It means the act of throwing or jumping out of windows. As one social commentator, writing about the stock market crash of 1929, remarked wryly: "In Wall Street *defenestration* reached a new high." In the 1970s the head of the United Fruit Company conglomerate *defenestrated* himself spectacularly from a midtown New York City skyscraper when exposure of illegal financial manipulations seemed imminent.

deign/disdain. *Deign* (pronounced DAYN), like *dignity,* stems from the Latin *dignus* (worthy) and originally meant "to think something worthy of doing" in the sense of being consistent with one's dignity. In general usage it has the meaning of condescending to do something, of lowering oneself to act. The word *disdain* (originally spelled "disdeign") is no longer the direct opposite of *deign,* but now has the meaning of to scorn or to look upon with contempt. *Deign* can be used as either a transitive or an intransitive verb, as "He did not *deign to* come" or "He would not *deign* an answer." *Disdain,* always transitive as a verb, is also a noun.

Delaware was named for Thomas West, Baron De La Warr, a British colonial governor who never even saw the state or the river that bears his name. De La Warr was actually colonial governor of Virginia and visited that colony in 1610. The British claimed that the coast north to what they named the De La Warr Bay was part of their Virginia colony. The Dutch paid no attention, however, claiming it as theirs because of Hudson's explorations. Just to complicate things further, the Swedes were the first to establish a permanent colony in what is now the state of Delaware—but the old baron's name stuck.

delenda est Carthago. As every schoolchild used to know, and few do today, this was the phrase with which Cato the Elder concluded each speech he made in the Roman Senate. In his way he must have been as much of a bore as some of our own solons who repeat themselves year after year. His message was plain, though: Carthage must be destroyed so that it can no longer be a menace to Rome's empire. He maintained his preachments to the end of his career and in time, of course, Carthage was destroyed—in 146 B.C. However, Cato the Censor (as he also was called, because of his opposition to the acceptance of Greek luxuries and vices by the Romans) died three years too soon to see his challenge vindicated.

deleterious/delete. *Deleterious* (pronounced del-uh-TEER-ee-us) means injurious in the sense of being pernicious, detrimental to health or life. Some authorities believe it to be derived from the Greek word of almost the same spelling, *deleterios,* which means "to injure." Others give it the same origin as *delete,* which is the Latin *deletus,* past participle of *delere,* "to blot out or destroy."

demographics is a very big word in the communications industry but little used elsewhere. Briefly put, demography is a science (some would say "pseudoscience") which studies the size, growth potential, density and other characteristics of the population of a given area. On the basis of the statistics thus gathered, a "demographic profile" of a community, state or country can be drawn. These profiles are relied on heavily by advertisers and TV programmers in planning ad campaigns and designing TV programs to appeal to the broadest possible audience or, conversely, to zero in on a limited special-interest audience. *Demographics* comes from two Greek words: *demos,* "people," and *graphein,* "to write."

denigrate most commonly means "to defame," but its basic meaning is "to blacken," either literally or figuratively. *Denigration* may be of one's character or of one's flesh, as a bruise darkens after physical injury. It comes from the Latin *denigare,* meaning "to blacken."

dentophobia. From the Latin *dentis* (tooth) and the Greek *phobos* (fear), *dentophobia* acquires its meaning of fear of dentistry.

Denver sandwich is known in most parts of the country as simply the "Western" sandwich. It's a sort of small omelet with onions, green pepper and chopped ham, between slices of bread or toast. The guess here is that some Denver restaurateur, carried away by civic pride, renamed the sandwich in his town's honor.

derby/bowler. The *derby* hat, known in England as the *bowler* (which see), was named after the famous race held annually at Epsom Downs, England. The race, in turn, was named after the twelfth Earl of Derby. The American Kentucky Derby was named for its British counterpart.

de rigueur. That which is *de rigueur* (pronounced deh ree-GER) is a "must" —it is absolutely required by etiquette. Taken from the French, the phrase says that it would be unthinkable not to abide by the rules governing dress and conduct for certain occasions. When an invitation is formal, it is *de rigueur* that formal dress be worn by both ladies and gentlemen.

dernier cri/dernier ressort. Here we have three French words which make up two convenient phrases—and because they are convenient they have been adopted into English. *Dernier* is "latest or last"; *cri* is "cry"; *ressort* is "resort."

Hence, *dernier cri,* literally "the latest cry," is the latest fashion or the last word. Since all such "in" things are quickly replaced by another, *le dernier cri* is a fad that is apt to fade as quickly as it came. *Dernier ressort* is a last resort, as "He was determined to pawn his cameras only as a *dernier ressort.*"

derrick. The *derrick* that we see used to lift and move heavy objects has a very sinister origin indeed. The first *derrick* was a gallows invented in the early seventeenth century by the most notorious London hangman of the time, whose name was Derrick. See also GUILLOTINE.

derriere (pronounced deh-ree-AIR) is a word borrowed direct from French, where it has the meaning of "in back of or behind." It has had a degree of popularity, particularly among fashion writers, as a euphemism for backside, buttocks or rump.

derring-do means courage, willingness to take chances, daring to do something. The expression goes all the way back to the time of Chaucer, when the verb "dare" was spelled *durran* and "do" was *don.* Over the centuries these spellings changed slightly, with the *don* losing its *n* but with *durran,* now respelled "derring," sounding pretty much as it does today. What we have here is a case of a relatively little used word which, over the centuries, simply didn't change form as much as the more commonly used "dare."

derringer was the name for a pistol with a short barrel and large bore, reportedly the favorite weapon of self-defense of chorus girls in the Gay Nineties period. The name came from its inventor, American gunsmith Henry Deringer (one *r*), who made the first ones around 1850.

dese, dem and dose. Some people insist that the familiar *dese, dem and dose* are Polish idiom. Others maintain that these expressions are from Brooklyn's heritage of Dutch settlers. These exaggerated mispronunciations have long been associated in the public mind with the so-called Brooklyn accent. This is rather unfair to Brooklyn, where, as it happens, we lived for a couple of years. We did hear some extraordinary pronunciations while there. A newspaperwoman once spoke of a "toilet" as a "terlet." We thought she was kidding but realized in time that she was completely serious.

However, the *dese, dem, dose* syndrome is, we believe, the creation of writers like Damon Runyon, who, in an attempt to mirror the diverse and often strange accents of this metropolis, came up with a dialect that was clever and amusing but entirely artificial. So blame it on Runyon and his contemporaries, not on the poor long-gone Dutchmen.

desert/dessert. These two words—actually three—often cause confusion. *Dessert,* the last course in a meal, comes from the French *desservir,* and means the last course before "unserving," that is, taking the dishes off the table. Just *deserts* (pronounced like the meal-ending *dessert:* deh-ZERT) are what the villain gets. This *desert* means simply "what he deserves." The other *desert* is no relation to either word. It comes from the Latin *desertum,* meaning "that which has been abandoned," just as most *deserts* have been abandoned by living things.

Desert Rats were the British soldiers of the North African campaign of World War II. Like the Old Contemptibles (which see) of World War I, they took an epithet scornfully cast upon them by the enemy (in this case, by Benito Mussolini) and made it a badge of honor to be proudly borne into battle and ultimate victory. Their armored brigade even adopted divisional insignia showing a desert rat against a white background.

desideratum is from Latin and means "that which is agreed to be needed and wanted." Not every *desideratum* becomes a reality, however, as might be predicted by looking at the origin of the word. It comes from the Latin *desiderare,* meaning "to long for," which probably goes back to a combination of *de-,* meaning "from," and *sidus* or *sideris,* meaning "star."

desultory. If you think of *desultory* as meaning "erratic, disorganized, jumping from one thing to another," you are literally correct. It comes from the Latin *de-*, meaning "from," and *salire*, meaning "to jump." It can also mean "aimless or random."

détente (pronounced day-TAHNT) is a borrowing from what used to be the international language of diplomacy—French. It means a gradual easing of tension in a political situation where two great powers find themselves stalemated in what Washington calls "eyeball-to-eyeball" confrontation.

de trop. That which is *de trop* (pronounced deh TROH) is unwanted or superfluous. The literal meaning of this French phrase is "too much or too many."

deucer. Dictionary editors carefully enter *deuce* (from the French *deux* and Latin *duo*, both meaning "two") and give its meanings in card and dice playing, as well as in tennis. But they neglect *deucer*, which, in the popular tongue, has half a dozen meanings—a two-dollar bill being the most common. In underworld slang, it is a person serving a two-year term. Baseball players use *deucer* as meaning either a two-base hit or the second game of a doubleheader. In vaudeville and circus slang it's the second spot on the bill, and to racing enthusiasts it's the horse that finishes second.

deus ex machina (pronounced DAY-oos ex MAH-kee-nah) is a Latin phrase which is part of the language of the theater. When a Greek or Roman playwright got snarled up in a plot and couldn't work his way to the final curtain, he had a simple solution. He'd bring in one of the gods to straighten things out. This was the *deus ex machina*, literally the "god from a machine." The term is used nowadays to describe any tricky or improbable device used to unravel a plot.

devil's advocate originated in Roman Catholicism. A candidate for sainthood would be represented before the papal court by two spokesmen, the *advocatus diaboli* (devil's advocate), who would present every conceivable argument against canonization or beatification, and the *advocatus dei*, who would make as strong a case as possible in favor of canonization. Nowadays the term is widely used to describe any person who is usually found on the wrong or losing side in any controversy, especially one who takes such positions out of sheer cantankerousness.

devil's strip. Many communities come to feel that a particular idiom of colorful expression is restricted in use to their locality. A case in point is the term *devil's strip* for the grass strip between sidewalk and curb which seemed to be used only in Akron, Ohio. At least that was the claim made by an Akron reader. Later, other readers reported having heard it in Toledo and other parts of Ohio—but it still seemed a very local idiom.

Then, however, came word of the use of *devil's strip* in a somewhat different connection many years ago in Canada. "When I was a mere lad, in 1906," wrote Leighton M. Long of Bowling Green, Ohio, "my folks moved from off the farm to the city of Toronto. As you probably know,

Toronto is famous for its surface cars. I can recall very vividly being warned that when crossing the street I must be careful not to get caught on the *devil's strip*. This was the center path between street cars going in opposite directions. The cars passed so close to each other that there was simply no standing room between them. At that time Toronto was populated mainly by immigrants from England, Ireland and Scotland, so very likely the name *devil's strip* may have originated in the auld country."

Well, that's an interesting new light on this colorful expression. And it's a reminder that much of the vigor is being drained from our language. The similar strip of grass and concrete separating the two halves of the Connecticut Turnpike, for example, is known as the median divider. How dull that is by contrast to *devil's strip!*

dexterous is one of several words in the language that indicate a prejudice for right-handed persons and against left-handed ones. Derived from the Latin *dexter*, which simply means "right," *dexterous* now has the meaning of skillful, while *sinister* (from the identical Latin word for "left") means today ominous or evil. See also GAUCHE, SINISTER.

diagnosis/prognosis are two terms from the language of medicine that occasionally trip up the layman. The first, *diagnosis*, means the act of deciding, on the basis of analyzing symptoms, what disease is affecting the patient. It comes, like most medical language, from Greek, specifically from *dia* (between) and *gignoskein* (to know). The *prognosis* follows the *diagnosis*. It is the prediction made by a physician of the course and probable termination of the disease. It has the same root as *diagnosis*, of course, and the prefix *pro* means "before." Thus a *prognosis* is a "knowing before"—or prediction.

dicey is a borrowing from British slang. Roughly synonymous with "chancy," it was first popularized by RAF pilots in World War II, a gallant lot who went out on many a *dicey* mission.

"dictionaries are like watches," said Dr. Samuel Johnson, as quoted by Mrs. Piozzi in her *Anecdotes of Johnson*. "The worst is better than none, and the best cannot be expected to go quite true."

Die hard. The Fourth Battalion, Queen's Regiment, of the British Army has been known as "The Diehards," because their commanding officer at the battle of Albuera (1811), though himself badly wounded, called out to his men: "Die hard, my men, die hard." Though this is the most celebrated example of the use of this expression, the *Encyclopaedia Britannica* reports the death of George Washington thus: "He faced the end with characteristic solemnity, saying: 'I die hard but I'm not afraid to go.' "

die in harness. The idea of continuing in one's chosen line of work until death is not a very fashionable one in these days of enforced retirement, social security, Medicare, senior citizens' homes and the like. But time was when that was the way things usually worked out and when, moreover, there was a certain pride to be had in the thought of *dying in harness.* The idea was given most vivid expression, perhaps, by Shakespeare when Macbeth (Act V, Scene 5) says: "Blow wind! come wrack!/At least we'll die with harness on our back."

die is cast. There is a widely held misconception that this expression means that a die or pattern has been cast in metal to make a mold which cannot be changed unless melted and recast. The true explanation—that *the die is cast* refers to the casting of dice, as in shooting craps—is supported by centuries of evidence. Specifically, according to the *Oxford Dictionary, die* and *dice* as items used in games of chance appeared in print as early as 1548, while *die* and *dies* as molds in metalworking didn't appear until nearly 1700.

We can also call Shakespeare to testify. In *Richard III,* first performed in 1592, appear these lines: "I have set my life upon the cast,/And I will stand the hazard of the die."

When Caesar decided to cross the Rubicon (and that's a phrase in itself, of course) he is supposed to have said, *"Jacta alea est"* ("The dice have been thrown" or *"The die is cast"*). He was referring, in terms of the common game of dice, to having made an irrevocable decision. All his future would stand or fall on the results of that fateful judgment. In Caesar's case, the Rubicon was a river separating his province of Cisalpine Gaul from Italy. Once he crossed that river and marched on Rome with his troops, he became an invader, starting the civil war which in time brought him to power.

Dieu et mon droit. The British royal family's motto literally means "God and my right." It was reportedly first uttered by Richard the Lion-Hearted at the Battle of Gisors in 1198—though it did not become the royal motto until much later, during the reign of Henry VI. Richard's meaning was that he—as King of England—ruled by the mandate of God and owed no fealty to the French against whom he was warring. Incidentally, the British won the battle.

diffident (pronounced DIF-uh-d'nt) is the adjective form of the word *diffidence,* which is a combination of two Latin words, *dis-* (not) and *fidere* (to trust). We can literally and accurately translate *diffidence* as lacking in trust in oneself. Substitute the prefix *con-* (with) for the prefix *dis-,* and you have *confidence* or, again literally, "faith in oneself."

digger, an affectionate nickname for Australian and New Zealand servicemen, is more than a hundred years old, having first been applied to settlers in Australia who went there to dig for gold.

digs/diggings. These casual terms for one's quarters, especially the sort of small flat or apartment kept by a bachelor, are reported in *Brewer's Dictionary of Phrase and Fable* as an importation from California "and its gold diggings." This is one of the rare occasions when we have caught Brewer out, so to speak, because the *Oxford Dictionary* reports the word in print in England as early as 1838, whereas the first California gold strike was at Sutter's Mill ten years later. In any event, the term is, as the dictionaries say, "chiefly British."

dingbat is an odd little term, little more than a century old but already with a variety of meanings. Its most general use is as a sort of synonym for *thingamajig, doohickey* or *doodad* (see GADGET). It also has the more restricted meaning of any small object that can be thrown easily, and printers use it to mean any of a variety of typographical ornaments not easy to describe precisely. As you can see, the various definitions of *dingbat* are rather broad-gauged and cover a variety of characteristics, which may well be the reason why the best-remembered of all the long line of Morris family cats was one named Dingbat. She was a calico cat, wearing the proverbial coat of many colors. An eccentric of the wildest order, she was predictable only in her profligacy and in the profusion of her progeny.

In Australia, incidentally, delirium tremens—or even an acute hangover —is known as *the dingbats.*

Dinky goes back to the early days of railroading, when it was the name for the engines used to switch freight cars around in freight yards. They were tiny little chug-chuggers, about the size of the train youngsters read about in *The Little Engine That Could.* By contrast with the mighty long-haul passenger and freight locomotives, they were dinky indeed, so the word became a synonym for "small." Later it was used as an alternative name for the tiny caps, usually called "beanies," that freshmen in many colleges were once required to wear.

diploma. The certificate signifying completion of a course of study in school or college originally simply meant a folded piece of paper, from the Greek word meaning "something doubled." It has, of course, given us all sorts of extended meanings through such words as *diplomacy, diplomat* and *diplomatic,* wherein the original possessor of a piece of folded paper now is considered to be suave, tactful, discreet and politic.

discography is a word coined by analogy to "bibliography." It means a listing of records devoted to a single composer or performer. Occasionally you will encounter a *critical discography,* containing, in addition to the date and label for each performance, some commentary on the interpretation, quality of recording and other related data.

discothèque (pronounced dis-koh-TEK) is a French word borrowed into English. Formed by analogy to *bibliothèque* (library), it originally meant a collection of discs or phonograph records. Then it came to mean an intimate nightclub where the music was supplied by records drawn from such a collection.

disingenuous (pronounced dis-in-JEN-yoo-us) is made up of *dis-* (not) and the Latin *ingenuus.* Because of the Latin meaning of the second part of the word, which was "freeborn, frank, noble," *ingenuous* was originally used to describe one of honorable birth or character, but it came to mean "candid, straightforward, sincere." A *disingenuous* person is one who is not sincere but rather crafty and cunning.

dismal. Time has softened the significance of *dismal,* which is now mainly used as an adjective meaning "gloomy, depressing, foreboding." It was once a noun meaning "evil day" (from the Latin *dies mali,* "evil days"). There were two days of each month which the Romans deemed to be unlucky—usually anniversaries of great disasters—and it was felt unwise to begin any venture of importance on any of those days. This belief continued into the Middle Ages, and the days were actually marked on medieval calendars.

In case you're superstitious, here are the dates: January 1 and 25; February 4 and 26; March 1 and 28; April 10 and 20; May 3 and 25; June 10 and 16; July 13 and 22; August 1 and 30; September 3 and 21; October 3 and 22; November 3 and 28; December 7 and 22.

dismal science. *The dismal science* was Carlyle's description of economics.

disparage/parage. *Disparage* (pronounced dis-PAIR-ij) comes to us from the Old French *desparagier* (to marry one of lower rank), which in turn came from *des-* and *parage* (rank). The present-day meaning of *disparage* is to belittle or to lower in esteem. One speaks of another *disparagingly* when being critical of his worth or ability. While there is still such a word as *parage,* it is a noun, not a verb, and is not in common use. *Parage* is a legal term for equality in rank or in distribution of property.

dissipate comes to English from the Latin *dissipare,* "to squander" or "disperse." Both senses are common in English. A *dissipated* person is one who has wasted or squandered his talents and health through the intemperate pursuit of pleasure. The basic sense of scattering or dispersing remains in expressions like: "The fog *dissipated* by noon."

distaff in the sense of "female" goes back to medieval times, when much of a woman's time was taken up at the spinning wheel. The *distaff* was the staff, later a spindle, from which the wool or flax was unwound. As long ago as 1488 the word was in common use as a symbol of womankind and her role in the scheme of things. Now it continues chiefly in such expressions as "the *distaff* side," meaning the female side of a family.

distressed pecan/distressed pine. The terms refer to wood of the pecan or pine tree that has been artificially worked over to give it an appearance of age. When you "distress" a person, you cause him anguish and mental pain. Likewise, when an expert "distresses" a piece of wood or furniture, he gouges it with fake wormholes and mars it with phony scars of pipe and cigar burns. You might keep this in mind the next time you stop by a roadside "antique" shop and the friendly proprietor grudgingly indicates he might be willing to part with a cherished family heirloom. It could be a piece that had been "distressed" overnight—and the eventual distress will surely be yours.

diva is the Italian word meaning "leading woman singer or prima donna." The correct pronunciation is DEE-vuh. *Diva* comes from the Latin, where it means "goddess"—which gives you an idea of how highly Italians regard opera singers.

divan. A reader asked us to unravel a sentence that, to her, made little sense: "As a member of the chess *divan,* I sat on a *divan* and ate chicken *divan.*" The confusion results from the fact that different *divans* are involved. The first is a council and it gets its name from the Turkish *divan,* which was a high government body, the privy council presided over by the sultan. Next comes *divan* the backless couch, often set against a wall and provided with pillows to assure comfort. And the third? Well, that's a very delicious, if calorie-packed, dish. It consists of breast of chicken on a bed of broccoli, covered with Mornay sauce and grated Parmesan cheese, the whole thing nicely browned under the broiler. It gets its name from a now unhappily defunct restaurant, the Divan Parisien. Located in midtown New York, it was for decades one of the finest restaurants in the city and Chicken Divan was, of course, the specialty of the house. The restaurant got its name from the fact that its patrons were seated on divans—with backs, this time—facing the tables.

dive. Hands across the sea—and down a steep flight of stairs. If a London acquaintance suggests visiting a *dive,* don't jump to the conclusion that you're being taken to an extra-legal rendezvous to partake of forbidden revelry. Much more often than not, a British *dive* is an entirely respectable pub located below street level.

divinity, or *divinity fudge,* as it's sometimes called, is a white or cream-colored fudge made with egg whites, syrup and often nuts. It gets its rather odd name from the fact that mankind has for centuries associated the color white with things sacred and the color black with the forces of evil. So *divinity* got its name from the fact that it's white in contrast to the dark color of regular fudge. The fact that *divinity* usually turns up at church cake-and-candy sales may have been a contributing factor.

Dixieland. There are many stories about this word. Perhaps the most credible is that the phrase originally was *the land of dixies*—dixie being the popular name for ten-dollar notes issued in Louisiana and bearing the French-Creole word *dix* (ten) on one side.

Another fanciful story is that the original *Dixieland* was a slave plantation in New York City. According to a Southern newspaper of the immediate post–Civil War period: "When slavery existed in New York, one Dixie owned a large tract of land in Manhattan and a large number of slaves. The increase of slaves and of the abolition movement caused an emigration of the slaves to more secure slave sections. The Negroes looked back to their old homes where they had lived in clover with feelings of regret, as they could not imagine any place like Dixie's."

That sounds pretty farfetched to us. But one thing all can agree on is that the song "Dixie" was written in 1859 by the greatest minstrel man of his time, Dan Emmett. First performed in New York, it rapidly swept the country and was enthusiastically adopted as the favorite marching song of the Confederacy.

do a Brodie comes from the famous exploit of Steve Brodie, who either did or did not jump off the Brooklyn Bridge in 1886. He claimed that he did and achieved instant fame for the deed. However, since he had no witnesses to prove his claim—only wet clothing as he was fished from the water—skeptics soon voiced their doubts about the feat. So the word *Brodie* has come to mean either a suicidal jump (on the theory that if Steve had actually jumped he would have been killed) or a complete fraud.

do a bunk *To do a bunk* is British slang for "to depart in haste," especially under suspicious circumstances. It's roughly equivalent to such American slang expressions as *take it on the lam, hightail it out* or, simply, *scram.*

Dobbin was originally Robin, which, in turn, is a nickname for Robert. It has been a popular name for horses, especially workhorses, in England for longer than anyone can remember. In Shakespeare's *Merchant of Venice,* Old Gobbo remarks to Launcelot: "Thou hast got more hairs on thy chin than *Dobbin* my fillhorse has on his taile."

docile/docility. *Docile* (pronounced DOSS-'l) means "easily taught," as does the word from which it is derived, the Latin *docilis.* (*Docilis* in turn had its origin in the Latin verb *docere,* "to teach.") It also means "easily managed," and the noun form, *docility,* means "gentleness or easy manageability."

doctor. The first *doctors* were teachers, for the word comes direct to us from Latin and is the noun formed from the verb *docere,* meaning "to teach." Originally it was applied to any learned man. Indeed, in many parts of the world today *doctor* is simply an honorific for any wise man, whether or not he has graduate degrees. Believe it or not, one of your co-authors often gets letters addressed to him as "Doctor Morris"—doubtless an extension of this Old World courtesy. However, it was not until the late Middle Ages that the title acquired a specifically medical connotation. And as we all know from the proliferation of doctoral degrees in our schools of higher learning, there are today probably many more nonmedical men entitled to the label *Doctor* than there are within the medical profession itself.

Doctor Fell. One of the legends of Christ Church, Oxford, has to do with a seventeenth-century dean, Dr. John Fell, who expelled a wit named Tom Brown. After argument, Fell agreed to stay the sentence if Brown would translate a Latin epigram of Martial: *"Non amo te, nec possum dicare quare/Hoc tantum possum dicere non amo te,"* which, roughly translated, runs: "I do not love thee, nor can I tell you why; this much I can tell you: I do not love you." Brown is reported to have improvised this version on the spot: "I do not like thee, Doctor Fell,/The reason why I cannot tell;/But this I know, I know full well,/I do not like thee, Doctor Fell." The dean, with perhaps more grace than some of today's college administrators might show under such provocation, did remit the punishment. Brown wrote many verses and a collected edition of them was published posthumously. Yet, in the words of one authority, "Perhaps the best known of his satirical verses is the one beginning: 'I do not like thee, Doctor Fell.' "

Dodgers. Just how did the baseball team get the name *Dodgers* anyway? For the answer we have to turn back to the start of this century, when the chief means of transportation in the bustling borough of Brooklyn was the trolley car. So numerous were the trolleys, especially in the central area around Borough Hall, that all Brooklynites were labeled *trolley dodgers.* Later the label was shortened to *Dodgers* and applied to the ball team. In the mid twenties and early thirties the team was often called the Brooklyn Robins, after their famed manager Wilbert Robinson.

does not go on all fours. One of our leading advertising experts—an Englishman—once criticized a proposed campaign this way: "It does not go on all fours." This is another way of saying, "Let's put it on the train and see if it gets off at Westport" or "Let's leave it in the water overnight and see if it springs any leaks." It sounds like an expression from a Madison Avenue ad factory, but actually it is a British saying meaning that something does not go quite right, but limps as would a four-legged animal that does not have equal use of all its limbs. The distinguished historian and essayist Lord Thomas Babington Macaulay is even recorded as having used it in translating the Latin saying *"Omnis comparatio claudicat"*—the literal translation of which is "Every simile limps." Lord Macaulay's version was: "No simile can go on all fours."

dog days. This is the season Charles Dudley Warner probably had in mind when he remarked that "Everybody talks about the weather but nobody does anything about it." Despite the efforts of artificial rainmakers with cloud-seeding experiments, it still appears that nobody can do very much about what Webster defines as the "close, sultry part of summer."

There's nothing new about the phrase. In the days of the Romans, the six or eight hottest weeks of summer were known colloquially as *caniculares dies,* or "days of the dog." The Roman theory was that the dog star Sirius, rising with the sun, added its heat to the sun's and thus the period —roughly from July 3 to August 11—when Sirius's rise coincides with that of the sun was the hottest season of the year.

Humanity has suffered through *dog days* for quite a few centuries now.

So we may as well console ourselves with Don Marquis's advice: "Don't cuss the climate. It probably doesn't like you any better than you like it."

dogie. Probably the best book on the language of the range is *Western Words* by Ramon F. Adams. His comments on the origin of *dogie* are characteristically colorful:

> A dogie, in the language of the cowboy, is "a calf that has lost its mammy and whose daddy has run off with another cow."
>
> One version of the origin of the word "dogie" is that it started in the eighties after a very severe winter had killed off a great many mother cows and left a number of orphan calves. Grass and water were too heavy a ration for these little orphans, and their bellies very much resembled a batch of sourdough carried in a sack. Having no mother whose brand could establish ownership, and carrying no brand themselves by which they could be identified, these orphans were put into the maverick class. The first to claim them was recognized as the owner, no matter where they were found.
>
> One day on a roundup a certain cowman who was trying to build up a herd, drove a bunch in from along the river. "Boys, there's five of them dough-guts in that drive and I claim every dang one of them," he yelled excitedly.
>
> During that roundup all orphans became known as "dough-guts" and later the term was shortened to "dogie" and has been used ever since throughout cattleland to refer to a pot-gutted orphan calf.

dog in the manger, meaning a person who selfishly refuses to give to others things he himself has no use for, comes from one of Aesop's fables, the one about the dog lying in a manger full of hay. He snarled at and bit the ox who tried to eat the hay—despite the fact that he couldn't possibly eat it himself. Thus, down the centuries, *dog in the manger* has designated a person who neither enjoys a thing nor allows others to enjoy it.

dogmerd. As far as we know, *dogmerd* was invented by Anthony Burgess, who has quite a talent for wordplay and word invention, as anyone who has read or seen his *A Clockwork Orange* knows very well. In that novel he invented a whole new language—a blend of Russian and London street slang—to indicate what we might expect to hear in time to come. Anyhow, *dogmerd* seems a felicitous blend of "dog" and the common French vulgarism for excrement. The prevalence of such litter on the streets of Manhattan has been a source of vast annoyance to many residents and is a fairly common topic for letters to the editor of the metropolitan newspapers. Now Mr. Burgess has supplied a word which will at least lend a little variety to their endless complaints.

dog-trot log house is a log cabin—really two log cabins—connected by a covered porch or passageway. Presumably it's considered just long enough to let a dog trot during inclement weather.

dog watch. In seaman's parlance a *dog watch* is a two-hour watch period (customary watches are four hours long). They are often set at mealtimes,

so as to simplify serving at mess. *Dog watches* were originally "docked
watches," with "docked" meaning shortened. By folk etymology, the unfamiliar "docked" was soon replaced by the familiar "dog."

doily is a small ornamental napkin or mat, usually of lace, but sometimes of
linen or other cloth. Its chief function is to protect furniture from soiling,
as is notably the case with the kind of *doily* known as the antimacassar
(which see). The *doily* gets its name from the Doyley family, noted linen
merchants in London from 1700 to 1850.

doily/divot/rug. Advertisements for men's wigs invariably refer to them as
hair pieces, but in the trade a wig may be a *doily,* a *divot* or a *rug.* These
are three trade nicknames for men's wigs, according to size and use. A *doily*
is designed for the fellow who still has traces of his own hair on the sides
and back of his head. It covers the crown from front to back.

A *divot*—and somehow we suspect the hand of divot-wearing, golf-
playing Bing Crosby in the origin of this term—merely conceals a small
bald spot.

And a *rug?* Well, that's the works—a wig to conceal overall baldness.
And those—forgive the expression—are the bare facts of the wig business.

dolce far niente is one of our favorite expressions because, like most people,
we like to think that we'd be happier freed of all responsibilities, without
even a far-distant deadline to think about. We have always translated it as
"the sweetness of doing nothing"—but Bartlett's *Familiar Quotations* gives
a more literal translation: "sweet doing-nothing." The idea itself is far from
new. Bartlett also cites Pliny the Younger, a Roman writer of the first
century A.D., as commenting on "that indolent but agreeable condition of
doing nothing." An approximation of the Italian pronunciation would be
DOL-chay far nee-EN-tay.

dollar. In *Macbeth* (Act I, Scene 2) there is a line that has puzzled many a
reader: "Nor would we deign him burial of his men/Till he disbursed at
Saint Colme's inch/Ten thousand *dollars* to our general use." Macbeth
was king of Scotland from 1040–1057 and the question arises: was the
dollar a unit of currency in Scotland at that time? The answer is no, but
there's more to the story than that.

Today the dollar is generally regarded as the basic unit of U.S. currency,
but it was actually in existence, in one form or another, at least a century
before the first Pilgrims landed at Plymouth. Very early in the sixteenth
century, the Bohemian Count of Schlick set up a mint in the picturesquely
named Dale of Joachim or Joachimsthal. He began issuing silver coins
dedicated to Joachim, better known to us as Joseph, husband of the Virgin
Mary. The coins were called "Joachimsthalers," which soon was shortened
to "thalers." The Dutch took to calling them "dalers," from which comes
the English *dollar.*

Now to *Macbeth.* The account quoted is the report given to King Duncan by one of the noblemen who has just returned from an attempted invasion of Scotland by Norwegians under the command of their King Sweno. He's the one who was forced to ante up ten thousand dollars before the Scots would permit him to bury the men slain in the invasion attempt. While it's true that there were no dollars around at the time of Macbeth's kingship, it's equally true that they were the currency of Norway at the time, four centuries later, when Shakespeare was writing his play. And since one of the attributes of greatness is the ability to ignore trivia like anachronisms, Shakespeare made the payoff in dollars, not pelts or whatever actually would have been used as a medium of exchange in 1040.

dollar sign. Which is the correct *dollar sign*—a capital *S* with two vertical marks or with a single vertical line? Both are used.

There is a theory that the sign was originally made by superimposing a *U* over the *S*—combining the initials of the newly formed United States. That, obviously, would result in a double line through the *S*.

However, there seems to be no doubt that the dollar and its appearance were both strongly influenced by the Spanish *peso,* which we call "piece of eight" because it carried the figure *8.* President Jefferson, strongly anti-British, wanted to be sure that the infant United States used a unit of currency as far removed from the British pound as possible. So he wrote, in 1782, that our basic unit should be the Spanish dollar *(peso),* "a known coin and most familiar to the minds of the people . . . already adopted from South to North and therefore happily offers itself as a unit already introduced." The first dollars were not actually minted until 1794. It seems likely that the *dollar sign* evolved from a desire to retain the general appearance of the piece of eight, with the two vertical bars added to prevent actual confusion between the Spanish dollar (as the *peso* was widely called) and the American.

Be that as it may, the single line is now standard with the U.S. government, as shown in the *Style Book of the Government Printing Office.*

Domesday Book was not the first census ever taken, merely the first census held in England after the Norman Conquest. You will recall that Jesus was born in Bethlehem when Joseph "because he was of the house and lineage of David [went] unto the city of David which is called Bethlehem, to be taxed with Mary his espoused wife." The word "tax" in this quotation (from Luke 2:3-4) means to enroll—which is, of course, the function of a census. The *Domesday Book* (sometimes called the *Doomsday Book*) was the record of the census ordered by William the Conqueror in 1085–1086 A.D. It got its name from the fact that "it spared no man, but judged all men indifferently, as the good Lord in that great day will do."

done up brown comes from baking. When a loaf of bread or a batch of biscuits is *done up brown,* it is complete, finished, ready to serve. So when a project is *done up brown,* nothing more can be added to it.

donnybrook. A true *donnybrook* consists of a knock-down-drag-out brawl with anywhere from a handful to a mob of participants. It takes its name from the town of Donnybrook, a suburb southeast of Dublin. There, from medieval times up to the middle of the nineteenth century, were held annual fairs which for riotous debauchery rivaled the Saturnalian revels of Caesar's time. They always wound up in fisticuffs and worse—much worse.

Over the centuries the Irish have displayed a notable disinclination to avoid a good fight. Indeed, their hankering for a brawl is as legendary as their ability at handling their traditional weapon, the shillelagh. So it's hardly to be wondered at that the annual spectacle of thousands of Irishmen flailing lightheartedly about with splendid disregard for the Marquis of Queensberry rules should have made the name *donnybrook* synonymous with riotous brawling.

don't care a fig. The most likely meaning of this expression is simply that the fig serves as a symbol for something practically worthless, similar to the expression "I wouldn't give a plugged nickel for your opinion."

However, there's a theory that it may have been used by the Elizabethans as a translation of the Spanish *fico,* a gesture very much like our snapping of thumb and fingers when saying something like: "I don't care *that* about the game." Shakespeare spoke of "A *fig* for Peter" (*Henry VI,* Part 2) and "The *figo* for thy friendship" *(Henry V).*

don't count your chickens before they're hatched. The meaning of the *count your chickens* adage is obvious. Plans based on hopes rather than certainties have a way of falling apart. The expression is a very old one. According to the *Oxford Dictionary of English Proverbs,* it appeared this way in 1575 —about the time Shakespeare was in grade school: "Counte not thy chickens that unhatched be."

don't look a gift horse in the mouth. This is one of the oldest proverbs known to man. In fact, is has been recorded in a Latin version by Saint Jerome as far back as 420 A.D. Traditionally, the age of a horse is estimated by examining the condition of its teeth. So it has always been considered poor manners to inspect the teeth of a horse that has been given to you. By extension it means that you shouldn't inquire too closely into the value or cost of any gift.

don't look back. Someone might be gaining on you. This is a quote from probably the greatest black baseball player of all time, Satchel Paige. Here's the entire Satchel Paige prescription for keeping young: "Avoid fried meats which angry up the blood. If your stomach disputes you, lie down and pacify it with cool thoughts. Keep the juices jangling around gently as you move. Go very light on the vices, such as carrying on in society. The social ramble ain't restful. Avoid running at all times. Don't look back. Someone might be gaining on you." If anyone in our day has ever offered sounder advice, it hasn't reached our ears.

don't take any wooden nickels. Just who first used the expression *Don't take* *any wooden nickels* is not recorded—but certainly it was a long time ago. The United States minted five-cent pieces from the earliest days of the Union, but they were not known as nickels until 1866, because in that year the first five-cent coins containing nickel were minted. The practice of making commemorative tokens out of wood as centennial souvenirs developed and we can assume that wooden nickels actually were made during the nineteenth century for this purpose. Frequently such coins are accepted as legal tender while the celebration is in progress, but of course they cease to have value when the show is over. So the expression *Don't take any wooden nickels* became the popular equivalent of "Don't be a sucker."

doodle. We suspect that Scotsmen and Welshmen won't be happy to learn that *doodle* originated from the fact that a lot of unsympathetic people feel that playing the bagpipes is a frivolous waste of time. The word *doodle* comes from the German word *Dudeln,* meaning "to play the bagpipe," and is related to similar words in many other languages—the Polish *dudlic,* Turkish *duduk* and Russian *duda,* among others. The notion seems to be that a person who spends his time playing bagpipes would be guilty of other frivolous time-wasting activities—like scribbling aimlessly and abstractedly on scraps of paper. Incidentally, though the word has been around for several centuries, it did not come into widespread popularity in this country until Gary Cooper used it in the film *Mr. Deeds Goes to Town* in 1936.

dope. The first *dope* was originally the Dutch *doop,* which meant a sauce or other thick liquid. It was used to describe the thick glop that results when opium is heated and eventually meant any narcotic—especially the kind used to dope race horses. Then it was applied to not-quite-bright people, the kind who could be taken in by a race in which a doped horse was run. Then, too, the person responsible for doping the horse was in possession of secret information—and the expression "inside *dope*" was born. In more recent times, *dope* has acquired a usage very similar to the original Dutch meaning—to describe the varnishlike preparation that strengthens and tautens the cloth surfaces of model airplanes.

Doppelgängers. An alleged psychic phenomenon that your editors find fascinating is the theory of *Doppelgängers.* And that's not double-talk! Briefly, the theory is that each of us has, somewhere in the world, an exact double —a person entirely unrelated by blood but absolutely identical in physical appearance and voice. It's a notion that has long intrigued novelists. Only a few years ago one of the better mysteries, *The Man with My Face,* used the *Doppelgänger* theme. Like "poltergeist," *Doppelgänger* is of German origin, from *doppel* (double) and *gänger* (goer or walker).

do-re-me-fa-sol-la. These musical symbols are the notes of the "solfeggio" system. The elements are from Italian, though a very similar system, using *ut* in place of *do,* is French. So far as we know, they were first used by Guido of Arezzo in the eleventh century. When teaching singing, he used these lines from a hymn to St. John (this is in translation, of course): "UT-tered by thy wondrous story/RE-prehensive though I be./ME make mindful of the glory,/FA-mous son of Zacharee;/SOL-ace to my spirit bring,/LA-boring thy praise to sing." In case you're wondering about the seventh note, *si* or *ti,* that wasn't added until the seventeenth century. In Guido's time, the scale used was a hexachord, or six-note scale.

dornick, a variation of the Gaelic *dornog,* is a stone small enough to hold in your hand—usually a flat, smooth stone. Male Irishmen use them for throwing, but the females use them in the kitchen. When warmed, *dornicks* serve well to keep dinner rolls warm.

dossier (pronounced DOSS-ee-ay) is a collection of papers about one person or one matter. The word implies that the collection is detailed and complete. A company might, for example, make a *dossier* on a man it expected to hire for an executive position. In the *dossier* would be not only his record of education and previous employment, but also facts about his personal habits, hobbies, likes and dislikes.

dotage is derived from to *dote,* which has the twin meanings of "to lavish affection on" and "to be of feeble mind." A person in his *dotage* (pronounced DOH-tij) is in his foolish, feeble old age.

dots and dashes. An interesting question, but one to which there is probably no answer available, came from a column reader who wanted to know whether Samuel Finley Breese Morse, inventor of the Morse code, also invented the names *dot* and *dash* to describe the signals used. The answer had to be that he might have but that in any event the origins are obvious from the method by which code is represented visually: a dot for the short sound and a dash for the long sound. Actually, Morse operators never use these words. When referring to the sounds of code, they say *dit* and *dah.*

There is at least one wholly apocryphal theory about the origin of *dot* and *dash,* though. It was spun out of whole cloth by Bill Vaughan, the sage of Kansas City, whose "Senator Soaper Says" comments appeared in hundreds of newspapers and magazines. Bill found himself feeling sad one day about the plight of Millard Fillmore, whom Bill regarded, rightly, as one of our most neglected Presidents. In order to let Fillmore bask in at least reflected glory, Bill wrote that the President had encouraged Morse in the development of the first telegraph and that Morse, as a gesture of gratitude, had named the two symbols *Dot* and *Dash* after Fillmore's children Dorothy and Dashiell. Somewhat to Vaughan's bewilderment, his wild imagining was taken with utmost seriousness in some quarters, and the legend has been repeatedly reprinted as historical fact.

Vaughan's invention has not yet received as wide circulation as Henry L. Mencken's celebrated "bathtub hoax," however. That resulted from a deadpan effort by Mencken to prove that the "booboisie" would believe anything, provided it was buttressed with enough solemn "facts" and "dates." He wrote a piece titled "A Neglected Anniversary" about the origin of bathtub bathing in the United States of the 1840s. The practice of using bathtubs was frowned upon, even feared, he wrote, until one was installed in the White House and, with the seal of presidential approval, the bathtub soon found its way into many American homes. Mencken wrote the piece as a year-end filler article for the *New York Mail* in 1917. For decades thereafter he tried to explain that the whole thing was only a prankish hoax—but few people believed him, for the story had been widely reprinted and had even been recorded in several encyclopedias. As late as 1951, President Truman, commenting on the rebuilding of the White House under his administration, solemnly quoted the Mencken fable as though it were historical fact.

double entendre is a phrase with two meanings, one of which is usually risqué or improper. The phrase comes from the French, where it was originally *double entente,* meaning "double understanding"—a phrase that can be understood in either of two meanings.

double in brass is an expression common among musicians. It probably started with the "pit bands" traveling with musical shows, though it may be of even earlier vintage. In any event, it means that a musician who chiefly plays a reed or a stringed instrument is able also to "double" on a brass instrument when the occasion demands. Incidentally, one shouldn't jump to the conclusion that the person *doubling in brass* is anything less than expert at his second job. One of our good friends was Bobby Hackett, certainly the finest cornet player in the land. Only a handful of people, who knew Bobby as long as we, realize that his first instruments were stringed and that during the years he spent with the Horace Heidt and Glenn Miller bands, he was used only as a guitar player—not even allowed to *double in brass.*

As for ourselves, we guess we could be accused of *doubling in brass*—what with writing a newspaper column, editing dictionaries, making lecture tours, plus TV and radio appearances. But there's another, newer item of slang that we prefer to apply to ourselves. We simply call all that activity "moonlighting."

doublet/triplet/quadruplet/quintuplet. If you would find the origin of *triplet, quadruplet* and *quintuplet* you have to go back to *doublet* to find the answer, since the other words were all coined in imitation of *doublet.* That word came from the Latin *duo,* meaning "two," by way of Old French, where it appeared in the same spelling we use in English today, meaning something folded or doubled. There was even a man's jacket—of the sort worn by Sir Walter Raleigh—called a *doublet* perhaps from the fact that the front folded over a bit.

Anyhow, *doublet,* in the sense of a pair of anything, inspired *triplet,* meaning three of anything—the "triple" part coming from the Latin words *tri* and *plus,* meaning "threefold." From there it was an easy step to *quadruplet*—the "quadruple" coming from Latin *quadruplus*—and *quintuplet,* with the "quintuple" coming from the Latin *quintuplex.*

doubting Thomas. The first *doubting Thomas* was St. Thomas, one of the twelve apostles. According to Scripture, he expressed skepticism about Christ's resurrection and demanded to see the marks on Christ's body (John, 20:25–29). After Christ had appeared before him and convinced him, he said: "Thomas, because thou hast seen me, thou hast believed; blessed are they that have not seen, and yet have believed."

doughboy. The nickname *doughboy* for U.S. infantryman was popularized in World War I, but it was part of army slang for many years before that. Elizabeth Custer, widow of General George ("Custer's Last Stand") Custer, explains it this way in her memoirs of the general: "A doughboy was a small round doughnut. Early in the Civil War the term was applied to the large globular brass buttons on the infantry uniform, from which it passed by a natural transition to the soldiers themselves." You'll also find references to *doughboy* in Bruce Catton's *Glory Road,* one of the three volumes in his history of the Army of the Potomac. So though we usually think of *doughboys* as members of the AEF, the first American foot soldiers to bear that honored nickname served in the Civil War.

But John Berryman of Butler, Pennsylvania, sends evidence that the first *doughboys* may not have been American at all. He notes that following the battle of Talavera in Spain in 1809, Lord Wellington retreated to Almaraz, Spain. Food supplies were very short and one of the members of the rifle brigade wrote in his diary: "For bread we took the corn of the fields and, having no proper means of winnowing and grinding it, were obliged to rub out the ears between our hands and pound them between stones to make dough—from which wretched practice we christened the place Dough Boy Hill."

Mr. Berryman further notes: "The writer here was using 'corn' in the English sense of small grain—not our 'corn,' which they call 'maize'—and referred most likely to wheat." So there we have evidence that the first *doughboys*—far from being American foot soldiers on the Western Front in World War I—were actually British riflemen fighting a century earlier in the Peninsular War against the forces of Napoleon.

doughnut. An almost certainly apocryphal story of the origin of the *doughnut* credits it to a doughty down East sea captain named Hansen Gregory. According to legend, he designed these tasty rings so that helmsmen on watch could slip one or two over the spokes of the ship's wheel to eat while they steered the ship.

Douglas originally was a Celtic word meaning "one who dwells by a dark stream." Later it was chosen as the name of one of the greatest of the Scottish clans—resulting in its wide popularity as a given name. Though it is now almost exclusively a boy's name, it once was used in Britain as commonly for girls as for boys.

dove. The *dove* has been a symbol of peace ever since Biblical times. As a symbol of deliverance from care, we see the dove in Genesis 8: 8–11, when Noah "sent forth a dove from him, to see if the waters were abated from off the face of the ground . . . and the dove came in to him in the evening; and, lo, in her mouth was an olive leaf pluckt off: so Noah knew the waters were abated from off the earth."

down East. The expression *down East* is older than our nation. It goes back to Colonial times when Maine was, at least technically, part of the Massachusetts Bay Colony. In those years long before railroads, most of the traffic between Boston and Maine was by sailing ship. Since a ship plying that route in the northerly direction would be sailing "downwind," the expression "going down to Maine" or *down East* was commonly used.

That's one theory. The other is that the early colonists were influenced by British speech patterns—as indeed they were. To this day, an Englishman will speak of going "up" to London—no matter what direction is involved. Likewise, when he leaves London he goes "down" to whatever town is his destination. At the time, Boston occupied a position in the colonies just as important as London's in Britain. In fact, Boston was called, only half jokingly, "the hub of the universe." So it's little wonder that anyone leaving Boston for the provincial areas of Maine would be said to be going *down East.*

down in the dumps. *Dump* is thought to be derived from the Dutch word *domp* (meaning "haze" or "dullness"). During the Elizabethan period a *dump* was also any kind of a slow, mournful song or dance. In *The Taming of the Shrew,* Katherina, after her first lively quarrel with Petruchio, is asked by her father: "Why, how now, daughter Katherina! In your dumps?" So even in Shakespeare's time, *in the dumps* meant "out of spirits."

down in the mouth. The origin of *down in the mouth* is quite obvious. Take a look at the mirror next time you're feeling out of sorts. Notice how the corners of your mouth seem to turn down? Just the opposite of the smile you wear when you're happy!

down the hatch, which is common among patrons of bars, is from the jargon of sailing men, the mouth being regarded as analogous to the hatches down which cargo is lowered.

Doxology, the hymn sung at collection time in many Anglican churches ("Praise God from Whom All Blessings Flow"), comes from the Greek words *doxa* (praise) and *logos* (word). Properly speaking, it should apply to either the Greater Doxology ("Gloria in Excelsis Deo"—Glory to God in the Highest) or the Lesser Doxology ("Gloria Patri"—Glory to the Father).

draconian comes from Draco, an ancient Athenian lawgiver, one of the first to draft a written code. His penalties in most cases called for death—so a common observation of the period (seventh century B.C.) was that "The *Draconian* Code is written in blood."

draft/draught. Which is correct: a *draft* of ale or a *draught* of ale? Also, is there any connection between this kind of *draft* (or *draught*) and *draftsmanship* or *draughtsmanship?* There is indeed a connection between all the words mentioned. All come from the same Anglo-Saxon word, *dragan,* meaning "to draw." For many centuries the spelling *draught* persisted— as it still does in England—even though the pronunciation DRAFT became universal. During the present century there has been a strong tendency to spell the word as it is pronounced. Recent editions of American dictionaries, for instance, list *draughtsman* as an alternate spelling of *draftsman,* with the latter form the preferred spelling.

dragon. A fabulous beast, usually depicted as a sort of winged alligator or crocodile with the claws of a lion, the *dragon* gets its name from the Greek *drakon,* meaning "serpent." It was long regarded as the symbol of sin and St. George's slaying of the *dragon* was regarded as symbolic of the eventual triumph of good over evil, right over wrong. In ancient Britain the dragon was the symbol of war, and to this day it is the national symbol of Wales, for the Welsh flag shows a red dragon on a field of green and white. The Chinese and Japanese, by the way, take a very different view of the *dragon,* regarding him as a benevolent watchman and indeed a symbol of fertility.

drawing room, a term now virtually obsolete except as the name for a compartment on a Pullman (itself virtually obsolete), was in earlier times pretty much what we call a living room today. Its name comes from the phrase "withdrawing room" and refers to the now nearly forgotten custom of ladies withdrawing from the dining room at the close of dinner. That was done so that the gentlemen could enjoy their cigars, brandy and an exchange of masculine banter without offending the "delicate sensibilities" of any member of the "fair sex."

dressed to the nines means dressed in a very elaborate fashion. One of the great word sleuths of all time, Walter Wilson Skeat, thought that the expression originally must have been "dressed to the eyes." The way it might have appeared in Old English would have been: "To then eyne." It's easy to see how that could have been transformed into *to the nines.*

drollery started with a short, stout fellow whom the Dutch called a *drol,* a name which they also gave to a bowling pin. The French took the word, made it *drôle,* and used it as a name for a jester or buffoon. It came into English as *droll,* meaning amusing in a quaint or odd way, with *drollery* the word for quaintly amusing act or behavior.

drop the other shoe. This expression, meaning "end the suspense," has been around for many decades. There are various stories to account for its origin, but our own favorite comes from Kiyoaki Murata, managing editor of the *Tokyo Times.* "I was traveling in Germany and at a hotel my interpreter friend read me a joke out of a German magazine. It went like this: A traveler came to an inn late at night and asked for a room. There was only one available and he was told to be very careful because the guest in the next room was a timid fellow and a very light sleeper, disturbed by the slightest noise. So the new guest made every effort to be silent as he got ready for bed, but because he was so nervous he dropped one shoe, making a crashing sound in the silence of the night. Sure enough, it awakened the man next door and the new guest could hear him toss and turn. So he managed to get the other shoe off in silence and got into bed. Toward dawn he heard his neighbor still tossing about and finally, just about daybreak, he heard a pounding on the wall and a shout: 'When are you going to drop the other shoe?' "

Dr. Pangloss was the tutor in Voltaire's *Candide,* the one who preached that everything is "for the best in this best of all possible worlds." His philosophy, thus, was somewhat akin to that of another incurable optimist, Mr. Micawber (which see). *Pangloss* is made up of two Greek words, *pan,* meaning "all," and *glossa,* meaning "tongue or language." So *Dr. Pangloss* spoke many tongues, none of them especially lucidly, though invariably pedantically. The name of the guileless hero, Candide, comes from the Latin *candidus,* meaning "white or innocent." Ironically, from the same root we take the word *"candidate,"* few of whom can make much claim to spotless purity.

drumhead court-martial is a summary *court-martial,* held upon the field of battle in order to administer instant justice, so to speak. Its name, obviously, comes from the fact that it often was held by circling accused, accuser and judges around the head of a drum.

drunk as a fiddler has been common for many centuries and goes back to the practice of paying off the fiddler in wine when he performed at fairs and wakes. Since he got no other pay, he was likely to take in as much wine as he could hold—with predictable results.

drunk as a lord. Anyone who is *drunk as a lord* is very drunk indeed. The expression comes to us from the time of George III of England, the same who reigned during the American Revolution. In those days drunkenness was the mark of a gentleman. "Two-" and "three-bottle men" were commonplace among leaders in society and quite a few formal state dinners ended with many lords collapsed in drunken stupor—literally "under the table."

dry cleaning. *Dry* in this phrase has a meaning very different from the customary definition: "without moisture of any kind." Actually, *dry cleaning* is more accurately called, in some sections of our country, "French cleaning," for the phrase is a literal translation of the French *nettoyage à sec,* which means cleaning by the dry method, or cleaning without water. In other words, *dry cleaning* is "without water," which means that any of a large variety of liquid solvents—benzine, carbon tetrachloride and naphtha, for example—may be used in the process. The method was first developed in France midway through the nineteenth century and its great merits are that it causes no shrinking of the materials cleaned nor does it cause a garment to lose its shape.

dry fluids. French vintners for many a long year have been using the word *sec* (dry) to designate wines that are not sweet. The contrast between a sweet and a dry wine is perhaps most obvious in the distinction between sweet and dry vermouth. So, in American speech, a beer, gin, rum or even a ginger ale with little or no sweetness is labeled *dry*.

Duggan's dew is the name given the liquid lightning (illegally distilled spirits) which triggered many a Glencannon adventure in the famous stories by Guy Gilpatric. The name was as fanciful as the stories themselves were. However, in a neat instance of fact imitating fiction, an enterprising distiller has marketed a Scotch whisky under the name *Duggan's Dew* of Kirkintilloch. There is, sadly, no way of knowing whether Glencannon or his creator would have approved the product.

du jour. The listing of "soup *du jour*" on the restaurant menu is the most common use of *du jour* in this country. These French words mean "of the day," and "soup *du jour*" is simply the soup the chef decided to make for that particular day.

Dukhobors (pronounced DOO-koh-bors) are members of a sect of Russian origin who live in Canada. They have distinct beliefs and customs of their own, and a unique form of protest: they march around in the nude. This is understandably upsetting to Canadian authorities.

   Dukhobors is a name that literally means "spirit wrestlers," from the Russian *dukh* (spirit) and *bortsy* (wrestlers). They separated from the Russian Orthodox Church in 1785 because of their struggle against the doctrine of the Holy Spirit. In the 1890s many of them migrated to Canada in protest against military conscription, which they considered sinful.

dulce et decorum est pro patria mori. This quotation from Horace's *Odes* is literally translated: "Sweet and fitting it is to die for one's country." The motto appears often emblazoned on the walls of military schools and the like in sublime disregard—or, more likely, in utter ignorance—of the fact that Horace was writing satirically and meant nothing of the sort.

dun. There are two theories of the origin of *to dun*, both interesting and plausible. First, and most likely, is that it is simply a variant form of *to din*. In the days before the postman was used as a collection agent, the person to whom a debt was owed would send around a collector whose job was to get the money by fair means or foul. Naturally, this often led to loud quarrels, with much resulting din. Hence, *to din* or *dinning*—and later *to dun* and *dunning*. A more colorful theory traces it back to Joe Dun, a bailiff of Lincoln (England) in the time of Henry VII. Joe was such a relentless bill collector that he became a legend, and his name became part of the language. Instead of telling a collector to "make him pay up," people took to saying simply *"Dun* him."

dunce comes from the name of John Duns Scotus, one of the most brilliant scholars of the Middle Ages. He was a very conservative thinker and soon attracted many followers who were strongly opposed to the changes brought by St. Thomas Aquinas. In a sense they might be likened to the conservative elements in the Roman Catholic Church today who find themselves distressed by the many changes introduced after Pope John's ecumenical congress. However, after the death of Duns Scotus, as he was generally called, his followers—called "Dunsmen" or "Duncemen"—persisted in blind opposition to change of any kind and in time came to be considered a pretty dull and stupid lot. So with the passage of centuries, the word *dunce* acquired a meaning precisely the opposite of the brilliant man who first bore the name.

dundrearies is a style of whiskers, somewhat akin to muttonchops, but which are allowed to grow much fuller and silkier and are worn with a clean-shaven chin. They get their name from a character, Lord Dundreary, a dull old coot, good-natured but bumbling, who appears in Tom Taylor's play *Our American Cousin.* E. A. Sothern created the role in the London company and the play was regarded as one of his most notable triumphs. However, it would long have been forgotten had it not been for the fact that it was the play watched by President Lincoln in Ford's Theater, Washington, the night he was assassinated by John Wilkes Booth.

dungaree. More than 250 years ago, traders began to bring back from India to England a coarsely woven cotton cloth which was known in Hindustani —the trade language of India—as *dungri.* At first it was used chiefly for sails and tents, but seamen, noting its long-wearing qualities, began fashioning it into work clothing. As time passed, *dungri* picked up another syllable, becoming *dungaree.* What's more, *dungarees* became the standard work uniform of the navy and the merchant marine and it's a fair guess that the present popularity of *dungarees* can be traced, at least in part, to the fact that millions of young Americans wore them for the first time during World War II. The textile industry prefers to label the fabric "denim."

Dutch auction is one that proceeds directly in reverse of an ordinary auction. Instead of starting with a low bid and attracting progressively higher bids, the auctioneer in a Dutch auction starts with a high figure, reduces the price by regular stages and finally sells to the first person who accepts his price quotation.

Dutch courage/Dutch treat/Dutch love/etc. Probably no nationality has come in for so consistent a torrent of verbal abuse from the English as their

neighbors across the channel the Dutch. *Dutch courage*—the kind of courage that comes out of a bottle—is surely an unflattering phrase. When
you're invited to a *Dutch treat* or a *Dutch luncheon,* the host expects each
guest to pay his own way. *Double Dutch* is a kind of talk deliberately
intended to deceive the listener. And *to do the Dutch* is to commit suicide.

In these few phrases—and there are dozens more—the English have
implied that the Dutch are cowardly, niggardly and deceitful. Yet the rest
of the world sees Holland and its people as a land of tulips, windmills,
sunny-faced skaters and brave fellows tending the dikes. Why should the
British take such a contrary view?

It was not always thus. Until well after Shakespeare's time, the Dutch
were usually well regarded in all literary references by British authors. But
during the seventeenth century the two nations became rivals in international commerce. For a while, at least, the Dutch colonial empire loomed
as a real challenge to Britain's. So the disrespectful references began. One
of the earliest—a reference to *Dutch courage*—was penned by the poet
Edmund Waller in 1665: "The Dutch their wine and all their brandy lose,
Disarmed of that from which their courage grows."

Today, of course, Great Britain and the Netherlands have lived in peace
and fellowship for many years. But the damage done by the derogatory
phrases created in a time of wars and rivalry remains. To this day one hears
of *Dutch reckoning* (guesswork), *Dutch defense* (retreat or surrender), and
a pigheaded or stubborn man is one whose *Dutch is up.* It surely does beat
the Dutch!

An American invention is *Dutch love,* as in the expression "hotter than
Dutch love in an Irish kitchen." A Wisconsin reader explains: "The Irish
kitchen referred to the many immigrant Irish girls working as cooks and
'hired girls.' *Dutch love* refers to the German (not Dutch) boys that wooed
them. Many of my schoolmates had German fathers and Irish mothers.
How else would a boy get a name like Kevin Patrick Schmidt?"

Dutchman. *Dutch,* from the German *Deutsch,* originally applied to Germans,
but since the seventeenth century has been applied to natives of the Netherlands. The word originally meant simply "of the people" and can be traced
back to a Gothic word meaning simply "tribe."

The confusion between *Dutch* and *Deutsch* has resulted in such ironies
as "Pennsylvania Dutch" to describe folk of Germanic descent who till the
farmlands of Pennsylvania's Lancaster and neighboring counties.

Dwight was originally an English surname and meant "white or fair." One of
the early migrants to New England was John Dwight, and his numerous
descendants are believed to have popularized *Dwight* as a given name.

Dysmas is the name of the penitent thief who was crucified with Christ. His
name is sometimes transliterated *Dismas* or *Desmas.*

dysphemism is the precise opposite of "euphemism" (which see). It's from two

Greek words: *dys,* meaning "diseased, faulty, bad," and *pheme,* meaning "speech." As an example of *dysphemism* you might think of a truckdriver in a diner calling for a "mug of mud" instead of a "cup of coffee" or referring to butter as "axle grease."

early on is a phrase borrowed from British English. It doesn't say much more than *early* alone says: "He expects to arrive *early on.*" We rather like the expression, though, so right on, say we, to *early on.*

earmark. To *earmark* something is to give it a particular classification, especially something set aside *(earmarked)* for future consideration. The expression comes from the practice common among animal breeders of placing a distinctive identifying mark on the ear of each animal.

ears are burning. The common expression to the effect that if someone is talking about you, your ears will burn is at least as old in English as Chaucer. In *Troilus and Criseyde,* he wrote: "And we shall speak of thee somewhat, I think, when thou art gone, to make thine ears glow." The belief goes back, indeed, to classical times, for Pliny wrote: "When our ears do glow and tingle, some do talk of us in our absence."

Easter eggs. Eggs have been, since prehistoric times, a symbol of fertility, and hence of the return of life to the land with the coming of spring. However, the elaborate decorations on today's Easter eggs have evolved only within the past two or three centuries and, like the Christmas tree, originated in Germany. The word *Easter* seems to have been derived from the Middle English *Eostre,* the name of the Anglo-Saxon goddess of spring.

eating high on (off) the hog. We often hear this salty expression used to refer to someone who has achieved a full, prosperous life. "Old Tom surely is living *high on the hog* these days." The expression is quite literally accurate, since you have to go pretty high on the hog to get the tender—and expensive—loin chops and roasts.

eavesdrop comes to us virtually unchanged from Anglo-Saxon days. In those times a house had very wide overhanging eaves, not unlike those that may still be seen on thatched cottages in Devon. Since rain gutters and spouts were unknown then, the purpose of the wide overhang was to allow rain to drip safely away from the house's foundation. So the *eavesdrip,* which later became *eavesdrop,* provided a sheltered place where one could hide to listen clandestinely to conversations within the house.

ebullient teen-agers, with their high spirits and exuberance, give a clue to the origin of this word. It comes from the Latin *ebullire,* "to boil."

eclectic had its origin with the Eclectic philosophers of the first and second centuries B.C. Rather than confine themselves to the precepts of a single school of thought, they held themselves free to choose such elements from the various schools as suited their personal preferences. Thus *eclectic* came to mean "selective, freely choosing or borrowing."

ecology—the study of the interrelationship between organisms, including man, and their environment—is not a new word. The *Oxford Dictionary* reports that it is at least a hundred years old. It is derived from Greek *oikos,* "house," and -*logy,* "science or study of."

ecstasy comes from the Greek and originally meant a sort of religiously inspired fervor in which a person could quite literally be out of his or her mind. It is ultimately derived from *existanai,* a Greek word meaning "to drive out of one's senses."

ecumenical. Not until Pope John XXIII called the Vatican Council in 1962 for the furtherance of Christian unity did the word *ecumenical* become part of the language of the average man. *Ecumenical* councils have been part of the history of the Church for centuries, but none had been held for almost one hundred years. *Ecumenical* means "universal" and refers to the Christian church as a whole. (It can also be spelled *oecumenical.*) Its origin is in the Greek *oikoumenikos,* meaning "of or from the whole world."

effete is a word which has strayed far in popular use from its correct meaning of "worn-out, barren, exhausted." Perhaps because it is a favorite adjective of society columnists, it is now often and not very accurately used as a synonym for "sophisticated" in phrases like "the *effete* social whirl of Monte Carlo." Pronounced eh-FEET, it literally means "exhausted from bearing young," and thus should properly be used to describe people or a society which once was productive but now is barren and uncreative.

efficacy/effiacacious. *Efficacy* (pronounced EF-ih-kuh-see) is a noun meaning "ability to produce the effects desired." It comes from the Latin verb *efficere,* "to bring to pass or accomplish." Its adjective form is *efficacious* (pronounced ef-ih-KAY-shus).

egghead was first used by Owen Johnson in one of the Lawrenceville novels beloved by boy readers of the early days of the century. Even then, the connotation was of a person who was quite bright, even though he might not, on all occasions, use his brains to their highest potential. The word was revived during the 1952 Eisenhower-Stevenson presidential campaign. There's no doubt that it was often used invidiously and disparagingly by commentators of an anti-intellectual stripe. But though Stevenson and his associates were lampooned as *eggheads,* we don't believe anyone using the term questioned that so far as brains went, the *eggheads* rated very high.

eggs Benedict. The legendary Delmonico's Restaurant in New York City has been the birthplace of several tasty and now-famous dishes, among them *eggs Benedict.* According to a well-founded report, two of the regular customers were Mr. and Mrs. LeGrand Benedict. One Saturday at lunch Mrs. Benedict complained that there was nothing new on the menu, so the maître d'hôtel asked what she might suggest. Out of their colloquy came the now internationally famous recipe: toasted English muffins topped with a thin slice of ham and poached eggs, with hollandaise sauce over all. Voila! *Eggs Benedict.* See also LOBSTER NEWBURG.

egregious (pronounced eh-GREE-jus), from the Latin *ex-,* "out of," and *grex,* "flock," originally simply meant someone who stood out from the crowd, often because of his superior abilities. However, it has long since passed through the process of pejoration and now means "outstandingly bad or outrageous."

86, and bartenders' number code. Practicing barkeeps of the nation aren't going to like this explanation, but indications are that *86* may well have come from a number code created by the comparatively effete soda fountain clerks of the nation. Originally, according to the *American Thesaurus of Slang,* it was a password used between clerks to indicate: "We're all out of the item ordered." The transition from this meaning—common enough in soda fountains of the 1920s—to the bartender's sense of "Serve no more because of the shape he's in" is fairly obvious.

The number code developed by soda clerks was very extensive, incidentally. The head fountain manager was *99,* the assistant manager was *98*—which also meant "pest." A hissed *"98"* from one soda-popper to another indicated, "The assistant manager is prowling around. Watch out." And for some reason, *33* meant a cherry-flavored Coca-Cola, *55* meant root beer and *19* was a banana split. And most cheerful warning of all, *87½,* meaning, "There's a good-looking girl out front!"

Eisteddfod is the great Welsh festival of singing and poetry. Indeed, there are several regional *eisteddfods* held in Wales each year to select the bards and choral groups to appear in the two great celebrations—the National Eisteddfod and the International Eisteddfod. The latter, as the name indicates, has competitors from all parts of the world, including representatives of Welsh descent from the United States and Canada. Pronounced eye-STETH-vod, these occasions combine the atmosphere of an American country fair with singing of a robust richness not to be matched anywhere else in the world and poetry that must charm the Gaelic bards but is rather rough going for the nonspeaker of the Welsh language.

élan was borrowed from the French to denote a quality of personality—a way of doing things with spirit and impetuosity and always with enthusiasm. In French it means "an outburst" or "impetuosity," but we have added to that the elements of vigor and imagination.

elephant tablets is a popular and mistaken name for Alophen tablets, a laxative pill once very common and still, we believe, available at drugstores. Ironically, Alophen tablets are anything but elephantlike in size, being tinier than a coffee bean. The process by which expressions like *elephant tablets* and "sparrow grass" for asparagus are created is known to language experts as "folk etymology"—the tendency of nonexperts to change an unfamiliar word to a well-known one. Other examples are "very coarse veins" for varicose veins, "high-bred" for hybrid and "reddish" for radish.

eleventh commandment, the coinage of an unknown cynic, comes in several versions: "Mind your own business" and "Don't get caught" or, as Brewer phrases it: "Thou shalt not be found out."

Elgin marbles. In the early years of the nineteenth century, while Greece was a province of Turkey, the seventh Earl of Elgin, Thomas Bruce, was British ambassador to the Sublime Porte, as Turkey was sometimes called. On visits to Greece he was much taken with the statuary that he found in the Parthenon and elsewhere and made arrangements with the Turks to take the marbles to England between 1801 and 1803. Later he sold them to the British government and they have, for a century and a half, been among the most admired objects on display in the British Museum.

The British, naturally, regard themselves as saviors and protectors of these cultural remains of the ancient Greeks. In recent years, however, the Greeks have made it clear that they do not precisely share this view and claim that they have been "raped" of this vital part of their cultural heritage. But the likelihood of the Elgin marbles being returned to Greece seems remote. Incidentally, the *Elgin* in this phrase is pronounced with a hard *g* (EL-gin), not, as is the case with Elgin watches, with a soft *g* (EL-jin).

elhi/K-12. For the past two decades, at least, *elhi* has been publishing-trade jargon for the divisions of textbook publishers that prepare texts for elementary and high schools. As a cant word it will probably never find its way into the general lexicons but will remain restricted in use to publishers and their educator customers. Still another voguish expression in textbook circles is *K-12,* covering the entire range of public school education from kindergarten through twelfth grade.

Emerald Isle. Anyone who has ever been to Ireland knows that it is famous for its lush green fields, due in part to the fact that it rains a lot there. What's more, the color green is prominent in the flag of Ireland and, especially in the shade called "Kelly green," turns up on all tourist promotional material from Ireland.

The emerald, of course, is a brilliant green gem, so it was no surprise that someone began to call the island of Ireland the *Emerald Isle.* Who did it first? That's hard to say, but we do know that the expression was used as long ago as 1800 by an Irish doctor and poet named William Drennan. He wrote a poem called "Erin," containing these lines: "Arm of Erin! Prove strong, but be gentle as brave,/And, uplifted to strike, still be ready to save,/Nor one feeling of vengeance presume to defile/The cause or the men of the *Emerald Isle.*"

emeritus after a title means simply that its possessor has been retired but retains a courtesy title identical with the one he held immediately preceding retirement. It comes from Latin and means, literally, "earned by service."

empathy (pronounced EM-puh-thee) is a psychological term meaning the projection of one's own personality into the mind or personality of another in order to understand him better. This special meaning is, of course, not at all the same thing as "sympathy," which merely means a sharing of similar emotions. *Empathy* comes from the Greek *empatheia,* meaning "affection or passion."

emulate (pronounced EM-yoo-layt) means "try to equal or surpass." It comes directly from the Latin *aemulatus,* the past participle of the verb *aemulari,* which has the identical meaning as the English word. Its noun and adjective forms are *emulation* (em-yoo-LAY-shun) and *emulative* (EM-yoo-luh-tiv).

enclave/exclave. You are most apt to find these two words in writings on political science or geography—but they are interesting as examples of the influence of Latin on our language. The prefixes *en-* and *ex-,* of course, mean "in" and "out" respectively. Add the Latin *clavis,* meaning "key," and you have all proper clues: An *enclave* is a territory which is "locked in" or completely surrounded by a foreign country. It has no access to the rest of the world except over foreign land. By the same token, this territory is the *exclave* of the country which owns it and from which it is separated.

encomium (pronounced en-KOH-mee-um) means high praise, especially praise of a formal nature. The word is derived from the Greek *komos,* meaning "revel," and originally referred to songs sung in village revels in praise of Comus, the god of joy. It is amusing that this word, which had its origin in the lusty atmosphere of Bacchanalian revelry, is now reserved for relatively staid and formal expressions of praise.

encroach/crochet/crochety. The two English words *encroach* and *crochet* have distinctly different meanings today, but they share a common heritage: an Old French word *croc* or *croche,* meaning "hook." *Crochet,* the diminutive of *croche,* means "a small hook," and it describes perfectly the instrument for that type of knitting. *Encroach,* however, was formed by adding the prefix *en-* to the root word and acquired the meaning of "to seize upon or take." Today it means "to trespass or infringe, to exceed the proper limits or boundaries of another's right or property." Still another word which you would not think of as being from the same source is *crotchety.* Here the idea of a hook has been applied figuratively in the sense of "hooked or twisted," giving us a word to describe a person who is eccentric or cantankerous.

encyclopedia. How did the *encyclopedia* get its name? From two Greek words, meaning "a circle of knowledge"—in other words, the complete range of learning.

English language—size of. Many people ask us how many words there are in English. The answer is that we don't know—and neither does anybody else. For one thing, the language changes constantly. As new inventions and discoveries are made—and nowadays that's every day—new words must be invented to describe them. Similarly, as the need for them disappears, so do some obsolete words.

But aren't dictionaries a good indication of the size of the language? Again, yes and no. If you are thinking of the body of words known and used by the average intelligent layman, the answer is yes. Today's unabridged dictionaries do record all of this basic language, plus many thousands of technical terms used chiefly by specialists. But even here the advertised number of entries is no indication of actual content. By government standards, any variant form of a word, such as the principal parts of a verb, may be counted as an entry. Thus the entry *"go, going, gone"* is not one entry but three. Thanks to this numbers game, a dictionary claiming 450,000 entries may have as few as 150,000 basic words defined.

Leaving this aside, however, there is the matter of special vocabularies of the sciences and industry. Many of these run into the thousands of words —few of them of use to the layman and so they go unrecorded in standard dictionaries. After a lifetime spent in the study of words, though, we think we are entitled to an educated guess, and it is that the English language must contain between three million and five million words, including all the special vocabularies and jargons.

enigmatic, a synonym for *"puzzling"* or *"baffling,"* has its origin in the language of the early Greeks, who took their puzzles very seriously. It is derived from the Greek *ainigma* and *ainissesthai,* "to speak in riddles." In early Greece it was believed that whoever failed to solve a riddle was bound in servitude to the person posing the riddle.

ennui. One of the many French words appropriated by English, *ennui* means "a state of boredom or listlessness from lack of interest."

Enoch Arden. The legend of a man who mysteriously disappeared from home and family only to return many years later to find his wife, though still in love with him, married to another is as old as human history. However, it was given lasting form in our time by Tennyson, whose poem "Enoch Arden" contributed this phrase—by now virtually the generic term for the protagonist in such a situation—to our language.

en rapport, a French phrase meaning "in harmony with," merits attention because it seems to be the source of the very common slang term "to rap." When two people are "rapping," they are in conversation, of course, but it's a rather special kind of conversation, about topics in which they find themselves in agreement or harmony.

entente/entente cordiale. *Entente* is a French word which has been adopted by the English and Americans as a term for an agreement, particularly between nations. It is the past participle of *entendre,* meaning "to understand." Curiously, *entente cordiale* (pronounced ahn-TAHNT kor-DYAHL), meaning more specifically "a cordial understanding," remains a foreign term in the eyes of dictionary editors.

enthusiast. An *enthusiast* originally and literally was a person inspired by a god. The word ultimately is derived from two Greek words—*en* (in) and *theos* (god)—so an enthusiast was one who had a god within him.

entourage is "that which surrounds"—be it people or places. The *entourage* of a public figure is made up of those with whom he constantly associates, including his staff. Technically, it may also mean "surroundings or environment," but it is not often used that way. The word comes from the French *entourer,* "to surround."

eon simply means any extremely long period of time—thousands and thousands of years. It comes from the Greek word *aion,* which meant an age or all eternity.

epicure. Every Christmas the post office handles many gift packages consisting of boxes of assorted food oddities, ranging from dried grasshoppers to thumbnail-sized packages of imported cheese. The labels often say the contents are designed for the true *epicure.*

We can guarantee that the first epicure would have been as distressed as you or we at the prospect of eating grasshoppers. He was Epicurus, a Greek philosopher of about 340 B.C. He took the view that life need not be as grim as his rivals, the Stoics, seemed to think. As a result of his stress on happiness as an important element of living, he came to be thought of as advocating luxury and sensual pleasure. This wasn't exactly what Epicurus meant, but like a lot of other wrong ideas, it took hold. As a result, an *epicure* today is a person noted for his discriminating taste in wines and foods—which still leaves grasshopper-eaters somewhere in the outer darkness.

epidemic/pandemic. An *epidemic* describes the spread of a disease which affects many people in a community at the same time. An *epidemic* may cover a wide area—even an entire country. A disease which is *pandemic* is one which affects many if not most people over a very large area, usually including many countries. *Pandemic* may be understood to mean "internationally *epidemic.*"

epitome came to English from Greek and literally means "a sampling representative of the whole." It may either be a summary or a sample section characteristic of the whole. In correct usage *epitome* has no qualitative implications. For instance, a piece of text can be "the *epitome* of graceless prose" just as another may be "the *epitome* of brilliant writing."

epizootic. If you were to define *epizootic* as an epidemic among animals, you might be closer to the truth that you think. "Epidemic," you see, comes from the Greek words *epi-* (among) and *demos* (people), and originally meant anything (such as a disease) that spread rapidly among many people in a community. In the same fashion, *epizootic* comes from *epi-* and *zoion,* the Greek word for animal. So an *epizootic* is a disease rapidly spreading among cattle. It is pronounced ep-ih-zo-OT-ik.

What's more, the word has a somewhat broader meaning among country folk. In some farm dialects, *epizootic* is used to indicate any of a wide range of human ailments, especially those vague aches and pains that are hard to diagnose. You will sometimes hear remarks like: "Hiram just didn't appear at all today. Must be the *epizootics* have caught up with him again."

E Pluribus Unum. This is the motto of the United States of America. Pronounced EE PLOOR-ih-bus YOO-num, it means "one out of many" and refers to the banding together of the independent colonies into the Union.

epoch. There is a seeming contradiction between the meaning of *epoch* and the Greek word from which it came. An *epoch* is an era, a period in history covering certain important events, trends or changes, as an *epoch* in social revolution. It can also be used to denote the beginning of such a period, as the invention of television marked an *epoch* in the field of entertainment. But if you go back to the origin of the word, you find it comes from the Greek *epoche,* which means "pause or cessation." So think in terms of an *epoch* being not only the beginning of one era but the end of an earlier one.

Epsom salts are no longer the cure-all purgative of grandfather's day, having been pretty much supplanted by newer, brand-name laxatives. But before they fade completely into history, it may be well to record that the name for this hydrated magnesium sulfate came from the mineral springs of Epsom, England, where, since the early seventeenth century, the cathartic effects of the mineral springs have been well known. Epsom is also famous as the site of Epsom Downs, one of England's premier horse-racing tracks.

equanimity (pronounced eek-wuh-NIM-ih-tee) denotes calmness or serenity of temper and is a combination of the Latin *aequus* (even) and *animus* (mind). One of its root words, *animus,* has—when used as an English word —acquired a meaning of enmity or ill will.

equivocate. Coming from the Latin, *equivocate* literally means "to speak with two voices": *aequi* (equal) and *vocare* (to call). From this has evolved the present-day meaning of hedging or using double-talk in an effort to mislead or deceive.

Erewhon is an anagram of "nowhere" and served as the title of a satirical novel by Samuel Butler, published in 1872. Butler, positing an ideal commonwealth, made it as completely the opposite of England as possible. In *Erewhon* disease was a crime and crime a disease, for example.

ergo is one of the many foreign words and phrases which have proved so convenient that they have become part of the English language. It is Latin for "therefore" and comes in handy when stating a conclusion which is beyond dispute.

Erin go bragh! Ireland forever! Pronounced EH-rin go BRAH, it is an ancient battle cry of Irish warriors.

esoteric. Anything *esoteric* is intended for a chosen few, the insiders. The word comes from the Greek *esoteros* (inner).

espionage (ESS-pee-uh-nahj) seems to embody all the romance that is inherent in popular fiction about Mata Hari, James Bond and their like. Taken almost exactly—except for the dropping of an *n*—from the French word *espionnage, espionage* is the business of secretly discovering or observing the plans of an enemy or of a potential enemy.

esprit de corps is a French phrase which literally means "spirit of the body" —the body being a group of people engaged in the same activity. If a group works well together and everyone has a great sense of pride and honor in the common endeavor, the group is said to have *esprit de corps* (pronounced ess-PREE deh KOR).

esquire/squire are actually the same, with *esquire* being slightly the older version, as taken into English at the time of the Norman conquest from the French *esquier,* meaning "shield bearer." The earliest *squires* or *esquires* were candidates for knighthood. While serving their apprenticeships, they carried the shields and otherwise served as flunkies for those who had already made the grade to knighthood.

After the flowering of knighthood had passed, the words *Squire* and *Esquire* (now with initial capital letters) were used to designate men slightly above the rank of tradespeople. They were men of prestige in the community, often substantial landholders like Squire Western in Fielding's *Tom Jones.*

Then, as they were looked to as leaders, they often served as magistrates in the local courts and the term *Squire* came to be used more and more as a form of address for judges and other local dignitaries. Today the term is rarely used—at least in America—except as a courtesy title for attorneys at law. "Alexander W. Throttlebottom, Esq." is a rather more flattering way of addressing a letter to a lawyer than simply "Mr. Alexander W. Throttlebottom."

Establishment. When schoolboys proudly reel off "antidisestablishmentarianism" under the delusion that it is the longest word in the English language, the *establishment* part refers to the state church. Nowadays, though, the Establishment, butt of humorous barbs in Britain and abroad, is considered to be the conservative force in English life generally—not only the Church of England but all the members of Britain's ruling caste. In the U.S. the *Establishment* is a rather amorphous group, sometimes called "power brokers," who by dint of their influence in financial and governmental circles are thought to control or, at least, greatly influence the national destiny.

étagère is a recent borrowing from French. Pronounced ay-tah-ZHAIR, it's what grandmother used to call a "whatnot," a set of light open shelves for the display of knickknacks and other ornaments and trifles.

Eternal City. This name for Rome goes back to the poets of antiquity—Vergil, Ovid and others. According to the *Oxford Dictionary,* the phrase appeared in English as early as 1609.

eternal vigilance is the price of liberty. This famous quotation is often credited to Tom Paine or Thomas Jefferson, but a careful study of their speeches and writings fails to locate it anywhere. The nearest approach to it at that time appears in a speech by a great Irish orator, John Philpot Curran. In 1790 in Dublin he said: "The condition upon which God hath given liberty to man is eternal vigilance." That's pretty close—but not an exact quote. According to George Stimson, whose *Book About a Thousand Things* is a delightful trove of such information, the great nineteenth-century American orator Wendell Phillips claimed to be the man who first expressed the sentiment precisely in the words quoted. Phillips made the statement in a speech before the Massachusetts Anti-Slavery Society in January 1852.

ethnomusicology is the study of the form and origins of primitive folk music. One of the major fields of research for the *ethnomusicologist* is, of course, the music of Africa. The word is formed by the use of the combining form *ethno-* (from the Greek *ethnos,* meaning "nation").

etiquette. Nowadays the term *etiquette* covers just about everything from proper clothing for members of the wedding party to the manner in which a young lady may or may not entertain a young man in her apartment. But it was not always thus. Originally *etiquette* was simply a card bearing formal instructions on how to behave at court, but gradually it came to mean any prescribed code of social usage.

etymologist/entomologist Everyone has trouble with words. Even the experts find occasional pairs of words—similar in sound or in meaning—which they never can quite seem to keep straight. One of America's most eminent dictionary editors once confessed that his tongue sometimes slipped when he tried to say the word *etymologist*—meaning a student of word origins. Occasionally it would come out *entomologist*—one who studies insects and their habits.

Etymology comes from two Greek words: *etumon* (true sense) and *logos* (word). *Entomology* comes from the Greek *entomon* (insect) plus the suffix *-logy* (study of), which ultimately goes back to *logos.*

euphemism. The word *euphemism* is derived from the Greek *euphemismos,* to use a good word for an evil or unfavorable word. A *euphemism* itself is a word substituted for another which is actually more precise or accurate. See also CALL A SPADE A SPADE, DYSPHEMISM.

eureka! There's quite a story involved here, with a star-studded cast of characters, the discovery of an important principle of physics, and even—as befits a tale told for today's broad-minded audiences—a scene in which the leading character disports himself in the nude.

It seems that King Hiero II of Syracuse (the Greek city, not the one in upstate New York) gave a certain amount of gold to an artisan for making a crown. When the crown was delivered, he suspected that some of the gold had been stolen and silver substituted. But how to prove it?

So he sent for his wisest philosopher, Archimedes, and turned the problem over to him. Archimedes, not knowing the solution, decided to relax and consider the problem while soaking in a tepid bath. As he climbed into the brimful tub, some of the water overflowed and Archimedes raced into the street, still in the buff, shouting: *"Eureka! Eureka!"*—which is Greek for "I have found it!"

What he had found is the principle of measurement of the volume of an irregular solid by the displacement of water. Since gold is heavier than silver, he realized that a pure-gold crown would displace more water than one in which some silver had been used. When he made the test, it proved that the goldsmith had indeed been cheating the king. Then, presumably, Archimedes put his clothes on.

Incidentally, *"Eureka"* is the state motto of California, in reference to the discovery of gold by the forty-niners.

Eurodollars are dollars held outside the U.S. by overseas branches of banks headquartered in the U.S. It is, obviously, a blend of "Europe" and "dollars."

evanescent/evanesce. *Evanescent* (pronounced eh-vuh-NESS-ent) stems from the Latin *ex* (out) and *vanescere* (to vanish), and from these roots it has come to mean fleeting, fading or on the point of vanishing, as a vapor would *evanesce.* The noun form is *evanescence.*

everyone talks about the weather . . . The most famous quotation on the subject of weather—"Everyone talks about the weather, but nobody does anything about it"—is usually attributed to Mark Twain. Maybe he did say it one time, but the best evidence indicates that his brother-in-law, Charles Dudley Warner, actually wrote it first in an editorial in the *Hartford Courant.* Perhaps, though, the whole matter may now be left aside and forgotten, for somebody *has* done something about the weather. His name was Willis H. Carrier and he invented air conditioning.

everyone to his own taste. The expression *"Everyone to his own taste,* as the farmer said when he kissed the cow"* is a variation on an English folk saying that goes back at least to the mid 1500s. The version then current went like this: "Every man as he loveth, quoth the good man, whan he kyst his coowe." A similar notion is contained in the well-known French proverb *"Chacun à son gout"*—"Everyone to his own taste."

evil that men do lives after them. There seems to have been a difference of opinion on this matter between William Shakespeare and the Greek writer Euripides. In *Julius Caesar,* Shakespeare has Mark Antony speak after Caesar's death as follows: "The evil that men do lives after them;/The good is oft interred with their bones." But Euripides, who lived in the fifth century B.C., stated it quite differently: "When good men die, their goodness does not perish,/ But lives though they are gone. As for the bad,/ All that was theirs dies and is buried with them."

evince (pronounced eh-VINSS) is a verb meaning "to make manifest, show plainly." Derived from a combination of the Latin *ex* (out, from) and *vincere* (to conquer), it is commonly used in relation to emotions, thoughts or qualities of a peron, as in "He *evinced* a knowledge of science which amazed me." Though it has lost its original English meaning of conquering, it now means "to show beyond a doubt" and, in that sense, some trace of conquering remains.

ex cathedra. This borrowing from the Latin literally means "from the chair," the chair in this case being the throne whereon the Pope is seated when he promulgates his papal bulls. Thus any statement *ex cathedra* is one issued with authority, especially an official pronouncement.

excelsior. When used to mean shredded wood, this word has a curious history. Apparently *Excelsior*—with the *e* capitalized—was first used as a trademark to denote a certain brand of this commonly used packing material. But behind this fact lies an interesting tale involving the now long-forgotten nickname of New York.

Although New York's present nickname, the "Empire State," was occasionally heard in the nineteenth century, the more popular designation was the *"Excelsior* State," from the fact that the state seal bears the word *Excelsior.* This Latin word is the comparative of *excelsus* and simply means "higher." It was apparently chosen as the state motto on the erroneous assumption that it was an adverb meaning "upward." However that may have been, the word enjoyed great popularity, especially after Longfellow used it as the title of one of his most popular poems. During the Civil War the New York troops carried the state motto on their campaign flags, and *"Excelsior!"* became a popular rallying cry.

Astute merchants began labeling their products *excelsior* under the common delusion that the word was a fine-sounding synonym for "excellent." Some of these old trademarks exist to the present day, of course—if memory serves, a favorite brand of Fourth of July sparklers bears this label—but most have been long forgotten. The state nickname, which caused all the excitement in the first place, has likewise long been superseded by the "Empire State" label. But the businessman who, about 1860, first labeled his new brand of thin wood shavings *Excelsior* wrought better than he could ever have dreamed, for his brand name became the generic designation for this packing material.

exchequer. Did you ever try doing arithmetic with Roman numerals? It's difficult, well-nigh impossible. Faced with the problem—and having no Arabic numbers to work with—accountants and administrators for the Norman kings of England devised a checkered table on which figuring could be done by using counters. This table, which was marked off in squares, looked so much like a chessboard that it was given the name *escheker,* the Middle English term for chessboard.

The whole treasury department of the English government of that time became known as the Court of the Exchequer and not only collected taxes and debts but ruled on disputes between the king and his subjects. By the fourteenth century, revenue collection and adjudication of disputes were made separate functions under the British government.

Just as *exchequer* came to mean the treasury of England, it has, by extension, come to mean the treasury of any organization or government —and can even be used to refer to your own bank account.

exculpate (pronounced EX-kul-payt) has literally retained the meanings of its Latin roots, *ex* (out) and *culpatus,* past participle of *culpare* (to blame). For example: "The story told by the eyewitness *exculpated* [freed from blame] the suspected man." The accent shifts to the third syllable in the noun *exculpation* and to the second syllable in the adjectives *exculpable,* "able to be freed from blame," and *exculpatory,* "tending to *exculpate.* "

exobiology. A far-out science term, both literally and figuratively, is *exobiology,* which Isaac Asimov, the famous science writer, calls "a science in search of a subject." It was named by Joshua Lederberg, a noted biologist, taking his cue from the Greek *exo* (outside of) and "biology." It concerns the study—perhaps "speculation" would be a better word—of life forms outside the earth.

exosphere, a creation of the space age, denotes the outer fringe of the atmosphere—out past the stratosphere and the ionosphere.

exotic, according to one authority, means "different" or "strange" only in the sense of "from a foreign land." This, of course, is the original sense of the word. It comes from the Greek *exotikos,* meaning "foreign or alien." But, over the past few decades, it has also come to mean, in the words of the *World Webster Dictionary,* "having the charm or fascination of the unfamiliar; strangely beautiful and enticing."

expeditious/expedient. *Expeditious* (pronounced ex-peh-DISH-us) has its origin in the Latin *expedire,* which literally means "to free one caught by the foot" (*ex,* "out," and *pedis,* "foot"). From the same Latin word come the more commonly known *expedite,* "to facilitate or speed up," and *expedition.* *Expeditious* is an adjective and means "in a speedy or prompt manner; efficient." (Adverb: *expeditiously.*)

This word should not be confused with another word of the same origin, *expedient,* a noun which means "an immediate purpose; a convenient or makeshift device." Used as an adjective, an *expedient* measure may contribute to an *expeditious* completion of a project—or it may have to do only with an isolated incident.

expertise is a borrowing from the French and means not much more than "expertness." Why, then, should such a word crop up so often in current writing? Simply because it is what linguists call a "vogue" word. It's not new. The *Oxford Dictionary* lists it as appearing in print as early as 1869 in the sense of "expert opinion or knowledge." Incidentally, the British pronounce it ex-per-TYSE, whereas the common American pronunciation is ex-per-TEEZ.

explode has a history in the theater, where its meaning was once quite different than it is today. Originally *explode* meant to drive an actor off the stage by means of clapping and hooting. It is made up of the Latin prefix *ex-* and *plaudere* (to applaud). The word still retains the sense of rejection, such as in the act of exploding a theory—exposing it as false—and in general use, there is still noise associated with things that explode. But there the similarity ends.

ex post facto, borrowed from the Latin, means "retroactive, or after the fact." Our Constitution specifically states that Congress shall not pass any *ex post facto* laws (Art. I, Sect. 9), so that a person cannot be punished for a crime if the law establishing it as a crime is passed after the deed was committed.

expostulate (pronounced eks-POSS-chuh-layt) is usually followed by "with" and means to reason (with another) and argue against the advisability of an act, intended or in the process of being committed. It has practically the same meaning as "remonstrate." "He *expostulated* with his friend about his reckless driving." As you see, its meaning today is slightly different from that of the word from which it stems, the Latin *expostulare,* which means "to demand vehemently, to require." In its noun form, *expostulation,* the accent shifts to the fourth syllable.

extirpate, meaning "to root out or destroy completely," comes from the Latin *ex* (out) and *stirps* (root).

eyes as big as bullets. Most of us have heard the expression "The baby's *eyes* were *as big as bullets,* " without wondering about the fact that it is odd to liken the eyes of an innocent baby to an instrument of death and destruction. Well, it did bother one of our readers—and now we have a sensible-sounding explanation, from Mrs. L. T. Emmerson of Tacoma, Washington.

"When I was a child in England," she wrote, "we had a special hard candy. It came in two colors, black and brown, was round, and about twice the size of a marble. The dark one was licorice flavored and the brown one tasted slightly buttery. If we wanted the dark ones we asked for 'black bullets' and the brown ones were simply 'bullets.' Every so often a child would swallow one and scare the parents out of their wits. Very often when we had something surprising happen to us, our parents would say that our '*eyes* were *as big as bullets.* ' "

eye service. A person who does *eye service* is working against his will and only when the eye of his employer is on him. It comes from the Bible (Ephesians 6:5): "Servants, be obedient to them that are your masters . . . not with *eye service* as men pleasers; but as the servants of Christ."

Eyes of the Army was the nickname given one of the authentic heroes of the Confederate Army, General James Ewell Brown Stuart, who had an uncanny ability to locate the enemy and take his troops right around them and attack from the rear. He did this twice to Union General George B. McClellan's army, accounting in no small part for McClellan's removal from command of the Union forces. Stuart was renowned for personal valor as well as for ability to command troops. He met his death leading his forces in the defense of Richmond against the numerically far superior forces of General Philip Sheridan.

Fabian socialists. The *Fabian Society,* founded in England in 1884, took its name from Quintus Fabius Maximus, a Roman general who managed to defeat Hannibal by avoiding direct contact. While the goal of the group was to achieve socialism for England, the approach planned was a gradual one, more intellectual than forceful. Members of this genteelly radical group included Sidney and Beatrice Webb, H. G. Wells, George Bernard Shaw and, would you believe it, William Morris. The other William Morris, of course.

façade. To an architect or a builder, a *façade* is only one thing—the front of a building. Actually, it can mean the front part of anything and is often used figuratively in the sense of a "false front."

Façade is a French word taken over unchanged by English-speaking people. It comes from the Latin *facies,* meaning "face or appearance." Two other English words come from the same root: "face," of course, and "facet." "Facet" is simply the diminutive of "face."

face the music lives in our memories chiefly as part of the title for an Irving Berlin song of the 1930s, "Let's Face the Music and Dance," which inspired one of the truly great Fred Astaire–Ginger Rogers dance numbers. However, the expression is much older than that—and there are two theories of its origin. One says it started in the musical theater. A nervous actor would have to summon up all his courage (for that's what *face the music* means) and face the audience across the orchestra pit. The other theory is that it goes back to the early military practice of "drumming out" a soldier who was dismissed from service for dishonorable conduct. He, too, would have to *face the music.*

factotum is a borrowing direct from medieval Latin and in turn from the Latin *facere* (to do), and *totum* (everything). So a *general factotum*—the way the term is usually used today—is or should be a chap who can do just about everything in the service of his employer.

fair dinkum. We replied to a reader's inquiry that the Australian phrase *fair dinkum* meant excellent, top grade, of very best quality. A clipping found its way into the hands of E. W. Smith in Australia, and he came forward with further information on the subject:

> *Fair dinkum* has all of the meanings you indicate, but by innuendo and implication it means just a little more. A person is *fair dinkum* if he or she is really trying ("He made a *fair dinkum* effort") or really means what he says ("Fair dinkum,

I'll deliver it tomorrow"). In addition, the phrase denotes that a person or thing is true to type. A "fair dinkum Aussie," for example, implies at least a second-generation Australian with accepted local attitudes as distinct from more recent migrants who may still display European characteristics. It is a rare honour for a foreign-born resident to be accepted as a "fair dinkum Aussie."

On the other side of the coin, the phrase can dramatically reinforce an expletive. There are few more incisive insults in Australian argument than "You're a fair dinkum bastard." Similarly, "It's a fair dinkum cow" implies the worst of business or agricultural tragedies—floods, crop losses, bush fires and such traumatic situations. [The *Oxford English Dictionary* records "cow" as Australian slang for "a distasteful situation."]

fairy ring is a circle of mushrooms in a grassy area, marking the outer limits of underground fungus growth. In olden times such rings were thought to be caused by fairies dancing in circles by the light of the moon.

falderal/falderol/folderol are variant spellings of the same word. Actually, *falderal* is the oldest, though *folderol* is now more common. The whole nonsense—for that's exactly what it is—started in British music halls early in the nineteenth century. Popular comic songs often had nonsense verses like our own "Hut-Sut Ralston on the Rillerah" of World War II vintage. These nonsense verses were called *falderal* and the term eventually came to mean any form of nonsense.

fall-back position refers to a previously prepared position to be resorted to if strategic retreat is necessary. By extension, in governmental jargon it can mean an excuse prepared in advance in case a plan or project falls through.

fall guy. We are all familiar with the expression "He's a *fall guy,*" meaning a chronic loser, a patsy, a schnook or a schlemiel. The first *fall guys* were professional wrestlers. Until the early decades of this century, wrestling was a reputable sport and its champions were as highly esteemed as the champions in boxing and other professional sports. But then rigging of matches became so widespread that the participants were lampooned in the public prints as "grunt-and-groaners," and various state courts decreed that the shows could no longer be called "contests" but must be labeled "exhibitions." And the *fall guy,* of course, was the chump who was rigged in advance to take the fall to make the "champ" look good.

familiarity breeds contempt. Many writers, including Shakespeare (*Merry Wives of Windsor,* Act I, Scene 1), have used this expression, but the earliest recorded appearance is in the *Maxims* of Publius Syrus. Perhaps the most trenchant comment about this saying was made by Winston Churchill when he remarked: "Without a certain amount of familiarity, you will never breed anything."

fan. Most scholarly opinion for years regarded this as a shortened form of "fanatic." Now the theory is set forth that it may have come instead from "fancy," a now outmoded term for gentlemen who frequent prize fights.

We are inclined to think that this comes closer to the true spirit of the *fan* as we know him today. While he is enthusiastic, he is not likely to be actually fanatical.

fanatic. Winston Churchill, so long and eloquently a foe of Hitler's "mob," as he once called the Nazis, was certainly well qualified to speak on the subject of *fanaticism*. Perhaps that's why we especially like his definition of *fanatic*—"one who can't change his mind and won't change the subject." *Fanatic* comes from the Latin word for temple, *fanum,* and meant mad as if inspired by a god.

Fanny May is the financial community's nickname for the Federal National Mortgage Association. It is so widely accepted that the financial pages of the *New York Times* carry top headlines such as: FANNY MAY TO SELL $800-MILLION TOTAL IN TWO OFFERINGS.

fantods is a dialect term roughly synonymous with "the fidgets." It may originally have been a seaman's term because it still is used to describe a fidgety, nervous ship's officer. Mark Twain used it this way in *Huckleberry Finn:* "They was all nice pictures, I reckon, but I didn't somehow seem to take to them, because if ever I was down a little, they always give me the fantods."

farce, originally meaning "stuffing," comes from the French verb *farcer* (to stuff). During the Middle Ages it was the custom of acting companies to insert a brief, rowdy and highly comic interlude between the acts of the main drama. These short pieces were figuratively stuffed between sections of the performances and hence were called *farces.*

A *farce* today can be an entire play, as long as it is based on broad humor and ludicrous situations. By extension, the word has also come to mean anything that is ludicrous or has the quality of empty show.

far from the madding crowd. Most of us remember Thomas Hardy's novel *Far From the Madding Crowd.* However, the phrase was not original with Hardy. He quoted it from Thomas Gray's famous "Elegy Written in a Country Churchyard," in which the following lines appear: "Far from the madding crowd's ignoble strife/Their sober wishes never learned to stray;/Along the cool sequestered vale of life/They kept the noiseless tenour of their way."

The distinction between *madding* and *maddening* is well worth observing, by the way. *To mad* is a verb, now almost wholly archaic, meaning "to act madly or insanely." A *madding* crowd, then, is one that is acting like a group of lunatics. However, a *maddening* crowd would merely be one that causes vexation or annoyance, like the crowd that fills all the elevators in an office building, forcing you to wait.

farm out. *farm* has, for the most part, lost the meaning it had in the Middle Ages. However, in the phrase *to farm out,* it comes close to its original meaning. *Farm* was once a term for payments, such as taxes or rent, which were collected at regular intervals (from the medieval Latin *firma,* meaning "fixed payment"). A *farmer* in those days was one who paid a set sum to be allowed to collect *farms* or taxes, with the understanding that he kept whatever he collected. It wasn't until the sixteenth century that the term *farm* was applied to the land on which taxes or rent was paid, and a *farmer* could also be the man who operated the *farm.* In those days, "tenant farmer" would have been a redundant phrase, but gradually *farm* and *farmer* acquired their present-day meanings. It is from the old practice of delegating to someone else the collection of taxes or rent that we have acquired the phrase *to farm out,* meaning "to pay someone else to do the work."

farrago is a medley, mixture or conglomeration. It originally referred to mixed fodder prepared for feeding cattle and comes direct from Latin. It is pronounced fuh-RAY-goh or fuh-RAH-goh. Though it is usually seen in the phrase *"farrago* of nonsense," Virginia Woolf once rang a change on this phrase, speaking of a *"farrago* of absurdity."

fascism had its origin in one of Aesop's fables, in which it was shown that while sticks could easily be broken one by one, they could not be broken if several were tied together in a bundle. The moral was, of course, "In union there is strength." The Latin word for a bundle of sticks was *fasces* and such bundles were borne as symbols of authority by the lictors of ancient Rome. When Benito Mussolini marched on Rome in 1922, he appropriated the symbol so proudly borne two thousand years previously and named his followers *Fascists* and his form of dictatorship *Fascism.*

fashion plate. The original *fashion plates* were the printing plates from which illustrations were printed in early magazines of fashions. Then came the expression, to describe someone who dressed in the latest mode, "She's an animated fashion plate." The final step, to the point where the person herself was described as a *fashion plate,* is obvious.

Father of His Country was probably coined by a printer in Lancaster, Pennsylvania, called Francis Baily. In 1779 he published a calendar in German for the German-speaking people of his area. In it appears a picture of George Washington called *Des Landes Vater*—"Father of the Country." The first version in English seems to be in a letter written to Washington in 1787 by Henry Knox, later to be his first secretary of war.

fat's in the fire doubtless originated in somebody's kitchen centuries ago. If you have ever spilled fat into a flaming fire, you know what the result is: a sudden flaring up—and a quick end to the fat. That's the meaning of the expression, of course—"the damage is done."

fatuous (pronounced FAT-choo-us) is useful in describing persons or actions which are asinine, silly or complacently stupid. (A person so described is guilty of *fatuity.*) It can also mean "empty or unreal." Its origin is the Latin *fatuus* (foolish).

Feast of Fools was a medieval revel, occurring on January 1, the Feast of the Circumcision. In honor of Christ's entry into Jerusalem on a donkey, this beast was the focal point in the frequently bawdy revels, and from time to time the participants would bray in unison.

February. The second month of the year takes its name from the Latin *Februarius,* referring to a festival of purification held on February 15.

fecit, the Latin word for "he has done this" was formerly used as part of an artist's signature to a work of art: *Goya fecit*—"Goya painted this."

feel one's oats, meaning "to feel frisky, playful and full of energy," has been in our American language for at least a century and a half. It originated as a farmer's expression, indicating how much more energetic a horse acts after it has had its meal of oats.

feet of clay originated in Daniel 2: 31–34, in which a figure in a dream of Nebuchadnezzar is described in this way: "This image's head was of fine gold, his breast and his arms of silver, his belly and his thighs of brass, his legs of iron, his feet part of iron and part of clay." A stone struck "the feet that were of iron and clay, and brake them to pieces. Then was the iron, the clay, the brass, the silver, and the gold broken to pieces together, and became like the chaff of the summer threshing floors, and the wind carried them away." The moral, of course, is that a fatal flaw can be the undoing of a man and his career.

feist in the sense of a small scrappy dog has been part of the language for at least a couple of centuries, George Washington used it in a diary entry in the year 1770. *Feisty* as an adjective meaning either "touchy and quarrelsome" or "spirited and frisky" is somewhat more recent.

fellow traveler is a term that was much bandied about in America from the period of the Popular Front in the 1930s at least through the time of McCarthyite repression in the 1950s. The phrase is reported to have been coined by Leon Trotsky to describe those who sympathize with the aims of a movement, particularly a leftist-oriented group, without actually taking membership in it. The Russian word for fellow traveler is *sputnik* (which see).

fell swoop/swell foop. *Fell* in the expression "one *fell swoop*" means "savage or deadly." So when we say a hawk snatched a chicken "in one *fell swoop,*" we have a graphic picture of the action. Eventually the phrase came to mean "acting quickly and savagely," or, at least, with abrupt finality. The *swell foop* version—which means the same thing—started as a "spoonrism"—that is, an accidental and amusing transposition of the beginning consonants of a pair of words or a series of words. The name comes from a High Church cleric, the Reverend William A. Spooner, who made many such slips of the tongue. See SPOONERISM.

femme fatale is a French expression, literally meaning "fatal woman." It's used to refer to the glamorous dame in mystery or spy stories who betrays

—or tries to betray—the hero. History's most famous *femme fatale,* we suppose, was Mata Hari, noted spy of World War I.

fenberry sauce. The sauce of the first Thanksgiving dinner in this country was undoubtedly called *fenberry sauce* at the time, since the cranberry was known in England as the *fenberry* and it was not until years later that the Dutch gave it the name of "cranberry" from their *kranbeere.*

ferninst. Coming from the relatively unexplored lexicon of Irish contributions to American folk speech, this word means "opposite, near or against." It is heard in such expressions as: "Put the table over *ferninst* the wall." In various other spellings—*fernent, forninst, fanent* and *fornent*—it was brought to America by the colonists from other parts of the British Isles, but *ferninst* seems to be the Irish form, brought over midway through the last century, when Irish immigration was at its peak.

Sometimes *ferninst* is made into a noun as *ferninster,* meaning one who is chronically "agin" everything. Back in the early forties, William Allen White, the late, great Kansas editor, noted: "The trouble with the Republican leaders in Congress . . . is that they are just *ferninsters.*"

Ferris wheel. That favorite amusement park ride the *Ferris wheel* gets its name from George W. G. Ferris, the engineer who designed the first one for the Columbian Exposition in Chicago in 1893.

fetid (pronounced FET-id) means simply "having a repulsive smell" and comes from the Latin *fetidus,* with the same meaning. It is used to describe the offensive odor of rotten matter.

fetish is a word which originally meant, in primitive tribes, a material object which was purported to have powers of magic. It has acquired a slightly broader meaning in general use today as descriptive of any object of irrational reverence or devotion. It came into English by way of the French *fétiche,* which in turn comes from the Portuguese *feitico,* meaning "charm or sorcery."

F.F.V. stands for the First Families of Virginia, self-styled leaders of Southern aristocracy.

fiddled while Rome burned. The notion that Nero fiddled while Rome burned is nonsense because the fiddle wasn't invented until many centuries after he ruled Rome, from 54 to 68 A.D. He may have toyed with a lute, but certainly not a fiddle. What's more, Nero seems to have been something less than all bad. For one thing, he was a pioneer in what we would now call "urban renewal." He planned to rebuild much of Rome and ran into a lot of trouble with property owners who resented his condemnation proceedings. When the big fire broke out in 64 A.D. (it burned nine days and destroyed two thirds of the city), Nero didn't do much to win the hearts and minds of his people by ordering some other buildings burned to stop the fire's progress.

But in the end, Nero proved to be a pretty smart politician. He blamed the fire on the Christians, who were then a much put upon sect and a handy scapegoat. The truth seems to be that while the Christians didn't actually start the fire, they didn't do much about putting it out either, because they saw it as the sign of the second coming of Christ.

Fido is indeed a noble name befitting man's most loyal friend, the dog. It comes from the Latin word *fidus,* meaning "faithful."

FIDO is the acronymic designation for a method of fog dispersal along airport runways (Fog Investigation Dispersal Operations).

fidus Achates, "faithful Achates," trailed Aeneas through his travels, always turning up when needed. The Latin term has been borrowed into English to mean "faithful companion, bosom friend."

fiasco comes from the same Italian root as "flask"—*flasco.* There is a theory that a perfect bottle was called by medieval glassblowers a *flasco* and an imperfect one a *fiasco.* There is not much evidence to support this theory, so we incline to think that *fiasco* may have got its meaning of "complete failure" from the fact the bubbly contents of primitive flasks may have lost their sparkle and become flat when opened for drinking—truly a *fiasco.*

fifth column. Ernest Hemingway deserves credit for having established *fifth column* as a term for secret subversives working within a country. The phrase was first uttered by General Mola, who said, during the Spanish Civil War, that he was commanding five columns in the assault on Madrid, four converging on the city from various directions "and the fifth column within the city." But it was Hemingway's use of the phrase in a play called *The Fifth Column* that established it permanently in our language.

fifth wheel is something useless, superfluous and sometimes burdensome. So if you're visiting with a group of people, all of whom know each other well but whom you don't know, you're very likely to find yourself pretty well excluded from the conversation and feeling like a *fifth wheel.* It's rather a curious expression today because, when you stop to think of it, the fifth wheel on an auto plays a very important role indeed. It's your salvation if you have a flat tire. But the expression goes back to the days when wagons and carriages operated without collapsible rubber tires, so that a fifth wheel would indeed have been burdensome.

54–40 or Fight. This slogan was coined in 1844 by William Allen, a Democratic senator from Ohio who was known as "Earthquake Allen," "Petticoat Allen" and the "Ohio Gong." In a fiery speech in the Senate he demanded that England agree to a northern boundary of 54° 40′ for what was then the territory of Oregon. Allen's cry was adopted by the 1844 Democratic National Convention as the slogan of the party, even though it threatened open conflict with England. The Democrats won the election, but the new President, James K. Polk, negotiated a compromise settlement at the 49th parallel. Actually, that was all that the United States had requested during the years when the territory was under the joint occupancy of the two countries, but Britain had always refused. In light of the threat to trade relations and the danger of war, Britain asked the United States to renew its original offer of the 49th parallel, and the Senate voted to settle for it.

fighting like Kilkenny cats. The Kilkenny cats were Irish, taking their name from the town and county of Kilkenny. There are two stories of the origin of the expression, so we'll serve them both up and let you choose the one you prefer. First, though, we should warn you that both are a bit gory.

Back a few centuries, the cats of Kilkenny had already won a reputation for rough-and-tumble scrapping. So some sportsmen decided to see if the reputation was warranted. They rounded up a thousand cats from all over Ireland and pitted them against a thousand Kilkenny cats. The battle lasted all night, and came the dawn, the Kilkenny cats were a bit battered but still alive—and the field was strewn with the bodies of the thousand visiting cats.

Then there's the story of the time when Kilkenny was occupied by Hessian mercenary soldiers, shortly after they had served their time in the American Revolution. Some of them, finding themselves bored, decided to start a cat fight. They tied two Kilkenny cats together by the tails and hung them over a clothesline. Naturally the cats scratched and clawed at each other, making a great racket all the while. The commanding officer, hearing the noise, went to investigate. The soldiers heard him coming, but didn't have time to untie the cats. With a quick swish of a sword, one soldier cut off their tails, and the cats raced into the night. Then he told the officer that the cats had fought so viciously that only their tails were left.

figurehead. We all know *figureheads* in business—those impressive-looking chaps who contribute little beyond ornamentation to the companies they nominally head. The expression originated with the ornamental *figure-heads* on clippers and other sailing ships. They looked mighty handsome but had nothing at all to do with the speed or other characteristics of the vessels they adorned.

filch. The jargon of sixteenth-century thieves gives us the word *filch.* A thief's *filch* was a rod with a hook on the end of it which enabled the thief to appropriate things furtively. Those who *filch* today do it without benefit of a hook, and the word has become a verb meaning "to pilfer or steal something, particularly something of small value."

file 13 is the W.P.B.—the wastepaper basket. It is also sometimes called "File 17." Both terms were World War II army slang, but what the numbers indicate is known only to army intelligence, as far as we can determine.

filibuster was originally a Dutch term and had nothing whatever to do with government. Indeed, it originally meant "freebooting"—private citizens' engaging in warfare against a state with whom their country is at peace, usually for personal gain. The Dutch word *vrijbuiter* literally meant "freebooter or pirate," and its derivative *filibuster* was first used in this country during the 1850s to describe adventurers who were running guns to revolutionists in Cuba and other Central and South American countries. However, the term *filibustering* has become so completely identified with delaying tactics in the Senate that the word is not used for gun-running or piracy any more.

The first use of *filibuster* to describe obstruction of legislation by invoking parliamentary delays and resorting to prolonged speechmaking appeared in 1853, when one member of Congress sharply criticized the tactics of his rivals as *"filibustering against the United States."*

filthy lucre usually brings forth two theories as to its origin: one, that it obviously means "dirty bills"; another, that it's just a figurative expression, indicating that money is the root of all evil.

Theory No. 2 is closer to the truth—and not just because the expression originated before paper money was known, either. It comes from the New Testament (I Timothy 3:2–3), in which the qualifications of a bishop are set forth: "A bishop then must be blameless . . . of good behavior, given to hospitality, apt to teach; not given to wine, no striker, not greedy of *filthy lucre.*" The word "filthy" in the Biblical sense means "dishonorable," rather than dirty or unclean. So *filthy lucre* really means "dishonorable gain."

fin, meaning a five-dollar bill, was originally underworld slang, derived from the Yiddish *finnuf* or *finnif,* meaning a British five-pound note. It first appeared in the argot of English thieves at about the time Charles Dickens was chronicling the adventures of Fagin and his band of child criminals. *Fin* first appeared in the language of our native hoods during the roaring twenties and was popularized by the gangster pictures of the 1930s era.

fine fettle. "In *fine fettle*" means "in good health and spirits." It comes from the old English *fetel,* meaning "belt," and refers to the generally healthier feeling one has when properly belted, ready to take on all comers in battle.

fine Italian hand is used to indicate the accomplishment of one's ambitions by devious, subtle and slightly disreputable techniques. But it is by no means always used in this derogatory sense. Many times the person using it is confessing a certain grudging admiration for the results obtained.

In truth, the origin of the phrase seems to have been of the highest and holiest. During the Middle Ages, papal secretaries used a type of handwriting—technically known as *cancelleresca*—that was easily distinguishable by its delicacy and grace from the cruder Gothic styles of Northern Europe. Hence the *Italian hand* was one noted for its finesse.

fink/ratfink. In grandfather's day, *fink* was one of the strongest terms in the lexicon of labor unions. To call a man a *fink* was to say that he was a strikebreaker, an informer and perhaps worse. *Fink,* in union circles, was most definitely a fighting word. In a theory put forth by H. L. Mencken in the late 1920s, it is an altered form of "pink" for "Pinkerton"—the strikebreakers hired in the infamous Homestead steel strike of 1892.

finnan haddie is smoked haddock, a delicious dish when baked in milk. The phrase was originally Findhorn haddock, a product of Findhorn, a fishing port in Scotland (but confused with Findon, a village in Kincardineshire —a county in East Central Scotland, which would seem to put Findon a fair distance from the sea).

first dibs is heard most commonly among children who argue as to who gets *first dibs* in taking turns or playing games. The traditional theory is that this goes back to a game, similar to jacks, played by British children. It involved rolling or tossing stones ("dibstones," they were called). Sometimes the objects played with were the knuckle bones of sheep, which sounds pretty alarming to us. Obviously the player who had *first dibs* would start with a competitive advantage over his opponent.

You can believe that if you want to. Our own feeling is that the usage among American children is a contraction of an expression very common in our own youth—"to divvy or divvy up." Whenever a youngster had an apple or some such easily divided item, his friends would be after him to "divvy it up" and the "first divvies" might well be the best. "Divvy" in this sense is, of course, just a slang version of "divide."

fisherman's ring is the ring of investiture of the Pope, bearing a representation of St. Peter drawing his net full of fishes. It is used by the Pope to seal formal documents and, at his death, is destroyed.

fish or cut bait. "Make yourself useful" is a free translation of the phrase *fish or cut bait.* It comes from the fact that there is no place for lazy men in the cramped quarters of fishing boats. In other words, "If you're not going to fish yourself, get busy and cut bait for your fellow fishermen."

fit as a fiddle means in tiptop condition. Its origin is obscure, but Charles Earle Funk, in his amusing book *Heavens to Betsey,* has the theory that two hundred years ago people thought of fiddles as instruments of great beauty—which, in the proper hands, they are. Anyhow, says Funk, "to have one's face made of a fiddle" was to be exceptionally good-looking. To "play first fiddle" was to occupy a leading position, and a man *fit as a fiddle* was beyond need of improvement in health.

fit to a T. The T involved is the familiar T-square used by draftsmen for establishing and drawing parallel lines. If you apply a T-square to the edge of a properly trimmed board, you will see that it does indeed *fit to a T.*

flabbergasted means to be astounded, practically struck dumb with surprise. It's a word that has been in the language since before the American Revolution, and nobody is quite certain of its origin. The best guess, and this is the opinion of the *Oxford Dictionary,* is that it is a blend of "flabby" and "aghast." We certainly buy the second half of that theory because "aghast" is precisely what a person is when he's *flabbergasted*. But we fail to see what "flabby" has to do with the situation. So there is half an answer, set forth in the hope that half an answer is better than none at all.

flack is a slang term common in the theatrical and popular-music fields, meaning "press agent." We have been familiar with it in this sense for years and suspect it antedates the World War II meaning of *"flak"* (which see); that of antiaircraft fire. However, it has never enjoyed the wide popular acceptance given, for example, to the term *"disc jockey,"* which became current in entertainment circles at about the same time. Perhaps the word is just too blunt and unlovely to find favor among practitioners of the fine art of "space grabbing." The best of them even frown on the term "press agent." Nowadays they are "public relations consultants."

flag down. You often hear the expression *"flag down* a cab"—even though it simply means waving one's hand to attract the driver's attention so he'll stop. Originally this expression came from the vocabulary of automobile racing, where the officials signal to the winner that the race is over by waving a flag up and down. This signal is also sometimes used to warn other drivers that they should stop or proceed with caution. Trains also are *flagged down* when emergency conditions warrant and timetables sometimes indicate flag stops, where through trains will stop only when *flagged* by the stationmaster.

flagstone. There's no connection between *flagstones* and patriotic flags. Actually, the *flag* in *flagstone* comes directly from the Norse word *flaga,* meaning "flake." A true *flagstone* is a hard stone split ("flaked") into flat pieces for use as paving.

flak was the generally used British term in World War II for antiaircraft fire. It was borrowed from the German *flak,* an abbreviation of *fliegerabwehr-kanone,* "antiaircraft cannon." The word was used earlier by combat fliers in World War I as a part of the jargon of the air arm of the services.

flake/finger job. In the jargon of policemen—at least of New York City policemen—*flake* means to plant evidence on a person who has been arrested. *Finger job* means the same thing. Such planting of evidence sometimes leads to a "shakedown" of the victim, which in turn may lead to an illegal payoff.

flaky, referring to unusual or eccentric behavior, originated in the slang of baseball players. A *flake* is a colorful, often eccentric, player of the type that in earlier years would have been labeled a "screwball." Perhaps the outstanding *flake* in big-league ball is the amazing pitcher Mark "The Bird" Fidrych, a brilliant youngster who talks to the ball, kneels to pat the pitching mound, calls words of approval to his teammates and, generally speaking, puts on a very *flaky* but often very successful performance.

flambé is borrowed from the French. You will find it on the menu in expensive restaurants. It means "passed through flame," and we use it to mean to douse with brandy and then ignite. The results are spectacular.

flaming youth. Shakespeare used the phrase in the memorable scene in which Hamlet castigates his mother for marrying his father's brother: ". . . at your age/The heyday in the blood is tame/. . . If thou canst mutine in a matron's bones,/To *flaming youth* let virtue be as wax/And melt in her own fire." "Mutine" is a now-forgotten verb form of "mutiny." All in all, a pretty elegant background for a phrase that most of us associate with the pleasure-mad *flaming youth* of the Scott Fitzgerald era of the 1920s.

flap. In Washington, *flap* has pretty well replaced "hassle" as the slang term used to describe a lively argument, especially one about an important matter. A bureau chief can—and often does—stir up a *flap* by calling a few subordinates on the carpet for an inquiry into methods and procedures of operation. But a truly monumental *flap* can develop when two departments become involved in a struggle to take over some newly defined area of government authority. For fairly obvious reasons, the Pentagon is sometimes nicknamed "The Five-Sided Flaphouse."

flapper. According to H. L. Mencken, *flapper* was in use in England during the 1890s to describe a young woman who, in the euphemism of the period, "was no better than she should be." By 1910 the word was common in this country, but without any derogatory implications. In America a *flapper* has always been a giddy, attractive and slightly unconventional young thing who, in Mencken's words, "was a somewhat foolish girl, full of wild surmises and inclined to revolt against the precepts and admonitions of her elders." The *flapper* was also noted for her revolt against conventions of dress. *Flappers* of the twenties used to delight in wearing their overshoes ("galoshes," they were sometimes called) with the hooks unfastened, so that each boot would "flap" against the other as the pretty thing made her way down the street. The practice sounds clumsy and noisy—and it was. But it was also attention-getting, and few pretty young ladies, in the *flapper* period or since, ever objected to attention.

flash in the pan is generally thought to have originated in the days of flintlock muskets. Just as an ineffective flash of the primer in the pan of the musket would result in no explosion of the charge, so a person who failed to live up to his early promise came to be known as a *flash in the pan*.

flat comes from the Anglo-Saxon *flat,* meaning "ground or floor." In England it designates any suite of rooms on a single floor. In America the word is now little used, but formerly it meant a single-floor lodging in an unpretentious or "tenement" building. See also PIED-À-TERRE.

flaunt/flout are two words which even some literate people use mistakenly. In a single session of the United States Supreme Court, two such distinguished jurists as Justices Black and White managed to use these words incorrectly. *Flaunt* means "to make a gaudy, ostentatious or boastful display," while *flout* has the very different meaning of mocking or scorning something accepted by society. The *Oxford Dictionary* speculates that *flaunt* may be a blend of "fly" and "vaunt," while *Funk & Wagnalls* guesses that it may have come from a Scandinavian word meaning "to gad about." In any event, it has been in the language since the sixteenth century. *Flout*—"to show contempt for or to scorn"—seems to come from a Middle English verb, *flouten,* "to play the flute." Presumably, when one plays a light and merry air one communicates something less than respect for the person or thing he is flouting.

flautist/flutist. In years past among symphony musicians the term *flautist* (pronounced FLAWT-ist) has been more commonly heard, though today the simpler *flutist* would surely be the layman's preference and probably the musician's as well. *Flautist,* like so many terms in the musical vocabulary, comes from an Italian word, *flautista,* referring to one who plays a *flauto* or flute.

Flutist evolves from the Middle English *floute,* which in turn was borrowed from Old French *flaute,* which brings us right back to the Italian *flauto.*

flea market is an open-air or street market that sells a wide variety of merchandise, most of it secondhand and some of it masquerading as antique. The first *flea market*—then called *marche aux puces*—was in Paris, but it is now common in all parts of Western Europe and in Great Britain as well. The reason for the name is simply that there are so many secondhand articles of all kinds for sale that they are believed to gather fleas.

Fleshly School of Poets. In a famous article in the *Contemporary Review* (1871), R. W. Buchanan attacked several prominent British poets, notably Dante Gabriel Rossetti, Algernon Charles Swinburne and William Morris. Buchanan considered them too much concerned with matters of the flesh, rather than of the spirit. Swinburne gave him his comeuppance in a sharply worded reply and eventually all was forgiven.

flibbertigibbet. This term for any garrulous, silly, scatterbrained person was one of the five fiends named by Edgar in Shakespeare's *King Lear.* It is also the name of a character in Scott's novel *Kenilworth.*

flivver. A *flivver* was a Tin Lizzie, and a Tin Lizzie was a Model T Ford automobile, certainly the most popular, most ridiculed and most affectionately remembered automobile in history.

Flivver is a dialect term of unknown origin. Originally it meant anything that was a failure or a flop. Perhaps amusingly, it lives on in the language as a nickname for a car that, whatever its shortcomings, was anything but a failure.

Florida. The Sunshine State was named by its discoverer, Ponce de Leon, in 1513. There are two theories for his naming it as he did. One is that he reached land on Easter Sunday—*pascua florida,* in Spanish. The other is that he was impressed with the abundance of flowers (*florida* in Latin).

flotsam and jetsam. The word *flotsam* is used in maritime law to describe goods swept from a vessel and found floating in the sea. *Jetsam* refers to cargo deliberately thrown overboard (or *jettisoned*) from a ship when it is in imminent danger of wreck, especially goods which sink and remain under water. *Flotsam and jetsam* is often loosely used to refer to wreckage, either floating or washed up on shore.

flour is taken from the French *fleur de farine,* which literally means "the flower, or finest, of the meal"—the meal of grain.

flower names. Many flowers, not surprisingly, have taken their names from the men who first developed the species. *Begonias* are named after an eighteenth-century French botanist, Michel Begon; *magnolias* after Pierre Magnol, a near-contemporary of Begon; *gardenias* after the appropriately named Alexander Garden, an American; and *dahlias* after A. Dahl, a Swedish botanist. See also CAMELLIA, FUCHSIA, POINSETTIA, WISTERIA.

fly off the handle implies a sudden wild outburst of wrath—much more than simply getting angry. It suggests the kind of trouble that would result if an ax head flew off its handle.

F.O.B. does not mean "freight on board." It means "free on board." It indicates that the price quoted includes costs and charges at the point of manufacture or shipment, but not transportation charges, which must be borne by the consignee.

fo'c'sle/forecastle. In the days of sailing ships, the *fo'c'sle* was the place where ordinary sailors slept. Even today the *fo'c'sle* is the name for the crew's quarters on merchant vessels. The original *fo'c'sles,* then called *forecastles,* were the foreparts of medieval fighting ships. They were built up like battlements on ancient castles. By hiding behind the protection of these *forecastles,* archers could shoot down upon the enemy.

foggy bottom. This designation of our State Department was invented in 1947 by James Reston, Washington correspondent of the *New York Times.* The expression originally applied to an area of the District of Columbia where a gasworks once stood. Its gaseous emanations gave the place its name. In 1947 the State Department moved into a new building in that area, and though the expression originally applied to various government agencies in the neighborhood, it gradually became restricted to State.

fold meaning to close down, especially from lack of funds, is far from a new usage. It started as theatrical slang and probably first saw print in the pages of the show business weekly *Variety.* It's labeled "informal" or "colloquial" in most dictionaries.

folk etymology. Etymology is what this book is all about—the search for sources of words. It comes from two Greek words: *etumon,* "true meaning of a word," and *logos,* "word," from which we take the suffix "-logy" meaning "the study of or science of a subject." Thus *etymology,* the study of the true or earliest meaning of words and of their subsequent evolution. But *folk etymology* is something else again. It is much more often the popular and incorrect notion of the origin of a word, usually based on faulty analogy to better-known words. In folk speech or dialect one can find many examples—"Johnnyquil" for jonquil, "high-bred" for hybrid, "cow-cumber" for cucumber, and "sparrowgrass" for asparagus. A variation, which might more properly be called "popular etymology" would include such widely believed but false theories as the one about "marmalade" (which see) being derived from "Marie malade." We Morrises have still a third variation: Instant Folk Etymology, a theory made up on the spur of the moment without regard for fact. See GINGERLY.

folklore, describing the traditional beliefs and legends of the common people, is such a staple item of our culture that it comes as a bit of a shock to learn that the word itself was coined as recently as 1846. Its creator was the editor of the British *Athenaeum,* W. J. Thoms.

food from the opera. Perhaps the most famous dish to bear the name of an operatic diva is *chicken Tetrazzini,* named after Luisa Tetrazzini, whose Lucia di Lammermoor thrilled opera lovers throughout Europe and North and South America during the early decades of this century. As might be expected of an Italian-born singer, her favorite dish contains *pasta*—spe-cifically, thin spaghetti—plus chicken and a rich cheese-and-mushroom sauce. Delicious—but not for anyone counting calories!

The greatest tenor of our era, Enrico Caruso, was also one of the notable gourmands of his time. He has left us *sauce Caruso,* which is marinara sauce with sautéed mushrooms and chicken livers added. Characteris-tically again, this is designed for service with spaghetti.

And topping off the menu, we have *peach Melba,* named after the great Australian soprano Dame Nellie Melba. This concoction involves peach halves, vanilla ice cream and a sauce of currants and raspberries. *Melba toast,* also named for Dame Nellie, is thin dry toast, recommended for the diets of those who have indulged in *peach Melba.*

foolish consistency. "A *foolish consistency* is the hobgoblin of little minds, adored by little statesmen and philosophers and divines." Ralph Waldo Emerson, one of the leading pundits of nineteenth-century New England, wrote it in one of his essays, the one on "Self-Reliance." It is very widely quoted, but almost invariably misquoted. Note carefully that Emerson is not putting down consistency as such, merely *foolish consistency.*

foolscap is stationery measuring from 12 by 15 inches up to 13½ by 17 inches. The most common size is 13 by 16 inches, which is often folded to make pages of 8 by 13 inches. Originally it was a printing paper used in England and it got its name from the ancient watermark of a fool's head and cap used to identify the paper. The earliest specimens of paper using the *fool-scap* watermark date back to before the time of Shakespeare.

foopah/faux pas/foxpaw. *Foopah* is a dialect version of *faux pas* (false step), a term we borrowed from French to indicate a blunder or error, particu-larly in etiquette. In some parts of the country another dialect variation, *foxpaw,* is heard.

foot, as a unit of measurement, is twelve inches. According to legend, King John (reigned 1199–1216)—the same who signed the Magna Charta—simply stamped his foot on the ground, pointed to the indentation and declared: "There is a foot; let it be the measure from this day forward!"

foot the bill simply means to sign your name at the foot or bottom of the bill. Obviously the one who *foots the bill* assumes the responsibility for paying it.

forcemeat is at least as interesting to a word expert as to a master cook. It comes from the same root as the dramatic term "farce," and both originally meant the same thing—stuffing. During the Middle Ages it was the custom of acting companies to insert a brief, rowdy and highly comic interlude between the acts of the main drama. These short pieces were figuratively "stuffed" between sections of the performance and so were called *farces,* from the French word for stuffing. *Farcemeat*—finely chopped and seasoned meat or fish used as stuffing—in the course of time came to be *forcemeat,* possibly through confusion with the totally unrelated word "force"—since, as anyone who has stuffed a twenty-pound turkey knows, a certain amount of force is involved in the operation.

forgotten man. While Franklin D. Roosevelt was surely the person who made this phrase popular, he was not the first to use it. Back in 1883 Professor William Graham Sumner, of Yale University, used it in a speech. What he said was: "Such is the *forgotten man.* He works, he votes, generally he prays—but he always pays."

forlorn hope means a cause that is hopeless or doomed. The odd thing about this phrase is that the expression really doesn't have anything at all to do with "hope"—or at any rate, it didn't originally. The phrase was Dutch, *verloren hoop,* and it literally meant "lost troop." It was used to describe the first wave of assault troops, the "expendables." When the phrase was taken over into English, *verloren hoop* became, by folk etymology, *forlorn hope.*

for Pete's sake is simply a polite version of a common and profane expression involving the name of Christ. We'd surmise that the original "Pete" was St. Peter.

forsythia, a large flowering shrub whose brilliant yellow flowers are among the earliest harbingers of spring, was originally native to China but was domesticated in Great Britain by William Forsythe, royal gardener under George III. The plant was named in his honor.

forte has two distinctly different uses and pronunciations in the English language, depending on whether the French or Italian version is followed. In Latin *fortis* means "strong or powerful." The Italians coined *forte* (pronounced as two syllables—FOR-tay) as a musical term to indicate that a certain passage should be played loudly. The French used *fort* as an adjective to mean strong and then added an *e* to make a noun (pronounced as one syllable) to denote a person's strong point, something he does particularly well. In English, both forms of *forte* are used, the distinction as to meaning being indicated by the pronunciation.

fortnight/sennight. The *fort* in *fortnight* is simply a contraction of "fourteen" —and who first abbreviated "fourteen nights" that way is not known to history. Anyhow, it must have been many centuries ago, for the terms *fortnight* (two weeks) and *sennight* ("seven nights" or one week) are at least as old as written English. Indeed, they are thought to have been borrowed from the ancient German method of measuring time by counting nights rather than days.

FORTRAN is a computer-programming language by which problems can be expressed in algebraic terms. It is an acronym of FOR(mula) plus TRAN-(slation).

forty/four There is a reasonable explanation of why the *u* is omitted in the word *forty* while it is used in *four*. In Middle English *forty* was *fourti,* and *four* was *foure.* Why, between then and now, did *fourti* drop its *u* and *foure* retain it? Probably the explanation is very simple: *forty* could not be confused with any similarly spelled word—and the dropping of the *u* would be a logical simplification of the spelling. But if *four* were to become *for,* confusion would result because the preposition *for* (*for* God and Country) and the conjunction *for* (*for* he's a jolly good fellow) have long been established.

for want of a nail. This is one of the oldest proverbs in English. A version of it appeared in Gower's *Confessions of a Lover* about 1390 and every collector of proverbs from Heywood to Ben Franklin has used it. Franklin's version, in *Poor Richard's Almanack,* runs: "A little neglect may breed great mischief . . . *for want of a nail* the shoe was lost; for want of a shoe the horse was lost; and for want of a horse the rider was lost." A French version carries it one step further: "The rider, breaking his rank, may molest the company so far as to hazard the whole army."

four-flusher. A *four-flusher* is a person who pretends to be what he is not. He's a phony or a bluffer. In poker a flush is a potentially winning hand, which must contain five cards of the same suit. A player who tries to bluff his way with only four cards of the same suit is, obviously, a *four-flusher.* As a lagniappe, we offer, free, gratis and for nothing, the information that in some sophisticated cardplaying circles, the four-card flush is known as a "bobtail flush."

Four Freedoms. The basic human freedoms, as enunciated by Franklin Delano Roosevelt in 1941, were freedom of speech and religion and freedom from want and fear.

Fourteen Points. These were the conditions laid down by President Woodrow Wilson in 1918 as the basis for a peace settlement with Germany. They included a return by Germany to its prewar borders, freedom of the seas, and reduction of armaments.

Fourth Estate. This term for newspapermen originated in a speech of Sir Edmund Burke in the British Parliament. He noted the various estates of the realm: the Lords Spiritual, the Lords Temporal and the Commons—the powers that hold in their hands the control of British governments. Then Burke added, pointing to the press gallery: "And yonder sits the *Fourth Estate,* more important than them all."

foyer. For American use the pronunciation FOY-er is preferred for this word, though the fractured French foy-YAY is often heard. The word comes from France, where it had the very different meaning of "hearthside." Its transformation to our meaning of "lobby or entrance hall," especially of a theater, came about gradually. First it was used to designate the greenroom (which see) of a theater—the place where actors retire for informal chitchat. Then it gradually moved far offstage and became the name for the lobby.

Franglais/Frenglish. Some French scholars are furious with Americans who, they claim, are sullying the beauty of the French language with words like "drugstore" and "barbecue," which young Frenchmen are picking up from movies and TV. They have even invented a name, *Franglais,* for this blend of English and French.

It is amusing to see English and American suddenly attacked as influences "corrupting" French since for so long the trend was the other way. Beginning with the invasion of William the Conqueror, French influences on English have been enormous. The simple rough-hewn tongues of the Angles and Saxons became exposed to the more graceful, more elaborate Romance languages, chiefly French. For many centuries, indeed until the establishment of the United Nations, the chief language of international diplomacy was French. And of course, important fashions and culinary triumphs have masqueraded under French labels seemingly forever.

So slavish was fashion's devotion to the lingo of the French designers, that there's even one classic case of a perfectly good English phrase being borrowed by the French and then being taken back into English in its French form. The term is "redingote," which started in life as the relatively prosaic English "riding coat."

With all these centuries of linguistic traffic from France to Britain and thence to America, it's remarkable to see how thin-skinned and—to use a word we borrowed from them—how chauvinistic the French seem to be when a few Americanisms like "gadget" and "football" and "scriptgirl" begin to find their way across the ocean and into the pages of French newspapers.

We suspect that this is symptomatic of a deeper malaise. The French writer Pierre Daninos reminds his fellow countrymen that "if Frenchmen can freely shake the hands of Mexicans, it is because young men from Arkansas, Missouri and Ontario gave their lives at Normandy in 1944.

What is happening today in the world is exactly, on the international level, what occurs in our private lives: the friend who owes us his job, money, his very existence, can no longer stand the sight of us."

But whatever the reason for the attempted rebellion of French scholars, it will not succeed. The history of languages throughout the Western world is one of unceasing borrowing one from the other.

In the late 1960s even Le Grand Charles de Gaulle joined in the attack by French linguists against *Franglais,* the use of English terms by Frenchmen—even though this simply continued a practice that has been going back and forth between Britain and France ever since the Norman Conquest. The British promptly dubbed the new language *Frenglish* and implied that the French were better off for the resulting improvement in their native tongue.

Frankenstein was the doctor—actually a medical student—in Mary Shelley's novel of this name. The monster that he created from bits and pieces of cadavers is properly called *"Frankenstein's* monster," not *Frankenstein.*

fraught is a fine old word, going back to Middle English. As you might guess, it was originally another form of "freight," and centuries ago historians wrote of "ships with ryches full yfraught." Nowadays, of course, it means "accompanied by or burdened with," as in "a situation *fraught* with danger."

freebe/freebie *Freebe* is a copywriter's somewhat eccentric spelling of what in *Variety* and other show business publications is known as a "freebie" —a free ticket. In earlier times these were known as "Annie Oakleys," from the fact that each ticket had a hole in the center to ensure that it would not be sold. And Annie, in case anyone has forgotten, was the famous sharpshooter of Buffalo Bill's shows.

free lance goes back to medieval times. Originally it referred to the so-called free companies, both Italian and French, of mercenary soldiers who were willing to serve under any banner—for a price. The word *free* has no reference to the rates they charged; it merely means that they were free of loyalty to any one standard and thus free to fight for whoever paid the best fee. (Change "fight" to "write" in that sentence and you have a pretty fair definition of today's *free-lancer.*)

French-fried potatoes. The *French* in *French-fried potatoes* does not refer to the country of origin of this particular method of cookery, but rather to a method—*Frenching*—of preparing meats and vegetables before cooking them. A lamb chop is *Frenched,* for instance, when it is cut close to the bone so that the narrow strip of bone may be more easily handled. Vegetables, notably stringed or stringless beans, are *Frenched*—cut into narrow strips—before cooking. Similarly, beef tenderloin is sometimes cut into strips as part of the preparation for cooking. So it was by logical extension of this procedure of *Frenching* foods that *French-fried potatoes* got their name.

French leave/AWOL To a man who served in the armed forces during World War I, *French leave* meant the same as *AWOL*—absenting oneself from a navy ship or army post without permission. The term is no reflection on the bravery of French soldiers, as some people think, but goes back to a convention common in seventeenth-century France. The practice was frowned upon by the British, but to the French it was perfectly proper then to leave a party early without bidding formal farewell to the host and hostess, hence *French leave*. *AWOL* is an acronym formed by the first letters of the phrase "absent without leave" (someone stretched a point here to get a vowel). When the phrase was first abbreviated, it was just to four individually pronounced letters—A.W.O.L.—but it soon became *AWOL* (AY-wol).

French toast, unlike *French-fried potatoes,* gets its name from the fact that it originated in France, where it was known variously as *ameritte* and *pain perdu.* It consists of slices of bread—often stale—dipped in egg and milk, fried crisp in butter and served with cinnamon or syrup. Ralph Hickok of the *New Bedford* (Mass.) *Standard-Times* notes that there are many French-Canadians in that area and they make French toast with salt instead of sugar and serve it plain, or with sauced dishes like chicken à la king over it. *"Chacun,"* as the saying goes, *"à son goût."*

freshman/sophomore. The origin of *freshman* is fairly obvious, simply *fresh* in the sense of new and inexperienced, and *man.* The only surprising thing about the word is its antiquity. The *Oxford Dictionary* traces it back to 1550—before the birth of Shakespeare. *Sophomore* is a much more interesting word, coming from two Greek words: *sophos* (wise), and *moros* (foolish). So the *sophomore* is literally the wise fool—and that's why the adjective *sophomoric* has long meant "pretentious, immature and superficial."

frieze/frise are two kinds of fabrics very similarly named. *Frieze* (pronounced FREEZ) is correctly used to designate a heavy wool cloth with an uncut, shaggy nap on one side. It is generally used as an overcoat material and is believed to have originated in Friesland, Holland. *Frise* is an upholstery fabric, however, and in its original French form, had an acute accent on the final *e*—thereby calling for the pronunciation free-ZAY. *Frise,* which comes from the French word *friser* (to curl), is a fabric with a thick pile made of uncut loops or a combination of cut and uncut loops.

fringe. While an American may have her hair cut with "bangs" across the forehead, the same haircut is, to the British, one with *"fringe."*

Frisbee is the trademark for a small plastic disk which provides exercise and fun for young and old when tossed to and fro. According to William Cole, writing in the *Saturday Review,* it all started when Yale students took to tossing about pie plates of the Frisbie Pie Company of Bridgeport, Connecticut.

from pillar to post comes from the old game of court tennis, which was more like our present game of squash than lawn tennis as we know it today. It was played in medieval courtyards, and pillars and posts served as natural complications to the play. Thus a ball going from *post to pillar*—the original version of the phrase—would be one that had gotten out of control and was skittering about hither and yon.

front runner originally meant a horse that looked fine as long as it was out in front, setting the pace, but which would fall quickly back into the ruck when challenged. In its application to politics, however, *front runner* usually is taken to mean the candidate who, in the opinion of pollsters and other self-anointed experts, is favored to win.

fruit salad, as a slang term, is used to describe the collection of service and combat ribbons worn on the chest of military personnel.

fuchsia takes its name from Leonhard Fuchs, a sixteenth-century German botanist.

full of the Old Nick. *Old Nick* in this expression is a euphemism for the devil, and the expression simply means "full of devilment." There are almost as many euphemisms for the devil as there are for liquor and drinking. Among the commonest names for the evil one are Old Harry, Old Blazes, Old Scratch, Old Splitfoot and Old Sam Hill.

fulsome is a word widely misunderstood and misused because it is often used to describe praise. However, *"fulsome* praise" is far from what most people think it to be. While *fulsome* came from the Middle English *fulsum* or *fulsom,* which meant "full or fat," its present-day meaning is more akin to that of *foul.* Used accurately, it means "sickeningly excessive; offensive, particularly because it is insincere." So *"fulsome* praise" is hardly complimentary.

funny as a crutch means not funny at all. It usually turns up when a person attempts a joke that proves so inept or in such poor taste that he is told he is as *funny as a crutch.*

funny bone. Actually, what causes that painful tingling sensation when you bump your *funny bone* is the impact not on any bone but on the ulnar nerve. However, the term *funny bone* has been part of the language for many a long year and is apparently here to stay. It results from a rather learned pun on the name for the bone running from the shoulder to the elbow, the humerus. Get it?

furbish lousewort is a wild flower long believed to be extinct. About thirty specimens of this extremely rare plant were found in Maine at the site of a multimillion-dollar hydroelectric project, which so interested the *Wall Street Journal* that an editorial was devoted to it. It seems the project was long opposed by private utilities interests, which regarded it as "the last of the New Deal boondoggles." And just when it appeared that politicians favorable to federal power projects were about to have their way, they were thwarted by the *furbish lousewort.* If they went ahead with the project, they would find themselves running afoul of the Federal Endangered Species

Act. As the *Journal* said, "this outcome is replete with irony." The plant is named for its discoverer, Catherine "Kate" *Furbish* (1834–1931). The *lousewort* comes from the fact that sheep feeding on it were believed to be especially subject to vermin—"louses" or "lice."

Furies. The Furies were three winged goddesses with snakes for hair. Their function was to pursue and punish doers of unavenged misdeeds. These "daughters of darkness" were called Alecto, Megaera and Tisiphone.

furtive (pronounced FUR-tiv), with its meaning of "stealthy or sly," is derived from Latin. From *furtum* (theft) the Romans made *furtivus* (stolen or hidden) and it was the latter meaning that carried over to English. Thus a *furtive* movement is one which the maker tries to conceal; a *furtive* glance is one stolen with the hope of not being seen. As an adverb it becomes *furtively,* and as a noun, *furtiveness.*

fuzz can be traced to the slang of narcotics users and dealers from the 1920s onward. The federal narcotics agents—called "narcs" nowadays—were then simply called "feds." The theory is that the whispered "Feds!" as a warning of an impending raid could easily be corrupted into *fuzz.* However, we feel honor-bound to report that one of our faithful readers, Stewart Beach of New York City, reports having seen *fuzz* used as a nickname for British policemen in a novel written by Edgar Wallace in 1915. So possibly our underworld simply borrowed the expression from the criminal elements back in Blighty.

gabardine/gaberdine. During the Middle Ages, Jewish merchants wore a loose-fitting coat or cloak called a *gaberdine.* Shylock refers to his costume by this name in *The Merchant of Venice.* The same sort of garment was worn by wanderers and pilgrims. Indeed, the word originally came from the Old High German word *walvart* (pilgrimage) via the Old French *gauvardine.* Although the *er* spelling for the second syllable is still acceptable in England for both the historical meaning of "loose cloak" and the present-day meaning of "twilled fabric," American authorities generally agree that the *er* spelling, if used at all, should be restricted to the historical sense of the word.

gadfly. The original *gadfly* was any one of several pesky flies that cluster around livestock and bite or otherwise annoy them. The word comes from an Old English word, *gadde,* meaning "to sting or goad," plus "fly." It has long since developed the added meaning of a person who repeatedly criticizes institutions or programs, often in the interests of civic betterment.

gadget. No one knows for certain where *gadget* began, but it has been in the language for many years and was popularized by sailors. It means any small mechanical device, particularly one whose precise name escapes the speaker. Originally it was a sort of seagoing equivalent of the landlubber's "thingamajig" or "doodad." It has long since been an accepted part of the landman's vocabulary, though, sharing honors with "doohickey" and "gismo." One theory of the origin of *gadget* is that it is an engineer's corruption of the now obsolete Scottish word *gadge,* a variant of "gauge," the measuring device. Still another possible origin is in the French word *gachette,* meaning "catch or staple." Take your choice.

gaffer and gammer. We're all familiar with the phrase "old *gaffer,*" though one doesn't hear much about "old *gammers*" these days—perhaps because *gammers* seem to be getting younger and younger. The two words are dialect contractions of "grandpa" and "grandma."

gall is the word for nerve, impudence, cheek or what you will. In this sense it goes back many centuries. Originally a person with *gall* was one who had —in the theories of medieval medicine—too strong a secretion of bile from the liver. As a result he was arrogant, bitter, rancorous—and very much given to unpleasant treatment of his fellow men. In a word, he *galled* them.

galley west appears to be simply a popular version of the British dialect phrase "collyweston." It seems that in some rural sections of England the expression "It's all along o' Colly Weston" is used to describe a day when nothing seems to go right—the kind of day when "you can't win for losing."

gallimaufry. Here's a splendid word, too little used nowadays, that we borrowed from the French in the late sixteenth century. It means a hodgepodge, a hash, a stew—any combination of ridiculously unmatched elements. There is a theory that the French made the word up from a combination of the words *galer,* "to live a gay life," and *mafrer,* "to eat voraciously."

gallivant/gallant. Press accounts of one of the periodic cleanups of New York's Times Square reported that the prostitutes were *gallivanting* in other parts of the city. This seemed an extension of the original meaning of *gallivant,* which is, in the words of the *Oxford Dictionary:* "To gad about in a showy fashion, especially with persons of the opposite sex." Our own *American Heritage Dictionary* brings matters a bit more up to date and, in a sense, reflects better the conduct of harlots, defining *gallivant* as: "to consort frivolously with members of the opposite sex; to flirt." The word is closely related to *gallant,* as used in the old expression "to play the *gallant,*" a term originally reserved for males who were overly flirtatious. *Gallant* itself comes from an Old French verb, *galar,* "to rejoice," from which we also get the word "regale." Just how males "playing the *gallant*" became transmuted into prostitutes, presumably female, *gallivanting,* is just one of those things that we will have to put under the heading of "semantic change." What a change!

galluses are suspenders, especially the wide, sturdy kind once worn by firemen and still often worn by outdoorsmen and men doing heavy labor. *Gallus* is a variant of "gallows," which once had the meaning of "suspenders."

galore. In English we are accustomed to thinking of adjectives as preceding the nouns they modify, though there are many instances (notably predicate adjectives) where they follow. Some adjectives are regularly placed "postpositively," as grammarians say. For example: "court-martial." These usually follow the French pattern. But *galore* (as in "He makes mistakes *galore*") comes from Gaelic.

galoshes—which sound like an item from hillbilly dialect—actually come direct from the royal courts of the French monarchs. In the days when shoes were made of silk and other kinds of cloth, *galoches,* which were a sort of wooden sandal, were worn to protect the shoes on wet days. Over the centuries these wooden clogs were transmuted into the rubber overshoes we know as *galoshes* today.

galvanic. A number of scientists have contributed to our language words which have both scientific and general meanings. Luigi Galvani was an Italian physicist and physiologist whose experiments led to the discovery that electricity could be produced by chemical action. So *galvanize* was invented to mean "apply electrical current to." *Galvanic,* with the scientific meaning of "producing or caused by electrical current," is also used popularly to describe anything so stimulating or shocking that it might have been produced by electrical shock.

galvanize, meaning to spur to action, comes from the name of an eighteenth-century Italian physiologist, Luigi Galvani. While experimenting with frogs and other animals, he discovered that he could *galvanize* them by subjecting them to electric shock.

gamesmanship was coined by the late Stephen Potter and appeared first as the title of a book whose subtitle really serves as the best possible definition of *gamesmanship:* "The Art of Winning Games Without Actually Cheating." See also PETER PRINCIPLE, PARKINSON'S LAW, ONE-UPMANSHIP, MURPHY'S LAWS.

gandy dancer. There are various theories of the origin of this colorful name for a railroad section hand. First there's the idea that a trackwalker's gait is likely to be somewhat waddly as he steps from tie to tie. So the reference may be to the way a male goose—a *gander*—walks. Next is the theory that early section hands used a tool called a *gandy,* a metal tamping bar. The third possibility is that the name may have come from the Gandy Manufacturing Company, a long-defunct Chicago firm which once made tools used by railroad laborers.

Since none of these seemed to be entirely persuasive, we put the question to readers of our column and, sure enough, an old-time railroader came up with the answer. "I was interested in your discussion of the term *gandy dancer* as a name for railroad section hands," wrote S. V. Fulkerson of Whitewater, Wisconsin. "The reason for the name is that they used a tool called a *gandy* and fashioned somewhat like a stilt. It was an iron bar about five feet long with a sort of horn projecting at right angles from it and about a foot from one end. Gravel was spilled around the railroad ties and, to settle it in tightly, the workman thrust his gandy into the gravel. Then, with one foot on the horn and one hand on the long end of the tool, he *danced* around and around, his other leg supplying the motive power." So now we know where the *dancer* in *gandy dancer* comes from.

gang agley. Here *gang* is a Scottish-dialect verb meaning "to walk or go" and *agley* means "awry." It's known and remembered almost exclusively because of Robert Burns's famous lines "To a Mouse": "The best laid schemes o' mice an' men/Gang aft a-gley,/An' lea'e us naught but grief an' pain,/For promis'd joy!"

gardenia isn't just any sort of garden flower, as its name might suggest. It's a shrub originally native to China, with shiny evergreen leaves and large fragrant flowers, most often white. It gets its name not from "garden" but from Dr. Alexander Garden, a Scottish naturalist and botanist, who lived a good part of his life in Charleston, South Carolina. A Tory, he remained faithful to the crown during the Revolution, returning to England at its end.

garlic. An aromatic plant, much admired by some cooks and equally loathed by others, *garlic* has loosed its pungent aroma in England at least since Anglo-Saxon times, for its name goes back to the Old English words *gar* (spear) and *leak* (leek), from the spear-shaped leaves of the plant. Actually, of course, *garlic* was known to the ancients as well and an article of faith with many authorities, including Ptolemy and Plutarch, was the belief that a really strong whiff of *garlic* would overcome the magnetism in a lodestone—so *garlic* was not favored aboard ships, where the lodestone was needed as an aid to navigation.

Garrison finish. The Garrison of *Garrison finish* was jockey Edward H. Garrison, usually called "Snapper" Garrison. He left the turf before the start of the twentieth century but, in the days when Diamond Jim Brady was living high on the hog, the Snapper was one of America's folk heroes. It was his almost invariable practice to hold his horse far back in the pack, moving up with a rush only when entering the home stretch. Since most of his races were won in the last furlong, the *Garrison finish* became part of American sporting language.

gasconade (pronounced gas-kuh-NAYD) is a French word meaning "bombastic boasting or bragging, usually without much basis for the boast." The French tell of one native of Gascony, a notably poor province, who was asked his opinion of the Louvre. "Very nice," he replied. "It reminds me of the back part of my father's stables."

That in turn reminds us of the story of the Texan—ah, there, Gascony! —who was comparing notes with an Irish farmer. "My farm," said the Irishman, "is so big that it takes me an entire day to walk from one end to the other."

"Interesting," replied the Texas. "My spread is so big that it takes me three days to go from one end to the other by car."

"Ah, yes. I understand," said the Irishman. "I had a car like that once, too."

gasser. In the jargon of jazz musicians, a *gasser* is a person or event that stimulates a very enthusiastic response.

gastrosoph/gastronome. A *gastrosoph* (from the Greek *gaster,* "stomach," and *sophos,* "wise") has precisely the same meaning as *gastronome*—one who is fond of good eating. *Gastrosoph* is, however, much less frequently seen in print. The word is pronounced GAS-truh-sof.

gat, an underworld slang term for gun, probably is a contraction of *gatling gun,* the name of the first machine gun, invented by R. G. Gatling. The first gangster *gats* were probably the Thompson submachine guns, called "Tommy guns," favored by Capone-era mobsters. In later years, however, *gat* became a generic term for any portable firearm.

gauche (pronounced GOHSH) means "graceless, tactless or socially awkward." In French, from which the word comes directly, *gauche* means "left, warped or clumsy." Here we have an example of the way language seems always to discriminate against left-handed people. Have you noticed that "dexterous" (from the Latin *dexter,* meaning "right") and "adroit" (from the French *droit,* also meaning "right") both have the connotation of skillfulness and cleverness, while the "left-handed" words like "sinister" (from the identical Latin word for "left") and *gauche* have derogatory implications? Even the word "gawky" originally came from the dialect phrase "gawk-handed," meaning "left-handed."

gauntlet/gantlet. When one is forced to *run the gauntlet,* he runs between two facing lines of opponents, each intent on administering as much bodily harm to him as possible in the time it takes to pass. This *gauntlet* (also sometimes spelled *gantlet*) is derived from an earlier word, *gantlope,* and comes from two Swedish words, *gata* (road or way) and *lop* (course). According to the *Oxford Dictionary,* this kind of *gauntlet* has been part of the language since 1646, lending credence to the theory that it may have been introduced to England during the Thirty Years' War. Since Sweden was an active participant in those religious wars, it would seem logical for the word and even the practice to have been borrowed at that time.

The second *gauntlet* has a much longer history, going back to the days of knightly chivalry and combat. A diminutive of the French word *gant* (glove), it was the kind of heavy glove worn by knights in armor. When one knight threw down the *gauntlet* before another, that was a challenge to duel. When the second knight picked up the *gauntlet,* he signified that he was accepting the challenge, and the contest was on.

gay Lothario. The eighteenth-century equivalent of today's "swinger," a chap who played fast and loose with the affections of many females, got his name from a character in the play *The Fair Penitent* by Nicholas Rowe (1703).

He is described as "that haughty, gallant, gay Lothario" and, predictably, seduces the heroine, Calista, the fair penitent. Lothario himself, of course, showed no signs of penitence, that being against the code of the fashionable and unscrupulous rake. The expression *gay Lothario* has been rendered meaningless by the popularization of *gay* as a synonym for "homosexual."

gazebo. "He's a big *gazebo,*" back in the 1920s, was as common as "He's a wheel" or "He's a real operator" on college campuses of a later day. However, dictionaries give only this definition: "a summerhouse; a projecting window or balcony." Just how a rather high-flown word like *gazebo,* which is believed to have been formed from the word "gaze" in pretentious imitation of a Latin form, could have come to mean "guy" or "chap" is a minor linguistic mystery. In the process, the pronunciation was altered from guh-ZEE-boh to guh-ZAY-boh and the word dropped from proper usage to slang.

gazette. This common word for newspaper comes from the Venetian phrase *gazeta de la novita,* a newspaper sold for a small coin. The *gazeta* was a small copper coin, and in the sixteenth century it paid only for a reading of the paper or the privilege of hearing it read aloud. Later the word was taken into English, fleshed out with an extra *t* and a terminal *e,* and used as the name of the first official court newspaper, the *Oxford Gazette* (1642). Incidentally, the term "gazetteer," for a compendium of geographical data arranged in alphabetical order, comes from the name of an early collection, *The Gazetteer's Interpreter,* meaning a guide for the use of gazetteers (men who wrote *gazettes*).

geezer, in and of itself, is about as flattering as "old coot"—which isn't very flattering unless said in honeyed tones, as "You lovable old coot!" Scholars claim that *geezer* comes from the Old English word *guiser,* a man in disguise, and refers to an odd, eccentric fellow. However, the new supplement to the *Oxford Dictionary* says it now doesn't mean any more than "chap" or "fellow."

gendarme. *Les gendarmes* are, quite literally, "men of arms," from the French words *gens* (people) and *d'armes* (of arms). Technically, the title *gendarme* may apply either to a member of the French national police department or to any rural policeman. In practice, the folk name is more likely to be "flic," just as "cop" is certainly more common in American folk speech than "police officer."

generic terms. Just about the most fertile coiners of new words are manufacturers and merchandisers searching for new and catchy brand names for their products. Each year thousands of names for new drug products, new synthetic fibers, new gasoline additives and new photographic processes are coined—and these are only a few areas in which fertile brains are working feverishly to coin new names. According to a survey by the *Wall Street Journal,* the search for new names with sales appeal has taken a new turn.

Today dozens, sometimes hundreds, of alternate names for each new product are being tested—well in advance of the product's first marketing—by market research firms. What's more, those twentieth-century Merlins of Madison Avenue—the motivational research fellows—are now knee-deep in trying to find out why you, the public, react favorably to certain combinations of syllables and unfavorably to other combinations.

The Ford Motor Company, for example, tested many names for a projected line of "middle-price" cars to compete with Oldsmobile and the now defunct DeSoto. Among the candidates tested and rejected were Saxon (people thought it meant English muffins), Belmont (sounded like a race track) and Arrow (people confused this with shirts). They persevered valiantly and eventually came up with—you guessed it—the Edsel. Still they were undaunted, for after all, they had tested five thousand names before they hit upon Thunderbird.

But you can be too successful in naming a product. If your name becomes overpopular, it runs the risk of becoming so much a part of everyday speech that it denotes all articles of a similar type, no matter who manufactures them. The word, in short, becomes a *generic term,* applicable to an entire category of products—and how the trademark owners dread the day that happens! Many large corporations maintain a staff of attorneys and public relations men whose sole function is to see that any infringers of their trademark rights are warned and, if the infringement continues, prosecuted.

The Technicolor people have spent many thousands of dollars over the years to protect the validity of their trademark and to convince the general public that every picture in color is not a Technicolor picture. Similarly, the Scotch Transparent Tape people—Minnesota Mining and Manufacturing Company—want you to know that other brands of cellophane tape are not Scotch. Their realization of the need to protect their name is especially acute, since *cellophane*—once a Du Pont trademark—has now become a *generic term* and may be used by anyone manufacturing the stuff without payment of royalty. *Aspirin* likewise was once a Bayer trademark, and *escalator* was originally the exclusive property of Otis Elevator Company.

A reader in Waterbury, Connecticut, Ralph Drapatin, has made a list of such words which many people mistakenly think are "general terms regardless of brand," as he puts it. They include Frigidaire for electric refrigerator, Kleenex for cleansing tissue, Victrola for phonograph, and Kodak for camera. These are all, of course, registered trademarks, and you should view with mistrust any dealer who uses these designations for a product other than that made by the trademark owner.

How, then, can the ordinary person distinguish between a trademark and a *generic term?* Usually, as with Metrecal, a trademark is capped, that is, spelled with the first letter capitalized. Thus you will see Coke—a trademark name for Coca-Cola—spelled with a capital *C*, while *coke*, the common household fuel, starts with a small *c*.

Here are a few other examples, from a useful list compiled by the Milwaukee Proofreaders Association for their paper, the *Stet-O-Scope*. *Generic terms: cotton, rayon, nylon, acetate, asbestos, polyester.* Trademarks: Acrilan, Byrd Cloth, Chemstrand, Dacron, Duralon, Jungle Cloth, Sanforized, Taslan and Zefran. All clear? Well, just look for the caps, and you'll have a good guide to a solution of the trademark–*generic term* dilemma.

gentle birth. The origin and implication of the expression "He is a man of *gentle birth*" is found in the language of courtiers. *Gentil,* was an Old French word meaning "noble," so a "man of *gentle birth*" was one born —legitimately—into the nobility. In the course of the centuries since the Norman Conquest, the word "gentleman" has lost the connotation of nobility, but it still indicates a man whose innate courtesy and decorous behavior stamp him as a person of good breeding.

gentleman. A reader queried the origin of the statement: "A *gentleman* is one who never unintentionally offends."

One version of this idea is ascribed to John Henry Cardinal Newman, the distinguished Anglican prelate who became a leader in the hierarchy of the Roman Catholic Church. Newman once wrote: "It is almost the definition of a *gentleman* to say that he is one who never inflicts pain." That doesn't quite hit the mark, though, so we also offer this from the table talk of Oliver Herford: "A *gentleman* is one who never hurts anyone's feelings unintentionally."

geodesic dome is a structure made of lightweight elements that form a dome with no interior vertical supporting members. It was invented and named by Buckminster Fuller.

Georgia cracker. A native of the state of Georgia is often referred to as a *Georgia cracker*. A *cracker* is, in the words of H. L. Mencken, "a low-down Southern white man and from the start it seems to have been felt that such persons were especially numerous in Georgia." There are various explanations of how *cracker* acquired its further meaning of "worthless braggart." The one that seems soundest to us traces it to the verb "crack," which we now hear chiefly in the expression "he's not what he's cracked up to be," meaning that he doesn't live up to his own boastful opinion of himself.

Incidentally, natives of Georgia bitterly resented this label for a long time, but nowadays they seem to accept it philosophically and even refer to themselves by it.

geriatrics (pronounced jer-ee-AT-rix) is the study of the problems of aging people. It encompasses consideration of psychological and emotional problems as well as the physical aspects of aging. Coined from the Greek word *geras* (old age) and the combing form *-iatrics* (treatment of disease), it is the old-age counterpart of *pediatrics,* from the Greek *pais, paidos* (child) and the same suffix.

Geronimo. From the earliest wars in recorded history, men have plunged into battle shouting battle cries. Indeed, our common word "slogan" was originally the Gaelic *sluggh-ghairm,* meaning the call to battle used by Scottish Highlanders and Irish clans. One of the most interesting of these cries is that used by the U.S. airborne paratroopers: *"Geronimo!"*

When we speculated in print on why our soldiers use the name of a dead Apache chieftain for their slogan, several alumni of airborne regiments reported stories of its origin. A plausible one came from Arthur A. Manion. "At Fort Sill, Oklahoma," he wrote, "a series of rather steep hills, called, I believe, Medicine Bluffs, was pointed out to all new arrivals. It was said that one day Geronimo, with the army in hot pursuit, made a leap on horseback down an almost vertical cliff—a feat that the posse could not duplicate. The legend continues that in the midst of this jump to freedom he gave out the bloodcurdling cry of 'Geronimo-o-o!' Hence the practice adopted by our paratroopers. I hope this helps. It's at least colorful, if not authentic."

Another correspondent, who once lived at Fort Sill, added the information that the bluff from which Geronimo made his daring leap "is a cliff overlooking a small river." So we know that Geronimo and his steed had water, rather than desert floor, to break their fall.

Now, this is indeed an interesting tale and one that may very well be the real inspiration for the paratroopers' shout. But one niggling uncertainty remains. Fort Sill was at the time the army's Field Artillery and Guided Missile School. Paratroopers were trained at Forts Bragg and Campbell. Why, then, did they reach to Fort Sill for inspiration for their battle cry?

R. Collier of Milwaukee offered a less glamorous but probably more accurate account of the origin of the call. "In the early days of the 82nd Airborne," he wrote, "the men used to go to the nearby movie in Lafayetteville. During the week scheduled for the division's initial jumps, they saw a movie named *Geronimo.* (If that wasn't the title, at least the Indian chief played a leading part.) Anyway, one guy hollered the name and one of those things no one can explain happened. The whole division took it up and from them it spread to the later-activated airborne forces."

gerontocrat/gerontocracy. *Gerontocrat* and its parent word, *gerontocracy,* have been around a long time—more than a century and a half, in fact. *Gerontocracy* merely means government by old men. The words come from the Greek *geron* (old man) and the suffix *-cracy,* indicating government.

gerrymander (pronounced with either a hard or a soft *g*) means to relocate the boundary lines of voting districts in such a way as to benefit the party in power. Every time there is a realignment of voting districts because of population changes, charges of *gerrymandering* are sure to surface. The first and most notorious instance of *gerrymandering* occurred in the early 1800s and the man responsible was Elbridge Gerry, then governor of Massachusetts. As a result of his redistricting, one county's boundaries were so contorted that they resembled the shape of a salamander. So *gerrymander* was coined as a blend of his name and the last syllables of "salamander."

gesundheit. One has only to sneeze in a public place and, almost invariably, someone will murmur, "God bless you" or *"Gesundheit."* The speaker may be a friend or a complete stranger, but you would be an ingrate indeed if you didn't feel a momentary twinge of gratitude for these kind words. Have you ever wondered about where and when this custom began? Well, nobody knows for sure. Certainly the ancient Greeks and Romans uttered very similar expressions. It is recorded that whenever he heard one of his followers sneeze, the Roman emperor Tiberius would say, *"Absit omen"* ("Let any omen or mischance be absent"), which is a rather backhanded way of saying, "Good luck!" The almost universal use of such phrases probably stems from the plague years of the Middle Ages. A sneeze was regarded as a probable indication that the sneezer had contracted the plague and thus was certainly in need of divine help. *Gesundheit* (pronounced geh-ZOONDT-hite) is the German word for "health" and, as a matter of fact, is often used as a toast (like *prosit, skoal* and "your good health") as well as in benediction to one who has just sneezed.

get a bead on or "draw a bead on," means to take careful aim. The *bead* is the tiny metal knob on the end of a gun barrel, used for sighting.

get a break. The *break* in such common phrases as "He got a good *break*" or "The *breaks* are against him" comes from the poolroom. At the start of a game of pool the balls are racked up in triangular formation. The first player then plays the cue ball and, depending on whether he gets a good *break* or a bad one, pockets several balls or none at all. Since this initial play is a very chancy thing, it can be seen how readily the terms *good break* and *bad break* could come to mean good or bad luck.

get down to brass tacks. There are several theories about the origin of this expression, but the first we found that sounds authentic appeared in *American Heritage* magazine. In an article on the wonders of the old country store, Gerald Carson wrote: "In general, the right side of the store might be called the ladies' department. . . . On the shelves [were] piece goods by the bolt. Brass tacks were driven into the time-smoothed counter to mark an exact yard. 'Don't hold it up and guess. Get down to brass tacks.' "

get one's back up. This expression, meaning to bristle with anger at a real or fancied affront, comes from the familiar reaction of cats when confronted by dogs.

get the sack goes back to the early days of the Industrial Revolution in England, when skilled mechanics were expected to supply their own tools

while working in the primitive factories of the period. When a worker was
dismissed, the manager gave him a sack to take his tools away in.

getting up on the wrong side of the bed. There is a centuries-old tradition—
perhaps superstition is a better word—that right is right and left is wrong.
The fact that right-handed people are numerically superior to lefties probably has a lot to do with this, but it's nevertheless a fact of life, as every born
left-hander can attest.

This expression is simply another case in point. It originally was "You
got out of bed the wrong way" or " . . . with the left leg first." The ancient
superstition had it that you'd be unlucky if you put your left foot on the
floor first. The same thing was true if you were foolish enough to put your
left shoe on first. Naturally, if your day was ruined before it had scarcely
started, you were bound to be grumpy and ill-tempered all day long. And
that's what people mean when they accuse you of having got up on the
wrong side of the bed.

get your goat, meaning to become fretful or irritated because of the actions
of another person, comes from the race track. It used to be fairly common
practice to stable a goat with a thoroughbred, the theory being that the
goat's presence would help the high-strung nag to keep its composure. If
the goat were stolen the night before a big race, the horse might be expected
to lose its poise and blow the race.

ghetto was a section of a city in which Jews were required to live, apart from
the rest of the population. Curiously enough, it comes from an Italian word
of the same spelling.

Ghost of Cock Lane. We report on this famous eighteenth-century hoax only
because among those hoaxed was none other than our distinguished predecessor, Dr. Samuel Johnson. In the Smithfield section of London in 1762,
a "luminous lady," supposedly the ghost of one Mrs. Kent, was reported
to appear, to the accompaniment of knockings and other strange noises,
in a house in Cock Lane tenanted by a man named Parsons. It got to be
quite the thing to do, socially, to get together a party and take in the eerie
phenomena.

Eventually it turned out that Parsons's eleven-year-old daughter, Elizabeth, used to take a board to bed and rap upon it, thereby creating the
mysterious noises. Johnson later claimed that he had never believed a word
of it, but at least one of his critics, the satiric poet Charles Churchill, gave
him quite a roasting in a long poem called "The Ghost" (1763). Parsons
went to the pillory for his crime and history doesn't record what happened
to the daughter.

ghost walks. *The ghost walks* is a common theatrical expression meaning "It's
payday," though we suspect that for a younger generation the expression
the eagle flies may be more familiar, having been common in both World
Wars (and sometimes heard with a rather less elegant verb than *flies*). *The*

ghost walks has a long and cherished history in the theater. The original *ghost* was the Ghost of Hamlet's father. In the first act of Hamlet, Horatio asks the Ghost if he walks because "thou has uphoarded in thy life/Extorted treasure in the womb of earth." So when pre-Equity payless paydays came around, the players would mutter that "The ghost won't walk today."

ghoti is a "phonetic" spelling of "fish": *gh* as in "rough" *(f), o* as in "women" *(i)* and *ti* as in "nation" *(sh)*. There were quite a few such ridiculous spellings concocted back in the early years of this century when the advocates of reformed or simplified spelling were trying to convince us that the inconsistencies of our English spelling could and should be eliminated. They came up with gems like "filosofy" and "fotografer," and one dictionary *(Funk & Wagnalls),* two newspapers (the *Chicago Tribune* and the *New York Daily News*) and one President (Theodore Roosevelt) encouraged the movement. But it never really caught on and, with the exception of a few useful shortcuts like "thruway," its influence is not seen today.

GI. Harold Hopkins, of Bethesda, Maryland, has some very interesting thoughts on the origin of the term *GI* for the army enlisted man. He notes that he has read a number of explanations, including the theories that it originated as an abbreviation for "government issue" or "galvanized iron," as in "GI can."

> I don't believe the average soldier thought of himself as being a part of the government as such, but as part of the military and particularly his own branch of the military. I joined the Army in July, 1940, and at that time "GI" was in regular use as referring to certain articles of equipment that were intended for use in the garrison, as distinguished from in the field. For instance, a soldier was issued two pairs of shoes. One pair was made of fine leather for dress wear and was designated on the official Quartermaster supply form as "shoes, garrison issue." The other pair was made of a rougher-textured leather and had thicker soles for everyday wear and was designated on the list, as I recall, as "shoes, service."
>
> The garrison shoes and other equipment (garrison cap and garrison belt, for instance) were designated on QM supply lists as "cap, garrison issue" and "belt, garrison issue" and so forth. Practically all garrison issue items, except the garrison cap (the one with the leather visor and the brass insigne in the front center), were discontinued in 1941–42 along with much other peacetime paraphernalia.

Gibson. Credit for naming this version of the martini, in which an onion or two substitutes for the olive, goes to Charley Connolly, long the master barkeep at New York's famous The Players. The story goes that Charles Dana Gibson ordered a martini, Charley found himself temporarily out of olives, substituted a tiny onion—and the *Gibson* was born. Gibson himself, of course, was the preeminent magazine illustrator of the early part of this century.

gift of gab. We all know people who have the *gift of gab,* the ability to discourse freely and fluently, if not always wisely, on any and every topic. The expression is apparently of Scottish origin, *gab* meaning "mouthful" or "mouth" in that dialect. However, a case can be made for *gab* as a back formation from *gabble,* "meaningless chatter." The latter comes into English from a Middle Dutch word, *gabbelen.*

giga- A few years ago our scientists adopted the prefix *mega-* to mean a million of something—and soon their conversations were sprinkled with terms like *megaton, megabuck* and even, in forecasting the results of World War III, *megadeaths.* But that's old hat today. The new vogue prefix is *giga-* and it means one billion of anything. It comes from the Greek *gigas,* meaning "giant." And how is it used? Well, ponder the implications of such words as *gigabuck.*

gilding the lily. One of the most common misquotations is the expression *to gild the lily.* Both *gilding* and *the lily* appear—but not as commonly quoted —in *King John,* Act IV, Scene 2. The correct version is: "To gild refined gold, *to paint the lily,*/To throw a perfume on the violet/. . . Is wasteful and ridiculous excess."

A similar widely misquoted phrase has to do with gold and glitter. The way Shakespeare wrote it (*The Merchant of Venice,* Act II, Scene 7) was: *"All that glisters is not gold."* It was not a new idea even in his time, for Chaucer had written, a couple of centuries earlier: "But al thing which that shyneth as the gold nis nat gold, as that I have herd it told." Apparently the translator of *Don Quixote* thought well of Shakespeare's version, for he used it (with only a slight switch) to translate a phrase in Part II, Book II of Cervantes' great work: *"All is not gold that glisters."*

gimmick comes to us from the slang of carnival midways. The first *gimmicks* were hidden devices by which a confidence man could control the stopping point of the wheel of chance. Magicians were next to take up the word. For them a *gimmick* was any small device used secretly in the course of an illusion. Then, about 1930, the word passed into our general language and came to mean any clever device or gadget.

There are two theories of its origin. One is that it comes from the German word *gemach,* literally meaning "a convenience." The other, and the one we are inclined to favor, is that it's simply an altered form of "gimcrack"—a term long associated with carnivals and circuses to mean any showy but useless object.

gin originally was Geneva. However, this Geneva (or "genever," as it was often spelled) had nothing to do with the Swiss city. It was the British translation of the French *genièvre,* meaning "juniper." As all veterans of the Prohibition era will recall, essence of juniper—"juniper juice," it was commonly called—was widely regarded as an essential ingredient of bathtub gin. Probably few concocters of that foul potion realized, as they added juniper juice drop by drop, that they were putting in the ingredient from which the drink itself got its name.

Mr. T. F. Warffemius, from the admirably appropriate town of Brandywine, Maryland, added this to our information on the subject: "Probably you would like to know that the Dutch name for the gin flavored with the juniper berry is *Genever* pronounced jeh-NAY-ver." Thus he supplied the link between the original French word for "juniper" and the name which the British, by folk etymology, converted first to "Geneva" and then to *gin.*

Incidentally, the cotton-cleaning machine that Eli Whitney invented takes its name, *gin,* from a Middle English contradiction of the Old French *engin,* meaning a mechanical contrivance.

gingerly. One of the features of the word-oriented Morris household is a game which we have come to call "instant folk etymology." If someone asks where a word comes from, the person asked is obligated to give an immediate answer, the more plausible the better, but not necessarily based on fact. A good example came up one day when one of the children used the phrase "proceed in *gingerly* fashion" and followed it with the question: "Where does *gingerly* come from?" Mimi, one of the more creative of the tribe, responded at once. "In the mid seventeenth century," she announced, "a fleet of spice ships returned from the Far East to England, bearing a shipment of ginger far more potent than any the English had ever had before. At first people used it in their recipes in the same proportion that they had been accustomed to, but the result was that many people found their lips and tongues burned by the powerful ginger. So soon they were warning their friends that they should use this more potent herb 'in a *gingerly* fashion.' "

We all agreed that this explanation was both imaginative and instantaneous. We wish we could also call it correct, but it's far wide of the mark. The actual origin of *gingerly* seems to be in the Old French word *genzor,* the comparative form of *gent,* meaning "delicate." There are other theories, including one that it comes from the Icelandic by way of Swedish. However, unfortunately for Mimi's glib and persuasive theory, all authorities agree that the ginger in *gingerly* is not the same as the ginger in your kitchen.

girl. It seems hard to believe that in the Middle Ages a *girl* could be a young child of either sex. Indeed, such phrases as *knave girl* to designate a boy child were common. In Middle English the word had various spellings: *gerle, girle* and *gurle.*

Gish. We once had the privilege of sharing a radio "talk" program panel with the legendary Lillian Gish. Recalling the days of the 1920s, when she and her sister Dorothy were outstanding box-office "draws," she told of their delight in discovering that their name had entered popular slang. The word

Gish was used as a synonym for "entice" or "persuade," especially in the phrase, "Don't you *Gish* me," when rebuffing another person's attempt to persuade you against your will.

gismo. There are many theories of the origin of this handy word that the GI used to designate any kind of gadget or "what-you-may-call-it." Perhaps the likeliest explanation was given by George Yost, Jr., writing in *American Speech* magazine. Yost thinks it comes from the common Arabic phrase *shu ismo,* which has the same meaning. And where did our GIs pick it up? In Moroccan bazaars during the North African campaign.

give a hoot. In the nineteenth century a popular expression in rural areas was "I don't care a hooter for him," varied with: "The money ain't worth a hooter." In these expressions "hooter" is thought to be a regional dialect variation of "iota," meaning "any very small amount." Gradually the *er* ending was dropped and "I don't *give a hoot,*" sometimes intensified to "I don't give a hoot in hell," became popular.

give a sop to Cerberus. *Cerberus* in ancient mythology was the three-headed dog who watched the gates to Hades. In order to guarantee easy passage, the ancients used to put a cake soaked in honey and poppy juice in the hands of a dead person. Nowadays the expression means giving a bribe to ease one's way out of an awkward or dangerous plight.

give a wide berth. To give someone *a wide berth* is to steer very clear of him, an expression which, in a literal sense, is used by mariners. One ship entering a harbor is careful to give another ship at anchor *a wide berth,* since the latter may swing in a fairly wide arc while at anchor.

"give 'em hell!" has been used in political and military campaigns almost ever since the republic was born. One of the early users of the expression was Zachary Taylor, twelfth President of the U.S. During the battle of Buena Vista in 1847, during the Mexican War, Taylor saw the Second Kentucy Regiment rally after a severe attack by the enemy. "Hurrah for old Kentuck!" he yelled. "That's the way to do it. Give 'em hell, damn them." The widespread popularity of the expression in later years, though, can be traced directly to Harry Truman's campaign for reelection in 1948. Entering the campaign an underdog—for Tom Dewey was leading in all the polls —he concentrated on a fiery series of attacks on the "Do-Nothing Congress." His partisans at his whistle-stop rallies loved the way he "poured it on." The cry "Give 'em hell, Harry!" was heard from coast to coast.

give him the mitten. This was a popular expression during the Civil War and for about fifty years afterward. It meant to reject a suitor. As long ago as 1848 James Russell Lowell used it figuratively in his poem "A Fable for Critics": "Here comes Dana, who'll be going to write what'll never be written/Till the Muse, ere he thinks of it, gives him the mitten."

give my eyeteeth. The teeth referred to are the canine teeth, which lie directly below your eyes. Other teeth in your upper jaw tend to loosen more quickly. So when you say, "I'd *give my eyeteeth* for that," you mean you would surrender something of great value—and probably find yourself a candidate for a denture.

give short shrift, meaning to give very little attention to a person or thing, comes from the medieval practice of allowing a condemned person a few seconds on the scaffold for confession of sins before execution. *Shrift* comes from the Anglo-Saxon *scrifan,* "to receive confession." It's closely related to the now archaic word "shriving," the act of hearing confession of sins and pronouncing absolution of them. So when we *give short shrift* to a person who is bothering us, we're giving him about as much time as a criminal once had for a gallows confession.

give the hook. The *hook* here is straight out of vaudeville. In grandfather's time, a weekly event at the local vaudeville house was Amateur Night, when local talent competed for modest prizes and an opportunity to get a start in show business.

Very bad acts were hooted vehemently and, when the boos reached a peak, the manager would reach out from the wings with a long pole bearing a hook at the end and unceremoniously jerk the ham out of the limelight. Nowadays anyone who gets or is given *the hook* is a person discharged for incompetence.

give up the ghost. This expression—meaning "to die" or, in colloquial use, "to surrender"—derives simply from the belief that life exists independent of our mortal bodies and that when death comes, the *ghost* or soul leaves the body and lives on. The phrase is at least as old as the King James version of the Bible, where (Job 14:10) we find: "Man dieth, and wasteth away; yea, man giveth up the *ghost,* and where is he?"

glee club comes from the Middle English word *gleo,* meaning "merriment, play and music." Back in those ancient times there were itinerant singers and entertainers known as *gleemen,* because the songs they sang—unaccompanied songs for male voices—were called *glees.* When they got together and sang in groups, they were called *glee clubs.*

globaloney—a blend of *global* and *baloney*—was coined by Congresswoman Clare Boothe Luce in 1943. She used it as a term of derision in reference to aid programs for some of our wartime allies. It's a good example of what linguists call "nonce words"—words created for a single occasion and then forgotten.

glottochronology and lexicostatistics. Our candidates for this century's ugliest words are two: *lexicostatistics* and *glottochronology.* And do you know who coined them? Linguists, that's who—the very people who should be concerned with maintaining minimum linguistic standards. These two gems were coined to describe a technique by which some language researchers claim to be able to "date" the age of a word, just as Dr. Libby's carbon 14 method has successfully dated ancient artifacts.

glove money, simply put, means "bribe." In ancient days it was the custom in British law for the client to present a pair of gloves to the attorney who agreed to handle his case. On one celebrated occasion, a Mrs. Croaker gave Sir Thomas More, then the Lord Chancellor, a pair of gloves which contained the sum of forty pounds. The Lord Chancellor retained the gloves, in accordance with prevailing custom, but returned the money.

glutinous/gluttonous. *Glutinous* (pronounced GLOO-tin-us) should not be confused with *gluttonous.* Derived from the Latin *gluten* (glue), *glutinous* means "sticky, tenacious or resembling glue." *Gluttonous* (pronounced GLUT-'n-us) stems from the Latin verb *glutire* (to devour) and is used to describe one who eats too much or too greedily.

go against the grain. Carpenters learn early that it is easier to plane a board with the *grain* rather than *against the grain.* Therefore something that goes *against the grain* is something hard to accept.

gob has rather an uncertain ancestry, but neither of the two possible origins of the word confers dignity on the word. As H. L. Mencken reports in *The American Language:* "Gob has been traced variously to 'gobble,' an allusion to the somewhat earnest methods of feeding prevailing among sailors, and to *gob,* an archaic English dialect word signifying expectoration. The English coast-guardsmen, who are said to be free-spitters, are often called *gobbies.*"

gobbledegook/gobbledygook, meaning inflated and obscure bureaucratic language, is often credited to Maury Maverick, one-time Texas congressman. It's true that Maverick made the word famous with a World War II memo denouncing the tortured language found in governmental reports and memoranda, but he did not invent the word. It had been a part of service (especially navy) slang for decades. Several of our correspondents have testified to its currency during World War I. Still, Maverick's memo on *gobbledegook* merits quotation. He directed all members of his department to: "Be short and say what you're talking about. Stop 'pointing up' programs. No more 'finalizing,' 'effectuating,' or 'dynamics.' Anyone using the words 'activation' or 'implementation' will be shot."

go by shanks' mare. So far as we know, there never was any Mr. Shanks connected with the phrase. The *shanks* referred to are simply a person's legs. Just how the *mare* got into the expression is not known, but chances are that, since mares generally are more slow-paced than stallions, their pace would more nearly resemble walking.

go by the board(s). One often hears the expression "he trod the boards," meaning "he was once an actor." However, *boards* in this phrase have nothing to do with the stage; rather they refer to the side of a ship. It's a term that originated in sailing-ship days. When, at the height of a storm, a mast was broken, it was up to the skipper to decide whether to attempt to salvage it or to let it *go by the boards*—fall over the side to complete and utter destruction. So today when we decide to let a matter *go by the boards* or *by the board,* we mean that we are washing our hands of it—are finished with it for good and all.

God Bless the Duke of Argyle. There's an old folk tale about a British lord who erected "scratching posts" around his estate for his tenants to use, with the proviso that when they wriggled up to the posts they had to say, *God Bless the Duke of Argyle.* A British-born friend reported that he had often heard the expression spoken jocosely and suggested that we try Brewer.* So to Brewer we turned and found this admirable explanation: *"God Bless the Duke of Argyle* is a phrase supposed to be ejaculated by Highlanders when they scratched themselves. The story is that a Duke of Argyle caused posts to be erected in a treeless portion of his estates, so that cattle might have the opportunity of rubbing themselves against them and so easing themselves of the 'torment of flies.' It was not long before the herdsmen discovered the efficacy of the practice and, as they rubbed their itching backs against the posts, they thankfully muttered the above words."

God bless you! goes back to the plague years of the Middle Ages, when a person's sneezes were thought to be signs that he was catching the dreaded plague. Still another version of the origin of the expression goes like this. During the Middle Ages, people were very superstitious. Some of them believed that when a person sneezed—at that very moment—his soul left his body for a few seconds and the devil, who was always looking for human souls, could snatch it out of the air, and so the person's soul would be lost. To prevent this happening, a friend or relative standing by would quickly say *God bless you!* in order to protect the soul while it was out of the body until it could return to the sneezer and safety.

God's in his heaven is from one of the most radiantly optimistic verses in all English. It's called "Pippa Passes" and was written by Robert Browning. Here's how the stanza goes: "The year's at the spring/And day's at the morn;/Morning's at seven;/The hillside's dew-pearled;/The lark's on the wing;/The snail's on the thorn:/God's in his heaven—/All's right with the world."

God will help those who help themselves was first written by Jean de La Fontaine, a French poet and writer of fables in the seventeenth century. When a political society was formed in 1824 with the purpose of encouraging the middle classes to resist the government, *"Aide-toi et le Ciel t'aidera"* was adopted as its slogan.

go for broke was originally gamblers' slang, though you'll often hear it in sports announcing. It means simply to stake everything on one last throw of the dice or hand of cards. If you lose, you're cleaned, out of cash, just plain broke.

*Brewer's Dictionary of Phrase and Fable.

Gog and Magog. Earlier on (*see* ALBION), we recounted the charming tale of the Syrian king with fifty daughters who celebrated a mass wedding by murdering all fifty husbands on the wedding night, then fleeing to an island they called Albion after the oldest of the girls, Albia. A variation of this legend has the thirty-three daughters of the Roman emperor Diocletian (reigned A.D. 284–305) similarly set adrift and similarly winding up in England. There they crossbred with some singularly infamous demons and reared a race of giants. Only two of this clan survived and they were called *Gog and Magog.* Statutes of these two stood in London's Guildhall until they were destroyed in a Nazi air raid in 1940. However, the *Gog and Magog* a few generations of New Yorkers have known with affection are a brace of giant metal statues, each bearing a mighty hammer and flanking a huge bell which they strike the appropriate number of times every hour on the hour. Originally they adorned the building of the *New York* World, but now they are located in Herald Square, where they attract an admiring throng, especially at midday, when their act takes a full twelve seconds to complete.

going to pot has been going on for years and years—in fact, for centuries. The meaning nowadays is that one who is *going to pot* is deteriorating rapidly and soon will be utterly ruined. Originally—and this goes back over three hundred years—when you went to pot you were dead. There are two theories of how the expression originated. One is the analogy of meat and vegetables chopped up for a stew and put into a pot for cooking. Obviously all life is gone from the ingredients. The other theory is that the expression refers to the ancient practice of putting a deceased person's ashes in an urn or pot.

goldbricking achieved its widest use as an item of military slang, but it has been in common use for many years as a term describing the avoidance of work or shirking. A *goldbrick* is anything worthless which is passed off as genuine, and it originally referred to a bar of worthless metal which had been gilded to make it appear to be solid gold.

Golden State is California, the site of the Gold Rush of 1849. Its lush and fertile valleys and its magnificent mountains and forests give further credibility to the nickname.

golf. Amazing as it seems, *golf* was introduced in America as recently as 1888. The first players were an immigrant Scotsman named John Reid and several friends, who set up the first golf course in Yonkers, New York. They came to be called the Apple Tree Gang because their third course, laid out in 1892, was on a thirty-four-acre apple orchard. The game itself dates back at least to the fourteenth century, however, and no one is quite certain where it started. As the *American People's Encyclopedia* discreetly puts it, the game is "possibly of Dutch origin, but generally identified with Scotland." The idea that it started in Holland derives from the theory that the word *golf* came from the Dutch word *kolf,* meaning a club for hitting balls. A more recent theory, however, traces *golf* to the Scottish word *gowf,* meaning "to strike." We incline to accept this latter theory.

gone coon. Put yourself in the place of a raccoon finally treed by the hunting dogs, and you'll see why this phrase is used for a person in dire peril of some sort—in a terrible fix or on the verge of disaster.

gonfalon. CHISOX SNATCH GONFALON, read a headline sent in by a Midwest reader who asked: "Just what is the word *gonfalon* doing in a headline on the sports page? I gather it means 'flag' but why can't they say so? I can't even find it in my dictionary." Well, the reader was right: *gonfalon* does mean flag, specifically a flag once used in medieval Italy and designed to hang from a crosspiéce instead of from an upright staff. For some reason *gonfalon* has long been a favorite of sportswriters, many of whom go to great lengths to use elaborate words where simple ones will do.

goober. The peanut was native to South America originally and came to America by way of Africa, during the era of slave trading. There it got the *goober* name, a variation of the Congolese word *nguba.*

Good Friday. It may seem strange that the saddest, most solemn day in the entire Christian year should be labeled *Good* Friday. The reason is that this is an archaic sense of *good,* synonymous with "holy." A similar use is found in the ancient description of Christmas as "the *good* tide."

"good night, sweet prince" is a line from Shakespeare's *Hamlet* which is spoken by Hamlet's friend Horatio very near the end of the play, as Hamlet dies: "Now cracks a noble heart. *Good night, Sweet Prince,* / And flights of angels sing thee to thy rest!"

There are two reasons why John Barrymore comes to mind in connection with this line. First, although he ended his career playing in second-rate movies and a third-rate play, he was generally acknowledged to be the greatest American Hamlet when he played the role on Broadway in 1924. Second, Gene Fowler, a brilliant writer and lifelong friend of Barrymore, chose as the title for his biography *Good Night, Sweet Prince.* The book is probably now out of print, but we earnestly suggest that you look for it at your public library. It stands out in our memory as a brilliant, sympathetic and enormously readable account of the career of a brilliant and profligate actor.

Incidentally, we cherish one story about Barrymore and Fowler. Many clubs make a practice of posting the names of recently deceased members on a notice board inside the entrance. One day, as they walked past the Lambs Club in New York, Fowler said, "Jack, let's stop in and see whose name is on the board." "Don't bother," replied Barrymore. "It's never the right one."

Goody Two-Shoes comes from a nursery tale, "The History of Little Goody Two-Shoes," supposedly written by Oliver Goldsmith, famed playwright and friend of Samuel Johnson. Whether Oliver stooped to writing children's stories or not, the piece was published in 1765 by John Newbery, first publisher of books for children. The tale is of a child who had only one shoe. Somehow she obtained a pair and dashed about the town buttonholing everyone she met and exclaiming, "Two shoes, two shoes!" Incidentally, if Goldsmith really was the author of this story, it's possible to read a few bits of psychological significance into it, since Oliver—though a brilliant and prolific writer—was always in debt, and forever spending more than he could afford on his clothing. Including, we suppose, shoes.

googol was originally a facetious coinage by the nephew of Edward Kasner, distinguished American mathematician. Asked to suggest a name for the number 1 followed by 100 zeros, the youngster said: *"Googol."* Today the word is accepted and used by mathematicians throughout the world. Incidentally, a *googolplex* is the figure 1 followed by a *googol* of zeros—and if you can follow that, you have left us a *googol* of miles behind.

goon/jeep. *Jeep,* now the name of an all-purpose motor vehicle, is believed to have developed from the letters *GP,* army shorthand for "general purpose," but undoubtedly its immediate widespread acceptance can be credited to the popularity of a comic strip character, Eugene the *Jeep,* a tiny creature of supernatural powers, created by E. G. Segar in the *Popeye* comic strip just before World War II.

Goon is a somewhat similar case. The word existed in labor union jargon as the designation for a strikebreaker, probably from the days of the Wobblies, the IWW of the late nineteenth and early twentieth centuries. But it unquestionably owes its later general popularity to Segar's use of it in the same cartoon strip.

goop started its career in our language as the coinage of Gelett Burgess, one of America's favorite humorists in the early years of this century. Burgess is the same chap, by the way, who invented *blurb* to describe the descriptive material on a book jacket that praises the book's contents. He also invented *bromide,* meaning a trite remark or cliché, whence we have the adjective *bromidic* to describe trite, unimaginative speech. Quite an inventor, this Burgess! Originally a *goop* was a silly, boorish, ill-mannered fellow, and the first *goops* appeared in Burgess's book *Goops and How to Be Them,* published in 1900.

Sometime later *goop* began to develop other meanings, but always with the connotation of something distasteful and frequently of something messy or unpleasant to handle. Auto mechanics took to calling lubricating grease *goop.* Beauty shop operators used the same label for the thick fluid used in making finger waves. And most recently, soldiers labeled the mixtures used in incendiary bombs *goop.*

goose hangs high. *The goose hangs high* is an old folk expression, meaning that everything is on the up-and-up, and prospects for the future look good.

There's a theory that the expression was originally "the goose honks high," because migrating wild geese fly higher in fine weather.

G.O.P. The Grand Old Party got that name around 1880, and the expression was used derisively at first. It's unclear just who originally taunted the Republicans with that label, but it made its first appearance in print in the *Louisville Courier-Journal* in 1887. Later on, of course, the Republicans adopted the label as their own.

gopher. Hal Prince, the Broadway producer of such hits as *A Funny Thing Happened on the Way to the Forum* and *Fiddler on the Roof,* is reported to have started in the theater as a *gopher.* A *gopher,* in theater slang, is the lowliest of unpaid hangers-on, the stage-struck youngster who is willing to do all sorts of small tasks just to be close to the theater and its people. His name comes from the orders which keep him scurrying. Invariably they begin, "Hey kid, *go for* some coffee"; "*Go for* some cigarettes"; "*Go for* the papers." Hence, *gopher.*

gopher ball, in baseball, is a pitch that the batter knocks for a hit, usually a home run. There are various theories of how the ball got the name *gopher,* but here's one from Ken Ohst of WHA Radio in Madison, Wisconsin. "My authority," he writes, "is one of the great pitchers of the 1930s, as well as one of the most witty and articulate, Vernon Patrick "Lefty" Gomez of the New York Yankees. In 1938 I asked him about '*gopher.*' 'It's an errant pitch,' he told me, 'that will sometimes go for a double, sometimes gofer a triple and too often *gopher* a home run.' About the same time an interviewer asked Buck Newsome what he had thrown to a batter who had hit a ninth-inning homer. 'I threw him a *gopher* ball,' said Bobo."

gorilla is an African word and describes the largest anthropoid ape of West Africa. It has also been used in underworld slang to denote a mobster, usually one who acts as bodyguard for a big-shot gangster.

gospel is the Old English word *godspel,* literally "good news."

gospodin is a Russian word, literally meaning "lord." It's a title of respect, roughly equivalent to our "Mr." Incidentally, it's pronounced gos-poh-DEEN.

gossamer is a word with romantic connotations, reminding one as it does of the light and delicate party dresses of young girls or young women. It has a romantic origin, too. *Gossamer* comes from the Middle English *gosesomer,* which literally meant "goose summer." Goose summer was the name given to the calm, warm days of autumn when goose was the favorite dinner dish. The name was then applied to the fine, filmy cobwebs floating on the calm air or appearing on the grass and bushes at that time of the year.

gossip. A *gossip* in the time of Chaucer was a godparent, usually the godmother. The word then was spelled *godsibbe—god,* of course, having the same meaning it has today and *sibbe* meaning kin or relative. Over the years the original meaning was extended to include not only godparents but any very close or intimate friends. Since it's the nature of friendship to entrust one's closest secrets to one's friends, and since it seems to be human nature to pass on such secrets, the evolution of *gossip* is fairly obvious.

Gotham. The name *Gotham* was originally applied to New York City by Washington Irving in *Salmagundi,* a series of satirical pieces, published in 1807. But that's only a small part of the story.

Gotham (pronounced GOT-um in England but GOTH-um here) was originally a village near Nottingham known as the "town of wise fools." The story goes that King John once made a trip to Gotham for the express purpose of acquiring land and building a castle. The shrewd burghers realized that, with the royal presence at hand, they would be subjected to frequent tax levies. Not to put too fine a point on it, the king could make life unbearable if he were a resident of their town. So they decided to play the fool, and when the king's outriders neared Gotham they found most of the townspeople running wildly in circles, obviously daft. Equally obviously, this was no place for his royal highness to take up residence, so he abandoned his original plan and betook himself elsewhere. The townsfolk then remarked: "More fools pass through Gotham than remain in it"—and Gotham's reputation for "wise fools" was established.

Washington Irving, in choosing this epithet for New York, intended to satirize the wiseacre, know-it-all attitude of its inhabitants. Though much about New York has changed since he first applied the label, obviously the "wise guy" attitude has not.

go to Halifax was an expression often heard in our youth and, while we realized that *Halifax* was simply a euphemism for Hell, we always thought that the *Halifax* involved was the one down East in Nova Scotia. Not so. The origin of the expression takes us back a few centuries and to the city of *Halifax* in Yorkshire, England. It seems that beggars of the sixteenth century and later had a proverbial expression: "From Hell, Hull and Halifax may the Good Lord deliver us." The order of the localities sometimes changed, but the three place names remained the same through the centuries. Why should these places be so dreaded? you ask. In the words of one T. Fuller (1732): "This is part of the beggar's and vagrant's litany. . . . Hull is terrible unto them as a town of good government . . . Halifax is formidable unto them for thieves stealing cloth are instantly beheaded with an engine." And as for Hell, well, as George M. Cohan used to say in another connection, "That goes without saying."

go to the ant, thou sluggard. The full proverb is "Go to the ant, thou sluggard; consider her ways, and be wise." It is from the Old Testament (Proverbs 6 : 6).

goulash owes its name to the shepherds of Hungary. Indeed, *goulash*—or *gulyas,* as the Hungarians spell it—originally meant simply "shepherd."

Then it came to mean the food the shepherds ate, specifically the stew made with beef or veal and vegetables—and lots of paprika.

gourmand/gourmet. The distinction between *gourmet* and *gourmand* is a nice one, but one worth observing. A *gourmet* is a person who is an authority on the selection and preparation of fine foods; almost invariably he or she is also a qualified judge of vintage wines. But a *gourmet* is not necessarily a heavy eater. Indeed, he is likely, by reason of the discrimination that he brings to his choice of viands, to eat sparingly. A *gourmand,* on the other hand, while he often shares the gourmet's liking for rare and unusual delicacies, is primarily a trencherman, one who loves good eating—and, usually, plenty of it. The word *gourmand* (pronounced GOOR-mund) was originally a French adjective meaning "gluttonous" and some slight vestige of this earlier meaning carries over into our language.

Both words, by the way, come from the same French source, *groumet,* which originally meant groom or stableboy. Gradually *gourmet* came to mean any manservant and eventually the term was reserved for the wine-taster or steward. Since the prime requisite of a wine steward is the ability to discriminate among the choicest vintages, the word *gourmet* came to have the meaning of "epicure," a person with a refined and cultivated taste in both eating and drinking—and that is the sense in which it is used most accurately today.

government by crony. This phrase was the creation of the "Old Curmudgeon," Harold L. Ickes, one of the pillars of the Roosevelt cabinet and a tireless public servant. When he resigned in a huff from President Truman's cabinet in 1946, he made his departing statement as blunt as any of the many that characterized his speeches and statements to the press: "I am against *government by crony.*"

go west. *"Go west,* young man, *go west"* is generally credited to the *New York Tribune* editor Horace Greeley, though he often said that John Soule, in an article in the *Terre Haute Express,* had created the expression. In any event, it was first written in 1851 when the Gold Rush had focused public attention on the vast potential of this part of the continent. As Greeley later amended his advice, the idea was *"Go west,* young man, and grow with the country." The other meaning of *go west*—to die—was common in World War I. Actually, though, it is many years, perhaps many centuries, older. It derives from the legend believed by many American Indian tribes and by primitive civilizations the world over that each day is newly born in the east and dies in the west. Thus the "land of the setting sun"—the west—is where a person goes when he dies.

go whole hog. There are two theories of the origin of this phrase. The more fanciful one is that priests of the Moslem faith professed inability to determine which part of the hog they were forbidden to eat by Mohammed's decree. Each tended to exempt from the stricture that part of the pig that he personally most cherished. So, in a verse by William Cowper: "The conscience free from every clog,/Mohammedans eat up the hog." The other theory—less colorful but more probable—is that this expression came from seventeenth-century England, where a *hog* was a shilling. Since the shilling was then roughly equivalent to today's dollar, it meant a moderately substantial investment if one were to spend a whole shilling— to *go the whole hog.*

grace (before meals). *Grace,* a short prayer of thanks for one's food, is actually a shortened form of *give graces,* meaning to "render thanks." Earlier versions include the French *rendre grâces* and the Latin *gratias agere.*

graft. When Doheny, Fall and other corrupt politicians of the Harding administration used their control of the naval oil resources at Teapot Dome to build substantial private fortunes for themselves, they were labeled *grafters. Graft* is the same word as the name of the shoot or bud of one plant which is *grafted* onto the stem or trunk of another, where it keeps on growing, eventually becoming a permanent part. The meaning of *graft* as money obtained fraudulently comes from the fact that it usually results from illegal practices *grafted* upon an officeholder's legitimate functions.

In the slang of carnivals and circuses, the word undergoes a slight change to *grift.* A *grifter* is a person who runs a crooked gambling concession. So in the great American game of politics, the double-dealer is known as a *grafter,* while on the carnival midway he's labeled a *grifter.*

granary/grainery. An oddity of language is that the name of the place where grain is stored is spelled *granary* rather than *grainery.* The reason is that *granary* came directly to English from the Latin *granarium,* while *grain* came by the way of the French *graine,* thereby getting a different spelling.

Grand Canyon State. Although Arizona has a long history of mining and raising of sheep and cattle, its principle attraction is the Grand Canyon, the mightiest of its many chasms. Since it has made tourism a major industry in the state, the nickname was an obvious choice.

grandfather/grandson. In Anglo-Saxon the word *ealde,* which later became "old," was attached to other nouns to indicate a rank of special distinction, usually due to age. Thus an *ealdorman* was a chief or prince—a tribal leader. The same word appears today as "alderman." With the coming of the Normans, this title was gradually changed by the substitution of the French *grand* for the earlier *ealde.* Thus *grandfather* became the label for the head of the clan, and the son of his son became the *grandson.* Nowadays the prefix *grand-* means a relative two generations older or younger than the speaker.

Grand Guignol (pronounced grahn GEEN-yol) was the name of a theater in Paris that specialized in horror plays. The original Guignol was a character in a French puppet play, first performed about 1800. These puppet shows were somewhat similar to Punch and Judy shows, with emphasis on knockabout slapstick that progressively became more violent. In 1897 the *Grand Guignol* was founded in a gaslit alley in Montmartre. It soon achieved a reputation for bloodcurdling—and bloodletting—dramas. Great emphasis was placed on murder scenes and, according to report, the first director even invented an artificial blood that would congeal, in order to add realism to his gory shows.

grand panjandrum is a pompous, stuffy, self-important minor official. The expression itself comes from a nonsense story by Samuel Foote, a British wit, actor and dramatist of the eighteenth century. It's a pretty dull story, we fear, notable though for the fact that it was also the source of a once popular slang phrase, *no soap,* meaning "nothing doing." One sentence went: "And there were present the Joblillies, the Garyulies and the Grand Panjandrum himself, with the little red button atop."

grangerize means to illustrate a book with pictures taken from other books or publications. By extension it also means to mutilate a book by cutting out pictures to use in such a book. The word comes from the name (James Granger) of an Anglican divine of the eighteenth century who in 1769 published a *Biographical History of England,* leaving spaces in the text where illustrations filched from other books could be inserted.

grass widow. There's a faintly dated sound to this phrase in a day when every second marriage (or every fourth, depending on whose statistics you believe) ends in divorce. But in grandfather's day a *grass widow* was that comparative rarity, a divorcee. Earlier she had been rather less than that, for the term was first used as a euphemism for a lass who had been delivered of child without the benefit of matrimony. The *grass* in the phrase refers to the grass or straw of the bed or pallet on which the illicit behavior took place.

gratuitous is most often encountered in phrases like *"gratuitous* insult." While the meaning "uncalled-for" and the opprobrious connotation of "without cause or justification" do attach to this meaning of *gratuitous,* it has still another meaning: "given or received without charge or obligation." This, indeed, is the meaning closer to its Latin root, *gratuitus,* meaning "free or spontaneous." In law *gratuitous* has the special meaning of "given without receiving any return value."

Graustarkian. When Richard Nixon briefly outfitted some of the White House drum and bugle corps in elaborate and exaggerated uniforms, some of the newspapers described the uniforms as *Graustarkian* in character and appearance. The original Graustark was an imaginary country in a novel of that name by George Barr McCutcheon. It was a principality rather like Monaco, populated by beautiful princesses and villainous princes and, as a result of the huge success of the novel and movie and stage adaptations, Graustark has become a symbol of a royal, romantic never-never land.

great Scott. This expression of surprise and wonder first became popular midway through the nineteenth century. That was the heyday of popularity of General Winfield Scott, hero of the Mexican War and probably our most admired general between Washington and Lee. It seems likely that *Great Scott* started as a tribute to his exploits.

Greeks bearing gifts comes from a famous line in Vergil's *Aeneid: "Timeo Danaos et dona ferentes"*—"I fear the Greeks even when they offer gifts." The Greeks, after besieging Troy for ten years, indicated that they had grown weary of the war and were ready to withdraw. As they loaded their troops and equipment into ships for the long voyage home, they offered a gift in the form of a great wooden horse to the beleaguered citizens of Troy. Though older and wiser heads counseled to "beware the Greeks, even when they bear gifts," the horse was accepted and taken within the walls of the city. Everyone knows the rest of the story—how the Greek soldiers, under cover of night, crept out of the hollow horse, slew the guards and set fire to the city. Ever since, the Trojan Horse has been a symbol of enemy infiltration, and the phrase *Greeks bearing gifts* or even *Greek gift* is used to indicate an insincere and possibly treacherous gift.

Greeks had a word for it. *The Greeks had a word for it—it* being love—is a phrase of recent origin. It appeared first as the title of a play by Zoë Akins, produced on Broadway in 1929. The ladies who supplied the *it* were hetaerae. The hetaerae were the ancient Greek equivalent of the Japanese geisha girls, young women specially trained to provide conversation and entertainment for a fee. In case you want to drop either word in conversation, the Greek word is pronounced hih-TIR-ee and the Japanese is GAY-shuh.

green-eyed monster. Like so many familiar expressions, the phrase *green-eyed monster* comes from Shakespeare, specifically from *Othello* (Act III, Scene 3) when Iago says: "O, beware, my lord, of jealousy;/It is the *green-eyed monster* which doth mock/The meat it feeds on." The reference is to cats, tigers and others of the feline tribe who are noted for toying with trapped birds or animals, "mocking" them before feeding on them. So jealousy—the adult kind of which Iago was speaking—is often a blend of love and hatred, and thus it seems to toy with its victim before consuming it.

greenroom is the offstage retiring room used by the acting company in a theater. Most Broadway theaters are so cramped for space backstage that *greenrooms* are nonexistent. However, the old phrase remains in such terms as *"greenroom* gossip," as loosely synonymous with "backstage." The *greenroom* took its name from the fact that its walls were often painted green to rest the eyes of actors after exposure to bright stage lights.

green thumb. Each spring our mail brings a rash of queries about where the expression "She has a *green thumb*" originated. None of the standard reference books gives a satisfactory answer, so we went to Norman Taylor, formerly curator of the New York Botanical Garden, for an explanation.

Mr. Taylor, we might note, was the friend of several hundreds of thousands of gardeners who swear by his perennial best-selling *Taylor's Garden Encyclopedia*. Well, Mr. Taylor put his best research to work and passes on this quotation from the *Rural New Yorker* magazine (date of publication unknown):

> In the old days there once lived in Italy a monk named Fra Antonio. One of his important duties was the care of the cloister garden. So successful was he in the growing of herbs, fruit trees, flowers and other plants that he became the wonder, and almost the envy, of all his brothers. When asked the secret of his success as a gardener, he always shrugged his shoulders and replied, "I'm sure I don't know except that I love the plants."
>
> One day he was working in his garden when two of the monks approached and watched him at work behind his back. When he finally turned and saw them, the senior monk smiled and said, "I know why Fra Antonio can make plants grow so well. See, he has a *Green Thumb!*" Fra Antonio looked down at his hands, and sure enough, his right thumb was green from the plants he had been handling. From that day to this all good gardeners have been said to have a *Green Thumb*.

greetin' meeting is a Scottish term for a wake, the vigil before burial. Although it is all too true that such occasions mark the only opportunities for distant relatives to *greet* each other, this is not the true meaning of *greetin' meeting*. The *greet* in this expression is a Scottish word for "weep or cry."

gremlin. British fliers early in World War II blamed faulty performance of their planes on *gremlins*, "fanciful creatures, something like poltergeists," who could turn a well-planned operation into a complete *fubar*—"fouled up beyond all recognition."

Gresham's law is the economic theory holding that if two currencies of the same nominal value but different intrinsic values are in circulation at the same time, the currency with the lower intrinsic value (the "bad" currency) will eventually drive out of circulation the money with the higher intrinsic value (the "good" money), since people will hoard the good money. This theory was first expounded by Sir Thomas Gresham, a sixteenth-century English financier.

Gretna Green marriages. The original *Gretna Green* was—in fact, still is—a village just over the border from England in Dumfries, Scotland. Until 1754, a couple wanting to get married in haste and with the least publicity would go to Fleet Prison in London, where they could simply exchange vows before a witness, with no need for posting banns of marriage, getting a license or going through any of the customary formalities. But in 1753, Parliament passed an act which took effect the next year requiring that all future marriages be performed by clergy of the Church of England, and only after proper publication of the banns. That made it next to impossible for a couple to elope. So impatient young lovers soon found that they could skip a very few miles across the Scottish border to Gretna Green, where the same sort of simple ceremony that had been performed at Fleet Prison awaited them. Matter of fact, the village blacksmith became the foremost witness to these marriages and many thousands of couples were wed standing before his anvil.

Midway through the nineteenth century, Scotland passed a law requiring at least one party to a marriage to reside in Scotland for three weeks before the wedding, but the young people found ways to get around it. Finally, in 1940, a law was passed requiring that all marriages in Scotland be performed by a minister or magistrate. That was the end of *Gretna Green marriages.*

In the 1920s and 1930s the town of Elkton, Maryland, was known as the *Gretna Green* of the U.S. East Coast. Like the original, it was just across a border (from Delaware), and its streets were lined with signs saying "Minister."

gridiron. The first *gridirons* were grills for cooking meat and fish over an open fire. Usually rectangular, with parallel bars, they had a pattern similar to that of a football field viewed from high in the stands. The term was first used—in print, at any rate—in a story in the *Boston Herald* in 1897 referring to the "intense enthusiasm aroused by a contest on the *gridiron* like the Harvard-Yale game."

grim. One reader speculated that the word *grim* might have come into the language from the names of the Brothers Grimm, "writers of those ghastly so-called fairy tales." This was an interesting guess, but several light-miles wide of the mark. *Grim* was part of our language during the period of Anglo-Saxon domination of the British Isles, long before the Norman Conquest. Interestingly, it was often spelled with two *m*'s, just as the nineteenth-century fairy-tale writers spelled their name. Actually, *grim* is traced to an Indo-European stem, *ghrem-,* meaning "to roar angrily"— apparently the usual reaction of the warriors of old when faced with a grim, harsh or forbidding turn of events. The same root gives us the common word "grumble."

gringo. A good story dies hard, and the legend that the Spanish-American term *gringo*—a pejorative label for an American—came from "Green Grow the Lilacs" is a good story. Here's one version, as reported by a reader of our newspaper column: "In my day," he wrote, "infantry traveled on shanks' mare and we found that singing not only raised their morale but made the march easier to endure. The marching song of the Mexican War was 'Green Grow the Lilacs.' As the columns of Scott and Taylor wended their way through the countryside, the soldiers sang this song repeatedly. Because the natives heard it so constantly, they described the singers as *green-grows*—only what went into their ears as *green-grows* came out of their mouths as *gringos.* "

A pleasant fable—and maybe some of the soldiers actually believed it. But the truth is that the word *gringo* was standard in Spain before 1787, half a century or more before the Mexican War. Frank Vizetelly, long the pillar of the *Funk & Wagnalls Dictionary* staff, reported it as appearing in a Madrid publication in 1787 and meaning "any person with a peculiar accent that prevents him from achieving the true Castilian accent." In fact, the label *gringo* was first pinned upon the Irish!

By the way, one very fine thing—besides the song itself—may honestly be traced to "Green Grow the Lilacs." It was the inspiration for a play of the same name by Lynn Riggs. Produced by the Theatre Guild to indifferent success, it was later made into a musical play—the first of those wonderful Rodgers and Hammerstein collaborations—*Oklahoma!*

grin like a Cheshire cat. In Lewis Carroll's *Alice in Wonderland* (Chapter 6) Alice asks: "Please would you tell me why your cat grins like that?" and the Dutchess replies: "It's a Cheshire cat and that's why." Amusingly enough, the Duchess's explanation is about the only one there is, because theories that some of the famed Cheshire cheeses were made in the form of grinning cats turn out to be groundless. A truly remarkable thing about this Cheshire cat, as we all recall, is that after the cat itself disappeared, the grin remained. However, the phrase is much older than *Alice in Wonderland.* The best theory is that one of the leading families of Cheshire, England, had the face of a lion as part of its coat of arms. In the hands of local sign painters, the lion's image gradually got to look like a grinning cat.

grog blossom. A beer garden is the only garden where you would be likely to find a *grog blossom. Grog,* you see, is the British sailors' term for spirits —usually rum—diluted with water. And a *grog blossom* is a facial blotch or blemish resulting from overindulgence in *grog.*

grog shop as a name for a bar and grill is a British term, as British as the Royal Navy. Originally *grog* was a ration of spirits, usually rum and water, issued to British sailors. This issue was first authorized by an eighteenth-century officer, Admiral Vernon, who was nicknamed "Old Grog" from his habit of wearing a coat made of grogram.

groundnut is nothing more than the common peanut or, in Southern dialect, the *goober.*

group names in the animal kingdom. Hunters—at least the more proper among them—speak of a *cast* of hawks and a *covey* of quail. A countryman speaks, of course, of a *swarm* of bees, but only the most adventurous souls have run on a *skulk* of foxes, a *sloth* of bears, a *cete* of badgers, a *down* of hares; and a *fall* of woodcocks—to say nothing of a *troop* of monkeys.

Most of these group labels are today obsolete or used only in regional dialects but, in days when the hunting of game for food was of vital importance, such distinctions in the labeling of animal groups were carefully observed. Today the collection and preservation of such labels is mostly the work of connoisseurs of word oddities.

A *sord* of mallard, a *wisp* of snipe and a *drove* of kine delight such word collectors. But who would know that elk—the animal, not the human variety—travel not in herds but in *gangs.* For veteran bird watchers, the eye is cocked for a *nye* of pheasants, a *watch* of nightingales, a *muster* of peacocks, a *covert* of coots, and—inspired phrase—an *exaltation* of larks.

Back in the animal kingdom, one finds a *shrewdness* of apes, a *labor* of moles; a *clowder* of cats, a *rout* of wolves and a *sounder* of boars.

Kittens, we're told, come in *kindles,* but around our house the word is still *litter.* And when the group label for mongrel dogs is given as a *cowardice of curs,* we strongly protest and are joined by the howls of our somewhat disreputable "Poopsie"—no blueblood she, but courageous just the same.

grubstake goes back to mining days of the mid-nineteenth century. It literally means to gamble (stake) food (grub). The way it worked was that a relatively wealthy man would gamble on the chances of a prospector's striking ore to the extent of supplying him with food and equipment to start out on his search. If the gamble paid off the *grubstaker* took a share of the profits.

grubstreet hacks are underpaid free-lance writers. ("Underpaid free-lance writer" must seem to many in the craft a redundancy—but let it pass.) The original Grub Street was a lane in the London ward of Cripplegate Without. Samuel Johnson once described the street as "much inhabited by writers of small histories, dictionaries and temporary poems; whence any mean production is called *grubstreet.* " If you go to London today, by the way, don't waste time trying to find Grub Street. Its name was changed more than a century ago to Milton Street—not out of deference to John Milton, the poet, but after the landlord who owned most of the houses on the street.

grue is the name devised by Robert Louis Stevenson—obviously as a back formation from "gruesome"—for the macabre little verses that were so much in vogue during the Gay Nineties and later. The most famous *grue* went like this: "Little Willie in the best of sashes/Fell in the fire and was burned to ashes./By and by the room grew chilly,/But no one liked to poke up Willie." Many wits of the time tried their hands at fashioning *grues,* but the master was Harry Graham, who wrote under the pseudonym "Colonel D. Streamer" and put together a book of the verses aptly titled *Ruthless Rhymes for Heartless Homes.*

guardhouse lawyer is a self-styled expert on all aspects of military rules and regulations. The extent of his true understanding of these rules is measured by the fact that he is usually under detention himself—in the guardhouse. A *latrine lawyer* is similarly voluble and authoritative on army regulations, with one important difference—he is not yet behind bars. A *sea lawyer* is a sailor who is notably loud-mouthed and argumentative. He also often reveals a shrewd talent for using the red tape of regulations to avoid physical labor.

guerrilla was originally a Spanish word, the diminutive form of *guerra,* "war." *Guerrilla* originally meant a fast-moving, skirmishing type of warfare. Gradually it came to mean a soldier engaged in that kind of warfare. Today *guerrillas* are members of small groups—usually volunteers—whose specialty is quick hit-and-run attacks on supply lines and installations of the enemy. Often their activity is carried on behind the enemy lines.

guillotine. Here is one of the wry footnotes to history: the inventor of the *guillotine* was a French physician (named Dr. J. I. Guillotin) who thought that his invention was a great humanitarian contribution. In a sense he was correct, for the guillotine was at least a speedier and more efficient method of administering the death penalty than the drawn-out tortures which had been used before his time. But—thanks to the bloody abuse of the instrument during the French Revolution—the very word *guillotine* is now synonymous with needless and brutal slaughter.

gung-ho is a Chinese phrase, meaning "work together." During the early phase of World War II, it was the slogan of the Second Marine Raider Division, which served with distinction in raids on Guadalcanal and the assault on Little Makin Island. The division, also known as Carlson's Raiders, was led by Lieutenant Colonel Evans F. Carlson, who had served as an observer with the Chinese Eighth Route Army during 1937–1939. Some of his guerrilla tactics, as well as the *gung-ho* slogan of the division, seem to have been derived from his experiences there.

gunnysack is not a colloquialism but a perfectly good expression which the *Oxford Dictionary* indicates has been around at least since 1711. It originated in India. The word *gunny* comes from the Hindi *goni* and refers to the coarse hemp fabric, like burlap, from which the sacks are made.

guru. Shades of Westbrook Pegler! When that once dreaded and widely read syndicated columnist was smiting the Roosevelt administration hip and thigh, there must have been very few newspaper readers unaware of what a *guru* was. Pegler's second favorite target (after Mrs. Roosevelt) was former Vice-President Henry Wallace, who was regularly pictured as a visionary and impractical dreamer. (He once predicted fifty million jobs in post–World War II America.) Wallace also had taken a flier in Oriental meditation. In the course of his research he consulted the Maharishi of that day, a *guru*—which is simply the Hindi word for "teacher" or "venerable one." But that was enough for Pegler, and to the delight of headline writers, who love short, colorful words, "Henry and his guru" figured in hundreds of columns.

gussied up means "dressed in one's finest clothes" and often is heard as "all *gussied up."* There are two theories of the origin of *gussied up*. *Webster's New World Dictionary* says that *"gussie* is a nickname for Augusta," which indeed it is. But what that has to do with dressing up is left to the imagination. Perhaps someone somewhere named Augusta had a reputation for never wearing anything but fancy clothes. This we doubt. The other theory —much simpler—is that *gussy* comes from "gusset," and a gusset, in case you have been neglecting your sewing lately, is a triangular insert used in making garments—chiefly with the aim of making them roomier but also, on occasion, to make a more elegant garment than one made without gussets. So a lady wearing a much-gusseted dress would be "all *gussied up."*

guy/man. The use of *guy* for *man* goes back to a British festival known as Guy Fawkes' Day. You have to be British to understand why they should celebrate the attempt by Mr. Fawkes to blow up the British House of Lords on November 5, 1605. But celebrate it they do—with parades and noisy demonstrations, the whole thing accompanied by much burning of effigies of Fawkes. After this had been going on for a century or two, *guy,* originally used only for the effigies, became a casual nickname for any male person. British schoolchildren, doing a sort of "trick or treat" performance, would turn up on doorsteps showing the effigy of Fawkes and asking for "a penny for the *Guy."*

guzzle. The *National Geographic* magazine reports that *guzzle* is Cape Cod talk for a small channel between two sand bars." That's all right as far as it goes, but it doesn't go far enough. A *guzzle* is also a small stream running through a marsh. That's Massachusetts talk, too, for we remember hearing it as far north as Ipswich (where the Ipswich clams come from) in our marsh-trotting youth.

haberdasher is a word seldom seen these days outside biographies of Harry S Truman, certainly the nation's most distinguished exemplar of a vanishing breed. A *haberdasher,* by definition, ran a *haberdashery* and that was simply a small store dealing in men's furnishings. Urban department stores and suburban shopping centers have very nearly eliminated such stores. There are two theories of the origin of *haberdasher*. One is that it's from Icelandic *hapurtask,* meaning "sack for oats." Though it can be argued that some items of apparel may bear some resemblance to sacks, we find this farfetched. More persuasive is the theory that it came into English by way of Norman-French *haberdasser,* which in turn came from *hapertas,* "fabric or cloth." In any event, *haberdashers*—who then sold cloth, ribbons and needles—were well enough established in the Middle Ages to form one of the great merchant guilds of London in 1448.

habitué. If a friend of yours were a *habitué* of a certain club and you were looking for him at lunchtime, you would know where to find him. He would be sitting in his accustomed place, talking with fellow club members and eating or drinking his lunch. *Habitué* comes from the French *habituer* (to accustom) and means a person who is accustomed to going to a certain club or restaurant on a regular basis.

hacienda usually brings up visions of leisurely, gracious life in a house in a warm, sunny climate, but this is a word with a background of hard work. It is a Spanish-American term which may mean an estate or plantation in the country, but it may also mean a stock-raising, manufacturing or even mining operation, particularly when the owner resides on the property. *Hacienda* comes from the Latin *facienda,* meaning "things to be done"—so at the true *hacienda* there is so much to be done that little loafing goes on.

hackie/hackney. The term *hackie* for cabdriver is pretty much confined to the New York area, where the licensing bureau is known officially as the Hack Bureau. This is a shortened form of *hackney,* which meant "horse or carriage (or a combination of the two) for hire." It comes from a place name in England, but whether Hackney is where the hire cab originated is not a matter of historic record.

hacking/coming up on. In our column we voiced our irritation at a radio newscaster who repeatedly said: "The time is now coming up on 6:24" instead of simply saying: "The time is now 6:24." Well, there is an explanation for the phrase and we're indebted to Colonel Charles H. Shaw, USAF (Ret.), for telling us about it.

> As a pilot in the 8th Air Force in WWII, based in England, I flew a number of heavy bombardment missions over Germany. (Statisticians called them "sorties" and headline writers called them "raids" but the flight crews never called them anything but "missions.") Each mission was preceded by a "briefing," a presentation at which maps, charts, slides and other media were used to illustrate the objectives of the mission.
>
> As the final act of the briefing ceremony, the group navigator, custodian of the master chronometer, arose to give us a "hack." . . . *"Hacking"* was a procedure for synchronizing precisely the watches of every member of the group with the master timepiece. The navigator would say something like "The time is *coming up on* zero seven four three in seventy seconds." Each member of the group would pull out the winding stem of his watch when its second hand reached "12" and would then set the other hands to read 7:43. The navigator would count down the remaining seconds to 7:43, calling out "Hack" when the second hand of the master timepiece reached "12." Thereupon each of the others would push in the stem of his watch; all the watches were thus synchronized to the precise second—and the combat mission was under way.

hack writer. Perhaps not surprisingly, there's a connection between *hack writing* and the hackie who drives a taxicab—and we don't mean merely that cabdrivers often sound like frustrated writers or orators. The first hacks (originally "hackneys") were half-breed horses, usually fairly small and used for rental purposes. Gradually the term came to be applied to anyone working for hire, including prostitutes and charwomen as well as the poor Grub Street hacks of Johnson and Goldsmith's day. It was the latter, incidentally, who half-seriously eulogized a departed hack in this verse: "Here lies poor Ned Purdom, from misery freed,/Who long was a bookseller's hack;/He led such a damnable life in this world,/I don't think he'll wish to come back."

Hades was the nether-world kingdom of the shades of the dead in Greek mythology. Over the centuries it has erroneously come to be considered synonymous with Hell, though the shades in *Hades* were not necessarily suffering any torment nor expiating any sins. The word comes virtually unchanged from the Greek *Haides*.

hail as in *"Hail* to thee, Blithe Spirit" has no connection with the *hail* that, in the form of frozen rain, pelts those of us in northern climes from time to time. Instead it comes from a Middle English expression *waes haeil,* meaning "Be healthy," from which we also get the familiar yuletide "wassail." So when we *hail* a person, ceremonially at least, we are greeting him with enthusiasm and wishing him well.

hair of the dog goes all the way back to ancient Rome. The theory is that the best cure for a hangover is a drink of whatever it was that you were drinking the night before. Since the Romans believed that the cure for a dog bite was the burned hair of the dog that bit you, they had a saying *"Similia similibus curantur,"* meaning "Like things cure like."

hairsbreadth means a measure as narrow as a human hair. It's very old. The *Oxford Dictionary* traces it to 1561 and that sprightly young dramatist, Will Shakespeare, was using it only a few years later. In *Othello,* he had the leading character reminisce about the story of his life and "most disastrous chances, of moving accidents by flood and field, of hair-breadth 'scapes i' the imminent deadly breach, of being taken by the insolent foe, and sold to slavery." In England, at one time, the *hairsbreadth* was recognized as a formal unit of measure—one forty-eighth part of an inch.

hairy. In 1974 the CBS *Evening News* reported that the press plane accompanying the Nixon party in Russia had engine trouble at 24,000 feet, with the result that the correspondents had a "hairy" experience when the plane suddenly lost altitude and plummeted earthward. It all turned out all right, of course. *Hairy* is a fairly recent addition to our slang lexicon, cropping up first in the mid 1960s. It means hazardous, distressing or—in this case —harrowing. We suspect it's simply a shortened form of "hair-raising."

halcyon (pronounced HAL-see-un) is an adjective meaning "calm and peaceful." It comes from the Greek word for kingfisher. Legend was that the kingfisher's brooding period was the seven days before and the seven days after the shortest day of the year. Since the kingfisher's nest was believed to be borne on the waves of the ocean, it followed that during this period the weather would surely be calm and peaceful—or *halcyon*.

half-seas over, which was originally *half sea's over,* goes back to before the time of Shakespeare—to 1551, to be exact. At that time it meant literally halfway across the sea, then came to mean pretty much the same as the Latin phrase *in medias res,* "in the middle of things" or "halfway through a task." About 1700 it acquired the meaning in which it's most commonly encountered today, "more than slightly drunk," perhaps from the fact that a person *half-seas over* in drink has passed the point of no return.

Haligonian is a native of Halifax, Nova Scotia—just as a "Cantabrigian" is a native of Cambridge, a "Liverpudlian" of Liverpool, and a "Glaswegian" of Glasgow. All these odd nouns and adjectives derived from place names in England, where, indeed, a *Haligonian* is still considered a native of Halifax, Yorkshire.

hallelujah. This expression of jubilation comes from two Hebrew words, *hallelu* (praise), and *yah* (short for Yahweh, the Lord).

hallmark. The Goldsmith's Company in the Goldsmith's Hall in London initiated many centuries ago the practice of stamping an official mark on a silver or gold item to guarantee that it was genuine. Thus was the *hallmark* born. It was adopted by other government assay offices and, in addition, acquired the figurative sense of meaning any evidence or outward proof of high quality or genuineness: "Courtesy is the *hallmark* of a gentleman."

Halloween is a contraction of "All Hallows Even" and is so named because it is the evening before All Saints' Day (November 1) in the Christian church. All Saints' Day is also known as All Hallows and Halloween is also All Hallows Eve. "Hallow" is derived from an Old English word meaning "holy person."

In pagan times Halloween was the last day of the Celtic calendar and was thought to be the night when witches and warlocks were roaming the land and when evil spirits and souls of the dead were abroad. When Christianity came to the British Isles, it became the eve of All Hallows or All Saints' Day, but the old traditions remained. That's why youngsters wear masks when they go out trick-or-treating and it is also why the hollowed-out jack-o'-lantern has a masklike face.

halve Hahn/Kolsche Kaviar are two items of German cuisine that roughly parallel our Welsh rabbit (which is not a rabbit at all) and Scotch woodcock (which is not woodcock, either). *Halve Hahn* is, literally, "half a chicken," but—at least in Cologne—it actually is a slice of Edam cheese on a dark caraway-seeded bun. *Kolsche Kaviar* isn't caviar at all, but blood sausage or Blutwurst. The reason why these oddities came to our attention is that they made news when tourists from other parts of Germany interpreting the names literally, screamed that they had been swindled when the actual dishes arrived. This whole matter may now be but a footnote in the history of the culinary art, since some of the restaurants, seeking to avoid trouble, dropped the items from their menus.

ham as a name for an amateur radio operator has spawned several theories as to its origin. One of the more ridiculous is that it is derived from the initials (H., A., M.) of the first three men to hold amateur operator licenses. The fact is that *ham* in the sense of an unprofessional operator goes back to a period long before radio was even invented. It was part of the language of telegraphers a hundred years ago, a time that H. L. Mencken called "The golden age of the craft, when its aristocrats were the newspaper telegraphers who not only had to be fast and accurate at the Morse Code but also had to master the Phillips Code, which changed almost from day to day." *Ham* is simply a shortened form of "amateur," a person who devotes himself to a sport or hobby for the love of it.

ham actor. *Ham* in this phrase has two distinct meanings. First, probably by analogy to "amateur," there is the use of *ham* to mean an actor who is incompetent or unskilled. That's the meaning intended in such phrases as "Hollywood *hams.*" Then there is *ham* in the sense of one who overacts or outrageously overplays a scene—especially when his intention is to center all attention on himself to the exclusion of other players. Such devices as upstaging other actors, grimacing at the audience and pointedly fiddling with one's pocket handkerchief during another player's speech are common practices of actors bent on *"hamming* it up."

In the days of blackface minstrel shows before the turn of the century, one popular song was "The Hamfat Man" and it clearly referred to second-rate actors of the type that appeared in such shows. But nobody knows for sure whether the song inspired the name "hamfatter" for these actors or whether the name preceded the song. We think that the name came before the song, probably from the minstrel's practice of using ham fat to remove the heavy black makeup used during performances. In any event, *ham actor* is an American expression which made its first appearance in print during the 1880s.

hamburger was originally "Hamburg steak" and took its name from the city of Hamburg, Germany. The dish was brought to this country at the time of the first great wave of German immigration, midway through the nineteenth century. With the passage of time, "Hamburg steak" dropped its capital *H*, acquired an extra *er*, lost the "steak" and moved from the platter to a place between the slices of bread or roll to become the *"hamburger* sandwich" we know today. Incidentally, *hamburger*, with the terminal *er*, is closer to the original German, since that ending is the way German converts proper nouns to adjectives. The German version would be *Hamburger hackfleisch*, ground meat à la Hamburg.

handsome is as handsome does, meaning that good looks alone are not enough, that performance is what really counts, is centuries old and has appeared in many slightly varying versions. In 1580, for example, a book of maxims called *Sunday Examples* had it this way: "As the ancient adage is, goodly is he that goodly dooth." The distinguished etymologist Skeat drew what we think to be rather too fine a point in his comments on the saying. "In the proverb *'handsome is as handsome does,'*" wrote Skeat, "'handsome' means 'neat,' with reference to skilfulness of execution." Well, maybe.

hand that rocks the cradle is a much-quoted line, though verging on the obsolete by now. The original version by an otherwise forgotten nineteenth-century American poet, William Ross Wallace, ran: "They say that man is mighty./He governs land and sea./But a mightier power and stronger/-Man from his throne has hurled./And the *hand that rocks the cradle*/Is the hand that rules the world."

handwriting on the wall is an expression often heard as a portent of doom. "When the candidate saw the early returns from normally 'safe' wards, he knew that they were the *handwriting on the wall* and that he was doomed to defeat." The expression was inspired by a line from the Bible (Daniel V: 25–31). Belshazzar learned that he was about to lose his kingdom when the words "Mene, mene, tekel, upharsin" magically appeared on the wall of the palace. "This," continues the Bible, "is the interpretation of the thing . . . God hath numbered thy kingdom and finished it . . . Thou art weighed in the balances and art found wanting . . . Thy kingdom is divided, and given to the Medes and Persians."

hangar, the structure used for housing aircraft, has a very humble origin. It's borrowed from the French word for "shed" and eventually goes back to the Medieval Latin *angarium,* a blacksmith's shelter. Apparently Bleriot and other French aviation pioneers simply put their craft in vacant sheds and—*Voila!*—*hangar* acquired a new meaning.

hang in effigy. The practice of venting one's wrath on a facsimile of the person hated is probably as old as the human race. In every society from primitive Samoans to certain of the Pennsylvania "Dutch" sects of the present day, people have believed that they can do harm to their enemies by sticking pins into images or effigies of them. Our word *effigy* comes from the French word *effigie,* meaning "likeness or copy." The practice of hanging a person in effigy dates back to a French tradition in the years before the Revolution. Then, if a wanted criminal could not be found, it was the duty of the public executioner to hang an *effigie* of him.

hangnail. Why do we say *hangnail?* After all, it's not the nail that hangs but a pesky and painful bit of torn cuticle. The word was originally *agnail,* an Anglo-Saxon word for a corn on the toe, which in turn came from *ang* (painful) and *naegl* (nail)—the whole thing coming from the appearance of the corn, which they thought looked rather like a nail's head. Then folk etymology took over and people, seeing the resemblance between *ang* and *hang*, simply added the *h*. Somewhere along the way the ailment moved up from the foot to the finger and that's why that bit of torn skin at the side or base of a finger has the seemingly silly name *hangnail*.

hang up your socks and go home probably originated in an athletic locker room. The meaning is quite clear: your help—such as it is—is no longer needed. Pack up and be gone with you!

hanky-panky goes back more than a hundred years and originated in the jargon of fairs and carnivals. It's a variation on the much older "hocus-pocus"—a term used by shysters and magicians while performing tricks. Since there was always something underhanded about such activities, *hanky-panky* has come to mean double-dealing or devious trickery.

hansom cab, a two-wheeled carriage with the driver's seat above and outboard of the cab's roof, was the favorite vehicle of Sherlock Holmes and Dr. Watson, if memory serves. Anyway, the *hansom cab* was invented by an English architect with a name that might well have come straight out of one of Conan Doyle's tales. He was Joseph Aloysius Hansom, and he did the deed in 1834.

happy as a clam has puzzled many people, who can't be blamed for wondering just what this particular bivalve mollusk has to be happy about. The reason for the aphorism becomes clear, though, when we give it in full: *"Happy as a clam* at high tide." Clams, you see, can be dug only at low tide, when the mud flats in which they grow are exposed.

hara-kiri. Two pronunciations are permitted for this Japanese term which literally means "a cutting of the belly." HAH-rah-KEER-ih is preferred, but the first syllable may also be pronounced with a flat *a* sound—the *a* in "cat." The word may also be spelled *hari-kari,* in which case the pronunciation becomes HAH-ri-KAR-ih. Incidentally, the term is seldom used by the Japanese themselves, who call the act *seppuku.*

harbinger. The robin, the traditional *harbinger* of spring, bears little resemblance to a German soldier—but the word *harbinger* has much to do with soldiers. It is derived from the Old High German *heriberga,* which meant "shelter for soldiers." Originally a *harbinger* was one who went ahead of any army or a royal party to arrange for lodging and other accommodations. Since then it has come to mean anyone who goes ahead to announce the coming of others—or a person or thing which hints of coming events. That's how the robin got into the act.

hard hat, originally referring simply to the reinforced plastic or metal hats worn by construction workers, became a faintly pejorative label for construction workers themselves after the Wall Street confrontation of spring 1970 when anti-Vietnam war protesters were attacked by bands of workers wearing such hats.

hard-nosed has a special attraction for politicians, who are forever taking a "hard line" so that the "thrust" of their arguments will reach their targets with plenty of "clout." Well, *hard-nosed* originally meant little more than stubborn or insistent. Now it seems to have added an aspect of pugnacious determination to see a project to successful completion—with delicacy and finesse cast to the winds. It also has a much older meaning of a dog deficient in sense of smell and, hence, useless for hunting. In football, before the advent of the face mask, a *hard-nosed* player was one who didn't flinch at getting his nose right into the action.

hard to buy. In *The Confessions of Nat Turner,* William Styron has the lawyer say to the imprisoned slave, "And that you killed only one and were reluctant to kill more is a line of goods mighty *hard to buy.*" However, the expression *hard to buy* does not seem to have been in use as early as 1831, when Nat Turner led a revolt of slaves in Virginia. The use of *buy* in the sense of "believe or accept as true" is unrecorded in any but the most recent dictionaries and no example occurs earlier than the 1940s.

harem. Originally a *harem* was a house set aside for the female members of a Moslem household, not the women themselves. Also, to contradict the evidence of thousands of Hollywood spectaculars, *harems* do not consist solely of beautiful women in diaphanous drawers. The *harem* includes many women of all ages, including wives, concubines, female relatives and women servants. The original Arabic word *harim* meant "sacred or forbidden place."

harlot. The first *harlots* were male, not female. The word comes from an Old French word of the same spelling and meant "a young fellow," especially a vagabond. As recently as Chaucer's time, he could write: "He was a gentil *harlot,* and a kinde: a bettre felaw shulde man no wher finde." For the past couple of centuries, though, *harlot* has been restricted in use to indicating what the *Oxford Dictionary* chastely calls "an unchaste woman."

harrier. The first *harriers* were a special breed of hounds, smaller than fox-hounds, developed to hunt wild hares. In this sense, the word goes back to before the time of Shakespeare. Later there developed a game called "hare and hounds"—also called "paper chase." In it, members of one team (called "hares") would run across fields and through woods, leaving a trail of scraps of paper. The second team (called "hounds") would pursue them, following the trail in an effort to catch up to them ("capture" them) before a prearranged goal had been reached. Cross-country or long-distance running may well have evolved from the hare-and-hounds game. At any rate, this is surely the origin of *harrier* as a term for such runners.

Harvard beets. A half century or so ago, when Harvard had some of the finest football teams in the country (don't laugh, boys, they really did!), Harvard crimson was a color known throughout the land. About that time, a chef, whose name unfortunately has been lost to history, confected a dish of cooked beets warmed in a sauce of vinegar, sugar and cornstarch, whose resulting deep red color was very close to the crimson in Harvard's then proud banners. Eureka!—an inspiration—and the name *Harvard beets* was coined!

hash. The French *hacher* means "to chop," and from that came our word *hash,* meaning "a dish of chopped meat and vegetables." An earlier ancestor was the French *hache,* for "ax." *Hachette,* its diminutive form, was adopted by us as "hatchet," "a little ax."

hassle. Though the origin of *hassle* in the sense of a heated discussion is uncertain, some language experts believe it is derived from a Southern dialect word variously spelled *hassle, hassel* and *hessel.* This term means "to pant or to breathe noisily," as "The dog is *hassling.*" Since the participants in a lively *hassle* (argument) might well lose their breath as well as their tempers, perhaps this is as good an explanation of the origin of *hassle* as we are likely to find.

hat trick is part of the vocabulary of hockey. A player "pulls off the *hat trick*" when he scores three goals in a single match. The expression didn't originate in hockey, though. It was borrowed from cricket. If a bowler in Britain's national game takes three wickets with three successive balls, he is said to have done the *hat trick.* The feat is so rarely accomplished that in the early days of cricket, any player who pulled it off was awarded a hat as bonus. The term is also used today in horse racing. It's not uncommon for a star jockey to win three races on a day's card, but he is said to have pulled off the *hat trick* only if he wins three races in succession.

havelock is the cloth covering for a soldier's hat with a long flap in the back to protect the wearer's neck from the sun. Nowadays they are seen mostly in period films about desert warfare, like *Beau Geste,* but in Victoria's time they were part of the standard issue, especially to troops stationed in India. It gets it name from General Sir Henry *Havelock,* who served more than thirty years in India until his death in 1857.

have your cake and eat it too is a very old proverb, appearing in print in 1546 in Heywood's *Proverbs.* But, obviously, it had been in circulation for centuries before that, since Heywood's book was simply a collection of well-known sayings. It's worth remembering that in those early days the word *cake* was used to mean any kind of bread baked in small pieces, as well as what we call cake today.

havoc (pronounced HAV-uk) has an interesting history. Its meaning today is "destruction or devastation," especially that resulting from a great catastrophe. But back in the Middle Ages, when we took the word into English from the Norman French word *havok,* it was a war cry—a signal for invading warriors to attack, sack and plunder a village. Perhaps the word is best known nowadays in Mark Antony's soliloquy over the body of the newly fallen Caesar: "And Caesar's spirit, ranging for revenge,/. . . Shall in these confines with a monarch's voice/Cry 'Havoc!' and let slip the dogs of war." Here, as in so many other instances, Shakespeare's use of a word in memorable context has been incomparably the best insurance that the word would remain a part of the living language.

hawk, as a name for various birds of prey, goes back to the Middle English *hauk* and the Old English *heafoc,* which the *Oxford Dictionary* finds analogous, via a common Teutonic base, to the Latin *capere* (to seize). The common characteristic of all hawks is, of course, their swift downward descent and ruthless seizure of less powerful animals or birds. *Hawk* also has long been in the language in the sense of offer for sale, especially to the accompaniment of street cries or, as in the case of carnival barkers, extravagant spiels extolling the sometimes nonexistent virtues of the product offered.

hawk from a handsaw. It was New York's Mayor Fiorello H. La Guardia who made the classic statement: "I seldom make a mistake—but when I do, it's a beaut." Well, here's the story of a fairly classic goof. In the course of a newspaper column, we answered a question about a Shakespearean quotation: "I know a *hawk from a handsaw*"—meaning "I'm a pretty smart fellow." The line appears in *Hamlet,* when the title character says: "I am but mad north-north-west; when the wind is southerly, I know *a hawk from a handsaw.*" The explanation we gave—and one supported by many scholars—is that *handsaw* here is a corrupt form of *heronshaw*—a young heron. So a person who knows *a hawk from a handsaw* knows the difference between a bird of prey and the bird being preyed on. Pretty farfetched, you say. Well, you're right—and a lot of scholars should be red-faced today. Here's a more logical explanation of the origin of the phrase, from Francis W. Sheridan of Washington, D.C.

> Plasterers and carpenters were as common in Shakespeare's time as they are today. Then, as now, the *hawk* was a basic tool of the plasterer and the *handsaw* a basic tool of the carpenter. The *hawk* is a small square of wood or metal with a handle on the underside. The plasterers use it to hold the plaster in one hand while they apply it with a trowel in the other. The *handsaw* is long and narrow with its handle on the end. The tools are quite easy to distinguish.
>
> I know that *heronshaw* is the classic answer but why go all round Robin Hood's barn for an answer to a simple comparison of common tools? I have long believed that the classic answer was developed by a scholar who, in the sanctuary of his ivory tower, was far removed from such mundane matters as plasterers and their "mud."

head shrinker probably originated as a derisory reference to efforts by psychiatrists to shrink or deflate the delusions of grandeur of certain of their patients. The *Dictionary of American Slang* (Wentworth and Flexner) records it as appearing in print as early as 1957, but we recall having heard it at least ten years earlier. It may well have started as service slang in World War II. Today it's often shortened to simply "the shrink."

Heart of Dixie is the nickname for the state of Alabama, and with good reason. First settled by the French in 1702, the territory later came under British control and, after the Revolutionary War, under United States control. It then became part of the Mississippi territory in 1798, became a separate territory in 1817 and achieved statehood in 1819. It earned its nickname by being a leader in the movement to secede from the Union. Montgomery, its present capital, served as the first capital of the Confederate States.

heat's on originally meant intensive police pressure on organized crime as a result of pressure from reform groups. While the heat was on, criminals would "blow town," returning when the word went out that the *heat was off.* Nowadays it merely means that "trouble is brewing."

Hecate (pronounced HEK-uh-tee) might be termed a triple threat among Greek goddesses. Originally a fertility goddess, she later became the goddess of Hades and of the dead. In addition, she was the patron goddess of witches. Shakespeare, in *A Midsummer Night's Dream* (Act V, Scene 1), writes of "We fairies, that do run,/By the triple Hecate's team/From the presence of the sun,/Following darkness like a dream." The most recent literary evocation of Hecate was probably the appearance of her name in the title of Edmund Wilson's collection of short stories, *Memoirs of Hecate County* (1946). Apparently her power to hex mortals continues unabated, for that volume was officially banned by censors. The allegation was that certain passages in one of the stories were calculated to arouse prurient interest. Amusingly enough, the only passages that seemed to our eyes to come even close to this definition of obscenity were written in French. One would think that the ability to read Edmund Wilson's French would presuppose a certain sophistication on the part even of censors, but apparently this was not so.

hector as a verb is commonly used to mean "to bully or torment"; as a noun it refers to a bully or to a blustering, swaggering fellow. The original Hector was one of Holmer's heroes in the *Iliad,* who was killed by Achilles. In early drama he was portrayed as a swaggering bully.

heebie-jeebies/hotsy-totsy/horse feathers. These examples of obsolescent (if not obsolete) slang were all created by Billy De Beck, a comic strip artist who also created such famous characters as Barney Google and Snuffy Smith. *Heebie-jeebies* may be roughly translated as "the creeps," as in "He gives me the *heebie-jeebies.*" *Hotsy-totsy* is an exclamation of approval, as in "That girl is really *hotsy-totsy!*" *Horse feathers* is an expression of derisive disapproval, similar to "Baloney!" or "Nuts!"

heeler. The *Dictionary of American Slang,* by Wentworth and Flexner, defines *heeler* as "one who toadies before superiors; one who curries favor with superiors or social groups in order to increase his own status." The authors also indicate that it means the same as "apple polisher." They seem to have overlooked the very common—and not at all derogatory—use of *heeler* on college campuses. There a *heeler* for the college newspaper, for instance, is simply a beginner or apprentice legman. If his performance freshman year is commendable, he gets a staff appointment in later years. The first reference is clearly from the practice of training a dog, or in the case of royal couples, a consort, to follow the master or mistress closely behind or at the heels.

heinous is a word often misused and even oftener mispronounced. Meaning "hateful" or "atrocious," it is a word of Teutonic origin which came into English through the Old French *hainus,* "hateful." Pronounced HAY-nus, it was used with notable effectiveness by Cole Porter in his "Brush up Your Shakespeare" number in *Kiss Me, Kate,* wherein he managed to rhyme *heinous* with Coriolanus.

heirloom is any valued possession which has been passed on within a family for several generations. Originally, however, it was much more closely related to the family's traditional trade or occupation. For the *loom* in *heirloom* was not necessarily the loom used in weaving. In Anglo-Saxon times (when the word was spelled *geloma*) the loom was any kind of tool or implement. Not until after the Norman Conquest did *loom* come to mean specifically the weaving apparatus that we call by that name today.

helicopter. The Greeks gave us the makings of the word *helicopter*—*helix* and *helikos* for "spiral" and *pteron* for "wing."

hell, like the idea it represents, has been around a long time. Back in Anglo-Saxon days it was spelled with a single *l,* and earlier it was taken from a Germanic word, *haljo,* meaning "the underworld or a concealed place." In Old Norse the word was also spelled with a single *l,* and it meant, in the words of Webster, "The heathen realm of the dead."

hell-bent for. Expressions involving *hell-bent for* go back to our early frontier days. The idea, of course, is that anyone *hell-bent for* something is recklessly determined to get it, regardless of the consequences even if they be hellfire and damnation.

As it happens, *"hell-bent for* election" can be pretty definitely traced to —of all places—the down East state of Maine. Back in 1840 a man named Edward Kent was running for governor of that state on the Whig ticket. The national slate was headed by William Henry Harrison, the hero of the battle of Tippecanoe, and John Tyler. As it turned out, the Whigs won, carrying Maine, where they had used the slogan *"hell-bent for* Kent," leading their opponents to say that Kent was *"hell-bent for* election."

When the returns were in, some long-forgotten rhymester concocted a victory song which included these less than immortal lines: "Oh, have you heard how old Maine went?/She went *hell-bent for* Governor Kent,/And Tippecanoe and Tyler, too!"

hell is paved with good intentions—which also appears as *The road to hell is paved with good intentions* and even, euphemistically, *The road to Hades is paved,* etc.—has been a favorite theme of writers from the time of Vergil onward. A seventeenth-century divine named Baxter is credited with having said it first in English—at least, Coleridge says he did. But then in the eighteenth century Boswell says that Johnson said, *"Hell is paved with good intentions,"* too. Sam, like all reference-book editors, tended to soak up some of the copy he edited, so it's not surprising that some of the wittiest of his bon mots can be traced to earlier writers. As a sort of topper to all this wit, be our guest as we quote a nineteenth-century writer, Robert Southey, who wrote:,"It has been more wittily than charitably said that *hell is paved with good intentions;* they have their place in heaven, too."

hello. At a guess, there's probably no other word (excepting "I") so much used in English as *hello.* Practically every phone conversation opens with it, and that alone must account for millions of uses every day. But where did it come from? The earliest English ancestor seems to be *hallow,* a word of greeting common in the time of Chaucer. It was pronounced with the accent on the second syllable. By Shakespeare's day, it had become *halloo* —a form still used by fox hunters and perhaps by more plebeian hunters as well. Then we come closer to the present form, because by the nineteenth century our fellow countrymen were greeting each other with *hullo.* Legend has it that Thomas Alva Edison himself was the first to say *hello* over the telephone—and this is one instance where legend may well be accurate. It is indeed true that *hello* came into widespread popularity within a very few years of the introduction of the telephone. Amusingly enough, the very first telephone exchange, set up at New Haven, Connecticut, in 1878, did not use *hello, hullo* or even the "View halloo" one might have expected from Yale's sporting bloods. Instead the phones were answered "Ahoy, ahoy!" The person responsible for this salutation was the inventor of the first practical telephone, Alexander Graham Bell, who is reported to have used "Hoy" or "Ahoy" all his life, rejecting "Hello," perhaps because his rival, Edison, was credited with it.

hello, Sucker. Nightclub hostess Texas Guinan was famous for greeting ring-siders at her club with the brash salutation *"Hello, Sucker!"*—and they loved her for it. Her other contribution to the slang of the 1920s was "big butter-and-egg man," to describe a well-to-do small-town businessman trying to prove himself a big shot in the big city by buying drinks for chorus girls.

Hell's Corner was a section of the British coastline along the English Channel near Dover. It got its name from the fact that during the trying months of the Battle of Britain (1940) it was under shellfire from German cross-Channel guns and under constant air threat because much of the fighting between the *Luftwaffe* and Britain's Spitfires was right overhead.

helpmeet/helpmate. The male co-author of this book once referred to his female co-author as his *helpmeet* and was promptly challenged as to his choice of words. *Helpmeet* is a "ghost word." It was created through a misreading of the Bible. In Genesis (2:18) you will find this: "And the Lord God said, It is not good that man should be alone; I will make him an *help meet* for him." The word *meet* simply meant "suitable or appropriate," so the meaning of the phrase was that the Lord planned to create a suitable helper for man. But when the Bible was read aloud the two words *help* and *meet* were consistently blended and read as one: *helpmeet.* Still later the word *helpmate* was formed with the idea that *mate* made more sense than *meet* in this combination.

hemming and hawing goes back at least to the seventeenth century. It's an "echoic" phrase, meaning in this case that the words involved attempt to duplicate the sound made by a person who is stammering, especially when he is trying to stall for time because he has no clear answer ready. Under such circumstances, the first thing one does is to clear one's throat *(Ahem!)* and then one stammers a bit until inspiration arrives (that's the *hawing*).

heroin. A staff member of a famous hospital sent us this query: "We have found that among the feelings drug addicts get, particularly with *heroin,* is one of being heroic or capable of performing in a heroic manner in certain areas, including the sexual. *Webster's Collegiate Dictionary* defines Hero as a priestess of Aphrodite, the love goddess. This leads us to ask whether or not there is possibly some connection between this Hero and the element *hero* in *heroin.* As you know, very often the reaction or effect of a drug is inherently a part of its trade name. For instance, Diuril is a diuretic, Equanil (implying equanimity) is a tranquilizer, and so forth."

To which we replied: "You have an ingenious theory—but not a very sound one, we're afraid. *Heroin* was originally a trade name—a German trade name—for this narcotic. But the coiner of the name seems to have been inspired by another Greek word, *heros* (from which we get our "hero") rather than by the name of the love goddess. We suspect that the rest of your theory holds, however, since the idea in the namer's mind was that one effect of the drug is to make its user feel, however briefly, like a conquering hero."

hero sandwich. *Hero* is the name given in the New York area to the kind of sandwich known in other parts of the country variously as "grinder," "poor boy," "submarine," and "hoagie." It consists of a small loaf of French bread, sliced lengthwise and containing a variety of meats, seasonings, and usually lettuce. The best explanation for the *hero* name is that one has to be something of a hero to work his way through it. The "submarine" name is obvious from the shape of the sandwich. "Poor boy" also needs no explanation—lots of food at a relatively small price. "Grinder" may get its name from the grinding of teeth as one battles the salami or what have you—but this is just a guess. We once asked Hoagy ("Stardust")

Carmichael if the *hoagie* sandwich was named for him, but he disclaimed responsibility.

herringbone. To most people the term *herringbone* refers to a twilled fabric which is woven in the pattern of the skeleton of a herring. Traditionally it has been used primarily for men's suiting. Long before it came to be used to describe a fabric pattern, however, *herringbone* referred to a type of stitch used either to decorate fabric or to fasten down heavy fabric. As such it was called "*herringbone* work." Half a century later, "*herringbone* work" came also to mean a method of masonry or paving in which stones were set in parallel lines of diagonally laid stones. Carpenters then applied the term to an arrangement of struts used in X form between joists to increase their strength. It wasn't until the middle of the nineteenth century that *herringbone* came to be applied to fabric. Somewhere along the way skiers took the word *herringbone* to describe—for obvious reasons—the method of climbing a steep slope by walking with the skis pointing outward, thus leaving a herringbone pattern in the snow.

he's a riot. *Riot,* in the sense of a major outbreak of violence, is nothing to laugh at. But the word *riot* has many other meanings. There is a "*riot* of color," meaning an unlimited profusion of colors—as in the colorful displays put on by trees in Northern states when the leaves change with the coming of fall. What's more, the original *riots* were debauched revels—not necessarily at all violent—in which fun and games played a major role. So the expression *He's a riot!*—while somewhat slangy—has a perfectly legitimate history.

he that runs may read. This appears in the Old Testament Book of Habakkuk (2: 2): "Write the vision, and make it plain upon tables, that he may run that readeth it." The version most commonly heard today is from the British poet Cowper, who wrote: "But truths, on which depend our main concern/ . . . Shine by the side of every path we tread/With such a lustre, he that runs may read."

he who fights and runs away will live to fight another day is such a truism that we'd guess that the first expression of it was grunted by a caveman weary of battle. One of the first recorded expressions, though, is credited to Demosthenes, the famous Greek orator and political leader. When Philip of Macedonia, Alexander the Great's father, attacked, Demosthenes took flight. Reproached for his seeming cowardice, he replied: "A man who runs away may fight again." And a poem by our favorite poet, Anonymous, appeared about the middle of the eighteenth century. It ran like this: "*He that fights and runs away/May turn and fight another day;/*But he that is in battle slain/Can never rise to fight again."

hex signs/hexagon. The colorful *hex signs* painted on barns in the Pennsylvania Dutch country to ward off evil spirits are sometimes six-sided (hence, *hexagons),* but this is mere coincidence. There is no direct connection between *hex* and *hexagon.* The former comes from an Old German word, *hagazussa,* from which the Anglo-Saxon word *hag* also comes. *Hexagon,* on the other hand, comes straight from the Greek *hexagonon,* "a six-sided figure."

heyday goes back to an Anglo-Saxon use of *hey* as an expression of great enthusiasm and happiness. So a person's *heyday* is the period of his greatest· vigor and success.

hi! as a greeting is generally considered a contraction of *hiya,* which is a corruption of *How are you?* Or so goes the conventional wisdom. However, etymologists working on our *American Heritage Dictionary* report finding virtually the identical greeting—*Hy!*—as early as the twelfth century.

hide. Ad men with their calculated assaults on the language—"like a cigarette should," for example—have often been targets for our fire. Occasionally, good writing turns up in ads and then we applaud. Even less frequently, though, do we find the ad writer who ventures into the word-origin field in an effort to plug his product. One such sortie that we didn't mind at all was an advertisement by one of New York's department stores aimed at selling fur coats to men. With a tongue-in-cheek air, the ad writer gives us "the story behind men's furs" as follows: "Man first used furs as a defense . . . and not just against the cold. By concealing himself in the hide of a wolf, he not only absorbed its courage; he also (hopefully) scared his enemy to death. And that's how we got our verb 'to hide.' "

How successful the ad was we don't know. But give the ad man his due. There is at least an element of accuracy in what he says. Both the verb and the noun *hide* can be traced back to Anglo-Saxon words, the verb to *hydan,* which means the same as our verb, and the noun to *hyd,* meaning "skin." The reconstruction of earlier Indo-European bases has brought scholars to the conclusion that the basic sense of the verb was probably "to cover with skin."

hide your light under a bushel. The *bushel* in this phrase is the container, usually made of earthenware or wood, used to measure a quantity (four pecks, as a matter of fact) of grain, vegetables or fruit. The phrase *hide your light under a bushel* now means to display excessive modesty about one's abilities. The phrase first appeared in the Bible (Matthew 5:14–15) when Jesus, after urging his disciples to be "the light of the world," added that "A city that is set on a hill cannot be hid. Neither do men light a candle, and put it under a bushel, but on a candlestick."

highball comes from bartenders' slang of the 1890s, when they called all glasses *balls.* Naturally, the tall glass used for whiskey and soda became the *highball.* Its popularity is doubtless partly due to the meaning *highball* has for railroaders: the signal to speed up on a clear track.

highbinder was in fairly widespread use as early as 1802. Then it meant, in the genteel language of the *Oxford Dictionary,* "rough," or as the *Dictio-*

nary of Americanisms has it, "a ruffian or rowdy." In fact, the first *high-binders* seem to have been New York scoundrels. At the start of the nineteenth century, the *New York Post* reported that in the lower part of the city there existed a "desperate association of lawless and unprincipled vagabonds, calling themselves 'highbinders.' " Later it came into use on the West Coast to refer to Chinese assassins, members of a secret society or tong, who would hire out to kill or perform lesser acts of violence.

high dudgeon. We have a neat problem here since *dudgeon* has two distinct meanings. The less common is "a kind of wood used for dagger hilts and, hence, the handle of a dagger." The second and only frequently heard use of the word today is in the phrase "in *high dudgeon,*" meaning in a state of irate indignation. *High* is here used in the sense of great or intense. Though most linguists contend that there is no direct connection between the *dudgeon* of the dagger hilt and the *dudgeon* of deep resentment, it seems to us that they are blinding themselves to a simple fact of medieval life—the period when this phrase first gained wide currency. What would be more likely than that a man of noble birth, feeling indignant over an insult to his name or reputation, would reach for his dagger as the first gesture of avenging the damage? How probable, indeed, that the dagger—instrument of vengeance—became by extension the term used to describe the high degree of wrath which would lead to its use! So *dudgeon,* in today's meaning of wrath or resentment, almost surely came from the medieval name of the instrument commonly used to avenge the cause of wrath.

highfalutin/highfaluting was originally an American slang word, first recorded in print about 1850. It was part of our frontier language and was used to disparage high-flown, bombastic orators. As a matter of fact, some language students think *highfalutin* is simply another form of "high-flown" or "high-floating"—to refer to the puffed-up phrases used by old-time Fourth of July orators.

high man. To circus and carnival folk, the *high man* is not the boss of the circus but the man who winds up on the top of a human pyramid.

high mucky muck/high-muck-a-muck. The dictionaries usually give the spelling *high-muck-a-muck,* and that's a bit closer to the original Chinook version, *hiu muckamuck,* meaning "plenty of food." In the Alaska of a century or more ago, a person with plenty to eat was a pretty important fellow—and that's what the expression means. A *high-muck-a-muck* is usually not only a person of authority, but one who likes to be sure that everyone knows how important he is.

high noon. How does *high noon* differ from simple noon? If you say, "I'll meet you at noon," the meaning can be precisely at noon or in the general area of noontime—give or take ten or fifteen minutes. *High noon,* by contrast, means precisely at 12 noon—not a minute before or after.

high seas applies to the oceans of the world beyond the three-mile jurisdictional limit allowed each coastal nation under international law. The *high seas* form the free waterways of the world.

high tea. British *high tea* may be served in the early evening hours as well as in late afternoon. But more than that, it's often very elaborate and constitutes a meal more comparable to a Scandinavian *smorgäsbord* than to what we call *tea*. Here's a description of an 1890s *high tea* from a British newspaper of the period: "*High tea* should have cold roast beef at the head of the table, a cold Yorkshire pie at the bottom, a mighty ham in the middle. The side dishes will comprise soused mackerel, pickled salmon, sausages and potatoes, etc. Rivers of tea, coffee, and ale, with dry and buttered toast, sally-lunns, scones, muffins and crumpets, jams and marmelade."

hijack. A number of sources say that *hijack* comes from the greeting with which hobos accosted intended victims of robbery. In considering the real meaning of the word *"hobo"* (which see), we feel that this is not a very persuasive theory. We prefer the one that Stewart Holbrook suggested back in the 1920s, when *hijacking* trucks loaded with illicit liquor was an everyday happening. " 'Hijack,' " wrote Holbrook, "comes from 'High, Jack'—a command to throw up the arms."

hillbilly is exactly what the word implies—a rustic from the hills. The *American Dialect Dictionary* by Harold Wentworth defines *hillbilly* as "an uncouth countryman, especially from the hills." The earliest examples of its use come from the turn of this century and from the vicinity of Arkansas. Then its use spread throughout the South and it became especially common in Kentucky and West Virginia.

hip/hep. *Hip* is a latter-day variant of *hep*. During the early big-band swing days of the 1930s, bands like Benny Goodman's and Count Basie's were labeled *hep*—meaning that the musicians, arrangers, et al., were "in the know." For a brief period about that time, devotees of jazz were popularly known as *hep cats,* a term that was never very popular with musicians themselves. *Hep* first appeared in soldier slang around 1900 as a borrowing from the drillmaster's cadence count: "*Hep,* two, three, four. *Hep,* two, three, four." The troop that always hit the beat properly was in step, hence *hep*. About the end of World War II, new voices were heard in the jazz world. "Bop" flourished for a while, later giving way to "cool" jazz. With these transitions, a new jazz argot came in, a new form of verbal communication between musicians themselves. *Hep,* in the words of one musician friend, "wasn't *hip* any more."

his name is mud/Mudd. A reader of our column, reading of efforts to obtain a belated presidential pardon for Samuel A. Mudd, the doctor who set the broken leg of Lincoln's assassin, John Wilkes Booth, raises the question of whether the popular expression *His name is mud* should not actually be *His name is Mudd,* referring to the fashion in which the doctor's name was blackened. In truth, it has been well established that Dr. Mudd was not a part of the conspiracy to kill Lincoln.

That's a most ingenious theory, and it wouldn't surprise us a bit if the story of Dr. Mudd and his claim of ignorance may have contributed to the popularity of the expression during the nineteenth century. However, *mud* in the sense of scandalous or defamatory charges goes back to a time well before the Civil War. In fact, there was an expression, "the *mud* press," to describe newspapers that besmirch people's reputations by throwing mud, as long ago as 1846. So it seems most likely that the expression *His name is mud* was well established before Dr. Mudd met his unhappy fate.

his nibs first appeared late in the eighteenth century as *his nabs,* and *nabs* was a variation of an even earlier word, *nob.* This might have been a shortened form of "nobleman," though there is no clear evidence for this theory. Or it might have come from *nabab,* a Hindi word for "governor," from which we get "nabob," an important person, and Nob Hill, a hill in San Francisco where many of the wealthy live. Anyhow, *nob, nabs* and *nibs* all meant, in the words of the *Oxford Dictionary,* "a person of some wealth or social distinction."

history is bunk. An irate reader (angry at the source books, not at us) protested that Henry Ford was misquoted as saying that *history is bunk,* and that what he said was: "History as taught in schools is bunk." The latter version she agreed with: "I do not think it would blow the children's minds to discover that Lincoln was a politician, not a saint, and that Benedict Arnold wasn't always a traitor." However, all the sources readily available on our bookshelves indicate that Ford *did* say *"History is bunk"* while testifying on the witness stand at Mount Clemens, Michigan, in his libel suit against the *Chicago Tribune* in July 1919. This is the quotation recorded in the *Home Book of American Quotations,* F.P.A.'s *Book of Quotations,* Bartlett's *Familiar Quotations* and the *Oxford Book of Quotations.*

hit a brace is from the idiom of the service academies. At the command of an upperclassman or officer, a cadet must *hit a brace,* that is, assume an exaggerated position of attention, shoulders drawn so far back that the shoulder blades almost touch, chest high and chin drawn tightly against the collar.

hitchhike evolved from the fact that a hitchhiker has to do some hiking between lifts and, at least in the early days, used to have to *hitch* (catch on to) a slowly moving vehicle.

hitting on all six comes straight from the slang of auto fans of about 1915. In an age when most cars had only four cylinders, a six-cylinder car was something pretty special. So if all six cylinders of a car were functioning properly *(hitting on all six),* the car and its driver were cutting a very fancy figure indeed. The phrase came to be used to apply to any person whose performance was better than usual.

hobby is a contraction of "hobbyhorse" and originally meant a small or medium-sized horse. Then it came to mean a light wicker frame-work, draped with colored cloth to simulate a horse, which was used by dancers in the medieval English country dances called Morris dances. In the course of these revels, various characters from the Robin Hood legend were depicted, so the function of the hobbyhorse as an instrument of make-believe is pretty obvious. Later the hobbyhorse came to be a child's play-thing—what Yorkshiremen call "a stick with an 'orse's 'ead 'andle"—and the phrase "to ride a hobbyhorse" came to indicate the pursuit of a childish game with a zeal worthy of more adult interests. Readers of Laurence Sterne's *Tristram Shandy* will recall with delight the relentless hobbyhorse riding of My Uncle Toby. Quite possibly his endearing addiction to his hobby may have contributed greatly to the establishment of *hobby* in its present meaning of an occupation or pursuit bordering on the frivolous to which a person is devoted. *Hobby* has by now come a long way from the time when it meant merely a small pacing horse. But through all its changes of meaning, the element of fun has been implicit in it.

hobnob is a word of impeccable ancestry. In its present form it has been in our language since Shakespeare's day. In fact, it is found in at least one of his plays. Originally it appeared in Chaucer's time as *habnab,* meaning literally "to have and have not" or "hit-or-miss." In those days, and through the centuries since, the term was used to describe the social practice of alternating in the buying of drinks: one chap buys a round, then his friend buys the next. First he has, then he has not, the honor of treating. Gradually the term *hobnobbing* came to mean any form of social inter-course on easy, familiar terms—the sense in which the word is most often used today.

hobo. Opinions may vary about the precise origin of the word *hobo,* but all agree that a *hobo* is not a bum or a tramp. He is simply a worker who likes to travel. One source suggests that it comes from "hoe boy," a migratory farm worker. Another proposes that it comes from the sarcastic greeting "Hey, bo," the "bo" being a corruption of *beau,* the French term for a dandy (which a hobo emphatically is not). Still another dictionary theo-rizes that it comes from the call "Ho, boy" used in the Northwestern United States in the 1880s by railroad mail handlers as they tossed mail-bags from trains.

Jefferson ("Jeff") Davis, who reigned as king of America's *Hobos* for more than half a century, made his own distinctions. "The hobo," he once said, "does not believe that society owes him a living, but he does believe that society owes him a chance to care for himself. . . . Some men are born hobos, some achieve hoboism and others have hoboism thrust upon them." Tramps, he stated, didn't want to work and felt that the world did owe them a living. Bums, in his opinion, were like tramps but were drunkards as well.

Hobson-Jobson is the name of a trade language developed by British colonists and soldiers in India in order to communicate with the natives. It took the form of Anglicizing Hindi words, assimilating them into something approximating well-known English words. An example of the method is the phrase *Hobson-Jobson* itself, which is an Anglicized version of an Arabic cry of lamentation: "Al Hasan! Al Hosain!"

Hobson's choice. Toward the end of the sixteenth century, one Thomas Hobson operated the leading livery stable in the university town of Cambridge, England. Devoted to the welfare of his horses, he established a firm rule that each customer in turn must take the horse nearest the door when he arrived. He tolerated no picking and choosing, insisting that this strict order of rotation be followed. Thus, when someone offered you *Hobson's choice,* you were actually being offered no choice at all.

hocus-pocus. There is quite a widespread superstition that this phrase came originally from the Latin version of the Roman Catholic mass. Is this true? Not exactly, though many people believe that this magician's phrase is derived from *"Hoc est corpus"* ("This is my body"), a phrase used in the mass. More likely, the term is simply what the *Oxford Dictionary* calls a "sham Latin" phrase invented by a magician to distract the audience while working his tricks.

hodgepodge. The original English spelling for this word was "hotchpotch," meaning a kind of stew. Logically enough, the word in time came to mean any kind of jumble or mess.

hogging moment is the moment of stress to which a ship is subjected when she is waterborne amidships but out of the water at both ends. The opposite situation is the *sagging moment.* Either way, it bodes ill for the ship.

hoicks is a variant of the better-known "yoicks"—a call to the hounds in fox hunting.

hoi polloi (pronounced hoi puh-LOI) comes from the Greek. It means "the many" and is generally used to refer to the great mass of humanity, the common people. Purists shudder at the sight of *the hoi polloi* in print, pointing out that it is equivalent to "the the many." However, theirs is probably a futile struggle. Even such conscientious writers as John Dryden refer to *the hoi polloi,* and in British university slang that is the common designation for students who graduate without honors.

hoist by his own petard means "destroyed by his own trickery or inventiveness." A *petard,* in medieval warfare, was an explosive charge which daring warriors would affix to the walls or gates of a castle under siege. This action in itself was a most hazardous one, but the greatest danger came after the *petard* was in place. The explosive was detonated by a slow match or slowly burning fuse. Occasionally, of course, the explosive went off prematurely, in which case the warrior was *hoist* (lifted or heaved) *by his own petard.* It is unlikely that this archaic phrase would have persisted in our language, even in a figurative sense, had not Shakespeare conferred immortality upon it with this line from *Hamlet:* " 'Tis the sport to have the engineer *hoist with his own petard.*" Today it is chiefly used to describe a person ruined by plans or devices with which he had plotted to ensnare others.

hoity-toity, meaning "haughty or snobbish," has been in common use for nearly three centuries. Some scholars say it comes from an obsolete verb, *hoit,* meaning "to romp around noisily," but that seems to us very far-fetched. More possibly, it is a corruption of "haughty." This latter theory, at any rate, comes much closer to the present meaning of the word.

hokum/hokeypokey. *Hokum* can be traced back to the lingo of magicians in Shakespeare's time. In order to divert the attention of the audience from the mechanics of their trickery, they would call out some fine-sounding but meaningless mock-Latin phrases. The magicians usually started with *"Hokus-pocus, toutus talontus, vade celerita jubes."*

In any event, the expression in various forms came down through show business channels. As *hokeypokey* it even became the name of a cheap imitation of ice cream—shaved ice with syrup—sold by street wagon vendors. Always, though, there is the element of phoniness, of trickery, involved. So *hokum* in show business means artful stage business designed to stimulate a cheaply sentimental reaction from the audience.

holistic is derived from a theory put forward by Jan C. Smuts, best known as a general of South African forces in the Boer War and later prime minister of that country. Smuts evolved an idea that, in the words of *Merriam-Webster:* "The determining factors in nature are wholes (as organisms) which are irreducible to the sum of their parts and that the evolution of the universe is the record of the activity and making of these wholes." *Holistic* is a voguish word with the "in" group of ecologists today. It's pronounced with a long *o,* by the way (hoh-LISS-tik), in case you want to impress your ecologically minded friends.

holler in the sense of shout or call comes from the French *hola,* meaning "Ho, there!" Originally a cry to attract attention, it appears in various forms throughout the English-speaking world. The fox hunter's cry "View halloo" is one variation, as are "hollo," "hullo" and, the most common form, "hello."

holocaust (pronounced HOL-oh-kost) is a word we sometimes see in the headlines, yet it is not one that many of us find in our speaking vocabularies. Originally a holocaust was a sacrificial burnt offering to pagan gods in pre-Christian times. It is derived from the Greek words *holos* (whole) and *kaustos* (burnt). Nowadays it is generally used to mean slaughter and destruction on a very wide scale, especially by fire. Specifically—and usually with a capital *H*—it refers to the Nazi slaughter of Jews in World War II.

holt as a pronunciation for *hold* is especially common in backwoods New

England and in the area ranging from West Virginia south through Tennessee, the Carolinas and on to Florida. It's a dialect variation of the generally accepted pronunciation.

holy orders. When we say that a person has taken *holy orders,* we don't mean that he or she has accepted certain rules and regulations. Rather the phrase means that he or she has been accepted into the ranks (orders) of the clergy. In the Roman Catholic Church there are three major orders: priests, deacons and subdeacons. The Eastern Orthodox Church has five major orders: bishops, priests, deacons, subdeacons and readers. In the Anglican Church there are three: bishops, priests and deacons.

holy Toledo! This exclamation of surprise refers to Toledo, Spain, which became one of the great centers of Christian culture after its liberation from the Moors in 1085. Its thirteenth-century Gothic cathedral, one of the largest in Europe, is the seat of the Cardinal Archbishop of Spain.

homage. To pay *homage* to a person is to express publicly respect, reverence or honor due him for what he is or has done. It is a purely voluntary action and places no obligation on the person honored. In the Middle Ages, however, feudal law required a tenant to make public avowal of his allegiance to his lord by kneeling before him in front of all the other vassals and proclaiming that he would be his "man." The ceremony was named *homage* from the French *homme,* meaning "man." While the vassal was obliged to acknowledge the terms under which he would hold the land, the ceremony also obligated the lord to give his protection to the tenant—hence, *homage* then was a mutual matter.

home economics. If language were a perfect science, if words did not change but kept the meanings of their root words, the *home* in *home economics* would be superfluous. The word *economics* (from the Greek *oikos,* "house," and *nemein* "to manage") originally meant household management—just about the same thing as *home economics* today. However, the term was soon extended to mean the management of the affairs of a community or a nation as a whole, and in time came to mean the science of production, distribution and consumption of wealth. The original meaning is many centuries (and two languages: Greek and Latin) behind us in the evolution of language. So today we use the phrase *home economics* when we refer to the science or skills of homemaking.

home in is a phrase that has been common in aviation circles for decades, originally meaning to find one's way to a destination, usually with the aid of sophisticated navigational devices. Now it has the more specific meaning of "to be guided to a target automatically." Naturally it also has a broader, popular sense. You can say that in the search for the solution to a puzzle or problem, you are beginning to *home in* on the answer.

Homer nodded. The expression usually appears as *even Homer nodded*— meaning that even the wisest and most gifted of men, like Homer, the great

Greek poet, make mistakes. The first appearance of the expression is in the *Ars Poetica* of the Roman poet Horace, who wrote: "Sometimes even good old Homer nods."

homonyms/homophones. Remember the old nursery rhyme about Fuzzy Wuzzy, the bear? It went like this: "Fuzzy Wuzzy was a bear./Fuzzy Wuzzy had no hair./Fuzzy Wuzzy wasn't fuzzy, was he?/No, he was a bare bear!" Perhaps because it's a rhyme that has been repeated times without number in the Morris nursery over the years, it came to mind when we received this inquiry from a column reader. "Isn't there a word," she asked, "to designate words which sound alike but have different meanings, like *alter* and *altar,* or *road, rowed* and *rode?*"

There is indeed a word for such pairs of sound-alike words. In fact, there are two words for them—*homophone* and *homonym.* Technically speaking, a *homophone* (from the Greek *homos,* "the same," and *phone,* "sound") means a word which sounds like another word of different meaning, while a *homonym* (from *homo* plus *onyma,* "name") is one which has the same sound and spelling as another word of different meaning. However, this distinction is seldom observed and, to all intents and purposes, *homonyms* and *homophones* are considered the same.

Homophones, of course, are the source not only of confusion but of many of our puns. Note the "bare bear" of the nursery rhyme or the remark of a television entertainer that a famous golfer had invited him to "tee."

While *homophones* are not strictly a phenomenon of the English language, it's true that we have many more of them than are to be found in other tongues. The reason? Simply because English has borrowed so widely from a great variety of languages that it was inevitable that words of different meanings but of similar spelling and sound would come from different source languages. "Bear," the animal, comes from the German *bar* by way of the Old English *bera,* while "bear," to carry, comes from the Anglo-Saxon *beran* and has indeed been traced by some scholars back to the Sanskrit *bharati.* "Tea" and "tee" come from countries half a world apart, the former from a Chinese word *t'e* and the latter from the Scottish dialect word *teaz.*

honcho/honsho. The origin of *honsho* or *honcho,* which has come into some slang use as a synonym for "big shot" or "boss," is in the Japanese word *hancho,* squad commander. It was widely used by American service personnel in occupation forces as an adjective meaning "top," "big boss," and so forth. Popular in Japanese-American street and bar language—some English, some Japanese, with the Japanese corrupted—it was neither correct Japanese nor correct English, but it was effective.

honest Injun, from Tom Sawyer and Huck Finn, has been traced back to 1851, but it is probably much older than that. Originally it was probably an expression of sarcastic derision—"as honest as an Indian." But later it came to mean about the same thing as the British *honor bright* or the American *scout's honor*—a pledge of truth and honesty.

honeymoon. The explanation of the origin of *honeymoon* is, we fear, a bitter-sweet one. First as to the *honey:* It was a custom in ancient times for a newly married couple to drink a potion containing honey on each of the first thirty days—a *moon*—of their marriage. Attila, king of the Huns, was reputed to have drunk so heavily of this potion that he died of suffocation. The thirty days, of course, roughly correspond to the lunar month, but there is still another explanation of the use of *moon* in this phrase. According to the *World Webster Dictionary,* this referred "not to the period of a month, but to the mutual affection of newlyweds, regarded as waning like the moon." There speaks a disillusioned etymologist. Let's cast off his cynical interpretation and revert to the happier thought of the young couple steeped in bliss and honey, at least for the first thirty days of their married life.

honkie/hunkie/hunky. *Honkie* seems first to have gained wide circulation as the result of televised speeches and statements by black militant leaders. It appears to be a corruption of *hunkie* or *hunky,* a slurring term originally applied to white laboring-class men of Hungarian origin. The *World Webster Dictionary* says that *hunky* is a "vulgar term of prejudice and contempt"—a description that certainly fits *honkie,* too.

honyoker is a dialect term meaning pretty much the same thing as "galoot." According to Wentworth and Flexner's *Dictionary of American Slang,* this word in various forms *(hon-yock, honyock, hon-yocker)* has been around for about a hundred years, though never in very widespread use. They define it as "farmer or rustic." Obviously the term is unflattering.

hooch has been part of our slang ever since the early days of Prohibition as a term for crudely distilled spirits. It got its name from a tribe of Alaskan Indians, the Hoochinoo, which had a reputation for creating an especially powerful kind of firewater. Dr. Arthur Hull Hayes, Jr., of the Medical College of Cornell University, adds this comment.

> While certainly not disputing your origin of the word, I think you might be interested in knowing that some pharmacologists frequently cite another origin. Since homemade alcohol produced during Prohibition days frequently contained the lethal contaminant methyl or wood alcohol, an anagram of the chemical formula for this type of alcohol was used as a slang term for illicit booze. The chemical formula for methyl alcohol involves the letters CH and OH. Any amateur anagram player could rearrange those letters and get HOOCH. I'm afraid I can give no legitimate references for this story, but if you have not already heard it, you may find it amusing.

We find it very interesting indeed. It happens that the evidence for "hoochinoo" goes considerably further back in history. In fact, in 1899 a

Boston newspaper reported: "The name of firewater in Alaska is 'hoo-chinoo,' and recently the House gave its official sanction to the word by enacting that no whisky, beer or hoochinoo shall be sold in Alaska."

However, we think that the anagram developed by the pharmacologists might very well have influenced the popularization of *hooch* during Prohibition times. After all, men with degrees in pharmacy had a lot to do with the distillation and even, in some cases, the distribution of booze in those days. We know from experience. During the last days of the Volstead era, William often worked in his uncle's pharmacy in Boston—reputedly the only drugstore in the neighborhood that did *not* peddle illegal spirits.

hood is a contraction of *hoodlum,* an underworld slang term first reported in San Francisco, where it was used to describe gangs of rowdies who specialized in maltreating Chinese laborers in the latter part of the nineteenth century. There are a few fanciful theories of its origin, the most unlikely being that it was first a backward spelling of Muldoon ("noodlum") and gradually became *hoodlum.* Incidentally, sources with closer connections with the underworld than we report that *hoods* themselves pronounce the word to rhyme with "brood." The real *hoods,* apparently, never use the pronunciation given to *hood,* the head covering.

hooker. A gentleman of probity and prominence in our community approached us on the street and said: "Would you be good enough to settle an argument about hookers?" It seems the argument had to do with whether the first hookers—and we assume everyone knows who they are —were camp followers of General Joseph Hooker in the Civil War.

Our research indicated that the word had appeared in print at least once in 1859, the year before the outbreak of hostilities. But it seemed wise to get a really authoritative answer to the question, so we wrote our old friend Bruce Catton, certainly the nation's foremost authority on the Civil War. We noted that General Hooker's reputation was not the highest. Indeed, we quoted Charles Francis Adams, Jr., as calling him a "man of blemished character . . . whose headquarters was a place to which no self-respecting man liked to go, and no decent woman could go—a combination of barroom and brothel."

Here is Catton's comment:

That business about Joe Hooker and the soiled doves of Civil War Washington pops up every so often. I agree with you that the term 'hooker' did not originate during the Civil War, but it certainly became popular then. During these war years, Washington developed a large and segregated district—the word 'segregated' had a different meaning as used then—somewhere south of Constitution Avenue. This became known as Hooker's Division in tribute to the proclivities of General Hooker and the name has stuck ever since.

hooliganism. As you might guess, a lad or lads named Hooligan gave the word *hooliganism* its start. Ernest Weekley, in his charming *Romance of Words,* recalls that "The original Hooligans were a spirited Irish family whose proceedings enlivened the drab monotony of life in Southwark (a district of southeast London) towards the end of the nineteenth century." Undoubtedly some of the popularity of the term *hooligan* in this country can be traced to the famous comic strip *Happy Hooligan,* which recounted the slaphappy misadventures of a gawky chap with, as we recall, a tin can for a cap. It was created by Frederick Burr Opper, the cartoonist who also created Maude the mule, and Alfonse and Gaston.

Interestingly enough, the word *hooligan* is common in Russia, with precisely the same meaning it has in England and the U.S. Along about the turn of the century, when relations between czarist Russia and England were cordial, a czarevitch (future czar) spent some time in London, picked up *hooligan* and, on his return to Russia, made it popular there.

hoolihan has two closely related meanings in the colorful jargon of the cowboy. An untamed or unbroken horse may buck in any one of a number of different ways. If he *swallers his head,* he drops his head between his forelegs. If he *crowhops,* he pitches with short, stiff-legged jumps. If he *jackknifes,* he clips his front and hind legs together. But if he *hoolihans* or *wildcats,* he actually somersaults. So a rider able to "throw the hoolihan" would have to be as skillful as they come. *Hoolihan*—sometimes written "hooley-ann"—has a second meaning in ranching. Cowpokes use various techniques to rope and throw cattle at roundup time. *Bulldogging* a steer means to get a grip on its horns and twist its neck until it hits the ground. *Hoolihaning* a steer is a very similar operation—knocking it down by leaping on its horns.

hoosegow. A jail or prison, *hoosegow* is derived from the Spanish word *juzgado.* The earliest recorded use of the word in American English is given as 1920, but, almost without question, the word was picked up by American cowboys from their Mexican saddlemates back in the mid 1800s.

Hoosier, referring to a native of Indiana, derives from the Cumberland dialect word *hoozer,* meaning anything unusually large. It has been found in its present-day meaning of Indianan as far back as 1829. All sorts of variations have been created, including "Hoosierdom," "Hoosierism" and even "Hoosierina," meaning a woman who lives in Indiana.

hop the twig is a British expression meaning "to elude capture" or, more specifically, "to get away scot-free from one's creditors." The reference is to a bird who *hops the twig* just before the hunter shoots.

hornet's nest. "Stirring up a *hornet's nest*" is a serious business indeed. If you have ever had the misfortune to disturb a hornet's nest, you know that the fury of a swarm of the creatures means trouble to anyone in the path.

hornswoggle. There's not much light to be shed on the origin of *hornswoggle.* Experts agree that it's an American coinage that can be traced to the early days of the nineteenth century. One Australian word authority recently commented: "The only American coinage which has left us breathless with admiration is *hornswoggle*"—and this from a nation that coined "bonzer," "bushwhacker" and "billabong!" Some theorists hold that the *horns* in *hornswoggle* may refer to the traditional symbol of the husband victimized by infidelity and that this would account for the element of deceit and trickery implicit in the word.

hors d'oeuvre. The literal meaning of the original French phrase *hors d'oeuvre* is "outside the work" and it was originally an architectural term referring to an outbuilding not incorporated into the architect's main design. The phrase was borrowed by France's culinary experts to indicate appetizers customarily served apart from the main course of a dinner. Thus *hors d'oeuvres* are, quite literally, outside the main design of the meal. *Vraiment, c'est simple, n'est-ce-pas?*

horse latitudes may be either of two belts of latitudes located at about 30 to 35 degrees north and south. They are characterized by high barometric pressure, calms and fickle breezes—or no breezes at all. There are two theories about how they got their name. The first is that sailing ships transporting horses might, when becalmed for a long period, have been forced to cast the horses overboard to lighten the ships and take advantage of whatever wind might be stirring. The second theory is that *horse latitudes* is a translation of the Spanish phrase *golfo de las yeguas,* "gulf of the mares." This would indicate that the Spaniards were comparing the fickleness of the breezes in this area of the ocean to the well-known capriciousness of mares.

By the bye, one of our favorite humorists, the late H. Allen Smith, once wrote a delightful book titled *Lost in the Horse Latitudes.* It didn't have anything to do with the *horse latitudes,* of course, but then neither did his celebrated *Low Man on a Totem Pole* have anything to do with totem poles.

horse of a different color simply means a different situation entirely. The expression has a long history, going back at least to the time of Shakespeare, who used a punning change on it when, in *Twelfth Night,* he described some conniving plans of Toby Belch and Andrew Aguecheek as "a horse of the same color."

horseshoe (as symbol of luck) goes as far back as ancient times. In the second century A.D., Pliny the Elder recommended *horseshoes* as a healing agent, which tells something about the state of medicine in those days. During the Middle Ages *horseshoes* were nailed to the doors of barns to keep witches and warlocks from stealing horses at night. Then they came to be put over the doors of houses so that no evil spirits could enter. There's even a story that Lord Nelson had a *horseshoe* nailed to the mainmast of his flagship and another that Harry Truman put one over the door of his office in the White House. But why the *horseshoe?* Well, there was a belief that its resemblance to the lunar crescent in shape made it a sign of good luck.

Another theory is that it looked enough like a halo to ward off evil. And there are two schools of thought as to how to hang it. One says to hang it with the heel down so that it looks more like a halo. The other says hang it with the toe down so the luck won't run out. Be our guest—take your choice.

hospital. The first *hospitals* were pretty much what we would now call "hostels"—places where weary travelers could rest a bit before pressing on with their journey. Indeed, the very first *hospitals* were used by pilgrims to Jerusalem during the Crusades. The best-known early organization providing such shelter was the Knights Hospitalers, which still exists as a lay order of distinguished Roman Catholics called the Knights of Malta. The name is eventually derived from the Latin *hospitalis,* "of a guest."

After a while, though, *hospital* came to mean a place for the care of old people and then, over the course of many years, acquired the meaning it has today—a place for the care of the ill and infirm, both young and old.

hot dog. The first recorded appearance in print of the term *hot dog* is in 1903. H. L. Mencken did some very thorough research on the origins of *hot dog.* His findings: although sausages in rolls have been sold in this country for many years, the first person to heat the roll and add mustard and relish was Harry Stevens, concessionaire at the Polo Grounds, home of the New York Giants. And the coiner of the name *hot dog?* None other than the late T. A. Dorgan, "Tad," undoubtedly the best-known sports cartoonist of the era.

hotpants. "Pants"—a shortened form of "pantaloons"—has been part of American English since before 1840. The expression *hotpants* was common campus slang in the 1920s and was used to describe members of either sex who were more than ordinarily excited by the presence of someone of the opposite sex. In this sense, the term was considered inadmissible in polite society. Then, when the miniskirt vogue showed signs of waning, designers of women's clothing broke out their lines of abbreviated shorts and gave them the hitherto taboo label *hotpants.*

Hot Stove League. The reason you can't find the *Hot Stove League* listed in any of the baseball record books is that it never existed. In the years before the Japanese and Puerto Rican winter leagues, there was no wintertime baseball activity, though there was much discussion of the game among fans and occasionally a major trade would be made between clubs. Such off-season activity was often referred to by sportswriters as the *Hot Stove League,* in allusion to the cartoonists' favorite scene of a group of fans huddled for warmth around an old-fashioned stove.

hot walker is what virtually every jockey in history began as. It's the lowliest rung on the ladder to racing stardom. The *hot walker* is the chap who walks hot horses, gradually letting them cool off after practice runs. A variation of this idiom of the race track is: "He *walks hots.*"

housen as a plural for "house" is, or was, quite widely heard in many parts of the country during the nineteenth century and earlier. It's now labeled "dialect" or "archaic," but Harold Wentworth's *American Dialect Dictionary* reports it as "used by old people" from Cape Cod to as far west as Missouri during grandfather's day. At one time, English had a good many nouns that formed their plurals in *en,* but there are few left today—"oxen," "children" and "brethren" being the most notable.

hubris has been defined as "wanton arrogance arising from overbearing pride or from passion." It's a word from the Greek *hybris,* which meant simply "insolence or outrage," and it has enjoyed a modest vogue, especially among intellectuals, in recent years. Curiously enough, the adjective form, "hubristic," has been recorded in English since the early nineteenth century. But *hubris* seems relatively a Johnny-come-lately. It's pronounced pretty much as you would expect (HYOO-bris), in case you want to dazzle your friends—and display a little of your own *hubris* in the process.

hue and cry. In the Middle Ages, under common law, if someone called out for help in pursuing a thief or other criminal, people hearing the cry and failing to assist in the chase could be adjudged guilty of a misdemeanor. The expression *hu e cri,* as it was in Anglo-Norman, has, of course, long since become merely a synonym for loud outcry. Actually, the term always was somewhat redundant since *hue* comes from the Old French *huer* (to cry out) and *cry* obviously means the same thing.

hugger-mugger is a word seldom come upon these days. Elliot Paul wrote a better-than-average mystery, *Hugger-mugger in the Louvre,* some years ago, but if the word has been much in evidence elsewhere, it has escaped this writer's attention. It originally meant "secrecy or stealth," and Mr. Paul pretty obviously extended this meaning to something bordering on skulduggery. It has also the meaning of an untidy, disorderly mess. *Hugger-mugger* is thought to be a variant of *hoker-moker,* from the Middle English *mokeren,* "to conceal or hoard." Thus the meaning of secrecy is inherent in the root of the word—and strengthened by the repetition.

hullabaloo began as "halloo-balloo," "halloo" being the cry hunters shouted when urging their dogs to pursue the fox in English fox hunts. If you saw that splendid film *Tom Jones,* you'll recall that an eighteenth-century fox hunt was a very lively and noisy affair indeed, so it's not surprising that *hullabaloo* got the meaning it has today—a noisy, exciting uproar.

humble pie. Here we have a play upon words which dates back to the time of William the Conqueror. First, the *pie* referred to in "eating *humble pie*" was really *umble pie,* made from the umbles—heart, liver and gizzard—of a deer. It was made to be eaten by servants and huntsmen, while the lord of the manor and his guests dined on venison. Thus a person who had to eat *umble pie* was one who was in a position of inferiority—one who had to humble himself before his betters. The pun resulting from *umble* and *humble* is even more precise when you recall that in several British dialects

—notably Cockney—the *h* in *humble* would be silent. Actually, the two words come from quite different roots, *humble* from the Latin *humilis* (low or slight), and *umble* from the Latin *lumulus* (loin).

humbug for "hoax" or "fraud" first appeared during the eighteenth century as a bit of popular slang and quite possibly came out of the jargon of the underworld. At any rate, it is first recorded by the Earl of Orrery, who termed it a "new-coined expression which is only to be found in the nonsensical vocabulary and sounds disagreeable and absurd." Its great popularity during the nineteenth century can be credited to P. T. Barnum, who probably never said, "There is a sucker born every minute," but most assuredly did say, "The American people like to be *humbugged.*" Indeed, Barnum once lectured in England on the subject "The Science of Money Making and the Philosophy of *Humbug*"—which sounds remarkably like a more forceful and candid exposition of the same sort of pragmatic approach to business success that is peddled today under labels such as "Influencing People," "Positive Thinking" and the like.

hunky-dory. There are a couple of theories of *hunky-dory*'s origin and we'll start with the more colorful one. It seems that in Yokohama, Japan, there was (perhaps there still is) an important street named Huncho-dori. American sailors on shore leave would head for that street to find the sort of pleasurable relaxation that sailors always seek when first ashore. Then, since the street happily led directly down to the docks, they knew that they would have no trouble finding the way back to their ships. Thus, once they were on Huncho-dori Street, everything was *hunky-dory.*

So far so good. But there's another theory, that the whole thing started with a song sung by the Christy Minstrels during the Civil War. It was called "Josephus Orange Blossom" and contained a line about "red-hot *hunky-dory* contraband." The song was a great hit and *hunky-dory* became part of the popular slang of the period. Now this was, as we said, during our Civil War. Since Japan was not opened to foreign ships until Commodore Perry's visit in 1854, it seems a bit doubtful that the Yokohama theory will hold water. It's unlikely that a bit of esoteric sailor slang could catch on quite so quickly, though that remains a possibility. Our guess, though, is that *hunky-dory* was already an established slang term when American sailors first had shore leave on Huncho-dori Street.

And then, of course, there is the staid, sober theory, supported by some dictionaries, that the word is simply derived from a Dutch word, *honk,* meaning "goal" or "home," as in a game of tag. So once you reached *honk,* everything would be *hunky-dory.* Could be—but sometimes it seems that dictionary editors simply take all the fun out of life. As a one-time sailor who surely enjoyed his shore leave, the co-author of this volume still favors the Yokohama theory.

hunting the gowk. An April Fool's Day trick practiced by the Scots, *hunting the gowk* translates to "hunting the cuckoo bird."

hurrah's nest. The term *hurrah's nest* means any place that is a disorderly mess, a scene of wild confusion. But just what a *hurrah* is—whether it be bird, beast or human roisterer—nobody seems to know. The word *hurrah* —which sometimes appears without the final *h* in this phrase, as *hurra's nest*—is pretty clearly the same word we use as an exclamation of delight or applause. "We'll rally round the flag, boys. Hurrah, boys, hurrah!" Anyone who has had the onerous task of cleaning up the scene of a party or rally on the morning after the *hurrahs* have ended knows how appropriate the term *hurrah's nest* would be for such a scene of disorder.

hurst. In Anglo-Saxon *hurst* meant "wooded hill" and it appears in many English place names, Sandhurst, where the Royal Military College is located, being one.

husband. A *husband* in medieval England was literally the master of a household, whether or not he was married to the mistress of the establishment. The word comes from *hus* (house), and *bondi* (one who dwells). It also was often used to mean "manager," as of a wine cellar or tavern. We still see this sense of the word in the verb form today: "She has carefully *husbanded* her resources."

hush puppies. Throughout the South *hush puppies* are known as tasty bits of deep-fried corn-meal batter often served as accompaniment to fried fish. The most common theory of the origin of the term traces it back to the years immediately following the War Between the States. During those days of Reconstruction, food was shockingly scarce and a staple on all diets was corn meal in various guises. According to legend, many a mother fried up bits of corn batter to quiet the plaintive cries of hungry children—and dogs—with the words "Hush, child. Hush, puppy!"

Another and perhaps more authentic explanation was offered to us by a column reader who explained that he was born and raised in the South, and that the original *hush puppy* was the salamander, an aquatic reptile almost always called a "water dog" or "water puppy." "Over fifty years ago," he wrote, "my mother told me that no one wanted anyone to know they were reduced to eating water dogs. So 'hush, don't say anything about it and just eat it.' The water dogs were generally fried with the fish and the corn dough, which was formed into small sticks—so they could easily be called *hush puppies* too."

The salamanders were also called "hell benders" and "land pike." As long ago as 1687 an early visitor to America described the land pike as "another strange reptile so called from its likeness to that fish; but instead of fins it hath four feet." So it's easy to understand how it could have been used as a substitute for the genuine article—and why people would want to keep that fact hush-hush.

husky. For a number of years one of the favored members of the Morris household was a *husky* dog, flown down from Anchorage at the instigation of a long-time family friend, Colonel Henry W. ("Eskie") Clark. Colonel Clark had acquired his nickname at Phillips Exeter where he was the first native-born Alaskan in attendance. We fear he regarded our dubbing the *husky* dog "Eskie" as a somewhat dubious honor but he was mollified to know that the whole matter is rather neatly resolved by the recent decision on the part of word historians that the word *husky* itself is probably a corruption of "Eskie," short for "Eskimo."

hussy. When you dismiss a woman as a *hussy,* you obviously mean that, in the Victorian expression, she is no better than she should be. But things weren't always so. Until as late as 1800 *hussy* was sometimes used merely as an affectionate shortening of "housewife."

hustings goes back to the very earliest form of Anglo-Saxon government. *Hus* was the ancient word for "house" and the *husting* was the house in which the tribal assembly was held. Nowadays the word is always plural in form —*hustings*—but singular in grammatical construction. In England the *hustings* was the raised platform on which candidates for Parliament used to stand and make their speeches to their constituents. From this use of the word comes the expressions "take to the *hustings*" or "go on the *hustings,* " meaning to take part in political campaigning.

hyacinth. This varicolored fragrant plant with its attractive clusters of flowers —a delightful harbinger of spring—takes its name from a Greek youth of legendary beauty. Hyacinthus was so beautiful that he was beloved both by Apollo, god of the sun, and by Zephyrus, god of the gentle west wind. Hyacinthus preferred Apollo and this made Zephyrus uncharacteristically violent. While competing in games one day, Zephyrus hurled Apollo's quoit (a ring of iron) at the lad's head, killing him. From the spurting blood of the dying lad sprang a beautiful flower. That's an interesting, if some-what gory, tale. The only thing wrong with it is that the original *hyacinth* wasn't the flower we call *hyacinth,* but a lily.

hymn, perhaps not surprisingly, comes from Latin *hymnus,* "ode to the gods."

hypocrite. The original *hypocrites* were simply actors. The word comes from the Greek word *hupocretes,* "one who plays a part." And a *hypocrite,* of course, is one who pretends to hold opinions or feelings that he actually does not share. Literature's most notable hypocrite was Uriah Heep in Dickens's *David Copperfield,* and it is almost certainly no accident that his last name is virtually the same as the first syllable of *hypocrite.*

I. Ego has nothing to do with the capitalization of the pronoun *I.* Printing and handwriting have everything to do with it. In Middle English the first person singular was *ich*—with a lower-case *i.* When this was shortened to *i,* manuscript writers and printers found it often got lost or attached to a neighboring word. So the reason for the capital *I* is simply to avoid confusion and error. Of course, some writers refuse to be bound by this convention. Two of our favorites, the poet e. e. cummings and Don Marquis, author of *archy and mehitabel,* both favored the lower-case *i.*

"I care not who writes the nation's laws, so long as I can write its ballads." This was written by a Scottish politician, Andrew Fletcher, of Saltoun, who used it in a pamphlet published in 1704. His contention was that songs are much more widely listened to and heeded than most of the dry-as-dust pronouncements of politicians.

Ice Capades. In response to a question about the origin of the term *Ice Capades* for the famous ice extravaganza, we guessed that it might have been coined from elements of *ice* and *escapade.* John H. Harris, producer of the spectacle, wrote to give us the history of the name and, incidentally, a nice little example of serendipity.

"At the meeting in 1950 when we were organizing the company," wrote Mr. Harris, "it was our desire to find a new name, not like Ice Scandals, Ice Follies and the like, which were just copies of George White's Scandals and Ziegfeld's Follies. We were looking for a fresh, new name. Walter Brown, a vice-president of our company, was looking through a dictionary and reading out all the terms that began with ice: ice bag, ice cream cone, ice man and the rest. Looking up from the book for a moment he said 'Ice capades' but then immediately corrected himself, saying 'I made a mistake. It's Escapades.' I said, 'No, Walter, you're wrong. It's Ice Capades.' He tried to correct me again with 'Escapades' but when I insisted on 'Ice Capades,' he thought about it for a minute and he said, 'Hey, that's all right, isn't it!' "

ice cream seems to be a completely American invention. The English had something they called "iced cream," which they borrowed from France and Italy, but that was really a chilled custard. The first printed appearance of *ice cream* in the colonies was in 1744, when the *Pennsylvania Magazine of History* reported with enthusiasm on "fine *ice cream* which, with strawberries and milk, one could eat more deliciously." During the late years of our colonial period, it became very popular. Contemporary sources report that it was often served in Washington's home, Mount Vernon. All this time *ice cream* was a homemade delicacy; not until 1851 did a Baltimore milk dealer begin manufacturing it on a commercial basis.

ice cream pants was a term applied—usually derisively—to the white flannel trousers which with blue blazers formed standard dress for young men of the earlier years of this century, especially when they were "going out on a date." The expression first appeared in print in the *Saturday Evening Post* of 1908: "About half-past eight, Johnny ambled up, decorated with a blue coat, white vest an' *ice cream pants,* an' his hair all slicked down."

Why *ice cream pants?* The simple answer is that they were the color of vanilla ice cream. However, one reader of our column offers another explanation. "I grew up in a village in New Hampshire," he writes, "and in the early days, around 1912, ice cream was not a year-round commodity. The local drugstore would put in during the summer a supply of ice cream and tonic to trap the tourist's dollar." (Note for non–New Englanders: "tonic" is down East language for "pop.")

"Because of the increased trade the druggist would always hire a fair-haired, rosy-cheeked Mama's Boy, dressed in white, to tend the ice cream and soft drink counter. Because, then as now, most kids had an affinity for dirt, Mama's Boy couldn't engage in any horse play on his way to or from work, lest his lily white pants get soiled. Since he was, in a way, signaling that 'I can't have anything to do with you hooligans because I might get dirty if I do,' the term *ice cream pants* became the badge of a sissy and a term of derision."

iconoclast (pronounced eye-KON-uh-klast) is a word which has come almost unchanged from the Greek *eikon* (image) and *klastes* (a breaker). Literally one who shatters sacred images, it has come to mean anyone who scoffs at our treasured beliefs.

idiot comes from Greek *idiotes,* an ignorant person, also a private person. In English it has a much more pejorative meaning. An *idiot* today is an imbecile, a dunderhead. As a technical label in psychology, *idiot* describes a person of the lowest measurable range of intelligence.

idiot card/idiot sheet describe prompt cards or sheets placed out of camera range so that a person being televised can appear to be speaking ad lib, without notes, while actually reading key sentences. The Teleprompter has pretty much replaced the original *idiot cards,* but TV directors and their assistants still wave time-cue cards off camera, so that the program host will know how much time remains.

I disapprove of what you say, but I will defend to the death your right to say it. Some years ago the *New York World* used to carry a quote on the editorial page: "I do not agree with a word that you say, but I will defend to the death your right to say it." Generally attributed to Voltaire, this statement does not appear verbatim in his published works. The closest he came was in this letter to Madame du Deffand: *"I disapprove of what you say, but I will defend to the death your right to say it."* Apparently even this quotation was actually a paraphrase by one of Voltaire's biographers (S. G. Tallentyre) of these words from Voltaire's *Essay on Tolerance:* "Think for yourself and let others enjoy the privilege to do so, too."

if I had my druthers has been common throughout Southern and Western America at least since 1875, when Bret Harte used it in his book *The Argonauts. Druthers* is a corruption of "rathers" and the phrase simply means "if I had my choice or preference."

if the mountain will not come to Mohammed ... The common version of this saying goes like this: "If the mountain will not come to Mohammed, Mohammed must go to the mountain." When Mohammed was bringing his message to the Arabs, they demanded some miracle to prove his power. He then ordered Mount Safa to come to him. When it failed to move, he said that God was indeed merciful, for had it obeyed, it would have fallen upon them, destroying them utterly. He then proposed to go to the mountain to offer thanks to God for his mercy. Generally speaking, this proverb is used to mean that when a person tries and fails at an impossible task, he is wise to bow to the inevitable.

if wishes were horses, beggars could ride has been a much-quoted English proverb for many centuries. It first appeared in print in a collection of proverbs published by John Ray in 1670, but it certainly was widely quoted long before that time—or else it wouldn't have reached the status of "proverb." It remained in that simple form until the nineteenth century, when an extended version appeared in *Halliwell's Collection of Nursery Rhymes:* "If wishes were horses, beggars could ride. If turnips were watches, I'd wear one by my side."

if you can't lick 'em, join 'em. In a careful search through our reference library we find this saying in one of our favorite books, *The American Treasury* by Clifton Fadiman and Charles Van Doren. Unfortunately, the authors credit it simply as "American Political Saying," so who said it first is not recorded.

if you gotta ask what jazz is, you'll never know. These words are generally credited to Louis Armstrong, but we seem to recall hearing Fats Waller say them back in the 1930s. Anyhow, King Louis did at one time set down these thoughts about jazz: "There's only two ways to sum up music; either it's good or it's bad. If it's good, you don't mess about with it. You just enjoy it."

ignominy comes from the Latin *ignominia* (*in-,* "without," and *nomen,* "name"). Since it means public disgrace or dishonor, you might say that since you are literally "without a name," you have lost your reputation or your claim to being "somebody."

I have seen the future and it works, the common version of this saying, is close to the original but not precisely right. The creator of the phrase was Lincoln Steffens, and he was reporting to financier Bernard Baruch on his trip to Russia shortly after the Communists had taken over control of that country. As Steffens tells the story in his autobiography—one of the finest autobiographies ever written, by the way—it went like this: " 'So you've been over into Russia?' said Bernard Baruch, and I answered very literally, 'I have been over into the future, and it works.' " One of Steffens's journalistic contemporaries later claimed that Steffens thought up the phrase, realized it was a gem of purest ray serene and made the trip to Russia just so he'd be able to utter it.

IHS/I.N.R.I. *IHS* is an adaptation into Roman characters of the Greek letters spelling the name of Jesus. The letters, woven in a monogram, are often found on altar cloths used in Roman Catholic services. They are not, however, the letters seen at the top of the crucifix. Those are *I.N.R.I.,* from the Latin phrase *Iesus Nazarenus, Rex Iudaeorum* (Jesus of Nazareth, King of the Jews), a phrase used by the Roman soldiers in mockery.

I knew him when is a common expression, meaning "I knew him before he became rich [or famous]." Credit for this goes to a light versifier named Arthur Guiterman, who wrote, about fifty years ago: "Of all cold words of tongue or pen,/The worst are these, 'I knew him when.' " This was part of a parody of Whittier's "Maud Muller": "For of all sad words of tongue or pen,/The saddest are these: 'It might have been.' "

illegitimates. In Australian history a person "transported" is not one carried away into transports of ecstasy and rapture. Rather it is one of the original settlers who were "transported" from England—almost all of whom were sent to Australia from various prisons in the homeland. The *illegitimates,* by contrast, were those who went of their own volition, not *(il-)* because of law *(lex, legis).*

illeism/illeist. *Illeism* is the practice of referring to oneself in the third person and an *illeist* obviously is one addicted to the practice. Pronounced IL-ee-ism and IL-ee-ist, these words record consummate egotism. The words come from the Latin *ille* (he).

I'm all right, Jack. According to Eric Partridge, the British authority on language, this expression—in a somewhat more elaborate and less printable form—was British service slang prior to World War I. It seems to have been of British Navy origin—hence the *Jack,* short for *Jack Tar.*

I'm from Missouri. The state of Missouri is often called the "Show Me" state and the expression *I'm from Missouri* is widely used to indicate that the speaker is less than convinced by the arguments he has been listening to. It started with a speech by an otherwise unremembered Missouri congressman, Willard Duncan Vandiver, at a navy banquet in Philadelphia in 1899. "I come from a state," he declaimed, "that raises corn and cotton and cockleburs and Democrats, and frothy eloquence neither convinces nor satisfies me. I am from Missouri. You have got to show me."

impasse is a word which all too frequently in recent years has cropped up in accounts of labor-management negotiations concerning provisions of new contracts. It means literally "dead end" and comes from French, where it originally meant "a road or way open only at one end."

impeach, from the Latin *impedicare,* meaning "to fetter, catch or entangle," is one of the most commonly misunderstood words in our language. The act of *impeachment* merely implies bringing serious charges against a public official. The language of our Constitution is quite clear on this point: "The President, Vice President and all civil officers of the United States, shall be removed from Office on *Impeachment* for, and Conviction of,

Treason, Bribery, or other High Crimes and Misdemeanors." Note that *impeachment*—or accusation—is not enough. *Conviction* must follow, if the accused is to be found guilty. In the case of President Andrew Johnson, he was impeached, but the motion for conviction failed by a single vote.

impedimenta. Anyone who has loaded a station wagon to take the family on a vacation trip should know what *impedimenta* means—"supplies accompanying an army." At least, that is one of its meanings. In general, it means "that which impedes or hinders progress," hence baggage or equipment taken along on a trip. Logically enough, it comes from the plural of the Latin word for hindrance, *impedimentum*, which comes from *impedire* (*im-*, "in," and *pedis*, "foot")—literally "to hold the foot."

impugn/impute. It's not surprising that many people confuse these two "lookalikes." Even our learned brethren of the legal profession, who nowadays can lay almost sole claim to *impugn*, since it rarely is heard outside courtrooms and legislative chambers, have been known to mistake one for the other. *Impute* means to ascribe to another the credit or blame for an action or event. Usually it is used in a derogatory sense. *Impugn* likewise is often used in a deprecatory sense and means to assail with insinuations or accusations. Thus one occasionally will hear an attorney protesting to the judge that his "worthy opponent" is attempting to *"impugn* his veracity." For a means of keeping the two words straight in your mind, we suggest you remember that *impute* (literally "think against" from the Latin *in* and *puto*) obviously implies greater subtlety in discrediting an opponent than *impugn* (from the Latin *impugno*, "fight against").

I murmured because I had no shoes, until I met a man who had no feet is a traditional Persian proverb of anonymous authorship.

in Abraham's bosom, referring to the sleep of the blessed in death, is best known from its appearance in Shakespeare's *Richard III* (Act IV, Scene 3): "The sons of Edward sleep in Abraham's bosom," but the reference ultimately is to Luke 16:22–23: "And it came to pass, that the beggar died, and was carried by the angels into Abraham's bosom: the rich man also died, and was buried; and in hell he lift up his eyes, being in torments, and seeth Abraham afar off." There's an amusing old English proverb which runs: "There's no leaping from Delilah's lap into Abraham's bosom"—a lesson that the rich man of the Biblical parable learned to his pain.

in a pickle means "in an awkward or embarrassing situation." It comes from a phrase we borrowed from Dutch, *in de pekel zitten*—"sitting in the pickle," with "pickle" being the brine used years ago to preserve meats and vegetables. Certainly anyone sitting *in the pickle* would be mighty uncomfortable. Incidentally, we borrowed the phrase over five hundred years ago.

inch, as a unit of measurement, is one twelfth of a foot. It was originally the length of the knuckle of the thumb of King Edgar of England (A.D. 944–975). See also FOOT.

in chancery is both legal and sporting. Technically, it first meant having a lawsuit hung up in the London court presided over by the lord chancellor. *Chancery* is a shortened form of "chancellery." Such actions were often long delayed. Indeed, it may have been here that the legal maxim "Justice delayed is justice denied" was born. In wrestling, *in chancery* describes a headlock in which one wrestler's head is secured against the other's chest in such a way that the head can be pummeled at length and at will.

inchoate (pronounced in-KOH-it), derived from the Latin verb *incohare* (to begin), is an adjective meaning "just commenced" or "incipient." It has no relation to *chaotic,* which describes a state of confusion or disorder.

incipient. Meaning "just beginning to exist," *incipient* comes to us from the Latin *in* (in or on) and *capere* (to take).

incunabula is the plural of the Latin word *incunabulum.* Originally it meant books printed before 1500, but now it has been extended to mean the very first stages of anything, the beginnings.

indemnify (pronounced in-DEM-nih-fy) means either to secure against loss or damage or to compensate for such. Its roots are Latin: *in* (not) and *demnum* (hurt).

independent as a hog on ice is an expression that has puzzled students of the language for many years. At first thought, there's hardly anything less independent than a squealing porker sliding around on a frozen pond. One scholar, the late Charles Earle Funk, came up with the theory that the hog referred to is not the farm animal at all but a marker used in the Scottish game of curling, in which stones are slid along ice. This theory falls apart when you realize that the expression is widely used in America and completely unknown in Scotland. However, some years ago readers of our column sent in their theories. Here are a few.

"When a farmer wanted to get his pigs from one side of a stream to another," wrote a California reader, "he would wait till it froze over, then put a strip of sand on the ice to make a path. A helper would go to the opposite side with feed and call the hogs. If one got off the sanded strip, it would slip a bit, then lie down until the men got it back on the strip."

An Ohio minister wrote: "A hog doesn't go on ice until it's butchered. Then it needs nothing, wants nothing and is altogether independent of people and things."

An Ashtabula, Ohio, reader theorized: "Many farmers used to turn their hogs out to fend for themselves part of the year (as in the phrase 'root, hog, or die'). When roundup time came, some hogs might be clever enough to get out on thin ice, which would make their capture a difficult, exasperating and dangerous business. So you have a picture of an animal just out of reach, a hazard to go after but too valuable to be left to drown or freeze.

Our ancestors valued self-reliance highly but realized it can be carried too far. So anyone who steadfastly refused badly needed help or advice—perhaps to his own detriment—was said to be as *independent as a hog on ice.*"

Indian giver/Indian summer/Indian corn/Indian tea. Originally an *Indian giver* was one who made a gift in expectation of getting an even better one in return. It is only comparatively recently that an *Indian gift* became one that was itself to be returned. Actually, the term was one of several—*Indian summer, Indian corn* and *Indian tea,* for example—invented by the earliest colonists to describe something which resembled the genuine article as they had known it in England but actually was not the same. Thus *Indian summer* is the brief period in the fall when we have a temporary return of summer's warm climate. *Indian corn* is not what the British called "corn"—which we know as wheat—and so on. If you are willing to concede that the Indians occasionally employed trickery in their dealings with the whites, you will understand why the white man came to use the word *Indian* as a synonym for "bogus."

Indian summer is a season well known in England, though not by that name. The English refer to it by the names of various saints: St. Martin's summer, St. Luke's summer, etc.

"I never met a man I didn't like" is a remark attributed to American humorist, actor and writer Will Rogers. It seems well established that he made the remark originally in Boston in 1930 and repeated it in many subsequent appearances. So there's little question about the accuracy of the quote.

So much for accuracy; now to veracity. Not long before his death, H. Allen Smith, himself one of the great American humorists of this century, recounted his first meeting with Will Rogers. Smith was a cub reporter at the time, assigned to cover a rodeo. He and several other young reporters were enjoying a pleasant session of light banter in the press box when it occurred to Smith that it would be interesting if Rogers would join them for a moment or two. So he approached Rogers, saying that they would consider it a great honor if he would visit with them. Rogers reply was a scathing: "Get lost, kid!" So to H. Allen Smith, at any rate, there was precious little veracity in that much-quoted remark.

inexorable (pronounced in-EX-er-uh-b'l), meaning inflexible, relentless, merciless and unmoved by any plea, is a combination of the Latin *in* (not) plus *ex* (out) and *orare* (to pray).

in fine fettle. When you're *in fine fettle,* you're in good shape and spirits. The original *fettles* were belts or girdles bound on the body by warriors before they ventured forth to battle. So the soldier in fine fettle had girded his loins and was ready for action.

infracaninophile. Many years ago the late Christopher Morley coined the word *infracaninophile* to describe a person who favors the underdog. Pronounced in-fruh-kuh-NIN-oh-file, it is based on the following word elements: *infra* (under), *canino* (dog) and *phile* (one who loves).

infra dig is a shortened form of *infra dignitatem*, meaning "beneath one's dignity."

ingenuous/ingenious. *Ingenuous* (pronounced in-JEN-yoo-us) is not to be confused with *ingenious*, the more common word, meaning "inventive or resourceful." Though both originate in the same Latin verb, *ingignere* (to produce), *ingenuous* comes directly from the Latin *ingenuus*, which meant "freeborn, noble or frank." In English it has come to mean "candid, frank, straightforward or naïve."

in loco parentis (a Latin phrase meaning "in the place of the parent") is a term used by earlier generations of private school and college deans to describe their function as disciplinarians.

innocuous desuetude means, in plain English, "harmless disuse." It was coined by President Grover Cleveland and used in a message to Congress, March 1, 1886. The complete quote from President Cleveland runs: "After an existence of nearly twenty years of almost *innocuous desuetude*, these laws are brought forth."

input. One of the vogue words in Washington is *input*, a borrowing from computer language. One political figure is quoted as saying: "It's important for anyone concerned with the fate of this nation to make as much of an *input* as he is capable of making." Obviously, a simple, old-fashioned word like "contribution" would never suffice if one wanted to be considered "in" —*input*wise, that is.

inscrutable (pronounced in-SCROO-tuh-b'l) describes that which is beyond comprehension, mysterious, incapable of being understood. Stemming from the Latin *in* (not) and *scrutari* (to search), it is related to the English word *scrutiny*, which means "careful or close examination."

insouciant is a word we borrowed from French. It means "carefree or blithely indifferent." It's an attitude toward life admirably characterized by mehitabel, the alley cat in Don Marquis's *archie and mehitabel*, whose motto— the essence of *insouciance*—was "toujours gai, jamais triste, so whathehell, archie!"

insurance policy/underwriter/annuity. Your insurance *policy* gets its name from an Italian word, *pòlizza*, meaning "written and folded document." The Mediterranean traders of the Middle Ages, mostly Lombard and Venetian, insured their cargoes and recorded the insurance on folded foolscap. When the idea of insurance reached England—the first insurance "ad" appeared in a London paper in 1720—the word *policy* came along with it.

As is usually the case, the fact preceded the written record of it, so underwriting insurance actually began in England in Shakespeare's time. Vessel owners, importers and exporters would place their proposals for insurance on the tables of coffeehouses like the famous Lloyds of London, and persons willing to accept part of the risk would write their names under the proposal and indicate the percentage of risk they would assume. Thus, very logically, they came to be called *underwriters.*

An *annuity,* obviously, originally meant a sum payable once a year—it comes from the Latin word for "year," *annus.* But now it means any sum payable at regular intervals, so such expressions as "an *annuity* payable annually" are commonplace.

intelligentsia. The pronunciation of *intelligentsia* with a hard *g* is a snobbish affectation—not wrong, mind you, but not normal either. Here's how it comes about. *Intelligentsia* followed a very curious path in coming to English. It is derived originally from the Latin *intelligentia,* meaning "perceptiveness and discernment." From the beginning it appeared in Italian, logically enough, as *intelligenza* (intelligence), but then it detoured to Russia, where it became *intelligentsiya,* with the meaning it has today— people who are or regard themselves as being the intellectual elite.

When it arrived in the Russian language the soft Italian *g* became the hard Russian *g.* However, the soft *g* is much more commonly heard, and by analogy with related words (*intelligence* itself, for instance) which did not take the Russian detour, it is a more logical pronunciation.

interabang. When you have an expression such as "Where's the fire?!" which can be either a question or an exclamation, you could use both an exclamation point and a question mark. However, a combined sign to use in place of "?!" has been devised by one of the leading type-casting companies. It looks rather like an exclamation point superimposed on a question mark (?) and is called an *interabang.* The *inter* comes from "interrogation" and *bang* is printer's slang for the exclamation point.

internecine comes from the Latin *inter* (between), and *necare* (to kill). While it can mean any kind of brutal slaughter, it usually denotes a form of destructive combat that is mutually damaging—deadly to both sides. The accepted pronunciations are: in-ter-NEE-seen and in-ter-NEE-sine.

in the clink sounds slangy, but it has been part of our language since well before the time of Shakespeare. In fact, the original *Clink* was a prison in the Southwark district of London and dates back at least as far as 1550. Very possibly the phrase goes even further back into antiquity than that, for the expression may very well have come from the clinking noise of shackles worn by prisoners or from the clinking noise made by the barred gates on prison cells.

in the doghouse. As everyone knows, a person *in the doghouse* is one who has fallen out of favor with the powers that be, usually just for a short period of time. Here's how it began. If you remember *Peter Pan,* you'll recall that the father of the children, Mr. Darling, was punished for his shabby treatment of Nana, the Newfoundland dog who was also nurse to the children. And where did he spend his exile? In Nana's doghouse, of course.

in the groove was a slang term popular in the "swing band" era of the late 1930s and early 1940s. Presumably it derived from the fact that a phonograph record does not sound well unless the stylus is *in the groove.* In the latter years of the 1960s, a derivative slang adjective, *groovy,* was popular with youth as an indication of high approbation.

in the slam(mer). Just who coined this expression is, as is the case with most prison slang, impossible to determine. The reference is to the great slam when the doors on jail cells are closed. In most large modern jails all the doors in a cellblock can be opened or closed at one time. As a result the slamming noise of all those metal doors hitting metal doorframes at one time is truly horrendous.

in the sticks. *The sticks* was originally used in the latter part of the nineteenth century by loggers to designate timberlands. Gradually it has come to mean any rural district, especially, but not necessarily, a backwoods area.

intramural means simply "performed within the walls" and has been in use in England since 1848, according to the *Oxford Dictionary.* It has long been used, in both England and America, to designate athletic contests played between teams made up of pupils in the same school or college.

intransigent (pronounced in-TRAN-suh-junt) is both a noun and an adjective. It is used to describe or identify a person who is uncompromising or who refuses to be reconciled, particularly politically. From the Latin *in* (not) and *transigere* (to come to an understanding), it gained its political significance in Spanish, when the name *los intransigentes* was the term applied to the extreme Left (Republican) party.

inveigle (pronounced in-VEE-g'l) means to entice or persuade by flattery or other deception. It is the English version of the French word *aveugler* (to blind) and goes back in Latin to *ab* (from) plus *oculus* (eye). The word *inveiglement* applies to either the act of *inveigling* or that of being *inveigled.* He who commits the act is an *inveigler.*

Inverness cape. There are several garments and fabrics which bear place names, rather than names of individuals, like cardigan and raglan. The *Inverness cape,* beloved of Sherlock Holmes enthusiasts, is one of these. This combination overcoat and outer cape is named after Inverness, a county seat in Scotland where the winters are surely such as to make a man appreciate the added warmth of his *Inverness.*

inveterate, meaning "firmly established or habitual," stems from the Latin *in* (in) and *vetus* (old).

I pledge allegiance to the flag. Four hundred years after Columbus discovered America, the Pledge of Allegiance first appeared in 1892 in a magazine called *The Youth's Companion* as part of a program for schoolchildren throughout the nation. It was first recited at the dedication of the World's

Columbian Exposition grounds in Chicago. There was some dispute for years regarding the author. Was it James Upham, an editor of the magazine, or Francis Bellamy, an ordained Baptist preacher and a member of the editorial staff? It was finally determined that Bellamy had written it at the suggestion of Upham. Three changes in the text have been made over the years. The pledge originally read: "I pledge allegiance to my flag and to the republic for which it stands; one nation, indivisible, with liberty and justice for all." In 1923 "my flag" was changed to "the flag of the United States" by the National Flag Conference and, one year later, the words "of America" were added by the same body. In 1954 the words "under God" were added by Congress, to follow "one nation."

ipso facto is a commonly heard Latin expression used in bolstering an argument or making a decision. It means "by that very fact; by the act or fact itself," as: "He was the only one who had intimate knowledge of the terrain of the land and, *ipso facto*, was put in charge of the search party."

irade, a word now found chiefly in crossword puzzles, comes almost without change from the Arabic word *iradah,* meaning "will or desire." As used by Turkish sultans, it meant something very close to the will of the ruler and so had the effect of a decree or law.

Irgun/Haganah. *Irgun* (full name: *Irgun Zvai Leumi*—"National Military Organization") was the name of an underground organization in Palestine especially active during the trying period immediately following World War II. According to the *Columbia Encyclopedia,* when the British in 1946 set quotas for the immigration of stateless Jews, "secret organizations attacked British military installations.... The most violent were the Irgun Zvai Leumi.... Haganah, the large and well-trained secret defense army of the Jews, abstained from violence." *Haganah* means "defense."

Irish as Paddy's pig. *Paddy* is the symbolic Irishman, just as Taffy is the typical Welshman and John Bull the prototype of the Englishman. The *pig* in this expression is included mostly for alliteration because, though Irish hams and bacon are deservedly famous, there's nothing notably Irish in pigs as pigs.

Irish—bog-trotting/lace-curtain/shanty. The Morrises have always regarded themselves as *bog-trotting Irish* and proud of it. Our pride was given support by a reader who, with uncharacteristic Irish modesty, asked to remain anonymous.

"During my childhood more than fifty years ago," he wrote, "we American Irish in the Middle West understood '*bog-trotters*' to be laborers or peasants in Ireland's bogs. Later the name gained dignity when accounts were read of British soldiers pursuing rebellious Irishmen across bogs, where the fugitives attempted concealment but all too often were discovered and bayonetted until 'the bogs ran red with Irish blood.'

"As for '*shanty Irish,*' a little understanding of history will help clarify that term, too. The Irish people were so oppressed by their English overlords that any improvements on their 'cottages' meant an increase in taxes. Naturally this policy destroyed ambition and led to a slackness in maintaining their homes.

"But things were different in America, where the *'lace-curtain Irish'* term was born. How those old-timers sacrificed and endured and worked to achieve even that small status in a British-oriented, American Protestant society which believed at that time that Irishmen and dogs should not be allowed in certain public places."

Irish confetti is simply the bricks tossed by a spalpeen at an omadhaun in the course of a donnybrook.

"Donnybrook" is the Irish version of a knock-down-drag-out brawl. "Spalpeen" (pronounced spal-PEEN, with a rising inflection) is the Irish term for rascal or scamp, and "omadhaun" (pronounced—and watch this now—OM-uh-thon) simply means fool, idiot or simpleton.

Irish potato, long a staple of the American diet, seems to have been somewhat misnamed, if you go back in history. It is true that the Irish depended on the potato so greatly for food that when disease destroyed the potato crop in the 1840s, famine resulted and thousands of Irishmen left their homeland for the New World. But the potato was first cultivated in South America, where the Indians had grown it for many centuries before it was introduced in Europe around 1570.

irony comes to us from the Greek *eiron,* meaning a person who dissembles (pretends) in his speech. Thus *irony* is the speech of one who says the opposite of his true meaning. Grammarians classify this figure of speech in two ways: *light irony,* which is humorous banter, and *severe irony,* which is usually sarcasm or cutting satire.

I swan has been around at least since Revolutionary War days and probably comes from a much older British dialect expression. All it means is "I swear!" The earliest example of its use found in print in America goes back to 1784 in a Boston magazine which, with the smugness traditional among Bostonians, reports: "Well, I swan (as the old saying is) we of Boston are better off after all than those of New York." It is thought to be a corruption of one or the other of these expressions: "I'se warn ye," "I's wan" and "I'se warrant." Take your choice.

itching palm. The exact origin of this phrase is unknown, but it derives from a superstition that if your palm itches, you're about to receive money, usually from some unexpected source. The expression goes back at least to the time of Shakespeare, for in *Julius Caesar* he writes: "Let me tell you, Cassius, you yourself/Are much condemned to have an itching palm."

itmo is an odd word and worth at least a casual glance. It is a Tagalog name for the betel vine and nut. In case you're still mystified, Tagalog is the native language of the Philippines and betel nuts are the mildly narcotic nuts chewed throughout Southeast Asia.

it's an ill wind that blows no good—meaning that no matter how dreadful an event appears to be, some good may come of it—has been around for many centuries. George Heywood in his *Proverbs* (1546) wrote: "An ill wind that bloweth no man to good." Shakespeare used the idea over and over again in his plays with slight variations ("Ill blows the wind that profits nobody" and "Not the ill wind which blows no man to good," for example). In each case *ill* has the now archaic meaning of "evil." A somewhat similar thought appears much earlier, in Vergil: *"Forsan et haec olim meminisse iuvabit,"* "Perhaps in the future we will remember with pleasure these things which now so much distress us."

it's no skin off my tail simply means that "the matter is no concern of mine and I don't intend to become trapped in a situation where I might be in trouble or suffer dire consequences." The reference, we suspect, is to an animal who has escaped a trap with *no skin off his tail.*

ivory tower, meaning a place where intellectuals go to think and get away from the world, was coined by a nineteenth-century French literary critic, Charles Augustin Sainte-Beuve. His version, of course, was *"une tour d'ivoire."*

Ivy League. There are two theories of the origin of the term *Ivy League* to designate a group of Eastern colleges almost equally noted for their academic achievements and their athletic embarrassments. Here is the first and more widely accepted theory: During the mid-1930s the football team of Fordham University was running roughshod over many of the big-name college teams of the country. One day in the sports department of the *New York Herald Tribune* the relative merits of Fordham, Princeton and Columbia were being discussed. Caswell Adams, a sportswriter, remarked disparagingly that the latter two were "only *Ivy League."* The sports editor, Stanley Woodward, noted the remark and used it the next day. Thus, as Adams later noted, he had "unconsciously" contributed a phrase to the language.

Not until after World War II did the *Ivy League* become an actuality. In order to balance sports schedules, so that the "egghead" colleges would not continue to have their teams trampled on by the "powerhouse" universities, several Northeastern schools banded together to form the *Ivy League.* It now includes Brown, Columbia, Cornell, Dartmouth, Harvard, the University of Pennsylvania, Princeton and Yale.

But hear Wallace L. Minto of Westwood, New Jersey, who proudly signed himself "Columbia, Class of '42": "Please be advised that the origins of *Ivy League* go much farther back than you indicate. An interscholastic league for athletic competition was formed about a century ago, comprising four schools: Harvard, Yale, Columbia and Princeton. This league was known officially as the *Four League* but, in the academic tradition of the day, the Roman numeral *IV* was used. You can see this on trophies of these schools dating well back into the last century. This, then, was the origin of the IV league. When referred to vocally it became the *Ivy League.*

"In the 1920s and '30s, these four schools were the big names in football. (Hear, hear, Notre Dame!) Their major opponents, Brown, Dartmouth, Cornell and Pennsylvania, were included by custom in that group, which is today referred to as the *Ivy League,* although it no longer consists of only four schools."

Well, that's a new and fairly plausible theory, even though Mr. Minto's counting these four teams among the "big names" of the 1930s indicates that his scholarship is tempered by a touch of old-grad enthusiasm.

Jabberwocky. Lewis Carroll, creator of *Alice in Wonderland,* invented the language he called *Jabberwocky* by blending two words into one and creating such words as *slithy,* made up of "lithe" and "slimy," and *mimsy,* made up of "miserable" and "flimsy." Carroll termed the words *portmanteau words* because they were "packed together" as in a portmanteau (suitcase). *Jabberwocky* itself was doubtless inspired in part by the verb *jabber,* "to babble on meaninglessly."

jackanapes is today a somewhat uncommon term for an impudent fellow, an upstart. But some centuries ago, it had great vogue. It began as a proper name, really a nickname, *Jack Napes,* and one theory holds that it was originally used as a term of endearment for a pet monkey. Lord Chesterfield writes scornfully of "dressing him out like a *jackanapes* and giving him money to play the fool with." Another theory is that *Jack Napes* was a nickname for the first Duke of Suffolk, William de la Pole, whose symbol was the figure of an ape, with ball and chain.

Jack Armstrong, the all-American boy. During the 1930s a very popular afternoon serial show on radio was called *Jack Armstrong, the All-American Boy.* The announcement fanfare, with a glee club hymning the virtues of a popular breakfast cereal, soon became the butt of juvenile humor and *Jack Armstrong* took his place in folklore and in the language, just as Frank Merriwell had a generation or two earlier. Abe Lincoln had a celebrated rough-and-tumble fight with a Jack Armstrong who later became his friend, but this does not appear to be the origin of this common American expression.

jackass. The word "ass" is widely used in all English-speaking countries except America to refer to any of several kinds of four-hoofed animals similar to the horse, even to wild species like zebras, as well as our familiar donkey. The "jack" part of the word *jackass* merely means that it is the male rather than the female animal.

jacket was originally used, in the form of *jaque,* to describe a short garment worn by French peasants, who were called *jaques.*

jack-o'-lantern. The hollowed-out pumpkin with a candle inside which we regard as the chief symbol of Halloween has a name originally applied to a variety of luminous natural phenomena. Also called "ignis fatuus," "will-o'-the-wisp" and "friar's lantern," these were the phosphorescent lights that hover over swampy ground at night. Modern scientists, lacking the imagination of our forebears, tell us that these lights result simply from the spontaneous combustion of gases formed by rotting organic matter. *Ignis fatuus,* by the way, is simply the Latin phrase for "foolish fire."

jackpot goes back to draw poker, where stakes are allowed to accumulate until a player is able to "open the *pot*" by demonstrating that among the cards he has drawn he has a pair of *jacks* or better.

Jack Tar. The *tar* in *Jack Tar,* an old-fashioned nickname for a sailor, comes from "tarpaulin," a waterproof cloth impregnated with tar. It was just about the first truly water-resistant fabric and so was often used by old-time sailors for caps and other articles of clothing. In *Two Years Before the Mast,* Richard Henry Dana describes himself as wearing "loose duck trousers, checked shirt and the tarpaulin hat of a sailor . . . and I suppose that I should pass very well for a *Jack Tar.*"

Jacobites were followers of the House of Stuart. They lost the throne of England, though they made several attempts to regain it, including an invasion of England from Scotland midway through the eighteenth century. They were disastrously defeated in the battle of Culloden (1746) but their leader, "Bonnie Prince Charlie," escaped. Largely because of the writings of Sir Walter Scott, the *Jacobites,* so called because they had supported James II—Jacobus being New Latin for James—hold a high place in the romantic legends of Great Britain, especially in Scotland.

Jacob's ladder is a ladder made of rope or cable, usually with wooden rungs. It is dropped over the side of a ship to enable people to ascend from or descend to small boats alongside. Harbor pilots usually come aboard via a *Jacob's ladder.* The *Jacob's ladder* gets its name from an incident in the Book of Genesis (28:12). The patriarch Jacob falls asleep and has a vision: "And he dreamed, and behold a ladder set up on the earth, and the top of it reached to heaven; and behold the angels of God ascending and descending on it." *Jacob's ladder* has been used in at least two other quite earthly meanings. A small plant with a flower-and-leaf formation resembling a ladder bears this name. In England, what Americans call "runs" in hosiery were formerly called *Jacob's ladders.* Nowadays they are simply *ladders.*

jaded is an adjective, the past participle of the verb *jade.* In the Old Norse language *jalda* meant "mare" and in English *jade* means "horse," particularly one which is old and tired. Thus the verb *jade* came to mean "make or become old and tired."

Janus/January. The Romans had gods for nearly every purpose, including one for gates and doors—and that was *Janus.* He is depicted on ancient

Roman coins as facing in two directions at once. That made him a natural for the deity after whom the first month of the year should be named since it was, in a sense, guarding the portal of the year. Hence, *January*.

jargon. In the French of the Middle Ages *jargoun* meant "twittering" and, later still, "meaningless chatter." It was in the latter sense that the word came into English and it was still being so used in the time of Thomas Carlyle, who called for "a blessed time when *jargon* might abate and genuine speech begin." By the twentieth century, though, *jargon* had become well established as the term used to designate the special vocabulary shared by members of a trade or profession. Thus "musicians' *jargon*," "educators' *jargon*" and the like. Virginia Woolf spoke for many of us when she remarked that she "could not follow the ugly academic *jargon*."

jawbone. The service slang term *jawbone* was reported to us by an Ohio reader who said that he had heard it often when on duty in the Canal Zone, especially referring to buying on credit. When a serviceman did that, he was paying *jawbone* or buying *jawbone*. Just how the expression originated was unclear until another reader straightened us out:

> *"Jawbone"* originated in the Philippine Islands around the turn of the century. In accordance with a "custombre del pais," a "lavandera" (native washerwoman) would always ask for a dime for soap ("una peseta para jabon") when she picked up the week's wash. It was always given, although all hands knew it would not be spent for soap or used to reduce the laundry bill. It was the lavandera's graft or cumshaw.
>
> In Spanish, "jabon" (soap) is pronounced "hah-bon," but the Americans substituted the English "j" and "jabon" became *"jawbone."* In so doing, it lost the original meaning of "soap" and took on a new meaning of "an advance of credit." How do I know? I lived in the Islands for eight years about that time and have paid out many "pesetas para jabon."

However, that's not the way it's used in Washington today. Now it simply means to persuade by threats or cajolery rather than by the use of force. This new sense of *jawbone* developed during the 1960s, and we're inclined to credit its widespread use to Lyndon Johnson, one of the master *jawboners* of all time.

jaywalker dates back to the early part of the century, when *jay* was a popular slang term meaning "countrified" or "rustic." A *jay* was pretty much the same as a "rube" and was so used by George M. Cohan in the lyrics of one of his most famous songs, "Forty-five Minutes from Broadway." A farmer, strange to the ways of the city and perhaps frightened by the newfangled automobiles churning down the streets at fantastic speeds up to fifteen or twenty miles an hour, might have been expected to cross the street in an erratic fashion, without paying too much attention to signals. Hence, *jaywalking*.

jazzmen's jargon. Some of us in the thinning hair and thickening paunch set can remember way back to the early thirties when jazz was a furtive thing heard only in a handful of nightclubs and speakeasies. Never were the raucous, wailing notes of jazz and the blues allowed to sully the nation's airwaves and seldom did a recording company stoop to record what was then known as "race" music. Indeed, almost the only time the dedicated jazz fan could hear his favorite music was when he was fortunate enough to be allowed to sit in on an after-hours jam session where the musicians made their kind of music for their own mutual enjoyment. Things have certainly changed, but one thing has changed little, the argot spoken by the musicians themselves. Like all secret languages, the talk of the working musician exists chiefly because he wants a way to communicate with his fellow musicians without the general public (*squares,* to musicians) knowing what is going on.

Any instrument may be labeled the *ax*—though the term is usually reserved for one or another of the horns. A *bash, gig, hame* or *bake* is an engagement where the musician works. But a *ball* to a jazz musician is never a formal dance; it's an occasion for exuberant enjoyment, a real good time. *Ball* is also used as a verb: "I'm going to *ball* tonight." A *benny* is a pawnbroker and a *bill* is a hundred dollars. Money, generally speaking, is *bread,* and for the most part, *bread* comes from the *bossman,* who may be booking agent, bandleader or music contractor.

A *cat* is *dragged* by a dull, boring experience, but a stimulating, enjoyable occurrence will *gas* him—sometimes to the extent that he will *flip.* When low in funds, the musician may speak up for a *taste*—meaning an advance upon the *bread* to come. If the *taste* is big enough, he might treat himself to a new *set of threads*—a suit.

JB King. These days writing on walls, which used to be considered minor vandalism, has been exalted to the point where lengthy collections of graffiti are appearing in book form and psychologists write weighty articles explaining just what impels people to scribble on walls in the first place.

It's nothing new, of course. Much mural writing was found in Pompeii when that devastated city was excavated. Indeed, wall drawings and inscriptions are probably the oldest evidences of human life. Still the mania for inscribing slogans or signatures persists, from the walls of Greenwich Village coffeehouses to the steps of the Pentagon.

Everyone who served in World War II remembers the simple line drawing of an idiot peering over a fence with the legend "Kilroy Was Here," certainly the most famous single graffito in history. A Pittsburgh reader, Rube J. Long, wrote to ask if anyone remembers a similar character from an earlier time in our history—one *JB King.* Mr. King, so the story goes, wrote his name on just about every piece of railroad rolling stock west of the Mississippi in the early years of this century. He didn't just write his name, either. He inscribed it in the most elegant Spencerian script, omitting periods after the *J* and *B* and linking all letters with a single stroke of the chalk or crayon. Sometimes, as a special gesture, he made the graffito read *JBKingEsq*—all without a break in the line. A poem was rife at the time, one which some loose-footed tramp improvised: "Who is this man, this JBKing,/Who writes his name on everything?/He may be poor or may be rich,/But in my book he's a S.O.B."

Well, we had never heard of Mr. King, but lots of readers from coast to coast sent us samples of the script which they well remembered seeing on boxcars. Many reported that the original King was the self-styled "King of the Hoboes" and one reader asserted that he offered a standing bet: "Any non-hobo could purchase a first-class railroad ticket coast to coast—and King would beat him there."

The most surprising letter of all, though, came from Joseph A. Abbott of St. Joseph, Missouri, who claimed to have been the first to write this legend on freight cars when he went to work for the railroad in Atchison, Kansas, in the earliest years of the century. He reported he took the signature *JBKing* from a Spencerian writing book and first began writing it "with switchman's chalk about as big around as your thumb and five inches long." Later, he reported, "I went to work for the St. Joseph and Grand Island [railroad] and, during World War I, I put *JBKing* on every piece of war machinery I could reach, even a large cannon on a tandem load on which I put *JBKing* on both sides. . . . After years with the UP, I was called back to St. Joseph in 1948 by which time we were getting a few all-steel cars with nice smooth sides which made nice writing on. . . . On nice days now, I go down to the yards as I am retired, and recently ran across a car on which I had written *JBKingEsq* on Aug. 12, 1914. It was pretty dim but could be read, so I just put another right over it."

So *JBKing* stands unmasked as the creation of Joseph A. Abbott and the anonymous author of a Spencerian handwriting textbook. Or does he? Anyway, it's a fine story and Mr. Abbott is, if nothing else, one of the most indefatigable graffitists of all time.

Recently a distillery has publicized another version of the *JB King* story to publicize a drink called The Hobo's Wife. The story runs that King was actually a very wealthy man who became a hobo because he had inherited rather than earned his wealth. He owned stock in many railroads, so felt free to sign his name on cars he believed he owned. The story is labeled "apocryphal," as indeed it is.

jeep is generally believed to have developed from the letters GP (for "general purpose"), used by the army as the code designation for this vehicle. Undoubtedly its immediate widespread acceptance can be credited in large part to the popularity of a comic strip character, Eugene the Jeep, a tiny creature with supernatural powers, created by the late E. C. Segar, a cartoonist syndicated in the years before World War II.

Jekyll and Hyde. This phrase, to refer to a person who alternates between charming demeanor and extremely unpleasant behavior, comes from Robert Louis Stevenson's tale *The Strange Case of Dr. Jekyll and Mr. Hyde.* Jekyll (pronounced in England JEE-kil and in America JEK-ill) was a doctor of repute who discovered a drug that would change him almost instantly into an evil dwarf. He was able to reconvert, but after repeated dosages, the drug began to lose its effect and he became more Hyde than Jekyll. Eventually Hyde committed murder, and after a trial in which Jekyll's lawyer revealed the secret, Hyde committed suicide. The term *Jekyll and Hyde* is often loosely used to refer to a case of "split personality," more accurately termed "schizophrenic" or "schizoid" personality.

je ne sais quoi. If you are at a loss for a word to express an indefinable quality of a person, try substituting *je ne sais quoi* (pronounced jeh neh say KWAH), a French saying which translates "I don't know what." Although it is a complete sentence, it is used as a noun, as "She has a *je ne sais quoi* which attracts the friendship of all."

jerkwater. Small towns are often referred to as *"jerkwater* towns." The general meaning of the term is obvious, its origin not quite so much so. In the days when most trains were powered by steam, it was necessary for them to stop at regular intervals to refill the water tender, the first car behind the engine. Since the water requirements of the trains did not always coincide with the regularly scheduled passenger stops, they often paused briefly in small way stations, where the fireman would jerk a cord attached to an enormous spigot hanging from the water tower and fill the tender with water. Hence, *jerkwater* to describe a hamlet with no other reason, from the railroaders' viewpoint, for existence.

jeroboam. A word occasionally met in champagne advertisements is *jeroboam,* pronounced jer-uh-BOH-um. The first Jeroboam (I Kings 11:28) was the "mighty man of valor who made Israel to sin." The measure of a *jeroboam* today is somewhat vague, but it's generally thought to be about one gallon.

jerry-built. A *jerry-built* building is one that is constructed unsubstantially, as the *Oxford Dictionary* puts it, of inferior materials. Most of the word books duck behind the "origin obscure" label when it comes to explaining the source of the term—but not us. We offer not one but three theories. First, that it is an allusion to the Biblical city of Jericho, whose walls came tumbling down at the sound of a trumpet. Second, that it is derived from the name of the prophet Jeremiah, whose prolonged lamentations would be echoed by tenants in a *jerry-built* house. Third—and candidly, you can forget the first two—is that the expression was originally a shipbuilding term, first used in the shipbuilding yards of Liverpool midway through the nineteenth century. It is probably a corruption of "jury" as in "jury rig" or "jury mast," meaning something hastily contrived for temporary use.

Brewer's estimable *Dictionary of Phrase and Fable* cites those first two Biblical possibilities but, noting that the *Oxford Dictionary* records the first appearance of the expression as 1881, we suggest skepticism.

jersey, a knitted fabric, is so called because it was originally produced on the island of Jersey, one of the Channel Islands.

Jerusalem seems to be derived from two Hebrew words, *yarah,* meaning "city," and *shalem,* a variant of *shalom,* meaning "peace." So *Jerusalem* means "City of Peace."

Jesus bug. The only *Jesus bug* recognized by standard reference books is the water strider—and that's the familiar long-legged bug that can move about on the surface of water. It gets its name from the Biblical reference (Matthew 14:25) to Jesus' ability to walk on water ("And in the fourth watch of the night Jesus went unto them, walking on the sea").

jew's-harp is a small metal instrument held between the teeth and plucked with a finger. It produces a twanging noise which bears about the same relationship to music as the sound of bagpipes. The origins of the *jew's-harp* are indeed ancient, however. It was known in France as the *jeu tromp,* literally "play trumpet." Then Beaumont and Fletcher, the Elizabethan dramatists, converted the *jeu* to *jew* to make the phrase *jew tromp.* Still later the "trumpet" idea gave way to the "harp"—which the instrument in a very remote way does resemble—and the term *jew's-harp* came into being.

jig is up, meaning "Your game has been exposed," was first heard during Shakespeare's time. *Jig* was then a slang word for "trick," so the phrase simply meant your trick or deceit has been found out.

Jim Crow. The original *Jim Crow* was a white blackface comedian named Thomas D. Rice who, in 1835, devised a song and dance whose theme went: "Wheel about, turn about/Do just so/Every time I wheel about/I jump Jim Crow." The act was a great success. Rice changed his billing to "Thomas 'Jim Crow' Rice" and was a smash hit the following year in London. The expression came to symbolize, for the American black, every form of segregation and discrimination imposed upon him by the predominantly white power structure. For more than a century expressions like *"Jim Crow* laws" and *"Jim Crow* schools" were widely heard.

Jimmy Higgins, in the jargon of the early labor union movement, was any conscientious, hard-working member of the rank and file, the sort of fellow who could be counted on to work selflessly at the drudgery of union work. The *Jimmy Higginses* never made headlines and they were seldom thanked for their labors, but they could be counted on to do the jobs nobody else wanted.

jitney/jitney bus were common expressions early in this century to refer to the early motorbuses. Earlier the word *jitney* was used as a slang term meaning "nickel." It may have been derived from the French word *jeton,* meaning "token." Since the French were among the earliest makers of autobuses, we may simply have imported the word along with the vehicles.

job action has to be the most asinine linguistic invention of the 1960s. The expression literally interpreted means exactly the opposite of what it describes. It's truly something out of *Alice in Wonderland* or, more ominously, out of George Orwell's *1984*. Clarence Barnhart's admirable *Barnhart Dictionary of New English* gives the earliest appearance of *job action* as 1968 and defines it as "a protest by workers without undertaking a general strike, such as a slowdown or a work-to-rules action." But the term now is used to describe complete work stoppages. The only explanation we have ever heard for the use of this euphemism is that in many areas, what we laughingly refer to as "public servants" are specifically forbidden to strike when it is against the public interest. So they call it a *job action* and strike anyway.

As Humpty Dumpty said to Alice: "When I use a word, it means just what I choose it to mean—neither more nor less." And there are those among the general public who may find it in their hearts to hope that the bureaucratic manipulators of language who coined *job action* will meet the same end as Humpty Dumpty.

Job's comforter is the kind of friend for whom the saying: "With friends like you who needs enemies?" was invented. Just as the Old Testament friends of Job seemed to commiserate with him while reminding him that his plight was largely of his own making, so today's *Job's comforter* is likely to leave you feeling worse off after getting his message of sympathy than before.

jock, for an athletically inclined young man, is simply borrowed from the word "jockstrap," the name of an essential piece of a male athlete's underwear that often is euphemistically called an "athletic supporter."

jockey is borrowed from a Scottish version of "Jack" and was simply a favorite nickname for young men who rode well.

jockeys—bench/disc/et al. The *disc jockey* (or *D.J.*) is a familiar figure on the radio scene, the chap who plays records interspersed with comment and commercials. Writing in *American Speech* magazine, Dr. Ruth Aldrich of the University of Wisconsin reported that the term *disc jockey* goes back "at least until 1946." William can attest that it appeared in a dictionary he edited *(Words: The New Dictionary)* in early 1947. Taking into account the time involved in getting a dictionary ready for publication, this means that it must have been current in the early 1940s.

The date of its first appearance is not nearly so interesting, though, as the remarkable collection of variations Dr. Aldrich has collected. Most of them are self-explanatory, and all reveal that genius for improvisation that makes the American brand of English the lively and often bewildering language it is. Here are a few: *bus jockey* (bus driver); *typewriter jockey* (typist); *plow jockey* (farmer); *car jockey* (parking lot attendant); *jet jockey* (jet pilot); *chopper jockey* (helicopter operator); *slide-rule jockey* (airplane's navigator or research engineer); *motorboat jockey* and *switchboard jockey.* Baseball, of course, has used the phrase *bench jockey*—a player who heckles the opposing team from the safety of his own dugout. And amusingly enough, elevator operators—a vanishing breed, judging from the popularity of automated elevators—are honored in Dr. Aldrich's collection with two separate listings: *elevator jockey* and *vertical jockey.*

Some authentication of the origin of *jockey* in such connotations came from a Washington, D.C., correspondent, who wrote that in the early 1920s ball players were already being called *bench jockeys.* One of the sportswriters of that era referred thus to Fritz Maisel, Baltimore Orioles third baseman. The logic behind the term was that a *jockey* does the riding and directing, with the help of his reins and whip, and Maisel was—metaphorically, at least—applying the same tactics to the opposition. To *jockey a fall guy* into an undesirable position seems to be an outgrowth of this same sense, somewhat different from *jockeying* a bobsled or motorcycle. It would be this latter sense, we guess, though the distinction is not great, which led to *disc jockey,* but trying to catch the exact connotations of such a phrase is like trying to put a rubber stamp on a slippery ghost.

jocose. Derived from the Latin *jocus* (joke), *jocose* is a synonym for "humorous or facetious." It's a favorite of *Oxford Dictionary* editors, who label any mildly amusing entry *jocose.*

jodhpurs/dhoti. These are two items of dress of Indian males. *Jodhpurs* take their name from Jodhpur, a state in northwestern India. As adapted in the form of riding breeches, they are associated in the minds of some Hindus with their one-time overlords, polo-playing British colonials. The *dhoti,* by contrast, is a nearly knee-length wraparound garment, somewhat resembling a bed sheet. It was the garment invariably worn by Mahatma Gandhi. *Jodhpurs* may be pronounced JOD-perz or JOHD-pers. *Dhoti* is pronounced DOH-tih. It is borrowed direct from Hindi.

Joe Miller. The original *Joe Miller* was a comedian of early-eighteenth-century England. In 1739, the year after Miller's death, a man named John Mottley collected some of Miller's jokes and put them into a book called *Joe Miller's Jests.* Nowadays the label "a *Joe Miller*" is used on jokes so old that they might have appeared in that book.

Joey is the backstage name for a circus clown, chosen in honor of the first great modern clown, Joseph Grimaldi, who charmed children and grownups alike in England more than a century and a half ago.

john. One of our readers questioned the origin of the word *john* to indicate a privy, latrine, water closet or toilet. Practically all the terms used to refer to any of these facilities are euphemisms to cover up embarrassment at any need to mention them: "bathroom" when there may be no tub or shower, "rest room," "men's room" or "ladies' room." All these have more or less logical explanations—but not *john*. The first appearance of *john* in print in this sense was in an official regulation of Harvard College published in 1735: The expression in full was "Cousin John" and signified what was more commonly called a privy. The regulation read: "No Freshman shall go into the Fellows' Cousin John."

John Bull as a nickname for the typical Englishman appeared in print first in a satire by John Arbuthnot, *Law Is a Bottomless Pit,* published in 1712. The author was court physician to Queen Anne and the pamphlet was intended as a satire on the Duke of Marlborough. At first it was thought to be written by the savage satirist Jonathan Swift, author of *Gulliver's Travels.* After Arbuthnot was established as the author, the work was reissued under the name *The History of John Bull*—and the nickname was forever established. In the pamphlet, *John Bull* was shown as hearty, bluff, good-natured and slightly pigheaded—characteristics that some might feel are still to be found in today's Englishmen.

John Doe/Richard Roe. Whether or not there actually was once a *John Doe* is not known. What is known is that the names *John Doe* and *Richard Roe* have been used since the fourteenth century in legal documents. In his fascinating book *Information Roundup,* George Stimpson tells us that the first use of these names may go as far back as the Magna Charta (1215), which required that two witnesses be produced in every legal action. Prosecutors soon fell into the habit of using these fictitious names when they couldn't find two bona fide witnesses or when they wished to protect the names of the actual witnesses. Later the names came to be widely used in lieu of the actual names of unknown parties to a suit, *John Doe* usually being the plaintiff and *Richard Roe* the defendant. At this time, and for many centuries thereafter, women had few rights in courts of law, especially in civil courts, so it is likely that the companion name *Jane Doe* did not come into use until much later. When it did become needed, the *Jane Doe* form was so obvious as to suggest itself.

John Henry/John Hancock. As every schoolboy knows, the biggest, boldest and most defiant signature on the Declaration of Independence was scrawled by John Hancock of Massachusetts. So completely did it overshadow the autographs of the other founding fathers that the term *John Hancock* has become synonymous with "signature" and each of us at one time or another has spoken of "putting his *John Hancock*" at the bottom of a document.

In the West, a half century and more later, the phrase became altered to *John Henry,* and nobody knows quite why. Suffice it that, in the words of Ramon Adams's excellent collection of cowboy jargon, *Western Words:* "John Henry is what the cowboy calls his signature. He never signs a document, he puts his *John Henry* to it!"

Incidentally, there seems to be no connection between the John Henry of cowboy slang and the fabulous John Henry of railroad lore, who was so powerful that he could outdrive a steam drill with his hammer and steel. This legend has been traced to the drilling of the Chesapeake and Ohio Big Bend Tunnel through West Virginia in the 1870s—substantially later than the first use of *John Henry* by cowpokes of the Old West.

johnnycake/hoecake. Where *johnnycake,* the name for flat corn bread cooked on a board or griddle over an open fire, came from nobody seems to know for sure. There's one widely held theory that it is a corruption of "journey cake," since corn bread lasted longer in the saddlebags of early travelers than bread made of wheat flour. More likely, however, is the theory that it was originally "Shawneecake"—from the Shawnee Indians, who certainly knew and used corn in cooking and baking long before any white men came to America. In the South the cakes were sometimes held in place with the metal head of a garden hoe. Hence, *hoecake.*

joie de vivre (pronounced jwah deh VEE-vruh) is French for "joy of living" —and it is not just contentment but a zestful expression of the joy of just being alive. One who possesses *joie de vivre* possesses gaiety and happiness and enjoys every minute of life. He has a love of doing things, going places and being with people—and so brightens the world around him.

joint. In British English a *joint* is any roast meat dish, such as ribs of beef or a leg of lamb.

Jolly Roger. The earliest pirate flags were simply squares of plain black cloth. In time, some prankish pirate decided to add a symbolic grinning skull and crossbones in white. In thieves' underworld cant of the time, beggars and rogues were called *Rogers.* So the *Jolly Roger* became the symbol of a shipful of rogues who would come "begging" for booty.

Joshua tree is a large treelike plant, *Yucca brevifolia,* found in the Southwestern United States. It has sword-shaped leaves and greenish-white flowers and gets its name from a Biblical allusion (Joshua 8:18). The branches of the *Joshua tree* extend widely and they reminded early settlers in the Southwest of the Biblical passage: "And the Lord said unto Joshua, Stretch out the spear that is in thy hand toward [the city of] Ai."

journey to Canossa. The first *journey to Canossa* was made in 1077 by Emperor Henry IV to Pope Gregory VII. Henry had been acting up a bit, making appointments of laymen to positions of high clerical authority. Since this was long before the era of ecumenical tolerance, the Pope took a very dim view of what he regarded as Henry's meddling. The order went out that Henry—king or no king—was excommunicated and could be restored to grace only by doing severe penance. So Henry journeyed to Canossa, where the Pope was castle guest of Matilda of Tuscany. Then he was made to stand in the snow outside the castle for three days before the Pope would rescind the sentence of excommunication. So making a *journey to Canossa* came to mean truckling down to a superior whom one has previously scorned.

juberous is rather more than just a synonym for "dubious." It *is* "dubious."

Actually, *juberous* started as a joking mispronunciation of "dubious" and figured prominently in humorous writing of the early and mid-nineteenth century. In that period, the days when Bill Nye was the ranking American humorist, mispronunciations and misspellings were the chief characteristics of our humor.

Juberous, according to Harold Wentworth's *American Dialect Dictionary,* is still very widely heard in many parts of the country, chiefly in rural regions. He reports that it is also sometimes spelled *jubous, duberous* and *jubious.* Sometimes, instead of being used subjectively to describe a state of mind ("I'm *juberous* about our chances"), it is applied to the object of the anxiety ("That car looks mighty *juberous*"—in poor shape for the trip ahead).

Judas priest! Judas was, of course, a priest, in the sense that he was one of the apostles, the one who betrayed Jesus. The expression is merely one of several used by people who want to express strong feelings without actually swearing.

Judas sheep (goat). In a letter to the editor of a Milwaukee newspaper, the county clerk of courts was referred to as a *Judas sheep* for suggesting drive-in windows for convenient payment of alimony. The *Judas sheep* (or *goat*) is the animal that leads other animals to slaughter. The writer of the letter obviously didn't believe in alimony at all, let alone facilitating the payment of it.

jukebox. The earliest *jukeboxes* were known as "juke organs" and were coin-operated devices which produced sounds like those heard from barrel organs or hurdy-gurdies. They got their name from the "jukes" or "jooks" —brothels—in which they were found. *Juke,* not surprisingly, is Gullah dialect and means "disorderly," as in "disorderly house."

Jukes and Kallikaks. Two lengthy case histories of U.S. families studied to determine the influence of heredity referred to them by the pseudonyms *Jukes* and *Kallikaks.* Since popular interest in both reports centered on the alleged feeble-mindedness of many members of both families, the phrase soon came to be a sort of catchall pejorative label for allegedly inherently stupid people. The playwright Maxwell Anderson, in high dudgeon after New York City's drama critics had turned in adversely critical notices on one of his plays, labeled them the "Jukeses and Kallikaks of journalism."

July. The seventh month of the year is dedicated to Julius Caesar (*Julius mensis* in Latin).

June. The sixth month of the year takes its name from the Latin *Junius mensis,* the month consecrated to the goddess Juno.

junk (Chinese and otherwise). Chinese *junks* are used for more than just fishing. They are often used for transshipping freight, especially from large oceangoing freighters to shore, in ports where the big ships cannot tie up to a pier. In many parts of the Orient they serve, too, as houseboats with whole families living aboard. The name itself came into English from the Portuguese *junco.* The Portuguese in turn took it either from the Javanese word *jon* or the Malay word *dgong.* In either case the Chinese *junk* has no connection to our everyday word *junk,* meaning "worthless refuse or clutter." This word has been part of our language for many centuries, going back to the Middle English *jonke,* which was a term used by sailors when referring to useless bits and ends of rope. Gradually *junk* came to be applied to anything that had served its useful time and was ready to be discarded.

junk/junkie. As a label for miscellaneous trash and as the name of a kind of Chinese sailing vessel, *junk* has long been in the language. Latterly, however, it has added the slang sense of narcotics, especially heroin. A *junkie* is a narcotics addict, especially one "hooked" on heroin.

junket. Congressmen's pleasure trips, a custardlike food, and market baskets made of rushes are all mixed up in the history of *junket.* The original *junket* was a custardlike food made of sweetened and flavored milk which had been curded. It was so named because it was taken to market in baskets made of rushes (from the Latin word for rush, *juncus*). Later it came to mean a picnic or a feast—then a pleasure excursion, particularly one at public expense. With or without any implication of graft, it's an excursion whose primary purpose is having fun.

Juno was the reigning queen of the hierarchy of Roman deities. She managed the rather remarkable feat of being both wife and sister to Jupiter. She was also considered the patroness of marriage, though the epithet often bestowed upon her—"venerable ox-eyed queen"—doesn't sound like much of a warrant of marital bliss.

junta comes to us from Spanish, where it is pronounced HOON-tah, but it has been a part of English long enough to have acquired the common pronunciation JUN-tah. It means an assembly or legislative body, when applied to a permanent division of a Spanish or Latin American government. Most recent *juntas,* though, have been factions, usually opposed to the powers that be, that undertake to seize control of a city or country. Technically, such groups or cabals should be called *juntos,* but the *junta* form is more common in the American press.

just deserts has been around a long time. We took the word over from the French *deservir,* the same word that gives us "deserve." So *desert* simply means "what he deserves."

Kafkaesque is an adjective derived from the name of the Austrian novelist Franz Kafka. His subject was man rendered powerless by bureaucratic red tape, struggling in vain against faceless authority. So a *Kafkaesque* form letter might be something along the order of those computer-dictated letters you get from credit card companies when they fail to record your payment and, despite letters and phone calls, continue to threaten dire penalties.

Kali was the Hindu goddess on whose behalf thugs committed all sorts of mayhem and whose worship degenerated into the foulest kind of bloodletting. A prettied-up version of a sacrifice to *Kali* was filmed as part of Mike Todd's version of *Around the World in 80 Days.* In this picture the human sacrifice, a suitably beautiful young lady, was just about to be immolated on a funeral pyre when the gallant hero came to her rescue. In actuality the story was far different, as may be gathered from this description of the goddess herself—"a grotesque creature wearing a garland of skulls and dancing on the inert body of Shiva [her husband]." Called "the black one," she symbolizes death and destruction, and why she should have a vast cult of worshipers is quite beyond our comprehension. Nonetheless, her festival is still celebrated in India in October and November.

kangaroo court is an illegal mock or sham court, usually one set up by inmates of a prison to levy fines and punishment on other inmates who violate the "code." Such organizations, usually very informal in nature, exist in most large prisons and are even encouraged by some wardens as a useful device for maintaining order. The name probably originated at the time when Australia, land of the kangaroo, was the penal colony for the British Empire.

kaput comes from German *kaputt.* It means "spoiled, done for, broken down." Apparently Yankee soldiers in World War II picked it up from their German counterparts, for whom the war did indeed go *kaput. Kaput* is pronounced "kuh-POOT."

katy/cady/kady. *Katy,* sometimes spelled *cady* or *kady,* is a name for a derby hat or bowler and has been around a long, long time. In fact, it appeared in print in 1846. It is also used, in the East at any rate, to refer to straw skimmers, sometimes called "boaters." *Katy* is believed to be derived from "caddie," which originally meant any young man or cadet, from the fact that such hats were once worn by youngsters.

katzenjammer/Katzenjammer Kids. *Katzenjammer* was originally a German word meaning "hangover"—and a hangover of the most painful kind. In German the word literally means "lamentation of cats," the idea apparently being that—in German anyway—it's not hair of the dog that will cure hangover, but hair of the cat. It has also acquired the meaning of "noisy, disruptive commotion," and this may very well be attributed to the *Katzenjammer Kids* of the comic strip, who were forever driving their parents and other adults to the verge of insanity by their outrageous and noisy antics.

keelhauling, as a figure of speech (which is the only way *keelhauling* is used these days), refers to a long and sometimes torturous examination or series of aggravations by a superior—in other words, a process which you cannot escape as long as you are on the spot. Originally it meant that a man was literally hauled under the keel of a ship as a form of punishment—which was, in many instances, fatal. Many years ago the practice existed in the Dutch navy of disciplining sailors by tying them to the yardarm, attaching weights to their feet and then, by means of a rope, hauling them from one side of the ship under and across the keel to the other side of the ship.

Keeping Up with the Joneses was originally the title of a comic strip by A. R. Momand, first released in 1913 and—perhaps ironically—a casualty of the depression year of 1931. The author says that he originally planned to call the strip *Keeping Up with the Smiths,* but changed the name to *Joneses* as being more euphonious. Apparently the Smiths, then as now, were quite as well-to-do as the Joneses.

"keep the faith!" has been credited to Henry VIII, the first of the British monarchs to bear the title of Defender of the Faith. There is an earlier use, however. In II Timothy 4:7, St. Paul charges Timothy as follows: "I have fought the good fight. I have finished my course. I have kept the faith."

kegler comes from the Old German word *Kegel,* meaning a ninepin or tenpin. The game and, with it, the origin of *Kegel,* "cone," goes back to the Middle Ages. Bowling began—believe it or not—in cathedral cloisters as a diversion for monks. These medieval German monks devised a game in which a single pin (the *Kegel*), similar in appearance to the present-day bowling pin, was set up at one end of the cloister. Then the monks would take turns hurling something—usually a stone—from the other end. The objective, of course, was to knock down the *Kegel,* and if you succeeded it was considered proof that you were leading a pure life.

Kelmscott Press was established by William Morris, British poet, designer and typophile, at Hammersmith, London, in 1891. Morris, concerned about the low standards of commercial bookmaking common in the Victorian period, undertook to lead a return to higher standards of book production, with special attention to paper and binding as well as to typographic excellence. Although the press went out of existence in 1898, two years after Morris's death, its influence is still felt by book designers. The Kelmscott folio-sized Chaucer, for example, is widely considered one of the most beautiful editions ever issued in English.

ketchup/catsup. There really is no difference at all between *catsup* and *ketchup.* Both words are the English equivalents of the Chinese word *ke-tsiap,* which came to us by way of the Malay *kĕcap.* Originally these words meant "taste" and our *catsup, ketchup,* and even *catchup* all refer to a tomato-base, spicy sauce which we use to add taste and flavor to other food.

Kewpie doll was invented early in the twentieth century by one Rose O'Neill and had a vogue certainly rivaling that of the Teddy bear and the more recent "Barbie." Miss O'Neill chose the name as a baby-talk version of

"Cupid" and the first illustration was of a chubby baby fairy, complete with topknot.

khaki, the name for the olive drab cloth used in soldiers' uniforms, comes from the Urdu word of the same spelling meaning "dusty or dust-colored." And how did the name for such a commonplace item come from such an exotic, faraway land as India? Well, by way of the British army, of course. It first used cloth of this color during the Sepoy Mutiny of 1857 in India.

kibitzers/tsitsers. The term *kibitzer* has been borrowed from the Yiddish, which in turn took it from the German *Kiebitz,* meaning "meddlesome onlooker." Mention of this, together with the pronunciation kih-BIT-zer, in our newspaper column brought a letter of reproof from a man who certainly should know, Dr. Henry Stone of New Castle, Pennsylvania, who has been editing a monthly newsletter called "The Kibitzer" for years.

"I have played bridge and pinochle for many years," he wrote, "and I have been tormented by many *kibitzers.* That word is of Jewish or Yiddish origin and is never accented on the second syllable. If it is, the *kibitzer* is not worthy of his name.

"And that brings me to a favorite *kibitzer* story. Do you know what a *tsitser* is? Well, a *kibitzer* is of the upper class and he is permitted to speak up and criticize at card games. He is permitted to sit very close to the card table. But there is a lower class who must sit behind the *kibitzers* and are not permitted to speak out with criticism. However, they are permitted to voice their disapproval with *ts, ts, ts, ts.* Try forcing your tongue against your upper teeth, and you have it!"

But we're afraid that we have to report that while KIB-it-zer is still the preferred pronunciation—the *only* one for Yiddish speakers—our original pronunciation, with stress on the second syllable, is widely heard. Indeed, the Webster *Third New International* enters it as an acceptable second pronunciation. That's the sort of change that is bound to occur when a word leaves the isolation of a special "in" group and becomes part of the common speech of the general public.

kibosh. There are two theories put forward by the experts about the origin of *kibosh* and they couldn't be more dissimilar. A leading dictionary avers that it is "probably Yiddish in origin" and indicates that it comes from a Middle High German word, *keibe,* meaning "carrion." On the other hand, the famous Irish poet Padraic Colum believes it comes from the Gaelic *cie bais,* meaning "cap of death." At any rate, today's meaning of "put the *kibosh* on"—to put an end to something—is well known and has, according to H. L. Mencken, been widely used in America for more than a century.

kick the bucket. There are two theories about the origin of *kick the bucket.* The first, and less likely, traces it to England, where, centuries ago, the frame from which a newly killed pig was hung was called a bucket. Presumably the pig would thrash about a bit and *kick the bucket.* The second, more likely, theory of origin is simply that the bucket referred to is the pail traditionally used by the suicide to stand on while tying a noose around his neck. Then, with a kick of the bucket, the fatal deed is done.

kid as a pet name, or hypocoristic, for "child" has been well established in the language since the time of Shakespeare. Originally—and still—*kid* meant "young goat." Some language students believe that the wide use of this word to designate human children may be due in part to its resemblance to the German words *kind* and *kinder,* meaning "child" and "children."

kidnap(p)ed. *Kidnap* has long been part of our language, and may in part be credited to America for its first widespread use. *Nap* was a common word in the seventeenth century, meaning "seize or snatch," just as the related word *nab* still does. A *kid* then was just what it is now—a child. But the first *kidnapings* were just as dreadful as those of today, for they involved the seizure of English children, who were sold to sea captains, who in turn sold them to plantation owners in the American colonies.

NOTE: Just about the only major American publication still holding to the double-consonant spelling *(kidnapped)* is *The New Yorker* magazine, which in this and other matters of printing style has long been a pillar of rectitude.

kidney. A book reviewer wrote: "It may not be quite in the class of Nicholas Monserrat's *The Cruel Sea* or C. S. Forester's *The Good Shepherd* but it is of that *kidney."* *Kidney,* as thus used, has come to mean "sort or kind, temperament, likeness or nature." Most commonly it is used to refer to "men of another *kidney*" or "men of the same *kidney."* It all goes back to the belief of ancient Hebrews that the kidneys (or "reins," as they were originally called) were the seat of the affections or passions—and of knowledge, pleasure and pain. In Proverbs 23:16, we find Solomon saying: "Yea, my reins shall rejoice, when thy lips speak right things." The belief has long since been abandoned, but the figure of speech remains.

kill the goose that laid the golden eggs means to act greedily and thus curtail a steady source of revenue, and is taken from the ancient fable of the farmer who had a goose that laid eggs of gold. Consumed with greed, he killed the goose, thinking to get lots of golden eggs at once. Needless to say, he didn't.

kill with kindness. In Shakespeare's *The Taming of the Shrew,* Petruchio explains all the measures he intends to take to curb his headstrong Kate. He plans all sorts of tricks to keep her awake night after night. Then sums up by saying: "This is a way to kill a wife with kindness. And thus I'll curb her mad and headstrong humour."

king's disease or *king's evil* is scrofula, a tubercular infection of the lymphatic glands, which usually causes swelling of the neck. It was very common, especially in young people, during the Middle Ages and later. First known in Middle Latin as *regius morbus,* it derived the name *king's evil* from the widespread belief that a touch from the royal hand would cure it. From the time of Edward the Confessor to the reign of Queen Anne, reigning monarchs touched great numbers of persons afflicted with the disease. One king (Charles II) reportedly touched nearly 100,000 sufferers during his reign. The number of cures, if any, is unreported.

kismet. "It is *kismet*"—meaning that something is fate or destiny and couldn't be avoided or changed—comes to us from the Turkish *qismet.* The Arabic form is *qismah,* meaning "portion or lot." Thus *kismet* is one's share of fortune—or misfortune.

kissing kin. A person is *kissing kin* if he or she is a relative whom one knows well enough to greet with a kiss when met on social occasions.

kit and caboodle. *Kit,* meaning a collection of anything, comes from the kit bag of a soldier, in which he had to carry all his belongings. The earliest record of its use is in England in 1785. Combined with *boodle,* it came to mean a collection of people. There's a difference of opinion as to where *boodle* originated, some authorities attributing it to *buddle* (which in turn was probably Old English *bottel*), meaning "bunch or bundle." Others think it came from the Dutch *boedel,* meaning "property." In this sense it has long been used by New England longshoremen. How did it become *caboodle? Caboodle* is said to be a corruption of *kit and boodle.* All of which certainly makes *the whole kit and caboodle* an all-inclusive phrase.

kitchen police/KP. The *police* in *kitchen police* (more commonly referred to as *KP*) has nothing to do with the law-enforcement duties of regular policemen. It's a service term deriving from the verb meaning "to keep neat and tidy." One of the first things a recruit learns is that he can't toss away a cigarette when he finishes with it. He must find a "butt can" to put it in, or shred it so that it can be carried away by the wind. Otherwise he'll be assigned to *police* the area, meaning to "clean it up." So a member of *kitchen police* is one assigned to dishwashing and other menial and tedious clean-up chores in the kitchen. Incidentally, there's an old army instruction covering the proper way to *police* the grounds of a camp: "If it's small, pick it up. If you can't pick it up, paint it. But if it moves, salute it!"

kith and kin. *Kith* in Anglo-Saxon was *cyth* and earlier *cuth*—the same root we see in the word "uncouth." It simply meant "known," so a *cyth* or *cuth* person was an acquaintance or friend. Thus *kith and kin* equals "friends and relatives."

kitsch is a word which had a quick vogue at the start of the 1970s although, like such other voguish words of the period as *empathy* and *charisma,* it was not at all new. *Kitsch* can perhaps be loosely defined as Middle European "camp." Originally it meant a literary or musical composition of inferior merit but wide popularity. The operettas of Sigmund Romberg and the verse of Edgar Guest might be considered examples of American *kitsch* of the 1920s era. The word is German in origin, being a back formation from the verb *kitschen,* a dialect word meaning "scrapings from the gutter." A *kitsch* production is usually sentimental, often somewhat sensational, and always successful—at least with the general public.

kitty-cornered is a colloquial variation of *cater-cornered,* meaning "diagonal." *Cater-cornered* comes from the French word *quatre* (four) and "cornered." It has a long history, having appeared in print as early as 1519, so it probably was well established in the popular tongue not long after the Norman Conquest.

kiwi (pronounced KEE-wee) is a nearly extinct New Zealand bird whose most remarkable characteristic is a complete inability to fly. A very odd-looking creature with large four-clawed feet and a disproportionately long beak, it lives—when in captivity—on a diet of earthworms and drinks fluids only when it is sick. It is almost unknown outside New Zealand, where it is considered the national bird. Whether the use of the nickname *kiwi* to designate flightless aviation cadets originated with the Australian and New Zealand armed forces is not certain, but the phrase has been in general use with U.S. forces at least since World War I.

klatch/klatsch. An informal gathering, usually of women, to gossip over coffee and cakes is often called a *coffee klatch,* a term derived from the German *Kaffee* (coffee) and *klatsch* (chat).

klutz has enjoyed considerable vogue in recent years as a synonym for "bungler." A reader noted that Czechs have a similar word, *klutzek,* which means "stick." Usually it's applied to persons whose personality isn't much warmer than a stick, she notes, and asks if the two words are related. Quite possibly, although the direct route by which *klutz* entered English is from the German *Klotz,* meaning "clod," by way of Yiddish. According to the *American Heritage Dictionary,* a *klutz* is a "clumsy or dull-witted person."

knee-walking drunk. Here's a tangy dialect phrase contributed by Clinton J. Maguire of Washington, D.C. It's one we had never seen before, and that's not surprising, for the variations of slang expressions for "drunk" must number in the thousands. This seemed so expressive, though, that we thought we'd share it with you.

knickerbockers. These baggy men's trousers, gathered below the knee, had a very considerable vogue, especially among golfers, during the 1920s. Despite several efforts to revive them, they appear destined to live in memory as one of the characteristic items of costume in that era of magnificent nonsense. The first Knickerbocker seems to have been Diedrich Knickerbocker, a character created by Washington Irving for his comical *History of New York.* Diedrich was supposed to be a typical Dutch settler of the Peter Stuyvesant era, and his name supposedly is made up of Dutch words meaning "baker of fancy cakes." All of which has little to do with men's trousers, except that a British edition of Irving's books was illustrated by the great comic artist Cruikshank, who also illustrated much of Dickens. He portrayed the male Dutch settlers as clothed in baggy britches, gathered below the knees. Thus were *knickerbockers* born.

Knight of La Mancha. The *knight* is the chief protagonist of Cervantes's *Don Quixote,* a book which, incidentally, added the word "quixotic" to our language. This tragicomedy of an idealist beset by the realities of a materialistic world has been read throughout the world since its first appearance in Spain in two parts (1605 and 1615).

knock a chip off his shoulder comes from a boyhood game at least a century and a half old. In the words of a New York newspaper of 1830: "When two churlish boys were determined to fight, a chip would be placed on the shoulder of one and the other demanded to knock it off—at his peril." So anybody who goes around *with a chip on his shoulder* is spoiling for a fight, or at least an argument.

knocked into a cocked hat. Arguing that the phrase *knocked into a cocked hat* was used as early as our colonial times, one amateur lexicographer contended that it refers to the cocked hat worn by generals as part of their uniforms in the Revolution. It seemed to him likely that enlisted men in the Revolutionary army were as unimpressed by generals (Washington excepted, of course) as today's GIs. So something *knocked into a cocked hat*—ruined beyond repair—would be something bungled by a know-nothing general. Perhaps. Revolutionary War generals did indeed wear three-cornered, *cocked* hats, but the reference is probably not to the hat but to a bowling game known as "three-cornered hat." It was a form of ninepins in which three pins were set up in a triangle. When only these three pins remained to be bowled, the game was said to be *knocked into a cocked hat*—hence, worthless.

knock off work originated in the days of slave galleys. To keep oarsmen rowing in unison, a man beat time rhythmically on a block of wood. When it was time to rest or change shifts, he would give a special knock on the block, signifying that they could *knock off work.*

knock on wood. There are several theories about the origin of this very common practice. One goes back to the child's game of "tag." In one version of this game the child who is able to touch a tree, thereby touching wood, is free from capture.

Then there is the Biblical theory that the wood symbolizes the cross on which Christ was crucified. In Galatians (6:14) we find "But God forbid that I should glory, save in the Cross of our Lord Jesus Christ." The theory here is that if you have made an exaggerated boast you will be forgiven if you turn your thoughts to the Cross.

Still another notion is that *knocking on wood* goes far back into ancient times, when druids and other spirits were thought to live in trees. So should danger threaten, simply rap the trunk of a tree and summon up the aid of the good spirit within.

There is an Irish belief that you *knock on wood* to let the leprechauns know that you are thanking them for a bit of good luck.

A Jewish version says it originated during the Spanish Inquisition under Torquemada during the 1490s. During that time Jews were in flight and since temples and synagogues were built of wood, they evolved a code to use in knocking on doors to gain admission. Since this resulted in lives being saved, it became commonplace to *knock on wood* for good luck.

Take your choice of these five theories—but be sure to *knock on wood* so you will pick the right one.

knock the spots off of is an expression more than a hundred years old and means "outdo, surpass or defeat decisively." Just what spots were originally knocked off is not clear. However, the first appearance of the expression in print in this country is in a sports report, so we may assume that it began in prize fighting and the idea may well be that one fighter beat the other so thoroughly that he even knocked his spots—meaning freckles—off.

knockwurst is a common variant spelling of *knackwurst* and refers to a sausage short and much thicker than a frankfurter but quite similar in flavor. It is usually steamed, rather than fried or broiled, and is often served with sauerkraut. The word comes from the German *knack* (make a sudden cracking sound) and *wurst* (sausage). Perhaps the earliest *knackwurst,* in animal tissue casing, made a sudden sharp noise when cut into.

knuckle down to. You may take your pick of two theories of the origin of this phrase. *Knuckle,* which we use nowadays to mean the knuckles of the hand, once meant any bone joint, including those of the human spine. Thus to *knuckle down* meant to "put one's back into the job, to work as hard as one could." But the other theory pleases us more. It's taken from the game of marbles. A boy can play marbles fairly casually, but when the issue is drawn and a lad is keenly contesting a match, he *knuckles down* with his fist to the earth to direct his shot better. This use of *knuckle down* is recorded in the *Oxford Dictionary* as going back at least to 1740, so its claim to historical sanction is pretty sound, too.

knuckle-dusters. Perhaps better known as "brass knuckles," these are links of chain into which the fingers of the fist fit, greatly intensifying the effect of a blow. *Knuckle-dusters* were and still are a favorite weapon of thugs, and the term was originally part of American thieves' slang. One notorious New York gang of the nineteenth-century Tenderloin was called the "Hudson Dusters" from their frequent use of *knuckle-dusters* when working over their victims. Carleton R. Reid of Wilbraham, Massachusetts, informed us that many of the handguns of the post–Civil War period were also known as *knuckle-dusters* because they sprayed powder on the knuckles of those who fired them—presumably because the chambers were not completely tight. He also reports on an interesting seven-shot handgun named "My Friend," which was patented by his grand-uncle. One fascinating aspect of "My Friend"—an example of which is still on exhibit in the Springfield (Mass.) Armory Museum—is that after all seven shots were fired, it could be used as a set of brass knuckles. A friend indeed!

kosher. Originally, and still, something *kosher* is food prepared in accordance with Jewish dietary laws. The word has also acquired the extended sense of "correct" or "legitimate": "He runs a completely *kosher* enterprise."

kowtow comes from the Chinese *k'o-t'ou* and koh-TOU nearly approximates the original Chinese pronunciation. However, the word has long been completely Americanized, and while that pronunciation cannot be called wrong, it is surely far less often heard, even in the speech of literate people, than KOU-TOU. To *kowtow* to a person, of course, means to show great respect to him. Originally, in the China of the mandarins, this respect was shown formally by kneeling before a superior and touching the ground with the forehead.

kraut/krauthead. The word *kraut* has, since World War I, been used derogatorily in reference to Germans and people of German descent. In fact, toward the end of World War II, the army newspaper *Stars and Stripes* announced that it would use *kraut* in its stories of enemy action because "it gives less dignity to the enemy." The epithet *krauthead* was also fairly common among U.S. servicemen of World War II and was always used unflatteringly in referring to German soldiers. Incidentally, the terms *kraut* and *krauthead* come from the belief that Germans invented sauerkraut and eat lots of it.

kudos. A fairly common error, especially in headlines, is the use of this word as if it were plural: MAGNATE WINS MANY KUDOS. But *kudos* (from the Greek *kydos*) is singular. If you want to say that a man received many honors, you must say that he has many *kudoses*—a repulsive word if we ever saw one. There are many ways out of the dilemma posed by *kudoses,* of course. The simplest is merely to avoid the word completely and use "fame," "honor" or "glory"—all perfectly good English words well established in our tongue long before *kudos* became used as British university slang in the early 1800s.

Kudos would probably never have enjoyed any vogue in America had not *Time* magazine used it frequently during the 1920s and 1930s. Indeed, *kudos* and *tycoon* are about the last vestigial remnants of the *Time*-style vocabulary evolved by Henry Luce and his staff when that magazine was a brash upstart just beginning to challenge such well-established organs as the *Literary Digest.* Besides odd words dredged from the small print of unabridged dictionaries, *Time* style also favored an inverted sentence structure, now happily abandoned. Its death knell was sounded by the late Wolcott Gibbs, who, in a classic *New Yorker* parody of *Time,* observed that after several paragraphs of *Time* prose "backward reels the mind" and "where it all will end, knows God."

kumatage, meaning "a bright appearance on the horizon, under sun or moon, arising from the reflected light of those bodies from the small rippling waves on the surface of the water," can be found in an 1847 edition of the *New American Practical Navigator,* by Nathaniel Bowditch, LL.D. After a lot of searching we have come to the conclusion that this extremely rare word may well have been coined by the great Dr. Bowditch himself. It is not, of course, to be found in any current dictionary, nor is it listed in such lexicons contemporary with Bowditch as the long-dead *Worcester's Dictionary. Kumatage* is based on the Greek *kyma,* meaning "wave," with the suffix *age,* meaning "collection of." There is in this origin, then, no hint of the element of light reflected from the waves. But it's worth noting that Bowditch was perhaps the most eminent American astronomer of his day and he may have coined this term by analogy to some other astronomical term.

kvetch/kvetchy. *Kvetch* is a Yiddish expression and one that, according to our friend Leo Rosten, is very versatile. In his excellent and amusing book *The Joys of Yiddish,* Rosten gives four slightly different meanings for the noun *kvetch.* It can be applied to anyone who is a chronic complainer or griper. It can be used to describe a person who is a very slow or inefficient worker. It means a person who is forever making excuses for poor performance. And it also applies to a chronic wet blanket ("Don't ask him to the party; he's such a *kvetch*"). As a verb, *kvetch* can mean to fret, complain, gripe, grunt or sigh, or to squeeze, quite literally. As you can see, it is indeed a versatile word. *Kvetchy* is the adjective form.

labanotation is the first satisfactory method for noting down by diagram the various movements and positions of a ballet. In the past choreographers have had to base their revivals of classic ballets on old pictures or the memories of dancers who had appeared in previous performances of the ballets. Now, thanks to *labanotation*—named after its creator, Rudolf Laban—every dance director can have at his fingertips the dance equivalent of the score an orchestral conductor follows. Perhaps of equal importance to the creators of ballets is that by transcribing their works by *labanotation,* they will be able to have them copyrighted and thus enjoy the same sort of protection from plagiarism which writers and composers have had for many years.

laches is a legal term meaning "failure to carry through an action at the proper time"—especially if such failure to act results in loss to a party in an action. An attorney who is engaged to bring an action but, through inexcusable delay, fails to do so until such time as the action is disqualified by the statute of limitations would be guilty of *laches.* Pronounced simply LACH-iz, it has been a common term in law for centuries. It is derived from the

Latin adjective *laxus,* meaning "lax or negligent," and it came into Middle English shortly after the Norman Conquest in the form *lachesse.*

lachrymatory comes from the Latin *lachrima* (tear). It has two meanings, first, as a vase designed to contain tears, found in the sepulchers of the ancient Romans and so called from a notion that tears of the deceased person's friends were collected in them. Second, *lachrymatory* is used humorously to mean a handkerchief.

lackadaisical, meaning "indolent, languid or slow-moving," comes from the early English *alackaday,* an exclamation implying lighthearted dismissal of cares and worries.

laconic. Laconia, which gives us the word *laconic,* was in ancient Greece, the native land of the Spartans, who have contributed their name to the language as a synonym for courage. Laconians were noted for their terse and succinct habits of speech. On one occasion Philip of Macedon threatened to invade their land and sent this message: "If I enter Laconia, I will level Sparta [the capital city] to the ground." The Spartan leaders replied with a single word: "If."

ladybug, ladybug, fly away home. The *ladybug* of this famous children's rhyme is a beetle so called after Our Lady, the Virgin Mary, and it received its name as a tribute for its valuable work in devouring harmful insects such as aphids and scale insects. In England it is known as the "ladybird" and the most popular version of the rhyme there runs: *"Ladybird, ladybird, fly away home,/*Your house is on fire, your children at home;/One is upstairs making the beds,/The others downstairs are crying for bread." Incidentally, British schoolchildren regard finding a ladybird on the way to school as an omen of good fortune for the day. Still another British version is: *"Ladybird, ladybird fly away home!/*Your house is on fire and your children will burn!/Little girl, little girl, what do I care?/My house is insured, and my children aren't there!"

lady-or-tiger situation. The reference is to one of the most famous nineteenth-century short stories, "The Lady or the Tiger?" by Frank Stockton. It told of an ancient monarchy in which the king had invented a novel way to dispense justice. A prisoner was taken into an arena and ordered to open one of two unmarked doors. One of them led to a tiger—which promptly chewed up the prisoner, who was then considered guilty. The other led to the boudoir of a beautiful lady. The prisoner who found her was judged innocent and usually married the lady.

So the decision facing one in a *lady-or-tiger situation* is one filled with peril—the wrong choice may mean disaster. In the story by Stockton, the hero falls in love with the beautiful daughter of the king. For this he is doomed and given the choice of doors. The daughter, reciprocating his love, undertakes to discover the secrets behind the two doors and signals her lover to open the right-hand door. Then, concludes the tale: "I leave it with all of you. Which came out the open door—the Lady or the Tiger?"

lagan. Most of us know the difference between flotsam (debris of a ship floating in the sea) and jetsam (cargo thrown overboard to lighten ship). But *lagan* (pronounced LAG-un) may be a new one to you. It means goods sunk but with an identifying buoy attached.

lagniappe, pronounced lan-YAP, is a Creole term derived from the Spanish *la napa* (the gift), and means a trifling present—a "bonus gift"—formerly given by New Orleans tradespeople to their favored customers. At first it was something as simple as an extra cookie or doughnut added to convert a routine dozen into a "baker's dozen," or thirteen. Apparently it was also used in Huey Long's time to refer to routine, small-scale bribery. In a history of the Huey Long era in politics, one Louisiana legislator is quoted as saying that it was the wide-scale bribery and corruption that bothered him, but that nobody worried about a "little *lagniappe*" now and then.

Lakshmi is the Indian deity of beauty, wife of Vishnu, and the goddess of abundance and prosperity. Nice person to know.

lallygag/lollygag/lollygog. No one knows for sure where *lallygag* came from, except that it has been a part of folk speech for about a century. Its primary meaning is "loitering, especially enjoying oneself while doing nothing in particular." It's a term we remember well from our own youth because, especially in the first fine days of spring, it was a great temptation to *lallygag* on the way to and from school. Like many dialect words that seldom appear in print, this one assumes a variety of spellings on the rare occasions when it does, two others being *lollygag* and *lollygog*. It also had the meaning of "to kiss or to spoon," but this use is now considered obsolete.

lame duck. Until 1933 a congressman who was defeated or failed to run for reelection in November remained in office until the following March 4. During this period of nearly four months these *lame duck* congressmen could make a good deal of mischief, especially if there were enough of them and they felt bitter about their rejection at the polls. The nickname seems to have come from an old hunter's maxim: "Never waste powder on a *dead duck.*" Since these *ducks* would not be entirely dead until March 4, some wit called them *lame ducks,* and the name stuck. Incidentally, the term goes back at least as far as the Civil War.

lampoon, nowadays most often encountered as part of the name of the Harvard College undergraduate humor magazine, is not a new word. Indeed, it's almost as old as Harvard itself. The *Oxford Dictionary* traces it to 1645, nine short years after John Harvard guaranteed his fame by donating a few books to a fledgling school in England's youngest colony.

The practice of writing bitingly satirical pieces *(lampoons)* flourished during the seventeenth and eighteenth centuries. And who were the first *lampoonists?* Appropriately enough, students—and drunken students at that. The word *lampoon,* you see, comes from the refrain of a drinking song popular in the early part of the seventeenth century: *"Lampone, lampone,*

camerada lampone," which, translated, means "Guzzler, guzzler, my fellow guzzler."

land-grant college (university) is a state institution whose founding was aided
by the granting of land by the federal government under the Morrill Act
of 1862 (see LAND-OFFICE BUSINESS). Among the stipulations attached to
the grant was the teaching of agricultural and mechanical-arts subjects.

landlubber. Most people think that *landlubber* is a corruption of "land-lover"
and means a person unhappy to be aboard ship and yearning to be back
home on shore. But no. A *landlubber* quite conceivably could love the sea
and still merit that label, for a *landlubber* is an awkward novice aboard
ship—a stumbling, bumbling greenhorn, whose lack of experience is apparent in everything he does. Nor does *lubber* come from "lover." It's a word
derived from the Anglo-Saxon *lobbe* and means a slow, clumsy, inexperienced person. Apparently the original intent of the sailors' derisive
label *landlubber* was a "person so awkward that he'd be clumsy even back
on land."

land-office business means a volume of business so great that customers very
nearly have to be turned away. The term became widely popular after the
federal government set up land offices to allocate homesteads to citizens
qualified for such land. Homesteaders were so eager to get their allocations
that long lines were queued up before the offices even opened their doors.
So the term *land-office business* has ever since been a synonym for "turna-
way trade."

Like many others, we had suffered under the delusion that *land-office
business* dated back only to the end of the Civil War with the real opening
up of the West. Mr. John Mattoon, chief of the Office of Information of
the Bureau of Land Management, Interior Department, pointed out that
this is an error. "The first land offices," he noted, "were established in Ohio
under the Act of May 10, 1800, which created land offices in Chillicothe,
Cincinnati, Marietta and Steubenville. By the time the Homestead Act was
passed in 1862 these and other offices had already disposed of hundreds of
millions of acres of public domain lands. There are still thirteen land offices
in the Western States and Alaska, and one in Silver Spring, Maryland. And
they still do a *land-office business* now, mainly in oil and gas leases. The
offices have the original land records indicating transfer of title from Uncle
Sam to private citizens, states, railroads and so forth, involving more than
a billion acres of what is now privately owned land. They do a steady
business with individuals searching these records."

land of milk and honey. This reference to a land rich in resources comes from
the Bible (Exodus 3: 8): "And the Lord said . . . I am come down to deliver
them out of the hand of the Egyptians, and to bring them up out of that
land unto a good land and a large, unto a land flowing with milk and
honey."

Land of Opportunity. This nickname for the state of Arkansas seems to have been more fitting in its earlier years than in later ones. Early in the nineteenth century a cotton boom brought prosperity to the state, and with it, the plantation system. Owners of large plantations, with slaves as their source of labor, pushed for secession from the Union in the 1860s and, after the Civil War, many of them lost their holdings. Then drought and depression brought the collapse of the cotton market in the 1930s. Today the state's economy depends on mining, farming and manufacturing.

land on your keister. The *keister* is the buttocks. A fall on the *keister* (also called a "pratfall") is a device as old as show business and virtually guaranteed to draw a laugh. In turn-of-the-century burlesque, one of the celebrated comedians was "Sliding Billy" Watson. He was known for his prodigious slides from one side of the stage to the other, always ending with —you guessed it—a pratfall on his *keister.*

Lane is one of a group of Old English "residence" names and is common today both as a boy's given name and as a family name. Many centuries ago some long-forgotten Englishman was first called "John o' the *lane.*" In time this became *John Lane,* and following the custom which still exists of using the mother's family name as a child's given name, *Lane* came to be used with considerable frequency as a first name for boys.

lark and larriken. In a column we mentioned the fact that *to lark* in the sense of "to frolic, especially in the company of members of the opposite sex," originated in the Middle Ages. Groups of lads and lasses would go into the fields early in the day—before sunup, usually—in order to catch larks, which were considered very tasty. Boys being boys—and girls girls—they didn't spend all their time chasing larks, and that's how *larking* got its frolicking meaning.

Henry F. Hebley of Pittsburgh told us how this expression acquired still another meaning in Australia and New Zealand: "An interesting extension heard in both these countries is the word *larriken,* commonly used to describe what in this country we class as 'young punks.' In the tough Surrey Hills section of Sydney, Australia, a young Irishman was brought before a Stipendiary Magistrate for disturbing the peace by his drunken and disorderly conduct. When asked what excuse he had to offer, he replied in a rich Irish brogue, 'Shure and may it plaze yer honor, I was only *larrikin.*'"

That phrase "Stipendiary Magistrate" which Mr. Hebley tossed off so casually is a very elegant British term for a judge holding just about the lowest echelon of the bar. Indeed, the S.M. differs from an ordinary justice of the peace only in that he gets paid (hence *stipendiary*) and the J.P. doesn't—at least in Britain.

larrup is a word of respectable ancestry, originally a British dialect term, and it means "to whip, beat, flog or spank."

laser/maser. *Laser* (pronounced LAY-zer) stands for Light Amplification by Stimulated Emission of Radiation. Similarly, *maser* is Microwave Amplification by Stimulated Emission of Radiation. The *laser* is a device that, under the necromancy of today's science, converts the energy of diffuse multicolored light into a beam of single-colored light of extraordinary intensity and energy with many uses in space, chemical and industrial research and technology.

last in the expression "Cobbler, stick to your *last*" is an Old English word meaning the sole of the foot or footprint. Bootmakers today use *last* as the name for a form shaped like a foot and used in making and repairing shoes.

latigo is the rawhide thong at the bottom of a pistol holster, tied around the leg to keep the holster from flopping up when the pistol is drawn. Pronounced LAD-ih-goh, it's a word that American cowboys undoubtedly borrowed from their Mexican counterparts, the vaqueros. It's also used as the name for the long strip of leather that tightens the cinch on a saddle. In the original Spanish, *latigo* means whip and, since jockeys often resort to the whip near the end of a race, the word has also come to mean exactly that—the end of a horse race.

Latin Quarter. Paris's Quartier Latin, famous as the locale of student life and Bohemian ways, got its name during the Middle Ages because tutors and students of the University of Paris, located there, conversed in Latin.

launching of ships. The custom of breaking champagne on the bow of newly launched ships is not exclusively American. It began in ancient times when animals were sacrificed as a gesture to the gods to invoke their protection for the new ship. Then, during the Middle Ages, red wine was substituted for the animal's blood. Later, champagne was used because it was more expensive and thus considered more worthy of such a formal occasion; the practice was common in England and France before Americans took it up. In our personal view, breaking a champagne bottle is not nearly as colorful as the Japanese custom of releasing doves when a ship is launched.

laurel is a shrub native to the Mediterranean area. It has aromatic leaves, which appear in our kitchens as bay leaves. Its chief claim to fame, though, is that wreaths made of *laurel* were used to crown citizens of Rome who had made significant contributions to the public weal or had displayed outstanding intellectual prowess. From this tradition we get the term "poet *laureate,*" for Great Britain's court poet, and "conductor *laureate*" for Leonard Bernstein of the New York Philharmonic.

According to ancient legend, a Greek nymph, Daphne, was fleeing from Apollo's unwelcome advances. She called upon the gods to help her and they promptly turned her into a *laurel* bush. For reasons not entirely clear, Apollo thought this was commendable and henceforth let it be known that the *laurel* was his favorite tree.

lavaliere. Originally, and still, a *lavaliere* (pronounced la-vuh-LEER) was an ornament, usually of jewelry, hung on a narrow chain around the neck. The name comes from the Duchess de La Vallière, who was, as the news magazines would euphemistically say, the great and good friend of France's King Louis XIV.

Law of Martinis. Ever hear of the scuba diver's *Law of Martinis?* Well, we hadn't either, until our good friend, the world-famed linguist, Charles Berlitz mentioned it in conversation. Pressed for an explanation, he told us that the further one goes beneath the surface of the water, the greater the sense of euphoria or well-being one feels. When the diver gets suffi- ciently far below the surface, a condition not far removed from drunken- ness sets in, with results that may be distinctly harmful, even fatal. The diver—like his intoxicated terrestrial counterpart—loses his sense of direc- tion and sometimes his other senses, too.

So why the *Law of Martinis?* Well, someone decided that the descent of one atmosphere—approximately thirty-two feet—had the effect on the human system of imbibing a single martini cocktail. Two atmospheres, two martinis, and so on. Curious, we asked Berlitz what was the deepest scuba dive yet recorded. It was, he told us, nearly one thousand feet in a Swiss lake. "Good Lord," we exclaimed, "that would be more than thirty mar- tinis." "Exactly," he replied. "Of the two men who reached that depth, only one returned alive."

laws and ballads. An often-quoted line runs like this: "I care not who makes the nation's laws, so long as I can write its ballads." The originator of the idea seems to have been one Andrew Fletcher of Saltoun, a Scottish politi- cian, and the passage appeared in a pamphlet published in 1704. The thrust —to use a word popular with today's politicians—is that songs are much more widely listened to and heeded than the dry-as-dust statements and writings of lawmakers. Some scholars have tried to show that Confucius and other Chinese sages made statements similar in intent, if not in precise phrasing, to Fletcher's, which, incidentally, ran like this: "If a man were permitted to make all the ballads, he need not care who should make the laws of a nation." The closest any Chinese sage came was: "If the king loves music, there is little wrong in the land."

lax. There is such a verb as *lax,* from which the forms *laxed* and *laxing* come. It is so little used, however, that it is not even entered in most American dictionaries. Here is the definition as given in the *Oxford Dictionary:* "to make lax; to unloosen, relax; to purge." In this verb form *lax* has been part of the language since before 1685.

lay an egg originated in the very British game of cricket. When a player failed to score, he was said to have "achieved a duck's egg"—an allusion to the resemblance between a duck's egg and the figure zero. As baseball became popular in this country, the term was domesticated as "goose egg," and in the days when sports-page prose was more luxuriant than it is today, you might read of Walter Johnson setting down the opposing team for "nine consecutive goose eggs." Gradually the "goose" dropped out of the expression and it became a favorite of vaudevillians in such expressions as: "The new comic opened in one and really *laid an egg.*" From vaudeville to radio and TV was the shortest of jumps and *to lay an egg* is now a common slang expression for "to fail utterly."

layover to catch meddlers is a dialect variant of a very common answer used by adults to evade a direct answer to children's questions. Instead of saying to the child, "It's none of your business," he would be told, "It's *layover to catch meddlers.*" So what's a *layover?* you ask. A *layover* is a trap for bears or other unwary animals, made of a pit covered with boughs. And a *meddler,* of course, is a person who interferes in other people's business. The phrase was recorded in Eastern and Southern states as long ago as 1890. It also appears as *larovers for meddlers, layos to catch meddlers* and even as a single word, *larofamedlers.*

lb. is the abbreviation for the Latin *libra,* meaning "pound." The original phrase was *libra pondo,* "a pound in weight." Over the centuries *pondo*—"in weight"—acquired the meaning of "pound" and *libra* was lost, except in *lb.*

leading question. Many laymen think the legal phrase *leading question* is used to describe questions that deliberately entrap a witness. Not so. Actually a *leading question* is simply one that suggests its own answer, such as: "Wasn't he flushed and breathing hard?"

lead-pipe cinch is something that is remarkably easy to do. Over the years we have had many suggestions—some wildly fanciful—from readers about its origin. The *cinch* part is clear. *Cinch* was borrowed by cowboys from the Spanish-Mexican *cincha,* the saddle girth which assured a rider that his saddle wouldn't slip. Securing the *cincha* was an easy job, so "It's a *cinch*" became popular to express the idea "It's easy." The most persuasive explanation of *lead-pipe* comes from an old-time plumber, who writes: "Before the days of modern plumbing, plumbers used a short piece of lead pipe to fit rigid piping to water closets and sinks to simplify 'out of line' connections, because lead pipe could be easily bent in almost any shape."

leap year occurs every fourth year, when the month of February has 29 days instead of the customary 28. This is to compensate for the fact that the year in the Gregorian calendar is actually one fourth of a day shorter than the astronomical year, so that every fourth year it is necessary to have a year of 366 days, rather than 365. One result of this is that while the days in ordinary years move forward only a single day, in *leap year* they jump ahead two days in the months following February. Thus if in normal years March 1 falls on a Tuesday in one year, it will fall on a Wednesday in the year following. But when *leap year* comes, the first day of March would "leap" to Thursday instead. Every *leap year* falls in a year whose number is divisible by four, except for centennial years, which are *leap years* only when divisible by 400. Thus the first centennial *leap year* since Shakespeare's time (1600) will fall in A.D. 2000.

The custom of women proposing to men in *leap year* is a very old one. Going back almost to the last centennial *leap year,* we find a pamphlet published in London in 1604 entitled "Love, Courtship and Matrimony," which states: ". . . as often as leap year doth return, the ladyes have the sole privilege during the time it continueth of making love, either by wordes or lookes, as to them seemeth proper; and, moreover, no man will be entitled to benefit of clergy who doth in any wise treat her proposal with slight or contumely." The practice is, however, probably much older than this would indicate. After all, wasn't it Eve who nudged Adam into taking the apple? In the words of Genesis (3:6), Eve "took of the fruit thereof, and did eat, and gave also unto her husband with her; and he did eat."

leatherbreeches/leatherbritches. A lad who grew "like a string bean" might well be dubbed *leatherbreeches* or *leatherbritches* by an affectionate grandmother—especially if he grew up in the South. *Leatherbreeches* or *leatherbritches* is particularly common in Tennessee, Kentucky and North Carolina, and it means string beans, especially beans which have been dried in the pod and later cooked "hull and all."

leatherhead. During the nineteenth century watchmen and policemen were often called *leatherheads,* apparently from the fact that many "men of the watch"—the earliest policemen in many towns and cities—wore leather hats. The term *leatherhead* was once used as a nickname for natives of Pennsylvania, though no one now seems able to recall the reason.

leatherneck originated as an epithet in the lively intraservice rivalry between sailors and Marines. During the middle years of the nineteenth century the Marine uniform jacket had a leather-lined collar or stock. In hot weather it became very uncomfortable, and was finally eliminated in 1875—but not before it had given sailors a handy weapon in the not-so-lighthearted badinage which took place whenever Marine and sailor met off duty. The sailors contended that *leatherneck* really meant a neck long unwashed. Indeed, they coined *leatherneck wash* and *Marine wash* to describe a method of washing one's face without taking one's shirt off.

leave no stone unturned goes back to a battle between forces led by the Persian general Mardonius and the Theban general Polycrates in 477 B.C. The Persian was supposed to have hidden a great treasure under his tent, but after he was defeated the victorious Polycrates couldn't find the valuables. So he put his problem to the oracle at Delphi and was told to return and *leave no stone unturned.* He did—and found the treasure.

And that reminds us of the small boy who stood by the seashore firing stone after stone toward a flock of birds at the water's edge. When an adult reprimanded him for his cruelty, he blithely remarked that he was fulfilling his lifelong ambition "to leave no tern unstoned."

lebensraum. Pronounced LAY-benz-rowm, this German word, which literally means "room or space for living," achieved a degree of infamy during the Hitler years, when it was used as a slogan to justify Nazi claims to the Sudetenland and other territories they planned to occupy.

lees of defeat. One of our acquaintances once sent us a copy of the *Bulletin* of the Harvard Club of New York, marking for our attention this sentence: "The Club's chess team can neither drink the wine of victory nor the *lees of defeat.*" In the margin is the scribbled notation: "What does it mean?" What the sentence means is that the chess team hasn't done either well or badly. The drinking of wine in celebration of victory is a custom which goes far back into classical antiquity. The *lees* of wine are the dregs, the bitter sediment which settles to the bottom of the wine vat in the aging process. Obviously, to the victors go the choicest portions of wine, while the vanquished must be content with the dregs or *lees.*

left-winger. *Left, leftist* and *left-wing* came to their present meaning of "radical" from the practice of most European legislatures of seating conservative members to the right of the chair and liberal and radical members on the left. Very likely this resulted from the ritual of always seating honored guests on the host's right at formal gatherings. Since the most distinguished and noble members of a parliament would almost invariably be politically conservative in their views, their parties became known as the parties "of the right" and the more radical groups were the parties "of the left."

legitimatist means "one who supports the legitimate or lawfully constituted authority." It's a term with origins dating back to feudal times. Indeed, we borrowed it from the French *légitimiste*. Then it meant "one who supported a monarchy based on rights of heredity."

leitmotif was originally a musical term, used to describe a device employed by Richard Wagner in his music dramas. A specific musical phrase was associated with the first—and each recurring—appearance of a character, situation, idea or emotion. Then, by extension, a *leitmotif* (pronounced LITE-moh-teef) came to have the general meaning of a recurring and often dominant theme in writing or in life itself. The original sense of the German word, incidentally, was "leading or guiding motive."

lemmings are the subject of a famous legend often referred to as the tale of the "Rats of Norway"—small creatures who journey in a dense pack through a country doing great damage and finally destroying themselves by marching into the sea. They are a breed of mouselike rodents who propagate at such a fantastic rate that every three or four years they are forced to make a great migration from hills and mountains to the sea. Just what impels them in this mad course is not precisely known. One theory has it that they are following a blind instinct inherited from the time, many thousands of years ago, when the Baltic and North seas were dry land and could offer a safe refuge.

lemon sole does not mean that lemon is squeezed on the fish before it is cooked. The word *lemon* in *lemon sole,* in fact, has nothing to do with the fruit. It is a translation of the French word *limande,* meaning any kind of flat fish. Incidentally, it adds up to a redundancy, for who ever heard of a sole that was anything but flat?

leonine contract, more common in British usage than American, harks back to the ancient fable of the lion and his fellow beasts. As Aesop told the story, several animals went along with the lion on a hunt. When it came time to divide the spoils, the lion announced that he would demand one-quarter share as his due as king of beasts; another quarter because of his superior bravery; the third quarter to feed his dam and cubs; and "as for the fourth, let he who will dispute it with me." So here we have the origin of the common expression "the lion's share," meaning the greater part or all of a reward. Here, too, is the origin of *leonine contract,* any agreement which is entirely one-sided.

leotard is often used by ballet dancers, chiefly as a rehearsal costume, not for actual performance. It is a close-fitting garment, usually of knit fabric, covering the entire body from wrist to ankle and having a fairly high neckline. The costume originated under the big top. One of France's most famous aerialists in the nineteenth century was Jules Leotard, who designed and introduced the garment—still worn by trapeze artists—which was tight-fitting, low at the neck and sleeveless but otherwise very similar to the ballet dancer's *leotard.*

leprechaun. The *leprechauns* (pronounced LEP-reh-kons) are a race of Irish elves, usually portrayed as cobblers. One theory of the origin of the name holds that since they are often depicted as working upon a single shoe, the name comes from the Celtic words *leith,* meaning "half," and *brog,* meaning "brogue or shoe." However, more recent research indicates that the word comes from the Old Irish *luchorpan,* which in turn comes from *lu* (small), and *corp* (body), from the Latin *corpus.*

let'er go, Gallegher. Every so often a silly expression sweeps the country. It could be *twenty-three skiddoo* or *so's your old man* or *wanna buy a duck.* This particular one was a popular nonsense expression during the late 1880s. It is possible that *Gallegher* was the newspaper-boy hero of Richard Harding Davis's famous short story published in 1891. However, there seems to be evidence that a popular song of this title was published in 1887, written by another newspaperman named James Ryder Randall.

let the devil take the hindmost first appeared in a play, *Philaster,* by the Elizabethan playwrights Beaumont and Fletcher. Today the common meaning is that if a member of a group drags his heels, either literally or figuratively, the other members may as well forget him and press on. In medieval times there was a superstition that the devil conducted a training school in Toledo, Spain. As part of what might be called the graduation ceremonies, the pupils had to run through a hallway under the earth. The last one was *the hindmost* and was captured by the devil and required to remain as his slave. Today *let the devil take the hindmost* is sometimes used as equivalent to "let the chips fall where they may."

Levant, a term used as far back as the time of Shakespeare, meant the eastern part of the Mediterranean Sea and the islands and countries of that area. It was so called because the sun rose there, *levant* being the present participle of the Latin verb *levare* (to rise). Thus *Levant* (pronounced leh-VANT) literally meant "a rising." Naturally the makeup of the *Levant* varied over the centuries as the political fortunes of its countries changed. Generally, though, the *Levant* was considered to consist of the regions from Greece to Egypt, including Syria, Lebanon and Palestine.

lewd—or, in its Anglo-Saxon spelling, *laewede*—originally simply meant "ignorant" or "uncultured." With the passage of centuries, it came to be used to describe the lower orders of society, the "vulgar" herd. ("Vulgar," incidentally, originally meant "belonging to the common people.") Then *lewd* came to mean base, unprincipled and vicious.

The meaning of obscene or lascivious for *lewd* is not recorded until about 1712. Today, however, this meaning is practically the only one heard.

liar's bench. In the days before radio, television and the supermarket, the country store was often the center for exchange of news, information and gossip. Usually there was a long settee in front of the store where customers could linger awhile and converse. Apparently a goodly number of customers failed to stick to facts in the accounts of their own doings, for, in New England at least, such a settee became known as a *liar's bench.*

libel comes from the Latin *libellus,* "little book," and it refers to what one Roman did when he wanted to defame another. He issued a little book setting forth the other fellow's alleged misdeeds. These "little books" could also be posters or broadsides designed to be read by the public at large and passed from hand to hand.

Liberties. In some of our cities—for example, Norfolk and Baltimore—there are sections known as *The Liberties.* In earlier times—the *Oxford Dictionary* says "until 1850"—a *liberty* was a section of a country over which a person or corporation had jurisdiction, usually under a special grant from the crown. Therefore the person or group were *at liberty* from the normal law-enforcement methods of the sheriff.

libertine, now defined as "a dissolute, licentious and immoral man," once had a more honorable meaning. In the days of the Romans, *libertus* (from which the word is derived) meant "a freedman, a man who had been freed from actual slavery." In the sixteenth century there flourished in France, the Netherlands and elsewhere a freethinking sect known as the *Libertines,* who asserted that God was the only being, that the whole universe is God and that, ergo, man cannot sin. Theory was followed by practice, no distinction was made between good and evil by the *Libertines*—and eventually the word became a generic term for one who considered himself free from all control, including moral codes.

lick and a promise was common in England at least two centuries ago. It refers to a cat who gives its dirty face a fast lick, with the promise to complete the job later. So giving something *a lick and a promise* is giving it "a once over lightly."

lickety-split. We've heard the expression "He's going at quite a lick," meaning at a fast pace. *Lickety-split* is what dictionary editors call a "fanciful formation" based on this sense of "lick." Our old friend Harold Wentworth, in his *American Dialect Dictionary*, found that it had been used on Nantucket Island as early as 1848. He records a lot of even more fanciful variations, like "lickety-brindle," "lickety-cut," "lickety-scoot," "lickety-tuck," and even "lickety-Christmas."

lick one's chops. No matter how you slice them, there are two different kinds of chops. The first—a cut of meat—is simply derived from the verb *to chop*. Doubtless it gets its name from the chopping motion used by the butcher. The *chop* in phrases like *licking your chops* is from a different Anglo-Saxon root entirely and means the mouth or jaws of a person or animal. *Licking one's chops* means "drooling in anticipation of a special treat." *Down in the chops*—a phrase more common in England than America—has the same meaning as *down at the mouth*.

lief. The sentence "I had *lief* go to the movies as watch television" is a correct one, despite the tendency of some persons to convert it to "I had as leave go. . . ." There is no connection between *lief* and *leave,* and substituting *leave* in this expression is wrong. The word *lief,* while heard nowadays only in informal speech, dates back to the Anglo-Saxon *leof,* meaning "beloved." Nowadays it means "willingly" or "gladly." The meaning of the sentence quoted above is: "I would as willingly go to the movies as watch television."

life of Reilly/Riley/O'Reilly. There are several theories of the origin of this popular expression. A person living the *life of Reilly* is one able to live luxuriously without working. One odd result of our research through the various theories of its origin was the discovery that the original Reilly was actually O'Reilly. Here's how it went. There's little doubt that the popularity of the phrase began when Pat Rooney—the founder of the line of vaudevillians who brought so much delight to so many Americans—sang a song, "Are You the O'Reilly," during the 1880s. It was an audience-participation song, a sort of pie-in-the-sky song, painting the pleasures that would be everyone's lot once O'Reilly struck it rich. "A hundred a day will be small pay" and "on the railroads you'll pay no fare" were two of the promises made in the lyrics. At the end of each verse, Rooney would turn to the audience and call out a line like: "Last night while walking up Broadway, the crowds shouted loud and clear . . ." and the audience would join in singing the chorus: "Are you the O'Reilly who keeps this hotel?/Are you the O'Reilly they speak of so well?/Are you the O'Reilly they speak of so highly?/Gor blime me, O'Reilly, you're looking well."

light a shuck goes back to the latter years of the nineteenth century and simply means to light out or depart in a hurry. There's a theory that it may also have reference to the speed of fire in dry cornstalks (shucks) in a wind.

lightning pilot. In Mark Twain's *Life on the Mississippi,* an observer says of Captain Horace Bixby (Twain's tutor): "By the shadow of Death, but he's a *lightning pilot."* A *lightning pilot* was a riverboat pilot who got from his ship every bit of speed possible.

like a house afire, meaning "with great speed," probably refers to the sudden, violent and utter destruction of a house by fire in the days of wooden walls and thatched roofs.

likewise is not only not a "colloquialism," as some assume it to be; it has been well established—according to the *Oxford Dictionary*—at least since 1449. It was originally a contraction of "in like wise," meaning "in the same way"—which is still its basic meaning. What may have led to much misunderstanding is the use of the phrase "*Likewise,* I'm sure" by radio and TV comedians in answer to such salutations as "Glad to meet you." In such use, the line is always delivered with a Bronxish accent, so that it sounds slangy even though it actually is not.

limelight. The *lime* in *limelight* has nothing to do with the fruit from which the color lime is derived. *Limelight* gets its name from calcium oxide, popularly known as lime, quicklime, slaked lime and so on. Calcium oxide was first isolated in 1808 by Sir Humphry Davy, famed British chemist, who soon demonstrated that it would give off a brilliant white light when heated. The phenomenon inspired Thomas Drummond to devise methods of concentrating and projecting the light for theatrical use. The light, first called the "Drummond light" and later used in lighthouses, gradually became known as *limelight.* It has long since been supplanted by arc and Klieg lights, but a man *in the limelight* still is a person center stage, so to speak, receiving the full intensity of the public spotlight.

limerick. Despite the fact that the *limerick* undoubtedly derives its name from Limerick County, Ireland, the Auld Sod cannot claim credit for the origin of the verse form. It was first used by Edward Lear, an English writer, whose *Book of Nonsense* remains popular today, more than a hundred years after its publication. One of his earliest *limericks,* appearing in 1846, was: "A flea and a fly in a flue/Were imprisoned, so what could they do?/Said the flea, 'Let us fly!'/Said the fly, 'Let us flee!'/So they flew through a flaw in the flue." Interestingly enough, Lear did not call these verses *limericks*. That name was first attached to the verse form more than fifty years later, when, about 1898, it became a popular taproom fad to bawl out the line: "We'll all come up, come up to Limerick" between verses of *limericks* rather more robust and indelicate than the one quoted above.

limey originated as a derogatory nickname for a British sailor. He was so called because of the long-standing custom in His Majesty's Navy of serving lime juice to the crew to prevent scurvy.

limousine has a curious history. In French it means literally "hood" and was used as the name of a flowing hooded garment worn by inhabitants of Limousin, a region of west-central France. Then it became the name of an automobile with an enclosed passenger compartment and a roof over the open seat for a chauffeur. It is not certain whether the name was chosen because of the costumes worn by the original chauffeurs or because the enclosure for the passenger compartment constituted a "hood."

liner notes. The comments printed on the back of record albums are known in the music trade as *liner notes*. The original *liners* may have been the paper sleeves that fit inside the slipcase and that occasionally carried descriptive copy. The first LP "albums" were very stark in appearance, in notable contrast to the four-color montages that are commonplace today, so the copy may well have been on the inside liner. Incidentally, most "albums" really aren't albums, if you hold to the original meaning of that word—a collection of photographs, phonograph records or the like. In the days of 78-rpm records, an album really *was* an album, since it had to contain three or more records to cover the amount of material now recorded on a single LP.

lingerie. The pronunciation of *lingerie* as lahn-jer-RAY is a good sample of "bargain-basement French." In truth, it's not French, English or American. It's as utterly senseless a pronunciation as any we know. The correct French pronunciation closely approximates lan-zh'-REE. Note that there's no *ay* sound in that last syllable. Best American pronunciation is—or should be—lahn-zhuh-REE. Incidentally, the word *lingerie* itself is an oddity. Its American meaning has nothing whatever to do with its French origin. In France *linge* means "linen" and *lingerie* means "linen clothing or linen closet."

Linnean taxonomy. Carolus Linnaeus, a prodigiously talented eighteenth-century botanist and physician, founded a system of taxonomy by assigning two names, both in Latin, to the species and genus of all then-known living organisms. It was he, for example, who first labeled man *Homo sapiens,* "wise or sapient man." He pronounced his name lin-EE-us and the adjective, *Linnean,* derived from it lin-EE-an. Nonetheless, the grade school your male co-author attended in Cambridge, Massachusetts, was located on what the natives firmly insisted was LIN-ee-un Street. But perhaps the Cantabs (which see) should not be blamed, since *Linnaeus* wasn't actually the botanist's name. He was born Carl von Linne, and changed his name when he got deep into assigning Latin names to plants and animals. Linne, converted into an adjective, would indeed produce the pronunciation LIN-ee-an.

Listerine. One of the most widely sold mouthwashes, *Listerine,* takes its name from Lord Lister, the English surgeon who is generally considered the father of aseptic surgery. H. L. Mencken reports in *The American Language* that Lister was unhappy about this use of his name and objected to it, but to no avail.

little bit on is British slang for "a trifle intoxicated." "His lordship is a *little bit on* tonight" means he's slightly spiffed but by no means plastered.

Little Egypt. The *Little Egypt* section of Illinois is a deltalike region, formed by the junction of the Ohio and Mississippi rivers. Along with such characteristically American place names as Buncome and Mound City, one finds there other names of indisputably Egyptian influence, such as Karnak and Thebes.

One theory of the origin of the *Little Egypt* label is that in the early nineteenth century, farmers from northern Illinois were struck by a serious crop failure and so migrated south to the more fertile soils of this area. The migration, seeming to parallel that in the Bible, was called a "journey into Egypt." Another notion is that the area, frequently flooded in the early days of its settlement, reminded the early settlers of the floods of the Nile. Paul Angle, of the Chicago Historical Society, told us that a clear-cut explanation of the term *Little Egypt* is probably impossible to determine at this late date. Most likely, he felt, the name evolved from the existence of the place names Cairo, Karnak and Thebes and the fact that the region is a delta, somewhat similar to the famed delta of the Nile.

little green men. Some time ago we wondered in print whether anyone could tell us who first used the expression *little green men* to describe creatures from outer space who come to earth. One rather fanciful explanation comes from James Anderson of Paterson, New Jersey. "One Sunday morning in 1926," he writes, "I had an appointment with an Irish dentist named Dr. O'Grady. Obviously this was not during the regular office hours. When I arrived the dentist had another patient in the chair, but all the doors were open and I could hear the conversation between the patient and the doctor, both of whom were Irish. The patient was stating that leprechauns were very real. In fact he said he had seen the little green fellows and they had pulled the covers off his bed. The doctor was not superstitious and tried to change the thinking of his patient without success. He was absolutely convinced that he had seen the little green men. It's not hard to believe that today's description of men from outer space actually started with those little green men, the leprechauns."

An interesting tale—especially that Sunday-morning part. We can well believe that a patient who had spent Saturday night in a local speakeasy, guzzling what passed for liquor in those Prohibition days, could easily believe that the *little green men* were after him. And they were probably pursued by a herd of pink elephants.

little man who wasn't there. One of our favorite old songs is called "The Little Man Who Wasn't There." Maybe you remember it: "Last night I saw upon the stair/A little man who wasn't there./He wasn't there again today./Oh, how I wish he'd go away." The original verse, called "The Psychoed," went: "As I was going up the stair/I met a man who wasn't there./He wasn't there again today./I wish, I wish he'd stay away." That version was written by Hughes Means, one-time chairman of the Department of Creative Education at New York University, who seems to have had his wish granted, because he lived to the age of ninety, presumably without seeing the little man again. The popular song version had lyrics by an old friend of your authors, Harold Adamson, who also wrote "Time on My Hands," "Around the World in 80 days" and many other hit songs.

Little Neck clams are widely considered to be among our choicest seafood delicacies. There is some dispute as to the reason for their name. Most reference books credit *Little Neck,* Long Island (now a community in the borough of Queens), as the birthplace of the first *Little Necks.* Your authors beg to differ. Every New Englander knows that the finest clams are to be found in Ipswich, Massachusetts, and by no accident at all, the two best clamming areas in Ipswich are known as *Little Neck* and Big Neck. More years ago than he cares to remember, William trod the mud flats of *Little Neck* in quest of clams in the true place of their origin. It was a memorable occasion, for he gathered buckets of clams and a torrid, unforgettable sunburn all at the same time. So the back of our hands to Little Neck, Long Island, and a great huzza to Little Neck, Ipswich, Mass.

little people achieved a certain popularity during the days of the New Deal. The idea was that programs like WPA were designed to help the *little people,* that is, the rank and file of the population, most of whom were jobless as a result of the depression. Joseph Mitchell, one of the most talented writers on the staff of *The New Yorker* magazine, once collected a number of his pieces into a book entitled *McSorley's Wonderful Saloon.* It's a book that we have reread many times with undiminished pleasure and one of the things we most like about it is Mitchell's dedication. It reads: "The people in a number of the stories are of the kind that many writers have got into the habit of referring to as 'the little people.' I regard this phrase as patronizing and repulsive. There are no little people in this book. They are as big as you are, whoever you are." And those are our sentiments —precisely.

little pitchers have big ears, a proverb which is as old as the English language, refers to the fact that the handles of pitchers somewhat resemble a person's ears. No matter how small the pitcher, its "ear" is relatively large. So small children may be expected to hear things not intended for their ears.

Liverpudlian is the name for a native of Liverpool. With the subtlety characteristic of British humor, some wit centuries ago substituted "puddle" for "pool" in Liverpool, came up with *Liverpudlian,* and the name stuck. Other odd names for natives of British cities are *Glaswegian* (pronounced glas-WEE-jun) for inhabitants of Glasgow and *Cantabrigian* for residents of Cambridge. The latter comes from the Latin name of the town, applied during the Roman occupation of England. See CANTAB.

loaded to the gills. A person who has obviously imbibed an inordinate amount of alcoholic beverage is said to be *loaded to the gills.* Why? Because he "drinks like a fish"—but the fish has several advantages over such a drinker. The fish drinks water for the purpose of getting oxygen which is dissolved in the water. After the oxygen is extracted, the water is expelled through the gills, openings on either side of the neck. The word *gills* has come to be used in a humorous way to refer to the flesh around the chin and jaws of a person, so if a man is *loaded to the gills* he has consumed a lot of liquor.

loaded to the guards is the nautical version of *loaded to the gills.* In this instance the *guard* is part of the Plimsoll mark or Plimsoll line found on the sides of all cargo- and passenger-carrying vessels to indicate the maximum depth to which that vessel may be loaded.

loaf/loafer. *Loaf* appeared first in the rural dialect of western New England in the late 1700s. Farmers used the term *loafer* as a disapproving label for a man who owned a farm but didn't work it himself. The word may well have been borrowed by the Yankees from their nearby Dutch neighbors in New York State. *Loaf,* meaning "to laze about," was a back formation of *loafer.* Much later came *loafer* the casual moccasin-type shoe.

lobbyist. The first *lobbyists* were men who hung around lobbies of statehouses and other places where legislators assembled, in order to persuade them to pass legislation favorable to the interests the *lobbyists* represented. Today, and for a good many decades past, the *lobbyist* has moved upward in the social and political world. To buttonhole a senator in the lobby would be gauche in the extreme. Nowadays the legislator may be wined, dined, entertained, asked to speak before a trade association for a sizable lecture fee, or influenced in a great variety of other subtle ways.

lobsterback. The epithet *lobsterback* is a very unflattering label for an Englishman, dating back to the American Revolution. You will recall that the British and Hessian soldiers of that conflict wore uniforms with red jackets, so that they were commonly called "redcoats." In New England, where lobster fishing was and still is an important industry, the hated foe was called *lobsterback,* from the resemblance to the red shell of a cooked lobster. A contemporary account of a pre-Revolutionary squabble in Boston in 1770 states: "The mob still increased, calling out 'Come you rascals, you bloody backs, you lobster scoundrels! Fire if you dare.' " And at least one account of the famous Boston Massacre says that it was provoked in part by one citizen who was "harassing and abusing the sentry, poking him rather severely with a stick, and calling him 'lobster,' a popular reproach."

lobster Newburg. A favorite supper dish that may possibly have contributed to this morning's indigestion is *Lobster Newburg.* It's a staggeringly rich concoction, involving heavy cream, sherry, egg yolks, cayenne and, of course, lots and lots of lobster meat. It was the invention of a West Indies ship captain named Ben Wenberg, who supplied the magic ingredient—cayenne—to the legendary Delmonico's Hotel, where the dish made its first appearance. Messrs. Delmonico and Wenberg had a falling out and Delmonico, as revenge, reversed the order of the first three letters in what had until then been listed as Lobster Wenberg. *Voilà—Lobster Newburg!*

lobster shift. In our column we wondered aloud about the term *lobster shift,* used for many a long year in newspaper circles to refer to the staffers who come to work after the main edition has been put to bed, usually in the early morning hours, and keep matters under control until time to start work on the next edition. Over the years we have asked many newspapermen, syndicate editors, even a brace of news service chiefs, and though everyone was familiar with the expression, none could give its origin.

But, as we expected, our readers did not let us down. Don Anderson of the *Saginaw News* weighed in with the most plausible explanation. "It is my understanding," he wrote, "that it was first picked up by New England newspapermen who went to work at the same time the lobster men were going out in their boats."

And then there was the comment from Max Sonderby, a retired reporter for the *Chicago Sun-Times,* as forwarded to us by George Johnson of Wausau, Wisconsin. "I have heard the expression frequently," he wrote, "and can only guess that it refers to the red complexion of the drunken editors assigned to it—or maybe to their crabbiness." Drunken editors, Mr. Sonderby? That strikes too close to home. Drunken rewrite men, perhaps, but drunken editors? Heaven forfend.

Mike Gann of Colonial Beach, Virginia, said the term originated in New York City early in this century. "Printers congregated in a Lobster House across from the Times building and whenever additional printers were needed, the foreman of the composing room sent over to the Lobster House to hire additional help. This occurred generally late at night. Therefore the name *lobster shift* for the late shift on any newspaper."

Horace B. Cooke of Reston, Virginia, came up with the explanation we're inclined to credit, if only because it explains why the term is known in every part of the country and is far from being a New York regional expression. "It occurred to me that my friend from Thurber Country, Joel

Sayre, might know the answer, so I turned to him. Joel tells me that years ago the word 'lobster' was synonymous with 'sucker.' The boys who had to work the late shift were considered to be just that. Hence the origin of the term. As an old newspaperman, he should know."

But just how much truth is there in Sayre's etymology for *lobster shift?* The answer is: plenty. According to the Merriam-Webster Second Edition (1934), "lobster" may be used as "a term of opprobrium or abuse . . . a gullible person." So unless and until a more persuasive explanation comes along, Joel Sayre has the last word.

lock, stock and barrel. The meaning of this phrase for the whole of anything should be instantly apparent to any huntsman, for the lock, stock and barrel are the three parts of a firearm and together they make up the whole gun.

loco was often used by railroaders themselves in the days of steam locomotives. There's no connection between the slang term for locomotive and the *loco* meaning "nuts". That's a shortened form of "locoweed," a plant once common on Western grazing lands, which could poison whole herds of cattle, after first driving them crazy.

Locofocos were members of the Equal Rights faction of the Democratic party in 1835 and later. They got their name in an interesting fashion. The original *locofocos* were the first self-igniting matches, and when the Equal Rights faction got word of a plan by their opponents to put out all the lights in Tammany Hall to prevent their holding a meeting, they rounded up great stocks of long *locofoco* matches and held the meeting anyway by matchlight. At about the same time an inventor, John Marck of New York, came up with what must certainly be the worst idea in the whole history of smoking. He invented a *locofoco* cigar ("segar," he called it). You simply struck the cigar against any handy abrasive surface, and it lit. Thereupon you smoked it—phosphorus and all.

locum tenens. This Latin phrase, literally meaning "one who is holding the place," is used, especially in Great Britain, for a clergyman or doctor who fills in for the regular pastor or physician when the latter is away.

log book. This started about the time of Columbus, when sailing ships kept track of their speed by means of a *log*—a thin quadrant of wood, loaded so as to float upright and connected to a line wound around a reel. The record of distance traveled was kept in a *log book* and that term, by extension, is applied to any record of travel. So the first *log* was actually made of wood.

loggerheads. Two people *at loggerheads* are involved in a quarrel, in an expression going back to Shakespeare's time. The first *loggerheads* were long-handled instruments with large metal cups on the end, used to melt tar over an open fire. In naval warfare during the Middle Ages, sailors would heat pitch and tar in *loggerheads* and then hurl or dump the contents on attacking craft. Thus the two crews would be *at loggerheads* with each other.

The *loggerhead* turtle gets his name from the fact that his chief characteristic, besides great size, is a remarkably big, knobby head.

logorrhea and its adjective, *logorrheic,* are derived from the Greek *logos,* "word," and *-rrhea,* "flow or discharge," familiar to us in the word "diarrhea." Technically speaking, *logorrhea* is a pathological condition in which the victim is quite literally unable to stop talking, even though his speech is often incoherent. By extension, *logorrheic* describes the person we all know who is everlastingly yakking on, saying more and more about less and less. Such a person, in someone's felicitous phrase, can be counted on to approach every problem with an open mouth.

logrolling goes back to the earliest days of Western migration. When a settler was clearing his land before building a home, he would often call on his neighbor for help in rolling heavy logs, with the tacit understanding that he would help the neighbor when he was in need. In politics it refers to the practice common among legislators of helping one another with favorite pieces of legislation.

loidman is a petty thief who uses a strip of celluloid to open doors. He slips the celluloid between the doorjamb and the spring lock, gradually forcing it open.

lollygagging/lallygagging is a term that has been part of American English at least since midway through the last century—and nobody has yet been able to pin it down to any one source. However, we like this example of its use in 1868: "The lascivious *lollygagging* lumps of licentiousness who disgrace the common decencies of life by their lovesick fawnings at our public dances." So you see, in those days *lollygagging* meant something more than simply dawdling or fooling around, as it does today. As one authority reported: "*Lollygagging* was Grandmother's word for lovemaking."

long in the tooth, meaning "aging," originally was applied to horses because their gums recede with age. It has long been applied to humans, both male and female. Thackeray used the expression way back in 1852, so it is well established in British English.

longshoreman, meaning a dockside worker who helps in the loading and unloading of ships, is simply a contraction of "along-shore-man." These workers are often also called "stevedores," a word taken from the Spanish *estivador,* "one who rams or packs things."

loo is British slang for "toilet." There are two theories of its origin. The first is that it's merely a typical British mispronunciation of the French *le lieu,* "the place." The trouble with this theory is that the standard French expression is *le w.c.,* borrowed from the British. The other theory, the one we prefer, is that it is a shortened form of "Gardy loo!," a cry of warning given by British housewives when, in the days before plumbing and sewers, they simply emptied their slop pails out the window. "Gardy loo!" is a corruption of the French *Gardez l'eau*—"watch out for the water."

loony bin, a slang term for "insane asylum," is a coinage from *loony,* a dialect form of "lunatic," and *bin,* a place where objects are stowed away.

Lord Home. When Lord Home served briefly as Britain's prime minister, American commentators had a bit of difficulty at first remembering that his name is pronounced as if it were spelled *Hume.* According to legend, one of his ancestors was a leader of Scottish forces in the battle of Flodden Field, which saw the defeat of the army of James IV in 1513. At a particularly critical point in the battle, Home sought to rally his battered troops and instill new bravery in them. So he resorted to the magic of his name to inspire them. "Home, Home, Home!" he cried, and—taking him at his word—the troops headed toward the road for home. The next day the third Lord Home, for so he was, decreed that henceforth his name should be pronounced "Hume."

Los/San. Both *Los* and *San* are Spanish words, the former meaning "the" and the latter, "saint." The use of them in the names of many Western cities reflects the influence of the early Spanish settlers, many of them missionaries.

According to George R. Stewart's *American Place Names,* Los Angeles is actually a shortened form of the Spanish phrase *Nuestra Senora (Reina) de los Angeles de la Porciuncula*—"Our Lady (the Virgin Mary) of the Angels of the Little Portion." The reason for this rather elaborate name is that the first expedition to camp there arrived on the feast day dedicated to Porciuncula.

lot lice. Nostalgic Americans who can remember gathering early in the morning to watch the big top go up would not have relished it so much if they had known the circus jargon name for themselves—*lot lice.*

Louis means "famed in battle" and comes from the name of the first of the Merovingian line of Frankish kings, Cholwig I. He was regarded as the first French king, and his name was Latinized to *Clovis* or *Ludovicus*—whence came our present spelling *Louis,* which was borne by at least eighteen French kings. It has long been a most popular name both in France and in England—where the spelling *Lewis* is perhaps more common.

lounge lizard. In the 1920s this term was popular slang used in reference to a chap who would like to regard himself as a Lothario but operated a bit on the cheap side. His idea of a great evening was lounging in the quarters of his lady fair, the target of his evil designs.

love as a term for zero in scoring tennis matches has caused some dispute among etymologists as to its origin. One theory is set forth by a reader of our newspaper column as follows.

"You are, of course, familiar with the U.S. slang term 'goose egg,' to mean zero. The same expression is carried over into French as *l'oeuf,* 'the egg,' which the French use to mean zero in a game. Having played tennis regularly in French-speaking New Caledonia, I heard the term regularly used there and used it myself, as in calling *'quarante-l'oeuf,'* and have also been told by others that it is regularly used in France in scoring tennis. The word *love* in the game of tennis as played in English is only our bad pronunciation of *l'oeuf.* I am sure if you will check further you will find that this is the origin of the term and that it has nothing to do with *l'amour.*"

That's an interesting theory, one that we have heard before. We're not going to dispute the fact that the French use *l'oeuf* for *love,* zero or zilch. The fact is that tennis, in the form of court tennis, seems to have been a French invention. But when the British got into the act, they converted *l'oeuf* to *love* for two reasons. First, the process of folk etymology was at work. That's the linguistic process by which an unfamiliar word is supplanted by a familiar one. Also *love* has long been synonymous with "nothing." Back in 1678 John Dryden wrote the play *All for Love or the World Well Lost.* So there's a case to be made for both theories.

love apples. Tomatoes were once known as *love apples.* Apparently some of our forefathers thought tomatoes were aphrodisiac, but that represents a distinct triumph of mind over matter, for science tells us that as a love potion tomato juice simply doesn't have what it takes. The whole idea comes from a mistake in etymology. Tomatoes originally grew in South America and were imported to Spain not long after Columbus discovered America. From there they were taken to Morocco and eventually were introduced to Italy, where they were known as *pomo dei Moro* (apple of the Moors). A romantic Frenchman mistakenly translated this as *pomme d'amour* (love apple) and a legend was born.

Love me, love my dog. This expression is at least a thousand years old. It first appears in the writings of a medieval saint—appropriately enough, St. Bernard, though not the one after whom the dogs are named. In his first sermon appears the Latin sentence: *"Qui me amat, amet et canem meum"* —"Who loves me will also love my dog."

lowbrow/highbrow/middlebrow. A *lowbrow* is a person of vulgar or uncultivated tastes. A *highbrow,* it follows, is one who at least aspires or pretends to a high level of cultivation and learning, while a *middlebrow* is a person of middle or mediocre cultivation. According to author Inez Haynes Irwin, her husband, Will Irwin, invented both *highbrow* and *lowbrow* for a series of articles in the *New York Sun* (1902–1903).

lower the boom. In maritime parlance, to *lower the boom* means to secure the cargo booms of a freighter at the time she leaves port and puts out to sea. The booms are lowered by means of block and tackle until they rest in a cradle and stretch parallel to the deck of the ship. Then, in maritime slang, the term can also be used to ask for a loan. "There's a poker game in the fo'c'sle. Can I *lower the boom* on you for ten bucks until the next draw?"

The "draw" refers to the money disbursed by the captain or purser and is made in local currency in port, not at sea.

low man on the totem pole is an expression that has enjoyed considerable popularity as a jocular reference to the lowest person in any organization. It is generally credited to H. Allen Smith, the American humorist, who used it as the title of one of his books. Actually, it was coined by Fred Allen in an introduction to an earlier collection of Smith's pieces, about what he called "the riff and the raff, those who slink through life fraught with insignificance." What Allen wrote was: "If Smith were an Indian, he would be *low man on any totem pole.*" Smith, who could spot a felicitous phrase a mile off (he also wrote *Lost in the Horse Latitudes* and *Life in a Putty Knife Factory*) promptly borrowed it for the title of his next book.

lox/heliox/oceanaut. *Lox,* to many people, is the smoked salmon that should be eaten with cream cheese on a bagel. (See BAGEL AND LOX.) To a child of the space age, however, *lox* has another meaning—liquid oxygen. He would also know that *heliox* is a blend of helium and oxygen used by oceanauts—and *oceanaut* is the word coined by Jacques-Yves Cousteau to describe the underseas adventurers who have lived and worked under the ocean for weeks on end.

loyalty laughter. The late Fred Allen coined this phrase to describe the kind of laughter that invariably greets jokes told by one's boss.

LSD/acid/acid heads/pot. *LSD* is the best-known of the synthetic hallucinogenic drugs, also called psychedelic (from Greek, meaning "mind-manipulating") drugs. It's a chemical called in the laboratory d-lysergic acid diethylamide tartrate. That's where its nickname *acid* comes from and why people who use it to go on "trips" are known as *acid heads.* The "trip" is, of course, an escape from the normal conscious world into a fantasy environment far removed from reality.

Man has been escaping from his environment almost ever since he has been on earth. Various forms of alcohol are the most socially acceptable vehicles for release from mundane affairs. In Latin America and other parts of the tropics, various kinds of mushrooms have also been used to provide mental escape. And for centuries hashish—the same marijuana that today's devotees call *pot*—has served to sublimate and at times inflame its users beyond reality.

luck out is one of those rare expressions that can have entirely opposite meanings, depending on the context in which it appears and, sometimes, the tone of voice in which it is spoken. In World War II it was commonly said that "So-and-so *lucked out*"—meaning that he was a casualty in a military action. The term was also used to indicate any misfortune or setback. It could be said of a loser in a poker game that he *"lucked out."* In current usage, however, it can mean that the person in question has had a run of good luck. *Merriam-Webster* cites such an example as "He *lucked* *out* on the exam." It also notes a use of the expression to indicate acting with complete reliance on luck, as *"lucking out* without any set plan of action." So *luck out* is a very versatile term and exactly what it means must be determined largely by the context in which it appears.

lucubration (pronounced loo-kyoo-BRAY-shun) comes from the Latin *lucubrare* (to work by candlelight) and has acquired the meaning not only of work done late at night but of any study or literary work of a laborious nature. It also applies to the product of scholarly work, particularly an elaborate one. The verb form is *lucubrate.*

Lucy Stoner. Lucy Stone was one of the most ardent women's suffrage leaders in the nineteenth century. She was so intent upon making the point of woman's equality with man that she refused to change her name when she married. Although legally Mrs. Henry Brown Blackwell, she would not answer to any name but Lucy Stone all the years of her married life. Her example was much emulated by "emancipated" women of the early years of this century. Heywood Broun's first wife, Ruth Hale, was a *Lucy Stoner,* as were many other literary and artistic women of the period. Perhaps the furthest point to which the crusade for women's equality in names was carried, though, was in the case of political commentator Raymond Swing. During more than a score of years of marriage to Betty Gram, he dutifully signed himself Raymond Gram Swing. When he married another lady, he reverted to Raymond Swing.

luddite is a person who attempts to halt industrial progress by tampering with or destroying the machines that may cost him his job. The first *luddite* was a Leicestershire village idiot named Ned Ludd, who in the late eighteenth century broke several stocking frames belonging to his employer. The name was taken by a group of workers who, between 1811 and 1816, tried to halt what came to be called the Industrial Revolution by smashing new labor-saving textile machinery.

lukewarm. *Luke* is simply the modern spelling of the Middle English *louke,* meaning "tepid," which in turn came from the Dutch *leuk.* Since "tepid" itself means "barely warm," *lukewarm* certainly seems redundant—but that won't diminish its popularity after all these centuries.

lulu is a bit of legislative slang, a corrupted form of *in lieu of.* It refers to a flat amount ranging between $2,000 and $15,000 given to a lawmaker *"in lieu of* expenses." The method of flat sum payment relieves him of the need to account for his expenditures item by item.

lumbermen's jargon. Ever hear of *flatheads, shavin' crews* or *swampers*? Would you recognize a *crummie, sky pilot* or *counter jumper* if you saw one? Well, these are all expressions from the jargon of lumbermen of the Northwest.

Lumbermen can be roughly grouped into three groups: the woods crew, the mill crew and the bunkhouse gang. There often is, as one veteran noted,

"quite a bit of brick-throwing between the woods crew and the mill crew."
But both are usually tolerant toward the bunkhouse gang because food and
shelter are involved. When cookie brings in a really poor meal, though, the
lumberjacks react by *walking the table*—which means that two lumberjacks mount the table, one at each end, and walk down it, kicking everything off. Cookie usually leaves by the next train.

But back to those words in the first paragraph. A *flathead* is a sawyer.
The *shavin' crew* are mill hands who plane the lumber. *Swampers* are the
lowest caste among lumbermen. They lob the limbs from the felled timber
and cut the roadways. A *crummie?* Well, he's the chap who manages the
bunkhouse, often called the *bull pen.* A *counter jumper* is merely a clerk
and a *sky pilot* is a preacher. Incidentally, should you hear a burly lumber-
jack suggest that he and his pal *go to Sunday school,* don't be misled. That's
lumbermen's slang for "Let's get up a poker game!"

lunatic, meaning "insane," comes from the Latin *luna,* "moon," and reflects
the beliefs of ancients and some moderns that prolonged exposure to the
moon renders one "moonstruck" or daft.

lunatic fringe was the invention of President Theodore Roosevelt. In a letter
to Henry Cabot Lodge in 1913 he commented on the defeat of the Bull
Moose party—a faction of the Republican party—in the previous year's
election. Somewhat morosely he noted that various groups of his supporters "have always developed among their members a large lunatic fringe."

lush as a generic term for beer and other intoxicating drinks has been British
slang for more than a century. It is supposed to have originated as a
contraction of the name of a London actors' club, the City of Lushington.
The use of *lush* to describe a drunken person and *lushed* or *lushed up* to
describe the state of intoxication has been common in America for at least
forty years.

lycanthropy. The name of the mania or disease that gets into those characters
in horror films and turns an ordinary man into a raging beast, usually a
wolf, is *lycanthropy*—from the Greek words *lukos* (wolf) and *anthropos*
(man). The legends of man-wolves are almost as old as man himself and
probably go back to the days of cavemen. In literature they appear in
Greek, Latin and all sorts of Gothic legends. Our English equivalent is the
"werewolf," from the Anglo-Saxon *wer* (man) and "wolf."

lynch law results in quick and violent death, usually by hanging, without any
of the niceties of legal trials. We can give you two theories of the origin
of the expression *lynch law.* Conveniently enough, both begin in Virginia
and in about the same period of time.

In 1780—so goes the first theory—Captain William Lynch organized a
group of his fellow citizens in Pittsylvania County who "having sustained
great and intolerable losses by a set of lawless men and abandoned wretches
are determined to inflict such corporal punishment as shall seem adequate

to the crime committed or the damage sustained."

Theory No. 2 sets the date at 1796 and has as its hero—if that's the word for it—a wealthy plantation owner and justice of the peace named William Lynch. He decided that due process of law was not moving swiftly enough for him, so he took the law into his own hands in dealing with persons he believed had supported the Tory cause during the American Revolution. Whether the original victims were hanged is not clear, but that was the customary form of punishment when later groups of vigilantes and the like resorted to *lynch law*.

In a travel guide for the British Isles we found an utterly fantastic account of the origin of *lynch* which takes it all the way back to the time of Columbus and locates the Lynches in Ireland. It seems the mayor of Galway, a man named James Lynch Fitzstephen, had a son named Walter, who was in love with a girl named Agnes. Returning from a trading trip to Spain, he brought with him a new-found friend named Gomez. After a while Walter became jealous of Gomez, who made frequent visits to Agnes's house. Little did he know that Gomez was innocent of any misdeed. He was merely tutoring Agnes's dad in Spanish. Then the inevitable happened. Tortured by jealousy, Walter killed his pal Gomez.

Now stay with us a bit. The centuries-old soap opera gets better. Walter, shaken by remorse, turned himself in to the police. His father, as chief magistrate, presided over the trial, and since Walter confessed his guilt, condemned him to death. But Walter was such a lovable lad—though a bit murderous at times—the official executioner refused to hang him. So—you guessed it—the mayor stepped into the breach and hanged his son.

Among the countless things wrong with that story is that it doesn't have anything to do with the actual meaning of *lynch law*, which is "execution without due process of law." And, just to be technical, even the *Oxford English Dictionary* says that the expression is of American origin and dates its first appearance in print more than three centuries after Columbus discovered America.

macadam. When we speak of a *macadam* road, we are unwittingly paying tribute to John L. MacAdam, the Scottish engineer who invented this method of paving highways. MacAdam, a Scot who came to America in the late eighteenth century, earned a fortune and returned to his native land. When he got back there he was appalled at the poor condition of the roads and put his time, thought and money into the development of new and better methods of paving them—with today's *macadam* roads the long-range result.

macadamia nuts are the edible seeds of the *macadamia* tree, native to Australia. The tree was named for its discoverer, a chemist named John Macadam, who, so far as we know, was no kin to the MacAdam of macadam road fame.

macaroni. We all know this as one of the staple pasta dishes. Because *macaroni* is usually mixed with sauces and condiments before serving, it's not surprising to learn that its Italian ancestor, *maccherone,* originally meant a jumbled-up mixture. From this we get the sense of *macaroni* as a jumbled-up verse form, usually a mixture of vernacular terms and Latin forms. Still another sense of *macaroni* is that of dandy, fop, or elegant coxcomb. This was the sense referred to in "Yankee Doodle" when he "put a feather in his hat and called it *macaroni.* " Matter of fact, there was even a regiment of Maryland militia during the Revolutionary War known as the "Macaronies" from the fact that they wore uniforms of a degree of splendor unknown in the nation.

mace is political slang for extorting contributions for political purposes from public employees, usually engaged in by political bosses. Most dictionaries list it as "origin unknown," but it may well be related to the earlier *mace,* a club or staff used as a symbol of authority by officials. Chemical *Mace* is the trademark name of a blend of chemicals sprayed under pressure, usually from a hand-held can, and used as a weapon to induce temporary blindness and other disabling reactions.

Mach is the term used to denote the ratio of air speed to the speed of sound. An airplane traveling at a speed of *Mach 1* is traveling at the speed of sound. *Mach* comes from the name of a noted Austrian physicist, Ernst Mach, who died in 1916.

Machiavellian cunning, derived from Niccolò Machiavelli, Italian political theorist and author of *The Prince* (1513), is synonymous with double-dealing and sly, underhanded political trickery. And that's scarcely fair because Niccolò actually was preaching nothing much more than the doctrine, now accepted by many allegedly civilized nations, that the end justifies the means. If the ruler had to resort to underhanded tactics and deception to maintain his authority, well—so the reasoning ran—his underlings were probably up to the same nefarious practices and it well behooved the chief to keep one step ahead of them.

mackerel snatcher (snapper). Back in Boston, in the days of our youth, we used to hear Roman Catholics called *mackerel snatchers,* though the *snapper* version seems to be more common. It simply refers to the fact that Roman Catholics of that era were sternly forbidden to eat meat on Fridays or other days of fast and abstinence, and mackerel was one of the favorite fishes substituted for meat.

mackintosh. The *mackintosh* raincoat bears the name of its inventor, Charles Mackintosh, the first man to make truly waterproof fabrics.

mad as a hatter. The explanation of this phrase that we find most believable holds that *hatter* is really a variant form of the Anglo-Saxon word *atter,* meaning "poison." *Atter* is closely related to "adder," the venomous viper whose sting was thought to cause insanity. This explanation has much to recommend it. For one thing, it explains why the phrase, in one form or another, was current before hatmaking became a recognized trade. Secondly, it removes the stigma from an otherwise honorable means of employment.

Another theory, which we consider erroneous, is that hatmakers, in making felt hats, used mercurous oxide and that inhaling this chemical over a period of years resulted in a disease very much like what used to be called St. Vitus's Dance—uncontrollable trembling. People so afflicted were often considered mad in the years before medical research found that the cause was physical rather than mental. The wide popularity of the phrase can be credited to Lewis Carroll, whose Mad Hatter in *Alice in Wonderland* is one of our most delightful comic creations. The phrase itself, however, was used often before Carroll's time, notably by Thackeray in *Pendennis.*

mad as a March hare. The theory is that hares are wilder than usual in March because this is their mating season. From childhood memories of raising Belgian hares, it seems to us that the mating season ran right straight through the year—and the hares were no more skittish in March than at any other time of the year. However that may be, the expression goes back as far as Chaucer, at least, for he alludes to it in "The Friar's Tale." We're inclined to believe that the expression may actually be a corruption of "marsh hare." At any rate, that was the theory expounded by the eminent Dutch theologian and scholar Desiderius Erasmus, who wrote: ". . . hares are wilder in marshes from the absence of hedges and cover." Still, the "March" version seems to have prevailed. As recently as the nineteenth century, Kingsley, in *Water Babies,* wrote: "A very clever old gentleman but . . . *mad as a March hare."* And of course, there is *the* March Hare who took part in the mad tea party with a Hatter, a Dormouse and Alice in *Alice's Adventures in Wonderland.* It was the *March Hare* who gave Alice a lesson in semantics.

> "Then you should say what you mean," the *March Hare* went on. "I do," Alice hastily replied: "at least—at least I mean what I say—that's the same thing, you know." "Not the same thing at all," said the Hatter. "Why, you might just as well say 'I see what I eat' is the same as 'I eat what I see!' "

Madison Avenue, as a generic term to describe advertising agencies and their employees, first came into use in 1944 when an article on advertising's contribution to the war effort appeared in the *New Republic* magazine, signed "Madison Avenue." In recent years some of the larger agencies have moved to Fifth and Park avenues, perhaps in a conscious effort to evade the opprobrium which now attaches to the *Mad Ave* label in the public's mind. Thus the label is rapidly becoming a misnomer as agencies show a marked inclination to locate their offices anywhere *but* on Madison Avenue.

Madras, when it is used as the name of the Indian city, is pronounced muh-DRAS or muh-DRAHS. The fabric *madras,* a kind of cotton cloth, usually striped, obviously derives its name from the name of the city where it is believed to have originated. Indeed, the fabric *madras* is still commonly used in India. However, in American usage at least, the common pronunciation of the fabric is MAD-ras.

maelstrom. The original *maelstrom* was much more exciting than a simple whirlpool. The Maelstrom (note the capital *M*) is located off the northwest coast of Norway and is caused by strong tidal currents capable of swamping and sinking small ships. In ancient days, so legend has it, two magic millstones ground out so much salt that the boat carrying them sank. The millstones continued to grind, even to this day, which is why the seas in that area are so turbulent—and why the oceans themselves are salty.

maffick. A "nonce word" is a word created for a single occasion—and *maffick* is the quintessential nonce word. It means to riot wildly and joyously, to engage in happy debauch as celebration of a wonderful and unexpected triumph. It refers to the wild celebration, especially in London but also in other parts of what used to be called the British Empire, when the siege of Mafeking was raised in 1900. Mafeking was a city in the South African British protectorate of Bechuanaland (now the republic of Botswana) and it was under siege by the Boers for more than six months. News of the lifting of the siege reached London on May 18, 1900, and the British were so exultant that they, in Jimmy Durante's notable phrase, "made the wall king ring," which, in less talented hands, usually reads "made the welkin ring."

mafia, also spelled *maffia,* comes from the Sicilian dialect of the Italian language—but it did not begin there. It originally was an Arabic word, *mahyah,* and meant "boastful or bragging." By the time it reached Italy—or Sicily, to be precise—it meant "boldness and lawlessness." It was first used as the name of a secret antigovernment terrorist society in nineteenth-century Sicily. Later the scope of its activities was expanded into organized crime and, under such names as the Black Hand and Cosa Nostra, expanded its scope to include the United States. *Mafia* in such expressions as "Irish *Mafia*" merely connotes a tightly knit and very powerful organization—not necessarily evil in intent.

Several readers have reported a theory that it is an acronym of the words: "Morte Alla Francia Italia Anela," with this translation: "Death to the French is the cry of Italy." That's a neat story, but we'll stand by the true one.

magenta. Back in 1859, Magenta, a town in northwest Italy, was the scene of one of the bloodiest battles ever fought. It was between the Austrians, who were beaten, and French and Piedmontese troops. The color—a sort of reddish purple—was named to commemorate the bloody battle.

magic. There is a widely held belief that the word *magic* is derived from the Three Wise Men (the *Magi*) who brought gifts to the infant Jesus at the Feast of the Epiphany. But this is only a half truth. The word *magic* is indeed derived from *Magi*—but there were many Magi besides the three who appeared on that occasion. Indeed, the Magi were a priestly caste in ancient Persia who, through sorcery, gained the reputation of having wonderful occult powers. The mumbo jumbo they performed in exorcising devils was called in Greek *magikē*—and from that word we derive our *magic.*

Maginot line mentality. André Maginot (pronounced mah-zhee-NOH), minister of war in France (1922–24, 1929–32), was responsible for the creation of the line of impregnable forts which would forever insure the French against invasion by Germany. The forts are still there, still superbly intact, because the Germans by a flanking maneuver invaded through Belgium. So *Maginot line mentality* has become a catch phrase to describe military minds—still all too common—who insist upon fighting the last war or the war before last instead of meeting situations that actually exist.

magnolia is an evergreen tree or shrub justly famous for its splendid display of white, purple or pink flowers. The flowers are fragrant and once were used in China to flavor rice. Its name comes from Pierre Magnol (1638–1715), a noted French botanist.

magnum opus. Latin for "great work," this phrase is usually applied to an author's or artist's most important work.

mahatma. Most Americans associate this title with the late Mahatma Gandhi, though there are a few of the more irreverent among us who recall that the legendary baseball figure Branch Rickey was often called "The Mahatma." The title actually is relevant to both men, for it simply is taken from two Sanskrit words, *maha* (great) and *atman* (soul).

mail was taken by the English from the Old French *male* soon after the time of the Norman Conquest. *Male* meant no more nor less than the bag or pouch in which letters were carried. At one time—about the time of Shakespeare—people spoke of a *mail* of letters. Indeed, in Great Britain today, according to the *Oxford Dictionary,* the word *mail* is used "to signify only the dispatch of letters abroad, as in 'Indian mail,' or as a shortened form of 'mail train,' as in 'night mail.' " The English use the word "post" the way we use *mail.* In Britain you put a letter "into the post," not "into the *mail.*"

main guy is not the circus owner but the guy rope that holds up the center pole in the big top.

Main Line, once synonymous with the suburban area where the first families of Philadelphia's social world resided, got its name in the simplest possible fashion: it is composed of communities located along the main line of the Pennsylvania Railroad. *Main line* has been used in a very different sense in the jargon of "junkies," as dope addicts sometimes call themselves. To them a *main liner* is an addict who takes heroin by direct injection into an artery *(main line)* in his arm.

Major Grey of chutney fame. With remarkable uniformity the basic books of biographical reference have ignored *Major Grey.* Indeed, after considerable fruitless search, your editors were almost ready to consign him to the limbo of corporate but incorporeal figureheads like Betty Crocker. However, we have the word of T. J. Finucan of the Crosse & Blackwell Company that there once was a living, breathing and, of course, eating Major Grey. He was a military officer who became acquainted with chutney—a relish made of fruits, spices and herbs—during his service in India. When he ended his tour of duty in the Punjab, he arranged to have supplies of the raw materials shipped home and set up the manufacture of Major Grey's Chutney in his home. After a while, the task became too great for him since, with his limited facilities, he couldn't keep abreast of the orders, so he made arrangements for Crosse & Blackwell to take over the manufacture and distribution of his product.

majority of one. The boss of one of our readers called a meeting about a proposed change in policy. He asked for votes of "yes" and "no" from the department heads. All voted "no" but he announced that the verdict was "yes" because "I am a majority of one." He claimed the phrase was original with him, but Thoreau, in his essay on "Civil Disobedience," wrote: "Any man more right than his neighbors constitutes a majority of one already."

make a clean breast goes back to the ancient custom (remember Hawthorne's *The Scarlet Letter?*) of branding a sinner on the breast with a symbol appropriate to the evil he or she had committed. Thus a person who confessed all would be one who had "come clean" or *made a clean breast of it.* By confessing he had purged himself of sin.

make a virtue of necessity. If events are beyond your control, there's no point in getting wrought up. Relax and enjoy things. This is a very old theory. Chaucer in *Troilus and Criseyde* wrote: "Thus maketh vertu of necessite!"

make no bones about it. We can offer two theories of the origin of this phrase. Theory No. 1 is that the *bones* in question are those found in stews or soups. A stew that "had *no bones about it*" would be simpler, more straightforward. And what we mean when we say we *"make no bones about something"* is that we are being plain, straightforward and candid. Theory No. 2 takes us into the gambling hall. The *bones* now are dice. Some gamblers make a great to-do over their dice before they cast them on the green baize table or blanket. They breathe on them, utter good-luck slogans and go through an elaborate ritual before making their throw. On the other hand, a true professional will *make no bones about* his cast, simply shaking them once and throwing them down.

make the grade. *Grade* in this phrase means an incline or slope and one who *makes the grade* has reached the highest point and reached his goal.

making a monkey out of goes back almost to the time of Shakespeare. Monkeys were used in carnival side shows as objects of ridicule and were teased or treated harshly in order to make them do tricks. So, if you were *making a monkey out of* another person, you were making a fool of him—or, worse, making him make a fool of himself.

making both ends meet was originally a nineteenth-century bookkeeping term. The bookkeeper's task was to make both ends mete (equal)—that is, make sure assets and liabilities balance.

making whoopee goes back nearly a century—perhaps longer. Walter Winchell used it a lot in his column and doubtless helped give it wide publicity, and Eddie Cantor once sang a song called "Making Whoopee." But neither coined the expression. Back in 1880 Mark Twain, in "A Tramp Abroad," wrote: "I propped myself up and raised a rousing Whoop-ee!" Still earlier, in 1862, a story in *Harper's* magazine contained this comment: "He yelled at the top of his voice, 'Whoopee. Whisky only 25 cents a gallon!' " So *whoopee*—and the elements involved in making it—have been around a long time.

malaise is the feeling that one is "coming down with something"—the vague sense of uneasiness or discomfort before developing an illness. It is made up of two French words: *mal,* meaning "bad," and *aise,* meaning "ease."

malapert. Although it is archaic, *malapert* is listed in dictionaries of the college size and larger. It is made up of two Latin parts: *mal,* for "ill" or "bad" and *apert,* meaning "clever." It means "impudent," "saucy," "pert."

Malaprop is the name of a character in Richard Brinsley Sheridan's comedy *The Rivals.* Mrs. Malaprop's utterances were highlighted by the affected misuse of elegant words, with hilarious results. As another character remarked, "She decks her dull chat with hard words which she don't understand." Incidentally, Sheridan did not have to look far for a name for his character. *Malaprop* is simply an abbreviated form of *malapropos,* a word we took directly from the French phrase *mal à propos.* It means "unsuitable, inappropriate, out of place."

malaria (from the Italian *mala,* meaning "bad," and *aria,* "air") originally meant the fetid and perhaps poisonous air rising from marshlands. The disease, which we now know is spread by the anopheles mosquito, was originally thought to be caused by foul swamp air.

malarkey has been a part of American slang at least since the 1930s. It means pretentious, exaggerated, high-flown language that finally adds up to nothing much at all. It's a latter-day synonym for "baloney" or "bunk."

maltworm is a heavy drinker, especially one who takes on large amounts of beer or ale. You'll find it in Shakespeare's *Henry IV,* Part 1 (Act II, Scene 1), when Gadshill says: "I am joined with . . . none of these mad mustachio purple-hued malt-worms, but with nobility and tranquillity."

mañana is Spanish for "tomorrow," but in English we have given it a meaning with a time element greater than a single day. Anyone who tells you he will do something *mañana* probably told you the same thing yesterday—and will tell you the same tomorrow. It's doubtful that he will ever do it.

Mancunian is a native of Manchester, England. The name comes from the Medieval Latin name for the city, *Mancunium.*

mandarin. Although the official national language of China is called Mandarin Chinese, the word *mandarin* itself is not Chinese. It is taken directly from the Portuguese and eventually can be traced back to the Sanskrit word for sage or counselor, *mantrin.* Originally the term referred to members of the nine highest ranks of bureaucrats in imperial China.

Manhattan/Bronx cocktail. As to the *Manhattan cocktail,* one theory is that it was invented in and named after the Manhattan Club, a men's social and political club in New York City. This theory dates the origin in the 1870s, but the *Dictionary of American English* records its first appearance in 1894. We suspect the earlier origin is more accurate. There is a *Bronx cocktail,* though it's seldom served these days, even in its native borough. It contains gin, orange juice and sometimes vermouth or bitters. Just why Brooklyn, Queens and Staten Island never had cocktails named for them is lost to history. Just possibly the residents of these boroughs knew better than to indulge in such high-octane tipple.

manifest destiny first appeared in an editorial written in 1845 in support of U.S. annexation of Texas. Written by John L. O'Sullivan, it referred to "our *manifest destiny* to overspread the continent allotted by Providence for the free development of our yearly multiplying millions." It was an argument curiously akin to the call of German journalists almost a century later for *Lebensraum,* "space to live in." Something closer to its present-day application can be found in an editorial by James Gordon Bennett in the *New York Herald* in 1865: "It is our *manifest destiny* to lead and rule all nations." More than a century later, there seem to be quite a few nations unwilling to accept Bennett's advice.

Man in the Gray Flannel Suit was inspired by the experience of a talented young writer who just didn't seem to be making the kind of progress he thought he had a right to expect. Finally he went to his superior with his beef. "I can't understand why other fellows who came in here about the same time as I did and who have actually had less copy get into print have been given raises and fancy titles while I get nothing. What am I doing wrong?" His superior told him that his problem was that he just didn't fit the Time, Inc. style. "For instance," he was told, "you're wearing jacket and trousers that not only don't match but clash colorwise. If you want to get ahead, go over to Brooks Brothers and get a three-button gray flannel suit, with a vest, and start to fit the established pattern." It proved to be good advice, for the young man did get the suit, and in due time he got the raise. But he also got a smashingly good book title from the experience. For the young man, who eventually left the Luce empire to pursue a career as a novelist, was Sloan Wilson and his first book took its title from that bit of advice: *The Man in the Gray Flannel Suit.*

man of the cloth was originally a term applied to anyone who wore a uniform or livery in his work. A baker's white jacket and trousers would be called "the baker's cloth." But by the seventeenth century, *man of the cloth* came to be restricted to the clergy and the expression *the cloth* meant clergymen collectively.

Man on Horseback is a term used to characterize a military man who puts himself forward as one chosen by destiny to rescue a nation if only the people will turn all power over to him. The first *Man on Horseback* was a French general in the latter part of the nineteenth century, Georges Ernest Jean Marie Boulanger. Born in 1837, he entered the army before he was twenty and, early on, served his country in far-flung quarters of the globe. Before he was twenty-five—in 1861—he was fighting with the French forces in Cochin-China—the name the French used for Vietnam.

man proposes, but God disposes. This proverb has been a part of English since the appearance of Langland's *The Vision of Piers Plowman* in the fourteenth century. It also appears in *The Imitation of Christ,* ascribed to Thomas à Kempis, published in 1418: *"Homo proponit, sed Deus disponit."*

mansard roof is one designed to provide an attic with a high ceiling. It has two slopes, the upper almost horizontal and the lower nearly vertical. Furthermore, windows in the vertical slope seem to jut out in a very distinctive manner. An odd thing about this roof is that, while it is named after its first deviser, it does not now follow the true spelling of his name, which was Mansart—with a *t.* He was a French architect (1598–1666) and this design for high-atticked roofs was very popular in America during the nineteenth century. To this day there are hundreds in brownstone and other dwellings in New York City and we well recall a somewhat idiotic sport of the early thirties called simply "Mansard!" It required for play at least six youths—preferably three of each sex—an open-top touring car or a roadster with rumble seat, and one or more flasks of potent spirits. The action took the form of driving through the streets of New York gazing fixedly at the rooftops. The first person to spot a *mansard roof* called out "Mansard!" and pointed to it. If the judge (usually the driver) agreed that the identification was accurate, the winner was rewarded with a pull at the flask. Naturally there were many mansard roofs and hence many winners at this featherbrained game.

man's home is his castle. This saying is as old as the basic concepts of English common law, and was stated in this fashion by the first great English jurist, Sir Edward Coke (pronounced COOK): "For a man's house is his castle and one's home is the safest refuge to everyone." Thomas Carlyle, in the nineteenth century, wrote: "My whinstone house my castle is;/I have my own four walls." Cervantes, in *Don Quixote,* wrote: "You are a King by your own Fireside,/As much as any Monarch on his Throne." Incidentally, one of the homeliest and most accurate observations about home is this from Robert Frost: "Home is the place where, when you have to go there, they have to take you in."

mantle of Elijah. When a person succeeds to a position of authority or power, he or she may be said to have assumed the *mantle of Elijah.* The phrase comes from Elijah's symbolic gesture of placing his mantle on the shoulders of Elisha when he named him as his successor (I Kings 19:19).

many-splendored thing. *Love Is a Many-Splendored Thing* was the name of a film and the film was based upon an earlier novel. But the novel took its title from a poem by Francis Thompson, first published in 1913. Titled "The Kingdom of God," it has a verse that ran: "The angels keep their ancient places;/Turn but a stone and start a wing!/'Tis ye, 'tis your estranged faces,/That miss the *many-splendoured thing.*" Note that Thompson, being British, spelled it "splendoured."

maraschino comes from *marasca,* the Italian name for the cherry tree whose fruit is used to make *maraschino* cherries.

March. The third month of the year takes its name from Mars, the Roman god of war.

march to the beat of a different drummer. This expression, often misquoted, appeared first in Thoreau's *Walden,* thus: "If a man does not keep pace with his companions, perhaps it is because he hears a different drummer. Let him step to the music which he hears, however measured or far away."

mare's nest. Actually, there never was such a thing as a *mare's nest* or "horse's nest," as the phrase ran originally. The phrase "find a *mare's nest*" means to happen upon what you think is a great discovery, announce it for all the world to hear—and then find out that your great achievement was no discovery at all. A celebrated instance of finding a *mare's nest* occurred in seventeenth-century England when a noted astronomer, Sir Paul Neal, triumphantly announced that he had discovered an elephant in the moon. It developed that a tiny mouse had crept between the lenses of his telescope —and had been mistaken for an elephant. So celebrated was Sir Paul's blooper that the phrase "you've found an elephant in the moon" was for many years almost as common as "you've found a *mare's nest.*"

By extension, a *mare's nest* is a hoax, either accidental or deliberate. By still further extension, it is now often used to refer to any hopelessly complicated situation.

margarine —properly "oleomargarine"—got its name from a misapplication of the term "margaric acid," a fatty substance in certain animal and vegetable oils. "Margaric" and its first derivative, "margarine," were pronounced "MAR-guh-rin." But by the time *margarine*'s use became widespread, the popular pronunciation of the word had become MAR-juh-rin. In the same fashion the pronounciation of "penicillin" started out as peh-NISS-ih-lin, but soon became pen-ih-SIL-in.

marmalade. There is a wild—and widespread—legend that *marmalade* is a contraction of *Marie malade.* The story goes that when Mary, Queen of Scots, was ill, this orange jam—then quite a rare delicacy—was one of the few things she could eat. This is ridiculous. Applying a French phrase like *Marie malade* (sick Mary) to the breakfast delicacy of a Scottish-born queen requires a really extraordinary imagination. The truth is fairly simple. *Marmalade* came into English from French at about the time of the Norman Conquest. But it can be traced to antiquity, to the Greek *melim-ēlon* (sweet apple). The preserve was originally made of quinces, but British housewives for many centuries have been making it with oranges.

married name. Most women take their husband's surnames at the time of marriage, although there have been exceptions. It all goes back to Roman times, when there were fewer names to go around and as a result, much confusion between the Octavias and Lauras. So when Octavia married Cicero, for example, she became Octavia Ciceronis (Octavia of Cicero). Before long the possessive case ending -*nis* dropped off, and she became simply Octavia Cicero—and that's the way it is today.

marrow (squash). *Marrow* is the British name for squash. In the words of the *American Heritage Dictionary,* it is the variety of squash that has "a very large, elongated greenish fruit."

marshal. The *field marshal* in many European armies is the officer senior in rank to all save the commander in chief—and that means that *marshals* have come a long way since their lowly beginnings in service. The first *marshals* were nothing but keepers of horses, for the name comes from the Old High German word *marah-scalc,* meaning "farrier" or "groom." Napoleon I proudly proclaimed himself Marshal of France and established the baton as symbol of the rank. In reference to his own relatively modest beginnings in the military, the "Little Corporal" is reported to have said, *"Tout soldat Français porte dans sa giberne le baton de maréchal de France"*—"Every French soldier carries a marshal's baton in his knapsack."

martinet. A strict disciplinarian who requires absolute adherence to a rigid set of rules is known as a *martinet.* The first *martinet* was Jean Martinet, a seventeenth-century French army officer who established a kind of military discipline under which even the effete dandies of the court of Louis Quatorze became efficient and disciplined officers. Some sources refer to Martinet as a colonel, others confer on him general's rank. As for us, we don't especially care and, after three centuries, doubt if M. Martinet does either.

martini cocktail comes by its name simply enough—from the name of the maker of one of its two ingredients, vermouth, the firm of Martini & Rossi. When the *martini* was young—about 1890—it was a very different drink from the one we know today. According to barmen's formularies of the period, it was made of one part gin and two parts of sweet (Italian) vermouth. This is very much the same thing you may encounter in British pubs today under the name "gin and it"—the "it" being a contraction of "Italian." Today's *martini* is made with dry (French) vermouth, and the less of it the better, according to connoisseurs. Movie director Alfred Hitchcock's recipe is deservedly famous as the ultimate in very dry *martini* concoctions. He insists upon a well-chilled glass, five jiggers of dry gin stirred with ice, and a bottle of extra-dry vermouth, which he taps lightly against the shaker three times. Then pour and serve.

mascot, which today might be anything from a teddy bear to a full-grown goat or mule, was originally a little sorcerer. And the sorcerer got its name from the French *mascotte,* the mask that sorcerers used to wear.

mashing a button. In one of his presidential press conferences, Lyndon Johnson spoke of *mashing a button,* meaning "to strike or push a button," which led us to inquire into the origin of this unusual expression. *Mash* in the sense of "beat or strike upon" is traced by H. L. Mencken to the Gullah dialect of the Georgia and South Carolina coasts, a dialect that some authorities think is simply an archaic form of English. In the past century, examples of this idiom, perhaps including *mash,* may well have spread throughout the South, even as far as President Johnson's home state of Texas.

Mason-Dixon line was named after its surveyors, Charles Mason and Jeremiah Dixon. It marked the boundary between Pennsylvania and Maryland and was regarded as the demarcation line between North and South in the years leading up to the Civil War.

Masons, Free and Accepted. There is a definite connection between the *Masons,* members of the secret fraternal order, and masons who lay brick. The first members of the *Free and Accepted Masons,* as the society is called, were actual stonemasons. Indeed, students of the order claim to have found many of their secret symbols and passwords chiseled in the stones of medieval cathedrals and other ancient buildings. The society existed in England before the seventeenth century, though tradition says that it goes back to the masons who built the Temple of Solomon.

Masscult is culture at the level of the masses. This term, together with Midcult (which see), was coined in 1965 by Dwight Macdonald, American essayist and social critic.

masthead on a daily newspaper is not, as is commonly believed, the paper's name in large type at the top of page one. The proper name for that is "name plate" or "flag." The *masthead* runs on an inside page, often the editorial page, and carries a smaller version of the name plate, together with names of top executives and editors, the address of the paper and miscellaneous information.

maudlin is generally applied to someone who is tearfully and weakly emotional or sentimental, particularly to one who goes on a crying jag after overimbibing. Its origin, however, is more serious than that. *Maudlin*, when capitalized, is a variant form or corruption of the name Magdalene, and depictions of the resurrection of Christ often show Mary Magdalene with eyes red from weeping.

mausoleum. Many a departed potentate rates a *mausoleum,* but the first and one of the grandest was the edifice erected to shelter the mortal remains of Mausolus, a satrap of Caria, who died in 353 B.C. It was erected at Halicarnassus and was considered one of the Seven Wonders of the (Ancient) World. The shrine was erected at the behest of his widow, Artemisia, but the record is unclear as to whether she, like Mrs. Grant in Grant's tomb, shared it with her departed husband.

mauve decade was roughly the period known more popularly as the Gay Nineties. The expression was coined as the title of a book by a relatively little-known American author, Thomas Beer. It reported on American life at the end of the nineteenth century, with chief emphasis on events from the Chicago World's Fair of 1893 to the Dewey Parade, with Theodore Roosevelt riding up Fifth Avenue at the head of the New York Militia, in 1899. Beer didn't think much of the direction the nation was taking during that period, believing it was deserting the stalwart New England traditions of Emerson, Thoreau and Channing and moving toward a period of "decay and meaningless phrases, 'the nobility of democracy,' 'social purity' and the like." Beer chose his title from a remark by painter James McNeill Whistler: "Mauve is just pink trying to be purple."

mavericks. Referring to unbranded calves on the open range, *mavericks* got their name from an early Texas rancher named Sam Maverick, who either *(a)* rounded up all strays and gave them his own brand or *(b)* let his own calves run unbranded so that many neighboring ranchers branded his cattle with their brands. The story is told both ways, so take your choice.

mavin, more frequently spelled *maven,* is a borrowing from Yiddish. Leo Rosten, in his *Joys of Yiddish,* defines a *mavin* as "an expert, a really knowledgeable person, a good judge of quality, a connoisseur." We first became acquainted with the word when a clever campaign for herring tidbits was launched in New York. Large-space ads proclaimed: "The herring *maven* strikes again!" and showed an empty herring jar.

May. The fifth month of the year takes its name from Maia, the Roman goddess of spring, daughter of Faunus and wife of Vulcan.

May Day, as used in radio communications, is merely the Anglicized spelling of the French phrase *(venez) m'aider,* meaning "(come) help me."

mayoral/gubernatorial. Both words come to us from Latin, but by slightly different routes. "Mayor," from which we get *mayoral,* comes from the Latin *major,* meaning "greater." It was a common title in Caesar's day and came simply enough into English by way of the French *maire.* However, though we have had "governor," usually spelled with the "-our" ending, in English for centuries, its Latin ancestor was *gubernator. Gubernatorial* came directly into English from Late Latin, with no detour through French.

Maypole. The custom of frolicking about a *Maypole* bedecked with multicolored streamers is, except possibly in a few women's colleges, now a thing of the past. Seemingly the most chaste and decorous of the rites of spring, it was not always thus. In fact, the *Maypole* itself was originally a phallic symbol, and in 1644 the Puritans destroyed the famous *Maypole* in the Strand in London in revulsion against the frivolous excesses it represented. At about the same time back in the colonies, Thomas Morton had succeeded in outraging the sensibilities of the proper Bostonians with a *Maypole* erected at Merrymount (now part of Quincy), south of Boston. There he plied the Indians with firewater and such merriment ensued that the horrified Pilgrims twice tore down his *Maypole* and twice sent him back to England. In a state of high indignation, they also burned down his house and confiscated all his property. Morton was a persistent chap, though, and he kept coming back, only to be tossed again into jail. Finally the powers that were gave up on him, decided it was costing them too much to keep him in durance vile, and turned him loose. He achieved revenge of a sort by writing *The New England Canaan of Thomas Morton,* which, while certainly not great literature, was a lot more readable than the average book of the time.

mazuma was originally a Hebrew word, *m'zumon,* which became the Yiddish *mezumen,* and eventually wound up in American English as *mazuma* (or *masuma*), a slang term for money. In the original Hebrew it meant "the ready necessary" and is said to appear in the Talmud.

meat and potatoes means "primary or basic." When you get right down to the *meat and potatoes* issues, you're dealing with what some would call the real nitty-gritty of a problem. The reference is to the fact that, to most American males, *meat and potatoes* constitute the basic elements of a meal.

meeting one's Waterloo. A person who *meets his Waterloo* is one who suffers a crushing defeat—just as Napoleon did in 1815 at *Waterloo,* Belgium, by the forces of Wellington and Blücher.

mega in classical Greek meant simply "big, great." Besides its original meaning in such medical terms as *megadont* (having large teeth) and *megaprosopous* (having a large face), it has also proven useful in other areas of science.

In physics, for example, *megacycle* is one million cycles. In electricity, a resistance of one million ohms is known as a *megohm*. So it's only natural that nuclear physicists, seeking a simple term to measure the most awesome force that man has ever conceived, would reckon the strength of blast of nuclear weapons first in tons, then kilotons (one thousand tons) and finally in *megatons*.

melee/mêlée. If you get involved in a *melee* (or *mêlée*), you are in the midst of a real fracas—a disorderly and widespread hand-to-hand fight. Sometimes what starts out as a quarrel between two men at a bar turns into a *melee* in which few people know whom or why they are fighting. *Mêlée* is a French word when the circumflex and acute accent are used, but most English-speaking people have dropped these marks and use the word in the rough-and-ready way it deserves.

melodrama. The first *melodramas* were more like operas than the melodramas of yesteryear. Complete with song and orchestral music, they were sensational, extravagant and romantic—but not as violent as later ones. Although the *melo-* part of the word comes from the Greek *melos* (song), the entire name *melodrama* was retained long after songs and music were eliminated.

melton cloth, from which many men's overcoats are made, gets its name from Melton Mowbray in Leicestershire, England.

ménage is a household. It usually means the persons who make up a household—the husband, wife, children and whoever else lives there—but it can also include the physical elements of the house and all its contents. It has the same spelling and meaning in French and comes from the Latin *mansio* (house or mansion). *Ménage à trois* is a voguish term for the "eternal triangle" comfortably ensconced under the same roof.

mendacity, duplicity, chicanery and corruption. The morning after Spiro Agnew's resignation, historian Henry Steele Commager appeared on CBS. In the course of the interview he made several general statements about Watergate and the Nixon administration. One phrase seemed to be worth remembering. Here it is: "Never has there been an administration so versed in *mendacity, duplicity, chicanery* and *corruption.*" Mendacity (pronounced men-DASS-ih-tee) means "habitual lying or untruthfulness." It's taken from the Latin *mendax,* meaning "lie," and it has been a part of the English language since the seventeenth century.

Duplicity means deception or double-dealing. This came into the language in Shakespeare's time as a borrowing from a French word of the same meaning, which in turn had come from Latin. It's pronounced doo (or dyoo)-PLISS-ih-tee.

Chicanery (shih-KAYN-er-ee) means deception by trickery, especially, as the dictionary reminds us, "the use of clever but tricky talk or action to deceive or evade, as in legal actions." It, too, has been around since Shakespeare's time and was borrowed from a French word, *chicanerie,* meaning "pettifog." And if there are any among you unfamiliar with "pettifog," be assured that as a verb it merely means "to quibble or deceive."

Corruption really needs no explanation. Unfortunately, examples are so abundant in public life today that it's doubtful that anyone over the age of six remains unaware of the meaning of the word. For the record, though, it comes from the Latin *corruptio,* of the same meaning, and came into the language from the ecclesiastical Latin spoken by medieval churchmen.

mene, mene, tekel, upharsin (pronounced MEE-nih, MEE-nih, TEK-'l, YOO-FAR-sin) were the words Daniel found written on the wall (Daniel 5:25). Translated from the Aramaic, they mean "numbered, numbered, weighed, (and) divided," which Daniel took to mean that God had weighed Belshazzar and his kingdom, found them wanting, and planned their destruction.

menial/mansion have common roots in the Latin word *mansio,* for "house or dwelling." While *mansion* is the more obvious derivative, *menial* wandered through Old French as *meisniée* or *maisnie* and appeared in Anglo-French as *meignal* or *menial* and in Middle English as *meynal* or *menall.* Since a *mansion* is a very large and pretentious dwelling and *menial* is a synonym for "servant," the common root does make sense.

men must garner the fruits of their labors is part of a statement made by Sir Roger Casement, who was either a great Irish patriot or a despicable English traitor, depending on which side you favored at the time of the "troubles" in Ireland. Casement, son of a British army colonel and himself a member of the British consular service, had been knighted for service above and beyond the call of duty to the crown. Notwithstanding, he felt that the cause of Irish independence was his paramount concern after retiring from the consular service. So he raised money for the Irish cause in the United States and then went to Germany in 1914, feeling that "England's difficulty is Ireland's opportunity."

He returned to Ireland via German submarine but was captured before being able to make contact with the Irish nationalists who were planning the Easter insurrection in Dublin. Taken back to England, he was hanged for his crime, but not before writing these lines from his prison cell (June 29, 1916): "Where all your rights become only an accumulated wrong; where men must beg with bated breath for leave to subsist in their own land, to think their own thoughts, to sing their own songs, to garner the fruits of their labors . . . then surely it is braver, a saner and truer thing, to be a rebel in act and deed against such circumstances as these than tamely to accept it as the natural lot of men."

A second possible source is the King James Bible (II Timothy, 2:6) where we find "The husbandman that laboureth must be first partaker of the fruits." The likelihood is great that Casement, perhaps unconsciously, was echoing this Biblical passage.

mercenary/mercy. It would not be accurate to call *mercenary* a derivative of *mercy*, though both words can be traced back to the same Latin root, *merces*, meaning "payment" or "reward." *Mercenary* has come to us almost unchanged from the Latin *mercenarius*, "one who works for wages," especially a soldier who serves a foreign power for pay, as did the Hessians who served under the British flag in the Revolutionary War. *Mercy* came into English by way of French *merci* and has several closely related meanings, of which the most common is the power or disposition to forgive—especially forgiveness in excess of what might be expected.

mercury/mercurial. Mercury in Roman mythology was not only the wing-footed messenger of the gods. He was also the god of commerce, travel, cleverness and thievery. His speed and elusiveness may be the reason why his name was given to the metal *mercury*. The adjective *mercurial* is defined as "having the qualities of both the god and the metal—as shrewd, clever and eloquent as the god and as quick, volatile and changeable as the metal."

meretricious (pronounced mer-uh-TRISH-us) is an adjective meaning "gaudy or deceptively attractive." It has its origin in the Latin *mereri* (to serve for hire) and *meretrix* (a prostitute). Its broader meaning is "tawdry or having false charms." Its noun form is *meretriciousness*.

meringue, a confection made of beaten egg whites and sugar, takes its name from the place of its origin, which was either Mehringen or Mehrinyghem, depending on whether you prefer the German or the Swiss version of the story. Anyhow, the confection came to England by way of France, where *meringues glacées* are notably delicious confections.

Merrie England. England of the Anglo-Saxon period and the Middle Ages was not a very happy place to be, let alone *merrie*. So why this phrase indicating revelry and joyous spirits, as if England were one perpetual Christmastime? The answer is that the word *merrie* originally meant merely "pleasing and delightful," not bubbling over with festive spirits, as it does today. The same earlier meaning is found in the famous expression "the *merry* month of May."

Merry Christmas around the world. One of the country's outstanding language experts, Charles Berlitz, is a mine of information about the different ways in which the various peoples of the world wish each other good fortune and good health at this holiday season. Here are a few examples he has given us.

In Arabia the appropriate greeting is *Milad Said* (Mee-LAHD Sah-EED), while in Norway one says *Gledelig Jul,* pronounced GLED-eh-leeg YOOL.

More familiar to most of us are the Christmas greetings voiced in the countries of Europe. *Joyeux Noël* (zhwah-yeu noh-ell) as the French say; *Buon Natale* (b'wohn nah-TAH-leh) from Italy; and *Froehliche Weihnachten* (FROY-lik-eh vy-NAHCK-ten), the German way of saying *Merry Christmas*.

Further to the north in Finland one says *Hauskaa Joula* (HOW-skah YOH-loo-uh), while in Sweden the greeting runs *God Yul* (gudt yool).

In Holland you would hear *Vrolijk Keerstfeest* (vroh-LYIK kehrst-FEEST), and in Portugal and Brazil it would be *Boas Festas*—BOH-ahs FESS-tas. In Greece one hears perhaps the loveliest-sounding syllables of all —*Kalla Xristouyena* (KAH-lah Krêes-TOO-yen-ah).

The Japanese, too, have a characteristic greeting for this holiday season. With them it goes *Kurisu Masu Wo Iwaimasu,* which is pronounced kur-EE-SOO MAH-SOO woh ee-waah-EE-mah-soo. Across the straits in Korea, the phrase runs *Chuck-syong-tahn,* while in those parts of Indonesia where this Christian holy day is still celebrated, they say *Selamat hari natal.* Nearer to our shores lies Hawaii, and there the words are *Mele Kalikimaka* (MEH-leh kah-lee-kee-MAH-kah).

mess, which today has the rather repulsive meaning of "a sloppy, confused mixture; a muddle," came to us from the Latin *missus* (a portion of food or a course at a meal). This was also its earliest meaning in English, as we know from the Biblical quotation: "Esau sold his birthright for a *mess* of pottage." Gradually *mess* came to mean any group of persons who regularly eat together—especially such groups as officers or enlisted men who by regulation are required to dine as a unit. The idea of *mess* as a muddle or hodgepodge came much later than these two earlier meanings, perhaps from the popular usage "to mix up a *mess* of food."

mestizo. A *mestizo* is a person of mixed Spanish or Portugese and American Indian ancestry. The word is derived from an Old Spanish word meaning "of mixed race."

Mexican standoff. So far as we know, a standoff is a standoff, whether it's Mexican, Norwegian or Indonesian. In other words, a draw is a draw and nationality has nothing to do with the actual situation. However, national pride has a great deal to do with the creation of derogatory epithets aimed at neighboring countries, especially those between which commercial or other rivalry may exist. Perhaps the classic case of such coinage of racially derogatory epithets was the rash of expressions coined by the English to put down their Dutch rivals during the eighteenth century, when commercial competition between the two nations was at its peak. That gave us "Dutch courage" (gained from the bottle), "Dutch treat" (pay for yourself), "Dutch defense" (surrender) and "do the Dutch" (commit suicide).

Something of the same attitude may be found in parts of the United States bordering on Mexico. The expression "Mexican athlete" is used to describe an athlete who goes out for the team but doesn't make it. A "Mexican promotion" is one in which an employee gets a fancy new title —but no increase in pay. And a "Mexican breakfast" consists of a cigarette and a glass of water. So a *Mexican standoff* is a situation from which nothing at all can be expected.

Micawber of Dickens's *David Copperfield* has become the prototype of the eternal optimist, the dreamer of great and everlastingly unfulfilled dreams, who moves through life with the absolute certainty that "something is bound to turn up"—though it seldom or never does.

Mickey/Mickey Finn is popularly but erroneously believed to be a potion of "knockout drops" designed to render a bar patron unconscious. Actually it is a potion surreptitiously added to a bar patron's drink to induce diarrhea. A moment's reflection will prove the point. No bar owner wants an unconscious man on his hands. He does want to render an objectionable patron so uncomfortable that he will depart the premises abruptly and, he hopes, permanently. Wentworth and Flexner in their *Dictionary of American Slang* claim that the original *Mickey Finn* was a laxative for horses.

Mickey Mouse rules. In the very early 1970s the armed services moved to dispense with a lot of traditional routine—predawn reveille, "butch" haircuts and the like. We're indebted to Martin C. Mooney of Arlington, Virginia, for explaining the origin of one of the phrases most commonly used to describe these traditions. "I'm sure that many readers will be asking for the origin of the phrase *Mickey Mouse* used in reference to certain petty rules recently lifted by Adm. Zumwalt, Chief of Naval Operations," he wrote. "It is known by many sailors that when a seaman recruit, in boot camp, cannot keep up on his military bearing and know-how, he is 'set back' and sometimes reindoctrinated in a special company. This company is known as the 'Military Indoctrination Center' or 'M.I.C.' Hence *Mickey Mouse*—a phrase every recruit fears until he's on that train or plane homeward bound."

microphone is made from the prefix *micro* (from Greek *mikros,* "small") and *phone* (Greek for "sound"), so it would seem to refer to a device to make sound smaller rather than to amplify it. But the prefix *micro* has several meanings. The first, "little or exceptionally small," is the most common. However, *micro* may also mean "enlarging what is small." Its most common appearance in this sense is probably in the word *microscope,* and it is thus that we find it in *microphone*—a perfectly accurate name for the device whose chief use is to intensify weak sounds.

Midcult denotes an intermediate state of culture, with elements of both high and mass culture. Like Masscult (which see), this was coined in 1965 by Dwight Macdonald in conscious imitation of "middlebrow."

mien (pronounced MEEN) denotes external appearance or bearing. Synonymous with *demeanor,* it probably has common origin in the Latin verb *minari,* which originally meant "to threaten" but later, as *minare,* meant "to lead." It is closer in meaning today to the French *mine* (look or air) and the German *Miene.* "She bore herself with truly aristocratic *mien.*"

migraine headaches must have been plaguing mankind for quite some time, considering the source of the word. Painful in the extreme and often accompanied by dizziness and nausea, a *migraine* headache is usually confined to one side of the head. Hence its name, from the Greek *hemikrania,* meaning "half of the skull" (*hemi-,* "half," and *kranion,* "skull").

military tattoo is an elaborately formal and impressive ceremony involving massed bands and marching by torchlight. It had a more common origin, though, for it started with pub-crawling by British soldiers in the Netherlands around 1700. In those days of relatively civilized warfare, it was common practice for both armies to withdraw at sundown to previously prepared rest areas. During the early evening hours the soldiers would hie themselves to nearby pubs—with the result that many of them would not hear or would choose to ignore the 9:30 P.M. summons back to camp (First Post). So searching parties, bearing torches, were sent out to round up the stragglers. Dutch barkeeps seeing the torchlights would call: "Tap toe"—meaning "Shut the bar" or "Turn off the taps." In time, "tap toe" became *tattoo* and the ceremony became a formalized spectacle.

militate (pronounced MIL-ih-tayt), derived from the Latin *militare,* "to serve as a soldier," originally meant to fight against in military fashion. Its meaning has changed over the centuries and *militate* now means "to operate or work," and is almost invariably followed by "against." Its subject should be circumstances, situation or facts. "The heavy rain *militated* against a speedy trip."

milk of human kindness is from Shakespeare's *Macbeth* (Act I, Scene 5). Lady Macbeth is talking to herself about her husband and her plans for his future, plans which—as we all recall—required a certain amount of ruthlessness to carry out. She rightly thinks him lacking in the necessary firmness and says: "Yet do I fear thy nature./It is too full of the *milk of human kindness*/To catch the nearest way. Thou wouldst be great/ . . . but without/The illness should attend it." The expression has been used thousands of times since, of course. The instance we like best concerns a British bishop who spent a day with another bishop of insufferable piety and sanctimoniousness. When they parted, the bishop remarked to a friend: "I have often heard of the *milk of human kindness,* but this is the first time I have met the cow."

milliner. Creators of ladies' headgear are seldom referred to as *milliners* these days, but this remains, nonetheless, the generic term for members of the breed. It is actually a corruption of "Milaner" and dates to the time when Milan was famous for the elegance of its laces and ribbons, both important in the making of women's bonnets in times past.

millionaire. Some very strange stories of word origins sometimes crop up in the writings of authors who do not bother to check their facts. One book on Wall Street makes this statement: "The term 'millionaire' was not coined until Pierre Lorillard, the cigar and snuff maker, died in 1843. At the time, an obituary writer, sweating out a deadline, minted the phrase and it passed into the language." A likely story! The obit writer may indeed have been sweating, though most of the ones we know are pretty cool characters. But he certainly didn't need to "mint" *millionaire*. According to the *Oxford Dictionary*, it had been appearing in print at least as early as 1826. What's more, it is a direct borrowing from the French *millionnaire* and was even spelled that way originally in English. Later it dropped one *n* to become the word we know today.

mills of God grind slowly is from Longfellow's translation of the poem "Retribution" by the German poet Von Logau: "Though the *mills of God grind slowly,* yet they grind exceeding small;/Though with patience He stands waiting, with exactness He grinds all."

mimeograph (from Greek *mimos,* "imitator," and *graphein,* "to write") was coined as the trademark of a particular process for duplicating written or typewritten matter. *Mimeograph* has been allowed to lose its trademark status and is now in the public domain. As a generic term, it may now be written with a small initial letter: *mimeograph.*

mind-boggling. *Boggle,* meaning "to startle or frighten," has been around since Shakespeare's time. However, the particular phrase *mind-boggling* is fairly recent. A *"mind-boggling* experience" is one that startles, astounds or stupefies a person. Incidentally, "boggle" is closely related to "bogle," which is none other than the well-known bogy man or goblin.

mind your p's and q's is most often used in advice to the young, warning them to be on their best behavior, especially to be careful of their words and actions. There are a variety of explanations of this expression, which dates back many centuries. The least likely version has it that the *p* refers to the jacket once worn by men and now surviving only in the navy pea jacket. In the sixteenth and seventeenth centuries men often wore their hair bound into queues or pigtails, often powdered. Thus a wife might tell her husband to *mind your p and q,* meaning to keep his queue from soiling the collar of his pea jacket. A more likely and more lusty explanation takes us to the pubs of the same period. There it was the practice to record a drinker's tab by chalking it on a blackboard under two headings: *Q* for quart and *P* for pint. Obviously each tosspot had best *mind his p's and q's* or the bill would greatly favor the house. Colorful though that explanation is, we fear it has to take a back seat to the simple, obvious explanation. Try writing the small *p* and the small *q* side by side. Note that the letters are identical save that the bulges are reversed. So the odds are that the expression *mind your p's and q's* originated with generations of writing teachers admonishing their pupils to special care in forming these two letters.

mingy. In an article by Dwight Macdonald on the 1968 election of Richard Nixon, he speaks of liberals taking "a resounding pratfall, but the least damaging within the *mingy* limits of their political ideas." *Mingy* is a fairly rare dialect term, meaning "niggardly, stingy or mean." "Pratfall" is a borrowing from showbiz language. It means a resounding fall on one's buttocks.

minion. Here is an example of a word whose meaning has changed considerably since its entry into English. In French, as *mignon,* it meant "darling" and was derived from *mignot,* meaning "dainty" or "wanton." Originally, in English, it carried much the same idea, meaning a servile, obsequious, fawning person dependent—as courtiers always were—on the favor of a king or ranking noble. Nowadays the sense has broadened to mean any subordinate, especially one with official or quasi-official status, such as a deputy or agent of a federal or state agency. The term is perhaps most commonly met in the phrase *"minion* of the law," a journalistic cliché for "policeman."

minister. Most of us have been reared to respect our *ministers* as men of God to whom at least token deference is due. So it comes as a bit of a shock to learn that the original meaning of *minister* is merely "attendant" or "servant." Indeed, in its original use the *minister* was simply the opposite of the "magister," the master. So how did the word *minister* come to be applied to the shepherd of the ecclesiastical flock? Simply because he is considered to be the servant of his congregation. Similarly, a minister of state, even the prime minister, is considered to be one serving the king or queen.

minstrel. The first *minstrels* were not unlike the first ministers (which see) in that they were servants of one sort or another. Indeed, the word *minstrel* comes from the same Latin root as "minister." However, the *minstrel* early on became a very special sort of court attendant, specifically charged with providing entertainment by song and story to the nobles.

mint. The place where money is coined gets its name quite properly from the Latin word for money, *moneta,* which, in turn, came from an epithet for Juno (Moneta), in whose house the original Roman *mint* was located. The Old English form was *mynet* and, by Middle English, it was *mynt.*

minutes. Although *minute* as a unit of time and *minutes* meaning "record of a meeting" come from the same Latin root, the senses in which they are used today are not related. The Latin word *minutus* meant "very little, small or tiny." Thus *minute* became the symbol for a very small unit of time.

But *minutus* also gave us a verb, *minute*—now no longer used—which meant to take down a record in very small handwriting to be rewritten later in a larger, more careful and complete version. This was called "engrossing"—a term still in use to describe the special large distinct writing sometimes used on legal documents. So the *minutes* of a meeting originally meant a record transcribed in tiny handwriting. Now, of course, it means the succinct official record of a meeting—no matter how it has been transcribed.

mirabile dictu/mirabile visu. *Mirabile dictu* (mih-rah-bih-leh DIK-too) is the intellectuals' version of "Believe it or not!" It's a Latin phrase, common in the epic poetry of Vergil, and literally means "wonderful to tell." There's a parallel term, *mirabile visu* (mih-rah-bih-leh WEE-soo), meaning "wonderful to behold."

mishmash/mishmosh. In the course of a political campaign some years ago, Pennsylvania's Governor William Scranton used the word *mishmash,* pronouncing it as spelled. This prompted comedian Groucho Marx to write him that he should change the pronunciation to rhyme with *slosh,* especially if he planned to campaign in Jewish neighborhoods. The next time he used the word, Scranton followed Marx's advice.

Now we'll take second billing to no one in our admiration for Groucho. After all, he's the creator of that immortal conspiratorial phrase "Let's go drop an eave." But in this case he's as wrong as he can be. *Mishmash* was part of the language two centuries before New York City (where *mishmosh* started) was even thought of. The *Oxford Dictionary* records *mishmash* as appearing in print in 1450—five full centuries before Groucho began giving pronunciation lessons to Scranton. And the pronunciation through all those centuries was mish-MASH.

As to Groucho's Johnny-come-lately mish-MOSH, this is a regional variation originating in Manhattan, Brooklyn and the Bronx and still commonly heard there. Many writers, reflecting Jewish or Yiddish speech patterns, actually spell it *mishmosh.* Damon Runyon once wrote of "the daily blats [papers] which made a big *mishmosh* of gamblers' welching on debts," and Billy Rose wrote of a foreign film thus: "a *mishmosh* from France called Passionnelle." So if Groucho wants to popularize his pronunciation, let him adopt the appropriate spelling. As to Scranton, the way of the politician is clear. In the future he should speak of "hodgepodge."

mitigate comes from the two Latin words *mitis* (mild) and *agere* (do), and in today's usage means "to make less severe or to give some excuse for," as in *"mitigating* circumstances."

Miznerisms. Wilson Mizner was a very remarkable chap. Primarily a press agent—as those fellows used to be called before they became "public relations counselors"—he and his brother Addison were important figures in the Florida land boom of the 1920s. Indeed, the two of them are credited with having given Palm Beach the characteristic Florida Moorish architectural style that still marks the town. However, Mizner's lasting fame is due to some of his remarks, which are still widely quoted decades after his death. "When you steal from one author," said he, "it's plagiarism. If you steal from many, it's research." And: "A good listener is not only popular everywhere, but after a while he gets to know something." Then there's the remark often credited to the late Walter Winchell but actually coined by Mizner: "Be nice to people on your way up because you'll meet them on your way down." And he once put down an objectionable fellow with this: "You're just a mouse studying to be a rat." Most memorable, perhaps, is a thought that we all can profit from: "Life's a tough proposition—and the first hundred years are the hardest."

mob is such a marvelously compact, expressive word that it sees daily service in the headlines of almost every paper, especially in times when *mobs* gather daily in all parts of the world. In view of its great popularity, it's almost amusing to note the long struggle *mob* had to gain acceptance by the self-anointed arbiters of language. Originally it was part of a Latin phrase, *mobile vulgus*—"excited or fickle crowd." Gradually it became shortened, during the sixteenth century, to *mobile* and eventually, in the late seventeenth century, to *mob*. But how the purists did howl at this "vulgarization" of the mother tongue. Richard Steele wrote in his magazine *The Tatler:* "I have done my utmost for some years past to stop the progress of 'mob' and 'banter,' but have been plainly borne down by numbers, and betrayed by those who promised to assist me."

mobile/stabile. *Mobile,* descriptive of a kind of sculpture having parts that move, especially in response to air currents, was coined by Alexander Calder, the American sculptor who created the genre. Calder was also the creator of the term *stabile,* which is an abstract sculpture of wire, sheet metal and sometimes wood that does not move.

modus vivendi/modus operandi. The first phrase (pronounced MOH-dus vih-VEN-dy) comes unchanged (except for the pronunciation of the last syllable) from Latin and means "manner of living"—especially a temporary arrangement pending final settlement of a dispute. The second phrase is pronounced MOH-dus op-uh-RAN-dy and means "manner or mode of working." It is often used in the sense of "procedure" in such a sentence as: "The director set up a *modus operandi* to be followed by all employees in fulfilling the contract."

mohair is a generic term (from the Arabic word *mukhayyar*) for the hair of the angora goat and fabric made from this hair. It's well thought of in fabric circles because it will outwear wool and is nearly three times as strong.

Mohave/Mojave. Who put the *j* in *Mojave,* as in Mojave Desert and River? Certainly not the Indians. The word originally came from two Yuman Indian words, *hamok,* meaning "three," and *avi,* meaning "mountain." Notice that *j* is nowhere to be found. However, mapmakers and dictionary editors all give *Mojave* as the preferred spelling, doubtless because this spelling was the choice of the government bureau which passes on spellings of place names. If you feel strongly that it should be *Mohave* rather than *Mojave,* you can find a whole county of people who agree with you if you will just go to Arizona. The name of the county? *Mohave,* of course.

Molly Maguires. The original *Molly Maguires,* who got the name because they sometimes disguised themselves as women, were a terrorist group

organized in Ireland in 1843 to prevent eviction of tenants from property
by the agents of absentee landlords. Their methods were direct and forceful
and they got quite a name for themselves—so much so that, half a century
later, the same name was taken by a group of Irish-American miners in
eastern Pennsylvania. What you think of these later *Molly Maguires* depends pretty much on where your sympathies lie in the labor-management
struggles of the period. To the bosses, *Molly Maguires* were "notorious for
criminal activities in the Pennsylvania coal region from 1865 to 1876" and
were guilty of "terrible crimes." To the mineworkers, they were valiant
fighters against unjust oppression, a society "which opposed oppressive
industrial and social conditions, sometimes with physical force." Whatever
the verdict, they now belong to history.

Molotov cocktail. The *Molotov cocktail,* which was used as an antitank
weapon during World War II, is a simple but effective device. It consists
of a bottle filled with a flammable fluid such as gasoline and covered with
a saturated rag. The rag is ignited and the bottle thrown against the side
of a tank or other target, thereupon bursting and spreading flames over the
target. The first *Molotov cocktails* were devised by the Finns for use against
the Russian invaders in the winter of 1939–1940. They got their name
because V. M. Molotov, Soviet minister of foreign affairs, was to the Finns
the hated symbol of Russian aggression.

Monday morning quarterback. Even an old Rugger Blue should be able to
fathom the meaning of this phrase. It's simply that anyone can be an expert
on strategy after the game is over. A *Monday morning quarterback* is a
chap who is quick to second-guess the man who is really doing the job.

Money is the root of all evil is a frequent misquotation of "For the love of
money is the root of all evil." The source is the Bible (I Timothy 6:10).

monicker, meaning "name," is not American slang. The word, which is sometimes spelled *monaker* and *moniker,* comes from the jargon of the British
underworld and has been used for at least a hundred years. Originally it
meant a mark left by a tramp on a building or fence to indicate to fellow
vagrants that he had been there. Each "knight of the road" developed his
own distinctive mark. Thus, a tramp's *monicker* identified him as readily
as his signature would and gradually the meaning developed of *monicker*
as one's real name—contrasted with one's alias. The word probably was
originally a corruption of *monogram.*

monitor. In the early days of radio broadcasting, *monitors* were engineers
whose job it was to check the quality of transmission and accuracy of
frequency of the broadcast stations. Similarly, wireless operators, especially those at sea, *monitored* the frequency used by distress calls so that
they could act upon or pass along any warnings of trouble. During World
War II, *monitor* stations were set up to check the propaganda content of

enemy broadcasts. All these fit in with the origin of the word, which can be found in the past participle of the Latin *monere,* meaning "to warn."

monkey jacket/monkey suit, slang terms for a uniform or a man's dress jacket, came into use because of the resemblance of such garments to the jackets worn by trained monkeys. The term *monkey jacket* was earlier applied to the short, tight jackets which used to be worn by sailors.

Monroe effect. The *Wall Street Journal* reported on an unexpected hazard encountered by pedestrians trying to navigate across the broad plazas surrounding the newer skyscrapers when the winds are high. For reasons not yet entirely clear to physicists, ordinary gusts take on gale force in these plazas, frequently blowing people off their feet and, at very least, tossing women's skirts high above their intended length. It's this latter characteristic that led engineers to choose the term *Monroe effect* to describe the phenomenon. The reference is to the celebrated publicity photo of Marilyn Monroe in the film *The Seven Year Itch,* in which she was shown standing on a subway grating just as a train passed beneath, blowing her skirt high in the air.

Montevideo is the capital of Uruguay, a Spanish-speaking nation. While the name of the capital comes from the Latin *montem,* "mountain," and *video,* "I see," the word is a Spanish one.

month of Sundays is a figurative term meaning "practically never." To those who would take it literally, it would mean thirty Sundays, not just four.

mooncussers got their name because they cussed the moon, and they cussed the moon for its interference with their trade—luring sailing ships to destruction on rocky shores. On the blackest, stormiest nights, the *mooncusser* would go out to a beach or promontory, light a bright oil lamp and wave it back and forth in hopes that a passing ship would see it, assume it was another ship—and follow the light to destruction on the shore. In the event of a shipwreck, the *mooncusser* would take what he wished from the cargo, as salvage. According to legend, there were *mooncursers* in England centuries ago. These charmers would offer to guide passing wayfarers to their destination by the light of flares or lanterns. Where they actually took them, of course, was to places where their partners in crime lay in waiting to rob the unwary traveler.

moon is made of green cheese is a very old proverb going back almost as far as the beginnings of our English language as we know it today. Its first appearance in English is in the works of Sir Thomas More (1478–1535). Shortly afterward it appeared in a collection of proverbs collected by Thomas Heywood: "The moone is made of a greene cheese"—and Heywood makes it pretty clear that anyone who believes this is a fool.

Heywood didn't claim to have created all his proverbs. He merely collected popular sayings and polished them up a bit, much as Benjamin Franklin did centuries later in *Poor Richard's Almanac.* Some people think that the French humorist François Rabelais, who was a contemporary of Heywood's, said this one first—but chances are they both merely wrote down an expression that had long been spoken by ordinary people.

By the way, *green* in this proverb does not refer to the color of the moon. A "green" cheese is one that is new, and has not had time to age properly. In the earliest days of cheesemaking, such a new cheese often resembled the moon in shape and coloring.

moonlighting. Remember when the word *moonlight* symbolized romance, when "Moonlight and Roses" was a favorite theme song of young lovers the country over? Well, in the world of business, *moonlight* now has a much more humdrum and unromantic meaning. Specifically, *moonlighting* is the term applied to the increasingly common practice of one person's holding down two jobs. More and more heads of families are finding it hard to make ends meet on the salary earned on one job. So they take on another part-time or full-time job to pad out the family income.

moonshine. The general belief is that *moonshine* as a name for illegally made whiskey originated because the distillers did their work under cover of night so as not to be detected by revenue agents. However, there is evidence in a dictionary published in London by the Rev. John Ash in 1785 that the word *moonshine* already existed and referred to liquor illegally smuggled by night from France into England. The booze involved was usually brandy and colorless, so that in appearance it would not have been unlike the "white lightning" of America's *moonshine* stills.

moot/much mooted. The verb *to moot* is not as familiar as the phrase *moot point,* but in essence the phrase *much mooted* simply means "much discussed." The expression comes from the Anglo-Saxon words *mot* (to meet) and *gemot* (a meeting). The earliest Anglo-Saxon parliament was known as the *Witenagemot,* the meeting of wise men. Since debates on current issues were commonplace in such assemblies, the word *moot* gradually came to mean "open for discussion or debate." Even today in many law schools the pupils and professors try theoretical cases in *moot courts* where, so far as is possible, the circumstances of an actual trial are duplicated. There's one big difference between *moot courts* and real courts, though: in the *moot court* the defendant, no matter what his alleged degree of guilt, always goes free.

morganatic marriage. A widespread belief is that *morganatic* in the term *morganatic marriage,* used to refer to a marriage of wealthy people, refers to people descended from, or as rich as, J. P. Morgan. Not at all. Indeed, the term was widely in vogue long before J. P. Morgan made his first million. The phrase comes from a Latin phrase, *matrimonium ad morganaticam,* and refers to the ancient custom by which a husband gives his bride a "morning gift" on the day after the ceremony. In a *morganatic marriage* the bride forswears all interest in her husband's worldly possessions and agrees that the children of the marriage will also not share in his estate. So the "morning gift" represents just about all she can ever expect to get of her husband's wealth.

moron was coined as a precise scientific term. Dr. Henry H. Goddard proposed it in 1910 to the American Association for the Study of the Feeble-minded and it was promptly adopted as the official designation for a mentally deficient person whose mental age is between eight and twelve years and whose Intelligence Quotient is below 75. *Moron* is the highest rating in mental deficiency, above "imbecile" and "idiot." But the word has long since been accepted in the popular tongue as simply synonymous with "fool." Since it was coined from the neuter form of the Greek word *moros,* meaning "foolish," this popular or colloquial meaning is really very close to the original Greek.

Morris chair was named after William Morris—not this William Morris, to be sure, but the famous English poet, typophile, Fabian socialist and furniture designer. That earlier William Morris would have a lasting reputation even had he never designed the chair or written a line of poetry, because his edition of Chaucer—the Kelmscott Chaucer—is universally admired as one of the greatest achievements of the graphic arts.

A distinguished authority on that William Morris, Professor Morris Bishop of Cornell, inclines to believe that this William Morris must be related to that William Morris, especially since we both are partly of Welsh descent. It's an interesting theory and one of these days we may find free time to check it out.

Morris dances were originally "Moorish" dances, brought to England from Spain about 1350. Adapted from Moorish military dances, they became very, very British, with the dancers miming various roles from the Robin Hood legends.

most unkindest cut of all. "This was the *most unkindest cut of all*" is from Mark Antony's speech to the Romans after the assassination of Julius Caesar and is found in Act III, Scene 2 of Shakespeare's play about the Roman emperor. The line remains immortal, despite the double superlative, *most unkindest.* Shakespeare, greatest of English poets and dramatists, was also one of the first. English as a language was still very young, and many of the conventions that we now call "rules" had not been established. That task was performed later by generations of schoolteachers, grammarians and dictionary editors. So the rich and glorious language of Shakespeare is studded with expressions that today's teacher of freshman English would mark with a red pencil.

motel. Gerald Carson, the distinguished American writer and historian, and we embarked on a joint search for the origin of the word *motel.* Mr. Carson, author of *Country Store* and many another book about America's past, wrote to ask if we could tell him when the word was coined—and by whom.

It was a good question, and one for which we had no ready answer. It seemed reasonable to date the origin of the word to the decade of the 1930s, for it was not recorded in either the Webster Unabridged (1934) or the *Merriam Collegiate* (1936) though it was appearing in print by 1940.

An appeal to readers of our column finally brought the complete and authoritative answer from Dr. Doris E. King, professor of history at North Carolina State University in Raleigh. She reported that the word "was first used in 1925 in connection with an establishment opened in San Luis Obispo, California. The name was coined by the architect and the place was first called and advertised as a *Mo-tel Inn.* The original *motel* consisted of a front administration building and a group of little cottages with a garage attached to each.

"The man who seemingly made *motels* respectable was a hotelman in California who built swank *motels* with full hotel facilities and services in Fresno and Sacramento, the El Rancho *motels.* Both the San Luis Obispo *Mo-tel* and El Rancho *motels* were Spanish Mission in architectural style, but the latter had rooms side by side in a ranch-style building which had a porch and a parking place in front of each door.

"Of course, in the East *motels* were known as tourist camps or courts until after World War II, when the word finally came into its own. As you can imagine, the hotel associations fought the newcomers to their industry tooth and nail, but when a few farsighted hotelmen went into the *motel* business, it suddenly became respectable as well as profitable—and the grand rush was on."

And how did Dr. King know all this? Well, she happened to have written an M.A. thesis on the subject and to be the author of a Harvard University Press book called *The Palaces of the Public, a History of American Hotels.*

Mother Goose. Like most of the rhymes themselves, the precise origin of the term *Mother Goose* is hard to pin down. One likely story, though, is that a Boston bookseller published a collection of nursery rhymes in 1719, calling it *Songs for the Nursery or Mother Goose's Melodies for Children.* The kicker on this story is that he named it after his mother-in-law, a Mrs. Goose, because her unmelodic singing drove him to distraction.

Mother's Day is the occasion when we all join in tribute to the leading ladies in our lives. It may be interesting to see where this celebration had its origin. According to Iona and Peter Opie's delightful *Lore and Language of Schoolchildren,* "A Miss Anna Jarvis of Philadelphia, who lost her mother on May 9, 1906, determined that a day should be set aside to honor motherhood. By forming a league of supporters, by persistent lobbying, and by what amounted to emotional blackmail (anyone who opposed her did not love his mother), Miss Jarvis quickly had her way. After one year's campaign Philadelphia observed her day; and on May 10, 1913, the House of Representatives solemnly passed a resolution making the second Sunday in May a national holiday, dedicated to the memory of 'the best mother in the world, your mother!' "

Actually, a somewhat similar tradition had existed in England for more than three centuries. The fourth Sunday in Lent was known as "Mothering Sunday" and apprentices and daughters "in service" were permitted by their masters to return home for the day. It was their custom to bring a gift, often a bunch of posies or a small cake. Sometimes, also, they showed their affection for their mother by doing the housework on this day. As a result of what some Britons call the "American Occupation" of Britain during World War II, the ancient tradition of Mothering Sunday became confused with *Mother's Day*. Today the Yankee version, complete with *Mother's Day* cards and specially inscribed cakes and boxes of candy, is observed throughout Great Britain.

Mother Shipton's prophecy. *Mother Shipton* was first heard from in 1641, when an article published in England claimed she had lived in the sixteenth century and accurately predicted the deaths of Wolsey, Cromwell and others not even living in her lifetime. From time to time thereafter enterprising publishers would update the dear lady and, as recently as 1862, a new edition of her life was published in which she was credited with predicting steam engines, the telegraph and other modern inventions. The "seeress" was also credited with predicting the end of the world in 1881, so it's safe to say that her foresight was slightly flawed.

mountain dew. The tradition of illicit distilling of spirits was once as strong in the Scottish Highlands as it is in the mountain regions of Kentucky and Tennessee even today. The product of our moonshiners is variously known as white mule, stump liquor, squirrel whiskey or Kentucky fire. But gleanings from Highland stills were always known simply as *mountain dew*. The classic version was Duggan's dew of Kirkintilloch, the liquid lightning which triggered many a Glencannon gala in the famous stories by Guy Gilpatric.

mountebank is a term for any quack or charlatan, but it originally referred to one specific kind. It is a combination of two Italian words, *montare* (mount) and *banco* (bench), and referred to a person who mounted a bench or platform, attracted crowds with jokes, stories and tricks, and then proceeded to sell quack medicines.

MOUSE. The full flowering of acronyms came during and after World War II with *radar* (Radio Detection and Ranging), *snafu* (situation normal, all fouled up) and *fubar* (fouled up beyond all recognition). Industry and government agencies soon added their contributions to the lists of acronyms. Space agencies have been using acronymic designations for all manner and variety of space "hardware," as multimillion-dollar rockets are known in the lingo of engineers. But perhaps the least felicitous acronym ever coined was among them. It was the label for the first planned

Minimum Orbital Unmanned Satellite of Earth—*MOUSE*.

Perhaps even more ludicrous is the word invented for the signal used, presumably, at Cape Kennedy when it's necessary to destroy a missile in flight. The system was named Electronic Ground Automatic Destruct System and the signal word, believe it or not—EGADS.

moxie. If you have ever lived for long in the New England states, you will surely be familiar with the soft drink *Moxie,* which has been popular in this area since 1884. Somewhat similar to root beer and cola drinks, it has a characteristic tartness which accounts for its popularity. In sports parlance, *moxie* has come to mean courage of a rather high order. It has also the secondary slang meaning of "nerve or gall." Just how a respected trademarked name came to acquire these slang connotations is a puzzle. One theory is that the original *Moxie* was so bitter that you had to have plenty of courage to drink the stuff.

Mr. and Mrs. *Mr.* is pretty obviously a logical abbreviation for *Mister,* being made up of the first and last letters of that title and form of address. If you were to follow logic, *Mrs.* would be an abbreviation for *Mistress,* a notion that might be a little shocking to those who translate "mistress" to mean only "paramour." Actually, *Mrs.* started out as an abbreviation for *Mistress* at a time when that word was reserved as a title and form of address for a married woman. (It was always capitalized then, of course.) Somewhere along the way, the abbreviation came to be pronounced "missis," and the original *mistress* lost its capitalization and its respectability except in such phrases as *mistress of the house.*

much is given, much is required is taken from John F. Kennedy's first and only inaugural address: "For of those to whom *much is given, much is required.*" The sentiment echoes these lines from Luke (12:48): "For unto whomsoever *much is given,* of him shall be *much required:* and to whom men have committed much, of him they will ask the more."

muckrakers were a group of American writers in the first decade of this century who were so affronted by the political corruption rampant in American cities and the venality characteristic of some sectors of American industry that they wrote many articles and a few books exposing the corruption as they saw it. Among the most notable of the muckrakers were Lincoln Steffens, whose *The Shame of the Cities* remains a classic of political invective, and Ida M. Tarbell, whose *History of the Standard Oil Company* was instrumental in bringing far-ranging reforms and legislation limiting the power of business monopolies. Magazines now long dead, like *Collier's, McClure's* and the *American Magazine,* published many articles by Steffens, Tarbell and such others as Ray Stannard Baker, Finley Peter Dunne ("Mr. Dooley"), Norman Hapgood and William Allen White. Theodore Roosevelt, no friend of the muckrakers because he thought their charges too sweeping and, in some cases, untrue, was the man who gave them their name. In 1906 he drew a parallel between them and "The Man with a Muck-rake"—a character in Bunyan's *Pilgrim's Progress* who was so intent on raking up muck that he didn't observe that a heavenly halo was being held over his head.

mugg. New York City must take the responsibility for the term *to mugg,* which is the base of the forms *mugged* and *mugger.* The *Dictionary of American Underworld Slang,* whose compilation was directed by two long-term convicts and a prison chaplain, gives a graphic definition of the verb *to mugg.* First meaning, according to these indisputable authorities, is "to assault by crunching the victim's head or throat in an arm-lock." (It also has the underworld meaning of "to rob with any degree of force, with or without weapons.") The second meaning is an earlier one, supported by Mencken's *The American Language:* "to photograph, especially for the Criminal Bureau of Investigation."

Mencken also places the term as originating in New York, describing the process of *mugging* as one in which one stickup man grabs "the victim around the neck from behind and chokes him while the other goes through his pockets. . . . This is called *mugging* in New York but *yoking* in most other places," he says. The urge for a lowly pun about no yoking is almost too great. We will quell it by pointing out that *mug* (with one *g*) has long been slang in America and England for the human face or, as a verb, "to grimace." It comes from Gypsy language, perhaps having its origin in *mukha,* Sanskrit for "face."

Mulligan. You're standing ready to tee off, you control the backswing nicely, chin in, eyes on the ball, the clubhead comes down, smacks the ball neatly —and off it spins into an unplayable lie just a few feet from the tee. What's the worst thing that can happen then? That's right. Your opponent says, "Too bad. Take a *Mulligan.*" That's the crowning humiliation, the condescension of a rival giving you a free shot when yours went bad.

Why is this hypocritical largesse called a *Mulligan?* Well, we didn't know either, so we asked the question in our column, and George Dressler, president of the Pennsylvania Public Golfers Association, sent this reply: "I feel sure that when I played as a youngster some thirty years ago, there was another term used to indicate that the player could replay the stroke without penalty. However, time has erased the earlier word and the increased use of *Mulligan* has probably replaced it forever. Milton Gross, in his book, *Eighteen Holes in My Head,* reported one theory of its origin, tracing it back to the saloons of yesteryear. According to him, in family-type saloons there was always a bottle called *Mulligan* on the bar. It was as standard as pretzels are today—and it was free. The basic ingredients were hot pepper seeds and water. If you were insane enough, you might swish a few drops of this concoction into your beer. It ate out your liver, stomach, bladder and finally your heart. In the psychological sense, this is precisely what happens on the tee when you accept a *Mulligan.*"

mulligrubs means "bad temper or sulkiness," so a person with a case of the *mulligrubs* would be a "sourpuss." It's a dialect term, heard, according to Harold Wentworth's *American Dialect Dictionary,* chiefly in the area running from Tennessee north to Indiana and Pennsylvania.

mumbo jumbo is generally used to mean any kind of gibberish or meaningless combination of words or syllables. Originally, however, it was a word in Mandingo *(ma-ma-gyo-mbo)* meaning "magician who makes the troubled spirits of ancestors go away." It referred to the belief of some Mandingo peoples in the western Sudan that a high priest called the *Mumbo Jumbo* had the power to protect his village from evil spirits.

mum's the word, meaning "Keep what I told you a secret," goes back to Shakespeare's *Henry IV,* Part 2: "Seal your lips and give no words but— mum."

Munchausen syndrome. Some people seem to like doctors and hospitals so much that they pretend illness in order to be admitted as patients. The name for this "sickness of the mind" is *Munchausen syndrome,* from the name of the famed Baron von Munchausen, the greatest liar since Ananias. *Syndrome,* of course, merely means "a number of symptoms which, taken together, characterize a disease."

mundane (pronounced mun-DAYN) denotes that which is of the world, worldly as opposed to spiritual or fanciful. It comes from the Latin *mundus* (world). "Now that the ballet has finished, let's turn our thoughts to more *mundane* matters—such as how we can find a taxi at this hour."

Murphy bed. Before "convertible" sofas came into vogue, the *Murphy bed* was a commonplace in small apartments. It was simply a bed which folded or swung into a closet for concealment during the hours when it was not in use. It was designed by an American named William Lawrence Murphy (1876–1950), whose other contributions to social advancement, if any, have gone unrecorded. Various forms of folding beds (but not ones that disappeared into closets) had been displayed at the Philadelphia Centennial Exposition (1876), and General Washington used a portable folding cot during the Revolution.

Murphy's Laws. A symposium by mail on the identity of Murphy, whose laws are better known than he, was started by the presentation as a graduation present of a box with *Murphy's Laws* engraved on it. They were:

1. Nothing is as easy as it looks.
2. Everything will take longer than you think it will.
3. If anything can go wrong, sometime it will.

The third law is well known to most scientists and technicians and has been quoted times without number. However, its creator seems to be as elusive as the famed "Kilroy," who was "here"—that is, everywhere—in World War II but never actually was seen.

Many readers offered suggestions as to the identity of Murphy. Robert

T. Nagler of Prairie du Sac, Wisconsin, offered these comments: *"Murphy's Laws* were not propounded by Murphy but by another man of the same name. (First Law: Nothing is as easy as it looks.) Although I have spent many years at the task, I have been able to discover nothing about the life and career of this great philosopher. (Second Law: Everything will take longer than you think)."

Then Gary M. Klauber of Silver Spring, Maryland, weighed in with this account of the origin of the laws: "One day a teacher named Murphy wanted to demonstrate the laws of probability to his math class. He had thirty of his students spread peanut butter on slices of bread, then toss the bread into the air to see if half would fall on the dry side and half on the buttered side. As it turned out, twenty-nine of the slices landed peanut-butter side on the floor, while the thirtieth stuck to the ceiling. Hence *Murphy's Law*—if anything can possibly go wrong, it will."

It remained for Andrew McCowan of Frederick, Maryland, to suggest that perhaps the inventor of the law was not the apocryphal Murphy at all but Queen Victoria's distinguished adviser and prime minister, Benjamin Disraeli, who once wrote: "What we anticipate seldom occurs, what we least expect generally happens."

In any event, Mr. Nagler, who opened this symposium, had the last word, as befits a man who can record Murphy's end. "I regret to say," he wrote, "that Murphy took a stroll along a country road one evening, being careful to walk on the left side of the road to face approaching traffic. He was struck and killed by an English driver who had just arrived in this country."

musical chairs is used figuratively to describe a change—such as a reshuffling of the President's cabinet—in which the people remain the same but their titles are different. It began with a parlor game in which people walked to music around a row of empty chairs, with one chair fewer than the number of players. At a signal, all would rush for chairs, and of course, one would be left standing and thus eliminated from the game.

music has charms to soothe the savage breast comes from a play, *Love for Love,* which William ,Congreve wrote in 1695. For some reason, it is generally misquoted as "music hath charms. . ."

mustache (the preferred spelling nowadays) comes from the Italian *mustacchio* by way of French *moustache.* Further back, in Greek, the word was *mystax* and referred to the upper lip or adornments growing there.

mustang. This wild horse of the Western plains, famed in lore, legend and, latterly, in motorcar advertising, gets its name from the fact that it's of mixed and indeterminate breed. The word *mustang* comes from the Mexican Spanish *mestengo,* meaning "stray animal," from *mesta* (a meeting of owners of stray animals). Indeed, the word can be traced even further back to the Medieval Latin phrase *animalia mixta,* referring to wild or stray animals that became mixed with and attached to a grazier's herd. One wonders whether the geniuses in Detroit realized, when they labeled their sporty car the *Mustang,* that they were—etymologically speaking—calling it a half-breed stray.

My name is Legion. *Legion* comes from the Latin verb *legio, legere,* "to gather or levy troops." Thus a collection of troops came to be called a "legion" and, in the Roman army, it usually consisted of from 3,000 to 6,000 foot soldiers and 100 to 200 cavalrymen. By extension it came to mean any considerable body of people, and the expression *our name is legion* comes from Mark 5:9: "And he asked him, What is thy name? And he answered, saying, *My name is Legion:* for we are many."

myrmidon. The first *Myrmidons* were loyal Thessalian followers of Achilles who fought at his side during the Trojan War. Nowadays the word has changed from upper to lower case and, as *myrmidon,* it now means—in Webster's pithy phrase—"a loyal follower, one who unquestioningly and pitilessly executes orders."

naïve. The central idea of *naïve* is simple, unaffected and unsophisticated innocence. It comes from the Latin *nativus,* from which we also get the word "native." As used by the Romans, it designated simple, untutored farm folk as distinguished from the cultivated, sophisticated dwellers in the capital of the empire.

naked truth, meaning truth plain and unadorned, goes back to an old fable. Truth and Falsehood went swimming together in a stream. Falsehood came out of the water first and dressed in Truth's clothing. Truth, not wanting to don the garments of Falsehood, remained naked.

name is mud. *Mud* in the sense of scandalous or defamatory charges goes back to a time well before the Civil War. In fact, there was an expression, "the mud press," to describe newspapers that besmirch people's reputations by throwing mud, as long ago as 1846, according to the *Dictionary of Americanisms.*

names for the baby—and where they come from. Wondering what to name the baby? Well, that's a problem all parents face from time to time. So, in our customary spirit of helpfulness, we'll run over some common and some unusual names and tell you where they came from and what they originally meant.

The most common girl's name in all Christian countries is *Mary,* because of the universal veneration of the mother of Christ. Did you know, though, that in its original Hebrew form it meant "bitterness or rebellion"? In the Bible you will find (Ruth 1:20) "Call me not *Naomi* [delight], call me *Mara* [bitterness]: for the Almighty hath dealt very bitterly with me."

This meaning has, except for its appearance in the Bible, long been forgotten.

Mary, likewise, has given rise to countless variants—*Maria, Marie, Marlene, Marilyn* (always knew those two had something in common!), *Manon, Moira, Molly* and many more. *Maribel* is simply a blend of *Mary* and the French *belle* (beautiful).

Looking for a more unusual name? How about one of the variations of *Ann*—a name almost as common as *Mary. Anitra, Annabelle, Nancy, Nanine, Nina, Nanon* and *Nannette* are only a few you can choose from. They all come from the same Hebrew word meaning "grace."

How about *Gretchen,* from the German for "little pearl"? *Maureen,* "the dark." *Melissa,* "the honeybee," from the Greek legend about the goddess Melissa, who first taught mortals the use of honey. Or *Roxana* or *Roxane,* from the Persian phrase for "dawn of the day."

Then there are the names derived from the Hebrew word for "lily"— *Sue, Susan, Susannah, Suzette* and so on. Or *Tabitha,* from the Aramaic word for "gazelle." Or *Eileen, Helen, Eleanor* or *Ellen*—all of them from the Greek word for "light."

And now a sampling of boy's names.

John is perhaps the most popular of boys' names—and with good reason, since it comes from a Hebrew word meaning "the gracious gift of the Lord." *Robert* is a name of Teutonic origin—appearing in German as *Ruprecht,* it means "of brightly shining fame," and has any number of variants—*Rob, Bobby, Rab* and *Robin,* to name a few.

Looking for something a little more off the beaten track? Well, how about *Reuben?* Admittedly this name fell into disfavor when the nickname "Rube" came to be synonymous with the stock hayseed farmer in old-time vaudeville. But all that has changed; today's farmer with his mechanized equipment and city comforts is anything but a hayseed. So why not restore the name *Reuben* to its one-time popularity? Few, if any, boys' names have as appropriate a meaning, for *Reuben* was the exclamation uttered by Leah when her eldest son was born (Genesis 29). It means simply: "Behold, a son!"

Or how about *Maximilian,* "the greatest." *Luther,* "famous warrior." *Luke* or *Lucas,* from the Latin word *lux,* meaning "light." *Sylvester,* "the forest dweller." Nor should we forget *David,* also from the Hebrew, and meaning "beloved one."

Nassau is a golf match in which the winner of the first nine holes wins a point or whatever was wagered. The winner of the second nine holes similarly scores a point or wins a wager, and a third point goes to the overall winner of all eighteen holes. *Nassau* takes its name from the capital city of the Bahama Islands, where it originated.

nation of shopkeepers. This is Great Britain, so labeled in derision by Napoleon. He took the epithet from Adam Smith, who wrote in his *Wealth of*

Nations: "To found a great empire for the sole purpose of raising up a people of customers may at first sight appear a project fit only for a *nation of shopkeepers.*" Napoleon might well have had occasion to paraphrase a famous remark of Winston Churchill: "Some shopkeepers!"

natter is a British dialect term which is making its way into American English. It originally meant "to fret or nag," but now, in the words of Webster's *Third International,* it has the sense of "to talk a great deal but say little —to chatter on." It seems to us a useful addition to the language, just right for describing the actions of people who "approach every new problem with an open mouth."

nature comes from the almost identical Latin word *natura,* which, in turn, comes from *natus* (born or produced). Thus it means "the essential character or qualities of a person or thing—what one is born with." Among its other basic meanings is the concept of scenery, including plants and animals, in their original state—or just as they were born.

navel orange got its name from the fact that this kind of orange has at one end a depression somewhat resembling the human navel.

nebby is an item from Scottish dialect. It means "nosy or prying" and comes from the fact that *neb* is a pointed object, like a bird's bill.

Nebuchadnezzar. "*Nebuchadnezzar* was the King of Babylon—Shadrach, Meshach and Abednego," runs the famous Negro spiritual. According to the Biblical source of the story (Daniel 3), the last-named trio refused to worship the golden idol built at the command of *Nebuchadnezzar,* were cast into a fiery furnace at his command, but miraculously emerged without harm thanks to the intervention of an angel of the Lord. According to less emotional historians, *Nebuchadnezzar* was one of the greatest of Babylonian kings, conquered Jerusalem on two occasions, carrying the Jews into captivity the second time (582 B.C.), invaded Egypt, took Tyre after a thirteen-year siege, built the Hanging Gardens of Babylon, one of the Seven Wonders of the (Ancient) World, and accomplished all sorts of other prodigies.

nebulous (pronounced NEB-yoo-luss) gets its meaning from the noun *nebula,* which is a mass of luminous gases in the sky, or a group of stars so far away that they cannot be distinguished and appear as a cloud. *Nebulous* thus has the meaning of "not clear, figuratively speaking; uncertain, indefinite, vague or obscure."

needle in a haystack is a lot older than Shakespeare and it was originally "a needle in a bottle of hay"—"bottle" being an early form of "bundle." The expression has been popular through the centuries because it gives a clear and precise picture of an almost impossible task. For the record, the first example of this idea in print was in the works of St. Thomas More in 1532: "To seek out one line in his bookes would be to go look [for] a needle in a meadow."

neither fish nor fowl nor good red herring (which sometimes also appears as "neither fish nor flesh nor good red herring") goes back at least as far as the Middle Ages. At that time the three chief classes of society (aside from nobility, a class by itself) were the clergy, lay people generally and paupers. Fish was food suitable to the clergy. Fowl (or flesh) was food appropriate for the mass of the common people. Red herring was food fit only for paupers. So something that was *neither fish nor fowl nor good red herring* would be suitable for no one. Nowadays the phrase is often used to characterize a plan or idea that is so vague, nobody can make anything of it.

neither hide nor hair. Meaning "absolutely nothing," this phrase probably came from the language of huntsmen. A hunter reporting a fruitless day might well report that he had seen *neither hide nor hair* of any game, referring to such smooth-hided beasts as bison or moose and to any of the much more common hair-coated beasts.

neither snow, nor rain, nor heat . . . For half a century or more the main Post Office building in New York City has trumpeted this proud boast from its chiseled frieze: "Neither snow, nor rain, nor heat, nor gloom of night stays these couriers from the swift completion of their appointed rounds." It's a quotation that these days is usually quoted in jest, but nevertheless there it stands. Its author is given as Herodotus, the ancient Greek historian generally called the "father of history." On at least one occasion it has been argued that the motto was dreamed up by an architect and attributed to Herodotus. However, the Penguin Classics edition of Herodotus's *The Histories* contains this: "Nothing stops these couriers from covering their allotted stage in the quickest possible time—neither snow, rain, heat, nor darkness." Allowing for a little freedom in the translation, that strikes us as pretty close to the inscription on the Post Office.

Nelson's blood was the name given by British sailors to their daily ration of grog—rum and water—discontinued by the British navy in 1970 after being a tradition for more than two hundred years. There's a story behind that expression, as you may well imagine. Admiral Horatio Nelson, England's greatest naval hero, scored his masterly triumph over the French and Spanish fleets in 1805 in the battle of Cape Trafalgar—and he gave his own life as part of the price of victory. Since modern embalming techniques were then unknown, the hero's body was put in a keg of rum to preserve it on the trip back to England. And that's how the rum ration—which had been an item of regular issue for forty-five years before Nelson's death—was renamed *Nelson's blood.*

nemesis. One often sees such sentences as "the previously undefeated team met its nemesis in the last game of the season." In this sense *nemesis* means unbeatable rival—but it was not always thus. The original *Nemesis* was the Greek goddess of retributive justice or vengeance. Indeed, her name came from the Greek word for retribution. While in theory a *nemesis* may dole out good fortune as well as bad, its use today is usually in the latter sense.

neologism is simply a "new word," a fresh coinage. It comes from the Greek *neos* (new) and *logos* (word).

nephew comes from the French *neveu,* and even though the word came over at the time of the Norman Conquest, the British haven't yet seen fit to make their pronunciation conform to the English spelling. So you'll still hear "NEV-yoo" very commonly in Britain, though the American preference is overwhelmingly for "NEF-yoo."

nepotism. The word used to describe the process by which officeholders place members of their immediate families in offices under them is known as *nepotism,* from the Latin *nepos* (nephew or grandson). In the Middle Ages, rulers of the Church were often thought to give special preference to their nephews in making appointments to office. "Nephew" in such cases was often a euphemism for "bastard."

nerd is a fairly new slang coinage. It means pretty much the same as the earlier "square" or "not hip." A *nerd* is defined as "an undesirable or unpleasant person, especially one who is not in the know."

nest egg. Poultry farmers formerly placed a porcelain or other fake egg in a hen's nest to encourage it to lay more eggs. From this came the sense of *nest egg* to mean a small sum of money set aside presumably to encourage the making of more.

nester was a term used derogatorily by cattle ranchers of the Old West to describe homesteaders or any other kind of farmer settling down on grazing land.

never give a sucker an even break. There seems to be some dispute as to whether Wilson Mizner, flamboyant press agent of the 1920s, or someone else actually created this expression. Clifton Fadiman, in *The American Treasury,* says it was coined by E. F. Albee, the great vaudeville impresario of the time, and Bartlett's *Quotations* agrees. However, Stevenson's *Home Book of Quotations* says that the immortal line was first uttered by W. C. Fields in the play *Poppy* in 1923. The play was written by Dorothy Donnelly, but the line was apparently ad-libbed by Fields, and no less an authority than Helen Hayes says she is sure he coined it. So we guess the conclusion must be that no matter who said it first, the immortal W. C. Fields made it famous.

New Deal/Fair Deal/New Frontier/Great Society. Some wit said before the 1968 election: "Roosevelt gave us the *New Deal,* Truman gave us the *Fair Deal,* but Johnson gave us the Ordeal."

Actually, of course, Johnson gave us what he termed the *Great Society.* Interestingly enough, he first tried out the phrase in a speech at the University of Michigan on May 22, 1964, and the text of the speech does not show the phrase to be capitalized. It reads: "The *great society* is not a safe harbor. . . . The great society is a place where men are more concerned with the quality of their goals than the quantity of their goods."

By January 4, 1965, he had adapted the phrase to his "State of the Union" address and added capitals. "The *Great Society* asks not how much, but how good; not only how to create wealth but how to use it; not only how fast we are going, but where we are headed. It proposes as the first test for a nation: the quality of its people."

His predecessor, John F. Kennedy, who gave us the *New Frontier,* did not capitalize the phrase that was to be the symbol of his administration. In his speech accepting the Democratic presidential nomination on July 16, 1960, he said: "We stand today on the edge of a *new frontier*—the frontier of the 1960s—a frontier of unknown opportunities and perils—a frontier of unfulfilled hopes and threats."

Dwight D. Eisenhower used *The Great Crusade* as his campaign slogan in the election of 1952.

Harry Truman had been President for nearly three years before he spoke of a *fair deal*—and then it was not campaign oratory, for he had already been reelected. On January 5, 1949, in his "State of the Union" message, he said: "Every segment of our population and every individual have a right to expect from our government a *fair deal.*"

Franklin Roosevelt said in a speech to the 1932 Democratic Convention, which had just nominated him as its presidential candidate: "I pledge you, I pledge myself, to a *new deal* for the American people."

newly rich. Two terms—both borrowed from French but both perfectly at home in English—*parvenu* and *nouveau riche,* mean a person who has suddenly risen to wealth but does not conform to the customs of the class he now belongs to.

news. One of the most prevalent and erroneous stories of the origin of a word —what linguists call a "folk etymology"—is that the word *news* is coined from the first letters of the points of the compass. Apparently the story got its start from the practice of some newspapers, especially those named the *Globe,* of putting a replica of the globe—complete with major compass points, N, E, W and S—on the masthead of the paper. Actually *news*— originally spelled *newes,* by the way—has been part of our language since the Norman Conquest and appears to be a translation of the French *nouvelles,* of the same meaning. As a matter of fact, the Latin *nova*—"those things that are new"—had exactly the same meaning. So, for that matter, did the Greek *neos.*

But this pat little story dies hard and we're certain that—though it couldn't be further from the truth—it will continue to be passed by word of mouth from generation to generation. Many years ago British children had an amusing bit of doggerel which doubtless helped popularize the legend: "*News* is conveyed by letter, word or mouth/And comes to us from North, East, West and South."

next to closing is an expression from the jargon of old-time vaudeville. It occurs in a popular song, "Charade," from the motion picture of the same title. The lyric runs: "Oh, what a hit we made./We were on *next to closing,*" and the question arises as to why that position on a vaudeville bill would constitute a "hit." In the ancient days of the Keith Vaudeville Circuit in the East, Gus Sun Time and Fox-Poli in the West, when eight acts of vaudeville made up a complete show, the prized spot was *next to closing* and it was always reserved for the star of the bill—George M. Cohan, Fred Allen or, to get closer to our time, Eddie Cantor or Jack Benny. The logic is obvious, if you think about it for a minute. The first six acts—acrobats, animal acts, secondary comics and the like—served to warm up the audience for the star. After he was finished, the closing act served simply to "play off" the audience—get them out of the theater.

nicety (NICE-uh-tee), like *nice,* has traveled far from the meaning of their common root, the Latin *nescire* (to be ignorant). Also like *nice,* it has many present-day meanings. Most of the meanings of *nicety* have an element of delicacy and minuteness. A *nicety* can be a minute distinction; exactness in treatment or management; delicacy or accuracy of perception; fastidiousness or acts in good taste.

nicknames have been common in English-speaking countries for many centuries. Back in Anglo-Saxon times, surnames were unknown and *nicknames* were frequently added to a person's name to help identify him. So you would have names like Long John or Barefoot Bill. These were first called *ekenames*—the *eke* meaning "also or added." Through a fairly routine linguistic change, "an *ekename*" became "a *nekename*" and eventually "a *nickname.*" In the same way "an apron" was originally "a napron" and "an adder" was first "a nadder."

   Nicknames didn't start in England, though. They were fairly common in ancient Greece and Rome, especially when used as affectionate terms for children. The Greeks had a word *hupokorisma,* meaning "calling by endearing names." We have even borrowed this word into English, so if you want to impress people you can talk about "hypocorisms," instead of "nicknames." One word of warning, though. "Hypocorism" is not the easiest word in the world to pronounce. Here's how it goes: hih-POK-uh-ris-um.

nick of time. This goes back many centuries before the computer age, when accounts and scores were kept on notched sticks of wood, called "tallies." In a contest—soccer, for instance—the tally stick would be nicked each time one side scored. When a last-minute score brought victory to one team, that nick was called the *nick in time.*

   The wooden tallies, by the way, were a very important part of the official bookkeeping of the British government for many centuries. Records were made of sums loaned to the government and the tallies were notched as each repayment was made. This practice was discontinued in 1826 and the frugal lawmakers decided to use the old wooden tallies to stoke the fires in the stoves in the House of Lords.

When this explanation appeared in our newspaper column, it brought an indignant complaint that soccer wasn't even invented until the nineteenth century, so how could ancients have been notching scores for a game that didn't exist? Well, it's a fact that rules for "association football," as soccer is properly named, were not codified until 1863. But—and it's a mighty big *but*—these rules merely "brought uniformity to a sport that had existed in diverse forms for many centuries." The words are those of the *Encyclopedia International*—an authoritative source, even if a chap named William Morris was the executive editor of it. In fact, the encyclopedia notes that the game in various forms was known in ancient Greece and in China, where they probably ran the score up on an abacus.

nicotine. The name of the drug found in tobacco comes from Jean Nicot, a French ambassador to Portugal. M. Nicot was presented with some seeds of tobacco brought from newly discovered America by Portuguese sailors. In 1560 he planted them in France, introduced tobacco to his native land and thus achieved fame.

nifty was a popular slang expression about the time that George M. Cohan, the Yankee Doodle Boy, staged his first flag-waving extravaganza. It's probably just a shortened form of "magnificent." However, Bret Harte, the short-story writer, claimed it was short for *Magnificat.* That's a little more elegant, but the first theory is probably sounder.

nigger. The *Oxford Dictionary* traces *nigger* to 1786, but it is almost certainly much older than that. It appears as early as 1700 in Samuel Sewall's *Diary,* spelled with a single *g*—as "niger." Ultimately, of course, it is a variant form and pronunciation of "Negro," a word which goes back to the Latin word *niger,* for "black." It is usually regarded as a disrespectful and derogatory term, though some claim that Joseph Conrad did not use it in this sense in his novel *The Nigger of the Narcissus.* However, as a leading black educator said to us many years ago: "The white man may not intend *nigger* to be derogatory—but to the black man it is always derogatory and demeaning."

nightmare. The *mare* in *nightmare* has nothing at all to do with a female horse. It comes from the Anglo-Saxon word *mare,* which meant "incubus," and an incubus was an evil spirit or monster which sat or lay on one's breast during sleep. Often in the Middle Ages, this demon was called the "night-hag." Nowadays a *nightmare* has come to mean any kind of frightening dream.

Nike. The *Nike* missile takes its name from that of the Greek goddess of Victory. It's pronounced NY-kee.

Nile of America was the name given to the Mississippi in the early years of the nineteenth century, and several cities and towns along the river were given Egyptian names, such as Karnak, Thebes and Cairo. (The last, by the way, is pronounced KAY-roh, not KY-roh.) Some think that the way it all began is that farmers in northern Illinois were struck by a severe drought and migrated south, where they found much more fertile soil. The migration, seeming to parallel that in the Bible, was called a "journey into Egypt." George R. Stewart, in his admirable book *American Place Names,* notes that such place names as Cairo "show the early 19th-century enthusiasm for exotic names, suggestive of grandeur."

nimrod. With the coming of fall and the hunting season, the sports pages always carry pictures of hunters returning with their kill and the headlines refer to them as *nimrods.* The reference is to Nimrod, grandson of Noah (Genesis 10:8–10), "a mighty hunter before the Lord."

nip (of whiskey) comes from a Dutch word, *nippertje,* which first appeared in English around 1690 as *nipperkin,* meaning a small flask or container holding less than a half pint. Gradually it was shortened to *nip* and the quantity shrunk also, so that now a *nip* is no more than an ounce or two.

nip and tuck. There are a very considerable number of theories about the origin of this expression, which means "closely contested or neck-and-neck": "It was *nip and tuck* whether the car or the train would reach the crossing first." Some authorities claim that the expression comes from tucking in an infant ("little nipper"?), but this seems much too tame to us. Still another word man, the late Charles Earle Funk, fantasied an elaborate theory based on the speculation that the expression really ought to be "rip and tuck," and said it had to do with ripping cloth and then tucking it together when making a patchwork quilt. Still pretty tame, say we.

So we note that *tuck* is an archaic name for a dueler's rapier (from *estock,* "thrusting sword," in Old French) and surely, to this day, duelers and other swordsmen speak of "nipping" their opponents. So we deduce that *nip and tuck* comes from the language of dueling or fencing and means that two opponents are very neatly matched.

Whatever the ultimate source, *nip and tuck* has always been a mighty popular term in these United States and, as Henry L. Mencken is our witness (*The American Language,* Supp. II, 534), there is or was in Texas a "surrealist community" named Nip and Tuck, which Mencken groups with the likes of Hog Eye, Black Ankle, Hot Coffee, Gourd Neck, Social Circle and—our own particular favorite—Wham, Louisiana.

nippity-tuck. Harold Wentworth's admirable *American Dialect Dictionary* records *nippity-tuck* as being widely heard in western Indiana, western North Carolina and upper New York State. That's a pretty wide distribution, so the likelihood is that it appears in other regional dialects as well. It means "very nearly even" and would occur in such a sentence as "the race went very *nippity-tuck.* "

Nittany Lions are not a new breed of cat, but the mountain lion (or cougar) which symbolizes the athletic teams of Pennsylvania State University. The practical—and undoubtedly true—explanation of the name is that Mount Nittany, a prominent landmark which can be seen from the Penn State campus, gave her her name.

Much more enchanting—though fanciful—is a bit of folklore sent us by a Pittsburgh correspondent. It seems that a Frenchman named Boyer fell in love with the daughter of an Indian chief, a gal named Nit-a-nee. Their romance was frowned on by Papa, with predictable results. Boyer was thrown into the waters of Penn's Cave and the Indians posted guard to be sure he couldn't get out of the only exit to the cave. He drowned, but according to legend, visitors to the cave can still hear the ghostly call— presumably with a French accent—"Nita-nee, Nita-nee!"

nitty-gritty means the basic elements of a matter, especially of a serious problem or challenge; the harsh truth. "Get down to the *nitty-gritty!*" It seems to be a borrowing from black slang and is probably a reduplication of "grit" and "gritty."

nix. This simple little word has quite a history. Meaning "no" or "stop," it comes from the German *nichts* (nothing), and ultimately from the Old High German *niwiht,* also meaning "nothing." There's still another *nix,* this one derived from Old High German *nihhus,* which is a water sprite, half fish and half human.

nixie. In any discussion of Christmas mail problems, post office officials often use the word *nixie.* The dictionary will tell you that a *nixie* is a "female nix"—which isn't much help, since a "nix" is defined as a goblin. Can it be that the Postal Service is blaming delays on leprechauns and mischievous little people? Without much doubt, gremlins do affect mail deliveries during holiday periods, else we'd never have those recurring stories about Christmas cards being delivered a year late. But the *nixies* referred to by the postal officials are not the little people of folk legend. These *nixies* are simply pieces of mail which are undeliverable, usually because of faulty addresses.

N.M.I. simply stands for "no middle initial." This book, for example, is written by William (N.M.I.) Morris and his wife, Mary D. Morris (who does have a middle initial). A somewhat similar, though less common, abbreviation is *I.O.,* for "initial(s) only." One of our former Presidents might be listed Harry S (I.O.) Truman, since the *S* doesn't stand for any middle name. A simpler way to write this is to regard the *S* as a middle name in itself and drop the period. Thus: Harry S Truman.

Nob Hill. San Francisco's *Nob Hill* traces its name to the fabled courts of Kubla Khan. It is derived, in fact, from the language of the ancient Mogul Empire of India. Before the tragic fire of 1906, the wealthiest of San Francisco's aristocrats—many of whom had made their fortunes in trade with the Far East—built magnificent homes on the steep hill overlooking the bay. So posh was the area that it soon became known as *Nabob Hill.* And a *nabob* (from the Hindustani *navah*) was originally a district ruler under the old Mogul regime. Later the word was applied to non-natives (English and Americans, chiefly) who went to India and became fabulously rich. So *Nabob Hill* it became, in the lingo of San Franciscans, only to be shortened to *Nob Hill* even before the terrible fire which wiped out the sumptuous homes that gave it its name.

noble names for ignoble items. As you well know, the Earl of Sandwich gave his name to perhaps the most ubiquitous item on the nation's bill of fare. There have been a few other names for common objects taken from names of former members of Britain's House of Lords. *Raglan,* as in raglan sleeves, is one of them. Also *Cardigan.* Here are a few more.

The twelfth Earl of Derby gave his name to the race which is still run annually at Epsom Downs, England. Our *Kentucky Derby* was named after it and thus, once removed, after the earl himself. Derby did not, however, give his name to the item of men's headgear known in this country as the *derby.* Back in Blighty that's known as a *bowler.*

Then there was the second Earl of Spencer, whose name comes down to us as the name for a short jacket, usually made of wool and worn by either men or women.

The really smashing contributor, though, was the Earl of Chesterfield, a nineteenth-century noble who managed to impress his name on a man's velvet-collared topcoat, a kind of heavily stuffed sofa with upright ends— and an American cigarette. This was not, incidentally, the Earl of Chester-field whose name has become synonymous with elegance and whose *Letters to His Son* are still widely read. That earl was an eighteenth-century figure.

noble science is one of the many euphemisms for the "manly art of self-defense" or fisticuffs.

noblesse oblige (pronounced noh-BLESS oh-BLEEJH) is the concept that persons of high social rank have an obligation to behave in a noble fashion to others less fortunate than they. It translates from the French as "nobility obliges," and today, when there are not many persons with the noble ranks of old, it is used mainly in speaking of the generosity of the rich to charity. With their resources, they can afford to exercise *noblesse oblige,* particularly if it is tax deductible.

noctiphile is a term referring to "night people"—those who claim to function better at night. They do their best work then, and their thought processes are at a peak of efficiency during the nighttime hours. Some years ago we worked on a book with one of the most complete "night people" we have ever known. He was Freling Foster and readers with long memories will recall that he contributed a sprightly column of odd and unusual facts to *Collier's* magazine. It was called "Keeping Up with the World." Foster flatly refused to make an appointment for any purpose whatever before 3 P.M. When he did show up, he was always pale, as only a man who never sees sunlight can be pale. Not surprisingly—for he was a fascinating chap with a fund of offbeat information—he was a great favorite on nighttime radio talk shows.

All of which is by way of background for Freling Foster's word to describe people, like himself, who function best during the nighttime hours. *Noctiphile* is based on the Latin *nox, noctis,* meaning "night," and the Greek *philos,* "love." There are some purists who contend that you can't coin a word by using elements of two ancient languages—that you must always blend two Greek roots or two Latin roots, never one Greek and one Latin. But our feeling is that what was good enough for Foster is fine with us. So *noctiphile* it is.

noctiphobia. A person afraid of night and darkness is a victim of *noctiphobia.* Roots of the word are found in the Latin *noctis* (night) and the Greek *phobos* (fear).

noggin. The experts who write dictionaries label the word *noggin* as "origin unknown." However, there are some things we do know about the word, and from them we may make a guess about how it came to mean "head." The word *noggin,* meaning "small mug or cup," is very old—about 350 years old, in fact. But it wasn't until about 1880 that it began to mean "head," and at first it was used only in expressions where it meant a head that was the object of beating or punching—in remarks like: "I'll give you a real sock on the *noggin.* " Now here's the theory of how a small cup came to mean a head. The idea is that a drink served in a very small glass would have a strong "punch" to it. Also *noggin* might be related to "knock" or "knocking" (forget the *k,* just think of the sound), and thus the contents of this small glass could knock somebody, just as a blow to the *noggin* would.

no host. In many parts of our not-so-wild West today, what Easterners call a "Dutch treat" lunch or dinner is called a *no host* affair. The expression is different, but the meaning the same. Everybody pays for his own portion and there's *no host* to pick up the tab.

noisome (pronounced NOY-sum), though similar in appearance to "noise" and "noisy," has nothing in common with them in terms of meaning or origin. *Noisome* appeared in Middle English as *noyesum* and stems from the same root as the word "annoy," which was the Latin *in odio* (in aversion). Its present meaning is that of being unwholesome and harmful to health. It also means offensive to the smell or the other senses.

no man was ever written down but by himself. This sentiment was first uttered by Dr. Samuel Johnson: "Depend upon it, *no man was ever written down but by himself.* "

nom de guerre. Literally "name of war," this French term has been anglicized to mean any fictitious name, especially a "cover" name adopted while involved in one particular activity. Originally all French soldiers adopted an assumed name when entering military service.

nom de plume. Literally "name of the pen," this French term has been taken into English as meaning "pseudonym." Mark Twain was the *nom de plume* of Samuel Clemens.

Nome (Alaska). According to George Stimpson, whose *Book About a Thousand Things* is one of the most fascinating collections of oddities in print: "Nome was originally called 'Anvil City.' The present name was suggested by Cape Nome, near which the town is situated. The cape itself was named in this manner: when a chart of the Alaskan Coast was being prepared by the British ship Herald, it was observed that this point had no name. This was indicated by '? Name,' meaning that the name was unknown. A draftsman carelessly copied it as 'Cape Name,' but the 'a' in 'Name' was so indistinct that in London the word was interpreted as 'Nome' and the name of the point was written as 'Point Nome.' There appears to be no foundation for the legend that 'Nome' is a corruption of Eskimo *Ka-no-me* ('I do not know'), the reply of natives when asked by Europeans what the name of the place was." One may be inclined to question whether such an error could creep into the transcribing of anything so carefully compiled as a coastal survey chart. But nobody who has had much experience with verbal renderings of artists and draftsmen will doubt that the incident could very well happen.

nonplus (pronounced non-PLUSS), a combination of the Latin *non* (not) and *plus* (more), is both a verb and a noun. As a noun it means "quandary or state of perplexity." However, it is more commonly used as an intransitive verb to describe being in such a condition that it is impossible to do any more thinking or take any further action.

non sequitur means that what a person has said has nothing to do with the matter under discussion—or it's an argument or statement that "does not follow," which is what this Latin phrase means. A *non sequitur* is a conclusion reached or an inference drawn that does not logically follow the facts or evidence. It is also something that is completely unconnected with what has gone before.

nor'easter. More properly called "northeaster," this is the kind of intense storm well known in New England: a gale coming from the northeast.

normalcy, indicating a state or condition of normality, has, as Mencken says, "been much derided by American intellectuals, though of respectable ancestry." When President Warren G. Harding called for a "return to normalcy" after World War I, he stirred up a controversy about the propriety of his word choice which hasn't settled yet. However, all carping to one side, *normalcy* has been in the language since the mid nineteenth century, according to the *Oxford Dictionary,* and is perfectly normally derived from the Latin *normalis,* "made according to the carpenter's square"—hence of standard or normal design.

normal schools derive their name from the French phrase *école normale.* These teacher-training institutions, the first of which was established in France by the Brothers of the Christian Schools in 1685, were intended to set a pattern, establish a "norm" after which all other schools would be modeled. The first *normal school* in America was established in Vermont in 1823. The name fell out of favor toward the end of the 1920s, when the influence of Columbia University's Teachers College became paramount in the field of public education. Most such institutions changed their names to "teachers colleges" during the 1930s. Now that the "progressive education" teachings of the Columbia group have been discredited, the Progressive Education Association itself has disbanded and most colleges have dropped "teachers" from their names. Thus we find that the *normal school* of grandfather's day became a "state teachers college" during father's youth, but today's sprouts are attending "state colleges."

no royal road to learning. The original statement was made by Euclid, the genius who developed the earliest theories of geometry in Alexandria, Egypt, in the third century B.C. King Ptolemy came to him one day and said that he was interested in knowing more about mathematical science but he was a bit pressed for time, so could Euclid teach him some shortcuts. "There is," pontificated Euclid, *"no royal road* to geometry." That last word has since been changed to *learning.*

nose out of joint has been around a long time. A person whose nose is out of joint is one who is vexed because he has been supplanted in another's affections. The earliest version of the saying that we have found goes back to 1895, when, up on Cape Cod, Massachusetts, the expression was "having your nose broke." The explanation runs: "The youngest child of a family is said to have its nose broke if another is born and it is therefore no longer 'the baby.' " We suppose that having your *nose out of joint* and having it "broke" come to pretty much the same thing.

nosh. This Yiddicism can be used as both noun and verb. In the latter case it means to munch on snacks between meals, while a *nosh* is a tidbit or snack so consumed. It is a shortened form of the Yiddish *nosherai,* which in turn comes from the Old High German *(h)nascon,* "to gnaw or nibble."

no show. The airlines hate this fellow; he's the one who makes a reservation for a flight, then fails to claim or cancel the reservation before the plane's departure.

no skin off my tail, meaning "no concern of mine," goes back to our Western frontier of the late nineteenth century.

nostalgia. For quite a few years, dictionary editors refused to concede that *nostalgia* had any meaning beyond the purely medical sense of "homesickness." The word came originally from the Greek words *nostos* (return) and *algos* (pain). The *Oxford Dictionary* gives the definition as "a form of melancholia caused by prolonged absence from one's country or home; severe homesickness." One salient fact about our language is that its devel-

opment is often completely illogical. The technical medical meaning of
nostalgia may well be the only one used in England today, but in this
country the popular, if illogical, meaning of "something to do with the
past" is so well established that dictionary editors enter it as completely
acceptable usage. Note this from the *World Webster,* College Edition: "a
longing for something far away or long ago."

Nostradamus is the Latinized form of the name of a French astrologer, Michel
de Nostre-Dame. In 1555 he brought out a set of prophecies which have
had seeming relevance to events occurring many centuries after his death.

nostrums were quack remedies, widely sold during the nineteenth century.
The name comes from the Latin *nostrum,* the neuter form of the adjective
noster, meaning "our." The idea was that each *nostrum* was "our own,"
exclusive to its maker, something invented and prepared by the seller.

not a fit night out for man nor beast was first used by W. C. Fields in a mock
temperance lecture called "The Fatal Glass of Beer." It was also Fields
who said: "It was a woman who drove me to drink—and I never remembered to thank her."

notarize, meaning to attest to the authenticity of a signature by a notary
public, is a word that somehow eluded the dictionary makers for many
years. Although it had been in general use for decades, it didn't appear in
many dictionaries until after World War II. Its root is the Latin *notare,*
"to note or mark."

notch in his tail. Used by cowboys in speaking of a man-killing bronc, *notch
in his tail* has the same connotation as the notched gun handles of gunfighters—one for each man killed.

not dry behind the ears literally means "as innocent as a newborn babe."
According to tradition, the last place where a newly born animal gets dry
is in the slight indentation behind each ear.

nothing to fear but fear itself. For many years, especially during the years of
World War II, we heard the statement "We have nothing to fear but fear
itself" attributed to Franklin D. Roosevelt. President Roosevelt was far
from the first person to express this thought, but the dramatic circumstances of his delivery of it during his first inaugural address, when the
nation was indeed in a mood of deep despair, made it lastingly memorable
for all who heard it.

Henry David Thoreau, in his *A Week on the Concord and Merrimack
Rivers,* observed: "Nothing is so much to be feared as fear." Much earlier,
in 1590, the French essayist Montaigne wrote: "The thing of which I have
most fear is fear." Even earlier, the anonymous author of the book of the
Bible called Proverbs wrote (3:25): "Be not afraid of sudden fear."

So there was nothing strikingly original in Roosevelt's phrase—no more
than there is in any other great and challenging concept, for in the words
of the cliché, "There's nothing new under the sun." However, for this

generation of Americans (another memorable Rooseveltian phrase), F.D.R.'s version marked an inspirational turning point in our lives and is assuredly the version we will remember longest.

not room enough to swing a cat goes back to sailing-ship days and the "cat" involved is the nine-thonged whip used to administer punishment to misbehaving sailors. More properly and fully called the "cat o' nine tails," it got its name from the fact that the welts left on a sailor's back after a whipping looked a bit like enormous cat scratches. Most such whippings took place on the open deck because in the cramped quarters belowdecks there was *not room enough to swing a cat.*

not up to par. *Par* is directly borrowed from Latin, where it meant "equal." Nowadays we use it to mean the accepted average, the normal standard. In golf, *par* is the number of strokes that a skilled player may be expected to take in completing an entire round of a course. So when a person is feeling *below par* or *not up to par* he is not up to the standard of health that he can reasonably expect.

not up to the mark. Anything that is *not up to the mark* does not come up to the established standard or is not quite good enough. The phrase comes from the standards of quality set by an assay office for articles made of silver or gold. Those items failing to meet the standards were not allowed to bear a hallmark.

not what it's cracked up to be sounds a bit slangy, but it has been part of American English for at least 140 years and, in slightly different form, has appeared in English ever since before the time of Shakespeare. The verb "to crack" formerly had the meaning of "to brag or boast" about something. According to the *Oxford Dictionary,* Joseph Addison (of the famous Addison and Steele duo) once wrote: "Thou art always cracking and boasting"—and he would have written that about 1700.

By the early days of the nineteenth century, the idiom *cracked up to be* was well established in American English and we find none other than Davy Crockett putting down Martin Van Buren with this remark: "Van Buren is not the man he is *cracked up to be.*" So today *not what he's cracked up to be,* meaning "not what he is believed to be" or "not what his boosters would have us believe," is well established in standard American speech and writing.

not worth a continental. During the Revolutionary War, the colonies were governed by the Continental Congress. It issued bank notes and other currency, but since there were no gold or silver reserves to back it up, the money was practically valueless. So something *not worth a continental* was something of no value at all and "I don't give a continental" was the eighteenth-century equivalent of "I just don't give a hoot."

not worth a damn originally came from the common phrase "not worth a tinker's dam," this *dam* being a pellet of bread used by old-time tinkers to block small holes in pots and pans while they poured in solder to fix the leak. When the patch was secure, the *dam* was discarded. So anything "not worth a tinker's dam" was something utterly worthless.

not worth two bits. *Bit* was originally British slang for any small coin. In the Southwestern U.S., as long ago as 1730, the term *bit* was applied to the Mexican *real,* a coin then worth about 12½ cents. *Two bits* thus meant 25 cents, from which the expression *not worth two bits,* meaning "practically worthless," came into being.

novel. The first *novels* in English were translations of Italian works like Boccaccio's *Decameron* and got their name from the Italian word *novella,* meaning "something new." Originally these works were collections of short stories, often racy and ribald, and usually centering on one character or group of characters. Gradually the longer, more integrated form developed, and though Richardson's *Pamela* and Fielding's *Tom Jones,* the first English novels, were more fully integrated than their predecessors, they carried the same name. Even today there are some publishers who feel that the chief reason for success of certain works of fiction is their "novelty" —the difference that sets one book apart from all the others and makes it a word-of-mouth best seller.

November. The eleventh month in the year takes its name from the Latin word *novem,* for nine, because it was the ninth month in the Roman calendar.

N.Q.O.S./P.L.U. These are two examples of a very "in" gimmick that has recently been in vogue—talking in a sort of initial code. It usually starts with one couple or group developing a series of such tricks or verbal shorthand. Gradually they spread. *N.Q.O.S.* stands for "Not Quite Our Sort." The reply, "Not *P.L.U.*" means "Not People Like Us."

nudnik. A *nudnik* may be, as one saying has it, a "no-goodnik," but this borrowing from Polish via Yiddish generally is used to describe a dull, boring fellow. It's from the Polish *nudny,* meaning "tedious or tiresome."

nut, as a theatrical term, means the investment required of a play's backers to put it into production and meet the payroll. Sometimes the term also means the "break-even point"—that stage in the show's financial operation when the initial investment has been recouped and the backers begin to make a profit.

Nutmeg State is the popular nickname for Connecticut, which is officially known as the Constitution State. A spokesman for the Greenwich Historical Society was not too happy to explain the origin of the popular tag. It seems that "many years ago some Yankee trader made wooden nutmegs and sold them around the country." *American Heritage Dictionary* puts it this way: "originally Wooden Nutmeg State from the reputed skill of Connecticut traders at such deceptions as selling wooden nutmegs." The official nickname derives from the fact that in 1639 the towns of Hartford,

Windsor and Wethersfield, which had been under the control of Massachusetts, declared themselves to be a commonwealth and adopted a constitution, which they called the Fundamentals of Connecticut. Some historians regard it as the first written constitution in the world and the basis for our present U.S. Constitution. During the Revolutionary War, Connecticut was dubbed the Provision State because it furnished so much of the munitions and food needed by the Continental Army.

nuts/nutty. Although *nuts* and *nutty* have been part of the language for more than a century, they have always been considered slang. The word *nut* first was used as a slang term for "head" back around 1820. Gradually it acquired the meaning not merely of "head" but of "something wrong in the head." So now a mentally ill person may be referred to as *nuts* or *nutty*.

oaf. One of the oldest superstitions is that concerning a changeling—a child whom the fairies have left in place of one they have stolen. In the Old Norse tongue, such a child was an *alfr* (elf). The word became *oaf*, and its meaning broadened to refer to any child who was abnormal, either mentally or physically. Over the years its meaning changed, and it now refers to any clumsy and stupid person, or a lout.

OAS is the Organization of American States, formed in 1948 to promote cooperation among the twenty-one American republics.

obfuscate (pronounced ob-FUS-kayt or OB-fus-kayt) has its origin in the Latin *ob* (to) plus *fuscus* (dark) and one of its meanings is "to darken." By extension it has come to mean "to obscure, confuse or stupefy."

obsession. In the days when people literally believed in evil spirits, *obsession* meant a state of siege by an evil spirit trying to take possession of a man's personality. (The Latin for it was *obsessio*.) The word still has a connotation of possession—but in the sense of being unduly preoccupied by an idea, emotion or desire.

October. The tenth month in the year takes its name from the Latin *octo* (eight), because it was the eighth month in the Roman calendar.

ods bodkins is a phrase that was heard for the first time by millions of Americans in the lyrics of "Brush Up Your Shakespeare," in Cole Porter's *Kiss Me, Kate.* In the sixteenth century, *ods bodkins* was a profane interjection, being a corruption of "God's bodikin" or "God's little body."

Oedipus, the protagonist of two plays by Sophocles, was a figure in Greek mythology, son of Laius and Jocasta. Abandoned at birth, he grew to manhood unaware of his true heritage and unwittingly killed his father and married his mother.

Oedipus complex is a term common in psychiatry to designate a person motivated by libidinal feelings for the parent of the opposite sex. Most commonly this manifests itself in an uncommonly strong attachment of a male child for his mother, accompanied by hostility toward his father. Although the term is sometimes used to designate the parallel situation with the sexes reversed (female child attracted to her father and hostile to her mother), this is more commonly called the "Electra" complex. Electra was the daughter of Clytemnestra and Agamemnon. With the aid of her brother Orestes, she killed her mother and her mother's lover, Aegisthus, because Clytemnestra had murdered Agamemnon when he returned from the siege of Troy.

oenophile/oenophilist/oenomaniac. *Oenophile* (pronounced EE-noh-file) is made up of the Greek words *oinos* (wine) and *philos* (love). This word has the added connotation of an "expert or connoisseur of wines." An *oenophile,* in other words, is no mere wine-bibber—that would be an *oenophilist,* who is, according to *Funk & Wagnalls,* "one who is too fond of wine." Then there's the *oenomaniac.* The Bowerys and skid rows of the nation have more than their proper quota of *oenomaniacs,* whom the police label "winos."

Off-Broadway. After World War II a number of small theater groups developed in New York City, such as the Circle in the Square. These devoted their attention to producing works by relatively unknown playwrights in theaters whose seating capacity was limited to 299 seats or fewer. In consideration of the smaller audiences and experimental nature of the plays, the theatrical unions made a number of concessions in their normally strict rules. As the *Off-Broadway* theater achieved a greater degree of commercial success, a still more experimental group of quasi-amateur companies developed what came to be known as the Off-Off-Broadway theater.

off-color was—and still is—a term used in various trades, notably the clothing and weaving industries, to indicate a color which deviates from the standard or norm. So an *off-color* story is one that deviates from the standards of good taste. If such stories are now being heard in mixed company and in polite society, we'd say the standards have changed, not the stories. A variant of this expression is the one used by professional entertainers, especially those who work in both nightclubs and TV. They speak of "cleaning up the act" for the tube, but "dipping into the blue" or telling "blue" jokes in their nightclub shows. When you hear an Englishman describe a person as *off-color,* it has nothing at all to do with humor, clean or otherwise. It simply means that the person referred to is not in the best of health and spirits.

off the schneider is a term used when a team scores its first run, especially after a series of scoreless innings. A *schneider* in Yiddish is a cloth-cutter in the garment district. To the bosses, *schneider* was a term of disrespect, rather like "schnook" and "schlemiel"—a born loser, in other words. So when the bosses gathered for their favorite pastime, gin rummy, they came to use *schneider* for a cardplayer who scored no points at all. To come *off the schneider* meant that a player had finally scored. There's still another variation of this expression—"to make [score] a *schneider.*" That's to run up a winning score before your opponent has won a single game.

off the top of your head comes from show business. It means unpremeditated. When you're talking right *off the top of your head,* you're ad-libbing or speaking without advance preparation.

oflag is a contraction of the German *Offizierlager* and means a World War II prison camp for officers only. Similar camps for enlisted men were known as *stalags,* and a few, known as *stalagluft,* were designed expressly for airmen and were run by the German *Luftwaffe.*

of the first water means "of top quality." This is thought to go all the way back to a term used by Arab gem traders many centuries ago. In any event, until midway through the nineteenth century, diamond merchants graded their gems in three classes: *of the first,* second or third *water.*

OGPU. Though now superseded by an intelligence agency known as the KGB, the *OGPU* was certainly the most famed and dreaded of Soviet Russian security organizations. Called either OG-POO or GAY-PAY-OO (from the last three initials), its name literally translated as Unified Government Political Administration. Its power lasted from 1923 to 1934. It was succeeded by the NKVD, which was dissolved during World War II (1943).

O.K./okay has probably been more discussed than any other item in the American language. Everyone from presidents to plumbers has his or her pet theory. Woodrow Wilson thought it was a Choctaw Indian word and should properly be spelled "Okeh." He persuaded a record company of the 1920s (the one that made the first Louis Armstrong records) to call their product "Okeh Records." But history fails to record that President Wilson converted many more people to his belief.

A distinguished Columbia professor, Allen Walker Read, announced in 1941 that the term originated as an abbreviation for the Old Kinderhook Club, a political organization supporting James Van Buren (The Kinderhook Fox) for the presidency in 1840. That theory was generally accepted until, in the mid 1960s, an equally distinguished scholar, Dr. Woodford A. Heflin, proved that *O.K.* had appeared in a Philadelphia newspaper in 1839 —a year ahead of Read's date. Professor Read then countered with evidence that a Boston paper had *O.K.* in print even earlier in 1839—and there the scholarly argument rests.

But not everyone agrees. Charles Berlitz, the eminent linguist, thinks it may well come from "Aux Cayes," a port in Haiti famous for its superior rum. This theory holds that American sailors were so enthusiastic about the rum that "Aux Cayes"—later *O.K.*—became their expression for approval.

There are various other theories of the origin of *O.K.* The most popular holds that Andrew Jackson, while a court clerk in Tennessee, marked *O.K.* on legal documents as an abbreviation for the illiterate "Orl Kerrect." In fact, Jackson was never a court clerk—he was a prosecuting attorney—and he was far from illiterate, serving as representative and U.S. senator before being elected President. Mencken once called *O.K.* "the most successful of Americanisms." It has certainly been successful in breeding theories about its origin.

O.K.D. These initials are always used in the negative—a Philadelphia expression used in conversation by two Main Line women about a third who is not. "She's nice enough, but not quite *O.K.D.,*" which means "not quite our kind, dear."

okey-doke. As noted above, *O.K.* first appeared in print some time before 1840. It has now achieved "colloquial" status in reference books, meaning that it is perfectly permissible in conversation and informal writing. *Okey-doke* and its variant *okey-dokey,* however, did not make their debuts in print until about 1930. Each is still considered slang.

Okie. During the years of the Depression, the *Okies* were migrant farm workers, many of them from Oklahoma—whence the name—who moved west to what they hoped would be the golden lands of California. Their migration was superbly recorded by John Steinbeck in his classic *Grapes of Wrath,* later made into an equally classic motion picture starring Henry Fonda. The image of the *Okie* memorialized by the book and film is one that has proved very long-lasting. The governor and the publicity agents of the state of Oklahoma have bent every effort to improve the public image of the *Okie*—but to little avail. Despite pressures brought upon the editors of at least one dictionary to upgrade the definition, it still remains true to the historical image: "an impoverished migrant farm worker; especially, one from Oklahoma forced to leave his farm during the Depression of the 1930's. Used disparagingly."

old Adam. As the founder of the race, Adam symbolizes original sin and man's enduring unregeneracy. So a person with "a touch of the *old Adam*" is, at the very least, no better than he should be.

Old Bill. The Bill Mauldin of World War I was a British cartoonist named Bruce Bairnsfather. His most famous cartoon showed a pair of British infantrymen (very like Mauldin's Willie and Joe) huddled in a shell hole knee-deep in water. One of the soldiers, Bert, complains of the inconvenience of their predicament and *Old Bill* replies, "If you know of a better 'ole, go to it." The cartoon and its creator became world famous and *Old Bill* became a household name throughout the English-speaking world.

Old Contemptibles. This was the first contingent of British troops to join the French and Belgian forces against the Germans in World War I. According to stories of the time (August 1914), the Kaiser ordered his troops to "exterminate the treacherous English and walk over [this] contemptible little army." The Kaiser learned, as did Hitler a generation later, that it's not wise to scorn the British. They turned the epithet into an accolade and styled themselves the *Old Contemptibles.*

Old Curmudgeon is an expression that enjoyed great popularity in the days of the New Deal, for it was the self-chosen nickname for Harold Ickes, Secretary of the Interior through all four terms of Franklin D. Roosevelt. Ickes was as cantankerous as he was incorruptible and, when F.D.R.'s final term was tragically cut short, he soon found that the new President, Harry S Truman, would not put up with his *curmudgeonly* tactics, so he resigned. His autobiography was called, of course, *The Autobiography of a Curmudgeon.*

The origin of *curmudgeon* is in dispute. Samuel Johnson thought it came from French *coeur mechant,* "evil heart," adding: "from an unknown correspondent." As a footnote to Johnson's etymology and as a commentary on how freely eighteenth-century dictionary editors (including Johnson) borrowed from each other, here's an indignant comment from *Brewer's Dictionary of Phrase and Fable:* "By a ridiculous blunder Ash (1775) copied this into his dictionary as 'from French *coeur* (unknown) and *mechant* (correspondent)'!" As a further, and somewhat irrelevant, footnote, the "Ash" referred to was an Anglican divine, the Reverend John Ash, whose 1775 dictionary was the last dictionary before the *American Heritage* (1969) to enter and define the so-called four-letter words which were banished from lexicons by Bowdler and other Victorians.

Another theory of the origin of *curmudgeon* is that it comes from a proper name common in medieval times, Curmegan. If so, the Curmegans would have been good people to avoid.

Old Diehards. During the Battle of Albuera (1811) during the Napoleonic Wars, one regimental commander, mortally wounded, exhorted his troops: "Never surrender. Die hard, men. Die hard." His unit, the First Battalion Middlesex Regiment, was thereafter called the *Diehards* or *Old Diehards.* The officer in command—the one who uttered the deathless words—was one Colonel Inglis and the seriousness of the situation may be measured by the fact that three-fourths of his battalion was killed or wounded. The British, incidentally, have long been famous for the colorful nicknames given to their military regiments. *Brewer's Dictionary of Phrase and Fable* devotes several pages to them, including such oddities as "The Devil's Own," "Pontius Pilate's Bodyguard" and "The Virgin Mary's Bodyguard."

Old Lady of Threadneedle Street is the Bank of England. It is so called because its headquarters is located on Threadneedle Street. *Old Lady* refers to its traditional conservatism in financial matters.

Old Man of the Sea is a character in the *Arabian Nights* story of "Sinbad the Sailor." The Old Man managed to climb up on Sinbad's shoulders and refused to get off. After a few weeks of this burden, Sinbad got a bright idea. He got the Old Man drunk and then easily slipped out from under. So you'll sometimes hear an intolerable burden referred to as an *old man of the sea.*

Old Nick. It may seem inconceivable that there is any connection between the names of *Old Nick,* the devil, and St. Nick, the embodiment of the Christmas Spirit. But some scholars do think that *Old Nick,* like St. Nick, may be derived from the name of St. Nicholas. He was a fourth-century bishop of Asia Minor whose feast day (December 6) was the children's holiday which, over a period of centuries, came to be celebrated on Christmas. "Santa Claus," incidentally, is derived from the Dutch name for St. Nicholas. However, a more likely explanation is that *Old Nick* got his name from Niccolò Machiavelli, Italian Renaissance statesman, who wrote *The Prince,* a book which gained its author a lasting reputation for political unscrupulousness. Macaulay, in his biographical study of Machiavelli, wrote: "Out of his surname they have coined an epithet for a knave, and out of his Christian name a synonym for the devil." So the probability is strong that *Old Nick* got his nickname not from the good saint, but from the evil genius of Renaissance statesmanship.

Old Scratch is a nickname for the devil. This has nothing to do with scratching to remedy an itch. The *Scratch* is derived from the Old Norse word *scratti,* meaning "devil" or "sorcerer."

oligopsony (Greek *oligos,* "few," and *opsonia,* "buying") is a word from the special language of economics. It means a market situation in which purchasers are so few that the action of any one of them can affect the price of a commodity so drastically that any other purchaser or seller is markedly affected.

olla podrida (pronounced ol-uh puh-DREE-duh) is a kind of Spanish stew, highly spiced and much more inviting than its name (which literally means "putrid pot") would indicate. The term is sometimes also used as a synonym for hodgepodge or mishmash (which see). The *olla* itself is an unglazed pottery jar. In the days before refrigeration and air conditioning, every patio in California and Mexico had an *olla* full of water and swathed in burlap. Evaporation kept the water cool for a refreshing drink in even the hottest weather.

olly, olly oxen free. We both recall this chant from the hide-and-seeks games of our childhoods, when it was used to call in any players who were holdouts at the end of the game. Mary, in rural Ohio, called out "Olly, Olly Octen Free." She has not the slightest idea what the "Octen" meant. William, in urban Massachusetts, called simply "Olly, Olly, all in free." The guess here is that both "oxen" and "Octen" are simply childish corruptions of the "all in."

The fact that the chant is common throughout English-speaking countries is shown in *The Lore and Language of School Children,* in which Iona and Peter Opie report that both "ollyoxalls" and "olly-olly-ee" are common "truce terms" among children in Britain.

The capacity of children of this age to confuse and corrupt common expressions is well known, like the child who recited "Deliver me not into temptation" as "Deliver me not into Penn Station." And William, reared in Boston, the home of the bean and the cod, vividly remembers a childhood game he called "Oyster Green Sail." Only many years later did he discover that its real name was "Hoist the Green Sail."

omadhaun is another word for "idiot, fool or simpleton." Dictionaries generally give the pronunciation as OM-uh-don, but we have heard the *thon* sound for the last syllable. It's a word which has come direct from Ireland with no change in spelling and is heard in families of Irish ancestry.

ombudsman is a Swedish word and originally meant "representative of the king." As used in Sweden and New Zealand and, recently, the United States, it means a person, usually on the public payroll, who serves as watchman for the interests of the common citizen. If you have a complaint about an unfair traffic fine or an unjustified increase in real estate taxes, you take your complaint to the *ombudsman.* He will cut through the layers of bureaucratic red tape and bring a speedy solution. One warning, however: if your complaint is not justified, the verdict will be against you.

omnibus. Usually contracted to "bus," this is the dative plural of the Latin adjective *omnis* (all), and literally means "for everyone." It has been used as a name for public vehicles since the late 1820s and has also been extended to cover all sorts of collections of similar items—*The Conrad Omnibus,* for a collection of the writings of Joseph Conrad, for example.

omnium gatherum (pronounced OM-nee-um GATH-er-um) is what one might call "dog Latin," meaning that it is an arbitrary coinage that the Romans would never have recognized, if only because the phrase wasn't invented until after A.D. 1500. It's made up of the Latin *omnium* (of everything) and the fake Latin *gatherum* (a gathering together). So it means a miscellaneous collection of people or things, usually the latter.

omnivorous words. Children learn early the difference between herbivorous and carnivorous animals—the first eat plants and the second eat fish or meat. One curious child, however, queried us about other *-vorous* words —that is, words describing the eating habits of other forms of life.

There are many such words, but they are hard to locate in the standard dictionaries. *Arachnivorous* (uh-rak-NIV-er-us) means "spider-eating," while *batrachivorous* (bat-ruh-KIV-er-us) would describe "one who eats frogs." That's a handy word to tuck away against the day when your dinner companion orders frog legs. How impressed he or she will be when you murmur: "I see you're *batrachivorous,* too."

Then there's the term for termites: *xylivorous* (zy-LIV-er-us), meaning "wood-eating." The mongoose, long famed for his hatred of the cobra, might qualify for the adjective *serpentivorous* (ser-pen-TIV-er-us), "snake-eating." If you are fond of seafood, the word for you is *piscivorous* (pis-KIV-er-us) or "fish-eating." You may never have thought of them this way, but your favorite household pets are probably either ossivorous or lactivorous —or both. *Ossivorous* means "bone-eating," while *lactivorous* is "milk-consuming." Your cat, when it has the chance, is also certain to be *rodenti-vorous*—"rodent-eating."

Practically everyone is *frugiverous* or *fructivorous*—both mean "fruit-eating"—and chances are that we're *panivorous* (bread-eating) and *phyti-vorous* (vegetable-eating) to boot. And we all know the voracious eater (that's right: *voracious* comes from the same Latin verb, *vorare,* "to de-vour") and he justly rates the descriptive *omnivorous*—"eating anything and everything."

once in a blue moon. The first appearance in print of this expression goes back to well before the time of Shakespeare—to 1528, in fact. In a little item called *Rede Me and Be Not Wroth* appears: "Yf they say the mone is blewe/We must believe that it is true." Making allowances for the fact that the pre-Elizabethans spelled differently from the way we do today, this makes the point that nobody really believed that the moon ever was blue. So *once in a blue moon* meant never. However, it appears that thanks to physical phenomena like dust storms, cloud banks and ice crystals in the atmosphere, the moon on very rare occasions may appear to be blue. So nowadays *once in a blue moon* translates best into W. S. Gilbert's famous line from *H.M.S. Pinafore:* "What, never? Well, hardly ever!"

Arthur A. Green of Windsor, Connecticut, told us of an experience he had some forty years ago when he shipped on a Panama Pacific liner from New York to San Francisco and back. "Sometime in midsummer," he wrote, "we were off the west coast of Nicaragua in the Pacific just out of sight of land. The moon must have been just about full as it rose just after dark and it was *blue.* I was so excited that I went around the deck pointing out the blue moon to members of the crew, who, being anything but an intellectual group, were not in the least interested. I have never again seen such a thing nor met anyone who has. Nicaragua has a lot of volcanoes. It may well be that they were the cause of this interesting phenomenon. Anyway, a blue moon *is* possible."

one fell swoop simply means one fierce, sudden onslaught, of the kind a hawk might make when swooping down on a defenseless small animal. *Fell* is a word rarely met outside of this particular phrase. It has no connection with "fall." This *fell* comes from the Anglo-Saxon word *fel,* from which we also get "felon," a person guilty of a major crime.

one foot in the grave. The origin of this phrase, meaning "hovering on the brink of death," is generally attributed to the emperor Julian, who said that he would "learn something even if he had *one foot in the grave.*" The Greeks, as is so often the case, had a very similar expression—"with one foot in Charon's ferryboat," referring to the means of transportation across the river Styx to the Elysian Fields.

one more stitch in the wildcat's tail. This odd expression came to our attention in a note from a reader who said that his grandmother, after finishing a difficult job, would say: "Well, that's *one more stitch in the wildcat's tail.*" We asked our column readers if any could tell us more about the expression and Frank Flanagan obliged. He wrote: "My late father, God rest his merry soul, would now and then come home smelling of strong drink and with a yen to sing. He had a very good voice and he could really belt out his favorite songs. One of them went like this, to my Jewish mother's disgust: 'Way down south in St. Augustine,/ A wildcat jumped on a sewing machine./ The sewing machine was going so fast/ It took 44 stitches in the wildcat's. . . .' Maybe the lady made a slight change in her version."

onerous/onus. *Onerous* (pronounced ON-er-us) is an adjective meaning "burdensome, tedious or troublesome." It is derived from the Latin word *onus,* meaning "load or burden"—a word which has, incidentally, come into English without change. Nowadays one might speak of the *onerous* duties of a street cleaner or say that the *onus* (burden of responsibility) for an international crisis is the aggressor nation's.

one swallow doesn't make a summer. The meaning of this phrase is simply that you mustn't think all your troubles are over simply because things have begun to improve. It originated with Aristotle, whose version was only slightly different from the one we use today: "One swallow doesn't make a spring."

one-upmanship, coined by the same Stephen Potter who gave us the classic "gamesmanship," means to keep a step ahead of one's competitor, even a friendly competitor, by recourse to claims, challenges or techniques that succeed whether or not they are entirely ethical.

on his uppers. A man who is *on his uppers* has met with serious misfortune and is so broke that he cannot afford a decent pair of shoes. Since the uppers are the parts of the shoes above the soles, he has worn through the bottoms of his shoes and is practically barefoot.

onomatopoeia. A word that sounds like whatever it refers to is an *onomatopoetic* word. "Buzz" and "cuckoo" are examples. Similarly, verse which echoes the sounds of its subject is called *onomatopoetic* verse. The best-known such verse in English is probably Edgar Allan Poe's "The Bells": "Keeping time, time, time,/In a sort of Runic rhyme,/To the tintinnabulation that so musically wells/From the bells, bells, bells, bells,/Bells, bells, bells." *Onomatopoeia* is a borrowing from the Greek and literally means "making a name or word."

on the blink. We theorize that this phrase might have come from the jargon of New England fishermen. A small mackerel—too small for profitable sale —was called a *blink*. A fishing expedition that pulled in only *blinks* would be notably unsuccessful—therefore *on the blink*.

on the drift. A cowboy *on the drift* is out of a job, riding from ranch to ranch until he can find work.

on the Fritz in the sense of not operating properly has been traced by the *Oxford Dictionary* back to 1902, though it is labeled of American origin. Our theory is that it all started with the comic strip known as *The Captain and the Kids* or *The Katzenjammer Kids*. It was one of the earliest strips and still appears in many papers. The customary Sunday sequence called for two madcap youngsters, Hans and Fritz, to cause all sorts of trouble for their elders, the Captain and his sidekick. By the end of the strip, their actions had the effect of putting whatever plans the Captain had made permanently *on the Fritz*.

on the house. The chances are that the original *house* was a British inn or tavern. In the years before Prohibition, it was the custom of most saloons, or as they are known in England, *public houses,* to give a free drink with every third or fourth one bought. This drink was *on the house*—meaning at the expense of the establishment.

on the lam. According to Mencken's *American Language* and the *Thesaurus of American Slang* by Berry and Van den Bark, *lam, lammister* and *on the lam*—all referring to hasty departure—were common in thieves' slang before the start of this century. Mencken quotes a newspaper report on the origin of *lam* which actually traces it indirectly back to Shakespeare's time. "Its origin should be obvious to anyone who runs over several colloquial phrases for leavetaking, such as 'beat it' and 'hit the trail' . . . The allusion in *lam* is to 'beat,' and 'beat it' is Old English, meaning 'to leave.' During the period of George Ade's *Fables in Slang* (1900), cabaret society delighted in talking slang, and *lam* was current. Like many other terms, it went under in the flood of new usages of those days, but was preserved in criminal slang. A quarter of a century later it reappeared." The Sage of Baltimore goes on to quote a story from the *New York Herald Tribune* in 1938 which reported that "one of the oldest police officers in New York said that he had heard *on the lam* about 30 years ago."

on the level is believed to have originated as part of the language of Freemasonry. Among members of the order the mason's level is a symbol of integrity. Therefore, a fellow Mason who is *on the level* is entirely trustworthy.

on the nose is not related to the horse-racing term "nose-and-nose," meaning that two horses are finishing at practically the same moment. *On the nose* originated in a sign made by radio directors who put a finger alongside the nose to indicate that a program was running precisely on schedule. There are quite a few similar items in the "sign language" of radio and TV—a language of pantomine made necessary because spoken instructions would go out over the air. The signal to stop, or "cut," for example, consists of the director violently pretending to saw his own throat with his right hand.

on the prod. Watch out, pardner. A cowboy *on the prod* is fighting mad and it's just not healthy to be in his vicinity.

on the q.t. A slang phrase for "on the quiet."

on the shady side. A person *on the shady side* of a date is on the far side of it. Thus a person *"on the shady side* of thirty-nine" may be presumed to be in his forties.

on the side of the angels. We sometimes say of a person whose intentions are good, even if his accomplishments may not be great, "At least he's *on the side of the angels."* When Darwin published *The Origin of Species,* starting the debate over his theory of evolution which has still not been settled in some quarters, a popular interpretation was that it signified that man is descended from the monkey. Britain's Prime Minister Disraeli made this comment: "The question is this: Is man an ape or an angel? I am *on the side of the angels."*

on the spot goes back to the days when pirates roamed the sea lanes of the world. Their chief symbol was the flag bearing a skull and crossbones. However, they had another symbol, just as dreaded. It was the ace of spades, which bears only one printed black spot. This was shown to a suspected traitor or informer as notice that he was to be executed. Centuries later, it was a common term in underworld slang. However, in recent years it has acquired a somewhat broader meaning. Today a person *on the spot* is in hazard, as the gamesters say, or in a precarious position. In its figurative sense, *on the spot* may merely mean in danger of being embarrassed.

on the wagon, meaning "abstaining from drinking alcoholic spirits," is a contraction of the older and more explicit "on the water wagon." It has been in the American idiom since at least the turn of the century, appearing in, of all places, *Mrs. Wiggs of the Cabbage Patch.* The corollary phrase *off the wagon* is of more recent vintage—if that's the word for it.

on tick is British slang for "on credit." Originally when a person took on a credit obligation he signed a contract known as a "ticket." In time this was shortened to *tick.*

on your own hook. The origin of this expression is credited to New England fishermen. On the fishing vessels operating along the Grand Banks, each fisherman was paid according to the size of his catch. Since early fishing was by hook and line, the individual fisherman would receive payment for what he had caught *on his own hook.*

oom. In Afrikaans, the language developed from seventeenth-century Dutch by the Dutch settlers in South Africa, *oom* means "uncle." It is chiefly known in the Western world as part of the sobriquet of Oom Paul Kruger

(1825–1904), leader of the Boer resistance to British encroachments in the Transvaal in the nineteenth century.

oompah is what dictionary editors call an "echoic" or "imitative" word. That is, it simply imitates the sound it describes. Just think of the sound the tuba makes in the bass section of a band and you'll hear that *oompah, oompah, oomp.*

oontz is an odd word which caused a bit of confusion in Louisville, Kentucky. It seems that Mayor Frank W. Burke found, on checking the state gambling laws, that there were strict prohibitions against games such as keno, faro, craps, cards and *oontz.* The only trouble was that no one there knew what *oontz* was and couldn't provide the necessary information for the police department. We finally located it in the *Dictionary of American Slang* by Wentworth and Flexner. The mayor can relax. It is defined there as "The usual game with dice; the standard dice game, craps." The word had some dialect use around 1900. Apparently it lives today only on the Kentucky lawbooks. Incidentally, *oontz* also turns up in an earlier work by Harold Wentworth, the *American Dialect Dictionary.* Defining it simply as "craps," he traces it to the Philogical Society of the University of Cincinnati. It adds up to a rather nice picture—all those dignified scholars playing craps with our language.

open city. Under international law a city, especially one containing shrines and other places of great historical value, may be declared an *open city,* by which the occupying army declares that it has withdrawn its troops and will make no effort to defend the city. During World War II Rome was declared an *open city.*

open season is the season of the year when hunting for certain specified game animals or birds is permitted. Loosely, the term is also used to indicate that some group is "fair game" for attack. "After the conventions were over, the editorialists declared *open season* on the candidates."

opera in one sense is merely the plural of "opus" and means "works or artistic creations." The more commonly used *opera*—the one often called "grand opera"—is an abbreviated form of the Italian phrase *opera in musica,* meaning "work set to music."

op'ry house. The top rail of the breaking corral where ranch hands sit and watch the bronc buster at work.

opsimathy is an elegant word which has been out of vogue in recent years but may be due for a revival. It means "learning late in life," something that adult education programs in schools and colleges are working hard to foster. The *Merriam-Webster* Second Edition (1934) marked it "rare" and it has disappeared entirely from the Third Edition (1961). It's pronounced op-SIM-uh-thee, and one who practices *opsimathy* is an *opsimath,* pronounced OP-sih-math. Both words come from the Greek *opsimathes.*

oracle was originally the place where or the medium by which ancient Greeks and Romans consulted their gods and asked their advice. The oracle of Delphi was the most famous. But the meaning of *oracle* today is "any person of great knowledge."

orange blossoms, plucked from the orange tree, are a favorite element in bridal bouquets. The white flowers are said to symbolize the presumed purity of the bride and the orange, a notably prolific tree, is said to insure future fertility.

ordeal. Back in the Middle Ages, an *ordeal* was something more than a trying experience. In those days it was spelled *ordal* and meant "judgment." If the courts lacked evidence of the guilt or innocence of the accused, an appeal was made to the "judgment" of God. Trial by *ordeal* meant exposure to physical dangers: carrying a red-hot iron for nine paces or plunging one's hands into boiling water. If no injuries resulted after three days, the accused was declared innocent. It leads one to wonder who was ever acquitted.

Order of the Garter is the most distinguished branch of the English peerage, the order to which retired prime ministers and the like are named. If this seems a commonplace name for such a distinguished group, there is a reason. It goes back many centuries to the reign of Edward III, around 1350. One of the great beauties of the royal court was Joan, Countess of Salisbury. While dancing at a royal ball, she lost a garter. In order to spare her the embarrassment of retrieving it and putting it back in place, the king picked the garter up, put it on his own knee and said: *"Honi soit qui mal y pense"*—"Shame to him who evil thinks." That has been the motto of the order ever since.

As might be expected, especially in these irreverent times, there have developed some rather ribald variations on the theme of this story. One goes like this: When the lady lost her garter, the king said: *"Honi soit qui mal y pense,"* which actually means, "Honey, your stocking is hanging down." Whereupon she replied: *"Dieu et mon droit,"* which means, "By God, you're right!"

Oreo is the trademarked name of a chocolate cookie with white cream filling made by the National Biscuit Company. It has enjoyed some vogue in black language as an opprobrious label for blacks who, in the opinion of their detractors, are playing the white man's game. *Oreo* in this use means "black outside but white inside." In Spanish *oreo* means "breeze or fresh air," but this has no connection with the name of the cookie, which seems to be simply an arbitrarily coined word.

orgy. This name for riotous debauch comes almost unchanged from the Greek *orgia.* The original *orgies* were secret ceremonies dedicated to the worship of such gods as Demeter and Dionysus and involved singing, dancing and all sorts of abandoned activities.

ornery. An *ornery* cowhand was one who was uppity, difficult and downright unpleasant to have around. Curiously enough, this colorful synonym for "stubborn" seems merely to be a corruption of "ordinary."

orpheum. This is a real oddity, a word we have been familiar with since childhood, yet one not to be found in the standard wordbooks—English or American. Its meaning is obvious enough—a shrine or temple to Orpheus, the Greek god of music. But it is not a Greek word and is, we suspect, a fairly recent coinage. The *Orpheum* circuit was an early chain of vaudeville theaters, most of which were later converted to movie houses. Thus it was a trade name, which appears to have become a common noun.

Orwellian. George Orwell, an English author whose real name was Eric Arthur Blair and who died in 1950, left two satiric masterpieces, *Animal Farm* and *1984.* The first was a devastating satire on totalitarianism, especially of the Stalinist variety. The second was a look into a future when society will be completely controlled by propaganda and when the language will be something called Newspeak, in which words will mean just what the government says they mean. In Orwell's view, the totalitarian conquest would be completed by 1984; hence the date of his title. Some commentators on the Watergate exposures of corruption in high places remarked that "1984 nearly came eleven years early." And that's a truly *Orwellian* thought.

Oscar is the name for the gold-plated statuette awarded in various categories of professional attainment each year by the Academy of Motion Picture Arts and Sciences. The statuettes were first awarded in 1929 but did not receive the nickname *Oscar* until 1931, when Mrs. Margaret Herrick, an official of the organization, remarked that it looked "just like my Uncle Oscar." This story has not been accepted without challenge. Merriam-Webster's *Third International* says that it is named after "Oscar Pierce, a 20th century American wheat and fruit grower," but whether this is the same person as Mrs. Herrick's Uncle Oscar is not recorded.

Brewer's Dictionary of Phrase and Fable reports: "When Helen Hayes was presented with the award, her husband, Charles MacArthur, a noted wit and playwright, said, 'Ah, I see you've got an Oscar,' and the name stuck." The implication seems to be that MacArthur may have coined the name—but that is demonstrably untrue, for she received the award (for her acting in *The Sin of Madelon Claudet*) in 1932, a year after the *Oscar* nickname appeared in print.

Miss Hayes, as befitted the first lady of the stage, took the honor very lightly, as we can attest from personal experience. One evening in the summer of 1936, William was a guest of the MacArthurs at their home in Nyack, New York. Dazzled by the charm of Miss Hayes, who was standing in the open doorway greeting her guests, William paid little heed to his feet and stumbled over the doorstop, landing crimson-faced at Miss Hayes's feet. The doorstop, need we say, was the *Oscar.*

oscillate. A little mask or face, suspended from a tree and swinging in the wind, gave us the English word *oscillate*. In Latin, such a swinging item was called *oscillum* (diminutive of *os,* "face"). The Latin verb *oscillare,* meaning "to swing," was formed, and from it we get *oscillate,* which can be literally "to swing to and fro" or, figuratively, to fluctuate, vacillate or be indecisive.

ostracize. Pronounced OSS-truh-size, this word comes from the Greek *ostrakon,* a "tile," the earliest form of ballot. When Athenians decided that a person had become a menace to the state, they would assemble to vote, by casting an *ostrakon,* on whether he should be exiled. If six thousand voted "yea," the victim was banished for at least five years—and thus *ostracized* very harshly indeed by his fellow citizens.

ottoman. This humble article of furniture, usually no more than a cushioned footstool, takes its name from the feminine form of the French *ottomane,* which in turn comes from the Arabic word for Turkish *Othmani.* The Ottoman Empire was quite something else again. For more than six centuries (1299–1919) it ruled, from its capital, Constantinople, vast land areas comprising southwestern Asia, northeastern Africa and much of southeastern Europe.

Ouija. The *Ouija* board is a device used by spiritualists, mediums and others trying to foretell the future. It consists of a large board with letters, numbers, symbols and a few simple words on it, plus a planchette with a pointer, resting on casters, which the communicator maneuvers until, by combinations of letters, it spells out answers to questions. The name is a blend of the French *oui* and the German *ja.* Since both words mean "yes," it's apparent that the board will tell you pretty much what you want to hear.

outage. One winter our town was hit by a particularly damaging sleet storm, with the result that we were without light and heat for five days. Partly out of understandable vexation at the hardships resulting, we expressed our displeasure at the term used by the electric light company to cover the situation. It was, they said, a "power *outage.*" We thought "power failure" would be more expressive—and said so. A knowledgeable reader wrote:

> An *outage* is not a synonym for "power failure." In the electrical-generating industry, the term covers any situation in which equipment is not functioning; it means simply "the equipment is out." It might be out for maintenance, improvement or replacement, as well as for breakdowns in service due to malfunction, accidents or acts of nature. Fortunately there are "scheduled *outages,*" or we'd find ourselves suffering even more from unpredictable, annoying forms of *outages.*
>
> I'm of the opinion that this bit of industrial jargon has moved from power plant usage to application throughout the industry and only recently into the vocabulary of the information media. Of course, the mass media's uses would

be during times when the public was inconvenienced and doubtless irritated by unplanned, accidental *outages*. Perhaps this more restricted application has resulted in the unfavorable connotation and impression, as you seem to have implied, that *outage* is a euphemism.

out of all scotch and notch. A distinguished British authority on the theater, speaking of certain trends in playwriting, said things had gotten *out of all scotch and notch.* This is an expression that comes not, as you might expect, from the pubs of Britain but from the child's game of hopscotch. It means simply "beyond all bounds" and refers to the boundary lines *(scotches)* and corners *(notches)* used in the game.

out of hand. If you reject an offer or idea *out of hand,* you do so without hesitation. However, this phrase has several different meanings, the oldest of them being "out of control," from the days when failure to keep a firm grip on the reins would result in a team of horses being *out of hand.*

out of the frying pan into the fire. This expression is as old as mankind—or, at least, as old as fire itself. The Greeks used to say: "out of the smoke and into the flame." Sir Thomas More wrote: "Leap they like a flounder *out of a frying-pan into the fire.*" Heywood in his *Proverbs* (1546) added a bit to this: "Leap *out of the frying pan into the fire* and change from ill pain to worse." And Shakespeare, in *As You Like It* (Act I, Scene 2) had it this way: "Thus must I from the smoke into the smother."

out of whole cloth. "Whole cloth" is cloth that runs the full width of the loom on which it is woven. Something that is made *out of whole cloth* is created entirely and completely fresh, without any connection with anything that may have gone before. So a story "fabricated *out of whole cloth*" is one that is completely untrue, without any basis of fact.

out-take. A "take"—and this is straight from the *American Heritage Dictionary*—is "the uninterrupted running of a motion picture or television camera or set of recording equipment in filming a movie or television program or cutting a record . . . a recording made in a single session." It's fairly common practice to "take" a musical number one, two or three times. In fact, especially if there is any slight fluff, the successive recordings are labeled "Take 1," "Take 2" and so on. One of the takes is selected for release and the others become *out-takes.* In recent years a number of albums of great stars of yesteryear like Billie Holiday, Bessie Smith and Louis Armstrong have contained such *out-take* material. For the benefit of laymen unfamiliar with the jargon of the recording trade, these are usually labeled "previously unreleased."

Out Where the West Begins is the title of a poem written by Arthur Chapman, the refrain of which runs: "Out where the handclasp's a little stronger/ Out where the smile dwells a little longer, / That's where the West begins."

overpaid, oversexed and over here. When British soldiers were asked the causes for their resentment of the Yank "army of occupation" during the months preceding the Normandy invasion in 1944, this was the common answer.

overt (pronounced oh-VERT) is an adjective derived from the French verb *ouvrir* (to open), of which *overt* is the past participle. In English it has the meaning of "manifest, openly done, unconcealed." For example, it is possible to suspect a person of malice toward another but, until he commits an *overt* act of malice, you might not be sure.

Over There was the title of the famous World War I patriotic song by George M. Cohan, in recognition of which he was awarded a gold medal by President Franklin D. Roosevelt in 1940.

over the top is widely used today, especially by fund-raisers who are forever beseeching contributors to add a bit more to put the campaign *over the top*. By now there are few among this group who know or care that this phrase had its origin in the trench warfare of World War I, when the command *"Over the top!"* meant that the infantrymen scrambled out of the trenches into no man's land. There was a famous novel of that war by Guy Empey, titled *Over the Top*.

Oxbridge, a composite term for the two leading British Universities (Oxford and Cambridge), was apparently first used by Thackeray in *Pendennis,* serialized during the years 1848–1850. Thackeray used it as the name of the university the novel's hero, Arthur Pendennis, attended. Then the word fell into disuse until Virginia Woolf revived it in lectures published in 1929 under the title *A Room of One's Own*. So Mrs. Woolf, though not the inventor of the word, may certainly be credited with having revived it and contributed to its popularity. Now it has broadened in application, so that it is used to describe the older, more traditional universities, as distinguished from the newer universities.

oxford (cloth). Colleges seem to play quite a role in the shirt business. At one time, for example, Scottish weavers invented four special fabrics for shirts and named them after the four great universities of the English-speaking world: Harvard, Oxford, Cambridge and Yale. Of the four, only *oxford* remains popular today.

Ozarkian language. This land of ours often seems, to a student of language, a country of many peoples and many tongues. So varied are the dialects of the New England farmer, the Texas cowhand, the Bronx cliff dweller and the Ozark mountaineer that each would have the greatest difficulty understanding the others. Yet in these regional tongues there is a color and vitality that make them a delight to those of us with ears to hear and the leisure to enjoy. One such observer is Mrs. Shelby Steger of Bear Camp Hollow, Van Buren, Missouri. Let us share with you some of the delightful expressions she has collected in ten years residence in the Ozarks.

Many are the words brought from England and Scotland by the Pilgrims which are still in common use here in the hills. Here are a few.

"Wash the baby's hands, they're all *gaumy* [or all *gaumed up*] from that candy." "The old henhouse is so *shacklety* it's about to fall down." "I bought the biggest *budget* of groceries." (Pronounced BOO-dget—that is, the *u* of "push," not "bud.") "Wal, I wouldn't exactly say he's lazy but he *is* right smart *workbrickle.*"

Many, of course, the dictionary has lost track of. The verb *to wool*—"The baby *wooled* that pore little kitten plumb to death." *Sull* as a verb, undoubtedly derived from "sullen"—"Pa whupped Old Ring for stealing eggs, and now the old hound's crawled under the floor and *sulled up* till he won't come even when you whistle to hie him out."

Plus so much picturesque speech that I regret I don't know shorthand. Rain? Why, hit was a "raining pitchforks and bull yearlings." "Another year of this drouth and the river'll be so low we'll have to start haulin' water to it." "I ain't ascaired of him. I ain't very big but if he messes with me, he'll think I'm a circle saw."

pachyderm most frequently appears in publicity releases as "parade of ponder-ous *pachyderms,*" heralding the arrival of the circus. So most people think that *pachyderm* is a synonym for "elephant." Not so. It may refer to any large, thick-skinned hoofed mammal, including the rhinoceros and hippo-potamus, as well as the elephant. The name, indeed, comes from Greek *pakhudermos,* "thick-skinned." One sage claimed he picked up small change by making and winning bar bets that the horse is a *pachyderm.* The *Merriam-Webster* Second Edition supports this view, saying that the clas-sification includes, besides the animals already mentioned, "tapirs, horses and pigs."

Pacific Ocean was named by the first navigator from the Western world to cross its vast reaches. He was the Portuguese navigator Ferdinand Magel-lan, leader of the Spanish expedition that was the first to circumnavigate the globe. After traversing the stormy strait between the southernmost tip of mainland South America and Tierra del Fuego, he found the wide ocean so relatively calm that he named it *Pacific* from the Latin *pacificus* (peace-ful).

package goods store. In the early days of Repeal, when liquor again became legal, euphemisms were much in vogue. Several state legislatures piously voted that the saloon must never return, so the saloons reopened as "tav-erns" or "lounges." The expressions "barroom" and "liquor store" were similarly taboo in many districts. So the euphemism *package goods store* became widely used—later cut down to simply *package store.* The meaning is simple: in such stores liquor is sold only in sealed containers (packages) for off-premises consumption.

pad was originally criminal slang meaning first a bed, later an apartment or, in jail, a cell. Teen-agers have picked it up from the jargon of jazz musicians and to them it now means "home."

paddle your own canoe. The word *canoe* has been traced back to the time of Columbus and is believed to be derived from a Haitian word, *canoa,* meaning a small handmade craft, originally one made from a hollowed-out tree trunk. The phrase *paddle your own canoe*—meaning "mind your own business"—has been traced back to the early nineteenth century, although canoeing as a sport did not become popular until around 1875. It was a favorite expression of President Lincoln and his frequent use of it probably did much to make it popular.

paddy wagon. This nickname for the police patrol wagon, used to tote lawbreakers off to jail, is a carry-over from the days when the Irish were low men on the social totem pole and hence fair game when a roundup of miscreants was needed to create favorable publicity for the law enforcers. *Paddy,* of course, was a common nickname for Irishmen.

pagan comes to us from the Latin *paganus,* meaning "villager" or "rustic." For many centuries it was thought that *pagan* got its meaning of "heathen" or "non-Christian" from the fact that early Christians were city dwellers and anyone not of the city was *paganus.* However, recent research shows that *paganus* was used by Roman soldiers as a slang term for "civilian." Since the early Christians considered themselves "soldiers of Christ," it was logical that they should adopt the soldier's derogatory label *paganus* to describe everyone who was not a member of Christ's army.

pageant. In medieval times religious "mystery" dramas designed to educate the people in the doctrines of the Christian faith were performed on stages called *pagents*. These rough scaffoldings, sometimes mounted on wheels so they could be moved from place to place, later gave their name, now spelled *pageant,* to the plays acted upon them.

painter. Probably because they used to spend many long months at sea, away from contact with civilization, seamen have always had a colorful language, one uniquely their own. Aboard ship, ceilings aren't ceilings, they're *overheads*. Similarly, walls are *bulkheads,* floors are *decks,* ropes are *lines* and drinking fountains are *scuttlebutts*. Another of these words is *painter* —the line by which a small boat is tied to a ship or mooring. Originally the *painter*—called in French *peyntour*—was the rope holding the anchor to the side of the ship. In this sense the word was used in the Middle Ages and can be traced back to the Latin word *pendere,* "to hang."

paint the town red. This colorful term for a wild spree, especially one involving much drinking, probably originated on the frontier. In the nineteenth century the section of town where brothels and saloons were located was known as the "red light district." So a group of lusty cowhands out for a night "on the town" might very well take it into their heads to make the whole town red.

Pakistan. Although an autonomous nation only since World War II, its name was created back in 1933, in anticipation of the eventual creation of the state. Like so many recently coined words, *Pakistan* is an acronym, made up of the first or last letters of a group of other words. Thus *Pakistan* contains these elements: *P* for Punjab; *A* for the Afghan border states; *K* for Kashmir; *S* for Sind; and *tan* for Baluchistan. By what is certainly more than just a happy coincidence, *Pakistan* also is composed of the Persian root *pak,* meaning "pure, unadulterated or holy," and *stan,* a common Urdu suffix meaning "land or place." Thus *Pakistan,* besides containing elements of the names of each of the states which made it up, also means "Land of the holy."

palindrome. A palindrome is a phrase or sentence that reads the same backward as forward. The word comes from the Greek words *palin* (again or back) and *dramein* (to run). The best-known specimen is certainly *Madam, I'm Adam,* the phrase with which the father of us all was supposed to have introduced himself to Eve. Then there is the statement ascribed to Napoleon: *Able was I ere I saw Elba.* Others include *Rise to vote, sir,* and, evocative of World War II: *A war at Tarawa.* An imperfect but memorable one is *Lewd I did live & evil did I dwel.* This cheats on two scores, the use of the ampersand and the imitation Old English spelling of *dwel.* Clark Kinnaird claims this one, from a sign observed on a beet root cannery: *Red Root Put Up to Order.* But the longest palindrome in English (Latin spawned some that were longer) is this couplet: "Dog as a devil deified,/ Deified lived as a god."

pallbearer. If we go back a few centuries we find that the *pall* was the *pallium,* a square of heavy cloth worn over the shoulders by Romans and also used by them as a bed covering. In life it was worn by freemen and slaves, soldiers and philosophers, but in death it was used only for men of prominence, as a covering for the coffin. "The poor," according to *Brewer's Dictionary of Phrase and Fable,* "were carried on a plain bier on men's shoulders." The *pallbearers* of those days were "men of mark" whose duties consisted of serving as attendants at the funeral, each of them holding a corner of the pall. Julius Caesar had magistrates as his *pallbearers.* Senators served as such for Augustus Caesar and tribunes and centurions attended Germanicus. Today the term means one who actually helps to carry the coffin, with or without a pall. The term is sometimes extended to those who serve in the honor guard for the coffin but do not actually assist in carrying it.

pall mall was originally the name of a game—a sort of distant cousin of croquet—imported from Italy to London's fashionable West End during the reign of Charles II. A high arch or hoop of iron was mounted at one end of an alley and the sporting blades of the time would engage in contests to see who could bat a boxwood ball through the arch most often. High man, of course, was winner. So popular was the game with members of the court that the alley where it was played eventually became a center of fashionable club life and *Pall Mall* became a symbol of elegance.

palomino. The *palomino* horse bears a name directly derived from the Spanish word for "dove"—*paloma.* Originally, in Spain, the word *palomilla* was used to describe horses of a dovelike color—something on the order of brownish gray. Early Spanish settlers in the American Southwest developed the future *palomino*—in the process, the name changed slightly— from a stock that was largely Arabian in ancestry. Incidentally, as our resident horse expert reminds us: *"Palomino* is a color—not a breed."

paltry, which today means "insignificant or trifling, as well as worthless or contemptible," is thought to come from the Low German dialect word *palt,* "rag." *Palter,* the verb from which it derives, means "to haggle or deal crookedly." It probably acquired that meaning as the result of haggling over the price of rags. With rags worth so little, *paltry* and *palter* arrived at their present-day meaning.

panache. Pronounced puh-NASH or puh-NAHSH, this word, long in our dictionaries (since 1553, in fact) has recently enjoyed a new vogue in the rather special sense of "dash, verve or swagger." We borrowed the word from the French, who had taken it from the Italian *pennacchio,* "tuft of feathers." Originally it was a plume worn on a fighting man's helmet—which would doubtless add swagger to his appearance.

Pancake Tuesday is an old British name for Shrove Tuesday, the day before Ash Wednesday, which starts the Lenten period of fast and prayer. The serving of pancakes on this day was once as traditional in Britain as eating turkey on Thanksgiving is here in America. Some think the practice started from the understandable desire of British housewives to clear out fats and other foods whose use would be forbidden during Lent.

The same day is widely celebrated as *Mardi gras,* a French term meaning "fat Tuesday." This name comes from an ancient French custom of parading a fat cow or ox through the village streets on this day to symbolize the passing of meat during the Lenten season to follow.

This symbolic fasting from the use of meat also gives us the word *carnival* (from the Middle Latin *carne vale*—"Flesh, farewell!"). Carnivals are still highlights of the Mardi gras observation in many countries of Europe, to say nothing of similar revelries in our own New Orleans.

panda. Actually there are two *pandas,* one—the giant *panda*—being a great bearlike carnivorous animal native to China and Tibet and notable for its distinctive black-and-white markings. This is the animal which, in toy form, has very nearly supplanted the teddy bear as the favorite nighttime companion of America's children. The other *panda*—the lesser *panda*—is much smaller, reddish in color, and has a long ringed tail. It looks more like a raccoon than like the giant *panda*. The name is from the native Nepalese word for the animal.

pandemic/epidemic. An *epidemic* is an outbreak of a contagious disease that spreads rapidly, but usually within a fairly limited area, while a *pandemic* is an *epidemic* that spreads over a very wide geographical area. A *pandemic* may even be worldwide in scope. *Epidemic* comes from Greek *epidemia nosos,* "sickness common among people," while *pandemic* comes from Greek *pandemos,* "disease of all the people."

pander. To *pander* to the vices of man is nothing new. Men have earned their livelihoods, quite literally, as pimps and procurers for centuries, and others, speaking figuratively, have debased their talents by appealing to the lowest common denominator of public taste. As our distinguished fellow student of words, Henry L. Mencken, once remarked in a somewhat parochial application of this principle: "Nobody ever went broke underestimating the taste of the American people." Pandare was a character in Chaucer's *Troilus and Criseyde* and, predictably, he procured Criseyde for Troilus. Among his historical antecedents were Pandara in Boccaccio's *Filostrato,* Pandarus in the *Aeneid,* and Pandaros in the *Iliad.* Except for the first-named, however, these were not involved in the business of procuring the love of fair ladies.

Pandora's box. There are many versions of the fable of *Pandora* and her *box*. According to ancient myth, Jupiter, king of the gods, had Vulcan create the first woman. She was named Pandora—"all-gifted." Then he told each of the gods to contribute one power that would eventually bring about the downfall of man. These were put into a box which she was to give to the man she married. Epimetheus married her and, against advice, opened the box she gave him.

At that point the accounts vary. One version says that out flew all the miseries that have plagued mankind. According to this version, the expression *Pandora's box* should be applied to situations in which it's wise to keep matters under control and under cover, lest a worse situation develop.

Another version has Pandora opening the box herself, letting out the evils before she could close the lid. Then she heard a voice inside, pleading to be let out. She opened the box to let out Hope. In yet another version, Pandora let all the blessings of the world out of her box, with Hope alone remaining inside.

panhandle. There are at least two famous *panhandles* in the U.S., the one in West Virginia—which is often called the *Panhandle State*—and the *Panhandle* section of Texas. Each area gets its name from the fact that a narrow strip of land extends out from the rest of the state, appearing on a map much like the handle of a pan formed by the rest of the state. There is absolutely no connection between this kind of panhandle and the *pan-handlers*—beggars and bums—who frequent the slum areas of our big cities. *Panhandlers* originally used tin pans when soliciting handouts.

panic is derived from the name of a figure in Greek mythology—Pan, the god of the fields and flocks. He was usually portrayed with human torso and the legs, ears and horns of a goat, playing the pipes of Pan. A frolicsome prankster, he was often reported as darting out from the underbrush to startle passers-by—driving them into a *panic.*

panic button. When you "hit the *panic button*" you are overreacting to a supposed emergency. The expression is said to have originated during World War II, when planes flying bombing missions had a system for warning members of the crew if damage to the plane was so extensive that they might have to abandon it. On occasion—happily rare—the pilot might hit the *panic button* when the damage was minor, thereby forcing the crew to bail out unnecessarily.

panorama, for a view over a very wide area with many objects visible, comes from the Greek *pan* (all, every) and *horan* (to see). It also is used to describe a picture or series of pictures representing a continuous scene, sometimes unrolled gradually before the eyes of spectators.

pan out. Old time prospectors are responsible for this expression. They would run water through a pan of dirt in which they hoped to find traces of gold. When efforts to find gold were not successful, they would say that the attempt had failed to *pan out.*

pansy is the common and prolific garden plant that we see in many colors. It has rounded velvety petals, which some of our ancestors likened to thoughtful faces. That's why they called it, in French, *pensée,* "thought." From there to *pansy* is no distance at all.

panther sweat is one of the more than a thousand slang words which have been invented over the years as synonyms for the word "liquor."

pantomime. True *pantomime* is complete dumb show, the actor playing many parts. The word comes from the Greek *pan* (all) and *mimos* (imitator). This form of theatrical entertainment first evolved in the times of Caesar Augustus. It was often accompanied by instrumental music and sometimes choral singing. During the Middle Ages it was an important part of the Italian *commedia dell'arte,* from which our own burlesque finally evolved.

pantophobia. The most inclusive of all phobias, *pantophobia* makes its victims thoroughly miserable all hours of the day and night. Meaning "fear of everything," it is derived from the Greek *pan* (all, every) and *phobos* (fear).

pants. Remember the expression: "You surely can tell who wears the *pants* in that family"? Already it sounds dated, almost quaint, in view of the revolution in women's wear which has made pant suits a commonplace item in the wardrobes of females from eight to eighty. The wholesale adoption by women of what had been male garb would probably be dated by a social historian to the days of World War II, when the fair sex by the hundreds of thousands took factory jobs previously held by men going into service. So the transition from "outlandish" to routine has taken remarkably few years—far less time than was needed for trousers to become acceptable attire for men in the first place. (Dr. Mary E. Walker, a surgeon in the Civil War and a militant feminist, created a sensation by wearing *pants* in the 1880s, but hers was an isolated phenomenon.)

About 1790 the first trousers—probably inspired by the *trews,* close-fitting tartan *pants* worn by certain Scottish regiments—were introduced in England. Most males were unenthusiastic, feeling that the breeches and silk stockings then in vogue were more flattering, for those were the days of male "dandies." Among military and naval men, though, the newfangled trousers soon won wide popularity since they were far better suited to rough wear. Still, for several decades no gentleman would dare be seen at a fashionable gathering dressed in what were mockingly called *pantaloons,* which was later shortened to the word we commonly use today—*pants.* Indeed, no less a hero than the Duke of Wellington was refused admittance to one of his London clubs in 1814 because he was dressed in plebeian *pants,* rather than in breeches and silken hose.

panzer divisions. The German *panzer divisions* of World War II, which, under General Erwin Rommel, dominated the early phases of warfare in the African desert and also played a major role in the invasions of France and Russia, consisted mainly of tanks and armored troop carriers. This is logical, since the word *panzer* is simply the German adjective meaning "armored." It can be traced ultimately by way of the Old French *panciere* (body armor) to the Vulgar Latin *pantica,* which meant simply "paunch."

papal bull is derived from the Latin *bulla* (knob or seal). Originally it referred to the seal affixed to official documents by a Pope. Now, while retaining the earlier meaning, it is more popularly used to refer to the official edicts or decrees of the Pope.

paperhanger, in police and underworld slang, is a person who passes bad checks.

paper tiger. In the language of diplomacy, a *paper tiger* is a nation that seems menacing and powerful but may in reality be quite weak. The expression is probably Oriental in origin.

Pap test. The name of this very commonly used test for the detection of uterine cancer comes from its originator, Dr. George Papanicolaou (1883–1962), an American scientist.

parasite. We still treasure the definition of *parasite* coined long ago by Ed Wynn, the legendary "perfect fool" of stage and radio. "A parasite," said Ed, "is the guy who goes through the revolving door on your push." By dictionary definition, a *parasite* is an organism or person who lives and feeds off another of his kind without contributing anything. In ancient

Greek it originally meant a professional dinner guest and came from *para* (beside) and *sitos* (grain or food). Put together, *parasitos* first meant "fellow guest" and acquired, even then, its present-day meanings.

paregoric, the name of a medicine commonly rubbed on the gums of teething infants, comes from the Greek *paregoros,* which was originally used to describe politicians who poured out soothing words to protesting citizens gathered in the marketplace. Eventually it was applied to anything that soothed or assuaged pain. More recently *paregoric* became the generic term for tincture of camphorated opium, very widely used in the late nineteenth and early twentieth centuries as a remedy for diarrhea and intestinal pain. Indeed, many experienced travelers still swear that you're out of your mind to visit one of the countries where you're told not to drink the water, unless you have a small bottle of *paregoric* in your medicine kit. It's the favored antidote for the ailments referred to south of the border as the Curse of Cortez and Montezuma's Revenge.

pariah. The original *pariah* was not a social outcast, as a *pariah* is today. *Pariahs* (capitalized) were members of one of the lower castes in India, who were formerly slaves to the higher castes but today are employed as domestic servants. The word comes from the Tamil *paraiyan,* meaning "drummer," since a member of the *Pariah* caste served as drummer at certain festivals.

Parkinson's Law. C. Northcote Parkinson, distinguished British author and for some years Raffles Professor of History at the University of Malaya, expounded in 1957 *Parkinson's Law:* "Work expands to fill the time allotted to it or, conversely, the amount of work completed is in inverse proportion to the number of people employed."

parquet flooring. The word *parquet* appeared in print in England at least as early as 1815, according to the *Oxford Dictionary,* and it existed in French long before that. *Parquet* originally meant "little park," then came to mean a special section of a courtroom reserved for the judges. Flooring of unique design was often used to indicate that this was a special section. Hence, *parquet* came to mean the patterned flooring itself. The term was also once used to designate special areas in theaters, usually the orchestra.

party symbols. Every election year the question arises as to how the Republican party acquired the elephant symbol and the Democratic party came to be caricatured with the donkey. It's sometimes pretty hard to figure out what the parties stand for—especially if you take the long view of history and realize that the present Democratic party started out as the Republican party, changing early in the nineteenth century to Democratic-Republican party and finally, about 1828, becoming the Democratic party. As to the origin of the donkey and elephant symbols, they are both often credited to the famous cartoonist Thomas Nast—but he really deserves credit for only one, the Republican elephant. The first recorded appearance of the donkey as the symbol of the Democratic party was in 1848 in a Chicago paper, *Field Piece,* published by the Whigs, then the opposition party. Nast later used the same symbol for a post–Civil War cartoon showing the Democratic "Copperheads"—symbolized by a donkey—kicking a recumbent lion, E. M. Stanton, who had been Lincoln's secretary of war. Nast—who, incidentally, also created the tiger as a symbol for Tammany Hall—first used the elephant as a Republican cartoon symbol in 1874.

pasquinade, pronounced pas-kwih-NAYD, means to lampoon or ridicule a person by posting a mocking cartoon or satiric attack on him in a public place. It's borrowed from the Italian Pasquino, the nickname for a statue in sixteenth-century Rome on which such lampoons were posted.

passel. Heard in such expressions as a *passel of people* or a *passel of greens,* this word is a variant of "parcel" and originated in regional Southern dialect. It has now, as these examples indicate, acquired the broader meaning of a group or a fairly large number.

passion for anonymity was coined by the late Franklin D. Roosevelt. Midway through his presidency, long after the original Brain Trust had broken up, he announced that he was going to appoint several "presidential assistants" who would serve him in an advisory capacity. Perhaps with a rueful recollection of the headline-grabbing antics of Tugwell, Ickes and others of his early associates, he noted that one of the first qualifications he would demand of the new assistants would be *a passion for anonymity.*

pasteurize, an eponymous term (a word made from a proper name), means to rid milk, beer and other liquids of most disease-producing microorganisms. It takes its name from that of its discoverer, French chemist Louis Pasteur (1822–1895).

pastiche, directly derived from the French and pronounced pass-TEESH, means a composition—literary, artistic or musical, or all three—imitating previous works of the same genre or type. Originally *pastiche* derived from the Italian word *pasticcio,* whose root is *pasta* (paste). Thus the earliest meaning of this word was a composition of bits and pieces of other people's work pasted together to make a new whole.

patent leather got its name from just about where you would expect—the U.S. Patent Office. The process by which this brilliantly polished black finish is applied to leather used in shoes and handbags was once protected by patent.

pathetic fallacy was coined by John Ruskin to describe the attribution of human characteristics to things. Such an expression as "a sad day" is an example of the *pathetic fallacy.* Similarly, this from James Thurber: "It's a naïve domestic Burgundy without any breeding, but I think you'll be amused by its presumption."

patient. Originally *patient,* which comes from the Latin *pati* (to suffer), was applied to one who was under the doctor's care because he was ill or injured. However, *patient* has long since come to mean anyone who is under a doctor's care—healthy or ill.

patio comes from Spanish and, when originally popularized in our Southwest, it was given the Spanish pronunciation PAH-tyoh. Gradually this was Americanized and the two syllables of Spanish became three: PAH tee-oh. With the expansion of suburban living in recent years, the ranch house—usually in hybrid variations no rancher would ever recognize—dominated the home-building scene. Since *patio* sounded more glamorous than "back yard," it became the custom to refer to almost anything in the way of outdoor recreation area as a *patio*. And since the flat, short *a* of "pat" is far more common, especially in the Midwest, than the broad *a* of the Spanish original, the pronunciation PAT-*ee-oh* became widely heard. So today all authorities accept both pronunciations, but all still indicate a slight preference for PAH-tee-oh.

Patriot's Day. April 19 is just another day to most Americans, but up in Massachusetts it is a very special day indeed: Patriot's Day, the anniversary of the day when the first formal encounter between colonial troops and British redcoats occurred at Concord and Lexington. It's a legal holiday in the commonwealth and the townspeople turn out to commemorate the colonists' valiant stand "by the rude bridge that arched the flood," in Emerson's words. Today's Bostonians also celebrate with the *Patriot's Day* marathon race of 26 miles, 385 yards. It draws runners from all over the world, and in recent years winners have come from Japan, Mexico and Finland.

patsy is usually a dull fellow who is the butt of others' pranks and often is used as the "fall guy" to take the blame for misdeeds by others. Most dictionaries list this simply as "origin unknown" but the *Merriam-Webster* Third Edition comes up with the somewhat ingenious—and logical-sounding—theory that it may come from the Italian word *pazzo*, meaning "fool."

pawnbroker as a name for a moneylender is simply a combination of *pawn* (a pledge given as security for a loan) and the familiar *broker* (agent). The *OED* records 1678 as the year when *pawnbroker* first appeared in print, but the symbol of the *pawnbroker*—three golden balls—is many centuries older, going back to the Middle Ages. The first moneylenders in London were Italians, including some members of the Medici family. This illustrious tribe, originally (as the name implies) medicine men, acquired its coat of arms when one of the Medici forebears, fighting for Charlemagne, slew a giant who attacked him with a weapon bearing three gilded balls. Thereafter the three shining balls were the Medicis' coat of arms, first in medicine, later in moneylending.

payola is anything but a new word. It has been part of the trade jargon of the music and recording industries for decades. Some years ago, for instance, *Variety*, the show business trade magazine, devoted many pages of several issues to an exposé of the *payola* practices which even then constituted a threat to the music industry. *Payola* appears to be a fanciful variant of "payoff," formed by analogy to at least two words well known in the music trade: "pianola" and "Victrola."

The practice of undercover bribery to assure success of a project is as old as humanity. Through the years bribery—for that's what *payola* is—has acquired some interesting and occasionally euphonious labels in the various trades. Politicians are said to be *on the take*. Ticket agents, handling "ducats" for top-rated Broadway shows, see to it that they get *ice* on *hot* tickets. Other variations are *schmeir, rake-off, grease, fall dough* or simply *the take*. Perhaps most ominous, for it seems an indication of how deeply the *payola* practice has infected the American business community, is the common phrase *do business,* meaning to obtain special favors through bribery.

pay through the nose. In British slang the word *rhino* means "money." *Rhinos* is the Greek word for "nose," as we see in rhinoceros, the nose-horned beast. One theory, then, is that the phrase *pay through the nose* evolved from the similarity of *rhino* and *rhinos.* More likely, it seems to us, is that it originated with the idea of being "bled" for money—via "nosebleed." That second theory has the advantage of sustaining the basic idea of the phrase: when you *pay through the nose,* it's a painful procedure because you're paying an excessively high price.

peacoat/pea jacket. The "pea" in these terms comes from an old Dutch word, *pij,* which was the name of a heavy coarse cloth originally used in making the garment.

peanut gallery. Back in the 1890s—and perhaps earlier—it was the custom of vaudeville audiences to eat peanuts during performances, just as today's moviegoers munch away on popcorn. Theaters in those days consisted of orchestra, balcony and gallery. The "gallery gods"—so called because their seats were nearest the ceiling, which often was decorated with allegorical paintings of the heavens—were a raffish, undisciplined crew given to direct action when they wanted to express displeasure at the entertainment. The most direct method, of course, was to rain peanut shells and, on occasion, pennies down on the heads of the hapless performers. Thus developed the practice of "playing to the galleries," since success and, occasionally, physical well-being depended on satisfying the denizens of the *peanut gallery.*

peasant —a term seldom used in America—is a man of the soil. His name came into English at the time of the Norman Conquest in the form of the French word *paisent,* which is directly derived from *pays,* the French word for "country." Further back, it can be traced to the Latin word *pagus,* "district or province."

pease porridge. *Pease* is simply the archaic plural of "pea." *Pease porridge* was what we would call a thick pea soup—and that's a favorite of ours served hot. But *"pease porridge* cold"? Ugh! The rhyme goes like this: *"Pease porridge* hot, *pease porridge* cold,/ *Pease porridge* in the pot, nine days old."

peccadillo (pronounced pek-uh-DIL-oh) is a petty fault or a minor sin. A Spanish word, it is the diminutive of *pecado,* which in turn is derived from the Latin verb *peccare* (to sin).

peculate. One who *peculates* is one who embezzles or one who misappropriates public funds or any property of another which has been entrusted to him. Originally it applied principally to cattle, since this was an important part of a man's fortune. Taken from the Latin *peculari* (to embezzle), it has its earlier origin in *pecus,* meaning "cattle."

pedagogue is a schoolmaster or a teacher—usually one who is quite dogmatic and pedantic in his methods. The word comes from the Greek *pais, paidos* (child) and *agein* (to lead). The *paidagōgus* of ancient Greece was a slave whose responsibility it was to accompany the master's son wherever he went.

pedestrian comes from the Latin word *pedester,* "one who moves on foot," and its first meaning is "walking or moving on foot." For centuries, though, it has had the figurative meaning—especially when applied to writing or speech—of "prosaic or dull."

peelers are British policemen, also often called *bobbies.* Both nicknames come from the name of the founder of modern London's police, Sir Robert Peel, who earlier also organized the Irish constabulary. In America, *peeler* is show business slang for striptease dancer.

Peeping Tom goes back to one of the most celebrated legends of the Anglo-Saxon period of British history. Leofric, Lord of Coventry, imposed exorbitant taxes upon his subjects. His wife, Lady Godiva, was sympathetic to the complaints of her subjects and repeatedly pleaded with him to reduce their tax burden. He refused but eventually, more to make her be quiet than anything else, said that he would cut taxes if she agreed to ride unclad through the streets of Coventry. To Leofric's astonishment, she accepted the challenge and, after asking that all townspeople stay indoors and close their shutters while she rode, she made the ride on a white horse. Everyone honored her request except the town tailor, Tom, who peeped through the shutters and, as legend has it, was stricken blind for his impudence. And yes, the taxes were lowered.

peer/peerage. The first and basic meaning of *peer* is "equal." It came into English, by way of Norman French, from the Latin *par,* meaning "equal." However, the word also has overtones of high living on a grand social scale. In the British Empire there were five ranks of nobility, collectively making up what was (and is) known as the *peerage.* These ranks are duke, marquis, earl, viscount and baron. All of them are entitled to sit and vote in the House of Lords.

pelican. This bird with the famous pouch under the lower bill has been hymned in song and story since the dawn of history. There is even a name for him in Sanskrit: *parasu,* "ax," from the resemblance of the lower bill to the blade of an ax. The Greeks called the bird *pelekan,* which is pretty close to our own version. By the Middle Ages, the *pelican* had acquired quite a few legends, chief among them one that her maternal instinct was so great she would rend her own breast to feed her hungry offspring with her blood. This led to Congreve's writing: "What, wouldst thou have me turn *Pelican,* and feed thee out of my own Vitals?" But by all odds the most celebrated recent tribute to the *pelican* was penned by Dixon Lanier Merritt in 1910: "A wonderful bird is the *pelican,*/His bill will hold more than his belican./He can take in his beak,/Food enough for a week,/But I'm damned if I see how the helican."

P.E.N. is the international society of members of the writing fraternity and it takes its name from some of the letters of its official name: International Association of Poets, Playwrights, Editors, Essayists, and Novelists. It was founded in London in 1921, with John Galsworthy as its first president. There are American chapters in New York City and Los Angeles.

penchant (pronounced PEN-chant) is a strong liking or inclination, and comes from the French verb *pencher* (to incline).

Penelope's web. Penelope was the wife of Ulysses, who remained faithful to him during his long absence at the siege of Troy, despite the pleas of a variety of suitors. In order to keep them at bay, she promised to make a choice among them as soon as she completed a knitting project that she had in progress. But every night she unraveled the day's knitting, so the task was never completed. So *Penelope's web* symbolizes a project which, by careful design, will never be finished. Shakespeare put it rather nicely in *Coriolanus* (Act I, Scene 3), when Valeria says to Virgilia, who is busy sewing: "You would be another Penelope; yet they say, all the yarn she spun in Ulysses' absence did but fill Ithaca full of moths."

penguin. These strutting birds in formal dress got their name from Welsh and Breton fishermen who not only never saw a penguin, but never got within thousands of miles of the South Pole. Here's how this paradox developed. The great auk was a flightless diving bird, commonly found during the seventeenth and eighteenth centuries on the islands of the North Atlantic. With its heavy body, webbed feet and short tail and wings, it was as incapable of flight as the penguin of the polar regions, which indeed it much resembled. Because of the white spots the great auk had near its eyes, it was known to Breton and Welsh sailors as the *penguin,* from *pen* (head) and *gwyn* (white). When, many years later, sailors in southern latitudes saw a similar kind of flightless bird, they applied the same name to it, though the label by now was inaccurate, since one characteristic of today's *penguin* is his black head.

penicillin, one of the first of the wonder drugs, was named by its discoverer,

Dr. Alexander Fleming. He favored the pronunciation peh-NISS-ih-lin, which is still used by the British to some extent. However, there as in this country the pronunciation pen-ih-SIL-in is the favorite.

Pennsylvania (literally Penn's Woods, from William Penn's name and *silva,* Latin for "forest") is not, as many believe, named after William Penn, founder of the original colony, but after his father. In 1681 Penn was quoted, in an authorized biography, as saying: "My country was confirmed to me by the name *Pennsylvania;* a name the king would give it in honour of my father. . . . I proposed 'Sylvania' and they added 'Penn' to it." We suppose it would be quibbling to note that Penn's father was also William Penn—Sir William Penn, that is, an admiral of the king's navy and a man made unhappy by his son's plans for a "peaceable kingdom." Still, father and son were reconciled before the father's death and it remains an ironic footnote to history that the first settlement in the New World specifically devoted to peace was named after a man of war.

penny wise and pound foolish, dating back at least to the time of Shakespeare, describes a person so concerned with minutiae that he loses track of truly important considerations. A contemporary version of the same idea is to be found in the Peter Principle (which see) in reference to the man who "takes care of the molehill and lets the mountains take care of themselves."

Pentagon committee. This is the way TV commentator David Brinkley described a *Pentagon committee:* "a group of the unwilling, chosen from the unfit, to do the unnecessary."

penthouse. The *pent-* in *penthouse* comes from the same Latin root as *appendix*—the verb *appendere.* Literally, an *appendix* is something that is attached to something else. So a *penthouse* is a structure attached to (usually on top of) another, larger building.

people who live in glass houses shouldn't throw stones. This expression is about as old as anything in written English. Indeed, Chaucer has a variation of it in *Troilus and Criseyde,* using the word *verre* for "glass" (as the French still do) and substituting "head" for "house." But he makes his point strongly: "And for-thy, who that hath a hed of verre,/For cast of stones war him in the werre [war]."

percent symbol (%) is simply a figurative interpretation of the mathematical formula $X/100$ expressing "by the hundred," which is what "percent" means.

perfidious Albion means "untrustworthy England." The British have had this reputation for many centuries, it seems. Though the expression is often credited to Napoleon—who would have had plenty of reason for using it —it actually has been traced to a French bishop, Jacques Bossuet, who wrote in the seventeenth century: *"L'Angleterre, ah! La perfide Angleterre!"*

perforce (per-FORSS), an adverb, means "of necessity." The *per-* in the word is Latin for "through," so we have a meaning of "through force," the force being that of circumstances or necessity. The word is found in Old French and Middle English as *par force.*

perfume, now connoting feminine delicacy and seductiveness, comes from two Latin words: *per* (through) and *fumus* (smoke). The first *perfumes,* then, were merely scented smoke—usually from fragrant logs added to a funeral pyre to conceal the smell of burning flesh.

peripatetic, meaning "ambulatory," comes to us from the practice of Greek philosopher Aristotle, who instructed his pupils through discussions held while wandering through the covered walks of the Lyceum in Athens. The Greek word for "walk about" is *peripatein,* so his system of philosophy became known as the *Peripatetic* School.

perk is political shorthand for "perquisite" (pronounced PER-kwih-zit), which roughly equals what nonpoliticians call "fringe benefits." It's any sort of payment or benefit received in addition to the basic salary. In the case of a congressman, it can include, besides his pension, special allowances for travel expenses, stationery and the cost of maintaining an office in his home state.

pernickety/persnickety —whichever way you spell it—means "fussy, fastidious or overprecise." The word originally came from Scottish dialect, perhaps from *pertickie,* a Scottish children's form of "particular."

per se (pronounced pur say) is derived directly from Latin. It means "by or through itself." When we say that a law does not *per se* make people obey it, we mean that the law by itself has little meaning. Until the agencies of law enforcement put the law into effect it has, *per se,* meant little.

persona grata. Pronounced per-SOH-nuh GRAH-tuh, this phrase comes directly from the Latin and is used in diplomatic circles to indicate that a proposed ambassador or other legate will be an "acceptable person" to the government of the country to which he will be assigned. One who is not welcome is *persona non grata.*

personality has been a part of English at least since the fifteenth century and, indeed, was taken by way of the Norman French *personalité* from the Latin *personalitas.* It has had a variety of senses, the best known being its use to sum up the various characteristics and attributes that make an individual distinct from his fellow man. As Willy Loman in Arthur Miller's play *Death of a Salesman* said: "It's not what you say, it's how you say it— because *personality* always wins the day."

Peter Principle. "In a hierarchy, every employee tends to rise to the level of his incompetence." This was originally enunciated in *The Peter Principle,* published in 1969 and written by Dr. Laurence J. Peter and Raymond Hull. The book also tells "why incompetence is no mistake in any area of human endeavor—why schools do not bestow wisdom, why governments cannot maintain order, why courts do not dispense justice, and why Utopian plans never produce Utopias." The volume, as *Life* magazine noted at the time, "is a minor cultural phenomenon and its title phrase, like Parkinson's Law, is certain to enter the language." We especially like its description of a minor functionary (there's one in every office) whose credo is to "take care of the molehill and let the mountains take care of themselves."

petticoat tails is the name of a particular kind of cookies found in Louisiana Creole cuisine, and we are indebted to Mrs. Margaret C. Williams of Tarentum, Pennsylvania, for an explanation of how they acquired their name.

"*Petticoat Tails* is the common name in Scotland," she wrote, "for a form of shortbread cookies—and it dates back to the French influence during the Stuart–Mary Queen of Scots reign. This particular form of shortbread was made with a scalloped edge—in French *petite gatelles,* or 'little scallops.' But, when taken into Scottish dialect, it became *petticoat tails.*"

This kind of alteration from an unfamiliar to a more familiar combination of words is, incidentally, very common. Other examples of what linguists call "folk etymology" are "sparrow grass" for asparagus and "Jimmy John" for demijohn, among many to be heard in rural areas of this country.

When numerous Highlanders left their homeland to come to this country, many of them settled in our Southern states and that's how *petticoat tails* came to Louisiana.

Philadelphia lawyer is an attorney who has great talent for exposing weaknesses of opposition witnesses and an uncommon knowledge of the law's intricacies. He need never have seen the City of Brotherly Love, though it was the shrewdness of colonial lawyers in that city that gave rise to the term. There was a saying, years ago, that three *Philadelphia lawyers* would be a match for the devil himself.

But that's not all the story. There was one preeminent *Philadelphia lawyer* whose achievements may have established the label for all time. His name was Andrew (not Alexander) Hamilton and it was his defense of the New York printer John Peter Zenger that struck the first blow for freedom of the press in America.

It's an interesting story, worth recalling especially in these days when freedom of the press has been threatened in many parts of the world, not excluding our own country. Zenger was a German immigrant who settled in New York in 1710. He was apprenticed to the great Quaker printer, William Bradford, and later established his own newspaper. It was what today we'd call an anti-Establishment or "underground" newspaper. Zenger was not happy about the performance of the provincial government and didn't hesitate to attack what he considered its abuses. So in 1734 he was arrested and tried for criminal libel. Enter now our *Philadelphia lawyer,* Andrew Hamilton. As one authority put it: "Hamilton's masterly defense of Zenger persuaded the jury to acquit him. Zenger was freed and the trial was instrumental in establishing a precedent for freedom of the press in America."

It further appears that the term *Philadelphia lawyer* was used during the trial "both in praise and opprobrium." The mayor of New York was so pleased with Hamilton's defense of Zenger that he gave him special honors, while "remarks on the trial by two lawyers defending the arguments of the Crown repeatedly use the expression in a disparaging manner." And that's the story of the first *Philadelphia lawyer*—one who truly struck a blow for freedom.

philanthropy comes from two Greek words, *philos,* "love," and *anthropos,* "mankind." Today the first two dictionary meanings are: "the effort to increase the well-being of mankind, as by charitable aid or donations" and "love of mankind in general."

philatelic jargon. Almost since the issuance of the first postal stamp, over a century ago, the collection of these colored bits of paper has fascinated young and old the world over. The word *philately* itself was coined from the Greek words *philos* (love) and *ateleia* (exemption from tax), alluding to the fact that the first stamps served as evidence that postage charges had been prepaid and thus the receiver was exempted from further charge.

Like all hobbies, *philately* (pronounced phil-AT-uh-lee) has a language all its own—one which its devotees bandy about freely and which contains enough odd and colorful lingo to attract the interest even of noncollectors. Here are just a few of the commoner items from the stamp collector's working vocabulary: *Mint condition* describes a stamp or block of stamps in the same condition as when first printed. A *sleeper* is a stamp more rare —and thus more valuable—than the catalogue listings indicate. A *first-day cover* means an envelope bearing a stamp used and postmarked on the day of official issue. A *cachet* (kash-AY) is the inscription, usually printed, on an envelope bearing a special issue commemorating some great event.

Philemon and Baucis. The tale of *Philemon and Baucis* comes from the *Metamorphoses* of Ovid, a Roman poet who lived and wrote at the very dawn of the Christian era and whose works were standard fare, along with Cicero and Vergil, in the classrooms of a half century ago. As Ovid told the tale, *Philemon and Baucis* were poor cottagers in Phrygia, a country in Asia Minor. They were visited by Jupiter, who was so pleased by their hospitality that he promised to grant them any wish they might make. So devoted were they to each other that they wished only to remain together in death as in life. Their request was granted and Philemon became an oak, Baucis a linden tree, growing so close together that their upper branches were intertwined.

phillumenist. A person who collects matchbook covers is a *phillumenist,* from the Greek word *philos* (love) and the Latin *lumen* (light). Incidentally, most word coiners prefer to have both elements of a compound word come from the same language rather than one part from Latin, one from Greek. But since there is already a national society of *phillumenists,* we suppose this word is probably here to stay.

phobias are those fears which, in greater or less degree, haunt all of us. Are you fearful of high places? Do you flee from subways? Do you tremble at the thought of being alone, or are you, perhaps, terrified of being in a crowd? Whatever your fear, there's a name for it—and by the time we run through a few of the *phobias,* the chances are that your day will have turned to gloom and you'll be snorting instead of smiling at the passers-by. Don't be too depressed, though. Remember that everyone has his own particular *phobia* in the weird gamut ranging from *acrophobia,* the fear of high places, to *zoophobia,* fear of animals.

Have you ever had stage fright? Well, that's a special form of *topophobia,* fear of being in a particular place. Don't confuse that with *tropophobia,* by the way; that means fear of moving or making changes.

Most of us are familiar with *claustrophobia,* the fear of being shut up in a closed space, but there is also a more extreme form of this particular dread. It's called *taphephobia* and means fear of being buried alive. One touch of *taphephobia* and you lose all love for cave exploring!

Stenophobia does not, as it happens, mean the awe amounting nearly to fear with which a boss regards an efficient secretary; *stenophobia* is simply the fear of narrow places.

Some years ago H. L. Mencken coined the word "ecdysiast" to describe striptease dancers. He might have saved himself the trouble by calling them *vestiophobes,* people with an aversion to wearing clothing.

Unless you are a victim of *sophophobia,* fear of learning, or of *verbophobia,* aversion to words, why not look at a few more common and uncommon *phobias?*

A child afraid of night and darkness is a victim of *noctiphobia.* By contrast, some people fear bright lights. They are victims of *photophobia.* If you blanch at the thought of going to the top of the Empire State Building, chances are you have a touch of *acrophobia,* fear of high places.

Practically everyone of sense has a touch of *anemophobia,* the dread of hurricanes and cyclones, but *ailurophobes* are relatively scarce. They are people who hate cats. Many soldiers, including some of the bravest, are victims of *ballistophobia,* fear of bullets, but it's a rare person who is prone to *botanophobia,* intense dislike of flowers and plants.

If you're a regular user of that soap that claims to stop "B.O.," chances are you have a touch of *bromidrosiphobia,* fear of body odors. And the makers of color television sets will certainly have no use for victims of *chromophobia,* dislike of colors.

Practically all of us have suffered at one time or another from a touch of *dentophobia,* fear of dentistry, but no subscriber to the philosophy that "man's best friend is his bed" ever succumbed to *clinophobia,* fear of going to bed.

Well, those are just a few of the commoner *phobias.* If none of them seem to fit your case, just possibly the reason is that you're a victim of *pantophobia*—fear of everything.

phonograph. It is seldom possible to assign a precise date to changes in language, especially when dealing with the names for such a popular item as the *phonograph.* However, while *graphophone* was in common use from about 1900 to 1930, it dropped out of the popular tongue at about the time when Victor introduced its first *Orthophonic* records in the late 1920s. *Phonograph* had been in common use all along, and after 1930 became almost the exclusive term for the instrument.

Thomas Edison gets credit for inventing the *phonograph,* though his original cylinder machine was never very successful and has long since been supplanted by the disc-playing machine. The latter was the invention of Emile Berliner, about ten years after Edison, and was first called a *gramophone.* This name, incidentally, is still the generic term in Great Britain. The first Berliner machine was marketed as the Victor Talking Machine. Then, as *phonograph* became a popular name for the instrument, someone —probably the Columbia record people—switched the elements in the word and got a trademark on the word *graphophone.* The more common word *phonograph* was not eligible for trademark because it had been used as early as 1835 to describe one of the elements in a system of shorthand.

Photostat was coined in 1912 and originally applied only to the original Photostat machine and copies made by it. Undoubtedly the owners of the trademark *Photostat* wish that popular usage were still limited in that way. But whether through failure to prosecute violations of their trademark or simply because of the wide popularity of the machine and its many imitators, the word *photostat* (with a small *p*) is now part of the common tongue —a generic term.

phrenology is a pseudo science which claims to read the mind and give an analysis of character by feeling the bumps on one's head. Its root is the Greek *phren,* meaning "mind."

Pic de la Mirandole. To call a man a *Pic de la Mirandole* is to imply that he knows everything about everything. The original *Pic de la Mirandole* was an Italian humanist and philosopher of the Middle Ages who was so brilliant and learned that he was condemned by the Pope for heresy, thereby joining a select group of geniuses headed by Galileo. Matter of fact, he was accused of heresy more than a hundred years before Galileo and was later cleared of the charges.

pickle, meaning "to preserve edibles like cucumbers in brine," commemorates one William Beukelz, a fourteenth-century Dutch fisherman, who is cred-

ited with inventing the process. Presumably he *pickled* fish first and it may
be to him that we owe a debt of gratitude for having *pickled* the first
herring. By the time his name had reached the English language it had
become *pickle.*

pickup of a leftover. Only one who is capable of carrying a grudge could be
guilty of a *pickup of a leftover.* It consists of taking up again an old, old
quarrel which supposedly had been given up.

picnic. The first *picnics* were BYOB (Bring Your Own Basket) affairs. The
word came into English about 1750, borrowed from the French *pique-
nique,* which meant the same thing but somehow sounds a trifle more
piquant. Nowadays a *picnic* is any meal eaten out of doors and usually at
a spot some distance from home.

pidgin English. *Pidgin* came from Chinese traders' mispronunciation of the
word "business." Originally *pidgin English* was a language developed by
British traders with China during the seventeenth century—a blend of
English words and Chinese syntax. The end result sounds very much like
baby talk, in that many short words are used to express the sense of a single
word not known to the natives. Thus "bishop" becomes "top-side-piecee-
Heaven-pidgin-man," and "Belly-belong-me-walk-about" means "I am
hungry."

There are today many varieties of *pidgin English* and, for that matter,
pidgin French, pidgin Spanish and so on. In Mediterranean seaports, a
hybrid language containing elements of Arabic, Turkish, Spanish, Italian,
French and Greek is spoken. It is called *lingua franca*—literally "the
Frankish language"—and the Franks, you recall, were a German tribe
that, during the Middle Ages, ruled over most of Europe. Thus the term
lingua franca originally meant the language through which the Moslem
world could conduct business dealings with the Franks.

One of the most interesting kinds of *pidgin* is that known as *bêche-le-mar*
or *bêche-de-mer,* a blend of English and Malayan spoken in Samoa, Tahiti
and other Polynesian islands. When traders talk together in the islands,
you hear such phrases as "Capsize him coffee along cup" for "Pour the
coffee," and "Shoot him kaikai" for "Serve dinner." A Frenchman is called
"man-a-wee-wee" (the man who says *oui-oui*) and a butcher is called
"man-belong-bullanacow."

pie. The origin of *pie* is complicated and hardly appetizing. First, remember
that the original pies—in the British Isles, at least—were very different
from what Americans usually refer to as pies today. Instead of dessert
dishes like apple *pie* and lemon *pie,* British pies were main dishes concocted of meat or fish and a variety of vegetables, under a pastry or potato
covering. Indeed, they really were stews in *pie* form. The magpie, a member
of the crow family, has long been famous for his habit of bringing all sorts
of useless odds and ends back to his nest. So the theory is that the first pies

were so called because they contained a miscellaneous mixture of meats and vegetables, not unlike the oddments collected by the magpie.

pie card/pie card artist. Union cards were often called *pie cards* or *bean sheets* because friendly storekeepers and restaurant owners would usually allow credit to cardholders. *Pie card artist* was a derogatory term for a union organizer, especially one who promised "pie in the sky" to the union members.

pied-à-terre, a French term meaning literally "foot to the ground," is rather a popular expression in England to designate temporary lodgings. Thus an actor in town for the brief run of a show might rent an unpretentious *pied-à-terre,* rather than take a lavish apartment or, as the British would call it, a "flat" on a long lease.

piedmont. The original Piedmont is in Italy. It's a division of the country that lies largely in the Alps and hence merits its name, literally "foot of the mountain." However, *piedmont* with a small *p* is a geological and geographic term designating any land at the foot of or lying between mountains. Like the word "mediterranean," which is sometimes used by geographers to designate any body of water enclosed or nearly enclosed by land, *piedmont* can be very confusing to the nonspecialist. We have often been vexed at finding encyclopedia references to *"piedmont* districts" thousands of miles from Italy or our own North Carolina, to say nothing of "mediterranean areas" in the wastelands of Russia.

Pied Piper of Hamelin. One of the most durable of folk legends tells of a hamlet in Germany overrun by rats. To the town one day came a piper dressed in multicolored *(pied)* costume. He contracted with the town fathers to rid the place of rats for a fee. The offer was accepted and he marched off, playing his pipes, and the rats followed him to their death. When he returned for his payment the officials reneged on their promise, so he picked up his pipes again and marched merrily off—this time with all the children of the town following. There are various versions of what happened then, but most agree that virtually all the children disappeared, never to return.

piggyback. As it happens, pigs have nothing to do with this expression. Originally it was *pick-a-pack,* from the way in which packs are picked up and carried on the shoulders, just as camping packs still are today. When fathers began carrying their offspring *pick-a-pack,* the children soon translated it into the more informal and expressive *piggyback.*

piggybacking is the method of long-distance hauling of loaded truck trailers whereby the trailers are fastened on railroad flatcars and thus travel to the railroad station nearest their destination.

pig Latin has been a childhood diversion for many decades, though completely ignored by students of language and not even defined in most dictionaries. It consists simply of transposing the initial consonant of a word from the front to the end and adding the sound *ay* after it. Thus "John went home" becomes "Ohnjay entway omehay." In their excellent book *The Lore and Language of School Children*, Iona and Peter Opie report that *pig Latin* was common in England before World War I. Our guess is that *ig-pay Atin-lay* is much older than that.

pile driver. In the colorful language of the West, a *pile driver* is a horse that, in bucking, comes down to earth with all four legs stiff.

piling Pelion on Ossa means "piling embarrassment upon embarrassment." The reference is to an incident in the *Odyssey* in which the Titans, attempting to attack the gods in heaven, piled Mount Pelion on Mount Ossa, and both onto Mount Olympus.

pinch hitter comes from baseball and, in correct use, refers to a person who is substituted in the line-up when a hitter more powerful than the one coming to bat is needed. The situation most commonly occurs when the pitcher (for pitchers are notoriously weak hitters) comes to bat with runners on base and runs are badly needed. However, the term has come to be loosely used to refer to any substitute, as: "An unknown tenor was rushed in to *pinch hit* for the star when the latter became ill."

Ping-Pong is a trade name for table tennis and was invented as an "echoic" term, reflecting the sounds made by the ball as it is volleyed back and forth.

pinkie, also spelled *pinky,* looks like a typical bit of nursery slang. So it comes as something of a surprise to learn that it has been around a long, long time and that we originally borrowed it from the Dutch. Their word is *pinkje* and it means the little finger.

pin money may have originally meant money set aside especially for the purchase of pins, which, in mid-seventeenth-century England and America, were very expensive because the manufacture of pins was controlled by a monopoly under grant from the crown. More likely, however, the term is merely a figurative one, meaning funds over which the wife alone has control. Since a husband would be scarcely likely to be buying pins, the term is not inappropriate. The phrase *pin money* is recorded in the *New English [Oxford] Dictionary* as early as 1697.

pinto pony is a horse with irregular spots or markings, sometimes called "piebald" or "paint." The word comes ultimately from the Latin *pingere,* "to paint," by way of Mexican Spanish.

pioneer place names. Americans have long showed remarkable individuality in choosing names for their rivers, towns and mountains. In the early days of the opening of the West, our ancestors were inspired to name some communities in wildly imaginative fashion. In Texas, for instance, there were Hog Eye, Black Ankle, Lick Skillet, and Nip and Tuck. Mississippi named one town Hot Coffee, Tennessee had a Gizzard, Oklahoma a Bowlegs, and Missouri a Peculiar. But, in the words of H. L. Mencken, "It was after the Plains and Rockies were crossed that the pioneers really spit on their hands and showed what they could do." In California alone there were Humbug Flat, Jackass Gulch, Red Dog, Lousy Level and Hangtown, as well as Chucklehead, Rat Trap, Gospel Swamp, Paint Fot, Poverty Hill and Git-Up-and-Git.

pippin, meaning a superior or highly admired person, seems to be based on the variety of apple called the pippin—so much admired by our forebears that as early as 1900, the expression "She's a *pippin*" was admiringly applied to many a pretty girl.

pithy (pronounced PITH-ee) is the adjective form of *pith,* which was Anglo-Saxon and has kept its original meaning of the central substance of certain plant stalks. It has acquired the further meaning of "strength, force, or essence." *Pithy,* when used figuratively, can be defined as containing the central substance in terms of meaning.

pizzazz comes from the slang of show biz, ad agencies, or both combined. It's usually heard in such expressions as "Give it the old *pizzazz,*" meaning approximately "Shine it up, give it a push and see if it will roll." It's a sort of all-purpose expression. In a sentence like "It's got lots of *pizzazz,*" the *pizzazz* can be synonymous with zip, force, power, flair, savvy or what you will. While we don't know its language of origin, we suggested in print that it might come from Italian.

Not so, reported William D. Kahl of Monongahela, Pennsylvania, who remembered the word from an early comic strip. "*Pizzazza* was a magic ointment invented by a comic-strip character which would make any mechanical device, whether broken down or not, get up and go. It may also be that the product could be taken internally with similar results, though I'm not sure. I recall also that in the late 1920s the expression 'put some *pizzazza* on it' was used by my father and his cronies in much the same sense that we younger people said 'put a nickel in it.' When I asked my father the meaning of *pizzazza,* he gave us the comic-strip explanation."

There's ample record of a slang term *pazzazz*—almost certainly the same word with slightly altered spelling. *Pazzazz* or *pazzazza* meant "money," and if you subscribe to the widely held theory that money is what makes the world move, it's obvious that that's plenty of the old *pizzazz.* But this is not all. "A good number of years ago," wrote a Milwaukee lady, "it was considered quite risqué to refer to the nether part of the anatomy as the *pazzazza.* We were going ice skating on the old pond and Dad wouldn't let me use my new Christmas club skates until he had filed down the burrs. I had to use my old wood skates, so I made it my business to do a lot of falling. When I got home sopping wet, Mother asked what had happened. I told her I kept falling on my *pazzazza* with those dumb ol' skates. Mother asked if I knew what 'that word' meant. I nodded and pointed and mother went for the bar of soap—naphtha soap it was, too!"

plain as a pikestaff. A pikestaff may be either a long spear or a walking stick tipped with a metal spike. In either case, the device is certainly "plain." But one wonders why this expression should have come to mean "clear and unmistakable." Well, the explanation is in part that it originally was "plain as a packstaff," not "pikestaff," and it referred to the simple staff on which a peddler carried his pack slung over his shoulder. Obviously such a stick or staff would soon be worn plain and smooth. The expression has been around for a long time and appeared in the writings of John Dryden back in the eighteenth century. "O Lord," he wrote, "what absurdities! As plain as any packstaff."

plantar wart is so called because it occurs on the sole of the foot. It's a word the medical profession borrowed from the Latin *planta,* meaning "sole of the foot."

plastic. An interesting item in the lexicon of youthful slang is *plastic.* No, not the way you usually use it. Rather as a synonym for "phony or untrustworthy." *"Plastic* people" are phonies and the term is sometimes applied by militant youth to such of their opponents as *"plastic* liberals."

play a hunch. We often hear the phrase *play a hunch,* meaning "act upon intuition or premonition." It goes back to the gamblers' superstition that good luck would follow if one touched a hunchback on his hump.

play hooky. According to the *Dictionary of Americanisms,* this is apparently from the verb *hook,* "to make off." But *hook* in this sense is not familiar to us, unless the dictionary editor means to "make off with something," as "he *hooked* an orange from the fruit stand." Anyhow, *playing hooky* is an old, if not exactly honored, American custom. The same source traces it back to 1848, and the phrase, understandably enough, crops up often in the writings of Mark Twain at a somewhat later date.

playing ducks and drakes is simply the literary expression for what we, as youngsters, called "skimming" flat stones across water. What the poet Samuel Butler wrote centuries ago is just as true today, as every child knows: "Flat figured slates are best to make/On watery surface *duck and drake."*

play in Peoria. The late Peter Lisagor, in commenting on a program of the Nixon administration, stated that "A lot more than that will have to be done before it will *play in Peoria."* In show business a successful act is sometimes referred to as one that "plays" or "plays well." In other words, it gets a good audience reaction. So Lisagor's meaning was that more must be done before mid-America would accept Mr. Nixon's proposal.

play it close to the vest is a phrase from the game of poker, where, as in any card game, it is wise to keep your own council and not let others know what cards you hold.

play it coony. *Coony* is a dialect term meaning "sly or cunning, like a coon." In colloquial speech *to play it coony* is roughly synonymous with "to play it cozy or clever or crafty."

playoff. That long list of credits at the end of many a television show, which gives the names of everyone from the cast to the makeup man, is, in television parlance, the *playoff.*

play possum means to feign sleep or even death to outwit an opponent. The theory is that this is a method often resorted to by *possums* (actually opossums), in order to avoid harm or capture.

play the sedulous ape. This phrase is used to describe people, especially writers, who slavishly imitate their betters. It was coined by Robert Louis Stevenson, who, in a reminiscent essay, once wrote: "I have *played the sedulous ape* to Hazlitt, to Lamb, to Wordsworth, to Sir Thomas Browne, to Defoe, to Hawthorne, to Montaigne, to Baudelaire, and to Obermann. . . . That, like it or not, is the way to learn to write."

please is often used in the Bible with the meaning of "to give pleasure to or satisfy." It wasn't until the 1620s that it was first used in requests or as an indication of politeness. When we say, "Pass the butter, *please,* " the *please* is simply a shortened form of "if it pleases you," as in the French *s'il vous plait* (see voo PLAY). According to the *Oxford Dictionary,* "this use of *'please'* appears to have been unknown to Shakespeare, whose shortest form is *'please* you.' " However, the word as we know it turns up very soon thereafter (in 1622, six years after Shakespeare's death, in fact).

Plimsoll mark. All cargo- and passenger-carrying vessels bear marks, usually on either side of the bow and stern of the ship, to indicate the depth of the ship's draft under various conditions of loading. The most important mark carried by ships, however, is the *Plimsoll mark,* sometimes called the *Plimsoll line.* It is distinguished from the ordinary draft markings by being not simply a line but a circle with a horizontal line drawn through it. It is located amidships on both sides of the ship and marks the maximum depth to which that ship may be loaded. Samuel Plimsoll, a member of Parliament, waged a long campaign against shippers who, during the early-nineteenth-century period of migration from the Old World to the New, persisted in sending to sea ships that were overloaded and undermanned. So infamous and so widespread was this practice that such ships came to be known as "coffin ships." In any kind of heavy gale, the ships' chances of survival were slight, but the owners, having heavily insured the ships, stood to make a handsome profit if they were lost at sea. This murderous practice was finally halted in 1876, when Parliament passed Plimsoll's bill, and from that day onward all British ships—and virtually all the rest of the world's shipping—have carried this symbol of safe loading, named in Plimsoll's honor. American flagships also carry what are known as A.B.S. (American Bureau of Shipping) marks. These, like the *Plimsoll line,* are carried amidships, but they are four in number and mark the maximum permissible load under four sets of conditions: fresh water—summer; fresh water—winter; salt water—summer; salt water—winter.

plug, in the sense of a free promotional pitch for a book, record or show, is one of the staple products of our TV- and radio-dominated society. However, *plug* in this sense is not new. John O'Hara used it in *Pal Joey,* appropriately enough a show-biz yarn, in 1939. However, in the phrase *plug away,* meaning to work hard in support of something, it goes back to the turn of the century. In a 1908 novel, called *Show Girl,* the heroine asks: "Is it considered *au fait* for a bride-about-to-be to do a little *plugging* for wedding presents this early in the game?"

plug-ugly goes back to nineteenth-century slang, when to *plug* a chap was to hit him with your fist, preferably on the snoot. A series of such *plugs* did not tend to beautify the features of the man on the receiving end. So, with his nose spread in various directions, he became *plug-ugly.*

pocketbook. Today's ladies' *pocketbooks* could never fit into any conceivable pocket and don't at all resemble books. Still, that's what the original *pocketbook* did—back around 1800. They were men's purses, for the most part, containing two or more compartments with hinged openings that were held together, when the purse was closed, by a clasp at the top. When open, the purse could, to an imaginative fellow, have something of the appearance of an open book. When closed, the purse was fitted into the owner's pocket. Hence, *pocketbook.* Incidentally, the British suffer no such confusion. To them a *pocket book* is a pocket diary or memorandum book. An Englishman keeps his money and credit cards in his wallet or purse.

podium/lectern. A *podium* is a dais, or raised platform. It is not the desk or small stand where the speaker assembles notes for his speech. That's a *lectern,* and if you hear people refer to it as a *podium,* credit it not to "usage" but to their ignorance. The differentiation is even clearer when you consider the origins of the two words. *Podium* has its roots in the Greek *podion,* which means "base or small foot," coming in turn from *pous,* the word for the human foot. "Lectern" is from the Latin *lectus,* past participle of the verb *legere* (to read).

poetic justice describes a situation in which a person receives his just deserts or, in the popular phrase, gets what is coming to him, in a way that is ironically appropriate. It could be used in the case of a trickster who is undone by having his own trick backfire. The expression has been around a long time. In 1679, the English poet John Dryden wrote: "We are glad when we behold his crimes are punished and that *poetic justice* is done upon him."

pogonotomy/pogonology/pogonotrophy. *Pogonotomy* simply means "cutting a beard, shaving." It's made up of two Greek words: *pogon,* "beard," and *tomos,* "cutting."

While we're on the subject, anyone writing a treatise on beards would be involved in *pogonology,* the study of beards, and the person who decides to let his facial hair grow long is indulging in *pogonotrophy* (poh-goh-NOT-ruh-fee), beard-growing.

poinsettia, the traditional Christmas evergreen plant with large, brilliant-red petal-like leaves, small greenish-yellow flowers and green foliage, is one of the many plants named after the people who discovered them. It was named for Joel Poinsett of South Carolina, who was United States ambassador to Mexico more than a hundred years ago. He discovered the plant, there and brought it to this country.

poky/pokey. Spelled without the *e*, this word appeared first in print in 1849 and was an adjective which, when applied to a place, meant "petty in size or accommodations," hence "confined." Spelled either way it is a slang term for "jail," which is fitting and logical. It is one of many slang terms for various kinds of prisons, but we'd say that *pokey* is more often used as a synonym for a place where a person is held in detention for a relatively short period of time, often while awaiting release on bail or until the money to cover a speeding ticket can be obtained.

polecat takes its first syllable from French *poule*, "chicken." The second syllable derives from a real or fancied resemblance to the domestic cat. *Polecat*, then, originally meant "chicken thief," for the European *polecat* had a reputation as precisely that. The European *polecat*, unlike the American skunk, its counterpart, does not have a stripe down the back.

political language. The language of politics, especially in the United States, is colorful and ever-changing. The contrast with the long-established terminology of Great Britain's political parties is, in a sense, symbolized by the different terms applied to a candidate for office. In England one *stands* for Commons, while in America a candidate *runs* for Congress.

With the establishment of a new nation and a radically new form of government after the Revolution, it was necessary to coin a great many words and phrases, for the reason that the customs and institutions being described simply hadn't existed before. Thus our founding fathers were responsible for such now commonplace political terms as *machine* (coined by Aaron Burr), *favorite son,* first used in reference to George Washington, and *platform,* which was in use as early as 1789.

Later ingenious inventions included the phrase *to send up Salt River* (to defeat a candidate), *to crawfish* (to backtrack from a position previously taken), *to straddle, to split the ticket, to boodle* and *to eat crow.* Then there are such phrases as *lame duck,* to designate an officeholder who fails to be reelected but still has a few weeks or months to serve, and *gerrymander,* to rearrange congressional or other electoral districts in order to benefit the party in power. The phrase *taking to the stump* pretty obviously goes back to the early days of our Western migration, when the campaigning politician would mount any platform—even a tree stump—where he could find a handful of voters willing to listen to his speech.

No primary campaign would be complete without the claim of the defeated candidate that his opponent's election was actually dictated by the *bosses in the smoke-filled room.* This phrase is a comparative newcomer to our political scene and is credited to a former Associated Press reporter, Kirke Simpson, who used it to describe backstage maneuvering for Warren Harding's nomination at the 1920 Republican convention.

The word *boss* is no stranger to the American scene. It comes from the Dutch word *baas,* meaning "master." Quite possibly, then, the first American political boss was none other than old Peter Stuyvesant.

Among native American political terms, few are more colorful than *Tammany.* You may be surprised to learn that Tammany Hall was originally an exclusive social club, founded in 1789 by a group of politically minded New Yorkers including Aaron Burr. It was named after a Delaware Indian chieftain, who, some historians believe, was the person who negotiated with William Penn the transfer of the territory which eventually became Pennsylvania.

political slang—nineteenth century. The relatively mild epithets exchanged by candidates for public office in recent campaigns contrast sharply with the brash, colorful and occasionally downright libelous language of campaigns in the nineteenth century. Perhaps we should be thankful that today's talk is of "social security extension" rather than of *boodle* and *boodlers* and that our candidates choose to address themselves to such topics as "better schools and teachers" rather than to *pork barrels* and *bulldozing.* But if our nation is the gainer for this more serious-minded approach to politics, our language is the poorer. Just as the torchlight parades have been replaced by sober, sedate television appearances, so the lusty language of old has given way to the polished platitudes of ghost writers.

Before they're all forgotten, though, let's look at a few of the terms popular in granddad's day. A *roorback,* for instance, is a defamatory lie about a candidate given wide circulation on the eve of election. Its success depends upon its timing, for if the libeled candidate has sufficient time to present the facts to the electorate, public opinion is likely to swing to his support and away from the candidate who stooped to vicious libel. The original *roorback* took the form of a printed account, back in 1844, of the alleged trip through Southern states of one Baron Roorback. He reported seeing a number of Negro slaves bearing the brand of James K. Polk, Democratic candidate for the presidency. Since no Roorback really existed and since Polk was elected anyway, one might say that the first *roorback* backfired. This hasn't kept unscrupulous politicians from attempting the trick many times since, however.

A *mugwump* is a political figure who refuses to follow faithfully the dictates of his party. The term, originally an Algonquian Indian word for "chief," first came into wide use in its political sense when many Republicans refused to support the party's candidate (James G. Blaine) in the election of 1884. An attempt was made to revive this term in the New Deal days to describe a fence-straddling politician—one who had his *mug* on one side and his *wump* on the other. The revival effort, not surprisingly, failed.

Carpetbagger is the term used for unscrupulous Northern politicians, adventurers who, carrying their meager belongings in the then fashionable carpetbags, roamed through the shattered South in the years immediately following the Civil War. The shameless way in which they took advantage of impoverished Southerners has made *carpetbagger* a lasting symbol of political trickery and venality.

A *boodle* was a bribe and a *boodler* one who dealt in bribes, especially in an effort to "fix" an election. The *pork barrel* was—and is—the device by which government appropriations are used for local political patronage, disregarding the interests of the nation as a whole. *Bulldozing* was an attempt to intimidate elected officials by threat of physical violence.

Nowadays, *grass roots* is usually considered to mean the rural sections of our country and *"grass roots* sentiment" is thought to be reaction arising spontaneously from the people, especially the folks on farms. It didn't always have that meaning, however. As long ago as 1876, *grass roots* was a mining term, meaning the soil just beneath the surface of the ground. To describe a mining site in North Dakota's Black Hills as one in which gold could be found even at the *grass roots* was a certain "come-on" for Eastern speculators. Later *grass roots* developed a new meaning, in the phrase "get down to *grass roots"*—getting down to basic facts. This may well have been because many of the naïve Eastern speculators found nothing but hard rock instead of dreamed-of gold when they reached the grass roots. In any event, the term in the political sense of "sons of the soil" seems to have been introduced about 1920 by the Farmer Labor party and it was taken over by the Republicans when, in 1935, at the nadir of their fortunes in this century, they held a "Grass Roots Conference" at Springfield, Illinois. The ill-fated Alf Landon presidential campaign of 1936 also stressed the *grass roots* theme and doubtless did much to bring the phrase to wide popular recognition and use.

politics/politician. *Politics* has its origin in the Greek words *polis* (city) and *polites* (citizen). From the same source, incidentally, came the word *police.*

Originally *politics* meant whatever had to do with the rights and status of a citizen. Gradually it has come to have at least two clearly defined meanings: the art and science of government, sometimes called "political science," and the day-to-day professional management of political affairs from the city precinct to the White House. An expert manipulator of political affairs, especially one who regards the great game of politics as his career, is known as a *politician.* This word has always had somewhat unsavory connotations, with, as one authority puts it, "implications of seeking personal or partisan gain." For this reason even the most skilled political operators often shun the label *politician,* much preferring to be called "statesmen."

politics makes strange bedfellows, one of the most widely quoted of American aphorisms, originally appeared in print in *My Summer in a Garden* (1870) by Charles Dudley Warner, editor of the *Hartford* (Conn.) *Courant* as well as brother-in-law and collaborator of Mark Twain. According to some authorities, it was Warner, not Twain, who first wrote: "Everybody talks about the weather, but nobody does anything about it."

polka dot. One dictionary, which shall here be nameless, suggests that *polka dot* may be "perhaps a respelling of 'poke a dot.'" Well, the story behind this expression is by no means as dull as that editor's imagination. It all started in the nineteenth century when dancing the polka was all the rage in America. Just as the Charleston swept the country in the 1920s and the Frug and Watusi in the 1960s, so the polka was once the dance for everyone with any pretensions to style. At the time, there was no radio or TV, not even phonograph records, so fashions in music as well as in dress tended to last much longer than they do today. Fabric manufacturers and dress designers often named their products after the songs most in vogue at the time. And so it was that those years saw "polka gauze," "polka hats" and fabrics printed with *polka dots.* Only the *polka dots* lasted, though.

poll. The first *polls* were elections held by counting heads, for *pol, polle* in Middle English simply meant "head." One still, of course, goes to the *polls* to cast ballots in elections. The first so-called straw or unofficial *polls* were held in the United States in 1824. They consisted chiefly of man-in-the-street interviews or door-to-door canvassing by newspaper reporters. Since the mid 1930s, with the debacle of the *Literary Digest* mail poll, which predicted a victory for Landon over Roosevelt, techniques have been greatly improved. Now such *polls* as the Gallup, Harris and Roper surveys are used not only to gauge probable election results but also to test public reaction to new products.

poltergeist —from the German *Polter,* meaning "uproar," and *Geist,* "spirit or ghost"—is a prankish sort of spirit, the Middle European equivalent of Erin's elves, leprechauns and little men.

pompadour is a style of hairdress affected by both men and women. In both cases the hair is brushed straight up from the forehead. It is named for its inventor, Marquise de *Pompadour,* mistress of French King Louis XV— the one who said, *"Après moi le déluge"* (which see).

pomp and circumstance, which Elgar used as the title of his composition so often heard at high school graduations, comes from a line in *Othello:* "pride, pomp and circumstance of glorious war." *Circumstance* comes from two Latin words, *circum* and *stare,* and originally meant "standing around." Then it came to mean an event at which large numbers of people were standing around. By Shakespeare's day, it meant any formal show or ceremony. This meaning is now archaic.

pooh-pooh goes back centuries. As simply *pooh,* it was an expression of disgust or contempt even in the time of Shakespeare. Then, back in the seventeenth century, people began doubling the *pooh,* presumably to make their feelings more apparent. Now it simply is a term used to express disdain or contempt for something other people regard highly.

poor as Job's turkey. If there were any comment on poultry in the Book of Job, it would not refer to *turkey*—at least not in the King James version —since the turkey is a uniquely American bird. The phrase *poor as Job's turkey* was coined in the early nineteenth century by a rustic humorist named "Sam Slick." It was intended to indicate someone who was even poorer than the Biblical Job, who was the very personification of poverty. Sam Slick's real name was Thomas Chandler Halliburton.

poor thing but mine own. John L. Lewis, fiery long-time president of the United Mine Workers of America, is credited with saying "A *poor thing but mine own."* We don't doubt in the slightest that John L. used this phrase, for he was a lifelong student of Shakespeare and the Bible. But it's a certainty that Lewis, steeped as he was in Shakespeare, borrowed from *As You Like It* (Act V, Scene 4) and paraphrased the speech of Touchstone to Jaques in which he describes his beloved Audrey as "A poor virgin, sir, an ill-favored thing, sir, but mine own." One of John L.'s most famous utterances came when F.D.R. quoted *Romeo and Juliet,* "A plague on both your houses," at a critical point in the labor-management battles of the 1930s. Lewis repaid with what Ed Murrow called "the lash of his biblical oratory." "Labor, like Israel, has many sorrows," said Lewis. "Its women weep for their fallen and they lament for the future of the children of the race. It ill behooves one who has supped at Labor's table and been sheltered in Labor's house to curse with equal fervor and fine impartiality both labor and its adversaries when they become locked in deadly embrace."

pope's nose/parson's nose. The best evidence seems to put this expression back at least to the time of King James II of England. Feeling was fairly strong among some sections of the public against any future occupancy of the British throne by a Roman Catholic. Someone fancied a resemblance of the fowl's rump to the nose of a pope, and the term was born—or so the story goes. The only trouble with this account is that the *Oxford English Dictionary* defines *pope's nose* as merely equivalent of *parson's nose.* This would seem to indicate that parsons had the dubious honor of being likened to fowl long before the label was extended to popes. The term *parson's nose* was also widely current during the nineteenth century in America, and no less a literary figure than Henry Wadsworth Longfellow used it when referring to what he termed that "epicurean morsel."

pop goes the weasel! From earliest childhood we remember with fondness the nonsense rhyme about the monkey and the weasel. Remember? "Every night when I come home,/The Monkey's on the table./I take a stick and knock him off/And *Pop goes the Weasel!*"

Here is the background of the original, and far different, British version of this rhyme—which turns out to be not such nonsense after all. It runs: "Up and down the City Road,/In and out the Eagle,/That's the way the money goes./*Pop goes the weasel!*"

And would you believe that the whole silly rhyme started with some drunken London hatters, the kind that today's sociologists would label "compulsive drinkers"? True. And here's the explanation. The City Road was a street in London where there was a much-liked tavern ("pub" in England, of course) called The Eagle. To it on Saturday nights, and maybe oftener, went many a hatmaker. If he was short of funds, as often happened, he pawned ("popped") his *weasel* (a hatmaker's tool). So there you have, unmasked, the sordid truth behind that simple nursery rhyme.

popinjay comes from the Arabic word *babaga* by way of the Greek *papagos,* meaning "parrot." One of the notable characteristics of parrots is their ability to chatter away without having a thought in their heads. Another is the dazzling beauty of their plumage. Put these two characteristics together and you'll see how easily we came to the present-day meaning of *popinjay*—a foppishly dressed chatter-mouth.

pork barrel. There is an old story that this expression dates back to plantation days in the old South, when the opening of a barrel of pork was the signal that "caused a rush to be made by the slaves." You can believe this story if you want to, but it seems to us that there is not much logic to it. First, many plantations raised their own hogs and the smokehouse where hams and bacon were cured was a familiar sight on most of them. So the opening of a barrel of pork would be no great cause of excitement. What's more, it doesn't seem likely that slaves "rushing" to raid such a barrel could have been a common sight in the antebellum South.

The more probable, though less colorful, origin of *pork barrel* is that it is simply an expression that developed from *pork,* which had been in common slang use in the sense of graft or patronage since the carpetbagger days of the Reconstruction. As long ago as 1879 the *Congressional Record* reports the use of the term: "St. Louis is going to have some of this *pork* indirectly."

Later, when legislation like the Rivers and Harbors bill became an omnibus vehicle in which patronage plums were distributed by many congressmen to their constituents, the analogy of packing all the *pork* into a single *barrel* became obvious. By 1913 "Fighting Bob" La Follette was writing about "*pork-barrel* legislation" and the chances are that the expression was in general use even before that time.

pork chops/pork chopper. *Pork chops* was the rough-and-ready term used to designate the benefits expected by unionized workers as a result of a strike.

Nowadays, the talk is more likely to be of "fringe benefits," the *pork chops* having long since been taken care of. Still, *pork chopper* remains as a disrespectful term for a union official who is chiefly interested in making a good living for himself.

port, the left side of a ship facing forward, is a fairly recent replacement of "larboard," meaning the side of the boat on which loading was customarily done. This was, in Middle English, the *laddeborde,* or lading side. *Port* probably replaced "larboard" because the latter sounded so much like "starboard." In the teeth of a howling gale, it can be very important to have commands interpreted correctly.

portholes. Ever wonder why the windows in ships are called *portholes* when half of them are on the starboard side? Well, in early sailing days, the only holes in the sides of the vessels were the ports for guns—called *portholes.* In those times, sailors were given little or no consideration below deck and had practically no air or light in their sleeping quarters. Gradually matters improved, and when holes were cut into ships' sides to admit light and air, they were given the same name as the earlier openings—*portholes.*

portico is an open porch or a walkway with a roof supported by pillars. It comes from the Italian word of the same spelling, which simply means "porch."

posh is a borrowing from British slang, meaning "smart, sophisticated or elegant." Thus one might be complimented on a "very *posh* party" or a well-turned-out sportsman could be applauded as "looking very *posh* today." There is a charming story of the word's origin. It dates back to the era when Great Britain was truly a seat of empire and her colonial emissaries were making regular trips from London by steamer to India, Australia and other far-flung territories. Preferred accommodations aboard ship were "away from the weather"—port side outward-bound and starboard side homeward-bound. And that is where *posh* came from—Port Outward, Starboard Home.

posting of the banns. *Banns* are a series of announcements of the intent of a couple to wed. Today's common meaning of "ban"—to forbid or prohibit —is nowhere involved in the *banns* of marriage. Yet the two words come from the same Anglo-Saxon root, *bannan*—"to proclaim or to summon." What has happened is that the word has acquired through the centuries the specialized meaning of to proclaim a prohibition. This probably resulted from the use of *bann* and later *ban* by church authorities to proclaim the excommunication of sinners. This most serious form of ecclesiastical disapproval soon diverted the word from its general meaning to the special sense of prohibition in which it is most commonly used today.

potatoes and point. At mealtime during the dreadful years of the potato famine in nineteenth-century Ireland, even salt was in short supply and often the salt cellar was empty. On such occasions, the empty cellar was put in the middle of the table and the children would be told to point their potato toward the cellar before eating it. Such a meal was called *potatoes and point. Brewer's Dictionary of Phrase and Fable* agrees with this definition. However, Bernard Bates of Milwaukee, Wisconsin, challenged that account, saying: "I learned about *potatoes and point* as a preschooler and the version I heard had nothing to do with the potato famine but was a regular part of Irish life in the old times. As in all societies, some members were wealthier than others, and one sure sign of wealth was a slab of bacon hanging over the fireplace. After dipping the potato in salt, it was ritually raised in the direction of the bacon. The potatoes naturally tasted better this way—and it also impressed the neighbors." It is possible that his version is true, but that by the time of the famine few families had salt, let alone bacon, and some didn't even have potatoes.

pot calling the kettle black. There are two slightly varying interpretations of this phrase, which is used figuratively to apply to persons. One theory is that such action is ridiculous because they are both black, presumably from standing for years on a wood-burning stove or in a fireplace. So the pot as well as the kettle is black (evil) and neither one is better than the other. This supports the explanation of the phrase as given in *Brewer's Dictionary of Phrase and Fable:* "Said of one accusing another of faults similar to those committed by himself."

The other theory is that the pot was black but the kettle was polished copper and the pot, seeing its own blackness reflected in the shiny surface of the kettle, maintained that the kettle, not it, was actually black. In any event, it seems that the best, if slangy, retort by the kettle may have been: "Look who's talking!"

Usually the source of the phrase is given as Cervantes' *Don Quixote* and simply as "The pot calls the kettle black," but another version of *Don Quixote* comes out as "Said the pot to the kettle, get away black-face!" Henry Fielding, eighteenth-century British writer, reverses the roles in *Covent Garden Tragedy:* "Dares thus the kettle to rebuke our sin!/Dares thus the kettle say the pot is black!" Even Shakespeare used the idea in *Troilus and Cressida:* "The raven chides blackness."

pot likker does not refer to homemade moonshine, brewed in the hillbilly sections of the country. Such moonshine may be called *silo drippings, mountain dew* or, perhaps, *stump liquor. Pot likker,* on the contrary, is an entirely respectable and assuredly nonalcoholic beverage. *Pot liquor,* to give it its formal spelling, is a sort of broth made from greens or field peas boiled with a fat meat, usually that cut of pork known as fatback. Its praises have been sung by no less an authority on Southern cuisine than the late Marjorie Kinnan Rawlings, whose *The Yearling* remains one of the authentically great books of our time. In *Cross Creek* she wrote: "Turnip greens cooked with white bacon, with cornbread on the side, make an occasion. *Pot liquor* and cornbread have even entered into Southern politics, a man addicted to the combination being able to claim himself a man of the people."

potter's field is a burying ground for destitute or unknown people. It has its origin in the Bible (Matthew 27:7), where the chief priests and elders of the people are faced with the problem of what to do with the thirty pieces of silver which Judas cast down in the temple. "And they took counsel, and bought with them the *potter's field,* to bury strangers in."

pound sterling. In medieval England the smallest unit of currency was the silver *sterling,* worth about the same as a penny today. The *sterling* got its name from the fact that a star (*steorra* in Middle English) was embossed on it. When a larger unit of currency was needed, it was originally fixed at one pound of these *sterlings.* Thus, *pound sterling.*

pox upon you! This expression comes straight out of the eighteenth century. In that era, when smallpox was one of the most widespread and deadly maladies, the expression *A pox upon you!* was a very serious oath. Today, thanks to the success of medical science in virtually eliminating smallpox, it is merely an archaic and amusing euphemism.

practical joke is a trick played upon another person. Usually it is intended to be funny, but occasionally the trick goes awry and the result is painful to both perpetrator and victim. Such *practical jokes* as the "hot foot" fall into this category. But the quality that distinguishes a *practical joke* from the ordinary jest is that it depends upon some "practical" action by the person perpetrating the joke. In the case of the "hot foot" it is the action of igniting a match previously inserted between the sole and upper part of the victim's shoe.

pragmatic/pragmatical/pragmatist. *Pragmatic* (pronounced prag-MAT-ik) is the adjective form of *pragmatism,* a form of philosophy based on the practical utility of any given function or conception. Stemming from the Greek word *prassein,* meaning "to do," it has the same origin as "practice" and "practical." *Pragmatical* has the meaning of meddlesome or officious, opinionated or conceited. These same meanings apply to *pragmatic;* however, this shorter form has other, broader meanings, including: practical, busy, pertaining to the civil affairs of a state, concerned with the historical evolution of causes and effects. *Pragmatist* is the usual word for a *pragmatic* person, although *pragmatic* alone is sometimes used as a noun to designate such a person. The term *"pragmatic* sanction" is applied to a royal decree that has the same force as fundamental law.

praise the Lord and pass the ammunition! is credited to a Navy chaplain, Howell M. Forgy, of the U.S.S. *New Orleans.* He is said to have used the expression as an exhortation to the ship's gunners during the Japanese attack on Pearl Harbor in 1941. It owes its popularity to a popular song of that title written by Frank Loesser, who delighted audiences in postwar years with such Broadway hits as *Guys and Dolls* and *How to Succeed in Business.*

pratt fall, meaning a fall on the buttocks in an effort to obtain laughs from an audience, is certainly slang, a part of the trade talk of show business for as long as we can remember. Just by the way, a commonly heard synonym for *prat* or *pratt* in show business circles is *keister* (pronounced KEE-ster).

praying mantis. A green or brown predatory insect *(Mantis religiosa),* the *praying mantis* gets its name from the fact that, at rest, it folds its front legs as if in prayer.

precarious. The person who chooses to live in *precarious* proximity to danger will do well to remember his prayers, for that is literally what *precarious,* from the Latin *precarius,* means—"dependent upon prayer." The ultimate Latin word for prayer or entreaty is *prex,* a form we also see in words like "imprecation."

prejudice. Some authorities on usage maintain that *prejudice* may only be used in an unfavorable sense—that is, one must always be prejudiced *against* something, never *for* something. The assertion was often made in the early days of this century—when language proprieties were perhaps more closely observed than they are today—that one might be *partial* or *predisposed* in favor of a person or thing but never *prejudiced.* Actually, there was never any linguistic basis for this "rule." *Prejudice* comes from the Latin prefix *prae-* (before) and *judicium* (judgment), and merely means a preconceived idea—either favorable or unfavorable.

prestige. In the business and literary worlds of today there is no certain method of acquiring *prestige,* but once acquired, it has an element of dignity which was lacking in the Latin word from which it comes. Its Latin root, *praestigiae,* meant "jugglers' tricks" and was made up of *praesto* (quick) and *digitus* (finger). It became *prestige* in French, from which we borrowed it. Today, of course, it means "importance or reputation based on success in a given field." The original meaning of its Latin root, however, remains in the word *prestidigitators,* the first of whom were jugglers in ancient Rome.

pretty kettle of fish is an odd phrase. Except to the devoted fisherman, there's no such thing as a *pretty kettle of fish*—and most truly sporting fishermen prefer to broil or fry their catch anyway. The phrase came from a custom common along the Scottish border. At the start of the salmon run each year, groups would gather for outdoor picnics along the banks of the streams. The main course at these affairs was salmon boiled in a huge pot of well-salted water and eaten in catch-as-catch-can fashion. Give thought for a moment to the shambles likely to result from dozens of people trying to eat hot boiled salmon with their fingers while sitting along the banks of a woodland stream—and you'll understand why the phrase *pretty kettle of fish* has long been synonymous with confusion, muddle and mess.

pretty penny. How did the expression *pretty penny* come about? "Pretty" has several meanings besides "pleasing to the eye." It also means "considerable," as in expressions like: "He won a pretty good sum of money at the race track." That's the sense in which *pretty penny* is used—a considerable sum of money.

prevaricate. To *prevaricate* is to be evasive for the purpose of deceiving. It is also used loosely to mean "to lie." It comes from the Latin *prevaricari,* which literally means "to walk crookedly." The *-varicari* in the word stems from *varus,* meaning "bent"—hence *prevarication* could be said to be "bending the truth," which in a strict sense is not the same as "to lie."

primordial (pronounced pry-MOR-dee-al) comes from the Latin *primus* (first) and *ordiri* (to begin) and is an adjective meaning "first in order, original, primitive or fundamental." "The first life developed from the *primordial* ooze."

primrose path. Like so many common sayings, this comes from Shakespeare —from *Hamlet,* in fact. Laertes, Ophelia's brother, has just been giving her a lot of well-intentioned brotherly advice. Ophelia is not impressed. "Do not," she tells him, "as some ungracious pastors do,/Show me the steep and thorny way to heaven,/Whilst, like a puff'd and reckless libertine,/ Himself the *primrose path* of dalliance treads."

pristine (pronounced PRISS-teen) comes to us directly from the Latin *pristinus,* "primitive." Properly defined as "earliest" or even "primeval," the word has come to mean "unchanged or uncorrupted." Thus an antique dealer might refer to a Victorian highboy as being in *"pristine* condition," signifying that it has been preserved by its previous owners so carefully that it is truly "as good as new." *Pristine* here is practically the same as a stamp or coin dealer's usage "mint condition," meaning his merchandise is as fine as the day it left the mint.

private (in the army) is one of so many that he certainly doesn't seem "separate or apart," as the adjective form of the word is usually interpreted. When you consider that the word comes from the Latin *privare* (to separate or deprive), the military term becomes more logical. A *private,* as any one of them will tell you, is certainly deprived of rank or office.

private eye. The *eye* part of *private eye* started with the letterhead of the Pinkerton detective organization, which featured a large all-seeing eye. The idea, of course, was that nothing could escape the always vigilant Pinkertons. Since the Pinkertons were detectives for hire—private detectives—the expression *private eye* quickly became underworld slang for any and all undercover investigators not on the public payroll. The first great fictional *private eye* was Sam Spade in Dashiell Hammett's *The Maltese Falcon.* In the memorable Warner Brothers film of *The Maltese Falcon,* Humphrey Bogart, under John Huston's direction, created the prototype of today's motion picture private eyes. The rugged tough-guy character of Hammett's book and the later film was undoubtedly authentic—if only because Hammett himself had been a Pinkerton *private eye.*

pro bono publico is a Latin phrase meaning "for the public good."

Procrustean bed. Procrustes was a fabled Greek giant and highwayman who fitted all his victims to an iron bed. If they were too short, he stretched them to fit; if too tall, he lopped off any part extending beyond the length of the bed. So *Procrustean bed* has come to mean any foreordained standard to which exact conformity is required.

prodigal is often but inaccurately interpreted as meaning "wandering or straying." It doesn't. It means "extravagant or wasteful." Many people know the word *prodigal* only through the New Testament story (Luke 15:13) of the prodigal son. You recall that the younger of two sons, taking his share of his father's goods, "took his journey into a far country, and there wasted his substance with riotous living." It's the "wasting his substance" that earned him the label *prodigal.* But many people tend to remember the "journey into a far country" and mistakenly think that's what *prodigal* means.

profile. A drawing in *profile* is usually simply an outline. The Italian word *profilo* is made up ultimately of the Latin elements *pro* (forward) and *filare* (to draw a line). During the 1930s and 1940s the word came into general use as the name for a casual, anecdotal biographical sketch of a celebrated person. In this sense it was first used by *The New Yorker* magazine.

Project Gemini. The second phase of America's manned-spacecraft operation was called *Project Gemini. Gemini* is the Latin word for "twins" and refers to the fact that the spacecraft was planned to carry two men into orbit.

prole is an item from British slang—a shortened form of *proletarian.* Thus a *prole* is a member of the working class.

proletariat. The *proletariat,* meaning the working class and especially the industrial working class, has an entirely different economic position in most countries today than it had in ancient Rome, where the word originated. *Proletarian* and *proletary,* both of which designate a member of the *proletariat,* also come from the Latin *proletarius,* which in turn comes from the Latin *proles,* meaning offspring. In ancient Rome a *proletarian* or *proletary* was a citizen of the lowest class, owning no property and regarded as serving the state only by having children.

prolix (pronounced PROH-lix or proh-LIX) is an adjective meaning "wordy, profuse, tedious or long-winded" and is derived from the Latin *prolixus* (extended). It becomes *prolixity* or *prolixness* as a noun, *prolixly* as an adverb. "Johnson's prose style was notable for its *prolixity.*"

promo, in the jargon of radio and television, is a short "promotional" plug. It's used to promote interest in another show on the same station.

propaganda. In today's battle of ideas and ideologies, what our side says is "information," what the opposition says is *propaganda.* It's curious that this word should have come to the point where its use today is almost wholly in derogatory connotations, for few words ever had more estimable sponsorship and few were ever coined with the idea of describing a more worthy cause. *Propaganda* was the coinage of Pope Urban VIII, who organized a *congregatio de propaganda fide,* a "congregation for propagating the faith." The original intent of the word *propaganda* was the spreading of Christian faith by missions throughout the world. Through the centuries *propaganda* came to mean any doctrine circulated on a broad scale, and late in the last century began to be used in what H. L. Mencken calls "the evil sense."

propinquity is pronounced pruh-PING-kwih-tee and is given three meanings in the *American Heritage Dictionary:* (1) nearness; proximity; (2) kinship; (3) similarity in nature. It comes to English almost unchanged from the Latin *propinquitas.*

prop man (girl). The person responsible for assembling the various properties required for a theatrical performance is usually known as the *prop man* or *prop girl.* These properties include virtually every item involved in the production, save costumes and scenery.

prosaic. It's easy to remember the meaning of *prosaic*—as well as its origin —if you are fond of poetry. *Prosaic* is unpoetic—prose as opposed to poetry —hence "commonplace, matter-of-fact and dull." As a matter of fact, it comes from the Latin *prosa,* which means "prose."

proscenium. In today's theater the *proscenium* is that part of the stage between the curtain and the footlights, but in the classical theater of Greece it included the entire stage, from backdrop or scenery to the orchestra. Hence its name, from the Greek *pro* (before) and *skene* (tent or backdrop).

protean, meaning "able to take on different sizes or shapes," comes from Proteus, a Greek sea god who could change his shape at will.

prothonotary warbler, the name of a bird, has quite a story behind it. *Prothonotary* now is chiefly used as an elegant legal name for a clerk in a court of law, but that's not the only meaning it has. In the Roman Catholic Church there is a group of high officials known as the College of Prothonotaries Apostolic. At important meetings they sometimes wear brilliant yellow robes and it's thought that the *prothonotary warbler* was so called because of the resemblance of its brilliant yellow head and breast to the ecclesiastical costumes. *Prothonotary* (sometimes spelled without the *h*) comes from the Latin word for shorthand, so it would appear that church scribes were using various forms of shorthand many centuries before the Gregg, Pitman and Speedwriting methods were invented.

protocol means to most persons the etiquette observed at official functions or in the relationships of heads of state, ministers and diplomatic corps. But it really means more than that. It comes from the Late Greek *protokollon* (*protos,* "first," and *kolla,* "glue"), which was a leaf glued to the front of a manuscript. On the leaf were notes as to the contents of the manuscript. *Protocol* still refers to the original draft or record on which a document is based. In diplomacy, *protocol* may mean a signed document which sets forth the points on which agreement has been reached by representatives of different governments and on which the final treaty or document will be based. Then, too, it may mean who sits next to whom at dinner.

prurient interest is a favorite phrase of lawyers and judges involved in questions of whether or not something is obscene. The legal position usually is that anything which arouses the *prurient interest* of the one viewing it should be considered obscene unless it has literary merit of considerable import. *Prurient* comes from the Latin *pruriens,* present participle of *prurire,* meaning "to long for or to be wanton." Webster's *New International Dictionary,* Third Edition, defines it as "marked with restless longing," "itching with curiosity" or "tending to excite lasciviousness."

psychedelic is coined from two Greek words and means "mind-manipulating." It was probably coined by Drs. Leary and Alpert, the two unfrocked Harvard professors who were the high priests of the cult of LSD and the other hallucinogenic drugs. And "hallucinogenic," of course, means "producing hallucinations" or wildly visionary dreams. The word was probably coined during the late 1950s.

psychosomatic. During recent years much has been written about *psychosomatic* medicine and many authorities have labeled it a great step forward in medical history. Put briefly, *psychosomatic* medicine is that branch of medicine which treats physical ailments caused by mental illness. Not only colds but many more serious physical illnesses—such as asthma—often may be caused by worry. They may, in medical language, be "of *psychosomatic* origin." As one doctor stated: "We have always known that illness can make us unhappy. Now we are beginning to realize that unhappiness can actually make us ill." Appropriately enough, *psychosomatic* is derived from the Greek words *psyche* (mind) and *soma* (body).

public be damned. William Henry Vanderbilt was an executive of the New York Central Railroad at the time when, in 1882, the road started a high-speed "flier" from New York City to Chicago to compete with a similar train on the Pennsylvania Railroad. He told a reporter that the road was losing money on the train but would continue to run it because of the competition. "But," asked the reporter, "wouldn't you continue it anyway for the benefit of the public?" "The *public be damned,*" roared Vanderbilt. "Railroads are not run on sentiment but on business principles."

pub names in Britain. Among the more unusual, yet characteristic, aspects of Britain are the pub signs to be seen in even the smallest hamlet. *The Pig and Whistle, The Rose and Crown, The Hare and Hounds,* and suchlike —usually with some coat of arms or other insignia—are to be found throughout the countryside. Nowadays most such town and country *pubs*

—short for *public houses*—are owned or controlled by one of the major brewers. But the feeling of intimate identity with the community is retained, and the manager and the barmaid, who is often his wife, are respected and substantial citizens, on a first-name basis with just about everyone in town. The pub has traditionally been the common man's club. Today it's his wife's as well.

The origin of these remarkable public-house names was an item of interest to us during a recent trip to England, and we found the research both stimulating and rewarding. For one thing, many of the oldest names go back to the days when the lord of the manor dominated a neighborhood, with most townspeople directly or indirectly obligated to him for their livelihood. So it's not surprising that many names reflect a loyalty or, perhaps, servility to him by being simply his name or that of the reigning monarch, *The Royal George, The Prince of Wales, The Albert,* and so on. Such names as *Fox and Hounds* reflect the favorite activity of the local lord. Similarly, pride in national conquest resulted in names like *Duke of Wellington* and *Waterloo.*

Still other names have changed through the centuries—with sometimes whimsical results. *The Bacchanals*—very properly classical—is now *The Bag o' Nails. St. Catherine's Wheel* became *The Cat and Wheel. The Plume of Feathers*—referring to the Prince of Wales—became *The Plum and Feathers,* and so on. *The Two Chairmen* does not, as you might think, designate a pub where board chairmen may be expected to meet to discuss weighty business deals. Rather it gets its name from the fact that in the eighteenth century it was a favorite stopping place for weary chairmen, carriers of the sedan chairs which were the taxis of the period. And down in London's Fleet Street there's a pub frequented by newspapermen. Its name dates back centuries and is perhaps symbolic of the place to which managing editors have been consigning ink-stained wretches since publishing began. It's called, simply, *The Devil.*

Puck is a mischievous sprite, also called Robin Goodfellow, of English folklore. He is the British equivalent of Germany's Til Eulenspiegel, Ireland's leprechauns, and other mythical pranksters. Immortalized by Shakespeare in *A Midsummer Night's Dream, Puck* also plays a notable role in one of Kipling's finest books, his account of Britain under the Romans, *Puck of Pook's Hill.*

Pudding and Tame, familiar to most of us because of a children's chant beginning with those words, has religious associations. It is, according to the Opies' *The Lore and Language of School Children,* "the name of the fiend or devil *'Pudding of Tame'* listed in Harnet's Popish Impostures," published way back in Shakespeare's time. The devilish implications of the name have long since been forgotten by the children who cheerfully chant: "What's my name, *Puddin' and Tame.* Ask me again and I'll tell you the same." Curiously enough, although the original name is English, the children's rhyme is said to have originated in Maryland. Wentworth's *American Dialect Dictionary* reports it as turning up all over the country—Arkansas, Mississippi, New York State and heaven (or the devil) only knows where else.

pugilist comes straight from the Latin *pugil* (boxer), which in turn came from *pugnus* (fist).

pug-nosed comes from the name of the *pug* dog, now a relatively rare animal but not so long ago a great favorite. The *pug* is a small, short-haired dog whose chief facial characteristic is a blunt snub nose. It was a great favorite with ladies of fashion a century or so ago and the name may be a variant form of "puck," a term of endearment.

pull chestnuts out of the fire. This goes back to the ancient fable, found in both Aesop and La Fontaine, of the monkey who wanted to get some chestnuts out of the fire so he persuaded the cat to do it for him. Result: one singed paw and one new word in the language: "cat's-paw," to describe a person who is easily duped into performing a dangerous task for someone else.

pulling the wool over his eyes. This expression goes back to the days when all gentlemen wore powdered wigs similar to the ones still worn by the judges in British courts. The word *wool* was then a popular joking term for hair—as it still is in some areas today, especially when referring to very curly hair. The expression *pulling the wool over his eyes* came from the practice of jokingly tilting a man's wig over his eyes, so that he'd be unable to see what was going on. From this came, of course, today's meaning of "to deceive or hoodwink."

Pullman. Before the last *Pullman* car leaves the rails, let's give a nod in the direction of George M. Pullman (1831–1897), who not only designed the first railroad sleeping car (the Pullman Palace) but was responsible for several generations of sleeping car porters' being called "George." Pullman was also responsible for a "model town" (the inhabitants called it a "company town," for good reason), which still exists as a community near Lake Calumet on Chicago's Far South Side. This was the scene of the legendary strike of railway workers led by Eugene V. Debs in 1893—one of the most bitter and bloody in American labor history.

pumpernickel. Three centuries ago, a *Pumpernickel* was a dolt, a fool or a blockhead. The word was made up of *Pumper,* the sound made by a person falling, and *Nickel,* a dwarf or goblin. Thus the original *Pumpernickel* was an object of derision and the butt of the heavy-handed and occasionally savage humor of the period. Why the name was later applied to loaves of dark rye bread is a matter for speculation. Possibly the characteristically round shape of the loaves reminded Westphalians of the expressionless moon face of the village half-wit.

punk, as a name for the slow-burning sticks used to light fireworks, comes from Algonquian, a family of North American Indian languages used by more than fifty tribes, including the Cheyenne, Fox, Chippewa and Blackfoot. So *punk* can be said to be a bit more "early American" than the Fourth of July itself.

pupil. School *pupils* and eye *pupils* have one thing in common—the Latin word *pupilla,* which is the diminutive of *pupa,* meaning "girl." Since *pupilla* meant "little girl," the Romans also used the word to refer to the figure reflected in the eye and hence to the *pupil* of the eye, since that was where the figure was seen. The Romans also had a word, *pupillus,* for "little boy," making it possible for today's school *pupil* to be either a boy or a girl.

purple cow. Just about everyone knows that Gelett Burgess wrote the quatrain running: "I never saw a *purple cow./*I never hope to see one./But I can tell you anyhow,/I'd rather see than be one." But did you know that years later he was moved to this thought: "Ah, yes, I wrote the *'purple cow.'*/I'm sorry now I wrote it./But I can tell you anyhow,/I'll kill you if you quote it."

push merchandise/P.M.. In many retail outlets, buyers and managers make special deals with suppliers whereby a premium in the form of special discount or rebate is made on articles called *P.M.*'s or *push merchandise* items. These are given special display, and often retail clerks are given small cash premiums for recommending the *P.M.* over competing items. *P.M.*'s are sometimes also called *spiffs.*

pusillanimous. A *pusillanimous* character gets no sympathy from anyone because he is so cowardly or timid and has no courage or conviction of mind. He literally has a tiny mind, from the Latin *pusillus* for "tiny" and *animus* for "mind."

put on the dog has been around for more than a century, so long that many dictionaries now label it "archaic." It first appeared in print in 1871 in a book by L. H. Bagg called *Four Years at Yale.* His definition is still a good one: "To *put on the dog* is to make a flashy display, to cut a swell."

put the kibosh on, in the sense of putting an end to something, is a well-known phrase that has been widely used in America for more than a century. Authorities differ widely, however, as to the origin of *kibosh* itself. One theory is that it is Yiddish in origin, coming from the Middle High German *keibe* (carrion); others believe it comes from the Gaelic *cie bais* (cap of death).

put up your dukes was originally a British slang expression, dating to the time (1870) when Britain still had a few good prize fighters. It comes from the peculiar rhyming slang of London's Cockneys. In this lingo the only resemblance between an expression and its true meaning is that it rhymes with it. Thus if a Cockney means "forks" he'll say "Duke of York's." "Forks" in Cockney jargon means "fingers" and "fingers" is used to express "hands." So, by a very involved route, *dukes* came to mean "hands or fists" in the slang of the underworld, which then, as now, was much involved in prize fighting.

Another, less plausible, theory of the origin of *dukes* meaning a man's fists traces it to the Duke of Wellington's nose. It seems he had one of a prodigious size, to rival Cyrano de Bergerac's. To spare the great man embarrassment, perhaps, men's noses in general came to be called *dukes*. From there it was an obvious step for a pugilist's fists to be labeled *duke busters,* and this in time was shortened, and fists became simply *dukes.*

put your best foot forward is an expression dating back at least to the time of Shakespeare. It means to make your very best effort, especially at the start of a new endeavor. A variation can be found in Shakespeare's *King John:* "Nay, but make haste; the better foot before."

put your money on the barrelhead goes back to an earlier day, when America's "general stores" sold commodities like sugar, flour and crackers directly from open barrels. Unopened or turned-over barrels often served as counters and the grocer might well insist on cash *on the barrelhead* before delivering the goods. Incidentally, since these stores were the places where neighborhood gossip and philosophy were exchanged, that's where "cracker-barrel humor" originated.

Pygmalion and Galatea. Few legends have intrigued more great writers than the story of a king of Cyprus, Pygmalion, who detested women but sculpted a statue of such surpassing beauty that he fell in love with it. Aphrodite, ever eager to aid the cause of romance, brought the statue to life as Galatea. Ovid gave the story a leg up on permanent fame and William Morris was one of two Victorians to polish it up for that generation of readers. His version was called *The Earthly Paradise.* His fellow Victorian W. S. Gilbert packaged the legend as a comedy. In his version Pygmalion had a wife and she took a dim view of the liaison between sculptor and sculpted. After she had stirred up sufficient ruckus, Galatea decided that the whole thing wasn't worth all the trouble she was causing, so she voluntarily returned to her place with the rest of the statuary. By all odds the most financially successful rendering of the theme was by George Bernard Shaw, whose *Pygmalion* (1912) first introduced us to the Cockney flower girl Liza Doolittle and the phonetics professor, Henry Higgins, who reshaped her from a pitiable drab into a social triumph. This version was made into Shaw's first film (1939) and later, in a musical version by Alan J. Lerner and Frederick Loewe, it became *My Fair Lady* (1956), one of the great triumphs of our musical theater.

Pyrrhic victory. This is a victory won at such staggering cost that it amounts to no victory at all. The reference is to Pyrrhus, king of Epirus (319–

272 B.C.), who defeated the Romans at Asculum (279 B.C.) in just such a battle.

Q.E.D. The abbreviation for the Latin phrase *quod erat demonstrandum* (kwod eh-raht dem-on-STRAHN-dum), it means "which was to be demonstrated."

Q.E.F.. The abbreviation for the Latin phrase *quod erat faciendum* (kwod eh-raht fah-kee-EN-dum), it means "which was to be done."

Q.S. is the abbreviation of the Latin *quantum sufficit,* meaning "as much as suffices." It appears chiefly on pharmaceutical prescriptions.

qsim. Here's an oddity. Occasionally you see a proper name in English beginning with *q* and having no *u* for the second letter. But look at this, from a newspaper story out of Tangiers: "As in the days of Hannibal, time meant little—the *qsim,* a span of time equal to five of our minutes, was the smallest unit known to the citizen dozing in a burnoose." A *q* without a *u* is almost unknown in English. During World War II we read much about the Qattara Depression in the Sahara, and the unabridged dictionaries list some fifteen or twenty words starting this way. Most of these, like *Qattara,* are proper names from Arabic or other Semitic languages. Some, like Qabbala (for Cabbala) are merely variant spellings. Then there is the name of Australia's national airline, QANTAS, an acronym for Queensland and Northern Territories Air Service.

qua is borrowed from the Latin, but it has been long established in English usage. It's an adverb meaning "in the function of," used in such an expression as "The President *qua* Commander in Chief."

quack—a medical quack, that is, not the noise a duck makes—is a charlatan who makes a lot of noise about his remedies. *Quack* is a shortened form of *quacksalver,* one who quacks loudly about his salves.

Quai d'Orsay. Just as "foggy bottom" describes the U.S. State Department because that is the traditional name for the part of Washington where it is located, so *Quai d'Orsay* symbolizes the French Foreign Office because it is located on this street on the left bank of the Seine.

quail is a game bird with mottled brown plumage, known in both Europe and the U.S., where one breed is called "bobwhite" or "partridge." For reasons entirely unclear, the *quail* has long had a reputation for what one source calls "an inordinately amorous disposition." In Shakespeare's time harlots were known as *quails* and he refers in *Troilus and Cressida* to Agamemnon, "an honest fellow enough and one who loves *quails.*" A variation on this sense of *quail* was common in midcentury U.S. slang. "San Quentin *quail*" referred to females below the legal age of consent. Misconduct with one such might lead to jail, San Quentin being one of the most notorious of the federal prisons.

Quakers. Americans tend to think of the *Quakers* chiefly as the people who founded Philadelphia and settled Pennsylvania and as a religious sect that got its name from the fact that some members, transported by religious ecstasy, would shake and quake in excitement. The first part of this belief is true. Indeed, the territory that came to be called Pennsylvania (Penn's Woods," from William Penn's father's name and the Latin *sylva,* "forest") originally also included Delaware. But the *Quaker* nickname came not from the antics of members of the Society of Friends (a notably reserved and tranquil group) but from a statement made by the founder of the sect during one of the many court actions instituted to legislate them out of existence in the seventeenth century. Wrote George Fox in his *Founder's Journal* (1653): "Justice Bennet of Derby was the first to call us *Quakers,* because I bade him quake and tremble at the word of the Lord."

quandary is a state of perplexity or indecision, particularly one in which several equally acceptable solutions are possible. In this it differs from a *dilemma,* which presents only unpleasant alternatives. Although its exact origin is obscure, it may have come from the Latin interrogative *quanda* (when) or it may be a corruption of the Middle English *wandreth* (evil, perplexity).

quantum jump. We have borrowed this term from nuclear physics and use it to mean any sudden and dramatic change, especially in the fields of scientific research, scholarship and learning.

quarantine. When one is isolated from contact with others for fear of spreading contagious diseases, one is said to be in *quarantine,* a word which comes from the Italian *quarantèna giorni* (forty days), from the fact that the original *quarantines* were of that length.

quarterback is the player in a football backfield who calls signals, takes most passes from the center and frequently throws forward passes. Why *quarterback,* since he often scrambles all over the backfield? The answer lies in the earlier days of football before "linebackers" and "flanker backs" made their appearance. In those simpler days the backfield consisted of four men: one man directly behind the center (actually behind and slightly to one side), two men flanking him but positioned several feet to the rear, and one chap quite a distance farther back and directly behind the center. This chap who was all the way back was called the "fullback" ("fully back from the line"). The two flanking backs were half the fullback's distance back and so were logically called "halfbacks." Equally logically, the man closest to the line was only one quarter as far from it as the fullback. So he became the *quarterback.*

quarter horses were originally developed by the earliest settlers in Virginia more than two hundred years ago. They got their name from the fact that, since there were no race tracks in those days, they were raced on short paths about a quarter of a mile long. Later they were crossbred with thoroughbreds to improve their quality and performance. Because of their remarkable speed for short dashes, they make ideal cow ponies and are widely used on Western ranches as "cutting ponies."

quasar was coined to describe what Walter Sullivan of the *New York Times* calls "incredible objects . . . which look much like stars, are strong emitters of radio waves. They seem to be scattered across the universe, separated from each other by enormous distances, the farthest lying beyond any other visible object. They are so far away that, if they were stars, they would not be visible." The odd semantic fact about *quasars* is that there is a difference of opinion among the experts as to whether they should be called by that name. While a majority of astrophysicists polled at a national meeting plumped for *quasar,* a highly vocal minority held out for *quasi-stellar radio sources.* Look closely at that more explicit phrase and you will see where *quasar* comes from. It's a somewhat scrambled acronym made up of letters in *quasi-stellar radio.*

quash. When the judge *quashes* an indictment, he sets it aside or annuls it. Thereby he, quite literally, is making the charge vacant, since the verb comes from the Latin *casses* (empty or void).

Queen's English today. A news story from London reports that a new edition of the *Oxford Dictionary* contains a number of words and phrases unfamiliar to Americans. An *ice-lolly,* it seems, is what we know best by the trade name Popsicle—frozen water ice on a stick. A *lay-by* is a parking strip beside a main highway, where motorists pull off for minor repairs and where truckmen sometimes stop for a snooze. In England a passer-by will stare at you uncomprehendingly if you speak to him about a billboard sign. To him it's a *hoarding.* A shoe is a *boot.* The mailbox is a *pillar-box* or *post-box,* and the office postage meter is a *franking machine.* One doesn't speak of a can of corn; it is a *tin of maize.* The drugstore is usually the *chemist's shop,* though the American phrase is beginning to appear, especially in cities. An elevator is a *lift.* The first floor (or *storey*) of a building is a flight higher than ours. What we call the first floor is known in England as the *ground floor.* British cars have *bonnets* where ours have hoods, and the British *hood* is the American *top* (of a convertible). Our sedan is their *saloon,* our fenders are their *wings,* and the generator is a *dynamo.*

queue up. *Queue* comes to us from French, where it means "pigtail" or simply "tail." In turn this comes from the Latin *cauda,* also meaning "tail." Now it is chiefly used as part of the British expression *queue up,* meaning to get in line for something—box office, bus or whatever. In America this is usually referred to as "standing in line," though New Yorkers, for reasons which defy our comprehension, insist on speaking of "standing *on* line."

quiche, pronounced KEESH, is a custard baked in an unsweetened pastry shell, often with bits of crisp bacon or grated cheese. We borrowed the word from French, where it usually appears on menus as *Quiche* Lorraine.

quick as you can say Jack Robinson is older than baseball's Jackie Robinson —about two centuries older, in fact. While no one knows for sure where the expression started, it was listed as early as 1785 by Francis Grose in his *Classical Dictionary of the Vulgar Tongue.* Grose gave the following unlikely explanation of its origin: "Before one could say Jack Robinson is a saying to express a very short time, originating from a very volatile gentleman who would call on his neighbors and be gone before his name could be announced."

quid custodiet custodes? is a Latin expression meaning "who watches the watchmen?"

quiddity originally meant the real essence of a thing, its essential nature. However, as a result of endless hairsplitting discussions among scholars as to what constitutes "real essence," *quiddity* came to mean a "quirk" or "quibble." It comes from Medieval Latin *quidditas,* which in turn came from Latin *quid* (what).

quidnunc. A busybody or, as the British say, a "Nosy Parker," can merit this rather elegant term borrowed from the Latin *quid* (what) and *nunc* (now).

quid pro quo, a phrase borrowed unchanged from Latin (literally "something for something"), is used in the sense of "an equal exchange."

¿quien sabe? (kyen SAH-bay) is borrowed from Spanish and means "Who knows?"

quinquennial. A *quinquennial* event is one that occurs every five years. Pronounced kwin-KWEN-ee-ul, the word comes from the Latin words *quinque* (five) and *annus* (year).

quintessence is the purest, most essential quality of any substance or concept. In ancient Greece philosophers taught that all matter took one of four forms: fire, air, water and earth. Pythagoras added a fifth essence—*quintessence*—from which heavenly bodies were made. It is now used, as the *American Heritage Dictionary* puts it, to mean the purest or most typical instance: "thou fiery-faced *quintessence* of all that is abominable!" (Edgar Allan Poe).

quisling, a traitor, especially one who is placed in a position of power by the enemy, gets the name from Vidkun *Quisling,* puppet leader of the Norwegian State Council during the German occupation in World War II.

qui vive (kee veev) was originally a French sentry's challenge, roughly equivalent to "Who goes there?" Its literal meaning is "who lives," but it has been taken into English in the phrase "on the *qui vive.*" A person on the *qui vive* is one who is very alert.

quixotic. An impractical dreamer, a chap carried away by romantic delusions and idealistic notions of chivalry and honor, is a *quixotic* man. The adjective comes from the name of the hero of Cervantes' *Don Quixote.*

quiz has become very popular in educational jargon and it's almost impossible to turn on TV or radio without getting some sort of a *quiz* show. Where did the word come from? Nobody really knows. Nearly all dictionaries list it as "origin unknown" or "origin uncertain." However, there is one pleasantly Gaelic story of its origin, and if it smacks a bit more of 100 proof Irish whiskey than of 100 percent accuracy, don't say we didn't warn you.

It seems that late in the eighteenth century one James Daly, the manager of a theater in Dublin, being somewhat in his cups, made a very rash wager. He bet that he could introduce a word into the language overnight—specifically within twenty-four hours. What's more, he wagered that this would be a word absolutely without meaning. There were takers for his bet —of that you may be sure. So it was up to Jim Daly to make good his boast and he did. He hired all the urchins in Dublintown, equipped them with pieces of chalk, and sent them out into the night with instructions to chalk a single word on every wall and billboard in the city. The word was *quiz*. And, as a result of Daly's enterprise, it was on the lips of all Dublin in the morning.

At first it became synonymous with practical joke—for that was what he had played on the citizenry. Gradually it came to mean making fun of a person by verbal bantering. In time, it came to mean what *quiz* means today—to question a person in order to learn the extent of his knowledge.

quonking is just what it must sound like to the sound men on television when a pair of bit players, unaware of an open mike, carry on a private conversation that interferes with the main dialogue of the show.

Quonset hut. Quonset Point, Rhode Island, is the place where the first semicylindrical corrugated-metal huts were prefabricated early in World War II. The great virtue of the *Quonset hut* was its ease of assembly. No thing of beauty, it did a great service in sheltering thousands of soldiers and pieces of equipment in every part of the globe. The British equivalent is the *Nissen hut,* named for its designer, Colonel P. N. Nissen.

R has been a symbol used by pharmacists since ancient times. The *R* in the symbol means *recipere* (take this). The slant bar across the base of the *R* is the sign of the Roman god Jupiter, patron of medicines. According to *Brewer's Dictionary of Phrase and Fable,* the sign can be paraphrased this way: "Under the good auspices of Jove, patron of medicines, take the following drugs in the proportions set down."

rabbit's foot. Ever since ancient times the rabbit has been a symbol of fertility —and in those days, long before Planned Parenthood and Zero Population Growth, a large group of offspring was considered good fortune, especially if you were a farmer. Also, the earth was a symbol of the source of life. Hence the part of the rabbit that came into closest contact with the earth became a good luck talisman.

rabbit tobacco, which is a slang term for balsamweed, is known to most children who live in the South because it is what they use to make their first do-it-yourself cigarettes. "All kids used to roll it and sit behind the barn and try it," a Southern-bred lady relative says. "It's harmless and it has a terrible taste."

You'll find reference to it in Uncle Remus: " 'den he drawd de rockin'-cheer en front er de fier he did, en tuck a big chaw terbarker.' 'Tobacco?' asked the little boy, incredulously. 'Rabbit terbarker, honey. . . .' "

It is also reported that in Ohio and elsewhere the would-be youthful smokers used to do the same with dried corn silk—but they called it just that: "corn silk." Any kind of raw greens or vegetables, especially lettuce, is understandably called "rabbit food" because the farmer's real problem is to keep the rabbits from eating them out of the garden. We can only surmise that *rabbit tobacco* got its name because it is a weed and grows where the rabbits run wild.

race is not to the swift. The original quotation, "The *race is not to the swift, nor the battle to the strong*," is from the Bible (Ecclesiastes 9:11). It was Franklin Pierce Adams, who, in his "Conning Tower" column in the old *New York World,* once observed: "The *race is not to the swift,* nor the battle to the strong; but the betting is best that way."

radical. In its precise sense, *radical* signifies a person desirous of getting to the root of matters, for the word comes from the Latin word for "root," *radix.* In today's political terminology, a *radical* is usually regarded as one sympathetic to leftist or even revolutionary causes.

radiosonde is a radio device borne aloft, usually by balloon, whose purpose is to gather meteorological data for weather forecasting. It's a combination of *radio* and *sonde,* French for "sounding line." The final *e* is silent, so it's pronounced RAY-dee-oh-sond.

Rae/Rachel. *Rae* is a shortened form of *Rachel,* from the Hebrew word for "ewe." Thus it denotes gentleness and innocence.

raft. The *raft* that means "a great number" is not related at all to the *raft* that carries people or their possessions in the water. The two words are homonyms—words spelled the same but of different origin and meaning. The *raft* used in a phrase such as "raft of presents" is from the French word *raffe.* It means "a large number or collection," and in theory at least, should be spelled "raff." However, it picked up the final *t* on its way down through the centuries, precisely because a lot of other people made the same mistake.

ragtime was a popular form of music in the early years of the twentieth century, a sort of precursor of jazz. Perhaps the best known authentic ragtime piece is "Tiger Rag," though the imitative "Alexander's Ragtime Band" by Irving Berlin is often erroneously referred to as a "rag." The characteristics of the style are an elaborately syncopated rhythm in the melody against a steadily accented accompaniment. The precise origin of the word is unknown, but it seems to be a slurring of "ragged time," referring to the then unconventional syncopation. *Ragtime* enjoyed a brief but spirited revival in the 1970s.

railroad as a verb has acquired two rather interesting colloquial meanings. Important legislation being put through in a rush is said to have been *railroaded.* And a person sent to prison after a speedy trial on trumped-up charges is said to have been *railroaded.*

railroad/railway. *Railroad* and *railway* are both nouns, but they also have adjective forms identically spelled. In years past the word *railway* was generally reserved for streetcar systems or other forms of rail transportation lighter than the full-fledged *railroads,* with locomotives and rolling stock. This distinction, which was never observed by the British, incidentally, has gone by the boards in America.

raining cats and dogs goes back many hundreds of years to the Dark Ages, when people believed in all sorts of ghosts, goblins and witches and even thought that animals, like cats and dogs, had magical powers. The cat was thought by sailors to have a lot to do with storms, and the witches that were believed to ride in the storms were often pictured as black cats. Dogs and wolves were symbols of winds and the Norse storm god Odin was frequently shown surrounded by dogs and wolves. So when a particularly violent rainstorm came along, people would say it was *raining cats and dogs* —with the cats symbolizing the rain and the dogs representing the wind and storm.

raise Cain. In the term *raise Cain,* the allusion is the brother of Abel, traditionally the world's first criminal. In earlier times, *Cain* was used by God-fearing folk as a euphemism for "devil" and the expression *to raise Cain,* meaning to create a loud disturbance or to cause a great deal of trouble, was used instead of "to raise the devil."

raison d'être is a reason for being or existing and can belong to either a person or a thing. In French it literally means "reason of to be."

rally stripes. When new car models are illustrated with a broad stripe running off center, over the top and from front to rear bumper, these cars are said to have *rally stripes.* They were originally used in European sports car road races—*rallies* or sometimes even *rallyes*—to aid in identifying the competitors.

-rama/-orama goes all the way back to the Greek word *horama,* meaning "sight"—but it never really hit its stride until General Motors named its exhibit at the New York World's Fair of 1939 the Futu*rama.* This was a breathtaking view into the future, with heavy emphasis—as might be expected—on superhighways to come. It was, with the possible exception of Billy Rose's Aquacade—which also gave a word to the language—the most popular exhibit in the show. Although such words as "pan*orama*" and "cycl*orama*" had long been in the language, the GM hit show led to countless imitations of the name, with "food*orama*" and "health*orama*" being characteristic of the lot.

rambunctious. An Irish contribution to American folk language, *rambunctious* (pronounced ram-BUNK-shus) means "wild, disorderly or unruly." The word's popularity is attested by the fact that it turns up in various forms in different parts of the country—*rambustious, rambuctious* and *rambumptious* being three variants often heard.

ramshackle comes from the Icelandic *ramskakkr,* meaning "badly twisted." Thus it comes to its present meaning of "about to fall to pieces."

Randall. A favorite Old English name is *Randall*—also found as *Randell, Randle,* and *Randal.* Equally common is *Randolph,* from which *Randall* is derived. This name comes from two Anglo-Saxon words—*rand,* meaning "shield," and *wulf,* meaning "wolf." Thus *Randolph,* the shield against wolves, came to mean "protector."

rank and file. Originally a military term, this has been applied in recent years to the membership of the labor unions in this country. *Rank and file* is the enlisted component of an army, as contrasted with the officers. The designation comes from the fact that ordinary soldiers are required to muster in *ranks*—drawn up side by side—and in *files*—one behind the other. Obviously the leaders—officers—are not required to assemble in such group formations.

rap. A word that seems to have considerable popularity among the "under thirty" set is *rap.* A daughter, asked why she was so late coming home from a date, might say, "It was perfectly harmless, just a few of us sitting around rapping." Somewhat to our surprise, *rap* seems to have been established in Broadway slang in the early thirties. Damon Runyon (whose *Guys and Dolls* is something of a classic) used the term in the sense of "speak to or recognize" in this sentence written in 1932: "I wish Moose a hello, and he never *raps* to me but only bows and takes my hat." The Runyon sense could have been simply a corruption of "reply," but we have the feeling that its present sense is strongly influenced by the word *rapport,* because it is usually used in reference to speaking to or with a group whose ideas and emotions are congenial—*en rapport.*

rappel, the rapid, jolting, but safe descent from a mountainside via rope, comes from the Old French verb *rappeler,* meaning "to summon or recall," and was apparently first used in the military as "to call to arms." Just how this came to mean "a method of descending from a mountainside or cliff by means of a double rope passed under one thigh and over the opposite shoulder"—to quote the *American Heritage Dictionary* definition—puzzles us. Perhaps a signal to descend became confused with the descent itself. But that's only a guess—and a guess made by ones who never climbed a mountain higher than the foothills of New Hampshire's White Mountains.

rasher has been a part of our language since the Norman Conquest, when it came into English from the French *raser,* meaning "to shave or slice thin." So not only does a *rasher* mean a single slice, it means a thin slice. It has no connection at all with "rash," meaning "reckless or hasty."

read as a noun, referring to the act of reading, is a British expression that has become a bit of a vogue. Phrases like "Tom's new novel is a smashing good *read*" flow freely in the three-martinis-for-lunch book-editor circles. Ironically, we first came across it in the rugged, rough-hewn prose of Brendan Behan's *Borstal Boy.* In recounting his literary discoveries while a pupil or inmate of Britain's Borstal schools, Behan would again and again report that he found a newly discovered classic "a splendid *read.*"

read the riot act. The original *riot act* was passed by the British Parliament in 1714. George I was new to the throne and the first of the German Hanoverian line to rule England. He was very unpopular with the masses of British people because of his brusque, domineering manner and the fact that he didn't bother to learn the language. In protest there were a number of disturbances of the peace and the *riot act* was designed to stop these outbreaks. The way it worked was simplicity itself. If a dozen or more people assembled unlawfully, any sheriff or justice of the peace could order them to disperse by reading this proclamation: "Our Sovereign Lord the King chargeth and commandeth all persons assembled immediately to disperse themselves and peacefully to depart to their habitations or to their lawful business." Anyone who refused or who continued to riot for an hour or more after the warning was given in the king's or queen's name would be guilty of a felony and would quickly find himself in jail. Since *reading the riot act* implied strong disapproval of the actions of the persons being read to, the expression came to mean any stern criticism of another's conduct.

real McCoy. Anything that is the *real McCoy* is absolutely bona fide, certifiably genuine. Theories about the origin of the expression are many. Mencken, in Supplement II to his *American Language,* records a half dozen or so, including one that goes all the way back to the Jacobite troubles of 1715–1745, but draws no conclusions. More recently Alistair Cooke, we're told, theorized that it was taken from the name of a great nineteenth-century cattle baron. There has even been a suggestion that the McCoy involved was a member of the McCoy clan, famous for its deadly feud with the Hatfields.

However, we feel that the *real McCoy* was originally the world's welterweight boxing champion "Kid" McCoy." One story of how he acquired the nickname has it that he was challenged in a saloon by a chap who refused to believe that he was the boxing champ. After prolonged argument, McCoy proved his case with a right to the jaw. When the challenger managed to get up from the floor, he muttered: "You're the *real McCoy,* all right."

That's a nice story and it may even be true, but we think there's a more logical explanation. Toward the end of the last century it was a fairly common practice for an aspiring young pugilist to adopt the name of a more famous fighter—at least so long as he confined his fighting to the tank-town circuit, where deceptions of this sort were at least as common as thrown fights. Surely the most celebrated battler ever to adopt another fighter's name was Jack Dempsey. Dempsey's real name was William Harrison Dempsey, but for ring purposes he adopted Jack Dempsey, which had long been famous in ring circles as the sobriquet of Jack "The Nonpareil" Dempsey. During the period from 1890 to 1900 the world's welterweight champion was Kid McCoy. His reputation inspired so many imitators that he eventually had to bill himself as Kid *"The Real"* McCoy.

rebarbative means "repellent, repulsive and downright nasty." It's a word that the *Oxford Dictionary* traces to 1892 but labels "rare." It's not in most of the desk dictionaries and even *Funk & Wagnalls'* Unabridged hasn't found it yet. *Rebarbative* comes from the same Latin root as "beard" *(barba),* and one might think it was coined by some gentle Victorian damsel who found beards repugnant. But why *re*barbative? Why not simply barbative? But there's more to the story of *rebarbative* than that, as we learn from Richard Monges of Tenafly, New Jersey, who reported that it was borrowed from the French *rébarbatif,* which means "surly, unprepossessing, or grim." This, in turn, was a word from the slang of scholastics derived from the verb *rebarber,* which in the Middle Ages meant to resist literally "beard to beard." So you see the Frenchman of the Middle Ages found such close-quarters debate as repulsive as many of us find the "eyeball-to-eyeball confrontations" common in Washington in recent times.

rebel yell. It's impossible to express in words the essence of the *rebel yell*— a prolonged high-pitched, blood-curdling cross between a yell and a scream. It was uttered (if that's the word for it—"roared" might be better) by companies of Confederate troops as they attacked the Yankee enemy. Richard S. Ullery of Longmeadow, Massachusetts, adds this: "Many Southern families are descendants of English people who emigrated to the colonies for political or religious reasons. The yell used by Confederate troops was wordless, but is said to have been a corruption of the old fox-hunting shout 'Tally-ho!' "

rebus is the kind of puzzle in which pictures of objects suggest words or phrases by the sound of their names. For example, a picture of a pair of gates and a head would be a *rebus* for Gateshead. The word is the ablative plural of the Latin word *res* (thing). So *rebus* literally means "by things." Originally the phrase was *rebus non verbis*—"by things not words."

recant (pronounced rih-KANT) is a verb meaning to retract, renounce or withdraw in a formal or public way a previous statement or belief. It is derived from the Latin *re* (again, back) and *cantare* (to sing). The act itself is called *recantation.* Interestingly enough, when an underworld character confesses to the misdeeds of himself and his accomplices, thus *recanting* his previous statements, he is said to "sing."

recap may mean to put a new rubber tread on a used auto tire, but not when used by a newspaperman: "Tomorrow I'll give you a *recap* of the whole thing." *Recap* in this context is an abbreviated form of *recapitulation,* meaning a review or summary of information previously transmitted. In this sense, it is in common use in newspaper offices, and an order familiar to every rewrite man is: "Give me a quick *recap* on this story," meaning: "Give me a shortened summary, omitting none of the essential facts."

receipt/recipe. The similarity between these two words is understandable since they both come from the same Latin word, *recipere,* "to take back or receive." *Recipe* is the present tense, imperative, meaning literally "Take!" From the earliest days of medicine, *recipe* has been used as the first word in prescriptions, either spelled out or, in recent times, abbreviated by the letter *R* with a slant mark across its base. Though *recipe* is still used primarily in this medical sense, it has also long been used to designate any list of ingredients, as in cooking *recipes. Receipt* comes from the past participle of *recipere* and originally meant "that which has been received." Since *receipts* are traditionally handed down from experienced to inexperienced cooks, these formulas are "received" by one from the other.

reclusion is a seldom-heard word, but it has been part of the language for centuries. It's a back formation from the noun *recluse,* a person who withdraws from the world to live alone, as hermits do.

red dog is a term much used and abused by football fans these days. Originally it meant a defensive tactic whereby a linebacker shot through the offensive line to hit the quarterback and stall the play before it got started. The *dog* part is fairly obvious, since the job of the linebacker was to "dog" or "hound" the passer. The *red* comes from a color code developed by Clark Shaughnessy, one of the game's greatest coaches. If one backer was sent through, the code would be "red"; if two, "blue"; if three, "green." No one today speaks of "blue dog" or "green dog." Only *red dog* remains, and it is carelessly used to mean almost any kind of shooting a gap in the offensive line.

redeye is another slang word for "liquor," one of the thousand or more synonyms invented over the years.

red herring. The original *red herrings* were dried salted herrings, called by the British "bloaters." The theory among fox hunters of Old England was that a red herring dragged across a fox's trail would divert the dogs to a false trail by destroying the fox's scent. This was known, in the language of the hunt, as "faulting the hounds." So, properly speaking, a political *red herring* is simply a charge used to confuse or divert the voter's attention from the real issues. The most famous use of the phrase in recent years was by President Harry Truman in 1948. Commenting on Whittaker Chambers's charge that Alger Hiss had been a Communist courier, Truman said that this and other charges of Communist influence in our government was "just a *red herring* to get the minds of the voters off the sins of the 80th Congress."

redingote, in the language of fashion, describes a long, light outer garment, worn open at the front to show the dress beneath. The name comes from the French pronunciation of "riding coat."

red letter day. Almanacs and calendars issued by religious organizations often print saints' days and holidays in red. Since these are days for special services, the expression *red letter day* came to mean any very special day, especially one that's lucky for you.

redneck is today a somewhat disparaging label for white rural laboring men of the Southern states. The origin of the expression is obvious: months and years of labor in the fields give any man a toughened, reddened neck. However, we were surprised to discover that this is a term of relatively recent origin. H. L. Mencken doesn't once mention it in *The American Language,* and the *Merriam-Webster* Unabridged published in 1934 says nothing about it, though it is properly recorded in the 1961 edition. So the evidence is that *redneck* gained its first widespread use during the years of the Great Depression. It does appear in the expression "a bunch of *rednecks*" in a book published in 1929, but it seems not to have been widely used until later.

In 1947 *Newsweek* magazine gave this explanation of the term: "The *rednecks* were the poverty-stricken white tenant farmers and sharecroppers who lived in the piney woods and barren red-clay hills behind the Delta." Since then the application of the *redneck* label has spread far beyond the state of Mississippi and now it is applied to white rural laborers throughout the South—but always in a derogatory or disparaging sense. But it was not always that way. One of the South's greatest editors, Jonathan Daniels, writing in 1938, put it this way: "But a *redneck* is by no means to be confused with po' whites. Lincoln and Jackson came from a Southern folk the backs of whose necks were ridged and red from labor in the sun."

Reds. The use of *Red* as a synonym for "Communist" derives from the *red* flag which has been the international symbol of Communism for a century or more and is now the official flag of the Soviet Union. Since the time of the French Revolution it has been a symbol of anarchy and rebellion, and the extreme partisans of that period were known—strange though this sounds to American ears—as *red republicans.* Reportedly their hatred of the nobility they had vowed to overthrow was so intense that they dipped their hands in the blood of their victim, then brandished them aloft in triumph—whence the label *red.*

It seems to us unfortunate that the word *red* has taken on such unpleasant connotations in the past century or two, because throughout history red has been a color associated with honor (note its use in royal and ecclesiastical robes) and good fortune and magic (for, as Yeats pointed out, "Red is the color of magic in almost every country. . . . The caps of fairies are well-nigh always red.").

red tape. The practice of tying official documents with tape of a reddish hue began in seventeenth-century England. By the nineteenth century its use to mean inaction or delay caused by official sluggishness had become well established. Early in the 1800s, Washington Irving described a bureaucrat thus: "His brain was little better than *red tape* and parchment."

red up has been widespread in the United States—especially in the rural sections of our country—for a hundred years. It is a dialect version of "ready up" and it's heard mostly in remarks like: "We'll have to *red up* the room before the company comes." The spelling *red up* is the most common but it sometimes appears as *rid up* or *redd up*. Harold Wentworth, in his *American Dialect Dictionary,* reports the expression as appearing at various times in areas as far removed as Maine and Florida and from Virginia to Kansas. As a matter of fact, it has even appeared in *Time* magazine; in 1941 it reported that "Russian troops were camped outside Teheran, *redding up* their tanks for a triumphal entry into the city."

reformer. New York's Mayor Jimmy Walker said it first: "A *reformer* is a guy who rides through a sewer in a glass-bottom boat."

regatta. Today any series of races between yachts or even sailboats or racing crews qualifies as a *regatta*. The first ones, though, were contests between the gondoliers of Venice, and *regatta* in Venetian dialect meant simply "gondola race."

regs. Here are a couple of examples of a term which appears more and more frequently in writings about tax matters: "The new *regs* do not cover this trouble spot" and "The May 15 cut-off in the *regs* is a break for those who make leases." This is an obvious back formation from "regulations."

relevant/relevancy/irrelevant. *Relevant* (pronounced REL-eh-vent) means pertinent to or applicable in a given situation or matter, as in "The only discussion permitted was that *relevant* to the major issue before the convention." It is derived from the same Latin words as the word *relieve* (*re*, "again" and *levare*, "to lift") but its meaning is quite different. *Relevancy* is its noun form and *irrelevant* its opposite.

remember the Alamo! The Alamo lives in American history, as a symbol of bravery, since its gallant defenders—including the legendary Davy Crockett—were slain to the last man by a force of Mexicans under Santa Ana. What is less well known is that the *alamo* is a kind of poplar tree also known as the "cottonwood tree" and the fortress called "The Alamo" got its name because it was situated in a grove of *alamo* trees. Originally a

Franciscan mission, it was used as garrison headquarters and, in 1836, some 160 soldiers were reputedly massacred by a force estimated at 4,000 Mexicans. The cry *"Remember the Alamo!"* was the rallying slogan for troops under General Sam Houston when they defeated the Mexicans later that year at San Jacinto.

reminder sike is a term that falls strangely on the ears of those not in show business, but once you know what it means you will realize that you see one within minutes after you turn on your television set. The *sike* part of the phrase is more than a century old in show business. Spelled out in full, it is *"cyclorama,"* but is usually abbreviated in stage directions to *"cyc."* and invariably pronounced *sike.* It is a large screen, sometimes curved, used as a background for stage settings. The phrase *reminder sike* simply refers to the cyclorama on which the sponsor's message *(reminder)* is projected.

remuda is the string of horses herded in reserve during a roundup. It's a term borrowed by American cowboys from their Mexican counterparts. Originally the word was Spanish.

reprehensible. That which is *reprehensible* is deserving of censure or rebuke. Its sources are logical Latin ones: *re* (back) and *prehendre* (take).

res gestae. Race JEST-eye is a fairly accurate phonetic rendering of *res gestae,* favored "legal Latin" phrase for "all the essential circumstances attending a given transaction." However, most lawyers would pronounce the phrase race JEST-ee. The long-*I* pronunciation is more characteristic of classical Latin than of lawyer's Latin.

rest on one's laurels. This is said of a person who has achieved great fame and feels that he or she can now relax and enjoy that fame without further exertion. The allusion is to the wreaths of laurel with which outstanding Roman citizens were crowned.

retort courteous is from Shakespeare's *As You Like It* (Act V, Scene 4). Touchstone, the wise clown, is explaining how one can criticize and even insult a person without the exchange resulting in physical conflict. The seven stages include: (1) the *retort courteous,* (2) the quip modest, (3) the reply churlish, (4) the reproof valiant, (5) the countercheck quarrelsome, (6) the lie circumstance, (7) the lie direct. "All these," says Touchstone, "you may avoid but the lie direct; and you may avoid that too, with an If." In other words, anything short of direct insult may be used without fear of physical consequences.

Rhodes scholar. The best-known, though not the only, *Rhodes scholars* are those who study each year at Oxford on scholarships endowed under the will of Cecil Rhodes (1853–1902), perhaps the greatest figure in the British colonization of Africa in the latter half of the nineteenth century. He left a fortune in excess of six million pounds, the income from which still maintains scholarships for, among others, thirty-two Americans each year.

rhubarb, meaning a heated argument, often between professional athletes in the course of a game, comes from the language of the theater, TV and movies. In the early days of films—and still today in the theater—when a crowd is supposed to be muttering in a surly or argumentative mood, the director tells them to say *"rhubarb"* over and over again.

rich beyond the dreams of avarice was first used by the playwright Edward Moore in *The Gamester* (1753). But it owes its lasting popularity to the fact that Dr. Samuel Johnson used it in talking to his biographer, Boswell. "We are not here," he said, "to sell a parcel of boilers and vats, but the potentiality of growing *rich beyond the dreams of avarice.*" Sam never made that kind of a fortune, of course, but then dictionary editors never do. As Dean Kenneth G. Wilson of the University of Connecticut once remarked to us: "Dictionary editors make a living. Dictionary publishers get rich."

ricochet words. Everyone who has even a nodding acquaintance with the English language knows what a quirky, confusing, oddball tongue it is. Every grade school child wonders why words like *bough, dough, cough* and *enough* are spelled similarly and yet sound so different. And the oddities of language continue to puzzle and sometimes delight word buffs of more advanced age and sophistication. One such stopped into our editorial sanctum to razzle-dazzle us with an extended demonstration of harum-scarum hokey-pokey. His name is Winthrop Wadleigh (which, not at all oddly, rhymes with "oddly"). By profession he is a highly successful attorney in Manchester, New Hampshire, and his hobby is collecting what he calls "Siamese-twin words." You have just seen three of them—and he has found dozens more, from *argy-bargy* to *zoot suit.*

The word experts call these "reduplicated words" or, in lighter moments, *ricochet words.* Their charm lies, of course, in the built-in rhyme and it's not surprising that the overwhelming majority of the 257 specimens that this hotshot has collected are lighthearted and slangy. Some are ancient. For example, the *Oxford Dictionary* reports that *hugger-mugger,* meaning secret or stealthy doings, was in print as early as 1526, while its predecessors *hoker-moker* and *hucker-mucker* (which Mr. Wadleigh missed on his list) go back centuries earlier.

But hell's bells, most of the hodgepodge of hanky-panky, fancy-pantsy, flipperty-flapperty fiddle-faddle our legal beagle has accumulated are of recent vintage. And such a mishmash, or should it be mishmosh? There is even a specimen of what must be double talk: rammis-frammis. And it's as up-to-date as the *boob tube.* The collection runs the gamut from *chalk talk* to *claptrap,* passing *chitchat* en route. There even is a suggestion of hokey-pokey in the mention of hoochie-coochie honey-bunnies. Well, jeepers creepers, if any jet-set bigwig or leadhead nitwit wants to know more about the subject of *ricochet words,* now you know whom to ask!

riffraff originally came to English from the French *rif et raf,* meaning "one and all." Later, thanks perhaps to the influence of a Swedish word, *raff,* meaning "sweepings," it came to mean the offscourings of society, the dregs of humanity.

rigadoon is a dance, lively and spirited, performed by two people. It originated in the eighteenth century. The dancers in a *rigadoon* spend most of their time pirouetting at some slight distance from each other.

right off the bat, meaning "speedily or instantly," is borrowed from baseball. A ball coming *right off the bat* is usually coming at great speed.

rill. "I was amazed," a woman from Wisconsin wrote us, "at hearing a well-educated woman on a quiz show get stuck on the question: 'What is the meaning of *rills* in "I love thy rocks and *rills,* thy woods and templed hills"?' I was even more amazed the next day when I told a couple of recent University of Wisconsin graduates and, instead of laughing, they gave me a blank stare. Neither had any idea of its meaning. I kept trying and found that few if any graduates knew this word. Finally, after about six tries, I found a man who knew it. He hadn't been to school much but he read because he liked to." It is indeed astonishing that so many well-educated people should be ignorant of the meaning of such a simple word as *rill*— especially one which is often on the lips of every schoolchild in the verse quoted from "America." A *rill* is a small stream or rivulet. It comes from the Dutch word *ril,* of the same meaning.

ringalevio. The child's game *ringalevio* is one of the "ring" games in which children gather in a circle, then break away to run and hide until members of the rival team find them. It's a variation of what, when we were children in Cambridge and Columbus, was simply called "hide-and-go-seek." The name comes from *relievo,* which probably simply referred to the time when the hiding children were released, or relieved.

ringer originated on the race track. When a horse of superior ability is entered in a race under the name of another horse which he resembles, he is called a *ringer.* The reason for such a maneuver is, of course, to take advantage of the longer odds the inferior horse would get. By extension, the word has come to be used to describe any athlete with experience at an advanced level of play taking part in competition on a lower level. For example, a ballplayer who had played on a minor-league team would be considered a *ringer* if he later played in college baseball. Incidentally, the presumed resemblance of the *ringer* in racing to the horse whose name he carries is the source of the expression "dead *ringer,*" meaning any close look-alike.

ringing the changes comes from the almost forgotten art of bell ringing. A set of bells (from three to twelve) tuned to the diatonic scale are rung in a series of variations from the regular striking order. Theoretically every possible variation is rung without any repetition. *Ringing the changes,* figuratively speaking, now means trying every possible way of doing something.

Rio Grande. Every so often a reader will challenge our statement that there is in Ohio a small town called *Rio Grande,* which is pronounced locally as RYE-oh GRAND. We know we're right because we have visited the town many times and are, indeed, the son-in-law and daughter of Dr. J. Boyd Davis, for many years chairman of the board of trustees of *Rio Grande* College. On a visit with Dr. Davis, he added this background: When the town was incorporated in 1848 the townsfolk wrote to the Post Office Department, making several suggestions for the name of the town. All were turned down because they would duplicate the names of post offices already in existence in Ohio. Finally, inspired by events of the then current Mexican War, somebody suggested *Rio Grande*—and the Post Office approved. Now, here's the important point. At that time the pronunciation used universally by soldiers engaged in the war was RYE-oh GRAND, so that's why the pronunciation was adopted that is still in use.

rip-off. We fear the origin of this term is all too obvious to anyone who has lived in crime-ridden sections of our major cities since the 1960s. In New York drug addicts who perpetrate most such thefts will often quite literally *rip off* the door of a flat to gain entrance—usually during the daytime hours when the occupant is at work. All manner and variety of special locks and bars and chains are resorted to by residents of the metropolitan areas, but none seems effective against the ingenuity and desperation of the addict driven by the need to feed his habit. The operation can be so successful and so complete that a TV, photographic enlarger, electrical appliances and the like are almost literally "ripped off" the walls. We recorded the term in the *American Heritage Dictionary* (1969), labeling it "slang" and adding that it had been extended in meaning to cover just about any kind of theft or swindle.

rise above principle. The cynical observation that "There are times when a politician has to *rise above principle*" is at least a half century old, perhaps much older, perhaps even as old as the traditional politician's preference for the expedient solution rather than the difficult course of following principles. In any event, the record shows that it was uttered by Representative Edward Quin, who represented a Mississippi district from 1913 to 1931.

risley act. A *risley act* is one in which an acrobat lies on his back and tosses objects or other people aloft with his feet, usually spinning them in the process. It gets its name from a famous American gymnast of the nineteenth century, Richard Risley Carlisle, who performed with his two sons as "The Risley Family."

Ritz/ritzy. César Ritz (1850–1918) was born in Switzerland and established three hotels which ranked as the world's most fashionable and elegant. They were located in Paris, London and New York. By the time the London hotel was opened in 1906, the word *Ritz* was internationally famous and represented the pinnacle of excellence in hotels, just as Cartier and Tiffany do in jewelry. However, *Ritz* was not as successful as Cartier and Tiffany in preserving his exclusive right to the name. By the 1920s, according to Henry L. Mencken, there were "Plazas, Astorias and *Ritzes* all over the hinterland." During that same period the word *ritzy* appeared. The 1934 *Merriam-Webster* Unabridged defined it as "ostentatiously and vulgarly smart in appearance and manner; ultrafashionable." Obviously the Merriam editors took a dim view of anything labeled *ritzy*. Perhaps this reflected the relatively sheltered lives they led in Springfield, Massachusetts, but their judgment that the original sense of true elegance implicit in *Ritz* had been cheapened by the adjective *ritzy* was sound. So it seems clear to us that the widespread use of *ritzy*—coined in America—would never have existed if the New York *Ritz* (properly the *Ritz*-Carlton) had not been widely recognized as a symbol of excellence.

rival. A *rival* was at one time only a neighbor—coming from the Latin *rivalis*, one living on the bank of the same stream as another. Presumably that was when the trouble started, because there was bound to be some conflict over the use of the stream. As a matter of fact, many such contests are found recorded in Roman law. Thus, as happens far too often even today, neighbors became *rivals* over common rights.

road to hell is paved with good intentions/hell is paved with good intentions. Both versions are commonly heard, so neither can be considered more "correct" than the other. And the idea is at least as old as the Latin poet Vergil. Samuel Taylor Coleridge, of "Ancient Mariner" fame, reported that a seventeenth-century clergyman named Baxter said it first in English. Then in the eighteenth century Boswell reported that Sam Johnson said it. But Sam, like all reference-book editors, tended to soak up some of the copy he edited, so it's not surprising that some of his wittiest remarks can be traced to earlier writers. And now, to top it all off, harken to these words of wisdom from Robert Southey: "It has been more wittily than charitably said that *hell is paved with good intentions*. They have their place in heaven, too."

Robin Hood. Is it true that Robin and his crew are only legendary? Wasn't there once a real *Robin Hood?* This is a hard question to answer, for leading authorities on the history and legends of pre-Chaucerian England are divided on the answer. Some hold that Robin was an actual outlaw, perhaps the Earl of Huntingdon, who harassed the Norman invaders, stealing from the rich and giving to the poor. Another theory is that he was a relatively obscure local hero of the thirteenth century around whom stories and legends handed down from Scandinavian mythology gradually gathered. And at least one eminent historian considers him merely the folk representation of traditional Saxon defiance of the Norman oppressors. While it may be impossible to show with certainty that an actual *Robin Hood* lived, the ballads, stories and legends associated with his name have entertained and inspired generations of English-speaking youth from his first appearance in the pages of *The Vision of Piers Plowman* before 1400 to the televised performances of today.

Incidentally, this reminds us of a practically immortal line by W. C. Fields in the play *Poppy,* in which he played the customary Fieldsian raffish rascal. At one point his daughter—the Poppy of the title—says: "Daddy, what do you do for a living?" Fields replies: "I'm a latter-day *Robin Hood.* I steal from the rich and give to the poor." Asks Poppy: "What poor, Daddy?" Replies Fields: "Us, poor, Poppy. Us poor!"

Robin Hood's barn. Robin Hood and his merry men, as noted above, were a band of medieval outlaws who stole from the rich and gave to the poor. Robin and his men lived in Sherwood Forest and the lands and fields surrounding it. Since there was no such thing as a barn there, the expression "by way of *Robin Hood's barn*" means wandering in a roundabout fashion.

robot. The first *robots*—mechanical men—appeared in Karel Capek's 1922 play *RUR* ("Rossum's Universal Robots"). This work, by a distinguished Czech novelist and playwright, gave a chilling forecast of a world in which automated machines could do the work of men. The word *robot* comes from the Czech *robota,* meaning "slave labor or drudgery." It is pronounced ROH-but.

rock hound is well established in the popular tongue as a name for geologists and especially for amateur geologists who collect specimens of rare rocks as a hobby.

rococo (pronounced roh-KOH-koh) is a word which frequently confuses even those who know its meaning and pronunciation, since the temptation to double the first or second *c* is almost irresistible. *Rococo* designates a style of architecture and decoration, originating in France in the early eighteenth century and characterized by curved designs, overall delicacy and much ornamentation. The word is believed to have come from the French *rocaille,* or "shellwork," used extensively as decoration during the reign of Louis XIV.

Roger —in the meaning of "Yes, O.K., I understand you"—is voice code for the letter *R.* It is part of the "Able, Baker, Charlie" code known and used by all radiophone operators in the services. From the earliest days of wireless communication, the Morse code letter *R* (dit-dah-dit) has been used to indicate "O.K.—understood." So *Roger* was the logical voice-phone equivalent.

Roland for his Oliver. Roland and Oliver were two of the twelve paladins or peers of the court of Charlemagne. As such they participated in many heroic adventures, and they repeatedly matched each other in feats of bravery. Eventually the two heroes met in hand-to-hand combat and fought for five consecutive days—to a draw. Thus the expression *a Roland for his Oliver* came to mean "tit for tat."

rollmops as we know them are marinated herring fillets, wrapped around gherkins or onions and served as an hors d'oeuvre. The word comes from German *rollen,* "to roll," and *mops,* "pug dog." Just what that pug dog is doing there baffles us, but that's how the Germans felt about rolled-up herrings.

roman à clef comes from French and translates as "novel with a key." Generally speaking, it means a novel whose leading figure or figures are only slightly disguised portraits of actual persons. For example, one of Nathaniel Hawthorne's novels, *The Blithedale Romance,* has as its leading figure a man named Hollingsworth, who is a slightly disguised portrait of Herman Melville.

romance languages are the languages that stem from Latin—the language of Rome. As normally construed, the group includes French, Italian, Portuguese, Spanish and Romanian. Other, lesser regional tongues derived largely from the same source include: Provençal, Catalan, Rhaeto-Romanic and Sardinian.

Rome wasn't built in a day. A good guess would be that this phrase originated in Rome itself. The meaning of the expression is, of course, that nothing of lasting value can be created in a very short time. It appears in English as early as 1546 in Heywood's *Proverbs,* but a French version goes back at least to A.D. 1100.

rooftree is used to symbolize the house as a whole. The *rooftree* is not a tree at all, but the ridgepole supporting the roof. Thus it is one of the most vital members in the support of a house and, by extension, is often referred to as symbolic of the roof and, indeed, of the house itself.

rookie is simply a variation on *recruit.* While it is most often used in reference to athletes, it probably started in the army as a derisive nickname for fresh recruits. Doubtless, also, the term was influenced by the much older expression *to rook,* thieves' slang dating back to Shakespeare's time and meaning "to cheat or dupe an unwary person."

roscoe is or was the underworld slang for a pistol or revolver. Our contact with criminal elements has never been what you would call close, but we suspect that *roscoe,* like "gat" and "heater," would be considered archaic by today's gangsters.

Rosetta stone. Perhaps the most important single discovery in the history of linguistic exploration was the deciphering of the *Rosetta stone*—a tablet inscribed with a decree of Ptolemy V of 196 B.C. It carried three versions of the decree, in Greek, Egyptian hieroglyphic and demotic. It was discovered near the town of Rosetta, Egypt, in 1799. Deciphered by Jean François Champollion, it proved to be the key by which other Egyptian hieroglyphics were subsequently deciphered.

rostrum, the raised platform for public speaking, came by its name in a very odd fashion. The Latin *rostrum* originally meant "beak" of a bird. Even earlier it was derived from the Latin verb *rodo,* "to gnaw," the same word from which we get "rodent," to describe animals, like rats and squirrels, that can only gnaw. They can't chew because they have no canine teeth, only incisor teeth. *Rostrum* then came to mean the bow of a ship. In ancient times these bows were carved in very intricate fashion, often resembling beaks of giant birds. When the Romans conquered the Carthaginians, they took the prows of some enemy ships back to Rome and used them to decorate the great Forum. Public speakers used these *rostrums* (Latin plural: *rostra*) as platforms and *rostrum* acquired the meaning it has today.

rotogravure is the name of a gravure printing process using rotary presses; hence, *roto* + *gravure.* The word is familiar to most Americans today because of its appearance in Irving Berlin's song "Easter Parade": "You'll find that you're in the *rotogravure.*" At the time Berlin wrote the song (1933), the four-color magazine inserts that are common in Sunday newspapers were practically unknown. Some of the most prestigious papers, including the *New York Times,* carried instead an insert, printed in a sort of sepia color, containing lots of pictures and, of course, advertisements. The insert was printed by the *rotogravure* method and was usually called the *rotogravure* section or, among newsmen, simply the *roto* section. To have your picture in the *roto,* as in the song, signified that you were a person of distinction, and if you were female, probably a real beauty. Coincidentally, a 1931 revue called *The Third Little Show* featured a number which we remember for its sheer undiluted awfulness. It was called "I'll Putcha Pitcher in the Paper" and contained the unfortunately deathless line: "I'll putcha photo in the *roto,* if you will be mine!" Don't let anyone tell you that today's songwriters have any sort of monopoly on bad taste.

Rotten Row. The magnificent bridle path in Hyde Park, London, is often referred to as *Rotten Row,* a corruption of Route du Roi (Route of the King).

roué. One of the tortures which eighteenth-century France practiced on her criminals was to literally break them on the wheel. And it is from the French verb *rouer,* meaning "to break on a wheel," that we get the word *roué,* a synonym for a dissipated and debauched man. When Louis IV was a minor and too young to rule France, a nephew of his—Philippe II, Duc d'Orléans—became regent of the country. He gathered about him a coterie of such disreputable and dissolute persons that the word *roué* was applied to them, the implication being that any or all of them were properly candidates for torture on the wheel.

round robin. The *robin* in this expression has nothing to do with the bird of the same name. This *robin* is derived from the French *ruban,* or "ribbon."

And here's the story of how this ribbon became a robin. During the seventeenth and eighteenth centuries in France, it was a brave man indeed who had the courage to petition the crown, even when he had a just grievance, because more than one monarch followed the practice of ordering beheaded the man whose signature came first on any petition distasteful to the king. Finally, some clever officers devised a *round robin,* which was attached to the document bearing their grievances. After each petitioner had signed the ribbon, it was joined into a circle in such a fashion that no one name headed the list—and thus no heads would roll.

Another way of signing *round robins* is for the signers to affix their names at the foot of the document like the spokes of a wheel. This method, one authority reports, originated in the British Navy, where, in the days of Lord Nelson and earlier, a ship's captain had the right to order hanged the man first signing a petition of grievance. The fact of his signature being at the top of the list was considered prima facie evidence that he was the instigator of mutiny. Nowadays *round robin* is a term widely used in sporting circles to designate a tournament in which each contestant plays every other contestant. *Round-robin* golf and tennis tournaments are common.

Round Table was the famous table given to King Arthur when he married Guinevere. The shape of the table was designed to eliminate any precedence among the knights. Each shared equal rank with the others and Arthur himself was *primus inter pares,* the first among equals.

Rowbottom and Reinhart. During the 1960s there was much student unrest, and demonstrations, some ending in violence, were common on college campuses. In earlier times student demonstrations tended to be more carefree, more an indication of youthful exuberance than of any politically or racially motivated antagonism. Two such frequently reprised demonstrations were the *Rowbottom* of the University of Pennsylvania and the *Reinhart* of Harvard.

Joseph E. Fleming, Jr., mayor of Titusville, Pennsylvania, tells us about the first of these: "In your column you discussed 'donnybrook,' a free-for-all brawl, which got its name from the famed Donnybrook Fair, formerly held near Dublin. That reminded me of an expression common at the University of Pennsylvania, the *Rowbottom,* pronounced ROE-bottom. It was a sort of student riot but not like our present-day student riots, which seem to denote an angry uprising of undergraduates who occupy and burn buildings. A *Rowbottom* was more on the order of a king-size pep rally. Damage was done, but it wasn't really malicious and the kids weren't demonstrating the way they do today. Traffic near the Penn campus was blocked, some autos were occasionally overturned, trolley cars were derailed and, of course, there was a lot of noise. But that's all.

"How did the name *Rowbottom* originate? Well, it seems there was a certain student who was quite a party boy, prone to return to his dormitory in the wee hours extremely inebriated. Unable to negotiate the stairs to his upper-floor room, he would stand in the yard and yell for his roommate, whose name was *Rowbottom,* to come and help him. His calls soon awakened other students, who would take up the cry 'Hey, *Rowbottom'* and fill the air with old shoes, bottles and the like. The whole thing could turn into a small-scale riot."

Harvard's *"Reinhart"* was a cry that was guaranteed to disturb the calm of the Harvard Yard and lead to all sorts of disorders, spilling out into adjacent Harvard Square. The story behind the cry was a bit different, though. According to hallowed Harvard legend, a wealthy young man named *Reinhart* came to the college expecting to become instantly popular because of his wealth. Instead he was shunned by the patrician Lodges, Hallowells and Cabots and, for spite, he determined to make his name famous in Harvard history whether they approved or not. So he hired various "townies" to stroll through the Yard night after night calling out: *"Reinhart, Reinhart!"* in the manner of old-time bellboys. Eventually the students took up the chant and it became the cry signaling a student riot.

Reinhart achieved fame of another sort through the inclusion of his name in the lyric George Frazier wrote for Count Basie's "Harvard Blues": *"Reinhart, Reinhart,* I'm a most peculiar guy!"

rubber, the substance of a thousand uses, from protective coverings for shoes to elastic bands, came by its name in a rather odd way. When the first samples were brought to England, there seemed to be no use for the stuff but to *rub* out pencil marks. In most languages other than English, *rubber* goes by a transliteration of "gum." Even in England, *rubber* boots are "gum" boots.

rubber/rubberneck. The verb *rubber* is a back formation from the noun *rubberneck,* originally applied to tourists who were forever stretching their necks in an effort to see all the sights. Indeed, buses with glass roofs and other devices to improve the vision of the occupants have long been known as *"rubberneck* buses."

Rube Goldberg. For many years Rube Goldberg's "inventions" were part of the household lore of all America. In essence each invention consisted of a preposterously complicated (but seemingly logical) method of performing a very simple operation. The diagrams illustrating his weird and wonderful contraptions were always ingeniously intricate and great good fun to follow. Long before his death, Rube swore off "inventions" and for two decades devoted his skills to political cartooning, winning two Pulitzer awards and a Presidential Medal of Honor. But, as Rube told us more than once, he ruefully had to admit that the public still associates *Rube Goldberg* with needlessly complicated gadgets to perform simple functions.

ruckus is a blend of "rumpus" and "ruction." Carrying this a step or two further, "rumpus" is said to have been originally a slang term among Swiss and German students, meaning a violent disturbance or uproar. "Ruction" means pretty much the same thing, of course, but it has a much more interesting history. The first "ruction" was an actual insurrection: the Irish Insurrection of 1798. This was an agrarian rebellion and, while not notably successful, it must have been noisy, for its name lives on.

rule of thumb means a rough or guesswork estimate, based more upon experience than on precise measurement, as in this example: "According to the supermarket manager, three out of every four shoppers, as a general *rule of thumb,* leave their shopping carts in the parking lot." There are two theories about the origin of this expression. The more logical theory is that it comes from the frequent use of the lower part of the thumb (roughly equal to one inch in the average adult male) as a crude measuring device. However, some authorities trace the phrase to a practice once common among brewmasters. In the days when beer was truly beer, not the pasteurized soft drink that passes for beer today, the chief brewer sometimes tested the temperature of a batch of brew by dipping in his thumb. This technique was neither so accurate nor so hygienic as a thermometer check would be, but based on the brewmaster's long experience, this *rule of thumb* would tell him how well the brewing was proceeding.

rumble seat. A now obsolete feature of the automobile was the *rumble seat,* called in Britain the *dickey* or *dickey seat.* For the benefit of today's youngsters, the *rumble seat* was a folding seat located in what is now the luggage compartment on most cars. It was unprotected by any roof and a *rumbleseat* ride to a late-season football game could be an invitation to pneumonia, unless the *rumble-seaters* were clad in the raccoon coats of the period. Like the running board, the *rumble seat* far antedates the autos. Indeed, it goes back to the early nineteenth century, when it was a feature of certain carriages. It got its name, obviously, from the fact that its occupants were all too aware of the rumble of the rear wheels.

rum fellow has nothing at all to do with rum or, for that matter, with intoxication of any kind. It is a corruption of *Romany,* a term used in England to denote a Gypsy. Since Gypsies are, by the standards of most people, "odd," the *rum fellow* expression came to be used to describe anyone who failed to conform to the standards of ordinary folk.

ruminate (pronounced ROO-mih-nayt) comes directly from the Latin verb *ruminare,* "to chew the cud," and carries the same meaning to the present day. An animal that chews its cud is a *ruminant. Ruminate* is most commonly used today, however, in the sense of contemplating a matter for some time, turning it over and over in the mind, meditating on it.

rummage sale. The *rummage* in *rummage sale* comes from the Middle French word *arrumage,* meaning to stow cargo in the hold of a ship. Since freighters usually carry a very varied cargo, considerable searching through—or *rummaging*— is often required before the desired lot is found. So a *rummage sale* is a sale of varied items of merchandise through which the prospective purchaser searches.

run amok/amuck. A headline on an account of student riots at a Western college read: RADICALISM RUN AMOK. A reader questioned whether this was the same as *run amuck* or a typographical error. Here we have a variant spelling of *amuck*—actually much closer to the Malayan word *amoq,* from which it is derived. The word was originally used to describe the actions of Malayan tribesmen who, frenzied by hatred and hashish, would rush furiously into hand-to-hand combat.

running boards. The original *running boards* extended from bow to stern on canal boats. Men walked (not ran) along them, propelling the boats with poles. The platforms along the sides of railroad locomotives were next called *running boards,* and the expression logically was applied to the boards along which conductors walked collecting fares on the old-time open trolley cars. From there it was a short and obvious step to the *running boards* which once distinguished such noble cars as the Pierce-Arrow. We believe the first American car to dispense completely with *running boards* was the classic Cord of the 1930s.

rushing the growler. The origin of this phrase may shed a little light on the social customs of our land in the years before Prohibition. In the old days it was the custom of laborers at lunch hour or the paterfamilias in the heat of a summer evening to dispatch someone to the corner saloon for a "bucket of suds." The person performing the errand was said to be *rushing the growler* and the *growler* was the pail itself. According to our informants —older, sager and more experienced folks than we—the typical *growler* held a half gallon when filled to capacity and the average price for the contents was 25 cents, with a nickel tip for the *rusher* unless he was one of the family, in which case he got nothing.

Naturally the barkeep didn't expect to provide a full 64-ounce half gallon for this relatively modest price, so the common practice was for him to put plenty of "head" on the beer—a technique not unknown to economy-minded bartenders today. The customers were not above matching guile with guile, though, and we're told that it was a common practice for some *growler-rushers* to wipe the inside lip of the can with a bit of bacon or salt-pork rind before bringing it in for refill. The thin film of grease thus deposited on the rim of the *growler* prevented the formation of the bubbles which made up the head, thereby frustrating the bartender and guaranteeing the thirsty patron full measure.

Russian roulette is the simple-minded stunt in which a person, usually responding to a dare, loads a single cylinder of a revolver, spins the cylinder, places the muzzle against his own temple and fires. The *roulette* element comes from the well-known gambling game in which bettors try to guess the color and/or number of the hole on a wheel where the little ball will come to rest. Needless to say, the odds in the gambling den are better than those (usually one in six that you lose—fatally) in *Russian roulette.* There is a possibility that the *Russian* in that phrase may come from the fact— if it is a fact—that this kind of sport was popular in czarist armies. More likely, since the phrase seems of much more recent origin, this element can be traced to the presumed fatalism attributed to Russians generally. Probably, also, the alliteration of the phrase contributes to its popularity.

sabbatical year. According to ancient Hebrew tradition, each seventh year fields were allowed to lie fallow for a twelve-month period to "rest" the soil. *Sabbath* and *sabbatical* both come from the Hebrew word *shabath,* "to rest." Nowadays the term applies to the year or half-year leave of absence granted at seven-year intervals to college and university teachers.

sabotage comes from the French word *sabot,* meaning "shoe or boot," and derives its meaning of deliberate delay or obstruction of work from some use of *sabots* for this purpose. We have never been much persuaded, however, by the story that workers threw their wooden shoes into factory machinery to cause damaging delays. You see, wooden shoes have traditionally been worn by peasants, rather than by city-dwelling factory workers. So it seems more likely that the first instances of *sabotage* were peasant revolts against oppressive landowners—rebellions or "strikes," if you will, that might well have taken the form of workers trampling down the landowners' crops. In any event, the word appeared in English around 1910 and attained its first popularity during World War I, when it acquired its other chief meaning—the calculated hindrance of an enemy nation's war efforts by destruction of bridges, machinery and railroads through the efforts of secret agents.

sack is a regional term for *bag,* which is the generic term including all sorts of containers from suitcases to Pliofilm refrigerator *Baggies.* One is just as good as the other, though *sack* is often used to mean a burlap bag or gunnysack. Another item of regional dialect is *poke* for a small bag whether made of paper or cloth. In Gold Rush times, a miner's stake was always kept in his *poke,* which is why Robert Service once wrote about "the woman that kissed him and pinched his *poke*—was the lady that's known as Lou."

saddler of Bawtry. During the eighteenth century it was the practice of a well-known tavern in York, England, to provide a farewell drink for all criminals condemned to death. The custom was for the condemned man and his guards to stop by the public house for this parting potion. But one man, the *saddler of Bawtry,* refused to stop for the drink and quickly was hanged. The irony of the tale lies in the fact that if he had tarried only a few minutes at the tavern, a reprieve en route from the king would have reached the gallows in time to spare his life.

sad iron. "Sad" is here used in the sense of "heavy." This meaning is now obsolete, except in some regional dialects. Why was it necessary to label this kind of heavy flatiron a *sad iron?* To distinguish it from the "box iron," which was heated by coals placed inside the iron. Today's dictionaries— edited by people who probably never saw a *sad iron*—describe it as "a heavy flatiron having points at both ends and a removable handle." True enough, but we seem to recall that the original *sad irons* were all of one piece—no detachable handles—and were pointed on only one end. The detachable handles came later.

sadism. There is nó connection whatever between "sad" and *sadism.* The adjective "sad" comes from the Anglo-Saxon word *saed,* meaning "full or sated." At first it described the feeling of being overfull of food. Now it means mournful or unhappy. *Sadism* and *sadistic* come from the name of Count Donatien de Sade, whose writings first brought to public attention the psychic aberration whereby one person derives pleasure from mistreating or hurting others.

saga today means any long, involved narrative, especially one chronicling deeds of bravery. Originally it was a medieval Norse legend celebrating the heroic exploits of one family. The most notable use of the elements of the *saga* in modern times is Richard Wagner's *Ring of the Nibelungs,* which draws heavily on the Old Norse Volsunga *Saga.* Notable also, perhaps, is the comment of comedian Groucho Marx, paraphrasing the famous statement of Vice-President Thomas R. Marshall: "What this country really needs is a good five-cent *saga.* "

sail under false colors goes back to the ancient days of piracy on the high seas, when a pirate ship would fly the flag ("colors") of a friendly nation until the moment of attack, when it would raise the Jolly Roger, bearing the dreaded symbol of the skull and crossbones.

salad days are the days of youth, when lack of experience and general naïveté make one appear "green" to mature oldsters. The phrase comes from Shakespeare's *Anthony and Cleopatra,* where, in Act I, Scene 5, Cleopatra speaks of "my *salad days,* when I was green in judgment."

Salisbury steak didn't get its name from a place but from a man. He was Dr. J. M. Salisbury, a British medico of the nineteenth century, who was a great advocate of dietary reform. The original *Salisbury steak* formula included eggs, milk, bread crumbs and other items designed to make the patty more nourishing.

salmagundi (or salmagundy, as it is sometimes spelled) is a salad of chopped meats, anchovies, eggs and onions. There are two theories about how the salad got that name. One is that it was named after a French noble woman who concocted it for Henry VI. The other, much more prosaic, is simply that it was derived from the Italian phrase *salame conditi,* meaning "pickled meat." Anyhow, it eventually came to mean any kind of mishmash or potpourri. When Washington Irving edited a magazine in the early 1800s, it seemed to him a good idea to give it the name *Salmagundi* to indicate the variety of articles, stories and poems it contained. Today the word lives on in New York as the name of a club whose membership consists entirely of artists and writers—the Salmagundi Club.

And then there is another Salmagundy—this one featured in a chant used by children jumping rope: *"Salmagundy,* born on Monday, christened on Tuesday, married on Wednesday, sick on Thursday, worse on Friday, died on Saturday, buried on Sunday, and that was the end of *Salmagundy. "*

salmonella is the name of a disease-causing bacteria commonly associated with food poisoning. It has nothing whatever to do with the fish, by the way, having got its name from Daniel Salmon, an American veterinarian.

saloon. Among the many efforts of lawmakers to legislate morality, perhaps none was less successful than the pious resolve to "eliminate the corner saloon" when Prohibition finally ended and the public drinking of liquor was again made legal. The *saloon* did not, of course, disappear. It's everywhere around us, disguised as "tavern," "club" or "café." In most states the only lasting result of the legislation is that no pub dares call itself a *saloon.* Two young New Yorkers, ignorant of this nicety, opened an attractive bar which they called "O'Neals' Saloon." In short order, the wrath of the law descended with demands that the offending word be removed. The resourceful proprietors, not wanting to pay for a new sign, simply changed a single letter on it. Now, to the distress of spelling purists and to the delight of all others, the sign reads "O'Neals' Baloon." *Saloon* came into English from French *salon,* "drawing room."

salt of the earth. Anyone regarded as the finest of his kind is the *salt of the earth.* The expression comes from Matthew 5:13, where Jesus, speaking to his disciples, says: "Ye are the *salt of the earth. . . .* Ye are the light of the world."

saluki is the oldest dog known to man. Carved replicas of it have been found in Near Eastern ruins dating back to 7000 B.C. It's a graceful hound, speedy and lithe, not unlike the greyhound in appearance. It is used by desert tribes to hunt gazelles, which will give you some idea of its speed.

Sam Browne belt. Sam Browne was, like the better-known Major Grey of chutney fame, one of the British soldiers who served his queen in India during the nineteenth century. At the time it was customary to wear a sword as side arm, and the weight of the sword had a tendency to drag down the belt on the left side. So Sam, being an ingenious sort, devised an over-the-shoulder belt which, fastened to the regular belt, held it even all around. If memory serves, the *Sam Browne belt* was part of the uniform of U.S. Army officers until World War II, when it, along with the somewhat foppish swagger stick that some officers used in imitation of their British counterparts, was abandoned. Today it is occasionally worn as part of a special ceremonial uniform.

However, though virtually abandoned by the armed forces, *Sam Browne's belt* has found a new and valued place in civilian life. As William C. Russell of the American Automobile Association pointed out: "The *Sam Browne belt* is currently worn by some 800,000 people in the United States, and to the persons with whom they are associated, it is a symbol of authority and respect. The group I refer to are the school safety patrols across the country, who are readily identified by their white *Sam Browne belts.* "

same old seven and six. A call for the meaning of the phrase *same old seventy-six* brought the following explanation from Colonel J. W. Bender (Ret.) of Alexandria, Virginia: "Unfortunately for you," he wrote, "the expression—which is as old as the hills—is 'The *same old seven and six'* which add up to the unlucky number of thirteen. Hence when you ask someone 'How are things?' and the answer is 'The *same old seven and six,'* it means 'No luck.' I have heard this expression, which is very common in the military, all my life—practically since Robert E. Lee was a second lieutenant."

Sam Hill is one of many euphemisms for "hell"—like "blazes," "Halifax," "heck," "Hoboken" and many more. This one was very popular with frontiersmen, especially when they needed to clean up their language in the presence of ladies. Will James records the comment of a cowboy who felt he had been insulted by an Eastern dude: "What the *Sam Hill* do you think we are out here, servants?" The first recorded appearance in print of *Sam Hill* was in 1839. Elmer Roessner, an editor friend, reported that turn-of-the-century Seattle newspapers made regular use of this expression. Jim Hill, the legendary "empire builder," whose railroads, including the Great Northern, remain his lasting monument, was a man given to notable rages when anyone dared to oppose one of his grandiose schemes. So frequent were these tirades, according to Roessner, that the papers carried as a standing head: JIM HILL MAD AS *SAM HILL.*

samurai. Pronounced SAM-oo-rye and spelled the same in both singular and plural, this Japanese word refers to members of the military class in feudal times. A *samurai* was usually the retainer of a noble, somewhat like the squires and equerries of European chivalry. Theoretically abolished in 1871 with the end of the Japanese feudal system, the code of the *samurai* continued to hold the allegiance of many military officers through World War II.

Sam, you made the pants too long. One of our columns had to do with an amusing Yiddish witticism by comedian Jack Gilford. We mentioned that we have known Gilford for many years and especially admire his rendition of "Sam, You Made the Pants Too Long." This prompted Jimmy Monsignore, of the Monsignore restaurant in New York City, to chide us for not mentioning that the late Joe E. Lewis had popularized the song first. This, in turn, inspired another reader to comment: "Perhaps your readers would be interested in the story behind Monsignore's story. 'Sam, You Made the Pants Too Long' was a parody of the lament, 'Lawd, You Made the Night Too Long,' a hit song with music by Victor Young (a Tin Pan Alley immortal) and lyrics by Sam Lewis. The special material was written by Fred Whitehouse and Milton Berle in 1940 for Berle. Miltie introduced the number, Joe E. Lewis revived it in the middle forties, and guess who revived the comic caper in 1966? Barbra Streisand!"

Well, as the little girl wrote in a report on a book about penguins: "This tells me more about penguins than I care to know." Certainly we now know all there is to know about the sad saga of Sam and his pants.

sandhog is a tunnel worker, one who works under air pressure in the early stages of excavation for tunnels and bridge foundations. His is dangerous work indeed, imbued with the obvious immediate hazards of drowning and "the bends," and the long-range threat of death from silicosis, the disease caused by inhalation of stone dust.

sandwich. Over the centuries, British nobility has made many contributions to the language. Perhaps the most famous was the invention of John Montague, nicknamed "Jemmy Twitcher," one of the most inveterate gamblers in the court of George III. Famous for his round-the-clock sessions at the gaming boards, "Jemmy" used to order his servant to bring him pieces of meat between slices of bread, so that he could continue gambling without loss of time. Very soon the bread-and-meat combination was given the name it retains to this day, the *sandwich.* "Jemmy Twitcher," you see, was more formally known as the fourth Earl of Sandwich.

sang-froid translates literally as "cold blood," but it really means the ability to stay calm, cool and collected in the face of any situation, even an emergency. It is French.

sanguinary/sanguine. *Sanguinary* (pronounced SANG-gwin-nehr-ee) is an adjective meaning "bloody, murderous or bloodthirsty," a definition that may seem highly illogical to those familiar with the word *sanguine,* which means "confident, cheerful and warm." The reason, if not the logic, lies in the fact that both words come from the Latin *sanguis* (blood). *Sanguine* originally meant "of the color of blood," hence ruddy, particularly as applied to the complexion. It acquired its present-day meaning in medieval physiology, when four fluids were held to be responsible for a person's disposition and health. Since a cheerful disposition and ruddy complexion were attributed to the strength of the blood, *sanguine* by extension means "warm, cheerful, confident and optimistic."

Sanhedrin (pronounced SAN-hih-drin) or *Great Sanhedrin* was the supreme council of the ancient Jews. It supervised both judicial and religious affairs of the Jewish nation. It had from seventy to seventy-two members. *Sanhedrin* comes from the Greek *sanedrion*, "council," which in turn came from *san*, "together," and *haedra*, "seat"—thus literally "a sitting together." *Sanhedrin* is sometimes used jocosely to refer to any potent "inner circle."

sans-culotte, a French phrase meaning "without knee breeches," was originally applied by French aristocrats to the revolutionaries, who wore pantaloons instead of breeches. In time it came to refer to the extreme "red" republicans of the French Revolution.

Santa Claus is a contraction of the Dutch "Sant Nikolaas," patron saint of children. His feast day is December 6 and originally gifts were given to children on the eve of that day. For more than a century, however, the celebration has been associated with the Christmas season in Western Europe and North America and *Santa Claus* is now believed by children to bring gifts to them on the eve of Christmas day. The much quoted "Night Before Christmas," incidentally, was originally titled "A Visit from St. Nicholas."

sardonic smiles or laughter may be mocking, derisive or sneering, but they are always bitter—and with good reason. Legend has it that *sardonic* comes from *sardanē,* a plant grown on the island of Sardinia, the taste of which was very bitter, so bitter, as to cause convulsions and facial contortions. Another version of its effect is that those who ate of it died laughing.

sartorial (from the Latin *sartor,* for "tailor") originally meant "concerned with tailors and their work." Now it can properly be used to refer to any aspect of men's clothing, from an individual item to the complete ensemble.

sashay is a popular form of the French *chassé* (pronounced shuh-SAY), meaning "to glide or move with a dancing step." It first became widely popular as a call in barn dances: *"Sashay* all, around the hall." Then it acquired all sorts of slightly variant meanings: to move on a diagonal or go kittycorner, to move with elegant airs, and also to rush in a great hurry.

Satan comes direct from the Hebrew *satan,* meaning "enemy or adversary." It has long been used as the name of the great enemy of mankind, Lucifer, the archangel who was cast out of heaven by Michael.

satrapy. A *satrap* originally designated the governor of a province in ancient Persia, and *satrapy* referred either to his government or to the province he ruled. The origin of the word is the old Persian *shathrapavan,* which literally means "protector of the land."

saucered and blowed is a rustic dialect expression meaning "all ready to be used or consumed." There is a story, going back a century or more, about a gallant gentleman whose manners were considerably better than his grammar. Seated in an inn at a stagecoach rest stop, he noticed that a lady who had ordered a cup of coffee seemed concerned that it would not cool quickly enough for her to drink it and get back on the stage before departure time. So bowing graciously, he said to the lady: "Here, take mine. It's all *saucered and blowed.*"

savoir-faire/savoir-vivre. *Savoir* means "to know"; *faire* means "to do" and *vivre* means "to live." Thus *savoir-faire* (pronounced sav-wahr FAIR) is the ability to know what and how to do or say—and when to do or say it. It amounts to tact or the smooth handling of any situation. *Savoir-vivre* is generally good manners or good breeding.

sawbuck is a ten-dollar bill. The name has been current in American slang since before 1850, having been especially popular on the Western frontier. The *sawbuck* originally was a kind of sawhorse with the legs also projecting above the crossbar, so that they formed X's at each end of the sawhorse. X, of course, is also the Roman numeral for "ten"—and that is how the ten-dollar bill came to be called a *sawbuck*.

sawed-off shotgun. The *shotgun* was an American invention, which first appeared in print in 1826. It's a shoulder-held, smooth-bore firearm that fires many pellets at once. The *sawed-off shotgun* made its first appearance as an instrument of gang warfare during the Prohibition era. We once saw a story in the London *Times* about three bank robbers who used *sawn-off shotguns*. Very British, but to our ears not quite right.

say it ain't so, Joe. This saying was an aftermath of the famed "Black Sox" scandal of 1919, when members of the Chicago White Sox were found to have sold out to gamblers. One of the great youth heroes in that day was outfielder "Shoeless Joe" Jackson—and this remark is said to have been addressed to him by an unknown boy as Jackson emerged from a courtroom after confessing his guilt.

scalawag is a worthless scamp, a reprobate, a person you are well rid of. There are a couple of versions of its origin, but the one we like best traces it to Scalloway, one of the Shetland Islands. We all know the famous Shetland ponies, beloved by generations of youngsters. Well, the ponies bred and reared on Scalloway are undersized, worthless runts, the original *scalawags*. Incidentally, the word has a very special meaning in American history. In the period of Reconstruction, immediately following the Civil War, white Republican Southerners who collaborated with Northern "carpetbaggers" were derisively called *scalawags*.

scam is underworld slang for a con game or swindle. It started as a part of carny talk—the private language of carnival workers. There a *scam* was a rigged concession (are there any other kind?) like the wheel of fortune, which always stops just one number away from yours. A recent version of the *scam* has a couple of characters taking a motel room for two or three days, advertising "genuine Indian jewelry" at bargain prices, then "taking it on the lam" before the local gentry finds out that the stuff is as phony as the proverbial nine-dollar bill.

scampi is the plural of *scampo,* the Italian word for shrimp, so theoretically at least, any shrimp can be called *scampi,* though no other seafood would be properly so called. However, in actual practice, the label is reserved for fairly large shrimp—also called "prawns"—that are cooked Italian style.

scapegoat is a person who is made to take the blame for the crime or mistake of others. Under Mosaic Law, the high priest of the ancient Jews would bring two goats to the altar of the tabernacle on the Day of Atonement. The high priest then cast lots to see which goat would be sacrificed to the Lord and which would be the *scapegoat.* After the priest had confessed the sins of his people over the head of the *scapegoat,* it was taken to the wilderness and allowed to escape, carrying with it all the sins of the people. The other goat was then given in sacrifice.

Scarborough Warning takes its name from the Yorkshire town of Scarborough, where, centuries ago, an offender caught in the act was summarily dispatched, usually by hanging. The method was not unlike the lynch law of our frontier West. The term was sometimes defined as "blow first, warning later." John Heywood, a sixteenth-century poet, put it this way: "This term *'Scarborough Warning'* grew, some say,/By hasty hanging for rank robbery there./Who that was met but suspect in that way/Straight he was trussed up, whatever he were."

scarce as hen's teeth is an old farmer's saying. Anything *scarce as hen's teeth* is scarce indeed—for hens have no teeth.

scarfing or, as it's more commonly spelled, "scoffing" simply means "eating." We first ran across it back in the early 1930s, when a common expression among Harvard undergraduates after midnight was "Let's go up to the Square and get something to scoff." *Merriam-Webster* adds to our definition slightly, defining "scoff" as "to eat greedily" and adding that its origin is unknown. However, Harold Wentworth, in his *American Dialect Dictionary,* gives an example of "scoff" used as long ago as 1909 on Cape Cod. The same author's more recent *Dictionary of American Slang* says that "scoff" originated in maritime and hobo use and seems to have more Negro than white use. He reports further that it is "said to have originated in Africa."

scarlet letter is the letter *A* that a woman convicted of adultery was required to wear during the Puritan days of early New England. Hawthorne's novel (1850) of this title tells the story of its heroine, Hester Prynne, doomed to wear the letter as penalty for adultery with her pastor.

scenario is a word that occurred often in the transcripts of tapes of the Nixon White House. It was a surprise to us, because we thought it had been forgotten along with most of the other Hollywood expressions of the 1920s and 1930s. *Scenario* was the term used for "screenplay" during the days when the Gish sisters, John Barrymore and Fatty Arbuckle were at the peak of their fame. The only reason for its resurgence in the White House records, so far as we can guess, is that a couple of Nixon's top advisers were alumni of an ad agency in Los Angeles and, presumably, had grown up under movie studio influence. It's a word taken from the Italian word for "scenery" and eventually can be traced to the Latin *scaena,* meaning "stage."

sceptre'd isle comes from the famous "This England" speech by John of Gaunt in Shakespeare's *Richard II* (Act II, Scene 1), in which Gaunt apostrophizes England as "This royal throne of kings, this *sceptre'd isle/* This earth of majesty, this seat of Mars,/ . . . This blessed plot, this earth, this realm, this England." In this speech Shakespeare merely uses *sceptre'd* as a more dramatic and evocative adjective than "imperial."

Scheherazade. In *The Arabian Nights,* the sultan plans to have a new bride every night, having her put to death at dawn. *Scheherazade* outwits him when she becomes his bride by telling such intriguing and suspenseful tales that, after one thousand and one nights, he changes his mind, takes her permanently to wife and declares her the liberator of her sex.

schlemiel is a very common word in the German and Yiddish languages. It refers to a man or person who is in bad luck all the time, for whom nothing is successful and everything goes wrong. It comes from the Bible, the Book of Numbers, Chapter 2. Shelumiel the son of Zurishaddai was the leader of the tribe of Simeon and it is said that whereas all other leaders were successful in battle, he was the only one who lost all the time. Hence, *schlemiel.*

schlep is a verb borrowed from Yiddish. It means "to tote or lug," especially something that can be carried only rather clumsily. We have heard one college-age youngster complaining, "I had to *schlep* two heavy armloads of books all the way from the student union to the dorm." *Schlep* also does duty as a noun and here it has a meaning rather close to "schlemiel," a clumsy or stupid person. As a noun it may also be used in a sense directly related to its verb meaning—a long or arduous journey. *Schlep* comes from the Yiddish verb *schlepen,* meaning "to drag or trail," and this in turn comes from the Middle Low German *schleppen.*

schlock means "spurious, fake or worthless." It originally was part of the slang of criminals, but in recent years it has become more and more common in the jargon of some areas of commerce, notably in the clothing and furniture businesses. The term *schlock shop* is also heard, meaning a store specializing in worthless or nearly worthless merchandise.

schmaltz is a very convenient slang word, which comes to us from the German by way of the Yiddish. In German, *schmalz* is literally "melted fat." So *schmaltz* is anything of smooth and oily sentimentality. It is used to apply to certain types of music or literature—and also to the act of buttering up someone, as "Don't give me that *schmaltz.*"

schmo. A borrowing from Yiddish, *schmo* is a stupid or dull clod. Yiddish took the word in the form *shmok* from a Slovenian word of the same meaning, *smok.*

schmoozing—loafing about and talking shop—comes from the Yiddish word *schmus,* meaning "to talk."

schnook, also sometimes spelled *schnook,* comes from Yiddish and means a person who is easily tricked or duped. You might say that a *schnook* is a Yiddish patsy or fall guy. In Yiddish the word is spelled *shnok* and is a variant of *shmok,* which also gave us *schmo.*

schnorrer is a leech, a parasite, sometimes an outright beggar. The word comes from the Yiddish *schnoren,* "to beg while playing a pipe or harp," and ultimately from the Middle High German *snurren,* "to whir or hum."

schnozzle. Probably no word has been so closely identified with a single performer as *schnozzle* or *schnozzola* with Jimmy Durante. For more than forty years his Cyrano-like nose was his trademark—quite literally, for each year he took an ad in the show business weekly *Variety,* with a sketch of himself in profile and no word of identification because none was needed. Everyone in the entertainment field knew from the *schnoz* that the ad was for the great Durante.

So it may come as a small surprise to learn that the word which became the trademark of this great Italian-American comedian is not Italian but Yiddish. *Schnozzle* comes from the Yiddish *shnoitsl,* meaning "snout," which in turn comes from the German *Schnauze,* also meaning "snout." In case you're wondering, the answer is yes, the schnauzer dog gets its name from the same source—and from the fact that its most prominent characteristic is a broad and blunt muzzle.

Schoolmaster of the Republic was Noah Webster—the same who wrote the first Webster dictionaries. He earned the title by writing, among many textbooks, the famous *Blue-Backed Speller,* which taught many generations of Americans to spell and, hence, to read. You may never have heard of this speller, which was originally published in 1783, but it sold many more than 100 million copies and is generally regarded as the largest-selling book by an American author in the nation's history.

schtick. Originally a term employed by Yiddish comedians to designate a routine or piece of business used in their acts, *schtick* now may mean a bit of action carefully repeated in episode after episode in a television series.

schwa. The upside-down *e* called the *schwa* first appeared as one of the many symbols making up the International Phonetic Alphabet (IPA), which is widely used by teachers of speech and constitutes the most accurate method of transcribing the sounds we make when we talk. Unfortunately, the great variety of symbols involved makes it impractical for use in general dictionaries. So the IPA remains usable primarily by the experts. However, when Clarence Barnhart was editing the first major college dictionary of the 1940s, the *American College Dictionary,* he decided to use the *schwa* for the first time in a dictionary intended for general readers. His reason: simply that it recorded the unstressed vowel sound better than any of the "Websterian" signs and symbols that had been used before. Perhaps because of its odd appearance, it caught on quickly and today practically all up-to-date dictionaries have it. We even used it in a new dictionary—the *Xerox Intermediate Dictionary*—designed for grade school children. *Schwa* comes from Hebrew, by way of German.

scissorbill, in the language of laboring men, was a nonunion worker, usually one with some sort of independent income. While not a militant strikebreaker, he certainly was no help to the union organizers. One Industrial Workers of the World song depicted him as not very bright: *"Scissorbill, he is a little dippy./Scissorbill,* he has a funny face./*Scissorbill* would drown in Mississippi;/He's the missing link Darwin tried to trace."

scofflaw is a most unusual word in many respects. For one thing, it is the only word we know of which was coined simultaneously by two different people, working entirely independently of each other. Here's how it happened. Back in 1923 many of the nation's law-enforcement officers were becoming distressed by the flagrant disrespect that many people were showing toward the newly enacted Eighteenth Amendment to the Constitution—the prohibition law. They felt, and rightly, that an attitude of defiance toward one of our federal laws might lead to a gradual erosion of respect for the whole body of our laws. So they sought a word to describe people who derided the National Prohibition Act.

A Massachusetts millionaire, Delcevare King, one of the foremost Prohibitionists of the time, announced a prize contest for the most appropriate word coined to meet this need. The prize was only $200, but it attracted more than 25,000 entries. In January 1924, King announced that the winning entry, *scofflaw,* had been submitted by both Henry Irving Shaw and Kate Butler, both residents of Massachusetts and both, presumably, ardent Prohibitionists.

scorched earth is an age-old custom in which invaded countries strip and pillage their own land in the path of an invader, leaving him nothing to sustain his troops. This practice was followed by Chinese troops at the time of the Japanese invasion during the 1930s and by Russian armies when the Nazis invaded their homeland in World War II.

Scotch verdict is a verdict of "not proven." Although in English and American law a jury in a criminal case is required to bring in a verdict of "guilty" or "not guilty," Scottish law allows this third alternative. In effect it says that while the jury strongly suspects that the defendant is guilty as charged, the prosecution has not adduced evidence sufficiently conclusive to justify a vote for conviction.

scot-free has nothing to do with Scotland or the Scottish people. In Shakespeare's day and before, a *scot* (or *sceot,* as it was originally spelled) was a municipal tax, one paid to the local bailiff or sheriff. Thus the present-day meaning of "without payment of a just penalty" can be traced directly back to the *scot-free* varlets of Elizabethan England who managed successfully to dodge paying their taxes.

Scotland Yard. For the strict precisionists among our readers, be it known that *Scotland Yard* is no longer located at Scotland Yard. Police H.Q. are now located on the Thames Embankment near the Houses of Parliament and are properly known as "New Scotland Yard." The Yard got its name from the street where Sir Robert Peel located police headquarters in 1829. And why was the street named Scotland Yard? Because in the years 970 to 1170, the kings of Scotland were required to come down to London once a year to acknowledge their indebtedness to the rulers of England—and the place where their castle was located became known, with typical British understatement, as *Scotland Yard.*

Scourge of God. Attila, leader of the Huns, earned the title *Flagellum Dei (Scourge of God)* during the Middle Ages because of his relentless pillaging of most of Europe between A.D. 433 and 453. Ironically, the name Attila is a baby-talk diminutive of *atta,* the Gothic word for "father." So it literally means "little father."

scrambled eggs is a highly descriptive, if somewhat disrespectful, term for the gold braid adorning the hats of top-ranking officers in the armed services.

scratchcake is simply a cake made entirely from scratch—not involving any sort of prepared cake mix. "Scratch" got the meaning of "a beginning" from the fact that the starting line of a race was often referred to as the scratch line or mark.

screaming meemies has been traced back to World War I, when it was used to describe certain German artillery shells with a high-pitched whine. Then it came to mean the disordered mental state of a person who had been exposed to the noise too long. Gradually during the 1920s, it became practically a synonym for the "heebie jeebies," something close to delirium tremens. During World War II it was revived in military service to name a small U.S. Army rocket launched from a multiple rocket projector mounted on the back of a jeep or truck.

screw as a term for a prison guard is based on the fact that *screw* was originally slang for "key." One of the most important functions of a prison guard, or turnkey, as he's often called, is to see that prisoners are locked up at the appropriate times—and that involves turning the "screw." Interestingly enough, Henry Mencken reports in *The American Language* that in the 1920s deskmen and bellboys in hotels used *screw* as a slang term for room key. Another theory is that *screw* refers to the thumbscrews used by jailers in ancient times to torture prisoners into confessing.

screwball was originally a pitched baseball which curved in a path similar to a corkscrew or just traveled erratically. Obviously it was hard to predict where it was going to go. Hence, a *screwball* is a person who behaves in an erratic or unconventional manner. The term is not always used in a derogatory manner and is not as opprobrious a term as *nut.* It was applied to eccentric ball players before it came into general use.

scrimmage line. The *line of scrimmage* is simply the theoretical line between opposing teams where the ball is put into play. In football, when the center bends over the ball, that open space between the contending players is the *scrimmage line*. The word is a corruption of *skirmish*.

scrod. A reader sent us a story with one of our favorite headlines: SCROD CALLED FISH FRAUD. The story has it that a Boston restaurant owner invented the word so that he could use it as a sort of generic label for whatever fish happened to be in good supply on any particular day. If pollack was running well, it appeared on his menu as *scrod*. If haddock was in plentiful supply, it was served up as *scrod*. And so on for a couple of other kinds of bland white fish. This way the restaurateur didn't have to change his menus every day.

That's a good story and you can believe it if you want to. But it just happens that we have spent many years in Boston and have visited most of that town's justly famous seafood restaurants. And one thing we can attest to is that you're not going to feed pollack to a Down East Yankee without his knowing what he's getting. No. The truth of the matter is that *scrod* is usually a fillet of cod cut from the thick part of the fish, near the tail. That's how it gets its name, for *scrod* is a borrowing from Old Dutch *scrood*, meaning "slice." It's true that you may—on very rare occasions— be served a small whole fish labeled *scrod*. In that case you're very fortunate indeed, because the fish being served is a very young and tender cod.

Scrooge, leading character in Dickens's *Christmas Carol,* has come to embody the traits of miserliness and greed so completely that his name has come into the language as a generic term for a very stingy person.

scrutiny. Coming from the Latin *scrutari,* "to search into carefully," *scrutiny* has the built-in meaning of close examination. Hence, the common phrase "close *scrutiny*" is redundant.

scuba is an acronym for "self-contained underwater breathing apparatus."

scunner is a word William learned many years ago from the late George Pierce Baker, the Yale and Harvard professor who numbered Eugene O'Neill, Thomas Wolfe and George Abbott among his many distinguished pupils. "G.P.," as he was known, had a striking and occasionally devastating vocabulary. When he mentioned that he had taken a *scunner* to the late Alexander Woollcott, no translation was necessary. He meant that he had a total aversion to the man. *Scunner* was originally a Scottish dialect word.

scuttlebutt means "gossip," but originally it referred to the lidded cask ("scuttled butt") from which the ship's company obtained drinking water. Just as personnel in offices and factories today gather round the drinking fountain to exchange the latest rumors, so sailors since the days of John Paul Jones have clustered at the *scuttlebutt* to pass on the latest rumor.

seagoing bellhops is a term for U.S. Marines used derisively by sailors and generally thought to refer to the Marines' elegant dress uniforms, much more colorful than those of the enlisted men in other services.

sea lawyer is a know-it-all, especially a sailor of an argumentative turn of mind. His volubility is usually exceeded only by his ignorance.

sea shanties/chanties, which sailors used to sing—the rhythmical songs originally sung in unison as sailors hoisted the sails—take their name from the French *chanter,* "to sing."

secretary goes back to the Middle Ages, when Latin was still the most widely used language, especially in communications between heads of state. Then a "secretarius" was a confidential officer, one who could be trusted with secrets of state. That word, in turn, came from the Latin *secretus,* "secret."

seeded. The special meaning of *seed* in sports has to do with the scattering *(seeding)* of the names of superior players in a tournament in such a way as to ensure that they will not meet each other in an early round. No tournament sponsor wants his stars to eliminate each other in the early rounds.

see red probably comes from the old belief that a bull seeing a red flag will become enraged and run amuck. Scientific researchers have now proved that a bull will rush at any brightly colored cloth that is waved at him. In fact, there is some evidence indicating that a simple white cloth will attract, and enrage, a bull more quickly than a red one. And thus dies another cherished illusion—cherished, that is, by everyone but the bull.

seersucker, a fabric with alternating stripes of white and a light blue, gray or tan color, got its name from the British colonial version of the Indian word *shirshaker.* This in turn was a borrowing from the Persian *shir-u-shakar,* which meant "milk and sugar," designating the alternate stripes.

segue (pronounced SEG-way) is a term common in the jargon of musicians. It means to move from one musical selection to another without modulation or interruption. *Segue* comes from the Italian and originally meant "to follow."

seiche. In Wisconsin there occasionally occurs a peculiar fluctuation in the water level of Green Bay. On a perfectly calm day with not a ripple and the surface glassy, the water will gradually rise three or four feet, then slowly return to its former level. The cycle may be repeated several times and each cycle may take about ten minutes. The phenomenon is called a *seiche.* People living in the area all pronounce it as though it were spelled "seech," to rhyme with "peach," "beach" and so forth.

Both *World Webster* and the *Pronouncing Dictionary of American English* give it as *saysh.* Webster's *Third International* agrees, as does *Funk & Wagnalls.* So the preponderance of learned evidence seems opposed to the local pronunciation. Nonetheless, we hope that the people of Green Bay will continue with *seech* because this is the established regional pronunciation and anything else would sound false and affected.

Just to complete the record, *seiche* is a Swiss-French word which was taken directly into English, with spelling unchanged.

sell like hot cakes. The best guess as to the origin of this phrase is that *hot cakes* used to be a favorite item of refreshment at carnivals and country fairs before the hot dog and, more recently, hamburgers and pizza, got the big play. Anyway, the cliché has been around a long time—at least since the early 1800s.

seltzer/club soda are two names for the same thing, a sparkling, flavorless, effervescent beverage, usually produced by charging plain water under pressure with carbon dioxide gas. *Seltzer* is much the older name. It derives from the name of a town in Germany, Nieder Selters, where a similar, naturally effervescent spring water was found. The terms "soda" and "soda water," which appear in English midway through the nineteenth century, derive from the fact that early versions were made by adding bicarbonate of soda to water.

The real question, though, is why the term *club soda* is becoming more widely used in many parts of this country than *seltzer*. Well, it's a fairly recent phenomenon. For the first three decades of this century, plain soda for use in homes or clubs was usually bottled in siphon bottles, and one asked for a *siphon of seltzer*. With the advent of repeal, bottlers of carbonated beverages found that they had a substantial domestic market for what they soon labeled "sparkling water" or "soda." The retreat from the word *seltzer* was doubtless influenced by widespread advertising of headache remedies with the word *seltzer* as part of their trade names. Obviously beverage manufacturers didn't care to associate the pleasures of party tippling with the horrors of the morning after, so the semantically infelicitous *seltzer* was doomed.

Other complications arose, moreover. In some areas of the Midwest the word "soda" meant a sweetish, lemon-flavored beverage. Many an Easterner has been startled to find that his whiskey and soda is served with a sickishly sweet soda mixed in, instead of the tasteless seltzer he expected. So a modifier was needed, and the modish and elegant *club* was added. Now the far traveler can ask for a drink with *club soda* anywhere in the land and be spared the traumatic experiences of seeking an adult drink and being served a child's.

separate the sheep from the goats. Down through the centuries goats have received rather a bad press. They were regarded as in league with the devil. Indeed, there was even one folk belief that every goat disappeared momentarily every day of its life for a brief communion with Satan to get its beard combed. That the goat was also a symbol of lechery is clear from the retention even today of expressions like "that old goat" to refer to a lecherous man past his prime. However, this particular expression comes from the King James Bible (Matthew 25:32, 33): "And before him shall be gathered all nations: and he shall separate them one from another, as a shepherd divideth his sheep from the goats." And then, as though that isn't insult enough for our goatish friends, the parable continues: "And he shall set the sheep on his right hand, but the goats on the left." The centuries-old prejudice in favor of "right" and against "left" is here exemplified yet another time.

Sepoy Mutiny. A famous mutiny of native *(Sepoy)* Indian troops against their British overlords in 1857–1858. It was touched off by the issuance to the troops of a new kind of musket requiring an application of grease to the cartridge. Since the soldiers were forbidden by their religion to touch beef fat, they rebelled and widespread massacres resulted. In the end, India became a crown colony, the East India Company was dissolved and many reforms of lands and laws were effected. *Sepoy* is from Urdu *sipahi* (soldier).

September. The ninth month in the year takes its name from the Latin word *septem* (seven) because it was the seventh month in the Roman calendar.

serendipity is the faculty of making happy and unexpected discoveries by accident. It was coined by the British author Horace Walpole, who based it on the title of an old fairy tale, "The Three Princes of Serendip." The princes in the story, he noted, were "always making discoveries of things they were not in quest of."

sergeant at arms. The word *sergeant* merely means "servant." It comes from the French *servire* (to serve). But early in British history, shortly after the Norman Conquest, *sergeant* came to be the term used for servants of the nobility, especially of the king. The *sergeants* in time assumed knightly rank, bore arms and served as an armed bodyguard to the king. Their job was to arrest anyone who attempted any traitorous action. Later, each of the two houses of Parliament appointed a *sergeant at arms* to enforce the decrees of each house and arrest offenders. When our Senate and House of Representatives were first organized, similar posts were provided for. Though the sergeants' arms are long gone, their authority remains.

setting her cap. In the Victorian era it was quite common for women to wear caps indoors. Remember Whistler's Mother? Usually they were simple affairs made of muslin, but some ladies, especially the younger ones, had fancy ones made of lace. When such a damsel put on her prettiest cap before her boyfriend called, the word quickly got around that she was *setting her cap* for him.

seven hills of Rome. The walled city of ancient Rome included these seven hills: Palatine, Capitoline, Quirinal, Aventine, Caelian, Esquiline and Viminal. As hills they never amounted to much, the tallest (Quirinal) being only 226 feet above sea level.

seventh heaven. *Seventh Heaven,* famous as the title of the unforgettable Janet Gaynor–Charles Farrell silent film, derives from an ancient theory of astronomy in which the seventh ring of stars was the highest and therefore represented supreme bliss.

Seward's Folly/Seward's Icebox/The Last Frontier. All of these are nicknames for the state of Alaska but the last one is the official one. The
Russians were the first to explore Alaska, in 1741, and before long Russian
fur trappers had moved in. When sea otters, from which they got fur,
diminished in number and Russia lost the Crimean War, Russia offered
Alaska for sale and W. H. Seward, who was then Secretary of State,
arranged to buy it in 1867, for $7.2 million. At the time, Americans
mocked this action, calling the territory *Seward's Folly* or *Seward's Icebox,*
but in 1880 gold was discovered there and Alaska became *The Last Frontier,* as it is now called. The discovery in 1968 of what is possibly the
world's largest reserve of oil brought more people and activity to the state
and the original nicknames were forgotten.

sewer service of a legal summons is no service at all. When a legal action is
taken to collect unpaid debts or whatever, the person being sued is supposed to be notified in writing to appear in court to defend himself. The
form used is known as a "process" and the person who delivers it is called
a "process server." Some unscrupulous process servers simply pocket their
fees and dump the summonses into the nearest sewer instead of delivering
them properly. Hence, *sewer service.*

shaggy dog story is one that starts with a fairly improbable premise, builds
suspense for a long time, adding detail upon detail, only to evaporate with
a final throwaway anticlimax. The first such tale began with an obscure ad
in the *Times* of London: "Personal: Wealthy, titled lord lacks only one item
to complete his collection of the world's outstanding oddities: the shaggiest
dog in the world. He is prepared to pay the sum of 5,000 pounds, together
with all travel expenses, to the person who will deliver to him the shaggiest
dog in the world. Deadline: New Year's Eve, midnight, next. Write Box
1313, Times."

The response to this ad was astonishing. At a time when most of the
world was trapped in a deep economic depression, 5,000 pounds was a very
considerable sum. Letters and calls began to come from all parts of the
globe. Soon the address of the noble lord was widely known and the path
to his house sometimes seemed as canine-packed as Madison Square Garden during the annual dog show. Applicant after applicant was turned
away, as often as not because the next dog in line was demonstrably more
shaggy. From Switzerland came mountain dogs—shaggy St. Bernards and
the like. From the hills of New Hampshire came a specially bred and
heavily maned Husky sled dog. Finally, as the year drew to its end, all
attention centered on one notable contender coming from Australia.

In those days the trip was made by ship, and at every stopping place a
Reuters correspondent would cable ever more exciting stories about the
throngs of thousands turning out to see the Australian candidate for the
shaggiest dog in the world. Finally, the day before New Year's, the ship

docked at Southampton, where a throng of 100,000 Britons massed on the docks in bitter-cold weather to catch a glimpse of the shaggiest dog in the world. Pressing on through the mob, the dog and his master caught the boat train, arrived in London—again to the roar of crowds in the railroad station—and caught a cab to the nobleman's address. As thousands cheered, they mounted the steps, were greeted by a footman, then ushered by a butler into a drawing room, where the man and shaggy dog waited before the fireplace.

After a moment, the lord of the manor appeared, took one look at the dog, and said: "I don't think he's so shaggy."

shampoo comes direct from the Hindu *champo,* meaning "press, knead or shampoo."

shanghai, meaning "to kidnap a person, especially to press him into service as a seaman," has a fairly obvious origin. It was first used to describe the practice of drugging a seaman and taking him aboard a ship in the China trade, especially nineteenth-century sailing ships plying the route from San Francisco to Shanghai.

sharper than a serpent's tooth occurs in a deeply touching scene in one of Shakespeare's greatest tragedies, *King Lear* (Act I, Scene 4). The full text is: "How *sharper than a serpent's tooth* it is to have a thankless child."

Shavian. The correct meaning of such words as "Shakespearean" and "Wagnerian" is "concerning or like the works of this author." There is certainly nothing more "Shakespearean" than a play or sonnet by Will himself. An adjective of this sort that we have always relished is *Shavian,* coined to refer to works by or in the style of Bernard Shaw. "Shawian" apparently sounded awkward or clumsy to this self-confessed genius, so he went to some pains to create his own adjective, inventing first the word *Shavius* as the Latinized form of Shaw and then deriving the adjective *Shavian* from it. Somehow this seems quite in character with this most Olympian—nay, Jovian—of twentieth-century wits.

she (for a ship). Ships through all recorded history have been referred to in the feminine gender. One theory is that to a sailor, his ship is nearer and dearer to him than anything save perhaps his mother. Less sentimental students of language, however, note that in many of the world's tongues, excluding English, all nouns have gender: masculine, feminine or neuter. In the Romance languages, the word for "ship" is always in the feminine gender. Thus seafaring men have been accustomed for centuries to using the feminine pronoun in referring to their ships.

sheik comes from the Arabic *shaikh,* which literally means "old man"—a title of respect used for the leaders of Arab tribes. The pronunciation *shake* is close to the original Arabic and is quite commonly used by Britons, especially those in the colonial service. However, since the days when Valentino's motion picture made *The Sheik* a household term throughout the

Western world, the common pronunciation has been *sheek.* All dictionaries prefer this pronunciation, and *shake* is usually labeled "rare." In fact, one pronunciation authority labels it "a Briticism seldom, if ever, heard in America."

Sheila is a variant of Cecilia, which, in turn, came from the Latin word *caecus,* meaning "blind." The reason why this name has been so popular for so many centuries is that it was borne by one of the most admired of the early martyrs, St. Cecilia, who sang while she was being cruelly tortured for her faith—and consequently became the patron saint of music.

shenanigans —meaning "mischief" and pronounced exactly as written—may or may not be of Irish origin. According to one theory, it comes from the old Irish word *sionnachuighim,* meaning "I play the fox." But there's another theory, this one more farfetched, that *shenanigans* comes from a German dialect word, *schinageln,* meaning "to work at hard labor." The idea here is that scamps who used trickery to avoid hard work succeeded in bringing to the word a meaning exactly the opposite of its original sense.

sheriff is properly the title of the chief law-enforcement officer of a county. It goes back to the earliest days of Anglo-Saxon England. In those days the country was divided into "shires"—a term that still exists in such county names as Devonshire. The king's chief representative and administrator of the law in each shire was called *scirgerefa,* from *scir* (shire) and *gerefa* (reeve, a chief officer).

shibboleth. Only a comparative handful of words have come direct from ancient Hebrew to English and of these perhaps the most interesting is *shibboleth,* the Hebraic word for "ear of corn." In our language today, *shibboleth* has the very different meaning of "test word" or "watchword," and behind that change of meaning lies an intriguing bit of Biblical history.

During a battle between the Gileadites and the Ephraimites at the Jordan fords, the men of Gilead took command of the fords and when any of the fugitives of the army of Ephraim asked to pass, they would be asked, "Are you an Ephraimite?" If the answer was no, then—in the words of *Judges* 12:6—"They said to him, 'Say now *Shibboleth,*' and he said '*Sibboleth,*' for he could not frame to pronounce it right. Then they took him and slew him at the passages of the Jordan." Thus the inability to pronounce correctly the Hebrew word for "ear of corn" was the distinguishing characteristic of the Ephraimites and one which the sons of Gilead were shrewd enough to use as their watchword, giving the word *shibboleth* the meaning it has today.

It is interesting to note that such *shibboleths* are still part of the equipment of the intelligence sections of most modern armies in the world today. During World War II, for example, our interrogating officers were careful to insist that each suspected Japanese spy read aloud several sentences containing words like "mellifluous," "unintelligible" and "lollapalooza."

Since the Japanese have great difficulty pronouncing our letter *l,* which comes out usually sounding much like *r,* a prisoner who talked of *rorraparoozas* was Japanese for a certainty—not the friendly Chinese he pretended to be. The Chinese, you see, have no trouble at all pronouncing the letter *l.* In fact, their weakness is just the opposite of the Japanese failing—they cannot pronounce *r.* And that's why generations of cartoonists have used with every picture of a Chinese the stereotyped phrase "Velly, velly solly!"

shill is a swindler's assistant. Most commonly he mingles with the crowd on sidewalk or carnival midway while the pitchman or peddler is making his sales talk to the crowd. By bidding or enthusiastic buying, he lures the unwary into the purchase of inferior merchandise or into fixed games of chance. *Shill* is short for "shillaber," a decoy.

shillelagh, pronounced shih-LAY-lee, originally meant "club or cudgel" and takes its name from the village of Shillelagh in County Wicklow, Ireland, a region noted for its oaks and blackthorns. These cudgels became somewhat domesticated and did duty as walking sticks as well.

shindig is thought to be a variation of "shindy," which, in turn, is believed to be a derivative of "shinny," a very simple version of hockey played by schoolchildren. *Shindig* today has two quite different meanings. It may describe a party, especially an uproarious jamboree. It may also mean a riotous brawl, just this side of a donnybrook. Mencken suggests that before the Civil War, it had the literal meaning of a kick on the shin and two correspondents report to us that *shindig* in the years around World War I was a kind of robust hopping and skipping dance that often resulted in bruised shins. Altogether a versatile word.

shirttail relative is a term that goes back to the days when people had large families and the children were less apt to move away when they grew up, but stayed around to marry the girl or boy next door. In time, half the people in the county could be related to each other in one way or another. According to *Merriam-Webster's Third International Dictionary,* a *shirttail relative* is a "distantly and indefinitely related person." *Merriam* gives this example: "He was a *shirttail relative* but we weren't friends." It's what we used to call a "sort of thirty-second cousin."

shitepoke/shidepoke is a name given to various birds, chiefly the green heron and the night heron, though Wentworth's *American Dialect Dictionary* reports it is used for the loon in Maine and the wild duck or pheasant in West Virginia. The birds get the name *shitepoke* from what *Merriam III* calls "their habit of defecating when flushed." For fairly obvious reasons, *shitepoke* has also acquired the extended meanings of "rascal" and "worthless, no-account person." It comes from a Dutch word of the same meaning, *schyte-poke.*

shivaree/charivari. The *shivaree* is an Americanized version of *charivari,* which was first a French and later an English word meaning tumultuous revelry and prankish mockery. The practice started in medieval times, and the raucous racket was originally designed to express disapproval of people who married a second time—especially widows who didn't wait what their neighbors considered a "decent" interval before remarrying. Common practice was to continue the harassment by noise and vituperation until the newly married couple provided food and drink for all. The custom was probably brought to this country by French settlers in Canada and Louisiana, though it has long been commonplace in the backwoods areas of the South and as far north as Ohio farm country. Nowadays the *shivaree* is part of the fun at first as well as second weddings, and while some of the horseplay may embarrass the newlyweds, it surely does not humiliate them. In some areas the *shivaree* is simply known as "belling" the bride and groom.

shoofly cop is one whose job is to spy on other members of the police department. The term comes from a nonsense song first popular during the Civil War: "Shoo Fly, Don't Bother Me." Plainclothes detectives have long been known, in underworld slang, as "flycops," so the combination *shoofly* may well have started as a whispered warning from one lawman to another, alerting him to the presence of a spy and telling him to "get lost."

shoofly pie is an open pie filled with a mixture of brown sugar and molasses that naturally attracts flies which must be shooed away.

shooting his cuffs goes back to the days when celluloid collars and cuffs were the salesman's answer to the laundry problem when on the road. With the high-buttoned jackets of the period, the collar and cuffs were all that showed, and since the celluloid could be wiped clean with a damp cloth, a drummer of the period could make a shirt last a week. One of the showy tricks of dandies of the day was to *shoot their cuffs,* which a dictionary of the period defines as "making a sudden and ostentatious display of one's cuffs." One must imagine that this was accompanied by a twirl of the mustachios, the tilting of a derby to a rakish angle—and the swift conquest of a demure maiden's heart.

short end is simply a shortened form of the rather vulgar slang expression "the *short end* of the stick." ·A person getting the *short end* is a loser, just as a person who draws the short straw is the one assigned to an unpleasant or dangerous duty.

shorthand. It is a common belief that Pitman or Gregg invented *shorthand,* but neither one did. The first *shorthand* system was devised some two thousand years ago, the creation of M. Tullius Tiro, who, in 63 B.C., used it to transcribe Cicero's speeches. During the Middle Ages there were various other *shorthand* methods devised by monks. Of the two modern methods, Pitman came earlier (1837) than Gregg, who published his system in 1888.

short shrift. *Shrift* (originally "shrive") can mean either confession or absolution after confession. The phrase *short shrift* started out to mean the short time a condemned prisoner is given to make a confession and receive absolution before execution. Its current meaning is quick and unsympathetic treatment of a person or proposal.

should of stood in bed. Back in the 1930s the most famous prize-fight manager was Joe Jacobs, who numbered among the stars of his stable heavyweight champion Max Schmeling, idol of Hitler's Germany, until Joe Louis knocked him kicking in less than a round. On one occasion the promotion for a fight in which one of Jacobs's fighters was engaged was poor and a distressingly small crowd turned out. Looking it over, Jacobs muttered the practically immortal line: "I should of stood in bed." "Stood" as a past tense of "stay" is grammatically incorrect, as is the use of "of" for "have." But "stood" for "stayed" is, as Mencken noted, fairly common in Yiddish-American speech and we have evidence that it is also heard in the speech of the Pennsylvania Dutch (Deutsch).

show must go on. For many decades one of the sprightliest innovators in our language has been *Variety,* the magazine of show business. Many of the terms coined by *Variety* staffers, usually called *muggs,* have entered popular slang. Such terms as *b.o.* for box office, *boffo* or *boffola* for a smash success, *whodunit* for a mystery story, *deejay* for disc jockey, *oater* for a Western picture and *soaper* for soap opera are part of the everyday idiom, as editor Abel Green wrote in an article noting its sixtieth anniversary (*anni* to *Variety,* which is no respecter of formality, even when it comes to its own birthday). It was also the thirtieth anniversary of one of its two most famous headlines: STIX NIX HICK PIX. The other head, of course, was the one used on the 1929 story of the stock market crash: WALL STREET LAYS AN EGG.

In the course of a nostalgic review of his magazine's contributions, Green *segued* (one of *Variety*'s favorite words) into a discussion of show biz contributions in general. "Over the years," he wrote, "the circus and carnival, later legit and vaudeville, Tin Pan Alley and Hollywood gave rise to phrases that caught the public fancy. When hypnotist 'Prof.' F. A. Mesmer did his stuff in the 19th century he sparked *mesmerizing* the audience. *Joe Miller* is the universal symbol for the stale joke. 'He *Barnumed* his show' speaks for itself. Annie Oakley's bullet-holes in theater tickets remain a symbol for passes. The *pink lady* cocktail came from the operetta of that name, much as *peach* (Nellie) *Melba* (also *Melba toast*), *chicken* (Luisa) *Tetrazzini,* and *spaghetti* (Enrico) *Caruso* are gastronomic hangovers."

One of the most interesting revelations Mr. Green made was that the famous slogan *"The show must go on"* had nothing whatever to do with the legitimate theater. As he put it, "Despite the early Warner Brothers *filmusicals* [the blend word is another *Variety* specialty], wherein Dick Powell conned and charmed Ruby Keeler that *'the show must go on'*—because it was a backstage tradition—it was fundamentally a circus phrase. It was meant to save lives, property and animals, and the ringmaster told the band to keep playing; *the show must go on* with all the available acts (except any injured) to divert the audience and to curb any possibility of panic as a result of whatever was the mishap."

shrapnel, which was named for British general Henry Shrapnel, was invented early in the nineteenth century. When the *shrapnel* shell exploded it showered metal balls with lethal effect. The original *shrapnel* shells are no longer in use, having been replaced by more sophisticated high-explosive fragmentation shells. However, *shrapnel* has become a sort of generic term for any of these fragmentation devices.

shucks. This expression, which the late Will Rogers made as much a part of his performing personality as the cowboy hat and lariat, is well established as a slang expression with distinctly "country-boy" overtones. It means practically nothing—about the same as such interjections as "pshaw" and "aw, fudge"—neither one of which one hears much any more. But *shucks* comes by its meaninglessness naturally. It refers to the outer covering of an ear of corn—also called the husk—which is discarded as without further value.

shuffle off this mortal coil is taken from the famous soliloquy "To be or not to be" in the third act of Shakespeare's *Hamlet:* "To die, to sleep;/To sleep: perchance to dream: ay, there's the rub:/For in that sleep of death what dreams may come,/When we have *shuffled off this mortal coil,*/Must give us pause." Many readers think *shuffled off this mortal coil* means "departed this world," but Shakespeare had more in mind than that. *Coil* is a now archaic word meaning "trouble, tumult and confusion." *Shuffle off* means simply "to get rid of" and *mortal* means "deathly." So *when we have shuffled off this mortal coil* means "when we have gotten rid of this deathly trouble; when we have shed the anguish that leads to death."

shun-pike is a detour around a toll-collecting point on a turnpike. A couple of centuries ago, when the first American toll roads were built, *shun-pikes* were the essence of simplicity. The owner of a farm paralleling the road where the toll station was established would arrange for vehicles to pass around the gate and over his property for a fee substantially cheaper than that charged by the owners of the toll road. Today, with most of our states crisscrossed by hundreds of well-paved roads, ingenious autoists frequently find that it saves them money to plot a route which will parallel the toll turnpikes for part of their trip.

shut my mouth is a very common expression of astonishment, especially among Southern blacks—at least those of an earlier generation. The idea is that one is so surprised that he is "struck dumb" or dumbfounded.

shy. The verb *to shy* in such phrases as "he *shied* a stone at the dog" probably goes back to a rather cruel sport common in the Middle Ages. Players tied a cock to a stake and took turns throwing stones at him. The best, and most deadly, marksman was the winner. Presumably he celebrated the victory with chicken-in-the-pot. This cruel sport was called "cockshying." One theory of the origin of this name is that most cocks would not fight until goaded into doing so. Pelting them with stones had the effect of making them less *shy.* So the adjective and the verb *shy* both had the same meaning originally.

sibling goes back to Anglo-Saxon times, though it had been very little used for centuries until psychologists and psychiatrists revived it in recent years as part of their trade jargon. Originally a *sib* was any relative. Indeed, in medieval times a *sib* was not even necessarily a blood relative. A *god-sib* (from which we get our word "gossip") was simply a godparent, a child's sponsor at baptism. Nowadays a *sibling* is one of two or more children having the same parents. More simply put, a *sibling* is a brother or a sister.

"*Sibling* rivalry" is the normal contention between children in a family, the sort of squabbling that is an inevitable part of growing up.

sideburns got their name from an illustrious American. He was General Ambrose Everett Burnside, one-time commander of the Army of the Potomac and the general in command when the Union forces suffered two of their most catastrophic defeats at the battles of Petersburg and Fredericksburg. Burnside was nearly drummed out of the army after a court of inquiry found his leadership deficient, but he went on to business success and served as Rhode Island's governor and senator. His muttonchop whiskers were a readily identifiable trademark and were widely imitated during the latter part of the nineteenth century. They were first called *burnsides,* but later, through a curious semantic shift, became *sideburns.*

sight for sore eyes is a very old expression and means "a very welcome sight," especially one that is unexpected, such as the sudden appearance of an old friend. The *Oxford Dictionary of English Proverbs* gives as an example this quotation from a book published in 1836: "What a *sight for sore eyes* it would be to see Garrick act." In Jonathan Swift's "Polite Conversation" (1738) he wrote: "The *sight* of you is good *for sore eyes.*" Incidentally, in the same work he used a line that we cherish: "She wears her clothes as if they were thrown at her with a pitchfork." That reminds us of the description of columnist Heywood Broun: "He looks like an unmade bed."

sigogglin. An old and valued friend of your authors is William Miller, long a contributor to the editorial pages of the *New York Herald Tribune* and *Life* magazine. Commenting on one of our earlier books, Miller wrote: "One item I looked for in vain. It's a word I have known since my boyhood in North Carolina: *sigogglin,* pronounced SY-gog-lin or sy-GOG-lin. In those days, long before the do-it-yourself craze, most farmers built their own barns and sheds simply because there was no other way to get them built. As a result, the lines weren't always in plumb. When the roof was too much on the skewgee, the neighbors would remark that 'That there barn sure is *sigogglin.*' Maybe next time you write a dictionary you can find space for this favorite word of mine."

And this is what we learned about his favorite word. *Sigogglin* is a regional variation of the somewhat better known *antigodlin* or *antigogglin.* In fact, there are a couple of other variant forms: *slantigodlin* and *sigodlin.* They all mean "crooked, askew, awry or out of plumb"—just as the North Carolina neighbors used it.

Harold Wentworth's valuable *American Dialect Dictionary* lists all these various forms and examples of their use. Interestingly enough, the earliest examples he gives—from around the turn of the century—are listed as "west or southwest North Carolina." One example of usage is: "You sawed that log off a little *sigodlin.* " From Arkansas he reported the same use that Miller heard as a boy: "The line of his barn roof is *antegodlin.* "

Just where the expression originated—or, indeed, how it got its meaning—is not clear. A clue may be found, however, in a secondary meaning given by Wentworth: "working against God." Possibly the idea was that any departure from the norm—such as a slaunchways or skewgee roof—was somehow against God's plan for an orderly universe.

silenced is not converted. The full expression, from the essay on *Compromise* by John, Viscount Morley (1838–1923), is: "You have not converted a man because you have silenced him." The quotation has been widely circulated in recent years, especially in the form of a poster memoralizing the Sacco-Vanzetti case, drawn by Ben Shahn (1898–1969). Lord Morley was a distinguished British public servant, though one of rather radical bent, and served as editor of the famous "English Men of Letters" series of biographies. Among his other notable observations, which may have a certain application to our troubled times, is this from his *Recollections:* "Excess of severity is not the path to order. On the contrary it is the path to the bomb."

silence gives consent. This axiom comes direct from Roman law: *Qui tacet consentire videtur*—"He who is silent seems to consent."

silence is golden. This aphorism, which gives the lie to the seemingly impeccable statement above, indicates that there are occasions—though possibly not in courts of law—when it's wise to remain silent. The full maxim reads: "Speech is silver; *silence is golden.* "

silly. One of the best examples of a word whose meaning is now very different from its original meaning is *silly.* In Anglo-Saxon times, a *silly* person was one who was "blessed and innocent." Then it came to mean "happy and unworldly." Gradually the last element dominated, and the present meaning of "foolish and absurd" developed.

Other examples of words whose meaning has changed are *lewd,* which originally simply meant "simple or uncultured," and *vulgar,* which first meant "belonging to the common people."

silo drippings is a term used, especially in rural areas, as a generic term for intoxicating liquor, rather like "hooch." But there's more to the story than that, for the *silo drippings* themselves literally were a potent liquor. One former farm boy put it quite colorfully when he wrote: "As you know, silos are used to store corn for the winter feeding of cows. As the silo became filled up, small doors on the side were closed up and the corn gradually settled. A liquid was formed by the slow warm fermentation and it settled to the bottom of the silo. It did not taste too bad when mixed with syrup and, believe you me, it was potent!

"In states like Kansas where prohibition was in effect from 1898 on, it was a common thing for some of the Rough Element to come to dances or box suppers with their jugs, filled from a hole in the bottom door of someone's silo.

"Sometimes a large rancher had two silos, one for green alfalfa, the other for green corn. The seepage from the two silos mixed together made an especially potent drink. But, you know something? You didn't have to drink the stuff to know its effect. Farmers sometimes used to have a man or two inside the silo stomping the alfalfa or corn down tight. If they stayed in there very long, they could get quite intoxicated from the fumes alone."

silver wedding/golden wedding. The designations *silver wedding* and *golden wedding* for the twenty-fifth and fiftieth wedding anniversaries respectively date back to medieval Germany. If a woman lived with her husband for twenty-five years, her women friends joined together in presenting her with a ring or wreath of silver. After another twenty-five years, she received a wreath of gold.

simoleon. To find the origin of this word meaning "dollar," we can go back to the days of the old West when frontiersmen coined a lot of slang terms for money—"kale," "grease" and "spondulix" among them. "Simon" was similarly coined to mean a dollar. That wasn't fancy enough for the roistering braggarts of the mining towns, so—perhaps influenced by "Napoleon" —simple Simon became *simoleon.*

simon pure. In New England in the 1920s there used to be lively competition in summertime between amateur and semiprofessional baseball clubs. Often it was hard to distinguish which was which, but the sports pages of newspapers used to refer to the amateurs as the *simon pures.* The original *Simon Pure* was a character in an eighteenth-century British play called *A Bold Stroke for a Wife.* The hero, named Simon Pure, has a letter of introduction to a man of substance. It is stolen by one Colonel Feignwell. The colonel not only tricks the wealthy man by pretending to be Simon Pure but marries his beautiful daughter. Then our hero has the devil's own time proving his real identity.

since Hector was a pup. Some people hold that W. C. Fields used this line in one of his early films—and that may well be true. Others contend that it was popularized by a comic strip of the 1920s called *Polly and Her Pals* —and this may also be true. But we have a hunch the expression is older than these two theories would indicate, and we have support in our notion from Mrs. J. Howard Gilroy of Beaver Falls, Pennsylvania. "My mother, if living, would be 110 years old," she writes. "And her mother used the same expression. Here's how it started. 'Hector' was a favorite name given to large dogs. My mother always said, 'Call a big dog Hector and he will wag his tail and smile,' since nine times out of ten his name actually was Hector."

That's an interesting story. Fashions in dogs' names change, just as in human names. In our youth most of the male mutts we knew were either Rex or Rover. More recently, practically all collies answered to the name Lassie, regardless of sex. So it well may be that large dogs at the turn of the century were called Hector, and all Fields and the cartoonist did was to further popularize an expression already well established.

sinecure, pronounced SY-nih-kyoor, comes straight from the Latin phrase *sine cure* (without care). Originally an ecclesiastical term, it meant a church position which paid a salary but did not require its holder to concern himself with the care of souls. Nowadays a *sinecure* is any job requiring little or no work, especially one obtained by political pressure.

sine qua non (SIN-ay kwah non) is a phrase borrowed from Latin, meaning literally "without which nothing" but more freely "that which is indispensable. The original Latin was *sine qua non potest esse*—"without which it is not possible to exist."

Sing Sing was originally the name of the town where the prison is located. It was the white man's version of the Delaware Indian name for the spot, *Assinesink,* meaning "At the small stone." By the end of the nineteenth century, the "small stone" had become "The Rock" and Sing Sing Prison was known as the toughest, cruelest penitentiary in the country. The townspeople were understandably unhappy that their charming community was regarded with such disfavor by the outer world, so in 1901 they officially changed their town's name to "Ossining."

sinister in Latin originally meant simply "left," but it soon acquired such meanings as "wrong, dishonest and corrupt." Vergil, Catullus and Tacitus —to name only three of the great Roman authors—used the word in the sense of "perverse, wrong, unfavorable and adverse." It seems to us that there is a very simple explanation for this and it is that right-handed people have always greatly outnumbered left-handers. In all areas of human activity there is the tendency for the majority to disdain and, if possible, suppress the minority. If this is not done by force, it may be attempted by semantic downgrading, so to speak. The same sort of bias is apparent in the implication of "left" as a political term. This started in the parliamentary bodies of Europe where the conservative and, usually, dominant party members were seated to the right of the chair and the radical or liberal members on the left. This practice is believed to have originated in the long-standing custom of seating the most important guest at a banquet at the right of the host. Again this reflects the deep-seated prejudice of the numerically superior right against the numerically inferior left.

sirloin. A legend that dies hard has it that King James I drew his sword and knighted a piece of beef "Sir Loin." This particular flight of fancy has been debunked so many times that one might expect people to know it for what it is—a wordplay hoax that has amused Britons for more than three centuries. Actually, *sirloin* came into English from French at the time of the Norman Conquest—long centuries before James I or any of the other monarchs who are credited with knighting this cut of beef. The word, in Old French, was *surlonge,* from *sur* (upon or above) and *longe* (loin). The transition from *surlonge* to *sirloin* evolved gradually, though one authority still stoutly maintains that *sirloin* is a "mistaken" spelling. Among the illustrious writers of the past who have accepted the fanciful legend of *sirloin*'s origin are Thomas Fuller, whose *Church History* (1655) credits Henry VIII with coining the word, and Jonathan Swift, who gave the honor to James I.

sirup/syrup. Your male co-author never saw the spelling "sirup" for *syrup* until he started editing his first dictionary in the 1940s. To his astonishment, he found that every dictionary current then seemed to favor the "sirup" that he had never seen before in print. Investigation indicated that this spelling was indeed closer to the source word (the French *sirop*) from which it was borrowed. But a different kind of investigation—along the shelves of the supermarkets—indicated that the bottlers of this flavorsome goo all spelled it "syrup." So your word man's first dictionary, almost alone among wordbooks of the time, indicated a preference for this spelling. Today, the new *Funk & Wagnalls,* the new *Merriam-Webster* and the still newer *American Heritage Dictionary of the English Language* all favor "syrup," with the earlier spelling given as a variant.

sitcom is an item of TV show biz jargon. It simply means "situation comedy."

sit-down strike is a strike of workers who sit down at their machines in their place of employment, thereby making it impossible for management to put new workers in their places. This form of strike originated in the United States during the 1930s.

sit-in. A technique of nonviolent resistance whereby victims of discrimination "sit in" at lunch counters, schools and churches to manifest their displeasure. Widely practiced by blacks and their sympathizers in the 1960s, it is modeled upon the teachings of Mohandas K. Gandhi.

sitz bath originated in Germany as *sitzbad,* from *sitz* (seat) and *bad* (bath). The treatment, which consists of immersing the body in water up to the waist and in a sitting position, was brought to this country late in the nineteenth century. First called by its German name, it quickly was Anglicized to *sitz bath* and now, in most American hospitals, has been further simplified to the form many nurses use: *sit bath.*

skeptic. The first *skeptics* were Greek philosophers who doubted the possibility of arriving at the truth or the real knowledge of anything. The school called *Skeptic* was founded by Pyrrho, who took its name from the Greek word *skeptikos,* meaning "thoughtful or inquiring." But however much the members of the school examined and inquired into matters which were generally accepted by others, they maintained that it was impossible to reach a judgment on any matter. The term *skeptic* has thus come to mean "a person who refuses to believe, particularly one who questions the Christian religion."

skewgee is one of a number of dialect terms used to describe something that is askew.

skid row/skid road. Each section of the country has its regional peculiarities of speech, expressions and pronunciations which the local residents cling to and know to be correct, even though those of us in the rest of the country may differ. Down Boston way, for example, anyone who pronounces the town name Quincy with anything other than a *zee* for the last syllable is regarded with the same suspicion afforded outlanders who desecrate clam chowder by adding tomatoes. In the same fashion, St. Louisans incline to take a dim view of people who pronounce their city's name LOO-ee rather than LOO-iss. And of course, natives of San Francisco regard with withering scorn barbarians who call their fair city "Frisco."

Similar passions seem to beat in the breast of the average resident of the Pacific Northwest when he hears the phrase *skid row.* The term, you are told politely but very firmly, is *skid road.* The first *skid road,* a hanging-out place for human derelicts, was in Seattle and was so named because it was made of greased logs over which lumbermen used to skid logs to the mills. Indeed, one editor of a respected lexicon of slang flatly labels *skid row* a "perversion" of *skid road.*

Nevertheless, the expression heard in the greater part of the country is *skid row* and this is the formulation found in the newer dictionaries. What, then, does the conscientious word student do—adopt what was apparently the original term or go along with the rest of the country? The best answer seems to be: "When in Rome, do as the Romans do."

In the words of the program director of a radio station in the Pacific Northwest: "Not being a native but being a word purveyor to many native Washingtonians, I feel obliged to conform. However, my argument is this: Perhaps *skid road* did originate in Seattle. Therefore, Seattle, Tacoma, Olympia, Longview and other northwest lumbering camps had their *skid roads.* However, Chicago, San Diego and many other cities which have had no logs to skid, in my opinion, have their *skid rows*—which term derives from the fact that they are frequented by men 'on the skids.' Am I right or wrong?"

Well, it's an interesting theory and, as we said above, "When in Rome . . ."

skiff/skift. A rather unusual expression, heard mainly in rural areas, is "a *skift* of snow." It means a light fall—and may apply to rain as well as snow.

skin of my teeth appears in the Book of Job (19: 20): "My bone cleaveth to my skin and to my flesh, and I am escaped with the *skin of my teeth.*" It appeared as *The Skin of Our Teeth,* a celebrated play by Thornton Wilder, in which, if memory serves, Fredric March, Florence Eldridge and Tallulah Bankhead appeared.

skipper swallows the anchor is an expression used by officers of the Cunard Line, and perhaps of other steamship lines as well, to describe the occasion when the captain goes into retirement.

skirl, the shrill and piercing sound made by a bagpipe, comes from the Old Norse word *skrylla* (to scream). With the possible exception of native-born Scotsmen, who hold the bagpipes in high regard, most people will agree that that derivation is highly appropriate.

skirmish and scaramouche. *Skirmish,* meaning a trifling and unimportant conflict, is one of the many words of chivalric warfare brought to England by the Norman conquerors. In Middle English it was often spelled *skrymishe,* the word from which the common football term "scrimmage" comes. In turn, the French had taken their word *escarmuche* from the Italian *scaramuccia.* From *scaramuccia* comes the proper name *Scaramouche* (skar-uh-MOOSH), which was the title of Raphael Sabatini's best-selling novel of the 1920s and the source of one of the most popular motion pictures ever filmed. *Scaramouche* was originally a stock character in Italian farce, a boastful braggart always skirmishing on the fringes of danger, but too cowardly ever to become involved in serious battle.

skirt came into English from Old Norse as the Anglo-Saxon word *scyrte,* which originally meant any short garment and, indeed, was more likely to mean a shirt than a skirt in those days.

skoal. If, when friends raise their glasses before drinking, one of them sings out *Skoal,* he is simply proposing a toast—"To your health." The word comes from the Danish and Norwegian *skaal,* meaning "cup or bowl."

skulduggery. Most source books label this word "origin obscure" or relate it to a now obsolete slang word, *skulduddery.* However, a plausible theory of its origin traces it to the Scottish dialect word *sculdudrie,* which has the meaning of "slipperiness and trickery." In present-day use—in such expressions as "I know there's *skulduggery* afoot"—the meaning is one of "underhanded, sly and evil trickery." So the Scottish origin makes sense.

skycaps, which refers to porters in airline terminals, was coined by analogy to "red caps," which for more than sixty years have been worn by baggage handlers in railroad stations. The first such red caps were designed to match the red carpet that was, until its final day, rolled out in Grand Central Terminal to meet America's most famous passenger train, the *20th Century Limited.*

sky pilot originally was a slang term for "minister or preacher." The allusion, of course, was to a minister's ability to pilot an errant soul to an eventual home in heaven, symbolized by the sky. One of the best-known and loved Canadian novels is *The Sky Pilot* by Ralph Connor, himself a one-time missionary to lumbermen and miners in the Canadian Rockies.

slang began as a slang term itself and its ultimate origin is in dispute. It is first recorded in print in 1756, but was probably common in the argot of the underworld before that date. One authority credits its origin to a Norwegian word, *slengjeord,* meaning "slang word," but in the next breath suggests it may be related to the English word "sling." From the way some people sling *slang* around, that last might be as good a theory as any.

slantindicular is a word you'll find only in special dialect dictionaries. It means, roughly, "slanting from the perpendicular," and what grandfather probably meant by it was that the supports were not squared properly, so that the whole structure could be easily tipped.

slapjack. Amid all the discussion of crime in the streets, police brutality and the like, the following nice distinction in weaponry might just possibly be helpful. We've all heard of the blackjack, the small, weighted bludgeon that has done service these many years on both sides of the law. Now we learn that there's a *slapjack,* which differs from its predecessor in having a flat lead weight instead of the blackjack's round lead weight. The *slapjack* is at least as damaging as its predecessor and has the advantage of being more easily hidden.

slapstick. *Slapstick* comedy, if done properly, can be hilariously funny even without the *slapsticks* from which this type of entertainment got its name. *Slapsticks* were literally two sticks bound together at one end which would slap together loudly when used by early comedians to strike other performers.

slipshod originally simply meant "shod with slippers." By easy and obvious stages it came to mean "down at the heels or slovenly." So anything *slipshod* is sloppy or careless in appearance.

slipstick is simply technicians' jargon for "slide rule."

slogan is derived from Gaelic *slaugh* (army) and *gairm* (shout). So the first *slogans* were literally battle cries.

sloid is a perfectly good, though now little used, term from the educational jargon of a half century ago. It's one of the comparative handful of words we have taken from Swedish—in this instance from *slojd,* meaning "skill." *Sloid* or *sloyd,* as it was often spelled, was a method of training boys in what used to be called the manual arts—wood carving, carpentry and the like.

slothful/sloth. *Slothful* (pronounced SLOTH-f'l) is an adjective which ascribes to a person the characteristics of the lazy, slow-moving animal that hangs by its feet from trees. *Sloth,* as a noun, is not only the name of the animal but is defined as "sluggishness, laziness and a disinclination to work." *Sloth* comes to us from the Middle English *slou,* meaning "slow."

slow match is a slow-burning brown stick, more commonly called "punk," used for lighting firecrackers.

slowpoke. *Poke* comes from a Middle English word, *poken,* and can be traced to Low German and Dutch. It has always had the basic meaning of "to prod or thrust." *Slowpoke* comes from a different meaning of the verb *poke* —to dawdle or loiter. Just how it got this meaning is not clear, except that poking one's nose into other people's business takes a good deal of time and this may have led to the idea of puttering about and dawdling.

slunk school is an old New England expression for "play hooky or play the truant." The early days of spring would find many boys who *slunk school* to go fishing or play ball.

slush fund, a term now used chiefly in political connotations, was first a bit of sailor lingo. The first *slush funds* were found on nineteenth-century ships. Sailors were allowed to sell excess grease or fat (which they called *slush*) and put the proceeds into a kitty to purchase luxuries they otherwise could not afford. The term came into political use because the bribes paid for votes enabled the persons who were bribed to buy things they wouldn't otherwise be able to afford.

slyboots may apply to any sly, crafty or cunning person—male or female— or to an animal. It's usually used in a joking fashion. It goes back at least to 1700 and originally had the rather more specialized meaning of a person who pretended to be stupid or unaware of what was going on while actually following events very closely.

small beer is an expression more often heard in England than in the U.S. to describe a matter of no great importance. The *small* refers to the beer's strength rather than the amount. In other words, *small beer* is beer of slight alcoholic content. The expression has been around since before the time of Shakespeare. In *Henry IV,* Part 2, he has Prince Hal say: "Doth it not show vilely in me to desire *small beer?*" And in *Henry VI,* Part 2, Jack Cade promises the citizenry that when he becomes king "I will make it a felony to drink *small beer.*"

smarmy may well have started as a variation of "smear," because the first smarm was a sort of slickum pomade used to smear down the hair on the heads of dandies in the early days of the Victorian era. Then it developed a related meaning of "slick, fulsome, unctuous flattery." As the *Oxford Dictionary* puts it: "To smarm means to behave in a fulsomely flattering or toadying manner." So in today's language, *smarmy* is ranked as a synonym for "gushing, unctuous or oily."

smart alec is a know-it-all, a conceited wise guy, usually endowed with a bit of the brassiness called in Yiddish "chutzpah." The expression has been common in America at least since midway through the last century. Its first recorded appearance in print was in a Carson City, Nevada, newspaper in 1862. But history doesn't record who the first *smart alec* was. Many years later there was a prodigiously vain figure on the New York literary scene called Alec—Alexander Woollcott—but the expression *smart alec* was well established long before his time.

smell a rat. To *smell a rat* is to suspect that something devious or improper is going forward. The allusion, obviously, is to a cat's ability to smell a rat it cannot see.

smog, a blend of "smoke" and "fog," was, according to one account, invented by Hubbard Keavy, one-time Associated Press news executive. When he worked on the *Des Moines Tribune* in 1923 the city was virtually under siege in winter by polluted air caused by heavy burning of soft coal and fog rising from the river. He wrote a headline involving "smoke" and "fog" for a front-page story but it would not fit into the space allowed. So, out of desperation or inspiration, he wrote this head: SMOG HITS/CITY ANEW. The managing editor called it a monstrosity, but the public seemed to approve.

snake in the grass is a hidden enemy, especially one who pretends friendship in order to betray you. The phrase comes from Vergil's *Eclogues: "Latet anguis in herba"*—"A snake lurks in the grass."

snark is a wholly imaginary creation of Lewis Carroll. The word is a blend of "snake" and "shark." In "The Hunting of the *Snark,*" the *snark* causes all sorts of mischief, so a band of hunters sets out to find it. When they succeed, they discover that what they tracked down was not a snark at all, but a "boojum." And what's a boojum? Originally it was just another figment of Carroll's wild imagination. But now its name has been given to a grotesque spiny tree found in lower California. It has the odd distinction of arching over so far that the tips of its branches sometimes touch the ground and take root.

snide has been current for years as a slang term meaning "sly" or "subtly derogatory." No one knows for certain where the word—most often heard in the phrase "*snide* remark"—came from. One theory is that it entered the language as a term of underworld slang derived from the German word *schneiden,* meaning "to cut" or "to make cutting or sarcastic remarks."

snit. We once quoted a letter from Mrs. V. Armentraut of Volga, West Virginia, asking what an apple *snit* is. Confessing our own ignorance, we asked for reader comment. And how it came—letters from nearly every state and even from Mexico. Here's one of the first to arrive, from E. B. Miller of

Arlington, Virginia: "I'm amazed that a lady by the name of Armentraut doesn't know what an apple *snit* is. Tell her to go to her grocery store, buy a bag of dried apples, tear it open and remove one piece. That piece is a wonderful good apple *snit*. *Snit* is a Pennsylvania Dutch word for slice of apple. The word is used in the Shenandoah Valley of Virginia, parts of West Virginia and of course in Penn-Dutch country—especially by a lot of persons named Armentraut!"

Floyd L. Fulk of Broadway, Virginia, added this personal reminiscence: "In late summer when I was a child, we would *snit* the apples and dry them and put them away in a bag in a dry place. Then we would have apple pies all winter made of the *snits*. If we had more than we could use, we could always sell them at the nearby country store for 3 cents per pound."

Here is an anecdote from Elsie Martin of Roaring Spring, Pennsylvania. "A teacher in a rural school was teaching fractions to a group of Pennsylvania Dutch youngsters," she wrote. "Cutting an apple in two, he asked, 'What do I have?' The class said, 'Halves.' Cutting a half, he said, 'What?' 'Quarters,' said the class. Cutting a quarter, the teacher asked, 'What?' And the class, with one voice, answered, '*Snits*.'"

snob. Most lexicons label *snob* "origin unknown," but from a Londoner came an explanation of the origin that seems quite logical. It seems that Oxford freshmen were required to register "according to rank." Those not of noble birth added after their names the phrase *sine nobilitate*, which was then abbreviated to "s. nob.," thus creating what our friend terms "a perfect definition for the commoner who wishes to mingle with the nobles."

snollygoster. When President Truman used the word *snollygoster* and defined it as "a man born out of wedlock," newspaper wire services were correct in pointing out that his definition didn't jibe with definitions found in the standard dictionaries. After quoting H. L. Mencken's *The American Language*, the wire service dispatches concluded that a *snollygoster* is "a fellow who wants office, regardless of party, platform or principles" and noted that the word was first recorded in a Georgia paper about 1895. For the record—and with no intent of supplying ammunition for either the pro- or anti-*snollygoster* faction—it should be noted that Wentworth's *American Dialect Dictionary* records its use as early as 1865 and defines *snollygoster* in a single word—"shyster." And to complete the record, *Funk & Wagnalls* defines *shyster* as "a lawyer who practices in an unscrupulous or tricky manner."

Snopesian This adjective comes from the Snopes family, who were characters in *The Hamlet* and other novels by William Faulkner. The *Encyclopedia International* describes them thus: "In contrast to the aristocratic Sartoris family, the vulgar Snopeses represent corruptive, opportunist elements in the Deep South."

snow. Who named *snow*? The answer is that no one really knows. In the earliest days of English civilization, in the time of the Angles and the Saxons, it was called "snaw." By the time of Shakespeare it had the spelling we use today. In other lands and in other times it has had various names. In German it is *schnee,* in Russian, *sneig,* and in ancient Rome it was simply *nix.*

snow job. You have heard the expression *"snow under,"* meaning to pile one thing on top of another until you reach the point of utter exhaustion. One can be snowed under with words, too—and that's where *snow job* gets its meaning. When a person asks a simple but embarrassing question and is answered by a flood of insincere flattery that somehow evades the issue, he is getting a *snow job.* He is being snowed under by pleasant but irrelevant blather.

snuck/snucked are regional dialect versions of "sneaked." "We *snuck* out of the house to go fishing" is the kind of thing you might find in *Huckleberry Finn,* where Mark Twain was carefully recording the speech of uneducated and only partly literate country folk.

soap opera goes back to the halcyon days of radio suspense serials, like *Mary Noble, Backstage Wife; Young Widder Brown* and *Our Gal Sunday.* There was nothing of the traditional "opera" about these sentimental, sensation-packed cliff-hangers, of course, but they had one thing in common: Practically all of them were sponsored by soap-makers.

soapy Sam is a suave, unctuous public speaker. The first *soapy Sam* was Samuel Wilberforce, Bishop of Oxford midway through the Victorian era. He got his nickname from his unctuous manner of speaking. Once when he was asked about the sobriquet, he smilingly assured his questioner that he was called *soapy Sam* because "I am often in hot water but always come out with clean hands."

soccer. The true name of *soccer* is "association football." Soccer is simply a shortened and altered form of "association."

sockdolager (pronounced sok-DOL-uh-jer) is from the frontier vocabulary of more than a century ago. It seems to be a combination of *sock,* meaning "a strong blow," and *dolager,* a corruption of "doxology," the brief hymn sung toward the end of many church services. Thus it means anything that is truly decisive—the ultimate of its kind.

socked in goes back to an earlier day in aviation, a day when such aids to pilots as radar and ground controlled approach were undreamed of. Early pilots had to rely for information about wind direction on a conical wind sock hung from a mast atop the biggest hangar. In a rough way, the sock also would give them an idea as to the wind's velocity. Naturally, when fog hung heavily over the airfield, the air sock would be invisible. Since planes would neither take off nor land under such "ceiling zero" conditions, the field was said to be *socked in.*

soigné(e). Two forms of this word are given—with and without the second *e*—because it is French and the ending changes, depending on whether it is applied to male or female. *Soigné* (pronounced swan-YAY) means well cared for or very well groomed.

sola topi. A *sola* (no *r*) *topi* is simply a sun hat, of the kind first worn in this country by animal trainers like Frank Buck and Clyde Beatty. It looks something like a helmet, with a curved brim, and is made of some light insulating cover, plus an inner lining. *Topi*—often spelled *topee*—is the Hindu name for the headgear. *Sola* is an East Indian herb whose pith was originally used in making the topis—also sometimes simply called "pith helmets." Because the adjective "solar" for "sun" is so close in spelling, the phrase often appears, erroneously, as *solar topi.*

soldier. Anyone who has worked hard during his stint in the army might well resent the dictionary definition of the phrase *to soldier.* A typical definition is "to shrink one's duty, as by making a pretense of working, feigning illness, etc." He might also question where that meaning came from. From the navy, that's where. During the nineteenth century and before, a *soldier* aboard ship acted as a privileged passenger—at least, he did none of the chores that are the daily lot of professional seamen. This naturally didn't sit well with the sailors, so they made *soldiering* synonymous with "goofing off."

solecism. The Greek colony of Soloi, far removed from Athens, developed a dialect of its own, much as Americans did when removed from the mother country, England. The Athenians, like the English, were shocked by what they called the colony's *soloikismos,* "speaking incorrectly," from which comes our word *solecism,* meaning "an error in grammar or the use of words."

Solon, a statesman who lived in Athens, Greece, five hundred years before Christ, might be called the headline-writer's friend, for his name has joined the host of words that are virtually indispensable to the newspaper copy-reader because of their brevity. The words "representative," "congressman," "legislator" and "lawmaker" are all long, and often as not, will fail to fit into a headline. So the name of Solon—now *solon*—comes in very handily to mean any lawmaker.

so long. Some of the wordbooks expound a theory that *So long* is formed by folk etymology from *Salaam,* an Arabic greeting related to the Hebrew *Shalom,* "peace." This seems to us wildly far of the mark. For one thing, *So long* is not a greeting but a farewell. For another, it's scarcely likely that even a handful of Yankees would know and use *Salaam* in talking to each other. But as an abbreviation for some such expression as "Don't let it be *so long* until we meet again," it makes perfectly good sense.

somebody said it couldn't be done. That's from the practically immortal Edgar A. Guest. The verse went: *"Somebody said it couldn't be done,/But he with a chuckle replied/That maybe it couldn't, but he would be one/*

Who wouldn't say so till he'd tried." Verse like that lends itself to parody, of course. The one we like best goes simply: *"Somebody said it couldn't be done*—and by golly, he was right."

some crust, an old-time slang expression applied to brash or presumptuous persons, is not heard frequently these days, but it is still around. Newer items, like "chutzpah," borrowed from Yiddish, are in vogue today. The way *crust* got this special sense is that it indicated a callous disregard for other people's feelings, a hard imperviousness that resembled the hard crust on some pies.

somersault/tumblesault. *Somersault* came into English by way of Old French, not long after the Norman Conquest. The Old French version was *somber-sault* and can be traced eventually to the two Latin words *supra* (over or above) and *salire* (to leap). Thus a *somersault,* as everyone knows, is a sort of topsy-turvy jump, heels over head and landing on one's feet. However, *tumblesault* or *tumbersalt* is a word well established in various regional American dialects. Harold Wentworth's *American Dialect Dictionary* reports it as occurring in the speech of Southerners all the way from Alabama to West Texas.

something rotten in the state of Denmark comes from the first act of Shakespeare's *Hamlet,* when the ghost of Hamlet's father suggests that he leave his friends Marcellus and Horatio, so that he and Hamlet can converse privately. His friends don't think it's a good idea, fearing that some harm may befall Hamlet, but he insists on going and Marcellus, still mistrustful, says *"Something is rotten in the state of Denmark."*

son of a gun goes back to the time when women were allowed to sail—usually with their husbands—aboard trading vessels and even aboard warships. In a book published more than a hundred years ago, called *The Sailor's Word Book,* we find this explanation: *"Son of a gun* is an epithet conveying contempt in slight degree and was originally applied to boys born afloat. One admiral declares he was literally thus cradled, under the breast of a gun-carriage."

sonorous (pronounced suh-NOH-russ) describes that which is resonant, vibrating or full-toned. Derived from the Latin *sonor* (a sound), it applies also to high-sounding speech, as in poetry or sermons. "The minister rambled on in *sonorous* platitudes."

sooney-sawney. *Sawney* was originally a British term, used derisively, meaning "Scotsman." In time, and this perhaps reflects the low state of British-Scottish relations during the eighteenth century, it came to mean "simpleton." Later, through the process known as reduplication, the adjective *sooney-sawney* was created, meaning simply "foolish."

sophisticated originally meant "adulterated," not pure or genuine. In this sense it was closely allied to "sophism," the technique of fallacious argument or reasoning, of pulling the wool over one's eyes, so to speak. This sense persisted until about the 1920s, when it acquired the chichi "smart set" connotation. Then, in the 1940s and 1950s, it came first to mean "more complicated" and then "more subtle." Now it is common to hear phrases like "*sophisticated* space probes," meaning probes that employ the most refined and advanced techniques. This is a long remove from the original sense of *sophisticated* as "adulterated," but the logic of the evolution in meaning can be seen if we bear in mind that the essential sense of "unnatural" or "removed from the natural state" is still very much a part of *sophisticated.*

sophistry. An argument or method of reasoning which appears clever and plausible but which is really misleading and fallacious is called *sophistry,* from the Greek *sophistēs,* meaning "wise man." Something went wrong with the Sophists (English plural for those who practice *sophistry*), who were professional teachers in ancient Greece. Some came to emphasize cleverness and speciousness in reasoning rather than soundness. Thus a sophist became less of a wise man and more of a "fast talker."

sophophobia is an aversion to wisdom or learning, from the Greek *sophia* (wisdom) and *phobos* (fear).

sort out. *Sort* comes from Roman times, when *sors* was a lot or chance drawn at random. Sometimes fortunes were told in this fashion. The true believer would go to a sorcerer (from the same root as *sort,* by the way) and draw his lot at random.

SOS/SSS. Many people believe SOS stands for "Save Our Ship," "Save Our Souls," "Stop Other Signals." Actually, the letters have no significance whatever. The first distress call used by the early Marconi Company was *CQD*—*CQ* being the general call to alert other ships that a message is coming and *D* standing for "danger" or "distress." For various technical reasons this proved unsatisfactory and in 1908, by international agreement, a signal made up of three dits, three dahs and three dits was adopted as the one most easily transmitted and understood. By coincidence, this signal is translatable as *SOS.* During World War II a new distress signal, SSS, was devised for use only when the cause of the distress was a submarine torpedoing.

soul, as an adjective, refers to a person or thing of Negro origin. The label *soul brother* on store windows usually serves to deter looting during times of trouble, since it indicates that the proprietor of the store is not only Negro but sympathetic to the black movement. *Soul food* describes the kinds of food common in the black belt areas of the South—black-eyed peas, chitlins, yams and the like. A perceptive comment on *soul* was made by black novelist Claude Brown: "*Soul* is being true to yourself—that uninhibited self-expression that goes into practically every Negro endeavor."

sourdough got its name from the practice of early Yukon and Klondike prospectors of carrying over a lump of sour dough from each biscuit baking to start fermentation of the next batch. It wasn't a very sanitary technique, but it worked. *Sourdough* as a nickname for early settlers is now as obsolete as the settlers themselves.

sour grapes comes from a fable of Aesop in which a fox tried to reach some grapes and, failing, said, "Well, they are probably sour anyway." So a person who is accused of taking a *sour grapes* attitude is one who is disparaging something because he knows it is beyond his capacity to attain.

Southern-fried chicken. In a letter commenting on the importation of petticoat tail cookies from Scotland to the Southern United States, Mrs. Margaret C. Williams wrote us from Tartentum, Pennsylvania, with her version of the origin of *Southern-fried chicken:* "When Boswell and Johnson visited Scotland, they were served fried chicken, for that was the standard way of cooking chicken in the Highlands. Since chicken in England at that time was either baked or boiled, the famous travelers made due note of being served fried chicken. From the early 1700s to about 1800, thousands of Highlanders had to leave their homeland and many of them settled in our Southern states. Doubtless, there they introduced what has come to be called *Southern-fried chicken.* And when 'petticoat tails' (which see) turned up in Louisiana, no doubt they came the same way."

southpaw, for left-hander, is a word that has long intrigued sports fans. We explained in our column that it started in baseball at a time when diamonds were laid out with the home plate to the west, so that a left-handed pitcher would face south. That explanation was all right as far as it went. But it didn't go far enough, as Finley Peter Dunne, Jr., of Washington reminded us: "According to the best authorities I know, including Prof. Elmer Ellis, who wrote my father's biography *(Mr. Dooley's America),* it was Finley Peter Dunne who originated the expression. The Chicago ballpark faced east and west, with home plate to the west, so a left-handed pitcher threw from the south side. My father, who covered sports for the *Chicago News,* and Charles Seymour of the *Herald* were credited with having introduced the modern style of baseball reporting, concentrating on the dramatic moments in the game and giving character to the players. According to Ellis, both Dunne and Seymour were using *southpaw* in 1887. My father was then 20 years old—and it was not until six years later that he started on the humorous pieces about Mr. Dooley that made him famous." So credit for coining *southpaw* seems to belong to one of our great political humorists, who, like Ring Lardner and many other outstanding writers, started out writing sports.

so vile a pun. John Dennis, eighteenth-century English playwright and coiner of the expression "steal one's thunder" (which see), had his lighter side. One evening he found himself in a coffeehouse with a fellow writer—an incurable punster—named Purcell. The latter rang the bell for a "drawer," as waiters were then called. When he failed to respond, Purcell rapped the table hard and asked what the table and the tavern had in common. The answer was: "There's no drawer in either one." Dennis gagged on the pun and remarked: "A man who would make *so vile a pun* would not scruple to pick a pocket."

sowing wild oats. *Wild oats* are tall weeds similar in appearance to oats but relatively worthless. So a person *sowing wild oats* would be planting a worthless crop, just as a young man does when he fritters away his time in fruitless dissipation.

sow the dragon's teeth. This expression goes back to a classical myth. A Phoenician prince named Cadmus killed a dragon and sowed its teeth. From the teeth there sprang up a band of fierce warriors called Sparti, who warred among themselves until only five remained. The idea behind the expression is that one can take a course of action that is peaceful in intent (disposing of the dragon's teeth by burying them) but actually leads to war. Incidentally, the phrase "Cadmean victory," meaning a victory won at nearly ruinous cost, comes from this incident.

spaceship earth is the coinage of Buckminster "Bucky" Fuller, the prodigious inventor and innovator who, well past his mid-seventies, captured the imagination of youth, especially that element of youth passionately interested in ecology and the survival of man and the planet on which he lives. That, of course, is the meaning of *spaceship earth.* In Fuller's thinking, the planet is the only place suitable for human habitation for the foreseeable future and we had better take all possible measures to eliminate pollution of the lands, sea and atmosphere, or we face extinction. And, so goes his dire prediction, that fate will be ours by the end of this century unless we act and act fast. Fuller is also the inventor of the geodesic dome, which in various mutations crops up just about everywhere these days. Perhaps the largest such dome was the one created for the United States building at the Montreal Expo. In our youth Fuller also devised a marvelous "dymaxion" three-wheeled automobile, but it never went into commercial production.

spanking/spanking new. *"Spank,"* meaning "to strike with an open hand," is a word formed in imitation of the sound it represents, an "echoic" word. "Blast," "slap" and "thump" are other words which probably originated in attempts to echo the sounds represented. *Spanking* as in *spanking new,* however, is thought to come from one of the Scandinavian tongues. Originally it was used to describe a fresh, lively breeze. Indeed, it probably was first a sailor's term, since it surely is related to the *spanker,* a fore-and-aft sail. Eventually *spanking* came to its present meaning—anything remarkable or outstanding of its kind.

spare the rod. The origin of the expression *"Spare the rod* and spoil the child" may be found in Proverbs 13:24; "He that spareth his rod hateth his child; but he that loveth him chastiseth him betimes."

spatial. Why is the adjective *spatial,* from "space," spelled that way? Because it was formed directly from the Latin word for space, *spatium,* while the noun "space" came to us by way of the French word *espace.*

speak/speakeasy. A *speak* or *speakeasy* was a clandestine saloon during the Prohibition era—so called because it was considered discreet to speak quietly to the doorman when telling him, through a peephole, "Joe sent me." It was this period that inspired Franklin Pierce Adams (F.P.A.) to one of his loftier flights of verse: "Prohibition is an awful flop. We like it./It can't stop what it's meant to stop. We like it./It's left a trail of graft and slime,/It's filled our land with vice and crime,/It doesn't prohibit worth a dime,/Nevertheless, we're for it."

speak of the devil is a very common expression, heard when a person who has been under discussion suddenly puts in an appearance. It's an American variation of a British proverb dating back at least to the seventeenth century: "Talk of the devil and he's sure to appear." R. C. Trench, Dean of Westminster, midway through the nineteenth century, took the whole matter with a seriousness perhaps befitting his ecclesiastical station. "The proverb "Talk of the devil and he is bound to appear,' " thundered Trench, "contains a very needful warning against curiosity about evil."

spectacular. In a column we commented on the decision of NBC-TV to ban the word *spectacular* in describing TV shows of unusual length or significance after the departure of its president Sylvester L. "Pat" Weaver, who had first used the word in that connection. Weaver saw the column and graciously added further background to the story. "I share your regret," he wrote, "over the silly move of NBC to eradicate the name *spectacular* for the big one-shots. I chose this name because advertising men used it in outdoor advertising to indicate the big, permanent installations, as on Times Square, and named by Douglas Leigh. This is because in outdoor advertising one also chose between spending funds in a wide dispersion of ads on 24-sheets, or spending in a single, big explosion. The name therefore helped me sell these shows when they were very difficult to sell and when the TV people and most ad people said that only continuity programming would work. The name 'specials' came from Max Liebman, who produced some of the early spectaculars and who would not accept my terminology because he knew that the critics would jump on the shows because of the name. My answer to this was 'So what.' " A glance at *Merriam-Webster* shows that *spectacular,* with specific reference to television, is entered, while "special" is not. So it would appear that, lexicographically at least, Pat Weaver is still one up on NBC.

spell. If asked to *"spell* me for a while," almost every American would know that he was being asked to relieve the other person of his duty temporarily. It's quite likely, too, that most people would consider the use of *spell* in this sense as a slang or dialect term. It is true that the phrase *to spell* as meaning "to relieve" is principally an American usage, but it can trace its lineage back to the Old English word *spelian,* which meant "to stand in place of," virtually the same thing. The noun *spell* in the sense of a period of time comes from the same root—but here again it is more common in America than in England.

spelunker is a cave explorer, more correctly called a "speleologist," from the name of the science of cave exploration, "speleology." Though *spelunker* has a disarmingly casual air about it—with more than an echo of "dunking"—it can trace its origin back more than two thousand years to the Latin word for "cave," *spelunca.*

Spelvin, George. The original *George Spelvin* was a theatrical myth—a name listed in theater programs to indicate an actor who was "doubling," that is, playing two or more parts. For the more important role he would be listed by his actual name; for the lesser roles, he'd be *George Spelvin.* In the now defunct magazine *Theatre Arts,* some of the wittiest and most penetrating comments appeared in articles signed "George Spelvin"—the pseudonym of John Chapman, for many years the drama critic for the *New York Daily News.*

spencer jacket. The short wool jacket known as the *spencer* and designed for wear by either men or women was first created by the second Earl of Spencer, whose chief claim to fame in his lifetime was the fact that he, as First Lord of the Admiralty, chose Horatio Nelson to command the fleet in the Mediterranean.

spick-and-span is a shortened form of *spick-and-span new,* a term originally used in the shipbuilding trade. A *spik* was a "spike" and a *span* was a "chip or shaving." Thus anything *spik-and-span new* would be sparkling new. As an example of how fashions in language change, note that Dr. Samuel Johnson entered this term very reluctantly in his dictionary (1755), for he felt that it was one he "should not have expected to have found authorized by a polite writer." Although he had to admit that writers as distinguished as Dean Swift and Samuel Butler had used it, Dr. Sam still growled that "*spick-and-span* is, however, a low word."

spider, as a name for a frying pan, goes back to colonial America, when most cooking was done on the open hearth. Frying pans in those days came with long handles, so the user wouldn't burn his or her hands, and three or four short legs, so that the pan could sit above the hot coals. The appearance, at least to a housewife with a good imagination, was not unlike that of a spider. For the same reason, trivets were often called *spiders.*

spike his guns means to thwart an opponent's plan of action. In early cannons the powder was set off by lighting a fuse which went through a breech or small hole. When it was necessary to retreat and abandon the cannons, a spike was driven into this hole so that the cannons could not be used immediately by the enemy.

spilled salt. From earliest times salt has played a part in religious ceremonies. Even today it is used in the Roman Catholic baptismal service as a symbol of purity. So it has long been considered "bad luck" to spill salt accidentally. An elaborate ritual, familiar to most of us, has been passed down through the centuries to exorcise evil spirits allegedly set loose when salt is spilled. One must take a pinch of salt between the thumb and first finger of the right hand and cast it over the left shoulder.

spinster goes back many centuries and originally included all unmarried women, regardless of age. Alfred the Great referred to the females in his family as "the spindle side." Each young woman was taught to spin and weave and was not regarded as ready for marriage until she had personally woven an entire set of household linens. Down through the centuries language changed to reflect changing customs. With maidens no longer required to spin and weave, the label *spinster* gradually came to mean only ladies who never married.

spit is a very old word, going back to the Anglo-Saxon *spitu,* meaning "point." In the sense of a thin, pointed rod, thrust through meat which is to be broiled over an open fire, it is at least five centuries old. The same word has also been applied to a narrow point of land jutting out into a large body of water, as a "sand *spit.* " There is no connection between this *spit* and "to eject from the mouth." That *spit* can be traced by way of Anglo-Saxon *spittan* to the Latin *sputum,* a word still used by doctors.

spitting image. There is far from complete agreement among students of language as to whether the "spit" in this expression comes from the same root (Anglo-Saxon *spittan*) as the common word meaning "to eject from the mouth." One authority, claiming that the phrase means "speaking likeness," quotes a source dating back to 1602 to support his claim that the two words are the same. However, one of our early collaborators on reference books, Harold Wentworth, suggests in his *American Dialect Dictionary* a different source. He notes that the phrase "He's the very spit of his father" is widely heard in the South and suggests that "spit" in this sense is probably derived from "spirit." Noting that the letter *r* is often indistinct in Southern speech, he suggests that the phrase may actually have started as "He's the very spirit and image of his father."

spizzerinctum. This oddity from rural dialect was discussed in our column and we mentioned that dictionaries define it as cold cash or hard money. The question that led to our discussing this word involved a minister who exhorted his followers to deliver more *spizzerinctum.* We implied that he was looking for a better-filled collection plate, but a West Virginia reader thought otherwise. "In this area," she writes, "the old people use the word to mean energy and enthusiasm. They say things like 'I wish I had his *spizzerinctum,*' when speaking about a young person. Undoubtedly this is how the minister meant the word. If you had attended an old-time revival meeting in my neck of the woods, you would know that joy, energy and enthusiasm are much more in abundance (and more desired) than cold cash!"

splice the mainbrace originated as part of the language of the sea but has now been adopted by landlubbers in the extended sense of "take a drink of intoxicating brew." The actual mainbrace is the line secured to the mainyard, which holds the mainsail. If you have followed us this far, we're sure you agree that the one thing certain about seamen who have been *splicing the mainbrace* in its figurative sense is that they are in no shape to perform the feat literally.

spoils of war. The earliest kind of *spoil* (in its Latin form *spolium*) was the hide stripped from an animal. Later *spoils* came to mean any kind of plunder or booty, especially arms surrendered by a conquered enemy, the *spoils of war*. The idea of *spoil* meaning to damage a thing so that it becomes virtually useless developed centuries later, from the fact that the stripped carcass of an animal is worthless.

spondulix is a bit of dated slang meaning money, specifically small change like nickels and dimes. It is one of many words coined in the mid-nineteenth century by humorists like Josh Billings and Petroleum V. Nasby in imitation of Latin and Greek words affected by the literati of the period. Mark Twain used it in *Huckleberry Finn* when he had a character say: "I'm derned if I'd live two miles out of town, not for all his *spondulix.*" We're told that it was one of W. C. Field's favorite words and that wouldn't surprise us a bit, for the great man doted on such verbal oddities.

spoof was created by a British comedian, Arthur Roberts, as the name of a game he invented about 1890. The invention, which earned him a footnote in the dictionaries, seems to have been a card game blended, as one might expect of a comedian's creation, with elements of pretense and humor. In the words of the *Oxford Dictionary,* "*Spoof* is a game of hoaxing and nonsensical character—a round game of cards in which certain cards when appearing together are termed *spoof.*"

spoonerism. The transposition of initial sounds, making "one swell foop" out of "one fell swoop," is called a *spoonerism* after the late William A. Spooner of Oxford, who made many of them in his time. One of his most celebrated *spoonerisms* came at the close of a wedding ceremony at which he officiated. Noticing that the groom was so nervous that he had overlooked an important part of the ceremony, the minister told him, "Son, it is kisstomery to cuss the bride."

These hilarious transpositions have been called *spoonerisms* ever since the memorable Sunday some seventy-five years ago when he approached one of his parishioners with this query: "Marden me, padam, aren't you occupewing the wrong pie? May I sew you to another sheet?" The good doctor also once chided one of his pupils for having "hissed my mystery lecture" and on another occasion startled clergy and laity alike by announcing that the next hymn would be "When Kinquering Congs Their Titles Take." Spooner lived to the ripe old age of eighty-six, though quite a few of his auditors would not have gambled much on his life expectancy when, at the height of Queen Victoria's reign, he referred to "our dear old queen" as "our queer old dean"!

Incidentally, Spooner was not the first victim of these accidental slips of the tongue which now bear his name. Grammarians had a name for them long before Spooner was born. In the turgid lexicon of grammatical terms, this was known as "metathesis," derived from the Greek word meaning "to place differently," and it described any form of transposition of syllables or letters of words, whether the effect was humorous or not.

With the advent of radio and television, announcers on both media committed more than their fair share of *spoonerisms.* Harry Von Zell, speaking from Washington, is reputed to have said "From the White House we bring you the President of the United States, Mr. Hoobert Heever." Ben Grauer once introduced famed suffragette Carrie Chapman Catt with this line: "We are deepful greatly that you could be here today." And Lowell Thomas, in a World War II broadcast from London, referred to British cabinet minister Sir Stafford Cripps as "Sir Stifford Crapps."

sport the oak is British university slang. The oak referred to is simply the outer door of a student's room or "digs." When it was closed, he was *sporting the oak* and this was the signal that visitors were not wanted.

spread misere. When Dangerous Dan McGrew played "solo" in the saloon, he said at one point, "I guess I'll make it a *spread misere.*" A reader asked what *spread misere* meant.

First, perhaps we'd better explain who Dan McGrew was. He was the hero, if that's the word for it, of a famous poem, "The Shooting of Dan McGrew," by the Canadian-born poet (if that's the word for him) Robert W. Service. The best-known lines go: "A bunch of the boys were whooping it up in the Malamute saloon;/ The kid that handles the music box was hitting a jag-time tune;/ Back of the bar, in a solo game, sat Dangerous Dan McGrew;/ And watching his luck was his light-o'-love, the lady that's known as Lou." The *spread misere* (pronounced SPRED mee-ZAIR) was a hand in solo whist which was so poor that the player decides simply to spread it out, face up, knowing that it is valueless. *Misere* is the French word for "poverty."

spree is usually thought of as a lively outing, especially one accompanied by considerable drinking and associated revelry. A related sense of the word occurs in expressions like "shopping *spree*"—again a rather carefree overindulgence. In recent years *spree* has turned up often in expressions like "The madman went on a shooting *spree*" or "The holdup man went on a bank-robbing *spree.*" Purists object to *spree* in such violent contexts, yet this may actually be closer to the original meaning than the fun-loving sense we have been accustomed to. *Spree* comes to us from Latin *praeda,* "spoils or bounty," by way of Gaelic Irish and Scotch *spreath,* "cattle taken as plunder in a raid."

spud. One of the most fanciful word origins was the one about this nickname for the potato. The story went that about one hundred years ago lots of people thought that potatoes were unhealthy and formed an association to discourage eating them. It was named the Society for the Prevention of Unwholesome Diets—and *spud* came from its initials. The truth is very different. The original *spud* was—and is—a sharp spade used to dig potatoes.

spurious comes to us direct from the Latin *spurius,* an adjective meaning "illegitimate, counterfeit or false."

sputnik. When the first Russian *sputnik* was launched, there was some speculation that the word might in time come to be the generic term for space vehicles. However, events have shown that while *sputnik* remains the common Russian word for space vehicle, English-speaking countries now use it only to refer to the first such orbital spaceship. The word *sputnik* in Russian means "one who travels the same path" or, in brief, "fellow traveler."

sputtsey is a dialect term for the common English sparrow. It is heard in Milwaukee and environs, where many people are of German descent. The *sputtsey* probably gets its name from German *Spatz,* "sparrow," pronounced shpahtz.

squalid (pronounced SKWOL-id) pertains to that which is filthy, foul, wretched and unkempt and is used most commonly to describe dwellings and environment. From the Latin *squalere* (to be foul or filthy), the condition it describes is *squalor.*

square deal/square meal. Besides the sense of "square" as "rectangular," the word has several related meanings, such as "fair, adequate and satisfying." Thus, "He got a *square deal*" and "She got a *square meal.*"

squash, the common garden vegetable of many varieties, gets its name from the Algonquian Indian *askutasquash.*

squaw, a term sometimes used humorously or disparagingly to refer to a woman or wife, is a direct borrowing from the Massachuset dialect of the Algonquian Indian language and originally meant any North American Indian woman.

squawk. Lewis Carroll, creator of *Alice in Wonderland,* gave to the English language many new words, each a blend of the sounds and the meanings of two words. Among these was *squawk,* from "squall" and "squeak."

squeaky wheel gets the grease. One of the leading American humorists of the mid-nineteenth century was a wit named Henry Wheeler Shaw, who wrote under the pen name Josh Billings. In a poem called "The Kicker" he wrote: "The wheel that squeaks the loudest/Is the one that gets the grease." Billings also said: "It's better to know nothing than to know what ain't so" and "There ain't much fun in medicine, but there's a good deal of medicine in fun."

squeegee is a device found in every service station in the land. It's a T-shaped instrument with a headpiece consisting of a rubber blade on one side and sponge on the other. The water-filled sponge is wiped across the windshield, followed by the rubber blade, which wipes off the water. *Squeegee* may be an echoic name, in that the rubber blade makes a noise not unlike the sound of the word itself. Less imaginative etymologists say it's simply an intensive variation of "squeeze."

SS Corps. The SS were the *Schutzstaffel*, "Black Shirts," the elite military and police corps of the Nazi Army, so named because they wore black shirts as part of their uniforms.

stalking horse goes back at least to the early 1500s, according to the *Oxford Dictionary*. Huntsmen of the period trained their horses so that they would approach unwary game while the huntsman himself, hidden behind the horse or under the coverings horses sometimes wore, got close enough to aim. Some imaginative hunters even built light portable dummy horses to hide behind. So *stalking horse* came to mean a sham front behind which the actual participant was hiding until the proper time to show himself.

stand the gaff. The *gaff* is the metal spur attached to the leg of a gamecock before "pitting" him against his rival. Obviously the one that can't *stand the gaff* is the loser.

starboard and larboard. For centuries these two terms were used to indicate the right and left sides of a boat, facing the bow. *Starboard*—a term still very much in use—has nothing whatever to do with the stars. Rather it comes from the fact that an oarsman sculling and steering a small boat usually stood on the right side near the stern. *Star* in this instance, then, comes from the Anglo-Saxon word *steor*, meaning "to steer." *Larboard* came from the Anglo-Saxon *leere*, "empty," referring to the fact that the steersman was not there. Because of the similarity of sounds in *starboard* and *larboard*—which some thought led to serious collisions—*larboard* is now obsolete and has been entirely supplanted by "port."

Star-Spangled Banner. Although Francis Scott Key wrote the verses for the song in 1814, it was not designated our national anthem until more than a century later. President Woodrow Wilson in 1916 issued an executive order to that effect, but his authority to make such a pronouncement was somewhat in question. However, in 1931 all doubt was removed and an act of Congress wrote into law the fact that *The Star-Spangled Banner* was indeed our national anthem. The music was adapted from the official song of a Masonic social club in London, the Anacreontic Society, and was originally titled "To Anacreon in Heaven."

start from scratch comes from the practice of giving handicaps to some competitors in racing. A contestant who *starts from scratch* (literally a line *scratched* on the turf or gravel) is the one who runs with no special advantages, while those with handicaps may be starting some distance down the track toward the goal.

stash. The original users of *stash,* vagabonds or hobos, used it to refer to hiding something for future use. Anything so hidden was usually improper or illegal. Harold Wentworth, in his *American Dialect Dictionary,* reports its first use was around 1929 and cites an early example of it in a remark heard in the Ozarks of northwest Arkansas: "Billy, he done stashed the jug in th' brash an' now the danged ol' fool cain't find hit!"

Most dictionaries indicate that *stash* is thought to be a blend of "store" and "cache," with the element of secretiveness a strong one. One word of caution—if you do *stash* anything of value, don't be like the "ol' fool" Billy and forget where it is.

As to Wentworth's date of its origin, Mrs. Miriam Staiger of Pittsburgh had these comments to make: "Did you possibly mean 1829? I know *stash* is far older than 1929. I remember my grandmother using it and my mother, who is eighty, says she has heard it all her life. It did not necessarily refer to anything improper or illegal, but rather to anything hoarded away for future use. Grandmother *stashed* fruitcake away so she would always have something handy to serve an important visitor. A good bottle of wine might so be held in reserve. Since these people were very close to the German and Pennsylvania Dutch people, perhaps the word stems from their speech."

Statue of Liberty. Originally called "Liberty Enlightening the World," this is the colossal statue of a lady holding a torch aloft at the entrance of New York harbor. It was a gift to the American people from the French in commemoration of the one hundredth anniversary of the Declaration of Independence. However, it was not formally dedicated until ten years later, 1886. It was the work of Frédéric Auguste Bartholdi, an Alsatian. Within the pedestal supporting the statue is the sonnet by Emma Lazarus, "The New Colossus," whose most famous lines are: "Give me your tired, your poor,/Your huddled masses yearning to breathe free,/The wretched refuse of your teeming shore./Send these, the homeless, tempest-tost to me./I lift my lamp beside the golden door!"

steal one's thunder, meaning to take credit for another person's accomplishments, is nothing new, as your authors have good reason to know. Here's the story of the first case on record of *stealing one's thunder.* John Dennis, an English poet and playwright, wrote a tragedy called *Appius and Virginia.* Produced in 1709, it laid an egg—as they would say on Broadway today. Just about the only thing the critics could find to praise about the show was a series of sound effects that thundered more realistically than any that had been heard before. After the Dennis show closed, he decided to take his mind off his worries by seeing a new production of *Macbeth*. When the famous witches' scene came on, with stage directions reading: "An open place. Thunder and lightning," Dennis stood bolt upright in the orchestra pit, shouting: "See how the rascals use me! They will not let my play run, and yet they *steal my thunder!*"

steatopygous (pronounced stee-at-oh-PIJ-us) means having a broad backside. It comes from two Greek elements meaning "fat rump." In some African tribes a *steatopygous* posterior is considered a mark of great beauty in a female.

stem to stern means "throughout"—as in "He studied the affair *from stem to stern.*" The stem is the bow of the ship. Technically, it's the member to which the ship's sides are joined at the prow, but it is loosely used simply as identical with "bow." The *stern* is the ship's rear.

stenophobia is a morbid fear of narrow places or things, from the Greek *stenos* (narrow) and *phobos* (fear).

step into the breach. The breach is a gap or rift, especially in a wall of a fort or in a dike. So jumping or stepping *into the breach* would be taking emergency measures to avert a dangerous situation or, in military terms, a disastrous defeat. Perhaps the best-known use of this phrase occurs in Shakespeare's *Henry V,* when the king rallies his forces with this call to battle: "Once more unto the breach, dear friends, once more;/Or close the wall up with our English dead!"

stepmother. The origin of this term goes back to furthest antiquity. In its present form, though with slight alteration in spelling, it goes back to the time of Chaucer and before. Originally the term *stepchild* meant "an orphaned child." Later the term was extended to mean the child of one's husband or wife by a former marriage. From that sense of *stepchild* the origin of *stepfather* and *stepmother* is obvious.

Stetson/John B., from the John B. Stetson hat manufacturing company, are both the accepted terms among working cowboys for the cowpuncher's ten-gallon hat. See also TEN-GALLON HAT.

sticks and stones will break my bones but names will never hurt me. This is a puzzlement. We went confidently to Bartlett's *Quotations,* sure we would find there the source of this old saying. No luck. Then on to Stevenson's compendious *Home Book of Quotations.* Again, no trace of the saying. And so on and on, and we realized with dismay that this expression which both of us have known since earliest childhood seemed to have escaped all the people who put together reference books.

But not quite all. The *Oxford Dictionary of English Proverbs* had found room for it but records it as first appearing in a book published in 1894 called *Folk Phrases.* The fact that it was in such a collection, of course, indicates that it is much older and that nobody knows who said it first. The listing reads: *"Sticks and stones will break my bones, but names will never hurt me*—said by one youngster to another calling names."

sticky wicket means an awkward and difficult situation. It comes from the language of the game of cricket. A batsman facing a *sticky wicket* is facing a difficult situation, one which demands cool and careful judgment on his part. In cricket—so we are told—a soft pitch can cause the batsman more trouble than one smartly delivered. We suppose that a parallel situation in baseball would have the batsman facing a *sticky wicket* when the pitcher resorts to his change-of-pace ball or "change-up."

stigma. Current meaning of *stigma* (aside from its use in botany or medicine) is "a mark of disgrace or a blot on one's reputation." In earlier days, however, it was far from a figurative thing. It was a brand applied to a slave or a criminal, either cut into the flesh or burned in with a hot iron. It goes back to the Greek word of the same spelling, which meant "to prick with a pointed instrument."

still small voice. A *still small voice* is a phrase from the Bible (I Kings 19:12): "And after the earthquake a fire; but the Lord was not in the fire; and after the fire a *still small voice.*" As to how a voice can be still and yet be heard —for the Lord, anything is possible.

"still stands thine ancient sacrifice" is from Rudyard Kipling's "Recessional" —a poem that makes especially interesting reading today, now that Britain has abandoned its empire and America seems bent on assuming what used to be called the "white man's burden."

stirrup cup was literally a drink given a guest as he sat, feet in stirrups, on his horse, which, quite unlike today's automobiles, could be counted on to bear him safely home, *stirrup cup* or no *stirrup cup.*

stooge has been part of show business talk for at least half a century and, may go all the way back to Shakespeare's day. One of the most famous *stooges* of this century was Dave Chasen, later an eminent Hollywood restaurateur, who served as foil for the late and beloved Joe Cook. Accordionist Phil Baker also employed a *stooge,* who heckled him from a balcony box. And Jack Benny used many *stooges,* of whom the most notable surely was Rochester, his butler. Thus a *stooge*—which probably originated as a variation of "student"—first meant a person who serves as foil for a comedian. Now, in general speech, it means any underling, especially an assistant held in low regard by the boss.

stormy petrel. This small sea bird was originally called *pitteral,* and there is a theory that this was a form of the Latin diminutive of Peter (Petrus), in allusion to the fact that the birds skim so close to the water they seem to be walking on it, as St. Peter was believed to have done. *Petrels* are also called "Mother Carey's chickens," and this name is thought to be a corruption of the Latin phrase *Mater Cara* (Beloved Mother), in allusion to the Virgin Mary, protector of seafaring folk.

story, in both of its most common senses—as a narrative and as the name of a level of a building—comes from the Latin word *historia.* Obviously our word "history" comes from the same source. Here's how it happened. Back in the Middle Ages, it was the custom in many parts of Europe to paint scenes or print legends on the outside of the various floors of a building. Thus each floor represented a different story and, before long, the levels themselves were called stories.

Some years ago when we were visiting in Lake Placid, New York, we found a large Swiss-style hotel called The Chalet. Each floor was decorated with large hand-lettered mottoes. We jotted down a few of them and they still make amusing and instructive reading. Here are four: "Horse sense is what a horse has that keeps him from betting on people." "The only way to multiply happiness is to divide it." "You can't keep trouble from coming —but you needn't give it a chair to sit in." And a memorable one credited to Albert Einstein: "Patriotism is good; nationalism is an infantile disease."

Storyville. Every history of jazz starts out with an account of how ragtime grew into jazz in a section of New Orleans known as *Storyville,* the red-light district that lasted until the start of World War I. The legendary home of barrel-house music and jazz got its name from the thoroughly prosaic fact that in 1896 New Orleans had a do-gooder alderman named Sidney Story. He was responsible for an ordinance that restricted the then legal activities of prostitutes to a thirty-eight-block area adjoining Canal Street. In 1917 the U.S. Navy cracked down and put *Storyville* out of existence.

straight from the horse's mouth comes from the old belief that the best way to tell a horse's age is to study his teeth, especially the lower jaw. Thus one finds the truth of a matter by getting an account *straight from the horse's mouth.*

strain at a gnat, and swallow a camel refers to the custom of becoming greatly exercised over minor sins but overlooking really major offenses. It comes from Matthew 23:24, where Jesus, rebuking the scribes and Pharisees for their hypocrisy, says: "Ye blind guides, which *strain at a gnat, and swallow a camel.*"

straw boss goes back to harvesting around the turn of the century. According to a writer in *American Speech* magazine: "The boss attended to the grain going into the thresher; the second-man watched the straw coming out and hence had little to do." So the *straw boss* is usually a foreman of a small group with little real authority to enforce his commands.

straw that broke the camel's back. In Charles Dickens's *Dombey and Son* (Chapter 2), you will find "As the last straw breaks the laden camel's back," meaning that there is a limit to everyone's endurance, or everyone has his breaking point. Dickens was writing in the nineteenth century and he may have received his inspiration from an earlier proverb, recorded by Thomas Fuller in his *Gnomologia* as " 'Tis the last feather that breaks the horse's back." (A gnomologia is a compilation of sayings.)

streusel, a topping for coffeecake made of a crumblike mixture of sugar, butter, cinnamon and often chopped nuts, comes from the German *Streusel,* meaning "something strewn together or sprinkled." The pronunciation STROY-zel is closer to the original German, but STROO-zel is heard often.

striffening is a dialect term describing an animal membrane, especially the membrane surrounding the abdominal viscera. It occurs in a variety of spellings—most commonly as simply "striffen" or "striffin"—and is fairly commonly heard throughout rural areas of the country from West Virginia to Kansas. *Merriam-Webster* suggests that it is probably derived from the Scottish-Gaelic word *streafon,* of the same meaning.

stringer. A staff member of one of the newspapers in which our column appears asked: "What is the origin of the word *stringer* as applying to a newspaper correspondent paid by the inches of type he produces? Our assistant managing editor says that it comes from the fact that such correspondents used to paste together their string stories in a long series to measure them. Is this it?" To which we could only reply: "Is an assistant managing editor ever wrong? Well, certainly not in this case. For evidence, we submit the testimony of Mary Morris, a *stringer* for the *Columbus* (Ohio) *Citizen* a few years longer ago than we care now to mention. Once a week she was expected to deliver her string of stories, pasted up end-to-end, to her assistant managing editor, who would measure them off and authorize the appropriate payment. She recalls her A.M.E. with gratitude because he used to pay for headlines, too. His theory was that though the *stringer* didn't write the head, there wouldn't be any head without the *stringer*'s story. There's rather a sad ending to Mrs. Morris's career as a *stringer,* though. After a while the kindly old A.M.E. discovered that she was making more on a *stringer* basis than most of the regular reporters. So what did the kindly old A.M.E. do? You guessed it. He put her on the staff at regular salary—about a third less than she had been making "on the *string."*

striped ties. An observant reader noted that the stripes on most ties designed for American men run from right downward to left and wondered whether there is anything sinister (which see) in this fact. That's an interesting theory, but we believe the answer is simpler and wholly without sinister implications. Most striped tie patterns originated in England as emblems of membership in a club, regiment or university. The designs are predominately made with stripes running from left to right. American tie-makers felt free to borrow the designs, but to avoid confusion with the original (and also to avoid the wrath of the genuine soldiers or clubmen), simply reversed the direction of the stripes.

strip to the buff, which has enjoyed something of a vogue in the theater and cinema in recent years, has a rather unflattering origin, for the original buff was undyed leather from the buffalo. Because of its light skinlike color, the term was extended to describe human flesh, so a person stripping to the buff is actually disrobing to reveal skin the color of undyed buffalo hide. That's a thought to quench almost any onlooker's enthusiasm.

struthious (pronounced STROO-thee-us) has been a part of the English language at least since the time of the Revolution. It's not what you would call a household word, though. In fact, until now it has been used chiefly by ornithologists—students of birds—because it literally means "pertaining to ostriches" and is eventually derived from the Greek word for ostrich, *struthion*. It seems to be a useful, if rather pretentious, addition to the current vocabulary in the extended sense of "acting like an ostrich."

stuffed shirt. One story has it that the first *stuffed shirt* was the turn-of-the-century stock-market plunger John "Bet a Million" Gates. The lady who applied the label to him was none other than the reigning queen of the musical theater of the time, Fay Templeton. Obviously she was underwhelmed by the self-styled financial genius.

stump. The use of the word *stump* in "take to the *stump*" and *"stump* the district" dates back to the earliest days of our nation. Specifically, the first recorded use of the word is in the *Memoirs of a Huguenot Family* by Ann Maury and the story it tells occurred in 1716. "I went down to the Saponey Indian town," runs the narrative. "There is in the center of the circle a great stump of a tree. I asked the reason they left it standing, and they informed me that it was for one of their head men to stand upon when he had anything of consequence to relate to them, so that being raised, he might the better be heard."

The tradition was one quickly adopted by the politicians among the colonists. As early as 1775 a popular patriotic song referred to the father of our country in these words: "Upon a *stump* he placed himself, Great Washington, did he."

sturm und drang is a German phrase meaning "storm and stress." It was first applied to the cultural awakening of Germany under the inspiration of Goethe late in the eighteenth century; it has been called the early phase of German romanticism.

St. Valentine's Day is the day when lovers traditionally exchange symbols of their mutual affection. It's a tradition at least as old as the English language, for Chaucer mentions it, but originally it was thought of as the day on which birds chose their mates for the year to come. St. Valentine himself had no direct connection with the romantic traditions we observe today. He was a priest in ancient Rome who was first jailed and eventually clubbed to death for his part in the rescue of early Christian martyrs. But thanks to the coincidence that the feast of the birds, with its romantic implications, fell on his birthday, the saint has been immortalized and become part of our common tongue in the word *valentine*.

subordination comes from the Latin word *subordinaire*, which means "to order under"—hence, to put a person under the power of another person or group.

subornation comes from the Latin *sub* (under) plus *ornare* (to furnish) and means "to supply or incite secretly." Thus the meaning of inducing a person to perform an illegal act by bribing him has been implicit in the word *subornation* since its earliest use in the courts and temples of ancient Rome.

succotash is the way the early Pilgrim settlers approximated the Narragansett Indian word *misickquatash*. The word originally meant "ear of corn" but in time came to mean the succulent dish, corn and beans cooked together, that we know today.

sudden death periods, which occur after the regular playing time has ended with both teams tied and in which the first team to score wins the game, are not unique to football. In fact, it is only relatively recently and only in the professional leagues that this method of deciding play-off games has been adopted. However, hockey and some other sports have used *sudden death* periods for a long time. Gamblers used the term even earlier to describe the final single throw of the dice or flip of the coin. Interestingly enough, the first appearance of the phrase *sudden death* had nothing to do with sports. Mark Twain reported it in 1865 as a frontier expression for rotgut whiskey.

suffer fools gladly. This expression appears first in the King James version of the Bible, I Corinthians 11:19: "For ye *suffer fools gladly*, seeing ye yourselves are wise." It also appears in a memorable quatrain of Lord Alfred Douglas: "I have been profligate of happiness/And reckless of the world's hostility,/The blessed part has not been given to me/*Gladly to suffer fools*."

suffragette was the label applied to early crusaders for equal rights for women. Their first battle was for "votes for women," which is how they came to be called *suffragettes*, from Medieval Latin *suffragium*, "vote." And that reminds us of our favorite liberated woman of the period, Mrs. August Belmont, who prided herself on being a "suffragist," which was one step above *suffragette*. One day she was organizing a protest march down Fifth Avenue in New York, demanding votes for women, when she noticed some of her young associates on the verge of tears. And well they might be, for street-corner rowdies were sure to taunt and ridicule them. So Mrs. Belmont waved her hand high above her head and cried: "Place your faith in the Lord, ladies. *She* will protect us!"

sui generis means "one of a kind, with a unique character." The Latin phrase, literally "of its own kind," is usually rendered in English as soo-eye JEN-er-is.

suits to a T. The *T* refers to the T-square used by draftsmen to make sure that their drawings of right angles, parallel lines and the like are precisely accurate. So anything that "fits you to a T" or *suits you to a T* is something that is exactly correct and very much to your liking.

sundae. The origin of the word *sundae*, according to H. L. Mencken, who devotes several pages of *The American Language* to the topic, belongs to the town of Two Rivers, Wisconsin. Here, in the early 1890s, was located an ice cream parlor run by E. C. Berners. One evening a customer named Hallauer was being served a portion of vanilla ice cream when he suggested that the proprietor pour over it some chocolate syrup ordinarily used in making sodas. Berners protested that the syrup would ruin the taste of the ice cream, but his customer insisted and the dish was born. It didn't, however, acquire its name at once. That developed in nearby Manitowoc, where George Giffy ran an ice cream parlor. Since he charged extra for the ice cream with syrup, he regarded it as a special item and sold it only on Sundays. One weekday a little girl demanded a dish of the new concoction. "I sell it only on Sundays," said Giffy. "Then this must be Sunday," replied the girl, "because that's the kind of ice cream I want." Thus inspired, Giffy decided to name the concoction a *Sunday.* Just how the spelling came to be changed to *sundae* is not known. Presumably the reasons were two: to avoid confusion with the day of the week, and to add a touch of elegance to the word.

Sunny Jim was one of the most successful trademark figures of the early days of American high-pressure advertising. His oversize vest protruded as though he carried a basketball over his thin stomach. His high collar was no doubt quite fashionable and his hair and coattails flared out behind him as though he were in a high gale. In those days—around the turn of the century—there were no such things as the singing commercials that we hear on radio and TV today. The prime advertising medium was print— magazines and newspapers. So the 1900 equivalent of today's commercials were rhymes and limericks extolling a product's supposed virtues. *Sunny Jim* was the hero of dozens of such rhymes, most of them created by a lady named Minny Maud Hanff (Mrs. Raymond F. Ayers in private life). The product being promoted was a cereal named Force, now long gone from the marketplace.

Here are a few of the more memorable rhymes: "Vigor, Vim,/ Perfect trim./ Force made him/ *Sunny Jim.* " "High over the fence/ Leaped *Sunny Jim./* Force is the food/ That raises him." And "Jim Dumps' young wife, while yet a bride,/ Some biscuits made with greatest pride./ Jim looked with fear upon the food,/ But to a bride one can't be rude./ Let's eat Force first, he said with vim,/ It saved the life of *Sunny Jim.* "

supercilious. Highfalutin, hoity-toity, condescending, disdainful, contemptuous and arrogant—all these are synonyms for *supercilious,* which, in its literal Latin derivation, means "with lifted eyebrow." It comes from *super* (over) and *cilium* (eyelid or brow).

supplicatory (pronounced SUP-lih-kuh-tor-ee) is the adjective form of the verb *supplicate,* which means "to implore, beseech or entreat; to request in a humble and earnest manner." It comes from the Latin verb *supplicare,* "to kneel down, to pray," which in turn is made up of *sub* (under) and *plicare* (to fold). All forms of the word *supplicate* retain the accent on the first syllable except *supplication* (sup-lik-KAY-shun). A *supplicant* is one who humbly and earnestly seeks.

supposititious. Derived from the Latin *suppositicius*—"something that has been substituted"—our word may mean either "hypothetical" or, more. commonly, "spurious" or "substituted with intent to defraud."

sure as shootin'. This expression comes from the Old West and it means that anyone who resorts to gunplay had better be sure of his own shooting because he's never going to get a second chance: the person he is shooting at can plug him first if his aim is bad. One example of the use of the expression goes back to 1851, in an account of a couple of hunters being attacked by a grizzly bear: " 'Hurry, Bill!' roared out Glass, as he saw the animal rushing toward them. 'We'll be made meat of, *sure as shootin'!* ' "

sure as tunket is an expression that used to turn up regularly in the wonderful Joseph C. Lincoln Cape Cod stories of years ago. *Tunket* is a euphemism for Tophet, the Old Testament name for a place where human sacrifices were made by fire. The expression *Sure as Tophet (Tunket)* was the salty New Englander's way of saying "Sure as hell."

surveillance. During an investigation of the New York City Police Department, one of the attorneys for the investigating commission asked an officer, "You mean you were surveilled all the time?" There is no such word as "surveilled" in English—except maybe what passes for English among New York lawyers. The proper term is "under *surveillance,*" meaning "under close watch." Curiously enough, the French have a verb, *surveiller,* from which our word *surveillance* was derived a couple of hundred years ago. There's no good reason why a verb "surveill" might not have come into English at the same time—but the fact is that it didn't. Apparently the simple phrase "keep watch over" was sufficient for our ancestors.

suspenders, in Britain, is the proper term for what we call garters. In turn, "braces" is the British term for what we call *suspenders.*

sutler. *Sutlers* since the time of Queen Elizabeth have been merchants who followed armies, selling food and liquor to soldiers. They were not an especially admirable group, as indicated by the origin of their name, the Dutch *soetaler,* "one who performs menial or dirty work."

Swanee. There never was a Swanee River and Stephen Foster was never within many miles of the Suwannee River, which, in a way, inspired his famous song. *That* river starts in Georgia near the Okefenokee Swamp, where Walt Kelly's beloved Pogo lived at a much later date, and it empties into the Gulf of Mexico.

Foster wrote his song in Pittsburgh in 1851 and he set out, as professional songwriters sometimes do, to write another "river" song. The first river he chose to immortalize was the Pee Dee, but the more he thought about that, the less he liked it. The Pee Dee, in case you care, runs through North and South Carolina. He then asked his brother, Morrison Foster, to suggest a better-sounding two-syllable name and he came up with Yazoo. Stephen decided that that sounded like a clinker, so he urged his brother to press on further in his atlas. He did and came up with Suwannee, which, since Stephen wanted only two syllables, was changed to *Swanee,* and musical history of a sort was made. Interestingly enough, though most people call the song "Swanee River," Stephen Foster himself always referred to it as "Old Folks at Home."

swan song. The legend that every swan sings one glorious song just before death is about as old as recorded legend goeth. The fact of the matter is that a swan never sings. But a romantic legend dies hard, especially when poets such as Shakespeare, Coleridge and Spenser hymn it in verse. Nowadays we often refer to the last great work of a creative artist, be he poet, writer, painter or musician, as his *swan song.*

swashbuckler today means a swaggering, romantic doer of deeds of daring. In American movies the two Douglas Fairbankses, Errol Flynn and Tyrone Power specialized in the type of role called *swashbuckling.* Originally the word came from *swash* (to dash against) and *buckler* (shield). It referred to swordsmen's practice of tapping their shields before attacking. As long ago as Shakespeare's time, though, *swashbucklers* had a bad reputation. John Florio in 1598 defined them as "braves that for money and good cheer will follow any man to defend him; but if any danger come, they run away the first and leave him in the lurch."

swatson. We hadn't ever heard of *swatson* until we fell to talking with the editor of one of our favorite weeklies, *The Village Gazette,* which is published in our home town of Old Greenwich, Connecticut. It's a paper that lives up to its name, by the way, in being a lively chronicle of the week's happenings in what is still in many respects a New England village.

Well, according to editor Wakeman Hartley, his grandfather, though a proper New England lawyer, delighted in using colorful and tangy Yankee sayings. One that lives on in his grandson's memory is "Come and sit down and let's *swatson* awhile." It's an interesting way to say "let's chat informally" and far nicer than "let's chew the fat"—but it's also a word that has so far eluded all dictionary editors, even the compilers of specialized works on dialect and slang.

When we mentioned *swatson* in our newspaper column, a number of readers came up with a very logical explanation—that the word is simply a Yankee variation of the colloquial German word *schwätzen,* meaning "to chat or gossip." Here's one comment, from Margarite Meyers of Oradell, New Jersey: "I can't claim to recall ever hearing *swatson* used in English but seeing it in print immediately brought to my mind the German *schwätzen,* pronounced SWAT-son. It would be interesting to learn whether the grandfather Mr. Hartley refers to came from Germany or from German stock, though a 'proper New Englander' himself."

Well, we checked this and other similar comments with Editor Hartley and learned that, while not of German descent, his grandfather was a very accomplished linguist and among his linguistic attainments was an ability to read and converse fluently in German. And so the mystery is solved.

sweet and fitting to die is a line from an ode by the Roman poet Horace: *"Dulce et decorum est pro patria mori"*—"It is sweet and fitting to die for one's country." Most people who quote the line have forgotten, if they ever knew, that Horace was writing a satire and actually meant nothing of the sort.

sweet singer of Michigan was Julia A. Moore (1847–1920), and she owes her fame not so much to her verse as to the comment made upon it by Mark Twain. "The one and unfailing great quality," he wrote, "that distinguishes her poetry from Shakespeare's and makes it precious to us is its stern and simple irrelevancy." Here's a sample: "And now, kind friends, what I have wrote/I hope you will pass o'er,/And not criticize as some have done/Hitherto herebefore." Had enough? No? Well, this next sample should satisfy the most ardent seeker for mediocrity: " 'Lord Byron' was an Englishman,/A poet I believe/His first works in old England/Was poorly received./Perhaps it was 'Lord Byron's' fault/And perhaps it was not./His life was full of misfortunes,/Ah, strange was his lot."

sword of Damocles is a peril or danger hanging over one. The reference is to the legend that Damocles, a courtier of ancient Syracuse, used to try to curry favor with his king by talking about the wondrous ease of the kingly life. In order to teach him the lesson that perils and responsibilities also accompany the privileges of kingship, King Dionysius invited him to a banquet, where he was seated under a sword hanging by a single thread. Damocles was so distraught that he could not enjoy any of the sumptuous repast set before him.

Sydney or the bush is a phrase of Australian origin, with the civilized comforts of *Sydney* contrasted to the rigors of life in the *bush* or Outback.

syndicate, in the sense of an association of financiers organized to gain control of the market in a certain commodity, is a borrowing from the French *syndicat.* According to some authorities, the legendary Jay Cooke was the first to use it in English.

synergy is a word borrowed from medical science and originally meant that a combination of two drugs often has a more powerful effect than the sum of their individual effects.

syzygy (pronounced SIZ-uh-jee) is a term used in several sciences, but most commonly in astronomy to indicate the precise conjunction or opposition of two heavenly bodies.

table d'hôte. Literally, in French, "the table of the host," this term originally meant the communal meal served to all guests at boardinghouses and the like. Nowadays it means a complete meal served at a fixed price. Sometimes also called *prix fixe,* this is in contrast to *à la carte,* in which each item chosen from the menu is charged individually.

taboo was originally a Tongan word, *tabu,* meaning "marked as holy." Tongan is a Polynesian language spoken in the Tonga island group of the southwest Pacific. The first *taboos* were prohibitions against the use or even the mention of certain things because of religious belief that to do so would invoke the wrath of the gods. The word gradually was extended in use to cover all sorts of prohibitions or bans based upon social convention. Thus in the nineteenth century the mention of a lady's "leg" was *taboo.* The only acceptable word was "limb." Similarly, words which had been freely entered in dictionaries of the eighteenth century became, thanks to the influence of the Rev. Thomas Bowdler and other reformers, *taboo* and have only in recent years been readmitted to public print.

tailgate is now most commonly used as a verb meaning to follow another vehicle so closely that you cannot avoid colliding with it if it stops abruptly. The *tailgate* referred to is the tail board of a truck or station wagon and the term obviously has been simply carried forward from the days of horse-drawn wagons. *Tailgate* has also given its name to a style of trombone playing popular in jazz bands. This came about from the practice at Negro funerals in New Orleans of having the marching band climb aboard the now-empty wagon after the funeral and play joyous ragtime tunes on the way back to town. Since the trombone's slide took the greatest space, the trombonist was usually seated on the *tailgate.* Incidentally, that's how the legendary trombonist Jack Teagarden got the nickname "Gate." Still a third use of *tailgate* is to describe picnics preceding football games at places like the Harvard Stadium and the Yale Bowl. Station wagon *tailgates* are lowered and serve as impromptu tables for the luncheon.

take a powder began as underworld slang. Originally the verb was simply *to powder* or *powder out,* meaning "to take it on the lam or flee." In this form it is recorded as appearing before 1925. Some theorize that it is a variant of the earlier "dust" in such phrases as "dust out of here." During the 1930s the phrase *take a run-out powder* was common in gangster movies, and in 1940 John O'Hara's Pal Joey wrote that he had to *"take a powder* out of here that day."

take down a peg comes from British Navy jargon of the eighteenth century. In those days a ship's colors were raised by a system of pegs; the higher the peg, the higher the honor. Conversely, if the flag was lowered a peg, the honor conferred was correspondingly reduced. So *to take him down a peg* meant to reduce the honor or esteem in which a person is held.

taken aback originally was sailor talk. When a sudden change in the wind blew the sails back against the mast, the boat's progress was momentarily halted and the sailors, needless to say, were somewhat surprised. So a person *taken aback* is one suddenly dumfounded by an unanticipated development.

take the bull by the horns. He who *takes the bull by the horns* is a brave man —whether he does it literally or figuratively. As a metaphor, it simply means "to face up to a very difficult or dangerous situation."

take the cake is a somewhat old-fashioned slang phrase which means "to deserve or carry off a prize." In former years, a form of entertainment among blacks in the South was a contest to determine the most graceful pair of walkers. Couples would walk in a circle around the cake, which was the prize, and the winners would, of course, *take the cake.* From such contests was developed the *cakewalk,* a form of dance generally popular during the early part of the twentieth century. Actually, the custom of having a cake as a contest prize goes back much farther than that. In ancient Greece, the cake went to the man who could stick with his drinking the longest. In Ireland, dancing contests used to be held in which the cake was the prize.

take with a grain of salt is a very old expression. In fact, the Romans used precisely the same expression, although their version, being in Latin, went *cum grano salis.* The idea is that you're approaching some suggestion or proposal with skepticism bordering on distaste. The basic concept is that you would take the same approach to an unappetizing meal which might be made palatable by the addition of a grain or two of salt.

talking through his (her) hat. This expression made its first appearance in print in 1888, as part of an interview with a streetcar driver in the old *New York World.* Management was trying to get the trolley men to wear white shirts, but one of them summed up the reaction of his fellow drivers this way: "Dis is only a bluff dey're makin'. Dey're *talkin' tru deir hats.* " We might note in passing that "dis" kind of writing would get any cub reporter fired from any paper in the land today. However, the fact that the expression was used in this fashion proves that most readers of the paper could be expected to know that *talking through one's hat* meant to utter boastful or nonsensical ideas. It could have developed as the counterpart of "keep it under your hat," meaning to keep something confidential.

talk turkey. Chances are you have used this phrase all your life to mean "talk serious business." Yet the odds are equally good that you don't know the rather charming story behind the expression. Back in early colonial days, a white hunter and a friendly Indian made a pact before they started out for the day's hunt. Whatever they bagged was to be divided equally between them. At the end of the day the white man undertook to divide the spoils, three crows and two turkeys. He first handed a crow to the Indian, then gave a turkey to himself; then another crow to the Indian and the second turkey to himself. At this point, the noble redskin complained, "You *talk all turkey* for you. Only talk crow for Indian."

tally. *Tallies* (from the Latin *talea*, "stick") have been used as records of accounts or scores for centuries. Originally a *tally* was a stick on which marks representing a debt were made crosswise. The stick was then split down the middle so that each half bore part of the mark, with the date alongside each half of the mark. The half given to the creditor was called the *stock*, and the half given to the debtor was the *counterstock*. When time came for payment of the debt, the two pieces were put together to make a *tally*. *Tallies* were used by the British Royal Exchequer from the time of the Norman kings to 1785 to record the debts of the state. When the *stocks* were redeemed by the state, they were fastened to the *counterstock* and stored by the treasury. After the practice was discontinued, the government ordered the *tallies* burned in the stoves of the House of Lords. It was a pretty spectacular occasion, since it resulted in the destruction by fire of all of the Houses of Parliament. *Tally* remains with us as "an account or a score" or, as a verb, "to match or correspond."

tam-o'-shanter is the familiar beret-like cloth or knitted cap, usually adorned with a feather, pompon or tassel and often simply called a "tam." It may well be the only piece of male headgear named after a poem, Robert Burns's "Tam o' Shanter," written in 1790.

tanbark is the bark of trees—usually oak trees—which is rich in tannin, a substance used in tanning hides into leather. After the bark has been used for this purpose, it is shredded and used to provide ground covering for circuses.

tangerine. The first *tangerines* came from Tangiers, the Moroccan seaport, and were called "*tangerine* oranges." The color *tangerine* is a bright reddish orange.

tank. When you give the matter a moment's thought, you realize that the military *tank* doesn't look the least bit like any other kind of tank you have ever seen. Here's why. The term *tank* is strictly British. During World War I, when armored vehicles were first introduced, they were "Most Secret" and were moved to the combat zone by rail. They were well camouflaged and were called *tanks* in military code. The code name stuck—and they are still *tanks* to the English-speaking world.

tantalize. Everyone knows the present meaning of *tantalize*—to tease a person, especially by holding something he or she wants just out of reach. But the first person to be tantalized, the man who invented the word, so to speak, was in much more dire straits than that. Tantalus, in Greek mythology, was a son of Zeus and king of Mount Sipylus in the ancient Aegean country of Lydia. Somehow he managed to infuriate other gods, perhaps by revealing some of the godly secrets. So he was condemned to stay forever in a deep and sunless abyss known as Tartarus. He was doomed to stand in water which receded whenever he tried to drink it. Above his head were clusters of luscious fruit, which receded whenever he reached for them. It sounds to us like the ultimate in frustration. Over the centuries the people have agreed—and that's how *tantalize* became part of the language.

taped. Expressions such as "you've really got it *taped,*" to mean "fully accomplished or rounded up," have become quite commonplace. The analogy is to a tape recording, which can be presumed to be the complete and faithful record of an event.

tap out, as in the expression *"tap out* a fire," started as a gambling term. When a bettor *taps out,* he has run out of money. He's finished. So a fire *tapped out* would be a fire extinguished.

taps. The earliest record of *taps* in print is in the *Congressional Record* for 1824, though it doubtless existed some time before that. Records go back to the sixteenth century of a British call, *tattoo,* to which our *taps* is probably related. In the days when the British and their Dutch adversaries were engaged in their seemingly interminable wars, they used to observe a charmingly civilized custom. At sundown they would knock off the fighting and head for the nearest pubs. The first summons back to camp (called First Post) was sounded about 9:30 P.M.—and went unheeded by many of the roistering soldiers. So search parties were sent, with torches, to round up the stragglers. When the Dutch barkeeps saw the lights, they would call *tap toe*—meaning "shut the bar" or "turn off the *taps."*

Taps itself was originally a drum roll and probably got its name, in part at least, from the tapping of the drums. However, the bugle call we now know so well did not have its beginning until the Civil War. According to one account, General Daniel Butterfield's troops were encamped on bluffs overlooking the James River in Virginia after the bloody fighting of the Peninsular Campaign. When the bugler sounded the call then known as "extinguish lights," Butterfield remarked to a fellow officer that it sounded too formal. The next day he called in the bugler, and together they worked out the haunting melody now played at the end of the soldier's day and at military funerals.

tar as a name for a sailor is a shortened form of "tarpaulin," a tar-impregnated cloth. In Lord Nelson's time sailors wore broad-brimmed hats made of this material. First the hats, then the sailors, were called "tarpaulins"—which gradually was shortened to *tars.*

tarantella. This Italian dance may loosely be said to have been named after the poisonous tarantula spider. During the fifteenth and sixteenth centuries, Southern Europe and especially Italy were the scenes of dreadful epidemics of a disease called tarantism, named after the town of Taranto, Italy, where the first epidemics occurred. Tarantism was a nervous disease characterized by extreme lethargy at the start and in later stages by a hysterical mania for dancing. For centuries people believed that this disease resulted from the bite of the tarantula, also named for the town. And in time they evolved a lively folk dance which—from its resemblance to the actions of victims of tarantism—they called the *tarantella*. So, while it is not strictly accurate to say that the dance is named after the spider, both derive their names from the common source, Taranto.

tarheel. In the *National Geographic* magazine the author of an article on North Carolina stated: "North Carolina was nicknamed the *'Tarheel* State' because the long-leaf pine forests of the coastal plains produced such an abundance of rosin, turpentine and tar." This is a fine explanation of the *tar* element, but where does the *heel* come in? Apparently the term dates from the Civil War period and was originally a derogatory reference. The earliest account of the origin (1869) records that "A brigade of North Carolinians . . . failed to hold a certain hill, and were laughed at by the Mississippians for having forgotten to *tar* their *heels* that morning."

Before long, though, the epithet was accepted by North Carolinians with no thought to its unhappy origin. In 1864 Governor Zebulon B. Vance visited some North Carolina troops serving with the Army of Northern Virginia. "I don't know what to call you fellows," he said. "I cannot call you fellow soldiers, because I am not now a soldier, nor fellow citizens because we do not live in this state. So I have concluded to call you 'Fellow *Tarheels.'* " According to reports, "There was a slight pause before the applause came, and from that time *Tarheel* has been honored as an epithet worthy to be offered to a gallant North Carolina soldier."

Henry L. Mencken, to whose *The American Language* we are indebted for this account, goes on to say: "Whatever the truth of all this, the fact remains that *tarheel* has now lost all its derogatory significance in North Carolina."

tarnal is simply a dialect version of "eternal" and is used in folksy expressions like "by the eternal" to avoid profanity.

tattersall. The dashing sportsman in his *tattersall* jacket would be less than happy to learn that the design he wears is, quite literally, taken from a horse blanket. The checked pattern that we call *tattersall* gets its name from Richard Tattersall (1724–1795), who ran a horse market in London. He devised the checkered blankets to distinguish his horses from others.

taut ship/tight ship is used to describe a ship whose crew is well disciplined and whose efficiency rating is high. In his years at sea during World War II, William always heard the phrase as *taut ship.* Presumably it comes from the days of sailing vessels, when lines drawn taut would be a sign of a shipshape craft and crew.

taxi is a borrowing from the French, a shortened form of *taximetre,* a device *(metre)* to measure the charge *(taxe)* for the ride.

taxi squad is a term used in professional football to designate players who are not listed on a club's roster but are available for quick call-up in an emergency. The term originated with a remarkable man, Arthur McBride, a man of many talents. He was a topflight newspaper circulation director, owned a wire service, published racing news scratch sheets, owned a taxicab company and founded the Cleveland Browns pro football team. The blending of the last two careers gave us the phrase *taxi squad.* McBride was relentless in his search for perfection, so he hired every good football prospect he could find—so many that there simply wasn't room for all of them on the club roster. Finally he hit on the device of having the spare players work out with the team—but be paid as employees of his taxicab company. And that's where the *taxi squad* was born.

tear up the pea patch. *Pea patch,* in the sense of a small garden planted in peas, is an old expression, especially common in the South. To *tear up the pea patch* means to go on a rampage or to upset the apple cart. The expression was popularized some years ago by a well-known sports broadcaster, Red Barber, who announced the Brooklyn Dodger games in the days long ago when there still were Brooklyn Dodgers. Barber used to liven up his play-by-play narrative with expressions like *tearing up the pea patch* and "sitting in the catbird seat," which meant sitting pretty—like a batter with three balls and no strikes.

teched, as in the statement "He's a wee bit *teched,*" is a dialect variation of "touched" and, as used in this sentence, is actually a short version of *"teched* in the head [haid]," meaning not quite right mentally.

teleran is an electronic device for transmitting pilot charts and other navigation data by television to planes in flight. *Teleran* (pronounced TEL-uh-ran) is made up from the first two syllables of *television* plus the first letters of *radar, air* and *navigation.*

tell it to the marines/horse marines One theory is that the marines referred to in this remark were the "horse marines"—a nonexistent outfit. While it's true that the expression is sometimes heard as *"Tell it to the horse marines,"* the simpler horseless version came first. As a matter of fact, it originated in the British Royal Navy, where marines were traditionally held in some slight contempt by sailors, who considered all marines green, lubberly and stupid. According to sailors, marines would believe any story told them, no matter how fanciful. There's no reason to believe that there was any particular truth in this idea, all services having a fair sprinkling of boobs. But it's indicative of the service rivalries which still exist, despite all talk of "unification," that seasoned sailors still sometimes call marines "seagoing bellhops."

When, in our syndicated column, we mentioned "horse marines" as a facetious nickname for a platoon of marines that never existed, our ears were pinned back by a fusillade of pan letters from ex-marines, all convinced that we were slandering the Corps, and presenting various bits of evidence to prove that there had indeed been units of U.S. "horse marines."

The only trouble was that none of our irate correspondents was able to cite any specific official unit, though all agreed (as we would, too) that marines have served on land, sea, in the air and even on horseback.

Then came an intriguing letter from John A. Childress of Washington, D.C., setting forth another story of the origin of "horse marines." He said:

As is well known, the War of 1812 resulted in the complete blockade of our Atlantic coast by some 300-odd warships of the British—to the extent that no ship could venture out of port. In the emergency, all trade along the eastern shore was conducted by wagons and they soon developed into a fleet. For example, a wagon full of shoes and hats would move from Massachusetts and Connecticut south possibly as far as Carolina and return with, say, cotton and rice.

Facetiously, those wagons became known as "ships," their drivers or owners became "captains" and soon were known as the "horse marines." For example, ads would appear in a Baltimore newspaper announcing that a shipload of articles from New England would "dock" at Lexington and Fayette Streets and "Captain Jones" would be glad to meet those interested, etc. Of course, those wagons would take on local freight from, say, Baltimore to Washington or Richmond and most of the wagons went along with the pretext to the extent of painting their names on the sides, like ships.

All of the above I read in a U.S. history some sixty years ago, with actual excerpts of local ads. It's strange but, in the intervening years, I have never run across another reference to that rather amusing episode in our history. Could it be because we rather like to forget the true facts of that unfavorable war and so even dismiss them from our records? I think that this handling of our disrupted trade was most ingenious—and certainly nothing to be ashamed of.

Agreed, Mr. Childress! And so, surprisingly enough, the first "horse marines" may actually have been "merchant marines" after all.

temper the wind to the shorn lamb does not appear in the Bible, though it does sound as though it might have appeared in the King James version. The first record we find of it is in French in the writings of Henri Estienne, a sixteenth-century Parisian printer and scholar. Its most famous appearance, though, is in Laurence Sterne's *A Sentimental Journey,* in which we find: " 'God *tempers the wind,*' said Maria, *'to the shorn lamb.'* "

tempest in a teapot first appeared in Cicero's *De Legibus* ("Concerning the Laws") as "He used to raise a tempest in a teapot." The actual Latin is *"Excitabat enim fluctus in simpulo."* Incidentally, *Brewer's Dictionary* makes it "storm in a teacup," which it defines with British understatement as "a mighty to-do about a trifle."

temporize (pronounced TEM-per-yze) is to compromise or seem to yield but always with thought of the time element involved. Derived from the Latin *tempus* (time), it may mean to avoid action at the given moment, to stall for time, to procrastinate, or to suit action to the time and place.

Tenderloin. A now almost forgotten district of Manhattan, extending from Madison Square (Twenty-third Street) to Longacre Square (Forty-second Street), the *Tenderloin* in the 1880s was the "wide-open" section of the big town. Indeed, some authorities say that every other building in the *Tenderloin* was devoted to vice of one form or another. Gambling was rife and the graft very substantial, so one police captain, being transferred there from a Wall Street precinct, remarked in eager anticipation: "I've had nothing but chuck for a long time but now I'm going to get some *tenderloin.*" And thus the district got its name.

ten-gallon hat. Some skeptics have expressed doubt as to whether the phrase *ten-gallon hat* has any connection to the hat's capacity. When the West was young, cowboys adopted this high-crowned, broad-brimmed hat for a variety of reasons, not the least of which was its water-carrying capacity. In his excellent glossary of Western words, Ramon Adams noted that "the crown makes a handy water bucket if a cowboy's horse cannot get to water, and the brim serves as his own drinking cup. He starts his fire with his hat by using it as a bellows to fan a sickly blaze, and he can use it as a water bucket again to put out that same fire when he breaks camp."

Obviously, the *ten-gallon hat* does not literally have a capacity of ten gallons. The *gallon* may well have been borrowed from Mexican-Spanish *sombrero galon,* "braided hat," an item from the costume of Mexican vaqueros.

Among working cowboys, by the way, the hat was generally called a Stetson or a John B. Both names derive from the name of the first and most famous maker of this kind of hat, the John B. Stetson Company of Philadelphia. As the Western writer Will James noted: "*Stetson* is the name the cowboy often gives his hat whether it is a 'genuwine' *Stetson* or not. The big *Stetson* hat is the earmark of the cow country. It's the first thing the tenderfoot buys when he goes west, but he never seems to learn how to wear it at just the right jack-deuce angle over his off-eye. . . . You may be surprised to learn that the cowboy's hat has more different uses than any other garment he wears. Often his life depends upon a good hat, for a limp brim of a cheap hat might flop in his eyes at just the wrong time. When he is riding in the scorching sun, the wide brim is like the shade of a tree, and the high crown furnishes space to keep his head cool. It also comes in handy to turn a stampeding bronc from dangerous ground by fanning its head when reins would be useless."

"tennis, anyone?" was reportedly the first and only line uttered by Humphrey Bogart in his Broadway debut. The show was a long-forgotten drawing-room comedy, light-miles removed from the sort of shows in which he made his later Broadway and Hollywood reputations.

tenterhooks. A tenter is a framework on which newly woven cloth is stretched, and a *tenterhook* is one of the hooks on the frame which holds the material taut. Thus a person *on tenterhooks* is in a state of great tension or suspense, with anxiety or curiosity "stretched" to the utmost.

tenuous/tenuity/tenuousness. *Tenuous* (pronounced TEN-yoo-us) is from the Latin *tenuis* (thin) and can be used to mean thin in either a physical or a figurative sense. In the physical sense it is applied to a thing slender and delicate, like a strand of a spider's web. More generally, though, it is used in such statements as "His was a very *tenuous* argument," in that it had no substance, was flimsy. *Tenuity* or *tenuousness* is the state or quality of being *tenuous.*

tenure comes to us from English law of centuries ago and originally meant the right to hold something, usually land, under certain terms and conditions. Since most Old English leaseholds were limited as to the number of years or lives they covered, the word also came to mean the time a *tenure* was in effect. It also became applied to office-holding, and even today we speak of a politician's actions "during his *tenure* in office." In each of these cases the right to hold land or office was clearly defined. Not so in the case of the teacher or professor until the principle of "academic *tenure*" was established to protect a member of a faculty from indiscriminate and often unfair firing. However, with that fight won and the right to keep a job established (in the absence of proven serious misconduct or incompetence), the phrase "academic *tenure*" has been shortened to simply *tenure.*

Terrible-tempered Mr. Bangs was an apoplectic character in Fontaine Fox's immortal *Toonerville Trolley* comic panel. He was forever blowing his stack, to use today's idiom, especially when the trolley, whose slogan was "We meet all trains," was late—as it invariably was.

thank-you-ma'am is a small bump in the road. Originally such bumps were created to divert rain water to the sides of the road. Today they are sometimes put into private roads in order to force drivers to go slow. In earlier times, if a young couple were out riding he was entitled to kiss her every time they hit one of these bumps, and the *"Thank you, ma'am"* was his joking way of acknowledging the kiss.

that's where the West begins is from Arthur Chapman's famous verse "Out where the West Begins": "Out where the handclasp's a little stronger,/Out where the smile dwells a little longer/*That's where the West begins."*

the buck stops here. Visitors to the Truman Library can see an exact replica of the late President's White House office. On the desk there is a sign that says: THE BUCK STOPS HERE. During the administration of President James Earl "Jimmy" Carter, the sign was returned, at his request, to the White House. "Passing the buck" is a phrase from poker, and since President Truman was an ardent player of the game, it is logical to assume that the sign on his desk was derived from his poker experiences. The original *buck* in card games was a marker placed before the poker player who was to deal the next hand. So "passing the buck" meant shifting the responsibility to another person. Obviously *"The buck stops here"* meant that Truman was assuming final authority. In the Old West, silver dollars were often used as bucks or markers—and that's how the dollar came to get the nickname *buck.*

theirs not to reason why, theirs but to do and die has to do with the famous Charge of the Light Brigade, immortalized in Tennyson's poem of that name. In the battle of Balaklava in the Crimean War, six hundred of her majesty's finest horse troops were given an impossible assignment—which they bravely tried to execute. Here's how Tennyson told the tale: " 'Forward, the Light Brigade!'/Was there a man dismayed? . . ./Someone had blundered./Theirs not to make reply,/ *Theirs not to reason why,/Theirs but to do and die* . . ./Into the jaws of death,/Into the mouth of hell,/Rode the Six Hundred." It was a relatively minor action in a relatively minor war. Historians generally regard the entire Crimean venture as folly. But the vividness of Tennyson's verses caught the imagination of the English people and they were quoted in generations of "elocution" and "declamation" classes both in England and here.

A slightly preposterous footnote to the whole tragic affair is that the two British officers involved in it—one running the entire campaign and the other leading the charge itself—were Generals Cardigan and Raglan. The former gave his name to the button-down-the-front jacket or sweater still popular and the latter designed the raglan sleeve. History rates them both as failures militarily speaking, but they surely did a lot for the clothing business.

theosophy —from the Greek *theos* (god), and *sophos* (wise)—as a general concept implies "divine wisdom" arrived at by intuition or philosophical speculation, sometimes based on historical revelation. Several ancient religions were considered *theosophical.* However, in today's use of the term, it applies chiefly to a movement founded in New York in 1875, called the Theosophical Society. The leaders soon moved to India and after the turn of the century the movement was led by Annie Besant, an Englishwoman who became an outstanding leader in the Home Rule for India movement.

there's a sucker born every minute was first said by the greatest showman of the nineteenth century, the legendary Phineas T. Barnum. It remained for Wilson Mizner, famous press agent and bon vivant of the 1920s, to top it. Mizner's version went: *"There's a sucker born every minute*—and two to take him."

these are my jewels was originally said by Cornelia, mother of the Gracchi, who later became leading statesmen in ancient Rome. One day she received a visitor, a woman from Campania, who insisted on flaunting her jewels, then asked to see Cornelia's jewels. Cornelia called her sons to her side and said to the visitor: *"These are my jewels,* in which alone I delight."

"they also serve who only stand and wait" is a line from John Milton's famous sonnet "On His Blindness."

things that go bump in the night. "From ghoulies and ghosties and longleggetie beasties/And *things that go bump in the night,*/Good Lord deliver us!" This seems to be an old Scottish prayer—author unknown. We did much research in hopes of finding the name of the author or even finding out how old the prayer is. The reason for our interest is that one of our favorite writers, James Thurber, wrote often about *"things that go bump in the night."*

thinking cap. The expression "put on your *thinking cap,*" meaning "give careful and thoughtful consideration to this," comes from the practice of judges in olden times of putting on a cap before sentencing a criminal. The practice is still followed in some countries, though not in the United States, when the death sentence is to be announced.

thin red line of heroes. In the poem "Tommy," Kipling's hero says: "We aren't no *thin red 'eroes"*—but that was not the first version of this famous line. In reporting the battle of Balaklava for the London *Times,* W. H. Russell, the greatest war correspondent of his era, wrote: "The Russians dashed on towards that *thin red-line* streak tipped with a line of steel."

third degree was originally the highest order of Freemasonry, the rank of Master Mason. Its use to refer to relentless grilling of a suspect by police officers is thought to come from the rigorous tests that, formerly at least, the candidate for the Master Mason rank had to pass.

third world is a term used to describe the underdeveloped countries of Africa, Asia and Latin America that have chosen not to ally themselves with either the Communist or non-Communist bloc nations. Therefore, the first world and the second world would be the Communist and non-Communist groupings.

30. In many newspaper offices the symbol *30* is used to mark the end of a piece of copy. There are several theories of the origin of the symbol. The most common is that *30* was simply taken over from the slang of old-time telegraph operators, who used that symbol to indicate the end of a day's or night's transmission. As one old-timer wrote: *"30* meant 'Good Night (GN), we are closing up the office and going home.' Another numerical sign that is still used by the telegraphic fraternity is 73. Its accepted meaning is 'Best regards and God bless you.' "

A typesetter disagrees with this theory, however, as witness this comment from Patrick Driscoll of Alexandria, Virginia: "May I suggest that the origin of the term *30* as a symbol at the end of newspaper copy is not, as stated in your column recently, from telegraphy but of more ancient lineage. The maximum line or length of slug on such composing machines as Linotype or Intertype is 30 picas, approximately 5 inches. When the operator reaches 30 picas, he has gone as far as he can."

three sheets in the wind The *sheet* referred to is not the common household bed covering; it is the line or chain attached to the lower corner of a sail. By tightening up on this line or by slacking it off, the set of the sail is controlled. When the sheet is allowed to run quite free, the sail is said to be *in the wind.* Thus, when all three sheets are *in the wind,* the sails are fluttering without control and the ship wallows and staggers like a person drunk. Hence the meaning of "very drunk" for *three sheets in the wind.*

throw in the towel/sponge. The rules of boxing provide that if a fighter's seconds throw any object into the ring while the fight is in progress, it is a sign of surrender, since the fighter is automatically disqualified. The objects customarily used as concessions of defeat are towels and sponges. So *throw in the towel* and *throw in the sponge* both mean "surrender."

thruway. Many communities and the homes in them have been affected by the building of vast *thruways*—modern versions of the king's highway. Where did this new word come from? Well, its origin is attributed to the original sponsor of the bill which authorized the New York Thruway. The story goes that State Assemblyman Abbot Low Moffat and his wife were out for a Sunday drive along one of New York's parkways and fell to discussing the name "parkway" as applied to the network of roads leading out of the city. Mr. Moffat objected to the name, feeling that it no longer suited roads which, originally intended for leisurely pleasure driving, had now become clogged with fast-moving through traffic. Searching for a name for the new superhighways he was to propose to the state legislature, he sought one which would express the primary function of the road—a two-way express artery uninterrupted by grade crossings. At that time the Queen Elizabeth Way, a four-lane limited-access highway, had just been opened in Canada. Mr. Moffat took "thoroughfare," modified it to "throughway," shortened that to *thruway* and had his name for the new highways.

thug is fascinating because, though it sounds as American as mom's apple pie, it's actually an Indian word—an Indian Indian word. The first *thugs* were worshipers of the Hindu goddess Kali, who waylaid innocent passers-by, stole their valuables and, more often than not, killed them on the spot. "Anything goes" seems to have been the motto of members of her sect— and that's all the more remarkable since she sounds like one of the most revolting goddesses in history. Called "the black one," she is described as "a grotesque creature, wearing a garland of skulls and dancing on the inert body of Shiva, her husband."

ticker-tape reception is peculiar to New York City, wherein celebrated persons (Charles Lindbergh was perhaps the first) are greeted at the Battery at the foot of Manhattan Island and taken in open cars up Broadway through the financial district to the city's official reception at City Hall. Along the way great showers of surplus paper tape from stock tickers is thrown out of the windows, making a confetti-like display over the heads of the hero or heroes of the day. Perhaps because the old stock ticker has been supplanted by electronic devices, *ticker-tape receptions* are now rare indeed.

ticket-of-leave man was roughly the same, in Great Britain and Australia, as our parolee—a man who had served part of a sentence and had been released from jail under conditions stipulating that he report regularly as evidence of proper conduct. One of the most successful nineteenth-century plays was *The Ticket-of-Leave Man* by Tom Taylor, first produced in 1863.

T.I.D. All of us at one time or another have puzzled over the curious hen tracks that doctors use in writing the prescriptions we take to the neighborhood pharmacist. Many of us feel, we're sure, that the chief purpose of this cabalistic calligraphy is to conceal from the patient the name of a drug which could be bought for less money were its generic name only known to the patient. That may occasionally be a correct guess, but more often the symbols—undecipherable by laymen—are merely time-honored abbreviations for the Latin phrases which have been used since the Middle Ages. When your doctor writes *"Sig.: T.I.D."* at the bottom of a prescription, he is telling the druggist: "Write on the label that the medicine is to be taken three times a day." Written out in full, the Latin phrase would look something like this: *Signum: Tres in die.* So you see, the abbreviation of the Latin phrase is actually designed not to confuse the patient but to save both time and space for doctor and druggist.

tilt at windmills. The allusion is to Cervantes' hero Don Quixote, who, accompanied by his faithful manservant, Sancho Panza, roams the countryside attacking windmills with his lance under the delusion that they are giants. So to *tilt at windmills* means to pursue a course foredoomed to frustration.

timber beast was a term widely applied to loggers and lumberjacks and not, we should guess, derogatorily. Mencken's *American Language* lists it as one of a number of slang terms for "logger," used in the lumbering industry; and Wentworth's *American Dialect Dictionary* reports that it was common in the states of Washington and Oregon as recently as 1918. Incidentally, one thing a logger would not stand for was to be called *lumberman.* As one authority notes: "Lumberjacks call themselves *loggers.* To call them *lumbermen* is an invitation to a brawl. To a logger a lumberman is a *sawdust-eater* down at the *macaroni-mills."* In other words, a sawyer in a sawmill.

timbromania is another name for philately—stamp collecting. This hobby is barely more than a hundred years old, and when it first started, no one quite knew what to call it. Just "stamp collecting" sounded too matter-of-fact. So a variety of high-sounding names were proposed, including *timbromania* and *timbrophily,* both based on the French word for "stamp," *timbre.* Neither one caught on, though, and throughout the English-speaking world the name for this engrossing pastime today is philately.

time is of the essence. In legal documents a date will be given, after which may be written: *"Time is of the essence."* This is a very old expression, credited by Bartlett's *Quotations* to Mr. Anon. It seems to mean simply that it is essential that the actions provided for in the legal document be completed by the date given.

tinhorn gambler/tinhorn sport. Most wordbooks content themselves with saying that these phrases get their meaning from "the flashy appearance and cheap quality of tin horns." Since a *tinhorn sport* is a pretentious fraud and an actual tin horn is a cheap imitation of the real thing, there is a certain plausibility to this theory of the term's origin. But why, when hundreds of items were made of tin in order to pass for gold, should the horn have been the only one immortalized in our language? George Willison, the Pulitzer Prize-winning historian, found the answer to that when he reported on the gambling ethics of the early West in his book *Here They Found Gold.* "Chuck-a-luck operators," reports Willison, "shake their dice in a small churn-like affair of metal—hence the expression *tinhorn gambler,* for the game is rather looked down on as one for 'chubbers' and chuck-a-luck gamblers are never admitted within the aristocratic circle of faro-dealers." It follows that a *tinhorn sport,* pretty obviously, would be one who patronized the *tinhorn gamblers.*

tinker's dam/damn is used to refer to something utterly without value. There are two theories about its origin. The first is that tinkers were itinerant menders of pots and pans who were generally held in low repute. Their speech was often profane—so it follows that a tinker would utter *damn* so frequently that it finally became meaningless. The other theory is that the word is actually *dam* and refers to a tiny pellet of bread used by tinkers to keep patching solder from running through the holes in pans being mended. When the patch was completed, the *dam* would be thrown away and hence was shown to be something utterly without value.

Tinker to Evers to Chance. Joe Tinker, Johnny Evers and Frank Chance were the "peerless trio" of the Chicago Cubs infield in the early years of this century. All were great players, with Evers and Chance ranking among the all-time great hitters of the game. But what assured them immortality and places in Baseball's Hall of Fame was their ability to make double plays. The line *"DP* [double play]: *Tinker to Evers to Chance"* appeared so often in box scores of the day that it became part of American folk idiom.

tin lizzie, also known as "the flivver" (which see) was Henry Ford's original Model T automobile. One cherished myth about the *tin lizzie* is that she got her name from Henry Ford's wife, Elizabeth. The trouble with that story is that his wife's maiden name was Clara Bryant. In truth, *lizzie* is simply a slang corruption of "limousine."

Tin-Pan Alley. Back around 1900, musicians' slang included the phrase *tin pan* for a cheap, tinny piano. Since those were the pianos used by song pluggers in music publishers' offices of the period, the area became known as *Tin-Pan Alley.*

tip. Most dictionaries dodge behind the label "uncertain" as far as this common word is concerned. A popular theory is that it is made from the first letters of the signs TO INSURE PROMPTNESS posted on coin boxes of tables in the coffeehouses of Dr. Johnson's day. This is one of those derivations that is just a bit too pat to be believable. More probably *tip* is a corruption of *stipend,* "a small payment of money," from the Latin word *stips,* meaning "gift."

Tippecanoe and Tyler too was the rallying cry of Whigs in the presidential election campaign of 1840. *Tippecanoe* referred to the victory by General William Henry Harrison in 1811 over Indians under Chief Tecumseh at the Tippecanoe River in west central Indiana. The ticket of Harrison and John Tyler was victorious, and since Harrison died shortly after inauguration, Tyler became the first U.S. President by vice-presidential succession.

tirade comes from the Italian *tirata,* "a volley of fire," which in turn came from the Latin *tirare,* meaning "to fire." So when a politician says he's going to "fire off a blast" at his opponent, he is very literally readying a *tirade.*

tit for tat, meaning retaliation, one stroke in return for another, is a very old expression. It goes back to the very first collection of English proverbs by John Heywood in the sixteenth century. It's probably borrowed from the Dutch expression *tip for tap,* "blow for blow," and is not unrelated to the Latin *quid pro quo.*

toady. *Toadying* is being unnecessarily flattering and obsequious. The verb *to toady* originally was "to toadeat" and refers to a custom common among traveling medicine men of a century or more ago. In those days the toad was popularly considered violently poisonous. So the mountebank would set up his pitch, displaying an obsequious assistant—usually a half-witted boy—who would swallow or pretend to swallow a toad. The medicine man then would purge the lad with some of his nostrums and, on the strength of this dramatic "cure," peddle his wares.

toast/toastmaster. One of the pleasanter and more civilized of our customs is *toasting* the continued good health of a friend. There is nothing new about the practice, for in all likelihood it began in ancient times, long before the Christian era. In those days the common practice was to pour a bit of the guest's wine into the host's glass and vice versa before either drank. The reason? Simply that few people trusted anyone outside the immediate circle of their family and one way to be sure the host hadn't poisoned your cup was to see to it that he drank some himself. With the passage of time and, presumably, the growth of goodwill among men, the practice of mixing the wine was abandoned and a ceremonial clicking of glasses took its place. The spoken wish "To your good health!" would logically accompany this ceremonial gesture.

The word *toast* seems incongruous these days, although the serving of beverages is often accompanied by varieties of toasted tidbits. In the time of Shakespeare and before, however, a piece of toasted bread was put in the bottom of the tankard or cup before the ale or wine was poured in. Chroniclers of the period say this was done to "improve the taste," but we suspect its chief purpose was to clarify the drink by collecting all sediment and impurities at the bottom of the cup. Thus the drink itself became a *toast.* A person who attained great popularity, so that his health was often toasted, soon became known himself as a *toast*—a usage that survives today in the phrase "toast of the town." Logically, also, the man in charge of introducing speakers at festive occasions was usually called upon to say felicitous words *toasting* each new speaker—and thus became known as the *toastmaster.*

to boot. The *boot* in *to boot* has nothing whatever to do with the boots we use on our feet. This other *boot* was originally an Anglo-Saxon word, *bote* or *bot,* meaning "advantage or profit." The word is now completely obsolete, except in the phrase *to boot.* However, in Milton's time it was commonly used. "Alas, what *boots* it with uncessant care," he wrote in "Lycidas," meaning: "What profit is there in unceasing worry." And Shakespeare wrote of *"bootless* errands,' meaning fruitless or profitless trips.

to err is human is credited to Alexander Pope, who lived from 1688 to 1744, but it appeared first as a saying in Latin: *"errare humanum est."* Pope did add one line: "to forgive divine." It appears in Part II of "An Essay on Criticism."

Toilet Paper Capital of the World is, believe it or not, the affectionate sobriquet bestowed on Green Bay, Wisconsin, by one of its most famous native sons, sportswriter Walter Wesley "Red" Smith. The reference is to the unquestioned fact that one of the city's two major industries is the manufacture of paper products. The other is meat packing, whence the name for the professional football team the Green Bay Packers, which some might rank as the city's third most important commercial product.

tolic is an oddity of regional dialect. It appears in expressions like "the whole kit and *tolic* of you," meaning pretty much the same thing as "whole kit and caboodle." Harold Wentworth in his *American Dialect Dictionary* reports hearing it before 1932 in Danbury, Connecticut, "especially by a 93-year-old woman."

toll has been well established in our tongue since Anglo-Saxon times in the sense of a tax levied for permission to pass along a road or over a bridge. It probably came from the Latin *teloneum,* meaning "tollhouse," a word brought to England by the Roman invaders under the Caesars.

tomfoolery nowadays simply means "nonsense, silly behavior." But back in medieval times it was considered great sport to watch the antics of insane people in asylums like Bedlam in London. The nicknames "Tom o' Bedlam" and "Tom Fool" were often used for male inmates who were favorites of the audience. Over the centuries the word *tomfoolery* evolved, eventually acquiring the relatively innocuous meaning it has today.

Tom Thumb golf, also known as "miniature golf," was very popular during the years of the Great Depression. Here's the story of the first such course, in Pinehurst, North Carolina. One of the millionaires who made Pinehurst their winter playground in those days fancied that it might be fun to be able to practice putting and the like right on his own front lawn. So he commissioned E. H. Wiswell, who had laid out many full-size courses, to create one for him in *Tom Thumb* scale. When Wiswell had finished his layout, the millionaire was not quite happy with it, so he asked further refinements. Wiswell, weary of the job by then, said: "No. This'll do." And as one historian puts it, "Someone with a flair for Scottish names supplied the burr and the course was named 'Thistle Dhu.' "

tongue in cheek is a truly odd expression, if you give it a bit of thought. Obviously, you can't say anything if you have your tongue lodged in your cheek. Perhaps the original idea was that, after saying something, you pushed out one cheek with your tongue as a gesture to indicate that you didn't really mean what you just said, like a wink to show "I hope you realize I'm just kidding." It first appeared in print in a book published in 1845 called *The Ingoldsby Legends,* in which the author, Richard Barham, reports a Frenchman as saying "Superbe! Magnifique!" (with his tongue in his cheek).

too late to whet the sword when the trumpet blows for battle is from Aesop's fable "The Wild Boar and the Fox" and is a comment that might be made to a child doing last-minute cramming for an exam.

top banana comes from the lingo of burlesque. In fact, it originated in a burlesque routine concerning a bunch of bananas. In time the chief comedian in a show came to be called the *top banana;* his foil or straight man was the *second banana.*

top brass. *Brass* in this phrase originated in the army and refers to the gold braid on the hats of military officers. Carried over into civilian life, *top brass* refers to top-ranking executives in the business as well as the military world.

top dog. Nowadays the business world often refers to the leader in any competitive enterprise as the *top dog.* The explanation is simple enough, if you don't mind drawing a parallel between business competition and a dog fight, the likely winner of which is the dog on top.

top mounter. In the language of the circus world, a *top mounter* is the man at the peak of a human pyramid. He is also known, logically enough, as *high man.*

torture by the boot. Mechanical devices such as the *boot,* which crushed the foot, and the *rack,* which painfully stretched the limbs, were used in England throughout the sixteenth and seventeenth centuries. So the England which gave us Shakespeare, Milton and the King James Bible was still using medieval instruments of torture to punish nonconformists.

Tory. The first Tories were seventeenth-century bog-trotting Irish outlaws. The word itself comes from an ancient Irish or Gaelic word, *toruidhe,* meaning "robber or pursuer." They were the first of many generations of Irish rebels who fought against the invading English soldiers and settlers. Later the word *Tory* came to be applied to relatively respectable Irish Catholics who supported the Royalist cause. The name came over to England during the period of the so-called Glorious Revolution (1688–1689), when King James II was deposed for attempting to restore Roman Catholicism as the official religion of England. That was when our namesakes, William and Mary of Orange, were invited to take the throne. Thereafter the *Tories* were one of the two official political parties in Great Britain, at first opposing the Whigs, later the Liberals and still later the Labourites. So it was only logical that the rightists or loyalists in the American colonies during the time of the Revolution should be dubbed *Tories*. Incidentally, while *Tory* remains a common newspaper term—especially popular with headline writers— the official designation of the party was changed long ago to "Conservative."

to the bitter end has nothing to do with *bitter* in the usual sense but was originally a nautical phrase. Aboard ship, a *bitt* is a post in the deck around which cables and ropes are wound. The ends of these ropes which are nearest the *bitts* are the *bitter ends*. If the anchor cable were let out *to the bitter end,* the ship would be much more subject to misfortune and possible shipwreck. Hence, the phrase came to mean "to the very end" or even "until death."

to the manner born. At first glance, it seems that there might be more logic in the phrase "to the manor born," if you merely mean "born to high estate or riches"—these being symbolized, of course, by the manor house. However, *to the manner born* is the correct phrasing, since the meaning of the expression is actually "fitted by birth or endowment for a certain position in life." As Hamlet puts it (Act I, Scene 4): "But to my mind—though I am native here/And *to the manner born*—it is a custom/More honored in the breach than the observance."

tour de force comes direct from French and means "feat of strength or skill." It is pronounced toor-duh-FORSS.

tournedos (note the final *s*) is a fillet of beef cut from the tip of the tenderloin, often bound in bacon or suet for cooking. It's pronounced TOOR-neh-doh, though the French put the stress on the final syllable. The plural is the same as the singular: *tournedos.*

towhead is a person—usually a young person—who has very blond hair, almost flaxen or pale yellow. "Tow" has for centuries been used as a name for flax or hemp prepared for spinning.

toxicologist comes from the Greek words *toxikon* (poison) and *logos* (word or thought). But there's more to the story of toxicology than that, for the Greek *toxikon* came from an earlier word, *toxon,* meaning "bow," and referred to the fact that the earliest poisons were those in which arrows were dipped before being shot at the enemy.

trade-last, or *T.L.,* is a bit hard to trace. Charles Earle Funk once reported that he had heard it first on Staten Island about 1890, but agreed that it was probably much older. Other authorities have reported it in Kansas shortly after the Civil War. Anyway, it means not merely a compliment but a flattering remark which the speaker will report if his listener will first give him a compliment. In other words, he is holding his compliment in reserve to "trade it last."

transistor gets its name from the first syllable of "transfer" and the last two syllables of "resistor." Its function is to control and amplify an electron current in a manner similar to that of a vacuum tube but without the use of a vacuum and with much lower power consumption. However, what makes the transistor the modern miracle of electronic science is its almost infinitesimally minute size. Scarcely any larger than a phonograph needle, it is less than one-thousandth the size of the vacuum tube whose functions it performs.

trifle tiddly. Some of the remarks made by actors in old British movies are puzzling to Americans who have seen these movies on television. If, for example, "Marybelle seemed just a *trifle tiddly,* " she had indulged a craving for spirits a bit too much and was giddy or spiffed but not plastered.

triphibious. A *triphibious* assault is an attack launched from land, sea and air. It's an improperly coined word, by the way. The *tri* for "three" is all right, but the word-makers fluffed on the second part. They took *phibious* from "amphibious," not realizing that the latter word in Greek was *amphibios,* "leading a double life," from *amphi* (on both sides) and *bios* (life). So the logical coinage would have been "tribios," omitting the "phi."

Tripos is a term used at Cambridge University to designate the three classes of honor ("honour" in England) students as ranked in competitive examinations for the A.B. degree in mathematics, natural science and the rest. *Tripos* originally was a three-legged stool on which a graduate sat during the commencement ceremonies and disputed in bantering fashion with the degree candidates. Later the verses created by the *Tripos* wit were published and, for reasons now obscure, the list of candidates qualified for the honors degree in mathematics was printed on the back of this sheet. Thus the three-legged stool finally became the symbol of the exam itself.

trip the light fantastic means to dance gaily, and comes from Milton's poem "L'Allegro." It's the one that begins "Haste thee, Nymph, and bring with thee Jest and youthful Jollity." Further on we come to: "Sport that wrinkled Care derides,/And Laughter holding both his sides./Come, and trip it as ye go/On the *light fantastic* toe." But the expression gained its greatest popularity in the lyrics of "The Sidewalks of New York": "Boys and girls together, me and Mamie O'Rourke,/*Tripped the light fantastic* on the sidewalks of New York."

triskaidekaphobia/triskaidekaphile. A reader queried whether there isn't a word for the fear of the number 13. Indeed there is. It's *triskaidekaphobia,* pronounced tris-ky-dek-uh-FOH-bee-uh. It's derived from the Greek words *triskaideka* (thirteen) and *phobia* (fear). Your word man happens to be a charter member of the Society of *Triskaidekaphiles,* people who dote on the number 13. As a matter of fact, he had little choice in the matter, having been born on the thirteenth of April in 1913. What's more, if you count the letters in William Morris, you will see that they total 13.

troll is a creature of Scandinavian mythology—indeed, the word is found in both Old Norse and Swedish. *Trolls* were first a race of giants; later—such is the flexibility of folklore—they became a race of little people who lived in caves.

truck farm. Many people share the notion that a *truck farm* is a farm close enough to urban centers that its produce may be transported by truck to the city. However, there is no connection whatever between truck farms and motor transportation. Long before motor trucks were even dreamed of—at least as far back as 1785—the word *truck* was used to mean garden vegetables intended for sale in the markets. In fact, we have here an excellent example of the confusion that can develop from homonyms— words which are identical in spelling and pronunciation but very different in meaning. Often, to unravel the complexities, one has to go back to the root of each word. In this case, the *truck* that is a vehicle for transporting freight comes from the Greek word *trochos,* meaning "wheel." However, *truck* meaning originally any commodities for sale and, later, garden produce for market comes from an entirely different root, *troque,* the Old French word for "barter."

trumped-up charges. The *trump* in this phrase comes from the same root as the word "trumpet," in that both owe their origin to the French word *tromper,* which once meant "to play on the trumpet" and now means "to deceive." Gradually—and perhaps by analogy to the card-game use of *trump* (from the French *triomphe)*—the word came to mean "cheat or deceive." Thus *trumped-up charges* are spurious, deceitful charges concocted out of whole cloth.

try out. *Trying out,* in the sense of extracting oil or fat from a substance by heating it, is not commonly heard these days but goes back to the Elizabethans. Perhaps the commonest use of the term in this country was in the whaling industry. As all readers of *Moby Dick* will recall, great *trying* vats were carried on some of the whaling vessels to reduce whale blubber to valuable and more readily transportable whale oil.

tryst. Not always has *tryst* had the romantic meaning of a clandestine meeting of young lovers. Spelled *tristre* in Middle English and Old French, it meant a hunting station or place of rendezvous for hunters.

T.S. slip. One treatment frequently indicated for the chronic complainers among World War II servicemen was the issuance of a *T.S. slip.* Roughly translated, that means "tough stuff slip." As it happens, William had occasion to issue more than one of these slips in his capacity as platoon leader, during the early training period of the war. Just recently, while inspecting moth holes in the old uniforms, he came across one of the slips. Here is its well-remembered text: "Your trials and tribulations have broken my heart. They are unique. I have never heard anything like them before. As proof of my deepest sympathy, I give you this card which entitles you to one hour of condolence from the nearest chaplain."

tsunami is a Japanese word meaning "storm wave." It is gradually coming into quite general use, especially in the Pacific area, where it is loosely used as a synonym for *tidal wave.* Pronounced tsoo-NAH-me, such storm waves start as a result of an earthquake or volcanic eruption. When they occur, they radiate in a way similar to the spreading of ripples when a pebble is dropped into a pond—except that they are monstrously more dangerous. *Tsunamis* are long and low and may travel as fast as 400 miles per hour. On the open sea they are almost imperceptible, but when they reach shallow water near shore they form waves twenty feet high. They have been known to cause great havoc in the Hawaiian Islands, Japan and India.

tulipomania started in the 1630s when the acquisition of beautiful tulips suddenly became a mad passion with Dutchmen. As they bid against each other for the choicest specimens, prices began to soar and speculators all over the continent and in Britain became involved. About 1636, when the rage reached its peak, a single bulb was sold at more than £500—and that, even at the most conservative estimate, would be at least five thousand of today's dollars. Soon brokers were selling "futures" in tulips and eager investors were buying prodigiously on margin. It couldn't last, of course, and when the market finally broke, disaster was widespread. That was the end of history's only recorded botanical boom and bust.

tune the old cow died of is a British expression meaning that advice is always in large supply, when it's really help that's needed. According to a relevant verse: "There was an old man and he had an old cow,/But he had no fodder to give her./So he took up his fiddle and played her the tune:/'Consider, good cow, consider./This isn't the time for the grass to grow,/Consider, good cow, consider.' " Presumably the good cow considered—and then keeled over.

tu quoque, a Latin phrase (pronounced too KWOH-kweh or too KWOH-kwih), simply means "You're another" or "You too."

turkey. We were talking with Albert Hague, composer of *Red Head* and several other Broadway musicals, and asked him his theory of the origin of *turkey,* meaning a show that flops. "Easy," he replied, showing his native talent for instant folk etymology. "Turkeys are shows that open on Thursday night." We restrained the impulse to remind him that his own show *Fig Leaves Are Falling* opened and closed on a Saturday night. But he saw from our expression that we had this fact in mind. "Being philosophical about that disaster," he remarked, "I bear in mind the fact that opening and closing on the same night is not the worst thing that ever happened on Broadway. There was one show we tried out at the Lambs. Club that folded after the first act."

turkey talk. Guinea fowl with *fenberry sauce* and a choice of *askutasquash* or *misickquatash* sounds like a bizarre menu, doesn't it? Yet the chances are that some or all of these foods appear on your table at least once a year. For these are the original names for the staples of the Thanksgiving Day feast: turkey, cranberry sauce, squash and succotash. The original settlers did not bring turkeys with them. They found a wild fowl somewhat similar in appearance to the guinea fowl they had known in England—a fowl that had acquired the common name *turkey* from the fact that it was at one time imported to Europe by way of Turkey. Thus a native American wild fowl acquired the truly exotic and rather inappropriate name of *turkey*.

But the early explorers had already set a pattern of blundering in the application of names to their discoveries. Amerigo Vespucci, the same who gave his name to our country, and Columbus himself were half a world away when they named the natives *Indians*, mistakenly thinking that our continent was Asia and that the inhabitants were natives of India. So the Pilgrim fathers can be forgiven a goof or two in their choice of names for the viands that grace our tables. And surely they did us all a favor by shortening *askutasquash* to just plain "squash" and *misickquatash*—both "Indian" names—to "succotash." And the *fenberry sauce?* Well, the cranberry was known in England as "fenberry." Not until the Dutch settlers came over many years later did the name "cranberry" come into English from their *kranbeere*.

turnpike. The pike, in olden days, was a pole, set on a vertical post, so as to bar movement along a road. When the fee was paid, the pike was turned and the traveler passed through and along his way. Because early toll roads were the most important highways, the term *turnpike* (often shortened to *pike*) came in time to be applied to any important road.

turtle/turtledove. The word *turtle* means a bird in the Bible and an amphibious reptile in modern English. Though spelled the same, these turtles are quite different. Let's take the bird first. This, more properly called the *turtledove*, was a small European and Mediterranean dove, notable for its white-edged black tail and its mournful coo. It was sometimes called the "mourning dove." Its name came from the Latin word *turtur*, which attempted to duplicate the sound of the dove's coo.

The other turtle, the one we see in swamps and soup, was originally called *tortuga* in Spanish—the same name as "tortoise," because the turtle and the tortoise are one and the same, though some people tend to think of the tortoise as only the dry-land version, probably from the popularity of the hare-and-tortoise fable. Anyhow, *tortuga* became *tortue* in French and then, when taken into English, became *turtle,* thanks to the influence of the *turtle(dove)* which had arrived in English a few centuries earlier.

tuxedo. Tuxedo Park, about forty miles north of New York City on the west bank of the Hudson River, was a famous and very exclusive residential community late in the nineteenth century. Astors, Goulds, Harrimans and the like were to be found there and lavish were the formal parties they gave. One dandy among the socialites—his name is lost to history—became irked with the awkward tails on his formal full-dress coat and had his tailor run up the first tailless dinner coat. It was an immediate sensation and, because of its greater convenience, soon replaced the tail coat on all but the most formal occasions. The new jacket, which *Harper's* magazine described in 1894 as a "hybrid garment," quickly became known as the Tuxedo coat, and by the turn of the century was simply called a *tuxedo. Tuxedo* comes from the Algonquian Indian word *p' tuksit,* meaning the "animal with the round foot"—the wolf. So a *tuxedo*-clad gay blade is a wolf in wolf's clothing.

twenty-one gun salute. Here is the official explanation of the *twenty-one gun salute,* from the chief of the news branch of the U.S. Army Public Information Division:

> The firing of gun salutes dates back to the early days of the British Navy. At that time guns could not be loaded quickly so the act of firing one in a salute indicated that the saluter had disarmed himself in deference to the person being saluted. The larger the number of guns fired, the greater the degree of disarmament. Since twenty-one guns was the number found on one side of one of the larger "ships of the line," firing all of them became the highest mark of respect, reserved for heads of state. Smaller numbers of guns were fired in salutes to people of lesser importance. But for all salutes only odd numbers are used, reflecting the old seagoing superstition against even numbers. This form of saluting was first recognized in the United States in 1875. As Commander-in-Chief, the President is accorded the highest salute of twenty-one guns.

twenty-three skiddoo. Here are two possible explanations of the old slang expression *twenty-thrée skiddoo.* The first is that a character in a play adapted from Dickens's *A Tale of Two Cities* counted off the number of people being guillotined in the final scene. The hero was number twenty-three—and the expression became a favorite of theater folk to indicate the time to leave, especially with *skiddoo* added. Another version dates back to the 1890s, when the Flatiron Building at Twenty-third Street and Broadway in New York was the town's first skyscraper and its most glamorous building. The corner was also considered 'he city's windiest, so gallant blades of the day used to hang out on Twenty-third Street waiting for the breezes to lift the skirts of passing ladies. But policemen, then as always, disapproved of such unseemly loitering. Hence their order: *"Twenty-three skiddoo."*

two bits. *Bit* was originally British slang for any kind of small coin. Thus a Cockney street vendor might speak of "a threepenny [pronounced thruppenny] bit." But in the Southwest United States, more than two centuries ago, Mexican currency was used interchangeably with the local coinage and the *real* (pronounced RAY-ahl)—a coin worth about twelve and a half cents American—was called a *bit.* So when the U.S. quarter-dollar piece was coined, it was quickly called *two bits.*

two shakes of a lamb's tail. This well-known farmer's expression occasioned a query from a reader. Why, she wanted to know, is it always a lamb's tail, never a pig's tail or a cow's tail? The answer would be obvious to anyone who had spent much time on a farm. The curlicue that passes for a pig's tail doesn't *shake* very well; it may squiggle and turn, but not shake. And the shaking of a cow's tail is a very model of tranquil ease and patient gradualness. Even when flies are most pestiferous on the hottest days of summer, the sweep of a cow's tail in the direction of her tormentors is a slow and easy motion. By contrast, the shaking of a lamb's tail is so brisk that it's over almost before you know it has started. As to the origin of this expression, it is reported as appearing in print as long ago as 1840, which means it must be much older than that. It is probably the rural American version of the expression *two shakes,* originally a gambler's expression. "I'll be finished in *two shakes"* meant "I'll be done in no time at all." The shakes referred to were *shakes* of dice in a cup or dice box.

Typhoid Mary. The original *Typhoid Mary* was an Irish cook named Mary Mallon, who lived and worked in New York and was found to be a carrier of typhoid. No date of birth is given for her, but she died in 1938. Her nickname is applied to any person who, according to *Webster's New World Dictionary,* "spreads any kind of disease, infection or corruption."

UFO/U.F.O., Pronounced YOO-ef-oh, this is an acronym for Unidentified Flying Objects, the so-called flying saucers.

umbrella is a borrowing from the Italian *ombrella,* meaning "little shade." We tend to think of umbrellas today as devices to protect us from rain but, especially in Mediterranean countries like Italy, ladies originally used them to protect their faces from the blazing sun.

unalienable/inalienable. One aspect of the Declaration of Independence that has long puzzled scholars is Thomas Jefferson's use of *unalienable* in the reference "that all men are endowed by their Creator with certain unalienable rights." The word appears virtually nowhere else in all our literature. Most dictionaries mark it "archaic" and define it with the single word *inalienable.* Why this curious aberration in the work of one of our finest prose stylists? Eugene F. Jannuzi of Beaver Falls, Pennsylvania may have the solution. "In facsimiles I have seen," he writes, "Thomas Jefferson clearly wrote *inalienable* in his rough draft. The word was changed to *unalienable* either by the Continental Congress, which made many changes, additions and deletions in the rough draft, or by the printer who put the Declaration on broadsides." Both words mean "not to be taken away" or "not to be transferred to another," and both come from the Latin *alienus* (other).

Uncle! is an expression commonly used to mean "Enough" or "I give up." The earliest record of it in print is around 1910, but it may be much older. We have turned up one theory, which you may believe if you want to. It goes all the way back to ancient Rome. When a Roman youngster got into trouble, so the story goes, he would yell *"Patrue mi patruissime"*—*"Uncle, my best of uncles!"*

Uncle Sam. The first characterization of our national spirit or tradition was in the figure Brother Jonathan, a shrewd Yankee in a play, *The Contrast,* by Royall Tyler, produced in 1787. It was our first comedy. Then, during the War of 1812, a meat-packer in Troy, New York, named Samuel Wilson was jokingly called "Uncle Sam" by his employees, in reference to the "U.S." stamped on food containers intended for the armed services. Gradually over the decades, *Uncle Sam* took over as the national symbol and Brother Jonathan faded into the footnotes of history. In 1832 a lithograph —unsigned—appeared called "Uncle Sam in Danger." It attacked the plan of Andrew Jackson to destroy the Bank of the United States, something he eventually accomplished—and without any lasting damage to the nation. However, the first picture of *Uncle Sam* as we know him today appeared in *Harper's* magazine in 1869. It looked forward to the first of the America's Cup races between Great Britain and the United States, which took place the next year. The cartoon showed Uncle Sam—top hat, striped trousers and all—holding the America's Cup aloft and smiling confidently while the British symbol, John Bull, glowers meancingly from across the ocean. The thrust of the cartoon is that America was bound to win. And that's the way it turned out—not only in that first race in 1870 but in every America's Cup race since.

Uncle Tom comes from the name of the chief character, a Negro slave, in Harriet Beecher Stowe's *Uncle Tom's Cabin,* the abolitionist novel (1851–1852) which Abraham Lincoln once credited with having helped start the Civil War. Blacks have long used the phrase as a term of opprobrium and abuse for members of their race who have sold out to the white man, who pander to "Whitey," so to speak. In fact, the term has become so common that it's usually used without the *Uncle* and an "establishment" black is simply a *Tom.*

unclubbable, meaning a person who would not fit well into a club, was used by none other than Dr. Samuel Johnson, a very clubbable type himself. A fellow member of his literary club was Sir John Hawkins, whose name lives today chiefly because Sam once put him down as "a very *unclubbable* man."

unctuous. Perhaps the most *unctuous* character in English literature was Uriah Heep in Dickens's *David Copperfield,* the very epitome of hypocritical flattery and smarmy sanctimoniousness. The sense of slipperiness always characteristic of Heep is readily understood when we look into the origin of *unctuous.* It comes from the Latin *unctum,* meaning "ointment" —and you can't get a substance much more slippery than ointment.

underground. The first general use of *underground* in the United States was in reference to the *underground* railroad which functioned from the early years of the nineteenth century until the Civil War, helping fugitive slaves to freedom. Various "stations" were set up along a variety of routes and as many as 100,000 former slaves found freedom in the North and in Canada. During World War II various *underground* newspapers were issued in countries occupied by the Axis powers and their contributions to sustaining the morale of the resistance fighters were reportedly very great. During the student revolts of the late 1960s a number of anti-Establishment papers sprang up. Some called them *underground,* but the editors of the few that lasted preferred "alternate press."

understander. Not the most spectacular but certainly the sturdiest one in the act, the *understander,* in circus slang, is the one whose shoulders carry the full weight of the acrobatic team.

under the hammer, meaning up for sale at auction, comes from the auctioneer's practice of tapping his hammer on the table when he regards the bidding as complete.

under the rose. Rather a romantic tale lies behind this expression, which is, incidentally, a direct translation of the Latin phrase *sub rosa.* According to ancient legend, the Greek god of silence, Harpocrates, stumbled upon Venus, the goddess of love, in the course of one of her amorous adventures. Cupid, Venus's son, happened along at an opportune moment and, by making a gift of a rose to Harpocrates, bought his pledge of secrecy. Since that time the rose has been the symbol of silence. During the Renaissance and later during the reigns of the pre-Revolutionary kings of France, the rose was a favorite architectural motif and often was sculptured on ceilings of dining and drawing rooms where diplomats gathered. The obvious implication was that matters discussed *under the rose* were considered to be held in confidence. A phrase often whispered at such diplomatic gatherings was: *Sub vino sub rosa est—*"What one says under the influence of wine is secret."

under the weather. When you're at sea and the weather becomes a bit rough and the ship starts to roll and your stomach feels a bit queasy, it's time for you to go below to your cabin—*under the weather.*

underwhelmed doesn't mean quite what you think. It's the opposite of "overwhelmed," to be sure, but it's usually employed when some device or presentation planned to make a big impression fails to have that effect. One story of its origin is traced to the late and legendary Mike Todd of *Around the World in 80 Days* fame. He was casting for a Broadway show and an agent promoted a new act with the customary line about how it was the greatest thing since the great Houdini, an absolute show-stopper and so on. When the act finished its audition, Mike murmured, "I'm *underwhelmed"* —and that was the end of it.

UNESCO. Acronym for United Nations Educational, Scientific and Cultural Organization.

unflappable. Most dictionaries define this word as just the opposite of "flappable," but there is more to it than that. "Imperturbable," "calm," "not readily excited or upset" are synonyms that come quickly to mind. The whole thing started in the 1950s with a slang meaning of "flap" which caught on quickly both in England and here. A "flap" was consternation, frenzied excitement or confusion. More often than not, the flap turned out to be much ado about nothing. Still earlier, British airmen at the time of the Battle of Britain had used "flap" to mean an air raid alarm—but that was in an entirely serious connection.

The term *unflappable* became widely used in the 1960s as an epithet applied to British Prime Minister Harold Macmillan, who seemed able to maintain unshakable calm no matter what dangers threatened his steadily eroding empire. "Mac the *Unflappable"* was his nickname—and there's no evidence that this rather disrespectful label ever caused him to flap either.

UNICEF. Acronym for United Nations Children's Fund. Originally United Nations International Children's Emergency Fund.

unicorn was the fabled beast of mythology resembling a horse but with a goatish beard and a lion's tail—and one horn sprouting from its brow. Its name comes from the Latin *unus* (one) and *cornu* (horn).

union suit/long johns/body suit. The expression was originally "union undergarment" and applied to both men's and women's underwear. The "union" comes from the fact that it's all one piece—top and bottom being joined in "union." Back in 1896 the famous *Godey's Lady's Book* was assuring its readers that in the higher levels of society, "Union undergarments of silk or wool are often substituted." The temptation is great to say that the *union suit* has gone the way of the union station—but a glance at the current Sears catalogue shows that *union suits* are still very much a part of the menswear picture. They're even being modishly styled with and without sleeves and with full or half-length legs. Rather a far cry from the *long johns* of grandfather's day. And why were they called *long johns?*

Well, a *long john* was originally any lean, lanky man. Quite possibly the undergarment got its name because a lean, lanky man looked especially incongruous in it. Today's feminine version of the *union suit* is called a *body suit,* is made out of synthetic fabric and covers the feet, too, which a *union suit* did not.

Mention of *long johns* always recalls to mind the New York stage debut of Jimmy Stewart, with whom William Morris did a stint in the old University Players. The play was George Abbott's production of *Three Men on a Horse.* Jimmy's role was wordless. At the end of the second act the three horse players are huddled over a poker game. Suddenly from downstage right Stewart emerges, clad only in *long johns,* races across the stage, exiting up left, while one of the players shouts: "Where do you think you are? The Park Central Hotel?" Curtain. It never failed to bring down the house.

United Nations. The term *United Nations* was first used during World War II to describe the alliance of nations—chiefly the United States, Russia and members of the British Commonwealth, plus various governments in exile —that were united in the war against the Axis powers, Germany, Italy and Japan. In 1945, when the war was drawing to a close, the international organization we now know as the U.N. was organized in San Francisco as U.N.O. (United Nations Organization), a name it still carries in many countries. Henry L. Mencken, in his *American Language,* quotes this account of the naming of the U.N.: *"United Nations* was coined by President Franklin Roosevelt. This was during Winston Churchill's visit to Washington at the end of December, 1941. He was a guest at the White House, and he and Churchill discussed the choice of a name for the new alliance. One morning, lying in bed, Roosevelt thought of *United Nations,* and at once sought Churchill, who was in his bath. 'How about *United Nations?'* he called through the door. 'That,' replied Churchill, 'should do it.' And so it was."

unmentionables. Today when this term is used at all it is as a joking reference to undergarments. In the Victorian era, however, with prudery rampant, *unmentionables* included men's breeches ("britches" in America) and trousers, and of course women's petticoats and the like.

until the last dog is hung. The earliest appearance of this phrase in print that we have been able to locate is in a novel by Stewart Edward White. Called *The Blazed Trail,* it was published in 1902 and contains this line: "They were loyal. It was a point of honor with them to stay *'until the last dog was hung.'* " White spent much of his early life on the frontier, first in the West, later in the Hudson Bay country. We would hazard the guess that the original "dogs" being hung were of the human species and that the reference is to the kind of vigilante lynchings known as "necktie parties" in the early West. Nowadays, of course, the expression is most often heard in reference to the inevitable two or three people at every cocktail party who hang around everlastingly—*until the last dog is hung* and the host shows them the door.

unusual words. Ten somewhat out-of-the-ordinary words were used as elements in the cover design of the paperback edition of one of our books, *It's Easy to Increase Your Vocabulary.* The words seem to have been chosen because they lie just on the outer fringes of the average vocabulary, representative of words you would like to have in your working vocabulary but may not quite have mastered. Let's look at the ten words.

Ameliorate (pronounced uh-MEEL-yor-ayt)—To make better, to improve. This comes direct from the Latin *ad* (to) and *melior* (better).

Culpable (KUL-puh-b'l)—Blameworthy, deserving of censure. Again, this comes from the Latin: *culpa* (blame).

Equivocate (ih-KWIV-uh-kayt)—To hedge; to use double-talk in an effort to mislead or deceive. Again from the Latin, this word literally means to speak with two voices: *aequi* (equal) and *vocare* (to call). So you see, our idea of "double-talk" is anything but new.

Esoteric (es-oh-TEHR-ik)—Intended for a chosen few, the insiders. This comes from the Greek *esoteros* (inner).

Extirpate (EK-ster-payt)—To root out, destroy completely, from the Latin *ex* (out) and *stirps* (root).

Incipient (in-SIP-ee-unt)—Just beginning to exist, from the Latin *in* (in, on) and *capere* (take).

Inveterate (in-VET-er-it)—Firmly established, deep-rooted. Again this is from Latin: *in* (in) and *vetus* (old).

Jocose (joh-KOHSS)—Humorous, facetious, from the Latin *jocus* (a joke).

Mitigate (MIT-ih-gayt)—Make less severe, from the Latin *mitis* (mild) and *agere* (do).

Reprehensible (rep-rih-HEN-sih-b'l)—Deserving to be censured or rebuked. Again our source is Latin: *re* (back) and *prehendere* (take).

Whether or not you agree with our editors that these ten words are enough out of the ordinary to be interesting, you must agree that this is a striking indication of the debt English owes to the classical languages of Greece and Rome.

upbeat is a term borrowed from music, where it means an unaccented beat on which the conductor's hand is raised—most especially the final beat of a measure. It's used by extension to mean happy or cheerful: "His novel has an *upbeat* ending."

upcoming/up-and-coming. *Upcoming* is a journalistic version of "coming up" and indicates futurity. Instead of "The Yankees have two big games coming up," you may find "The Yankees' two big *upcoming* games are with . . ." This kind of verbal shorthand is commonly used in "cablese," a style of writing notable for its compounded words and often used by newsmen to economize on cable charges for foreign dispatches. *Up-and-coming* is a well-established colloquial phrase meaning "enterprising, ambitious and promising." You'll hear it in sentences like: "That new salesman certainly seems to be an *up-and-coming* chap."

up Salt River is an old American political expression. When one campaigner takes his rival *"up Salt River,"* he has beaten him—usually decisively and sometimes by trickery. For many years it was believed that this expression came from an actual experience of Henry Clay during his 1832 campaign against Andrew Jackson. The story went that Clay hired a boatman to take him up the Ohio River to Louisville, Kentucky, where he was to make an important speech. The boatman—a loyal Jacksonian—took him *up Salt River* instead. So Clay never made the speech and, needless to say, never was elected President. However, scholars are never content to let a good story stand. So a few years ago Hans Sperber of Ohio State and James Tidwell of San Diego State reported in *American Speech* magazine that the expression was several years older than the Jackson-Clay campaign. The *Dictionary of Americanisms* also indicates that the expression appeared in a Cincinnati newspaper in 1830. So it appears that the ill-fated Henry Clay didn't even leave a good story for us to remember him by.

up the creek and its fuller form, *up the creek without a paddle,* are somewhat laundered versions of a very commonly heard expression. The meaning—to become trapped in an awkward or embarrassing situation—is obvious. Just who was the first person trapped *up the creek* is not a matter of record.

up the river was originally an underworld term for a sentence in a reformatory or jail. It probably derives from the fact that New York State's most famous prison, Sing Sing, is *up the river* from New York City.

up to snuff. Originally the expression *up to snuff* meant "sharp, keen, wise, all-knowing." Presumably it got this meaning because a person who has just sniffed some snuff would have a brief sense of exhilaration and might feel that he was a lot brighter than other people. Gradually the term came to be applied more and more to a person's physical condition. If you feel *up to snuff* nowadays, you feel that you're in good shape, in normal good health.

used-car dealers' jargon. Every trade has its own private language or jargon, whose chief purpose is to permit workers in the trade to converse with each other without an outsider's knowing what they are talking about. For example, if you hear one salesman talking to another refer to a used car as a *load,* an *orphan* or *a dog*—watch out! He may play you for a *schlemiel* and try to sell you a *load* which has *had its clock kicked.*

TRANSLATION: *Load, orphan, pig, dog, off-breed* and *iron* all designate poor cars. A *schlemiel* is an easy mark, a naïve and trusting buyer. And a car whose clock has been *kicked* is one whose speedometer has been set back. In the trade this is called a *fufnick.*

If you are a *flea* or a *murderer*—a person who bargains shrewdly and demands top value—you will be sure to check the *grippers* (brakes), the *juice box* (battery), the *glimmers* (headlights) and the *mill* (engine). Unless you have a large family you won't be interested in a *moose* (very large car). And while you're checking it over, take a good look at the *snortpipe* (exhaust) for signs of wear and, especially if you live in the North, you'll want to ask about *slushers* (chains) and *liquor* (antifreeze).

U.S.S. These three letters stand for "United States Ship," and may be used only with the names of ships of the U.S. Navy. The abbreviation *S.S.* (as in *S.S. America*) means "steamship" and is generally used for ships of all nationalities. Worth noting, perhaps, is that the initials *H.M.S.* appear only on ships in the British service and stand for "His/Her Majesty's Service." The initials *M.S.* designate a motor (rather than steam) ship.

usufructs is a word derived from the Latin *usufructus,* meaning the use and enjoyment of property that is not one's own, such as the many perquisites that go with presidential office—private jets, limousines, vacation retreats and a host of other special privileges. Incidentally, it's pronounced YOO-zuh-frukts.

V1/V2. These were the designations for two "robot bombs" used by the Germans in the last months of World War II to bomb London from bases across the English Channel. The *V1* was a relatively small, gyroscopically controlled winged missile, bearing explosives and propelled by jet fuel. The *V2* was much larger and more lethal, the first true ballistic missile. It was a long-range liquid-fuel rocket, a prototype of the rockets developed later for the exploration of outer space. The *V*'s in the names of these two weapons of war were abbreviations for *Vergeltungswaffe,* German for "retaliation weapon." The *V2* was a product of experimental research carried on at the German base at Peenemünde under the direction of Wernher von Braun. Years later he was the subject of a filmed autobiography, *We Aim at the Stars,* which moved British-born essayist Alistair Cooke to add wryly "and usually hit London."

vade mecum. As comment on the practice of ending sentences with prepositions, Professor Morris Bishop, one of our most distinguished teachers and past president of the Modern Language Association, wrote the following: "I lately lost a preposition;/It hid, I thought, beneath my chair/And angrily I cried 'perdition!/Up from out of in under there!'/Correctness is my *vade mecum,*/And straggling phrases I abhor./And yet I wondered, 'What should he come/Up from out of in under for?' "

Wondering about Professor Bishop's *vade mecum?* Well, it's a Latin phrase, literally translated as "go with me," and means something carried about for constant reference, such as a handbook.

vagabond has long had a romantic swashbuckling sound about it—witness Rudolf Friml's *Vagabond King*. But it was not always thus. The word, derived from the Latin *vagabundus* (one who wanders), originally meant an itinerant rogue, a disreputable idler, loafer or vagrant. Indeed, in the King James Bible (Genesis 4:12) the curse of the Lord upon Cain for the murder of Abel is "a fugitive and a vagabond shalt thou be in the earth." But now a *vagabond* is a figure of romance, not far removed from W. S. Gilbert's "wandering minstrel."

vagary (pronounced vuh-GAIR-ee) like *vagabond* is derived from the Latin *vagari* (to wander) and means "a whim or a wild fancy." In earlier use *vagary* meant "a ramble," but it is no longer used in this way.

vamoose came into our language from a source many hundreds of miles away from the habitat of the *moose*. Specifically, it is a word that early Texan cowboys picked up from the Mexican vaqueros. The word comes from the Spanish *vamos,* meaning "let's go." Most commonly it was used when there was some pressing reason for a hasty departure. Something along the lines of: "*Vamoose,* boys, here comes the law!"

vamp is thought by most people to be a word from the 1920s to designate the sirens of the screen who typified those days. Now it turns out that *vamp,* as an old-fashioned term for "volunteer fireman," must go back at least to the mid nineteenth century and be one of the earliest acronyms. Andrew Bernhard, who was editor of the *Pittsburgh Post-Gazette and Sun-Telegraph* for many years, wrote us as follows: "In 1940 when I became managing editor of the now gone *Brooklyn Eagle,* I was puzzled by the numerous stories of the *vamps* of this or that Long Island community. When several members of the staff were unable to explain the origin of the word, I took the matter up with our city editor, Howard Swain. Mr. Swain explained that the word was formed by the use of the initials of Voluntary Association of Master Pumpers, that being the name of the organization to which volunteer firemen belonged. If he was right—and the explanation does seem pat—it must go back a long time. Firemen have not, I believe, been called *pumpers* for many decades."

But how did *vamp* also come to mean a seductive woman? About 1914, Theda Bara played the part of a vampire in the movie *A Fool There Was.* Her mannerisms and dress led to the shortened form of *vamp* to mean "a woman who entices men" or, as a verb, to do so. It was Rudyard Kipling's poem "The Vampire" that supplied the movie's title (from the first line) and plot—such as it was. It went: "A fool there was and he made his prayer/(Even as you and I)/To a rag, a bone, and a hank of hair./We called her the woman who did not care—/But the fool he called her his lady fair —/(Even as you and I)."

There is also *vamp* as a musical notation—a short introduction before the verse of a popular song, usually marked "*Vamp* till ready," meaning that the accompanist will play certain short measures over and over until the singer or dancer is ready to start. *Webster's* indicates that it may have been originally a cobbler's term—a shoe repaired ("revamped") by changing its vamp—from which it came to mean any minor improvisation, including the vamping of a few bars of music. We can't say we're wild about that explanation, but it will have to do.

van, in the expression "in the *van,*" is short for "vanguard," which in turn is the English equivalent of the French term *avant-garde*—the advance guard. It originally meant that part of an army which moved into battle ahead of the main forces. Nowadays it means any person or group of persons that has moved well to the forefront of a mass movement.

vandal. The first *Vandals* were an East German warrior clan which sacked Rome in the year 455. So devastating was their destruction of the imperial city that their name has ever since been synonymous with reckless destruction.

vantage loaf is the thirteenth loaf in a baker's dozen. In medieval times some communities exacted severe penalties from bakers who had been found guilty of short-weighing their customers. So bakers adopted the practice of adding the thirteenth to every dozen loaves, rolls or whatever. *Vantage* at this time had the sense of "an additional amount or sum," a meaning that is now archaic.

varsity. Whenever William hears a reference to a high school *varsity* football team, it reminds him of a quixotic and wholly futile effort on the part of one of the masters at Exeter to preserve what he considered to be the true meaning of *varsity.* The venerable gentleman was named Tufts and was already in retirement. But each fall old "Tuffy" would come out of retirement at the start of the football season to deliver a lecture on the misuse of *varsity.* "Since *varsity* is a contraction of *university,*" he would declaim, "its use should be limited to college and university teams. We should proudly boast of our Exeter *school team,* not of our *varsity.*" The boys all listened with proper respect to the wise old man and turned out the following Saturday to cheer—of course—the *varsity.*

Vatican is synonymous with the Papacy, the home of the Pope, the world-famous center of the Roman Catholic faith. But long before the birth of Christ the *Vatican* was famed as one of the hills of Rome where soothsayers and prophets held forth. The Latin *vates* (prophet) is the word from which *Vatican* is ultimately derived.

vaudeville/variety. *Vaudeville* in its traditional form of a series of acts—usually eight—ranging from acrobatics to tap-dancing and comedy turns is dead, although there are those who feel that many TV shows are little more than *vaudeville* transposed from the theater to the television stage. The name *vaudeville* is a contraction of the French phrase *Chanson de Vau-de-Vire* (Song of the Valley of Vire). A noted minstrel of the fifteenth century, Olivier Basselin, composed many rollicking lighthearted songs which he labeled after the Vire section of Calvados in Normandy, his birthplace. Gradually the term came to be applied to an entire show made up of songs interspersed with other variety acts.

Variety as a synonym for *vaudeville* lives on chiefly as the name of the chief show business publication. It appears in two versions—a weekly published in New York City and a daily published in Hollywood. A typical recent issue of the weekly contained only three pages headed "Vaudeville," in contrast to twelve pages headed "Radio-Television" and twenty-four devoted to "Pictures." According to the *Oxford Dictionary,* the term *variety* as a shortened form of "variety performances" appeared in print as early as 1886. The *Dictionary of American English* records "variety troupe" as appearing in 1868 and Mencken notes that, in the form "varieties," it appeared as early as 1849.

Vendome. There were several *Vendômes* prominent in French history. In fact, the name was so prestigious that when Louis XIV laid out an especially elegant and imposing square in Paris north of the Seine he named it the Place Vendôme. Since then, the name *Vendome* has had a certain cachet of elegance, rather like "Ritz" as applied originally to hotels founded by the great Swiss hotelier César Ritz. His name even gave us the once-popular slang term *ritzy* (which see).

venison, from the Latin verb *venari* (to hunt), originally could be applied to any game animal taken in the hunt. Nowadays it is used only in reference to deer.

ventriloquism. The technique of throwing one's voice or, at least, making a voice seem to come from a dummy or object other than the person actually making the sounds gets its name from two Latin words: *venter* (belly) and *loqui* (speak). The old theory was that since the voice didn't seem to come from the mouth, it must come from the belly.

verb sap is short for the Latin phrase *verbum sapienti satis,* which means "a word to the wise is sufficient."

vernissage is used by art exhibitors and literally means "varnishing day." In earlier times the custom was to reserve the gallery on the day before the opening of an exhibit for the artist to use in touching up or varnishing paintings in his exhibit. Before long the artists fell into the habit of inviting a few friends along to keep them company. Now it simply means a preview reception for the artist's closest friends on the day before the exhibit formally opens.

vet. This rather odd verb has enjoyed a vogue among editors and teachers, in such phrases as "credit for *vetting* the manuscript" and "the plans may be *vetted* by your attorney." It is actually nothing more than a verb formed from the noun "veterinarian" and originally meant "to examine or treat as a veterinarian does." More recently it has come to be used—as the dictionaries say, "jocosely"—to mean any careful inspection of a document or manuscript.

vicissitude (pronounced vih-SISS-ih-tood) is "constantly occurring change," especially in fortune or condition. It is derived from the Latin *vicis* (a turn, change).

Vicki/Victoria. *Vicki* is the diminutive of *Victoria,* the feminine form of Victor. It comes directly from the Latin and means "victorious."

victuals/vittles. The word *victuals*—from the Latin *victualia,* meaning "food" or "provisions"—is pronounced VIT-t'ls, which has led to the erroneous spelling *vittles.* In the nineteenth century, when the word was much more common in America than it is today, such humorists as Petroleum V. Nasby and Bill Nye used to affect all sorts of deliberate misspellings in an effort to represent what they considered to be the dialects of farmers and frontiersmen. As a result, incidentally, their writings are all but unreadable today. One of the favorite misspellings of this school of humor was *vittles* for *victuals,* and since the word is rarely seen in print today, some people simply don't know the correct spelling of the word.

video, the name of the boob tube in the living room, is a direct borrowing from the Latin verb *video,* meaning "I see."

vigorish is the slang word for the percentage of a bet withheld by a bookmaker. The term is also sometimes used to mean the interest paid on a loan, especially one from a loan shark. *Vigorish* may have originated as a blend of Italian *vigoroso* and the German-Yiddish suffix *-ich.*

villain. There was a time when a *villain* was a poor but honest person, not the scoundrel he is today. In feudal England, the *villein* (as it was spelled then) was one of the many serfs of the lords who were the great landowners of the times. Although he was half free, he was a slave to his lord and master and could be sold as such. He got his name from the Latin *villanus* (farm servant), which in turn comes from *villa* (country seat or farm).

Vinland is the name given by early Norse voyagers to parts of North America visited by them in pre-Columbian times. There are any number of places claiming the honor of being the true *Vinland.* They range all the way from Nova Scotia to Rhode Island and even points farther south. However, to one of your authors there never has been the slightest question about the true location of *Vinland.* In his youth he often swam in the Charles River at a point called Gerry's Landing in Cambridge. There he often saw a small historical marker stating that on that precise point the Vikings had landed and named the spot *Vinland.* Who put the marker there and how much historical verification it had are entirely unknown at this late date. But the youthful memory persists and we'll need mighty powerful persuasion to be convinced that *Vinland* is anywhere other than at that precise point in Cambridge, Massachusetts.

visa. The *visa* is the document attached to a passport indicating that the traveler has official permission to visit and travel freely within a country. It comes from the Latin word *videre* (to see). *Visa* is, indeed, neuter plural of the past participle *visus* and thus literally means "things seen."

vitae/résumé. A practice which has been known to lead to arguments is that of some young men who use the term *vitae* in referring to their job résumés. Some argue that this is a plural form and that one résumé is a *vita.* The phrase which all of them are misusing is *curriculum vitae,* literally the running, course or career of one life. Just for the record, the plural form would be *curricula vitae.*

vituperate (pronounced vy-TOO-per-ayt) is a verb meaning "to berate, to revile, to speak to or about in abusive language." From the Latin *vituperare* (to blame), it has the variant forms *vituperation, vituperative* and *vituperator.*

viz. This abbreviation means "namely or to wit" and comes from the Latin *videlicet,* literally "to be permitted to." Thus, in a dictionary, *viz.* might be used to indicate that a certain word may be used as a certain part of speech. But where did the *z* come from? There's nothing in the Latin word to indicate such a letter. The explanation is that during the Middle Ages monks transcribing Latin often used the numeral *3* to denote a contraction. For example, *habet* became *hab3* and *omnibus* was *omnib3.* The *z* in *viz.* survives as the present-day substitute for the medieval *3.*

vocational comes from the Latin verb *vocare* (to call). *Vocation* was used as early as 1500, to mean, in the words of the *Oxford Dictionary,* "the action of God in calling a person to exercise some special (esp. spiritual) function, or to fill a certain position." The first "calling," or *vocation,* then, was to the priesthood. Gradually the term widened in meaning and one's *vocation* could be any of the learned professions.

vodka. Like several other names of potent spirits *(eau de vie, akvavit* and even *whiskey), vodka* is only a slight variation of "water"—linguistically speaking, that is. Anyone who has imbibed this colorless and virtually tasteless fluid knows that it is vastly more potent than water, *voda* in Russian. In light of its great popularity these days, we find amusing this comment in the *Funk & Wagnalls Unabridged Dictionary:* "The sale of *vodka* was suppressed Aug. 14, 1914." Presumably the suppression was by the Imperial Russian Government, but someone over at F&W ought to realize that things have changed a bit in that part of the globe.

vol au vent in French means "flight in the wind." It is a pastry shell made of puff pastry, filled with creamed meat or fish. The name refers, of course, to the pastry. Properly made, it is so light that a puff of wind will make it take flight.

volt/ampere/ohm/mho. Three terms, *volt, ampere* and *ohm,* commonly used in electricity are derived from the names of the scientists who first established their functions. *Volt* is from Alessandro Volta, an Italian physicist.

Ampere was named for André Marie Ampère, a Frenchman. And *ohm* comes from the noted German scientist G. S. Ohm, who has also achieved a curiously inverted fame through the word *mho.* A *mho* is the electrical unit of conductance—the opposite of *ohm,* the unit of resistance. As you have doubtless noticed, scientists in an unwonted burst of whimsy created the designation for the opposite of *ohm* by reversing letters in that word.

voracious (pronounced voh-RAY-shus) is an adjective meaning "greedy, gluttonous or rapacious." It stems from the Latin *vorare* (to devour) and is used not only in reference to eating but in the sense of being insatiable in other matters. The noun form is either *voraciousness* or *voracity;* the adverb, *voraciously.*

voyeur, originally a French word, means a person who derives pleasure from secretly observing others—a "peeping Tom." It still has this meaning, but it can be used merely as a synonym for "observer," as in the following statement in a magazine article: "American anthropologists insist on being participant observers (not *voyeurs*) when they go into the field."

vulgar comes from Latin *vulgus,* "the mob or the common people." A word labeled *vulgar* need not be obscene, although all obscene words are *vulgar.* A *vulgarism* is simply a coarse expression, characteristic of the lowest levels of society, culturally speaking.

waffle means to write, speak or act in a vague or indecisive fashion. If memory serves, it was often used to describe the actions (or lack of them) of British Prime Minister Harold Macmillan. In any event, *waffle* began as a Briticism, but has recently been widely used by our own Washington bureaucrats, whose prose it admirably describes. It fits the kind of writing in which public servants have excelled for decades, if not for centuries—weighty, seemingly important prose that actually says little or nothing. It is derived from Middle English *waffen,* "to wave," perhaps influenced by a now obsolete term, *waff, "to yelp."*

wake, meaning the period before a funeral, comes from the Middle English *wakien* (to be awake) and is cognate with the Latin *vigil,* which means the same thing. And this is a long way of telling you that *wake* simply means, traditionally at least, that someone stays awake all night at the side of the casket on the night before the funeral.

walk Spanish. In the days of piracy on the Spanish Main, a favorite trick of pirates was to lift their captives by the scruff of the neck and make them walk with their toes barely touching the deck. It was a painful experience, especially since the walk was punctuated with lusty blows from behind.

Walpurgis Night. Pronounced vahl-POOR-gis nite, this is the eve of May Day and is the night when witches, warlocks and the like revel in their satanic sabbath. The name comes from an English saint, Walpurga, who did missionary work in Germany. Her feast day is May Day.

wampum is a shortened form of the Algonquian Indian word *wampumpeag,* meaning "white strings," and referred to beads—especially white shell beads—on strings, used as currency by the Indians of New England.

War Between the States. Exactly who first used *War Between the States,* meaning the American Civil War, is not known for certain. However, one of the first to give the expression worldwide currency was the British government, which used the term in recognizing a state of "belligerency" in May 1861. This act was a great disappointment to the Confederate States, which had hoped to be recognized as an independent nation with the probability of overt support from Britain in the struggle.

warlocks/witches. *Witches* have been considered and depicted as females ever since the Dark Ages, when most people truly believed in them. Since that same period their male counterparts have been called *warlocks,* from two Old English words meaning "oath breaker," for *warlocks* were supposed to be demons who had broken with the true faith. *Witches* have always been more highly publicized than *warlocks.* For example, when Shakespeare wanted to set the proper mood for the sordid and murderous tragedy of *Macbeth,* he used three *witches,* not three *warlocks.* And when both sexes got together for an orgy, it was referred to as the *witches'* (not *warlocks'*) sabbath.

War of Jenkins' Ear. John Hay, secretary of state under Theodore Roosevelt, once called our Spanish-American War "that splendid little war." Nobody could apply the word "splendid" to the *War of Jenkins' Ear,* though it was fought in part in the same Caribbean area and one of the contestants, Spain, took part in both wars. *Jenkins'* was the earlier by more than a century and a half, running roughly from 1739 to 1741, though one of the oddities of this war is that it never really ended, being gradually merged in the more vital concerns of the War of the Austrian Succession.

There had been considerable rivalry between Britain and Spain with regard to trade with the southern colonies Georgia and Florida, and more especially with the islands of the Caribbean—an area Spain regarded as hers. The Spanish finally agreed to let Britain send one ship a year with supplies for her colonies, but then let out a loud yawp of protest when they discovered that the British had been reloading this one ship again and again at sea and then sending her on to America. Spain's protests, which took the form of armed attacks on British shipping, aroused the British populace, but Prime Minister Walpole managed to keep things under control until Jenkins, captain of a British ship engaged in smuggling goods to Florida, showed up brandishing his ear, which he said had been cut off by Spaniards. That did it. Nobody bothered to find out that the incident—if true at all—had taken place eight years before, and so the little *War of Jenkins' Ear* was under way. There were attacks on Cuba and Panama, and even some fighting in Florida and Georgia, but neither side cared very much and Britain was soon caught up in much more pressing affairs on the Continent. So Captain Jenkins, his ear, and his war became one of history's footnotes.

War of the Dictionaries. An erudite old railroader quoted a conversation, ostensibly between two learned men engaged in a construction project where a heavy beam was to be raised into position. The quote sounded something like: "You will either raise it with a LEE-ver or a LEV-er, according to whether thou useth Webster or Worcester." The reference is to one of the most fascinating and now all-but-forgotten episodes in nineteenth-century book business. Noah Webster's dictionary was, understandably, the first-ranking lexicon, especially after a brace of demon salesmen, George and Charles Merriam, took over its sale and distribution following Noah's death in 1843. But in 1859 a formidable rival appeared, this one edited by Joseph Worcester. Like Webster's tome, this one bulked large and was buttressed with careful scholarship. It was indeed a worthy rival.

There followed the *War of the Dictionaries.* Salesmen for both companies used every possible device to demean the competing book, resorting at times to devices that P. T. Barnum might have envied. In the end, of course, Webster won, and Worcester's name is now little more than a footnote in the history of American lexicography. And that's a pity, for if Worcester served no other purpose, he supplied the book which was used to prop up your male co-author at the Sunday dinner table when he was too small to reach the plate without help. A glance at the same Worcester dictionary, which we still cherish, shows that he recorded the LEE-ver pronunciation, while Webster preferred LEV-er. In this Worcester would seem to have been following British precedent, while Webster faithfully recorded the American.

warranty/guaranty. *Warranty* and *guaranty* are known to linguists as "doublets"—words derived from the same original source but traveling to today's English by different routes. Both can be traced to the Old French word *garantie* and thence, via *warant,* to the Old High German *werento,* "protector." The meanings of the two words are today quite similar, but not by any means interchangeable. *Warranty* has several special legal meanings that *guaranty* lacks.

wash one's hands. When you *wash your hands* of something, you have dismissed it from your attention and plan to pay it no further heed. The expression comes from the action of Pontius Pilate (Matthew 27:24): "When Pilate saw that he could prevail nothing, but that rather a tumult was made, he took water, and washed his hands before the multitude, saying, I am innocent of the blood of this just person: see ye to it."

watch and ward is an ancient English phrase meaning "everlasting watchfulness," *watch* being the guard by night (as in "night watch") and *ward* being protection during the daylight hours. It acquired quite another meaning in nineteenth-century America when Anthony Comstock was the moving spirit behind the organization of Boston's Watch and Ward Society in 1876. Comstock was a fanatical crusader against all forms of vice both real and imagined. Indeed, his name has come into the language—as "comstockery"—as a symbol of narrow-minded, censorious repression of thought. The Watch and Ward Society proved to be an ever-vigilant guardian of the morals of the good burghers of Boston and for several decades publishers sought to have their books "banned in Boston" because they knew that this label would be a spur to sales elsewhere in the nation.

Perhaps the most famous action taken against the Watch and Ward was by Henry L. Mencken, then editor of the *American Mercury*. When he published a short story called "Hatrack" about a small-town harlot in 1926, Boston's Watch and Ward Society moved quickly to suppress the issue. Mencken, showing a good journalist's flair for publicity, managed to persuade the secretary of the society, the Reverend J. Franklin Chase, to meet him on Boston Common and purchase from him a copy of the *Mercury* with the offending story. When Chase appeared and handed over a silver half dollar, Mencken bit the coin to be sure it was legitimate, handed over the magazine, and surrendered to the head of the Boston Vice Squad. The following day a fair-minded judge dismissed the charges against Mencken, and though the society continued its existence for many more years, it never again wielded the power of the original Watch and Ward Society.

weasel words is a phrase generally credited to Theodore Roosevelt but, though he popularized it, he didn't create it. First, though, what is a *weasel word?* It's a word that seems to have meaning but actually makes empty or equivocal the meaning of the sentence in which it appears. It gets its name from the fact that weasels are able to suck out the contents of an egg while leaving the shell virtually intact. So a statement studded with *weasel words* would seem to be meaningful but actually be virtually empty. Theodore Roosevelt used the term when attacking President Woodrow Wilson in 1916 for advocating something Wilson called "universal voluntary training." Said T.R.: "In connection with the word 'training,' the words 'universal voluntary' have exactly the same effect an acid has on an alkali—a neutralizing effect. One of our defects as a nation has been the tendency to use what have been called *'weasel words.'.* . . If you use a *weasel word* after another there is nothing left of the other. Now you can have universal training or you can have voluntary training, but when you use 'voluntary' to qualify 'universal,' you are using a *weasel word;* it has sucked all the meaning out of 'universal.' The two words flatly contradict each other."

weathervane/weathercock. In the dear, dead days before the ubiquitous TV weather forecaster began making life miserable for all of us by stretching out a simple two-line statement of his guess about the coming day's weather in order to fit in various commercial plugs, lots of people regarded wind direction as one of a number of indicators of what the weather would be. Farmers, in particular, paid heed to the direction in which the *weathervane* (originally and still often in the form of a cock and hence called *weather-cock*) was turning. The *weathercock* has been in standard use for more than eight centuries. Chaucer wrote: "as a wedercock that turneth his face with every wind." In some parts of the country—notably down East in New England—people describe and predict weather by referring to the direction of the prevailing wind. Ever hear of a "northeaster"? And the classic sailor's oilskin hat with the broad back brim to keep out the rain got its name from the storm that brought the rain—the "southwester."

Webster—what's-his-name. On an October day in 1758—the sixteenth, if you insist (as he would have) on accuracy—a man named Webster was born in the Connecticut town of West Hartford. His influence on the life and learning of every generation of American citizens from the founding of the republic until today is probably without equal. Yet this great man bore a name which, through one of the great ironies of our history, is still mis-called by most of our countrymen. The man was Webster—the Webster whose greatest accomplishment, though by no means his only achievement, was the creation of the first of the dictionaries that bear his name. But—stop for a moment and think—what was this Webster's first name?

Amazingly enough, though every American knows Webster's dictionary, polls show that four out of every five people think *Daniel* Webster wrote it. Thus, unwittingly, they deny to *Noah* Webster the honor that is due him for his great contributions to our culture.

For Noah Webster did much more than merely lay the foundation for what was the most influential of our American dictionaries. He was a devoted and eloquent spokesman for the patriot cause during the Revolution and the early years of the republic. As a schoolmaster he was aware of the need for improved teaching materials, and in 1783 he published his *Blue-Backed Speller*. This remarkable book is still in print and has sold more than 100 million copies, making it far and away the best-selling American book. During the great western migration of the nineteenth century, this speller was often the only book available for teaching the children of the pioneers. He would be a foolish man indeed who argued that the bombastic rhetoric of Daniel Webster had a greater influence on our nation's cultural growth than Noah's modest *Blue-Backed Speller*.

Add to this great work the creation of the first important American dictionary, and you have two contributions to our cultural development that are unparalleled. So let's give a thought to this relatively unsung genius, the "born definer of words"—and remember that Noah, not Daniel, deserves that proud label.

wedlock. The "lock" in *wedlock* has nothing whatever in common with that in, let us say, "padlock." It's merely an Old English suffix meaning "giving," and *wed* in this word means "pledge." So the original meaning of *wedlock* was merely the giving of pledges, specifically the wedding vows.

wee small hours. Why are the early morning hours called *wee small hours* when, especially for insomniacs, they seem anything but small? Well, the clock is the answer. Certainly the hours 1, 2 and 3 are smaller—mathematically anyway—than 7, 8 and 9.

weigh anchor means to haul it up, so that a ship may sail from the spot where it has been moored. This nautical use of *weigh* can be traced to its early Anglo-Saxon origin in the word *wegan,* which meant "to carry, bear or move." The concept of lifting or balancing objects in the hands to determine their weight came later and represents a somewhat more sophisticated sense of the original word. Incidentally, this matter of *weighing anchor* has led to confusion among sailors, many of whom use the phrase "under weigh" to indicate that their boats or ships are in motion. This is a variation of "under way," which most authorities regard as the simpler and more correct expression. Indeed, at least one British authority labels "under weigh" a solecism.

welkin, a word now archaic except in the phrase "making the *welkin* ring," literally means the heavens, the vault of the sky where clouds float, and it comes from the Anglo-Saxon word *wolcen,* meaning "cloud." So whether you raise Ned, Cain or the roof, you will be making enough noise to make the *welkin* ring.

welsh. To anyone with *Welsh* blood in his or her veins, the old nursery rhyme "Taffy was a Welshman, Taffy was a thief" is an outrage and a slander. There is no objection to the first statement: "Taffy" is a generic name for Welshman, a corruption of "David," the patron saint of Wales. But we greatly resent the implied slander on an entire nation in the second line: "Taffy was a thief." Even worse is the verb *to welsh,* meaning "to renege on a bet," thus impugning the honesty of all people of that country and their descendants.

The term *welsher* became common in Britain during the eighteenth and nineteenth centuries in the argot of race-track bettors. But from a reader came a comforting word for all Welshmen, one which gives a touch of logic to the use of the term: "It was *English* bookies who, having too many long shot winners against them, fled over the border to 'boondock' Wales to become the original *welshers* and escape irate bettors looking for their payoff." Signed: "Taffy" Hoxie. "P.S. You guessed it. I, too, had *Welsh* ancestors."

Welsh rabbit/rarebit. A widely held misconception is that *Welsh rabbit* is a vulgar form of *Welsh rarebit.* Actually the opposite is true, for *Welsh rarebit* is merely a mannered and affected corruption of a phrase that dates back nearly to Shakespeare's time. In those days only the wealthy in Wales could afford game from the royal preserves. So since rabbit itself was such a rarity, melted cheese on toast became known semihumorously as *Welsh rabbit*. In similar fashion, scrambled eggs on toast spread with anchovy butter came to be called Scotch woodcock. Up in New England even today, you may occasionally hear codfish called Cape Cod turkey. It's unfortunate that the editors of some cookbooks have helped to spread the nice-nellyism *rarebit*. Perhaps it's because the term has long been a favorite of restaurant menu writers—a curious breed who seem never able to say anything simply. H. W. Fowler, as usual, has a brusque and trenchant comment on the matter. *"Welsh rabbit,"* he writes, "is amusing and right, and *Welsh rarebit* stupid and wrong."

went (gone) for a burton. In every war servicemen invent euphemisms for death in battle. In World War I, the expression was "He has gone West." In the recent Vietnam war and earlier in the Korean conflict, servicemen used the expression "He bought the farm." We recorded a British expression identical in meaning, "He *went for a burton*," noting that it seemed to have originated with the RAF during World War II but that further information on its origin was not known. Then Anthony Bowdler of Okemos, Michigan, wrote: "I believe it possible that I may have identified a more certain origin for the expression. *Go for a burton* was used almost exclusively as a euphemism for being killed in action or, at best, to be missing in action. It was most characteristically used in the RAF. I distinctly recall a poster campaign in the late 1930s advertising a Burton, which was the name of a beer, in much the same way as one might now refer to a Budweiser. The posters would show a group with someone obviously missing, with the laconic legend: *Gone for a Burton*. I have little doubt that this was easily translated into common usage when its alternative meaning was increasingly required."

werewolf. This figure of fable, the man capable of assuming wolf's form, takes his name from the Anglo-Saxon *wer* (man) and *wulf* (wolf).

wetback is the slang term designating illegal immigrant farm laborers who enter California and Texas from Mexico. They are so called because most of them wade or swim across the Rio Grande under cover of darkness to escape detection by border patrol officers.

wet one's whistle. This expression for taking a drink goes back to Middle English and appears twice in Chaucer. A somewhat similar phrase, "wet the other eye," means "to take one drink right after another" and is traced by the *Oxford Dictionary* back to 1745. Still another British sense of *wet*, meaning simply "to drink intoxicating liquor," goes still further back. The *Oxford* gives this remarkable example of its use in 1687: "He was as Drunk as a Chaplain of the Army upon wetting his commission."

what is written without pain is read without pleasure. We don't know the author of that sentence, but the thought has been stated by many writers. Ernest Hemingway wrote: "Easy writing makes hard reading," and Samuel Johnson said: "What is easy is seldom excellent." But Mark Twain's Huckleberry Finn put it emphatically when he summed up the agony of writing this way: "There ain't nothing more to write about and I'm rotten glad of it, because if I'd a knowed what a trouble it was to make a book, I wouldn't a tackled it." (AUTHORS' NOTE: Amen!)

what the dickens has nothing whatever to do with the famous English novelist. It's simply a euphemism for "What the devil!" In fact, the expression was common centuries before Charles Dickens was born, having been used by Shakespeare in *The Merry Wives of Windsor* (Act III, Scene 2): "I cannot tell *what the dickens* his name is."

what this country needs is a good five-cent cigar. The fame of Vice-President Tom Marshall (in office 1913–1921) rests solely on his once having said: *"What this country needs is a good five-cent cigar."*

wheeler and dealer is typically American slang, doubtless having its origin in the gambling casinos of the West. There a "big *wheeler and dealer*" would be one who plunged heavily at the gambling wheels *(wheeler)* and at card games *(dealer)*. But there's more to the phrase than simply gambling lingo. As we know, it has the connotation of an operator (a *big wheel*) who takes over the direction of a business or enterprise and runs it according to his own whim, often with little or no regard for conventional rules or ethics. The expression probably evolved from the well-established slang verb *to wheel* and the noun *wheel,* as in *big wheel.* It may have originated as early as World War II, but its great vogue started in the mid-1950s. The element of rhyme makes the phrase an especially catchy one, of course.

when my ship comes in is an old expression, usually taken to mean the time when success and good fortune (not merely the tools for it) have arrived. One example given in the *Oxford Dictionary of English Proverbs* is a bit of dialogue from a celebrated novel of the nineteenth century, *John Halifax, Gentleman:* "Perhaps we may manage it sometime." "Yes, *when our ship comes in.*" The expression comes from the days when merchant commerce dominated the seas of the world. Then a wife waiting at home for her seafaring husband would literally be far better off when her ship came in, as would tradespeople receiving payment for a cargo shipped on the outbound voyage.

when St. George goes on horseback, St. Yves goes on foot. St. George was the patron saint of soldiers and St. Yves the patron of lawyers. So in the days when soldiers rode horses, this expressed the theory that lawyers did little or nothing in time of war.

where the MacGregor sits. In Barbara Tuchman's book about General "Vinegar Joe" Stilwell, the author used a phrase new to us. General Stilwell had just been relieved of command in Southeast Asia and wished for a new assignment on an active front. He decided to contact General MacArthur. "If there were to be any openings," wrote Mrs. Tuchman, "he judged the source would be *where the MacGregor sat* and he determined to go to the source if he could." According to Bartlett's *Quotations,* the expression *"Where the MacGregor sits,* there is the head of the table" is from Emerson. Apparently Emerson wrote "MacDonald," but Bartlett acknowledges that it is generally quoted as "MacGregor."

Then, by one of those odd coincidences that make research fun, we ran on a full explanation of the origin of the phrase in a long-neglected book called *Information Roundup* by George Stimson. It seems that Walter Scott, in his historical novel *Rob Roy,* had an outlaw named Robert MacGregor—sometimes called the "Robin Hood of Scotland" —use the expression Mrs. Tuchman quotes. It echoes a thought expressed centuries earlier by Don Quixote: "Let me sit wherever I will, that will still be the upper end." In other words, in General Stilwell's view, wherever MacArthur was, there would be the authority to give or deny him the position he sought.

where the woodbine twineth. To go *where the woodbine twineth* and the whangdoodle whineth—which means to disappear completely—comes out of the boastful talk of the American frontier in the mid nineteenth century. A more elaborate version is: "Gone *where the woodbine twineth* and the whangdoodle mourneth for his firstborn." Charles Earle Funk, of the dictionary Funks, reported that he and his brother knew the expression very well in their childhood days in Ohio. But he felt that it probably goes back to the early 1800s. Certainly the most famous use of the expression was by the robber baron Jubilee Jim Fisk. Interviewed by the *New York Tribune* in 1870, shortly after the notorious "Black Friday" stock market disaster, he was asked: "What became of the $50 million in gold carried for Mrs. Grant?" "Oh, that," replied Fisk, "has gone with all the rest— gone *where the woodbine twineth.* "

In an earlier and simpler world—and without the "whangdoodle"—the expression "Come *where the woodbine twineth*" meant simply: "Come where the beauties of nature are found in fields and forests." Shakespeare said it best, as usual, when in *A Midsummer Night's Dream* he wrote: "I know a bank whereon the wild thyme blows,/Where oxslips and the nodding violet grows/Quite overcanopied with luscious woodbine/With sweet musk-roses and with eglantine."

Whiffenpoofs. This is the legendary band of "gentlemen songsters" of Yale University, made up of the best singers among the senior class. In all the history of the *Whiffenpoofs,* from their first serenade around the "tables down at Mory's," there has been only one *Whiffenpoof* who sang with the group two years, our good friend Lanny Ross, who went on to a distinguished career in radio and musical theater. Part of the honor of being a *Whiffenpoof* is the right to carve your initials on the table at Mory's.

Lanny's are the only initials that appear twice.

The "gentlemen songsters" borrowed the refrain of their song from one of Rudyard Kipling's *Barrack Room Ballads,* "Gentlemen Rankers." There are two theories of the meaning of "gentlemen rankers," one that they are soldiers who receive battlefield promotions from the ranks, thus becoming, as officers, automatically "gentlemen." However, the other theory holds that in Kipling's version, the "rankers" were chaps of good birth and breeding who somehow had got into trouble and resorted to enlistment in the ranks to remake their lives. The Kipling verse runs: "We're poor little lambs who have lost our way,/Bah, bah, bah!/We're little black sheep who have gone astray,/Bah, -aaa -aah!/Gentlemen rankers out on the spree,/Damned from here to eternity,/God ha' mercy on such as we./Bah! Yah! Bah!"

Nobody is quite sure who wrote the original musical setting for the *Whiffenpoof* version, with credit, amusingly enough, being shared by Tod Galloway (Amherst) and Guy Scull (Harvard). The revision of the Kipling verses was the work of Meade Minnigerode and George S. Pomeroy—both Yalemen.

whim of iron. Around New York's famed club The Players, they still tell a story about one of their members, Oliver Herford. Herford, "the humorist's humorist," was known as an inveterate cigar smoker. In some thirty years of daily attendance at the club he had never been seen without a fine Havana set jauntily in the corner of his mouth. It was a matter of some concern to his fellow clubmates, therefore, when it was noticed that he had appeared two days in succession without his cigar. Pressed for an explanation, he told his old friend Franklin P. Adams that he had given up the weed because his wife had suddenly decided she couldn't stand cigar smoke. "Heavens, man," F.P.A. remonstrated. "You mean that you're giving up cigars after thirty years, just because of a whim of your wife?" "You don't know my wife, Frank," Herford replied gently. "She has a *whim of iron!*"

whip (legislative) is a term borrowed from the sport of fox hunting. The chap who assists the huntsman in handling the hounds is known as the "whipper-in." His job is to keep the hounds from straying by whipping them back into the pack. In the mid nineteenth century, the British Parliament adopted the term informally to designate that member of each delegation responsible for party discipline, for rounding up the members when a vote was to be called. These "whippers-in" soon became known as simply *whips.* Not long afterward our American Congress decided that it would follow British precedent. Today the chief job of the congressional *whips* is to keep party members in line—"whipped in," so to speak—especially when they show signs of straying from the prescribed party plan for voting.

whippersnapper. A fellow columnist asked: "Did a *whippersnapper* ever snap a whip and, if so, why wasn't he called a *whipsnapper?*" The answers are simple: he did snap a whip—and he was called a *whipsnapper.* The expression, meaning "an impertinent young person," was originally *whip snapper,* a cheeky chap who has nothing better to do than stand around snapping whips. Gradually, by a process the *Oxford Dictionary* calls a "jingling extension on the model of the earlier *snippersnapper,*" the word acquired the form it has today.

whipping boy, used in the sense of a person who is a scapegoat—a person punished for mistakes committed by someone else—comes to us from a practice common to European royalty four or five centuries ago. Each young princeling or royal personage was educated along with a boy of common birth—and the commoner was flogged whenever the young prince committed an act deemed worthy of punishment. So today when an office underling has to stand by and take the reprimand properly due his superior, he may at least take comfort in the thought that he is merely enacting a role once played by commoners at the courts of kings.

whiskey. The word *whiskey* comes from the Gaelic word *uisgebeatha,* meaning "water of life." This has been a favorite phrase for potent spirits ever since ancient Romans downed their *aqua vitae.* The Swedish brand of liquid lightning is called *akvavit,* while the French often refer to a choice brandy as *eau de vie.*

Both Scotsmen and Irishmen—but not the English—can claim credit for inventing *whiskey* and surely we are not audacious enough to mediate their respective claims. It seems clear, though, that *whiskey* first became widely popular during the reign of Henry VIII—a stalwart trencherman and two-fisted devotee of what, in his day, was called *whiskeybaugh.*

whistling girls and crowing hens. A Nebraska reader asked us about a line she had heard from her grandmother to the effect that *"Whistling girls and crowing hens* always come to some bad ends." A little checking in the *Oxford Dictionary of English Proverbs* showed that the expression was centuries old and had many variations, including "A whistling wife and a crowing hen will frighten the devil out of his den." So far so good, but what the Nebraska lady wanted to know was whether there might not be some suitable retort, something that the whistling woman might say to put the person kidding her in his place.

Marion A. Rivers of Pittsburgh seems to have the answer. "My mother was a *whistling girl* before the turn of the century," she writes, "and a woman doctor shortly after. Her father used to tease her with that *Whistling girls and crowing hens* couplet. Her reply, which I have always thought was original with her, was: 'A woman who whistles or a hen that crows/Will make her way wherever she goes.' That seems to me a fitting slogan for early Women's Lib!"

white elephant. Many centuries ago in Siam, now Thailand, the white or
albino elephant was so rare that each one born became automatically the
property of the king and none was permitted to work. So if the king took
a dislike to one of his courtiers, the punishment was swift, simple and
devastating. The king simply gave a white elephant to the victim of his
displeasure—and waited for time and the enormous appetite of the ele-·
phant to reduce the courtier to ruin.

White elephant may owe some of its popularity to more recent exploits
of P. T. Barnum. According to one story, Barnum was in his prime. The
circus business was competitive. A competitor spirited an albino elephant
from Siam and got a big play from the public. P. T. was not to be outdone.
He had his roustabouts whitewash one of his garden-variety gray elephants
and advertised so heavily that his competitor lost out and a *white elephant*
lost the charm of rarity. But worse, his competitor found no market for the
real article when he tried to dump it. Thus it was the original *white
elephant,* an article of reputed worth which no one wants. Just one thing
worries us about this story. What would happen to the whitewashed elephant if the circus parade were caught in a sudden rainstorm?

white feather has long been a symbol of cowardice. To give someone, literally
or figuratively, a *white feather* was to accuse him of cowardice. Many years
ago there was a celebrated motion picture—rather along the lines of *Beau
Geste*—about a young Britisher who "funked out" under pressure. Given
the *white feather* by his comrades, he had to spend the next eight reels
redeeming himself through acts of heroism. The film's name, obviously,
was *The White Feather.*

Where did the tradition start? Apparently in the cockpit. When two
fighting cocks were pitted against each other, the theory was that the cock
of pure breeding would have feathers all of a single color, while one of
mixed breeding might have a white feather in its tail. If the crossbred cock
lacked courage—was unable to stand the gaff—it would show the *white
feather* when it dropped its wings in defeat.

white horses. The white peaks of waves may be called whitecaps in America,
but in Britain they are known as *white horses.*

white man's burden was a popular expression during the later years of Queen
Victoria's reign, when the British Empire was an institution worldwide in
scope and fearsome in power. It referred to the duty of the British to
educate and govern the races they conquered. Whether or not Rudyard
Kipling created the phrase, he gave it fame in this stanza: "Take up the
White Man's Burden—/Send forth the best you breed,/Go bind your sons
to exile/To serve the captives' need."

white paper. A *white paper* is a government publication setting forth the
official position on any specific question. Such papers, by the very nature
of the auspices under which they are issued, usually present the govern-

ment as blameless. But that's not why they are called *white*. That term results simply from the fact that such documents are traditionally issued in white binding. Governments also sometimes issue "white books," which are more detailed expositions of governmental policies and procedure.

whodunit. The mystery in any good mystery story is, of course, who committed the crime—who did the fatal deed. By all rules of logic, these stories should be called "whodidits" rather than *whodunits*. But the one thing we know for certain about the word *whodunit* is that it was coined by one of the writers for *Variety*, the magazine of show business, whose writers for many years were encouraged to invent new and sprightly words. Just about anything would be accepted from a *Variety* "mugg," as the reporters called themselves, as long as its meaning was clear. There are two claimants for the honor of perpetrating *whodunit*. Abel Green, for many years *Variety*'s editor, claims his predecessor Sime Silverman coined it in 1936. But a one-time staff member, Wolfe Kaufman, says he invented it in 1935. So, as the old sideshow barker used to say: "Yer pays yer nickel and yer takes yer cherce."

whole ball of wax means some thing or some situation in its entirety. It's a phrase that was very popular along Madison Avenue in the 1960s and we have variously speculated that it may have originated as a reference to Madame Tussaud's waxworks or as a corruption of the phrase "the whole bailiwick."

Ken Bays of Louisville, Kentucky, weighed in with another suggestion, based upon his reading of the famous legal text *Coke on Littleton,* printed in 1620. Both Coke (pronounced Cook, by the way) and Littleton rank high in any list of Britain's most distinguished jurists. The section Mr. Bays cites has to do with the parceling of property, specifically land, among heirs to an estate. An example given is the partition of land among four female heirs. "Every part of the land by itself is written in a little scrawle and is covered by waxe in the manner of a little ball, so as none may see the scrawle. Then the four balls of waxe are put in a hat to be kept in the hands of an indifferent [that is, impartial] man and then the eldest daughter shall first put her hands into the hat and take a ball of waxe with the scrawle within the ball for her part and then the second sister . . . and so on."

"Now," added Mr. Bays, "can't you visualize one of the daughters drawing from the hat and not being particularly happy with her selection, hearing someone say: 'Well, that's the *whole ball of wax!*' " And that's a fascinating and very well documented theory. Our thanks to you, Mr. Bays, and we'll bet no Madison Avenue adman ever realized that his words had appeared centuries earlier in a British legal commentary.

whole shebang. The most logical explanation of this expression is that *shebang* is a variant of the Irish word *shebeen*. At any rate, its first recorded appearance in this country roughly coincides with the first major influx of

Irish immigrants early in the nineteenth century. A *shebeen* in Ireland was a very lowly public house, one where drinks were sold without a license. Indeed, a *shebeen* was very little better than the sort of establishment Americans of a generation back used to call a "blind pig." This being the case, a *shebeen* was regarded as a relatively valueless piece of real estate, and the expression "I'll give you so much for the whole *shebeen*" became current. Gradually the original reference to the lowly public house was lost and *shebeen*—now *shebang* after the trip across the Atlantic—came to mean any kind of trifling business affair or piece of property.

A reader tells us of several other uses that the expression has in her part of southeastern Michigan: "Here we use the word *shebang* frequently, but with three different though related meanings. We might say, 'I brought the whole *shebang*,' meaning a large group of people. Or we might say, 'That's the whole *shebang*,' referring to the entire amount of a large quantity of something. The other meaning we sometimes give it refers to a big party, such as a loud, crowded, happy wedding reception. For example, my husband and I are giving a 'big *shebang*' to celebrate my mother-in-law's nintieth birthday and our silver wedding anniversary. In fact, I might say, 'All of our neighbors—yes, the whole *shebang*—will help us celebrate at our big *shebang* by eating and drinking the whole *shebang!*' "

whole shooting match is a saying from the American frontier and means simply "the entire lot or crowd." Thus a ranch owner might say, "I don't want to buy just a few steers. I want you to give me a price on *the whole shootin' match.*" Obviously the expression must first have referred to the group of people gathered to witness a shooting match, but before long the expression came to mean, in the words of one frontiersman, "any kind of meeting from a church service to a dance." The expression "whole *kit and caboodle*" (which see) has the same meaning.

whom the gods would destroy. *"Whom the gods would destroy* they first make mad" comes from a little-known work of Henry Wadsworth Longfellow, "The Masque of Pandora." However, the idea he expressed is about as old as recorded history. According to James Boswell, in his *Life of Dr. Johnson,* this expression appears in the work of Euripides, the famed Greek dramatist of the fifth century B.C. The Latin version runs: *"Quos Deus vult perdere prius dementat"*—*"Whom God wishes to destroy, he first drives mad."* The first appearance in English of this idea is probably in John Dryden's "The Hind and the Panther": "For those whom God to ruin has design'd,/He fits for fate and first destroys their mind."

whopper-jawed. In our column we discussed the dialect term "cattywampus," meaning "cater-cornered or on the diagonal." One reader said that the same idea, especially when applied to something slightly out of alignment, was expressed by the term *whopper-jawed* in his part of the country. Another reader added: "We've lived in southeastern Ohio for most of our lives. We've said *whopper-jawed* all our sixty-two years. We think of it in carpenter's terms. A board sawed not quite straight or a table with one short leg is *whopper-jawed.* "

Who's Afraid of Virginia Woolf? Virginia Woolf was an English novelist and critic who was one of the leading literary lights of her time. The use of her name in the title of Edward Albee's play *Who's Afraid of Virginia Woolf?* was, so far as we know, just a sort of egghead pun on "Who's Afraid of the Big, Bad Wolf?"

widow's peak is the point formed by hair growing down in the middle of the forehead. According to old superstition, a woman having such a growth was slated for early widowhood.

widow's weeds. Originally *weeds* were any kind of clothing. The Anglo-Saxon word for "garment" was *waede.* Thus Spenser wrote of "A goodly lady clad in hunter's *weed.*" Over the centuries, though, its use has become chiefly restricted to mourning garments worn by widows.

wig. Now that ladies of fashion have a selection of *wigs* to match their gowns and moods, it's a bit startling to recall that the first *wigs* were worn almost exclusively by men and weren't even called *wigs;* they were "perukes." The word came, via French, from the Italian *parrucca* (head of hair). Gradually, in English, "peruke" became "periwig" and from there it was just a question of time until it was shortened to *wig.* When we speak of So-and-so as a "bigwig," meaning a person of prominence or importance, we are unconsciously referring to the times, notably the eighteenth century, when the larger the wig, the more important the man. And when, in the old British phrase, a person is given a "good wigging," meaning a sharp scolding, it is likely that this *wig,* too, refers to the fact that the person administering the scolding usually is in a position of authority and hence, in those earlier days, would have been a *wig* wearer.

wild and woolly West. Nobody is quite sure how *woolly* got into this phrase —though the alliteration of the three *w*'s is doubtless why it stayed there. One theory is that the wool of sheep allowed to graze on the open range grows coarse and rough—thus furnishing a parallel to the rough, coarse life of the frontier. The chief trouble with this theory is that the cattlemen who opened up the West held sheepherders in the same low esteem that Kentucky moonshiners reserve for "revenooers." So it's hardly likely that Western cattlemen would have rejoiced in a description which involved their pet hate, the sheep. More plausible is the theory that *woolly* refers to a kind of minor tornado, so called because the winds "beat the water into a wool-white foam"—according to a nineteenth-century authority. The trouble with this theory is that there wasn't much water around those parts of the West that were wildest and woolliest. So we come to our own surmise —that the word comes from the angora chaps worn by many cowpokes, the kind they themselves now call "hair pants." These angora chaps certainly qualify for the adjective *woolly* and were popular garb when the hands "duded up" for some special occasion like the trip to town after roundup.

willy-nilly has the sense of something unavoidable—"He determined to win the race *willy-nilly.*" But it also has the sense, as *World Webster* puts it, of "indecisive, vacillating, irresolute." It's a contraction of "will I, nill I?" —*nill* being an archaic word meaning "not to will" or "refuse."

wimpy. The hamburger is unknown as such in England. There it is wildly popular in cities but is known as the *wimpy,* after a character in the late E. C. Segar's comic strip *Popeye,* who was rarely seen without a hamburger in hand.

windfall as a term for an unexpected piece of good fortune goes back to medieval England, when commoners were forbidden to chop down trees for fuel. However, if a strong wind broke off branches or blew down trees, the debris was a lucky and legitimate find.

wine, women and song. In the Western world this phrase is traditionally associated with the romantic waltzes of old Vienna—the nineteenth-century Vienna of the Johann Strausses, father and son. Indeed, *"Wine, Women and Song"* is the title of one of the younger Strauss's most famous works. However, the actual coiner of the phrase was a German poet of a century or so earlier, Johann Heinrich Voss, who wrote: "Who does not love *wine, women and song*/Remains a fool his whole life long."

wisecrack/razzle-dazzle. During the earlier years of this century a comedian named Chic Sale had a fairly limited vogue, appearing mostly on rube vaudeville circuits. He wrote one book, a discussion of that once familiar American landmark, the outhouse. Called *The Specialist,* it had a very large sale and, indeed, is still in print. Sale has also been credited with having invented two words: *wisecrack* and *razzle-dazzle.* His title to the first is somewhat dubious, and there is no merit at all to the second claim.

However, we can report that at least one reputable dictionary—the *Dictionary of American Slang*—reports that "the late columnist O. O. McIntyre attributes this coinage to comedian Chic Sale." Now, this is a fairly slender reed upon which to hang one's claim to linguistic immortality, since McIntyre—known to his associates as "the very Odd McIntyre" —was not restrained when it came to imaginings and flights of fancy. What's more, the same dictionary suggests that the term, together with the closely related *wisecracker* and *wisecracking,* may have originated at the famous Round Table of New York's Hotel Algonquin. There a breed of humorists of a stripe very different from Mr. Sale used to congregate. Dorothy Parker, Robert Benchley, George S. Kaufman and Alexander Woollcott tried to top each other's best gags at daily luncheons. So whether *wisecrack* came from the earthy humor of Sale or the sophisticated jesters of the Algonquin is debatable.

There's no debate at all about *razzle-dazzle,* though. This dates back to the 1890s and probably comes from magicians' slang, since it means "planned deception and confusion, especially of a flashy, spectacular sort."

wishing on a wishbone. Nobody knows when the custom of breaking a chicken or turkey *wishbone* while making wishes began—except that it goes back at least to 1600. The English call this "merrythought" and the *Oxford Dictionary* says "the name has reference to two people pulling the furcula [the technical name for that bone] until it breaks; the notion being that the one who gets the longer piece will either be married first or will get any wish he may form at the moment."

wish is father to the thought. This expression, applicable to many credulous folk who believe, in the words of the popular song, that "wishing can make it so," comes from Shakespeare's *Henry IV,* Part II (Act IV, Scene 5). The Prince of Wales, finding his father, King Henry, on the verge of death, dons the crown and leaves the King's bedside. Recalled by courtiers, he says to the King: "I never thought to hear you speak again." To which the King replies: "Thy wish was father, Harry, to that thought./I stay too long by thee, I weary thee./Dost thou so hunger for mine empty chair/That thou wilt needs invest thee with mine honours/Before thy hour be ripe? O foolish youth!"

wisteria. When you admire the blossoms on a wisteria tree, you may not be aware of the fact that it is named after a famous American botanist of the nineteenth century, Caspar Wistar. Some years ago Joshua Logan, famed producer-director-playwright, embarked on a fruitless attempt to change the spelling of *wisteria* to *wistaria* on the ground that this spelling is closer to the botanist's name. In spite of the fact that his play *The Wistaria Trees* had a fair run on Broadway, Logan's quixotic attempt to bring belated fame to Wistar failed.

witch hazel. As so often happens, there are two theories of the origin of this medical term. First, though, you should know that the bottled *witch hazel* you get at the drugstore is an alcoholic solution of an extract from the leaves and bark of the witch hazel plant, a shrub with yellow flowers and easily bent branches. So one explanation is that *witch hazel* gets its name from the Anglo-Saxon *wice,* meaning "a tree with easily bent branches." That's probably the true origin, but we rather like the second theory—that the *witch* comes from the fact that branches of this shrub were often used as divining rods because of their mysterious, uncanny powers. These rods —often called *dowsing rods*—were widely used to locate hidden springs and thus find suitable locations for wells.

with a friend like you, who needs enemies? This witticism derives from a notion that has been commonplace for centuries. When leaving Louis XIV, Maréchal Villars is supposed to have said: "Defend me from my friends; I can defend myself from my enemies." And George Canning wrote: "Give me the avowed, the erect, the manly foe,/Bold I can meet—perhaps may turn his blow!/But of all plagues, Good Heaven, thy wrath can send,/Save, save, Oh, save me from the candid friend!"

with a grain of salt. If you take something *with a grain of salt,* you are viewing it with considerable skepticism. The phrase, a direct translation of the Latin *cum grano salis,* indicates that just as you would anticipate a very small quantity of salt in a dish served you, so you look for little truth in the statement made.

with all stops out. The reference is to the stops of an organ. With all stops out, the resulting sound would be fortissimo, so anything performed *with all stops out* is done without let or hindrance.

without rhyme or reason is credited to St. Thomas More, English statesman and author, who served Henry VIII as his Lord Chancellor and was eventually beheaded at Henry's order. As the story goes, an author submitted to St. Thomas a manuscript, hoping for his approval. "Take it back and rewrite it in verse," was St. Thomas's advice. When the writer had done so, he found himself the target for a bit of lordly wit. "Ay, ay," commented the Lord Chancellor, "that will do. 'Tis rhyme now, but before it was neither rhyme nor reason."

Wizard of Oz/Ooze. *The Wizard of Oz,* by L. Frank Baum, has been called the only truly original American contribution to the great fairy legends of the world. Published in 1900, it gave us such folk characters as the Cowardly Lion, the Tin Woodman, the Wizard himself and Dorothy, the Kansas farm girl around whom all the excitement revolved and who was portrayed so winningly by the young Judy Garland. Many years after the book and film had won their audiences, the late Senator Everett Dirksen of Illinois with sonorously cadenced recitations achieved a certain celebrity among his fellow solons as the *Wizard of Ooze.*

wobblies were (and are) members of the Industrial Workers of the World, a militant group that played an important role in the early years of America's union organizing. In newspaper headlines their name was usually shortened to I.W.W., which their opponents quickly translated as "I won't work."

woebegone. Here's an oddity, a word that means almost precisely the opposite of what you think it would mean from the sum of its parts. One would think that a *woebegone* chap would be all cheerful and devil-may-care, because his woe had been gone. Not so, however. In Middle English *wo* did indeed mean the same as *woe* now does, but *begon* was a word unto itself, meaning "beset." So a *woebegone* person is one beset by—not free from—woe.

wog, a term used derogatorily in reference to a person of Oriental or Middle Eastern ancestry, seems to have eluded most dictionary editors, though it was commonplace in the slang of U.S. soldiers in Viet Nam and William recalls hearing it on the docks in Egypt during World War II. Its origin is unclear, though Merriam III gives "golliwog" as a possible antecedent. An Omaha reader, recalling the origin of "posh" (which see) of the ships of the Peninsular and Orient Line in Queen Victoria's time, supplies another interesting, if dubious, word origin. "The term *'wog'* had its origin in P&O ships," he writes. "On the return voyage to England the ships often carried high-ranking Indians. If their behavior met with the approval of the pursers and stewards, the initials WOG were placed after their names, so the next P&O employe who met him would know he was a Wonderful Oriental Gentleman."

wok is a Chinese cooking utensil. Indeed, it may be called *the* basic, general-purpose pan used by Chinese cooks. It's a bowl—rather wide and fairly shallow—that sometimes sits upon a base placed over the source of heat.

woman is one of the more perplexing and unusually formed words in our language. It all starts with *mann,* the Anglo-Saxon word for "human being," to which was prefixed *wif-* for "female." (That's the same *wif-,* by the way, from which "wife" comes.) That gave us *wifmann,* which gradually became *wimman* and eventually *woman,* with the plural form *women.* But the pronunciation WIM-'n carried over from the earlier phase, when the plural of *wimman* was *wimmen.* Incidentally, both these words form plurals in accordance with an Old English form *-en,* which survives in very few other words today. Three that come readily to mind are "oxen," "brethren" and "children."

woman scorned. This was once the title of a motion picture—one of those three-handkerchief "women's pictures" that still turn up occasionally on late, late night TV. The expression originally came from a line in William Congreve's tragedy *The Mourning Bride* (1697): "Heaven has no rage like love to hatred turned,/Nor hell a fury like a *woman scorned.* "

woods colt, a term for a child born out of wedlock, seems to be a completely American expression. Wentworth's *American Dialect Dictionary* records it as having appeared in print as long ago as 1895, though most of the examples he gives of its use were in rural areas running roughly from Virginia to the Ozarks. He does give one example of *woods colt* cropping up in Maine, though. We first ran across the expression as the title of a book by Vance Randolph, who has written a number of delightful books about the Ozarks.

words for—and from—the birds. Our feathered friends, some of them not especially friendly when you stop to think about them, have made contributions to language and literature almost as numerous and varied as the worldwide population of birds themselves. Birds have supplied inspiration for writers from the time of Aristophanes. The Greek dramatist hymned "the swallow, the herald of spring" and even titled one of his comedies *The Birds.* Shakespeare invoked "the *lark* at break of day arising . . . sings hymns at heaven's gate."

Some birds, over the centuries, have had what might be called a "better press" than others. *Larks, doves, swallows* and *nightingales,* on the whole, do rather well at the hands of poets and writers generally, while *hawks,* *ravens, vultures* and *crows* are generally invoked as symbols of evil. "Who will not change a *raven* for a *dove?*" asked Shakespeare in *A Midsummer Night's Dream*—and we hear echoes of this invidious comparison in the labels *hawk* and *dove* to distinguish between political and military factions devoted to forceful or peaceful approaches to the solution of world problems.

And that is by no means all. Take sports, for instance. Birds are very big in sports, and have been since the days when cockfighting was a favored sport among the landed and blooded gentry. The *cockpits* of our fighting planes got their name from the pit into which *cocks* were dropped when two were *pitted* against each other.

Still earlier by a few centuries, a delightful outdoor sport gave rise to our word for a happy occasion, a *lark.* In Shakespeare's time the *lark* was highly regarded as a gourmet delight. Because of their tiny size, they wouldn't be hunted with bow and arrow, so were usually trapped in nets which were set out before daybreak. The custom was for young men and maids to join in the early morning pursuit of the elusive *lark,* and since they didn't always attend strictly to the business at hand, the whole business often took on the aspects of an outdoor frolic, and *larking* became as popular as drive-ins and discotheques are with today's youngsters. Other times, as they say, other customs—but the pursuit of maid by man, and vice versa, seems universal. And the birds had a word for it.

work like a Trojan. *Trojan* originally referred to the inhabitants of Troy, the ancient city besieged by the Greeks in their efforts to retrieve their queen, Helen, who had been abducted by the son of the King of Troy. According to legend, as recorded in both Vergil's *Aeneid* and Homer's *Iliad,* the Trojans were a hard-working, determined, industrious people. Hence: "He *worked like a Trojan.*"

work like a Turk. The *Turk* involved here is almost certainly not a person of Turkish birth or descent. It's much more likely that the *Turk* is a brawny Irishman. You see, the Irish themselves have a Gaelic word, *torc,* meaning "wild boar." So for centuries they have used this label—which gradually became *turk*—as a name for a strong, stubborn man, especially one quickly aroused to wrath. Among the Irish it became a common nickname for prize fighters, as well. The expression *work like a Turk* has the added attraction of a built-in rhyme.

world does move. One theory of the origin of the phrase *The world does move* ascribes it to Galileo. In 1633 he was hauled before the Inquisition and made to recant his belief in the Copernican theory of the rotation of the earth on its axis. As he completed his recantation, he is supposed to have murmured, *"Eppur si muove!"*—an Italian phrase meaning "And yet it does move!"

world, flesh and devil comes from the Book of Common Prayer—"From all the deceits of the world, the flesh and the devil, Good Lord deliver us."

world is my oyster came from Shakespeare. In the second act of *The Merry Wives of Windsor,* that peerless buffoon Sir John Falstaff asks one of his followers, a young braggart named Pistol, to do him a favor. Pistol refuses. Later Falstaff is approached by Pistol for a loan. Falstaff tells him: "I will not lend thee a penny." To which Pistol replies, brandishing a sword, "Why then the *world's mine oyster,* which I with sword will open." Ever since, the expression has been used to describe ambitious youth, for whom the future seems to hold unlimited possibilities. The oyster, of course, is valuable for what the young man hopes to find inside it—the pearl of success.

worm will turn. Like so many time-tested expressions, this one comes from Shakespeare. In Part Three of *Henry VI,* Clifford says: "Who scapes the lurking serpent's mortal sting?/Not he who sets his foot upon her back./ The smallest *worm will turn,* being trodden on,/And doves will peck in safeguard of their brood." The original meaning of the expression was that even the most humble creature will eventually turn to fight an oppressor.

worsted cloth. *Worsted* came first from the town of Worsted, now Worstead, England. We must say we prefer the warm, rich sound of such a centuries-old fabric to brisk but evanescent names like Dynel, Dacron and the other synthetics we see so widely advertised today.

worth his (her) salt. Quite literally, an employee who is not *worth his salt* is not worth his salary, for the two words have the same Latin root, *sal,* meaning "salt." Here's how it came about. The Romans realized that most foods are unappetizing without salt, so part of the wages of their soldiers was paid in salt. Later this was changed to a monetary allowance for the purchase of salt, and in time the word *salarium*—"of salt"—came to mean payment for services rendered, or "salary" as we use it today.

wouldn't touch it with a ten-foot pole, referring to a person or thing which is repugnant or distasteful, has been around a long time and apparently was used quite literally at first. The earliest record of the expression in print goes back to 1738. William Byrd in his *History of the Dividing Line betwixt Virginia and North Carolina* writes: "We found the ground moist, insomuch that it was an easy matter to run *a ten-foot pole* up to the head of it." Then, midway through the nineteenth century, the figurative sense of the expression appeared, but—again—not quite the way we use it today. A report from Nantucket went: "Can't *touch him with a ten-foot pole.* He is distant, proud and reserved." The present meaning is by now well established, though. Incidentally, the English version goes "I wouldn't touch him with a barge pole."

wowser is a word we have always cherished because it sounds so completely the opposite of what it actually means. At first glance you might well think that a *wowser* is a chap who spends most of his life kicking up his heels and having a wow of a good time. Not true. A *wowser*—the term originated in Australia—is a rather puritanical type, especially one who takes a public position in opposition to what most people would consider fairly minor vices. The term was popularized—if that's the word for it—by Henry L. Mencken when he was editing the *American Mercury* back in the twenties and making hash of Boston book censors and the like. *Wowser* is supposed to be an acronym of the name of an Australian reform group's motto: "We Only Want Social Evils Righted."

wrangle for an ass's shadow. The Athenian orator Demosthenes used this story to illustrate the futility of arguing over trifles—which is what this phrase means. One man hired an ass to take him on a journey and by noontime the sun was so hot that he dismounted and sat down to rest in the shadow of the ass. As he sat there, the owner came along (Demosthenes did not make it clear why) and demanded the right to sit in the ass's shadow. His contention was that while he had rented the ass, the shadow was not included in the bargain. While the two men wrangled and fought, the ass ran away, taking his shadow with him.

wreak/wreck. There is a fairly close kinship between these two words, and in the opinion of some word authorities, both come from the same Icelandic word, *rek*. However that may be, there is a clear distinction between the two today. *Wreak* (pronounced REEK) means "to inflict or to execute." Thus a hurricane *wreaks* (inflicts) havoc (destruction and devastation) along the New England shore. *Wreck* (pronounced REK) means "to destroy or badly damage." Thus, "A tidal wave *wrecked* the ship."

wreck of the Hesperus. To tell someone that he or she looks like the *wreck of the Hesperus* is to date yourself as someone who was in school in the 1920s or 1930s. In those days many of us were required to memorize the works of poets like Henry Wadsworth Longfellow and among them was his "Wreck of the Hesperus," which began: "It was the schooner Hesperus/That sailed the wintry sea;/And the skipper had taken his little daughter,/To keep him company." The phrase *wreck of the Hesperus* caught the imagination of schoolchildren of that time and became part of a figure of speech.

Wyoming. The original Wyoming was a valley in Pennsylvania, so named by the Algonquian Indians. The word in translation means "big flats." In 1809 a Scottish poet named Thomas Campbell wrote a poem called "Gertrude of Wyoming," which proved very popular. As a result towns in New York, Pennsylvania, West Virginia and other places chose Wyoming as their name. When it came time to name a new Western territory in 1868, an Ohio congressman, James M. Ashley, who had a lot of clout on the House Committee on Territories, insisted on calling it Wyoming. Some other members of the committee argued that it didn't make much sense to apply an Eastern Indian name to a Western territory, but Ashley finally won his point, partly by arguing that the "big flats" name was appropriate for a territory that was later to be known as one of the plains states.

x (for unknown quantity). Algebra is thought to have originated in Egypt, but the Arabs had a lot to do with its development. The Arabic word for "thing" or "something" was *shei,* and this was used in the Middle Ages to indicate a mathematically unknown quantity. The word was transcribed as "xei" and that was later simplified to *x*.

Xanadu. The reason *Xanadu* is not found in most dictionaries is that it never really existed. It was the invention of two English writers, Samuel Purchas and Samuel Taylor Coleridge. Purchas, a contemporary of Shakespeare, collected and published accounts of travelers and explorers in all parts of the globe. One of these was an account of a visit to the great Kubla Khan, a Mongol emperor who conquered all of China in the thirteenth century. According to literary historians, Coleridge was reading Purchas's account of Khan one night and fell asleep over the book. Awakening, he immediately set down, in a poem, the visions that had come to him in a dream. This poem, titled "Kubla Khan," begins: "In Xanadu did Kubla Khan/A stately pleasure dome decree:/Where Alph, the sacred river ran/Through caverns measureless to man/Down to a sunless sea." Incidentally, the pioneer work of literary detection on Coleridge was written back in 1927 by our favorite Harvard professor of English, John Livingston Lowes. It was called, appropriately enough, *The Road to Xanadu.*

Xanthippe. A shrewish, tart-tongued woman is often called a *Xanthippe,* after the wife of Socrates, who filled this bill of particulars in a spectacularly venomous fashion. Shakespeare had a word for her, too, appropriately enough in *The Taming of the Shrew* (Act I, Scene 2): "Be she . . . as curst and shrewd/As Socrates' *Xanthippe,* or a worse,/She moves me not . . ."

xenophobia, meaning fear or hatred of strangers or foreigners, comes from the Greek *xenos* (stranger) and *phobos* (fear).

Xerox is the trademark for a dry photocopying process, invented by Chester Floyd Carlson, developed in part by research at the Battelle Memorial Institute, and commercially marketed by the Haloid Company, later to become the Xerox Corporation. Carlson called his dry printing process "xerography," from the Greek prefix *xero-,* denoting dryness, and *graphein,* "to write." The Xerox Corporation has branched out into various other fields of activity, including educational publishing. Two of its subsidiaries, Ginn & Co. and Our Weekly Reader, have, indeed, published dictionaries designed for young readers and edited by your co-authors.

Xmas. Most people think that this is a sort of commercial shorthand for "Christmas" and while that is true enough as far as it goes, it doesn't go far enough. For *Xmas,* as a way of writing "Christmas," has a long and honorable history. The *Oxford Dictionary* indicates that *Xmas* appeared in print as early as 1555. The *X* is actually the Greek letter *X* transliterated as *K* and representing the Greek *Khristos.*

xylography, from the Greek *xylon* (wood) and *graphia* (writing), is the art of engraving on wood or the making of prints from wood engraving.

XYZ Affair. If we look back in our history, we can find any number of exciting episodes replete with secret agents, bribery, mysterious code messages and all the trappings of international suspense thrillers. One such is the mysteriously named *XYZ Affair.* It all began in 1797, when, after French pirates had been raising havoc with American shipping, President John Adams sent three envoys to Paris to seek peace. They were C. C. Pinckney, John Marshall, later to be a notable Chief Justice of the Supreme Court, and Elbridge Gerry, who later contributed "gerrymander" to the language.

The French foreign minister with whom they dealt was a canny character named Tallyrand, who was perfectly willing to make a peaceful settlement with our representatives—if they would turn over a million dollars as a loan to France, plus another quarter million to him for negotiating the deal. This begins to sound familiar, doesn't it?

Fortunately for our history, there wasn't that much loose cash available in the federal coffers, so Pinckney and Marshall headed home, leaving Gerry behind. He still thought he could make a deal with Tallyrand, but finally gave up when Adams ordered him home. During the negotiations, Tallyrand had used three agents, code-named "X," "Y" and "Z"—and that's how the episode got its name. When the story broke back home, native jingoists were all for declaring war on France and the slogan "Millions for defense, but not one cent for tribute" got its first airing. Pinckney was credited with saying it, but he claimed all he said was "No, no, not a single sixpence."

Yahoo is a creation of Jonathan Swift, in one of the seldom-read later books of *Gulliver's Travels.* He is the prototype of ugly, swinishly behaved, uncultured, vulgar human beings. By contrast, members of the ruling class, called "Houyhnhnms," have the bodies of horses but are cultured, educated and infinitely more intelligent than the *Yahoos.*

Yale University gets its name from a Boston-born British colonial governor of Madras, India. Jeremiah Dummer, a Harvard alumnus, persuaded Elihu Yale to help the struggling Collegiate School of Connecticut. He sent nine bales of fabrics, including muslins, calico, poplins, silk crepe and other items. These were sold at dockside in Boston and fetched the sum of 562 pounds and 12 shillings. He also donated some 450 volumes and a portrait of King George. His biographer, computing the value of the gift, reckoned that "It was about the same size as the gift John Harvard made to the college at Cambridge." His reward? The name of the Collegiate School was changed to *Yale.*

Yankee is any American in the eyes of the rest of the world; he is a Northerner, particularly one from New England, as far as the Southerners of this country are concerned. Originally, *Yankee* was *Jan Kaas,* a disparaging nickname for a Hollander (*Jan* meaning "John" and *Kaas* or *Kees* meaning "cheese"). Later it came to be used as a term for a Dutch freebooter. The Dutch, after coming to America and settling in what is now New York, applied the term to the English who moved into Connecticut. For a while *Yankee* was used generally in the colonies to apply to any northern neighbor who was disliked, but by the time of the Revolutionary War, the British had come to use it to apply to any colonist. In fact, the song "Yankee Doodle" was originally a song of derision sung by British soldiers to mock the poorly clothed colonists. But the colonial army gave the song new lyrics and adopted it as its marching song. The Civil War brought the term back to the meaning of a "disliked Northerner," but with the outbreak of World War I, all American soldiers became *Yankees* or *Yanks* to the rest of the world.

Novelist James Fenimore Cooper had a different theory of the origin of *Yankee.* He claimed that it was derived from the Indian pronunciation of the word "English." The Indians, said Cooper, pronounced "English" as *Yengees.* In our opinion Cooper is not much of an authority on word origins any more than he was any kind of a prose stylist. Despite his popularity in the nineteenth century, we have found his novels so ponderously written as to be practically unreadable.

Ranked very much higher as an authority on word origins is Professor Harold Bender, who contributed his vast and profound scholarship to the great *Merriam-Webster New International,* Second Edition. Here is Bender on the origin of *Yankee:* "Often derived, Indian corruption of *English,* or *Anglais,* but probably from a D[utch] derivative of *Jan* as applied by the Dutch of New York to the English of Connecticut." And H. L. Mencken, who devotes five pages of *The American Language,* Supp. I, to *Yankee,* calls it "perhaps the most notable of all the contributions of Knickerbocker Dutch to American."

Yankee Doodle. The first Yankees were Dutchmen and the expression "Yankee Dutch" was used as an expression of scorn by the British back in the early seventeenth century. During the French and Indian War, British General Wolfe was so disgusted with the appearance and lack of discipline of some New England frontier scouts under his command that he derisively nicknamed them "Yankees." The name stuck and when, a few years later, the colonists rebelled, the redcoats scorned them as "Yankee Doodlers" and sang a song deriding them. The colonists liked the tune and adopted

it—very much the same way American and British soldiers in World War
II adopted "Lili Marlene" from their German foes.

Yankee Doodle Dandy. The Fourth of July is the imaginary birthday of
George M. Cohan, the self-styled "Yankee Doodle Boy," who made his
debut in Providence, Rhode Island, on July 3, 1878. However, a little
miscalculation on nature's part was not likely to deter anyone so brashly
self-confident as "Little Georgie," as he was called when he joined his
parents' vaudeville act. Later, when he called himself "a real live nephew
of my Uncle Sam," he was simply expressing an earnest and sincere devotion to his American heritage. If the devotion also expressed itself in
commercially profitable songs and shows—well, that, too, is part of the
American tradition. Incidentally, the film biography of Cohan titled *Yankee Doodle Dandy* and starring James Cagney was considered by Cagney
to be the best of his many films.

Yarborough is a hand dealt in a bridge or whist game in which there is no card
higher than nine. It gets its name because Charles Anderson Worsley,
second Earl of Yarborough and a famous sportsman of the late Victorian
era, reportedly offered a standing bet of 1,000 to 1 against its turning up
in any game he played in. Lord Yarborough did not have access to present-
day analytical statistics on odds, but the fact seems to be that the actual
odds are 1,827 to 1 against the appearance of a *Yarborough.*

yard as a unit of measurement is three feet. It originally was the distance from
the tip of the nose of King Edgar of England (A.D. 944–975) to the tip of
his outstretched middle finger.

yclept. An archaic term for "named or called." It is now used only, as the
Oxford Dictionary might put it, "jocosely."

ye. The *y* in *ye* is only a representation of an ancient runic letter called the
"thorn," which is properly rendered by the sound *th.* So people who have
been going about talking of "Yee Olde Englishe Tearoom" have been
talking through their hats. *Ye* was never intended to be pronounced as
anything but "the."

yellow dog was once a bit of American slang widely used to designate any
worthless or mongrel thing. Today it survives chiefly in the phrase *"yellow-
dog* contract," a labor union term for the kind of contract which expressly
stipulates that an employee cannot join a union. In theory, at least, such
contracts were outlawed by the Wagner Labor Relations Act of 1935.

yellow jack is an acute tropical disease which long plagued our troops on
foreign duty, especially in Cuba during and after the Spanish-American
War. The story of the eventual conquest of the disease by Dr. Walter Reed
and several U.S. Army volunteers was graphically told in the play *Yellow
Jack* by Sidney Howard (1934).

yellow journalism, as a term descriptive of sensational newspaper treatment
of stories of crime, corruption and the like, goes back to before the turn

of the century. The first comic strip to run successfully in an American paper was *Yellow Kid* in the *New York World,* beginning in 1895. To attract attention to the feature, yellow ink was used, and the *World,* which was pretty sensational in those years, became known as the "yellow paper" —an epithet later extended in the term *yellow journalism* to any sensation-mongering newspaper.

yenta is a Yiddishism which has gained some currency in the general language. Our friend Leo Rosten, in his admirable book *The Joys of Yiddish,* defines a *yenta* as "a gossipy woman; a scandal-spreader; a rumormonger." And here is the definition given in our *American Heritage Dictionary:* "a gossipy woman, especially one who pries into the affairs of others and offers unsolicited advice."

yerba buena means "good herb" in Spanish. Yerba Buena was the name of an ersatz Dixieland band popular on the West Coast a few years ago. The name comes from an island in San Francisco Bay which connects two spans of the San Francisco–Oakland bridge. It was once known as Goat Island, and during the 1939 Exposition, as Treasure Island.

yes man. Like "hot dog," this is one of the creations of the great sports cartoonist TAD (T. A. Dorgan). *Yes man* first appeared in a cartoon in 1913. The cartoon was labeled "Giving the First Edition the Once Over" and showed a newspaper editor with his assistants looking over sheets fresh from the press. The assistants were all praising the edition—and each bore the label *yes-man.* The late Fred Allen added a phrase to the language which deserves to be better known. Describing the reaction with which smart young sycophants greet the boss's attempts at joke-making, Allen coined the phrase *loyalty laughter.* Both *yes men* and *loyalty laughter* are very much a part of the business scene today.

Yiddishisms. Leo Rosten, whose *The Joys of Yiddish* is the most entertaining and, at least to our knowledge, the most authoritative book on the subject, criticized our use of "Yiddicism" in our *Harper Dictionary of Contemporary Usage.* The proper word is *Yiddishism,* he contends, and—as you see —we bow to superior authority. Here are a few of these derivatives from German that have come into American use by way of Yiddish, itself a blend of Old German and Hebrew. Most of these terms were popularized by radio and TV comedians of the order of Milton Berle, Sid Caesar and many more. It's true that each has a special subtle overtone that is lost in translation, but nevertheless, let's give the English equivalents.

A *schlemiel* is an unlucky bungler, the perennial patsy. His name comes from Shelumiel, an Old Testament leader of the tribe of Simeon. While other leaders won their battles, he lost them all. *Schmaltz* is literally "melted fat," but now connotes excessive sentimentality. *Chutzpah* is nerve, brass or gall. *Kitsch* is anything of poor quality but wide popularity —like the "poetry" of the late Edgar Guest or the music of Lawrence Welk.

A *schnook* is a sucker, a dupe. One's *schtick* is one's trademark, like Jack Benny's stinginess. *Drek* or *dreck* is simply trash, junk or, in the clothing trade, a poorly made garment. To *schlep* something is to move it from one place to another, usually clumsily or with difficulty. And a *klutz* is a very dull person. In fact, it comes from the German word *klotz,* meaning "clod or blockhead."

yin and yang is a basic concept of Chinese philosophy. Here's the way the *Standard Dictionary of Folklore* puts it: "*Yin and yang.* The female (yin) and the male (yang) principles of the universe in Chinese philosophy and religion: assumed to be in eternal opposition. When in this opposition they achieve a dynamic balance, harmony has been achieved." The principle is sometimes illustrated with a circle bisected by a sine curve.

yoke. You don't get mugged in Baltimore, according to H. L. Mencken; you are *yoked. Yoke* was originally sailor slang and comes from the practice of catching a sailor from behind by the yoke of his tightly fitted collar. Then, by twisting his neckerchief, the mugger would quickly have him under control. Crooks who did this were sometimes called "jumper jacks" for obvious reasons.

Speaking of sailors, there's an ancient saying passed down from generation to generation of U.S. Naval Academy plebes: "When in danger or in doubt, Run in circles; scream and shout!" Good advice if you're being *yoked.*

Yorick was the King's jester in *Hamlet,* a fellow "of infinite jest, of most excellent fancy," whose skull Hamlet saluted (Act V, Scene 1) with "Alas, poor Yorick! I knew him, Horatio . . . Where be your gibes now? Your gambols, your songs, your flashes of merriment, that were wont to set the table on a roar? Not one now to mock your own grinning?"

you can't cheat an honest man is one of W. C. Fields's creations that we cherish. It's a simple statement of a truth we often overlook. In these days of hanky-panky and double-dealing on all levels of government, it's worth remembering that nobody gets involved in such trickery unless there's a little larceny in his soul.

you can't make a silk purse out of a sow's ear. Just who first said *You can't make a silk purse out of a sow's ear* is unknown. Like many proverbs, this has been used so often over the centuries—and in so many slightly varying forms—that the fellow who first uttered this homely truth has long been forgotten. In Laurence Sterne's *Tristram Shandy* the phrase turns up in this form: "As certainly as you can make a velvet cap *out of a sow's ear.*" At about the same time—the second half of the eighteenth century—a British versifier, John Walcott, who wrote under the name "Peter Pindar," said it this way: "You cannot make, my Lord, I fear, a velvet *purse of a sow's ear.*" Just when the velvet turned to silk would be anyone's guess, but the fundamental moral—that you cannot make a first-quality product from inferior material—remains as sound as the day it was first uttered.

zany is a word that may seem to be slang, but it dates back to the commedia dell'arte in Italy of the sixteenth to eighteenth centuries. In that form of theatrical production, the *zanni* (as it was spelled in Italian) was a buffoon who mimicked one of the stock characters, usually the clown. The English changed its spelling to *zany* and used it to refer to any simpleton or bumbling fool. Actually the first *zanni* was named John, since the word was a contraction of *Giovanni,* the Italian for John.

zealot. The first *Zealots* were members of a Jewish sect who made a defiant last stand against the Roman invaders at the fortress of Masada in A.D. 73. On the eve of Passover in that year, the Romans had very nearly destroyed their fortress by fire, so the 960 *Zealots,* facing the 6,000-man Tenth Roman Legion, elected to commit mass suicide—to die as free men rather than to live as slaves. A *zealot* today is a person fanatically dedicated to a cause.

zero hour. In World War I this term was used to designate the moment when an attack was to begin. In these years of the Age of Space the "countdown" has pretty much usurped the role formerly played by *zero hour.*

Zeus was the king of the gods in the Greek pantheon, and the progenitor of all the other gods and mortal heroes.

Z-gram is Navy slang for the terse memos written by former Chief of Navy Operations Admiral Elmo Zumwalt. They were—at least by customary Navy standards—models of concise, direct expression. The *Z-grams* which attracted most attention were those signaling a general relaxing of what servicemen call "Mickey Mouse" regulations. Under the Zumwalt code, long hair, beards and generally more casual dress, including the wearing of dungarees off the base, were permitted.

zinnia, a plant of variously colored flowers, native to tropical America, takes its name from a famous German botanist of the eighteenth century named Johann Gottfried Zinn.

zip has become a sort of voguish slang substitute for "zero." We'd guess that it owes its new popularity to the stress placed on "zip codes" by the postal service, though there's really no connection between the two. Wentworth and Flexner's *Dictionary of American Slang* records *zip* as common in student use as long ago as 1900. Apparently a pupil who drew an absolute blank on an exam would say "My grade was *zip.*" Amusingly enough, this same dictionary, published in 1960, reported that *zip* in the sense of "zero" was archaic—so today's sports and weather broadcasters are unwittingly restoring to life an expression their grandfathers buried long ago.

zip code is a method alleged to speed delivery of mail in the United States by assigning to each post office a numerical designation in addition to the city name and state abbreviation. The acronym represents the initial letters of the phrase (and this is pure governmentese) "Zone Improvement Program."

zodiac comes from the Greek word *zodiakos,* meaning "a circle of animals." The ancients believed that the heavens formed a circular belt with twelve parts, each symbolized by a figure such as Taurus, the bull, and Aries, the ram.

zoophobia victims experience a morbid fear of all animals. The prefix "zoo-" comes from the Greek *zoion,* which means "single animal." It is in the plural sense that "zoo-" is used in *zoophobia*—intense distaste for all animals. The American word *zoo,* meaning a collection of wild animals or menagerie, is actually an abbreviation of "zoological gardens."

zyzzyva is the name of a not especially important weevil found in tropical America and quite destructive of plants. It is pronounced zɪz-ih-vuh and appears here only because we rather like to end our reference books with this ultimate in pronounceable words. We closed out the *American Heritage Dictionary,* the *Grolier Universal Encyclopedia,* and now the *Morris Dictionary* of *Word and Phrase Origins* with *zyzzyva.* All hail!

Index